# PHYSICAL EDUCATION
## for the Elementary Classroom Teacher

Includes 3 CDs with music for dances and singing games!

DANCE

BODY MANAGEMENT

MANIPULATIVE ACTIVITIES

DEVELOPMENTALLY
APPROPRIATE GAMES

SPORT RELATED SKILL

PHYSICAL FITNESS

D1247402

Carol E. Plimpton ■ Victor..

# THIRD EDITION

000 7

Published in 2007 by

Huron Valley Publishing, Inc.
4557 Washtenaw Avenue
Ann Arbor, Michigan 48108
(734) 971-2135
(800) PRINT-01
E-Mail: publish@hvpi.com
Website: www.hvpi.com

# HURON VALLEY.

• PUBLISHING SOLUTIONS •

ISBN-10: 1-933377-20-8
ISBN-13: 978-1-933377-20-9

# Table of Contents

**Chapter Nineteen**     **Classroom Teacher and Physical Educator: A Dynamic Duo** .............................. **427**

**References and Suggested Readings** ................................... **433**

CHAPTER

# 1

# Why Teach Physical Education?

Welcome to one of the most exciting and interesting courses you will take en route to becoming a teacher! You have chosen a career as a classroom teacher, and you may be wondering why you are taking a course that prepares you to teach physical education to your future students! Although most schools have elementary physical education teachers, few schools offer physical education more frequently than twice a week for the children. As you will learn in this course, a strong physical education program can have major effects on the growth and development of the child in all three domains of learning: psychomotor, cognitive and affective. It is, therefore, very important that you, as the classroom teacher, understand and believe in the importance of physical education to ensure participation at an optimal level for your pupils, and, that you learn many ways to incorporate physical activity in the classroom for them as well!

The following document provides some startling facts regarding physical activity and the youth of the 90's. Read it carefully so you can compare it to the even MORE startling facts that you will find after the document.

## PHYSICAL ACTIVITY AND THE HEALTH OF YOUNG PEOPLE FACT SHEET

### BENEFITS OF REGULAR PHYSICAL ACTIVITY

- Helps build and maintain healthy bones and muscles[1]
- Helps control weight, build lean muscle, and reduce fat[1]
- Reduces feelings of depression and anxiety and promotes psychological well-being[1]

## LONG-TERM CONSEQUENCES OF PHYSICAL INACTIVITY

- Physical inactivity and poor diet together account for at least 300,000 deaths in the United States each year. Only tobacco use contributes to more preventable deaths.[2]
- Physical inactivity increases the risk of dying prematurely, dying of heart disease, and developing diabetes, colon cancer, and high blood pressure.[1]

## OVERWEIGHT AND OBESITY

- The percentage of children and adolescents who are overweight has more than doubled in the past 30 years; most of this increase has occurred since the late 1970s.[3]
- Of U.S. children and adolescents aged 6–17 years, about 4.7 million, or 11%, are seriously overweight.[3]
- Obese children and adolescents are more likely to become obese adults, overweight adults are at increased risk for heart disease, high blood pressure, stroke, diabetes, some types of cancer, and gallbladder disease.[6]

## PARTICIPATION IN PHYSICAL ACTIVITY BY YOUNG PEOPLE

- Nearly half of young people aged 12–21 do not engage in vigorous physical activity on a regular basis.[7]
- Participation in all types of physical activity declines strikingly as children and adolescents get older. For example:
- Regular participation in vigorous physical activity has been reported by 69% of young people aged 12–13 but only 38% of those aged 18–21.[7]
- Seventy-two percent of 9th graders participate in vigorous physical activity on a regular basis, compared with only 55% of 12th graders.[8]

## PHYSICAL ACTIVITY AMONG YOUNG PEOPLE IN THE UNITED STATES

| TYPES OF ACTIVITIES | 1992 NATIONAL HOUSEHOLD BASED SURVEY OF YOUTHS AGED 12–21 | 1995 NATIONAL SCHOOL BASED SURVEY OF STUDENTS IN GRADES 9–12 |
| --- | --- | --- |
| Regular vigorous physical activity | 54% | 64% |
| Almost daily light to moderate activity | 26% | 21% |
| Regular strengthening/toning activities | 46% | 50% |
| Regular stretching activities | 48% | 53% |

a. Participation in activities that make them sweat and breathe hard for at least 20 minutes on at least 3 of the 7 preceding days.
b. Walking or bicycling for 30 minutes or more on at least 5 of the 7 preceding days.
c. Participation in activities such as push-ups, sit-ups, and weightlifting on at least 3 of the 7 preceding days.
d. Participation in activities such as toe touching, knee bending, and leg stretching on at least 3 of the 7 preceding days.

## PARTICIPATION IN PHYSICAL EDUCATION CLASSES

- Forty percent of U.S. high school students are not enrolled in a physical education class; 19% of 9th graders and 58% of 12th graders are not enrolled.[8]
- The percentage of students who did not attend a daily physical education class rose from 58% in 1991 to 75% in 1995,8,9 in 1995, 59% of 9th graders and 87% of 12th graders did not attend a daily physical education class.[8]
- In 1991, 19% of students enrolled in a physical education class reported that they did not exercise for 20 or more minutes in an average physical education class; this figure rose to 30% in 1995.[8,9]
- Only 19% of all high school students are physically active for at least 20 minutes in a daily physical education class.[8]

# References

1. Centers for Disease Control and Prevention. Physical Activity and Health: A Report of the Surgeon General. Atlanta, GA: U.S. Department of Health and Human Services, 1996.
2. McGinnis, J.M., Foege, W.H. Actual causes of death in the United States. JAMA 1993: 270(18):2207–12.
3. Troiano, R.P., et al. Overweight prevalence and trends for children and adolescents: the National Health Examination Surveys, 1963–1991. Archives of Pediatric and Adolescent Medicine 1995:149:1085–91.
4. Casey, V.A., et al. Body mass index from childhood to middle age: a 50 year follow-up. American Journal of Clinical Nutrition 1992: 56:14–8.
5. Guo, S.S., et al. The predictive value of childhood body mass index values for overweight at age 35 years. American Journal of Clinical Nutrition 1994: 59:810–9.
6. Public Health Service. The Surgeon General's Report on Nutrition and Health. Washington, DC: U.S. Department of Health and Human Services, Public Health Service, 1988. DHHS publication no (PHS) 88-50210.
7. Adams, P.F., et al. Health risk behaviors among our nation's youth: United States, 1992. National Center for Health Statistics, 1995. Vital Health Statistics 10(192). DHHS publication no. (PHS) 95-1520.
8. Kann, L., et al. Youth risk behavior surveillance—United States, 1995. Morbidity and Mortality Weekly Report 1996: 45(88-4):1–86.
9. Centers for Disease Control and Prevention. Participation in school physical education and selected dietary patterns among high school students—United States, 1991. Morbidity and Mortality Weekly Report 1992: 41:597–601,607. Reprinted by permission of Centers for Disease Control and Prevention, Atlanta, GA 30341-3724

**U.S. DEPARTMENT OF HEALTH AND HUMAN SERVICES**
**Centers for Disease Control and Prevention**
**National Center for Chronic Disease Prevention and Health Promotion**
**March 1997**

And now here is the news that is even worse: The American Heart Association (AHA) has compiled some alarming facts that truly emphasize the need for physical activity for American children. Citing the National Health and Nutrition Examination Study 1992-2002, AHA states that the percentage of overweight teenagers reflects a **250%** increase from numbers gathered in 1970. In addition, children of today already possess many of the risk factors for poor health. Inactivity is one of the primary sources of this problem (www.americanheart.org/presenter.jtml?identifier=771). Just as research has shown that overweight teenagers tend to become overweight adults, our concern becomes that of the health status of overweight and obese children in the elementary schools. According to the President's Council on Physical Fitness and Sports, the number of children who are overweight has doubled since 1980. Citing studies, the President's Council indicates that children should be involved in physical activity for at least one hour per day. Quality physical education programs of at least 30 minutes per day should be implemented (Lee, Wechsler, & Balling, 2006).

The United States Department for Health and Human Services (USDHHS), in the document entitled "Overweight and Obesity: A Vision for the Future," states that there is a definite need for quality daily physical education at all grade levels in schools. This report reaffirms the information provided above regarding the need for 60 minutes a day of physical activity for school-age children (http://www.surgeongeneral.gov/topics/obesity/calltoaction/fact_vision.htm). We are currently in a crisis situation with childhood obesity and we need to address the issue as being partially a school related responsibility. Along with teaching children about proper nutrition, we certainly can be the site for exercise and physical education that these children need.

We also must keep in mind that children within typical body composition ranges also need the same amount of physical activity to grow strong and healthy. Physical fitness is essential for lifelong learning and wellness. As shown in the following paragraph, fitness and intellectual peformance go hand-in-hand: The schools must provide the resources to encourage healthy minds and bodies. It should be the goal of every school district to graduate physically educated individuals ho know the importance of physical activity to healthy lifestyles.

A recent study completed in California correlated the results of the 2001 Stanford Achievement Test and Fitnessgram scores of children in grades 5, 7 and 9. According to education officials in California, this study has established the evidence that there is a direct relationship between academic performance and fitness levels of youth today. Findings that were extremely important indicated that physically fit children made the highest gains in academic achievement as well. With statistics like these, it is hard to deny the importance of sound physical education programs to our children. The contribution that physical education can make to the total child is to motivate him/her to participate in physical activity for a lifetime.

Most states recommend quality daily physical education for elementary school students. Unfortunately, due to budget and facility constraints, school systems cannot provide space nor staff for full-time certified physical educators. Most situations call for the physical educator to teach 2–3 30-minute classes of physical education per week, per grade. At this point it becomes the responsibility of the classroom teacher to provide additional time in physical education or physical activiy for his/her students. Many classroom teachers do not feel comfortable in this role and often the supplementary physical education does not occur. Therefore, it is the intent of this text to provide you with a basic understanding of physical education and the role it plays in the growth and development of the child. Working within the framework of this text should help you to become comfortable in providing appropriate activity for your students, ensuring that they receive adequate levels of physical activity throughout their school days.

## Defining Physical Education

Physical education has been defined in many ways over the years. Current definitions remain varied. According to Nichols (1994), physical education is "the aspect of education in the schools designed to develop skillful, fit and knowledgeable movers through a series of carefully planned motor activities" (p. 4). Pangrazi and Dauer (1995) state that physical education is "education through movement" (p. 1). Kirchner & Fishburne (1995) state that physical education is an instructional program which contributes to the children's education to "enhance children's physical fitness and well-being and to teach them a wide variety of motor skills" (p. 4). Wall and Murray (1994) define physical education through the roles it plays in the education of the child. These roles include learning of motor skills, improvement of motor abilities, and enhancement of physical fitness. To be physically educated, according to Mueller (1990), is "to know the joy and exhilaration of moving well, and to experience the fun and freedom of any movement . . . it involves being whole, able and competent as a person, it is one aspect of becoming whole and progressing toward one's full potential" (pp. 100–101). Finally, the National Association for Sport and Physical Education (NASPE, 1995) which is a branch of the American Alliance for Health, Physical Education, Recreation and Dance (AAHPERD), has defined the physically educated person as "one who has learned skills necessary to perform a variety of physical activities . . . is physically fit . . . does participate regularly in physical activity . . . knows the implications of and the benefits from involvement in physical activities . . . and . . . values physical activity and its contributions to a healthy lifestyle" (p. 1).

The NASPE definition relates to the ultimate outcome: a positive feeling regarding physical activity and the physical education program will result in the students becoming a physically educated person. Since physical education is one of the important processes contributing to the evolution of the physically educated person, a combination of so many expert opinions yields the following: Physical education is a subject with the ultimate goal of developing a physically educated human being who possesses the physical coordination, knowledge, skills and level of fitness necessary to maintain a healthy lifestyle in which active leisure activities are important.

Keeping in mind that the ultimate outcome would refer to the "finished product," the high school graduate, you should note that elementary physical education represents the FIRST STEP in that process. By the end of the elementary years, children should have sufficient skill to be called efficient movers, should have a sound grasp of basic sport skills and should have the knowledge and means to become physically fit. The responsibility for these outcomes rests not only with the physical educator but with you as the child's most important influence during his/her time with you.

## The Three Domains of Learning

During your educational career you have heard about the three domains of learning: cognitive (intellectual), affective (emotional) and psychomotor (physical). All three domains are intertwined in most learning experiences, and therefore, you should consider each domain when creating learning activities in physical education. You should review the definitions of each domain before attempting to make the connection to the applicability of these domains to physical education.

### COGNITIVE DOMAIN

Learning in the cognitive domain has been defined as changes in the mental structure allowing for behavioral changes. These changes occur in the brain of the child and enable him/her to retain and use new knowledge. Perception is a key process in cognitive learning (Eggen & Kauchak, 1994).

### AFFECTIVE DOMAIN

The affective domain is primarily concerned with the child's value structure. Attitudes and feelings are developed and expressed within this domain (Eggen & Kauchak, 1994). The development of self-concept, or attitude toward self, is of primary importance in the affective domain.

### PSYCHOMOTOR DOMAIN

Learning in the psychomotor domain centers on acquiring the physical coordination and skill necessary to be successful in movement endeavors. These movement endeavors are to range from the fine-motor skills of writing or drawing to the large muscle activities involved in exercise or play (Eggen & Kauchak, 1994). The word itself, psychomotor, implies the relationship between mind (psycho-) and action (motor). Although other areas of the school curriculum directly affect development in the cognitive and affective areas, the psychomotor domain is principally influenced by physical education. Furthermore, the psychomotor area is further divided into two domains: fitness and motor skill.

## The Three Domains As Related To Physical Education

Since most people envision a physical education class as one in which students are constantly in motion, it is understandable that the psychomotor domain is recognized as being of primary importance. However, all that occurs in physical education is NOT physical! For example, the child THROWS (psychomotor) a ball at a target, he/she LEARNS (cognitive) through experimentation how much force to impart to the ball in order to hit the target, and when the ball does hit the target the child FEELS (affective) successful. Or, as the child progresses in gymnastics and BECOMES SKILLFUL (psychomotor) in numerous moves, he/she CHOREOGRAPHS (cognitive) a routine to perform with those moves, and RECEIVES PRAISE (affective) from parents and friends. Every accomplishment in physical education represents an intertwining of the three domains of learning.

Today's physical education should be designed to stimulate growth and maturation in each of the three domains. Physical skills must be taught that will enhance a child's ability to be an efficient mover, and, therefore, a good player: one who is readily accepted as a playmate or team member. Activities should be stressed that will lead the child to maintain good fitness levels, and through these activities the child should be able to learn about fitness concepts. Today's elementary physical education should be developmentally appropriate with activities and tasks selected that match the size and abilities of the child, allowing for a steady progression in learning in all three domains. Programs must be success-oriented so that the child will learn to enjoy and appreciate physical activity. Today's elementary physical education should recognize the child as an individual among many other individuals, and should center on the goal of creating the physically educated individual.

## Importance of Physical Education

Immediately after birth, learning by the infant occurs as a result of his/her interaction with the environment. During the Sensorimotor Period, the first stage of the cognitive development theory of Piaget, the infant spends the first two years of life learning through interactions with people and objects, through movement and exploration (Gabbard, 2003, 1992; Payne & Isaacs, 2001, 1995, 1991). At this time intelligence is not demonstrated through paper and pencil tests but, instead, through movement skills. Prior to formal schooling the majority of the child's time is spent learning through play. It is during this period that movement, exploration of the environment, and play are essential aspects of cognitive learning for the child.

Once the child enters the world of formal schooling, the mode of learning changes. The cognitive skill of reading replaces much of the physical exploration in learning about the world. Children remain sedentary for much of the day as they acquire and process new information. It seems as if this would be an abrupt transition from the active learning style experienced in the very early years.

It is commonly believed that if a child has fun while learning, that learning will be retained longer by the learner. Since play is a priority of children, learning through playful movement makes infinite sense. Teachers need to capitalize on the child's innate desire to play, to move, and to learn. Combining the three (playing, moving, and learning) will help the child to make the transition and to learn actively in the process. Cognitive skills are more likely to be retained if learned through activity: for example, jumping on colored squares, circles, triangles and diamonds will contribute to color and shape recognition as well as to the psychomotor skill of jumping.

Physical education itself allows the teacher to accomplish a number of goals. Daily physical education offers a balance between physical activity and less active deskwork. This balance helps the child to remain alert and ready to learn, whether in the classroom or in the physical education environment. According to Sylwester (1994) exercise creates an increase in endorphin release in the brain—this chemical response makes the child feel good about himself/herself and contributes directly to the ability to solve problems in possibly stressful situations. Sylwester suggests participation in whole body activity to relieve stress and to precede actually dealing with those situations, i.e. testing.

Through physical education the child will gain an understanding and appreciation of fitness. Fitness, in turn, results in positive feelings toward self as well as providing the energy resources to study efficiently. The development of efficient motor skills contributes to a positive self-concept of being a good player. Bass (1985) reported that a running program was found to increase attention span in learning disabled children each day the running was completed. It has been noted in the past literature (in Bass, 1985) that running has many psychological benefits, including relief of depression, anxiety, anger and aggression, as well as producing "a euphoric high." Most children love to run and physical education activities can lay the groundwork for a positive outlook on running as a health-enhancing mode of maintaining good health.

Physical activity in the appropriate amounts is necessary for bones and muscles to develop to their full potentials. Physical activity also provides many opportunities for children to learn about themselves, their own abilities, and the abilities of others. Play represents physical activity that contributes to the socialization of the child. This type of interactive participation is important to the child, especially during the growing and learning years. Physical education is a course that provides for learning both about and through physical activity.

## COGNITIVE DEVELOPMENT THROUGH MOVEMENT

Researchers have spent years trying to find a definite link between physical activity and cognitive growth. It has been determined that the performance of physical skills is related to academic readiness, but not directly related to the ability to read, as had been hypothesized. Therefore the relationship between physical activity and cognitive ability has proven to be indirect (Gabbard, LeBlanc & Lowy, 1987; Gallahue, 1987).

Before actual academic learning can take place efficiently, the child's perceptual systems must be functioning at appropriate levels. Children refine such perceptual systems through exploration and use in the environment as they progress through the initial learning stages. The more practice the child has in perceiving and in reaching to his/her perceptions, the more efficient the perceptual systems will become. Therefore, refinement of the perceptual systems is important for further cognitive development, and refinement is accomplished through active involvement with the environment.

Research has shown that children do learn academic concepts effectively through the medium of structured movement experiences (Gabbard, et al., 1987). Several books have been published regarding the relationship between movement and learning. Authors of these texts advocate teaching language arts, mathematics, social studies, and science through movement tasks and activities.

The physical education class itself can be used to promote cognitive learning. For example, scoring contributes to knowledge of mathematics, learning dances and games from different countries contributes to social studies, and learning about and refining of motor skills such as throwing, catching or kicking contribute to knowledge of physics as pertaining to force production, force absorption, and inertia (Gabbard, et al., 1987; Gallahue, 1987; Kirchner & Fishburne, 1995; Nichols, 1994; Pangrazi & Dauer, 1995).

## AFFECTIVE DEVELOPMENT THROUGH PHYSICAL ACTIVITY

The development of the self-concept of a child begins at birth when primary caretakers respond to the needs of the infant. As the child ages, he/she learns about self-worth through interactions with other persons. Since play is the primary medium for interaction during childhood, the child learns a lot about himself/herself while interacting with playmates. Children value other players who are skilled and competent; the child who is a good mover is more likely to be chosen as a playmate than is a poorer mover. Success in games allows the child to feel pride, contributing to his/her positive self-concept.

In the physical education class students are given the special opportunity to not only work on their own individual skills but also to work with others as a team. Getting along with coworkers and working together as a team in order to make a project successful are very important skills involved in the world of work. Students in the physical education setting are given the opportunity to develop these skills on an almost daily basis while participating in physical education activities.

Through participation in play, children have opportunities to practice sportsmanship as well as to follow precise rules. Transfer of learning should occur: learning to play by the rules of a game is similar to following the rules of society. In addition, moral judgment is often developed through physical education activities in which children need to interact and make choices (Gabbard, et al., 1987; Gallahue, 1987; Nichols, 1994; Pangrazi & Dauer, 1995; Siedentop, Herkowitz & Rink, 1984; Wall & Murray, 1994). These kinds of activities contribute to the child's growth in the affective domain.

## RELATIONSHIP OF PHYSICAL ACTIVITY TO PHYSICAL GROWTH

Physical activity is essential for physical growth to proceed at a normal pace and for the child to achieve his/her true potential as determined by heredity. When a child is born, bones are composed of a soft, cartilaginous material which ossifies (hardens) as a result of mild degrees of stress and strain from appropriate physical activity. Infants can often be seen in supine positions, waving arms and kicking legs repeatedly in rhythmic patterns. These actions serve as exercise for the infant. As the child ages and attains upright posture, physical activity causes the bones to strengthen and harden. Without such activity, growth may be stunted or retarded. Physical activity is necessary for bones to grow into their predetermined shapes and for ossification and mineralization to occur.

Crucial to bone growth is the growth plate that is located in the long bones of the arms and legs. The growth plate is situated between the shaft and the ends (epiphyses) of the bones. The plate consists of a layer of cells that continue to multiply as the bone increases in length. If damage occurs to the growth plate of the long bone, growth may be stunted. Growth plates finally close at the end of puberty, and growth itself is minimal after that time, although some changes will occur into the twenties. It has been found that one week of inactivity will result in the loss of 50% of the calcium from a bone.

Muscles will increase in size with physical activity that is appropriate for muscular development. Muscles grow in width and breadth as the size of the fibers increase. Although boys have greater muscle mass than do girls, the factor of muscular strength is really not of concern to the teaching of physical education until approximately fifth or sixth grade when the girls go through puberty. Girls undergo a strength spurt just prior to puberty, whereas the boys experience the strength spurt at the end of puberty. At these times the physical educator should equate teams, or individuals, by size and weight for many activities.

Gains in height and weight are largely dependent on bone and muscle growth. Therefore, it is essential that appropriate physical activity be provided for the creation of healthy bone and muscle tissue. Knowledgeable teachers will be able to provide developmentally appropriate activities to accomplish this end.

In light of this information, one may conclude that exercise is of utmost importance for healthy growth (Gabbard, 2003, 1992; Payne & Isaacs, 2001, 1995, 1991; Pangrazi & Dauer, 1995; Siedentop, et al., 1984).

## PHYSICAL FITNESS IN THE ELEMENTARY AGED CHILD

Due to information gleaned from a battery of tests in 1953 by Kraus and Weber, then President Eisenhower established the President's Council on Youth Fitness in order to help American youth become as fit as European youth. The Kraus and Weber studies had shown that American youth were out of shape and overweight. Many professionals and physical educators feel that today's situation is no better and, in fact, is getting even worse. The National Youth Fitness Study, a 1987 study by the Alliance for Health, Physical Education, Recreation, and Dance has shown that 40% of American Youth between the ages of 5 and 8 already demonstrate the possibility of having at least one of the risk factors associated with heart disease. Inactivity appears to be the most prominent problem. Unfortunately, for many students, physical education is the only time during the day that students partake in physical exercise. It is essential that children learn the importance of activity both within and outside the physical education class. Exercise not only reduces the risk of developing heart disease at a later age, but also helps reduce fatigue and obesity. Exercise also promotes normal growth and development of muscles and bones and helps prevent injuries through conditioning. Regular exercise has been found to promote self-esteem, self-discipline, and self-confidence. It has also proven to be helpful in dealing with tension, stress, and depression. There have been several studies relating exercise to a student's being able to become more alert and attentive to academics (Brzycki, 1995).

Physical fitness is a quality composed of the health-related components of cardiorespiratory (aerobic) endurance, muscular strength, muscular endurance, flexibility, and appropriate body composition. In addition, physical fitness includes the components of motor fitness: agility, balance, coordination, power, and speed.

A child who is born under normal circumstances is basically physically fit. The environment in which he/she grows will determine the maintenance of fitness. If properly motivated the child can participate in numerous healthful activities to increase and maintain the quality of overall physical fitness. It makes sense to conclude that the child who feels well (healthy body) will be able to function well in life.

It is widely known that individuals need to participate in appropriate physical activity at least three non-consecutive days a week in order to affect their fitness levels. Therefore, if physical education is scheduled 2–3 times per week, it cannot directly influence fitness levels due to the vast content, in addition to physical fitness, that needs to be covered. Physical education can, however, teach children about fitness and how to increase and maintain sound levels of fitness on their own (Gabbard, et al., 1987; Kirchner & Fishburne, 1995; Nichols, 1994; Pangrazi & Dauer, 1995; Siedentop, et al., 1984).

Students need to have the power and responsibility to implement the physical fitness principles which they have learned not only for now but throughout their lives. You, as the classroom teacher, along with the physical education specialist, have one of the greatest and most unique opportunities to make a difference in your students' present and future fitness through teaching and encouraging lifelong fitness principles.

## Summary

It is crucial that the classroom teacher understand the worth and importance of elementary physical education so that he/she will encourage participation by the children in healthy, active lifestyles. There are many benefits to physical education, and this belief needs to become a mutual understanding between the physical educator, the classroom teacher, and the students involved.

## References and Suggested Readings

Bass, C.K. (1985). Running can modify classroom behavior. *Journal of Learning Disabilities*, 18(3), pp. 160–161.

Brzycki, M. (1996). *Youth strength and conditioning for parents and players*. McGraw-Hill.

Brzycki, M. (1995). *Youth strength and conditioning for parents and players*. Masters Press.

Davis, M.G. (1996). Promoting our profession: The best of times . . . the worst of times. *Journal of Physical Education, Recreation and Dance*, 67(1), 48–51.

Eggen, P.D. & Kauchak, D. (1994). *Educational Psychology: Classroom connections*. Merrill, Maxwell MacMillan International.

Eggen, P.D. & Kauchak, D. (1992). *Educational Psychology: Classroom connections*. Merrill.

Gabbard, C.P. (2003). *Lifelong motor development*. Benjamin-Cummings.

Gabbard, C. (1992). *Lifelong motor development*. Wm. C. Brown.

Gabbard, C., LeBlanc, E., & Lowy, S. (1994). *Physical education for children: building the foundation*. Prentice-Hall.

Gallahue, D. (2005). *Developmental physical education for all children*. Human Kinetics.

Gallahue, D. (1997). *Developmental physical education for today's children*. McGraw-Hill.

Nichols, B. (1994). *Moving and learning: The elementary school physical education experience*. St. Louis: Times Mirror/Mosby.

Nichols, B. (1990). *Moving and learning: The elementary school physical education experience*. St. Louis: Times Mirror/Mosby.

Ogden, C.L., Flegal, K.M., Carroll, M.D., Johnson, C.L. (2002). Prevalence and trends in overweight among US children and adolescents, 1999-2000. *JAMA*, 288:1728-32.

Pangrazi, R.P. (2006). *Dynamic physical education for elementary school children*. San Francisco: Benjamin Cummings.

Pangrazi, R.P. (2003). *Dynamic physical education for elementary school children*. San Francisco: Benjamin Cummings.

Pangrazi, R.P. (1998). *Dynamic physical education for elementary school children*. Boston: Allyn & Bacon.

Pangrazi, R.P. & Dauer, V.P. (1995). *Dynamic physical education for elementary school children*. Boston: Allyn & Bacon.

Pangrazi, R.P. & Dauer, V.P. (1992). *Dynamic physical education for elementary school children*. New York: Macmillan.

Payne, V.G. & Isaacs, L.D. (2007). *Human motor development: A lifespan approach*. McGraw-Hill.

Payne, V.G. & Isaacs, L.D. (2001). *Human motor development: A lifespan approach*. Mountain View: Mayfield.

Payne, V. G. & Isaacs, L.D. (1991). *Human motor development: A lifespan approach*. Mountain View: Mayfield.

Siedentop, D., Herkowitz, J. & Rink, J. (1984). *Elementary physical education methods*. Englewood Cliffs: Prentice-Hall.

Solomon, G. (1997). Does physical education affect character development in students? *Journal of Physical Education, Recreation, and Dance*. 68(9), 38–41.

Sylwester, R. (1994). How emotions affect learning. *Educational Leadership*. October, 60–65.

U.S. Department of Health & Human Services. Centers for Disease Control and Prevention, March 1997, Information Packet on Guidelines for School and Community Programs to Promote Lifelong Physical Activity Among Young People.

Wall, J. & Murray, N. (1990). *Children and movement*. Dubuque: Wm. C. Brown

http://www.cdc.gov/nchs/products/pubs/pubd/hestats/overwght99.htm
http://www.cahperd.org/images/pdf_docs/CDE_News_release.pdf
http://www.cdc.gov/mmwr/preview/mmwrhtml/mm5233a1.htm
http://www.cdc.gov/nccdphp/dash/physicalactivity/promoting_health/calltoaction.htm

CHAPTER

# 2

# Effective Physical Education

According to Siedentop and Tannehill (1999) there are three components to teaching in physical education: instructing, managing, and supervising. When instructing, the teacher is providing information to the students in the form of lecturing, demonstrating with verbal cues, providing feedback on the students' performances, providing group feedback, or reteaching when necessary. Managing refers to the teacher's role in the structural content of the class: creating groups, planning for quick transitions, distributing and collecting equipment, organizing the students for drills or activities, and conducting such routine matters as taking attendance. The teacher, as supervisor, moves throughout the learning area, observing the students as they work and providing motivational feedback. The teacher is rarely still; the students are busily working.

In the environment of an effective teacher, learning is evident on the part of the students. It is necessary that the teacher use a well-planned sequence of learning activities, appropriate for the accomplishment of the curriculum objectives. A teacher needs to do this in such a way that the students find the learning to be meaningful (Nichols, 2001,1994).

The climate of the gymnasium should be a positive one, where children feel free to participate within a nurturing environment. Siedentop and Tannehill (1999) speak of the need for humane physical education. They describe this as a process in which children are treated equally and with respect for individual differences. Each child has the right to participate in physical education to the fullest extent possible. This, in turn, will foster self-growth for each student. It is important that the teacher provide success-oriented activities so that the children will increase in self-esteem while learning a pleasurable way to establish and maintain fitness for life.

# What's Happening In Exciting And Effective Gymnasiums

Perhaps the best way to begin to talk about effective teaching in physical education is to go into the gymnasiums of two different teachers. As you read each scenario, see if you can identify the things that the teacher says or does as instructor, as manager, and as supervisor to provide a warm, nurturing climate that results in active learning.

## A TYPICAL PHYSICAL EDUCATION CLASS FOR YOUNG CHILDREN

The second grade children enter the gymnasium and Ms. Fitness hands a yarn ball to each of three different children. As the group moves into the play area, Ms. Fitness says, "Time for Turtle Tag! Billy, Susan and Jimmy are 'Its'! Ready? Go!" The children begin to run around within the gymnasium while Billy, Susan and Jimmy try to tag others with the ball. If tagged, a child goes to the floor holding a push-up position until a classmate crawls underneath to free the tagged child. After three minutes Ms. Fitness stops the game, names three different "its," and the children play for another three minutes. She then blows a whistle to stop the game.

"Let's have all of you feel your pulses—remember where to find it, in your neck or on your wrist? Can everyone find it? What can you tell?"

"My heart is beating really fast!"

"My heart is on a race!"

"Good! That's what we wanted to do. We want to have our hearts work hard to make us strong and fit. Remember that a game like Turtle Tag will do this for you. "You can play it with your friends at home and get a good workout for your heart. Now I want all of you to sit in your squads please."

The children move to their pre-assigned places on the floor and focus attention on the teacher. There are four squad lines of six children each.

"Today we are going to work on our physical fitness by increasing our flexibility through stunts and tumbling. I would like squad 1 and squad 2 to form partners by pairing with the friend who is sitting directly across from you. Squads 3 and 4 may do the same. Good. When I say go, squads 1 and 2 will walk quietly to the pile of mats on the right side of the gym and take one for each set of partners. Squads 3 and 4 do the same on the left side of the gym. Remember you will need one mat for you and your partner. When you and your partner have your mat, place it in self-space where you can see and hear me. Go."

The children get the mats and arrange them on the gym floor. They make sure that their mat is not too close to any other mat. Ms. Fitness places a mat for herself where all the children can see.

"First we will review some of the stunts that you learned last year in first grade physical education. I am going to show you the log roll. I lie down on my back, arms stretched overhead so my body is as straight as a log. Then I roll sideways down the mat like this." Ms. Fitness rolls with control the length of the mat. "Now I would like you and your partner to take turns practicing the log roll while I come around to see how you are doing. Go." The children begin to work. Ms. Fitness walks around the mats, commenting to the children on their performances. She returns to the teaching mat and blows her whistle. The children stop moving and look to Ms. Fitness.

The lesson continues in the same sequence with Ms. Fitness' providing skill demonstrations followed by feedback as she walks through the learning environment. The lesson moves on with an egg roll, a forward roll from a squat position, a forward roll from a standing position, and animal walks to enhance flexibility: the inchworm, the bear walk, the lame puppy, and others.

Ms. Fitness blows her whistle. "When I say go, I want squads 1 and 2 to put their mats away on the right side of the gym and squads 3 and 4 on the left side. Be sure to stack them carefully and then walk to the door to line up. "Go."

"Today we worked on our stunts and tumbling skills to help us with strength and flexibility. Who can tell me what flexibility is?"

"Being able to stretch?"

"That's a good answer. Flexibility means that our muscles can move easily about our joints. Stretching helps us to develop flexibility. You can also work on your flexibility by practicing the animal walks that you have learned today."

## A TYPICAL PHYSICAL EDUCATION CLASS FOR INTERMEDIATE GRADE CHILDREN

As the fifth grade students enter the gymnasium, Mr. Muscle tells the students they are to jog around the outside lines of the gymnasium for 3 minutes. He reminds them to pace themselves so they can keep going for the entire time. As the students begin to jog, Mr. Muscle begins to set out equipment on the inside of the gymnasium lines for station activities.

At the end of three minutes, Mr. Muscle blows his whistle and tells the students to walk two more laps. They then will come to the center of the gymnasium and sit down to stretch out. As the students are stretching, Mr. Muscle reminds them to look at the charts on the wall that describe the stretches they should be doing. He then proceeds to talk about the day's lesson.

"Today, girls and boys, we are going to work on our individual skills in basketball. Each of you has had the opportunity to learn the basic skills in the past few classes. Now we will use a station approach so that you can work on refining those individual skills. As you look around the gymnasium you will see that there are six stations, one station for each squad. When you get to the station you are to read the instructions on the card placed on the traffic cone. Then go to work immediately. You will be at each station for four minutes. Be sure to work very hard on the assigned skill so that you will be ready when we play basketball games. When the whistle blows, leave your station with the equipment as you found it and begin to work at the next one. Move in a counterclockwise direction. Are there any questions?"

"Squads will report to the station that has the same number as the squad. Go."

The children, having completed their stretching during the introduction to the lesson, immediately disperse to their assigned stations. They read the directions and begin to work. Some have questions and Mr. Muscle goes to the stations to answer those questions. The stations consist of the following tasks:

> *STATION 1*: Using a basketball, practice your passing to the targets on the wall. Remember to use the chest pass, the bounce pass and the overhead pass. See how many good passes you can complete before the whistle blows. Rotate through the targets on your own.

> *STATION 2:* Using a basketball, practice your jump shots. There are Xs marked around the key: try several shots from each of the Xs. Remember to let the ball spin off your fingers. See how many baskets you can make in the time allowed.

> *STATION 3*: Work with a partner and use one basketball. One of you will dribble the ball and the other will guard. Keep moving in the designated space until the guard taps the ball away, then change positions. Remember to keep a low defensive stance and stay with the dribbler. Keep going for the entire four minutes.

> *STATION 4*: Using a basketball, hold the ball overhead and stand about 2' from the wall. Practice your rebounding skills. Jump, toss the ball to the wall and catch it before

coming back down! This will be a real challenge. Remember to keep your arms up. See how many rebounds you can get in the four minutes.

***STATION 5***: Using a basketball, practice taking your free throws from the mark indicated in the key. Line up around the key as you would do for a free throw. Change places after every four shots. Remember to stay focused: bend your knees, eyes on the rim, elbows extend, follow through.

***STATION 6:*** Using a basketball, work on the ball handling stunts we have done. Pass the ball around the head ten times, and weave the ball in and out of your legs ten times. Repeat this sequence as many times as you can before time is up.

As the students work at the stations, Mr. Muscle walks around to the stations and provides feedback and praise. Every four minutes he blows the whistle and the children rotate stations. After all children have completed all stations he calls "Stop!"

"When I say go, I would like each squad to take the equipment from its station and put it neatly away in the equipment room. Then come to the center of the gym, and sit down., Squads 1 and 2 go . . . 3 and 4 go . . . 5 and 6 go. . . ." When the equipment is put away and the children are seated, Mr. Muscle asks the children about the stations.

"Which station was the most difficult?" Most students indicated that the guarding station was the hardest.

"Why was that?"

The children concluded that it was because they had to work against an opponent whereas in the other stations they worked on their own skills. Some also felt the rebounding station was difficult.

"I'm glad that you worked so hard on your skills today. Remember that most of these skills can be practiced at home with almost any kind of ball. The more control you develop over the ball, the better player you will be. Next time we will begin to put our basketball skills together in some lead-up basketball games. Please walk to the door quietly and form a line."

These two scenarios have been designed to show you the classes of effective teachers. In most classes of effective teachers the students are busy and interested and do not often go off-task. Each of these teachers used direct style approaches to the classes, meaning that the approaches are teacher-centered: all decisions are made by the teacher. At the conclusion of this chapter you should have a good idea of how physical education is structured and how you can be effective in teaching physical education to your class.

# What Research Says About Good Physical Education

Siedentop and Tannehill (1999) provide a comprehensive review of research on teaching in physical education. Actual physical education classes were studied with the focus on teacher characteristics leading to learning effectiveness. As a result of the review of research, recommendations have been made for what would constitute good, effective physical education.

## TEACHER CHARACTERISTICS

Siedentop and Tannehill (1999) state that the effective physical education teacher should provide for adequate time in ALT–PE (Academic Learning Time–Physical Education). ALT–PE refers to the time that children have to work on designated learning content with a high degree of success. The theory is that students who are successful will continue to work and enhance their abilities whereas those who are challenged to the point of frustration will give up on the tasks. It is generally known that the more quality time spent on content in the classroom, the more children learn. The same principle holds true for learning in the physical education environment.

The effective teacher should hold high expectations for the students in the class. Pygmalion Theory tells us that students respond to teacher expectations by either rising to meet them or lessening efficiency to meet lower standards. Therefore the teacher who believes all of his/her students are capable of high performance will teach to them in such a way that they will rise to greater achievement levels.

Siedentop and Tannehill (1999) state that the good physical educator should be an efficient manager, therefore increasing time for ALT–PE. The teacher should be able to select appropriate content, and should be able to present it at a level that is developmentally appropriate for the class. In addition, the teacher should present information and keep the class flowing with good pace and momentum, free from long periods of waiting time on the part of the students. The active teacher supervises the class by interacting with students and by offering performance-based feedback to enhance skill development.

## GYMNASIUM CLIMATE

The climate for the good physical education class should present an atmosphere that invites the students to participate. The effective teacher should be sure the class provides for active learning, participation that is enjoyed by the students. There should not be long periods of waiting, i.e. inactivity. Children should feel as if they receive positive encouragement and they should well function within an atmosphere of success. It is difficult to separate the climate from the teacher characteristics as it is the teacher characteristics that actually create the climate.

## STUDENT RESPONSE

In good physical education the children are working, on task, and receiving appropriate feedback to aid in their achievement of optimum performance. They express interest in their learning by asking the teacher to "watch me!" and by asking for help in more difficult skills. When learning is occurring, good physical education is happening.

# How Children Learn In The Gymnasium

Learning in the gymnasium differs from that in the classroom. Whereas in the classroom the students may have their assigned spaces and desks, in the gymnasium the children must be moving in order to achieve competence in skills. Learned skills grow to become automatic motor programs that are essential to coordinated, efficient movement. The following discussion represents a combination of psychomotor learning theories as described by Kirchner and Fishburne (2001, 1998, 1995), Pangrazi and Dauer (1992, 1995), Nichols (2001, 1994), and Siedentop, Herkowitz and Rink (1984).

## MOTOR PROGRAM FORMATION

In the psychomotor domain, children learn best visually. The teacher should show the children the skill to be learned, demonstrating while verbalizing the teaching cues for the skill. A demonstration may be given by the teacher or by a student model. The children will then see what the skill looks like, will hear the cues, and will be able to try the skill on their own. The teacher should select cues that are significant aspects of the skillful performance and therefore relevant to learning.

For example, in teaching the children to jump for distance, the teacher may demonstrate while pointing out the important aspects of the jump: "crouch low, arms back; swing arms forward and out as you jump; bring legs through and land." The children watch the demonstration, and then try the skill. The teacher moves around the gymnasium offering performance-based feedback to the children. "Pull those arms through, Alicia! Try not to crouch so low this time, Ben. Great jump, Chris! You carried your arms through very well." As the children apply the feedback to their subsequent attempts, the skill comes to look more and more like the demonstration. The children are working in cycles: try, feedback, try again. The teacher may stop then and give some group-related feedback at any time. "I see that many children have been using a good strong arm swing. This is very important to your take-off. See if you can all swing through powerfully enough to carry you even further this time."

Once the children have been successful in producing the movement, they continue to practice the skill. This practice, similar to the component of rehearsal in cognitive learning, causes a motor program to be formed in the brain. The more the skill is practiced, the better ingrained the motor program becomes. This is very similar to long term memory but eventually the child will not think about how to jump, and the motor program will fire when necessary. Think about what you do when you are walking to class. Do you think about how you are walking? Do you tell yourself that you must contact the ground with the heel of the foot and roll up to the toe before lifting the foot? Surely you do not. You use your motor program for walking.

It is important that children establish automatic motor programs that will fire when necessary. Let's review the steps in the establishment of the motor program:
- the child SEES what is to be learned
- the child HEARS the auditory cues
- the child TRIES the skill
- the child RECEIVES feedback on the performance
- the child ADJUSTS the response to the feedback
- the child REHEARSES the skill correctly

The result may be referred to as the "ideal" of the skill and it is structurally embedded in the neural networks of the brain. The problem in learning comes if the child does not receive proper feedback, or is taught incorrectly, and the skill is learned so that it is inefficient. In this case, to then learn the skill properly, the learner must break some bad habits. While "relearning" is occurring, skill performance quality will often decrease and the learner may lose interest in the skill because success is hard to reach. The learner eventually will reach a level of success, but often must be patient. This is why initial demonstration and proper feedback are so important.

The initial demonstration should show the children what is to be accomplished, the expected end product. The demonstration should proceed at approximately the normal speed execution of the skill. It should represent a meaningful whole: the children see where they are headed, what the result of the learning will be. Then, if it is a complicated skill, it will be broken down into parts to be practiced. It is important, however, that the children know where the accomplishment of all the parts will lead. Some skills are simple enough that one demonstration and feedback cycle will be ample for success; for example, a jump in place. Others require work on different parts of the skill so that once each part has been achieved, the parts are then put together for the accomplished skill. For example, in order to learn a set shot in basketball the child would watch a demonstration. Using the basic principles of task analysis, the teacher would point out the specific parts of the skill: stand with knees comfortably bent, feet shoulder width apart, elbow of shooting arm parallel to the floor and arm bent at 90 degrees, ball resting on palm of hand, movement begins from knees and feet, elbow lifts, wrist snaps as ball is lifted upward off the fingers toward the basket. The children who are just beginning to learn this skill may begin by holding the ball in one hand and spinning it upward off the fingertips. They may then add the lift from the knees to initiate the push and spin, etc. Eventually, with sufficient practice, the children will be able to perform basketball set shots.

When the children have been successful in forming the motor program, they should be reinforced for their accomplishments. The learning of a complex skill (having many parts) calls for positive reinforcement throughout the learning experience. It is easy to incorporate social reinforcement with feedback: "That was a good try, Susan. This time let's see if you can spin the ball a bit higher."

Once the motor program is established, the child learns to extend the movement to adjust for different environmental conditions. For the original example of the jump, the child may be asked to jump farther, to jump higher, or to jump over obstacles. For the example of the set shot, the child may be asked to dribble and then shoot, or to shoot with a defender in the path. Each of these tasks requires a variation of the original motor program.

The child then learns to vary the use of the skill. Each of the above skills may be used in various game situations. In the variations, the skill will be used in such a way as to respond to the needs of the environment. The child will learn to alter the response in order to be successful with a new piece of equipment or a new situation. These skills can later be applied in a sport-related setting.

## DEVELOPMENTALLY APPROPRIATE EQUIPMENT AND ACTIVITIES

With the view of sport that society holds today, children are often expected to be skillful when using equipment designed for the adult. Children need to compensate for the comparable lack of strength and size and, consequently, they often develop inefficient and awkward psychomotor skills.

The term "developmentally appropriate" refers to the idea that children constantly grow and mature as they progress through the elementary education years. Whereas the 10' basketball rim of the high school gymnasium is appropriate for high school students, it is not appropriate for elementary school students due to physical size as well as strength levels. A rim placed at 8' would be developmentally appropriate for the typical fifth or sixth grade child. A rim at 7' would be developmentally appropriate for the 3rd and 4th grade child. In that same vein, a regulation basketball is too large for the elementary child to use in learning proper skill. A junior ball is developmentally appropriate. This fits comfortably in the child's hands and is lightweight so that strength is not a factor in learning the proper movements for ball-handling skills.

When learning psychomotor skills, children should have equipment that is appropriate for their size, strength and maturity levels. Foam or yarn balls should be used for throwing and catching activities; junior sized basketballs, soccer balls and footballs should be used in the intermediate grades as well as the sponge variety of ball for each area. Larger, lightweight foam or trainer balls should be used for volleyball. Baseball bats should be light and easy to manage. Targets for any games should be placed at levels and distances that complement the size and strength of the child.

Activities should be played in areas that are directly related to the size and stamina of the child. It is not necessary for 4th grade children to play on a 100 x 50 yard soccer or football field. Baseball diamonds may be reduced in size as well. Activities should be selected that meet the psychomotor skills and cognitive level of the children involved. Too much strategy at an early age will only confuse the child. Games of low organization for younger children will help them to participate successfully and to build skills in strategy development.

Teaching approaches should also be developmentally appropriate. When children are initially learning psychomotor skills, the teacher should present the skill as isolated from game-like situations. For example, to learn to strike a ball properly with a bat, the child should first work on hitting the ball off a batting tee. The tee should be set at the correct height for the child so that the ball sits at the center of the child's "strike zone," between the knees and the chest. In addition, the ball should be relatively large and lightweight. The child then practices the technique of striking in this format. Because the ball is stationary, and not pitched toward the child, this is termed a "closed" skill. The child does not have to deal with the effects of the environment and with the difficult perceptual task of contacting a moving ball. Once the child has established competence with the ball on the tee, the teacher may reduce the size of the ball to be hit. Once this is mastered, the teacher may pitch a slow, large ball to the child. Now that the ball is moving, the skill has become "open" and the environment has an effect. The fact that the pitched ball is slow and large reflects the principle that the equipment is developmentally appropriate. Progression from closed skills to open skills is essential in learning.

## PRINCIPLES OF PROGRESSION

Psychomotor skills are learned through appropriate progressions. In order to skip, a child must be able to hop. In order to hop, a child must be able to jump. And, in order to jump, a child must have sufficient leg strength to propel himself/herself off the ground. To provide skillful and meaningful learning for the child, the teacher must recognize prerequisite skills and teach them to the child in a logical order. The fundamental motor skills of run, jump, throw, kick, catch and strike form the building blocks for all subsequent motor skills. These are discussed in great detail in Chapter Four.

# Teaching Techniques For The Gymnasium

The gymnasium setting differs from that of the classroom in that it is large, children are often noisy, and movement is the mode of learning. Some might regard the physical education class as a less formal instructional setting in which teacher and children interact on a different basis from the stricter formality of the classroom. This is not to say that being less formal constitutes being less demanding of the students to learn, but rather that the approach is through the child's favorite medium for learning: play. The physical educator has the benefit of being able to capitalize on that favorite mode. Through this learning experience children become better movers and feel good about themselves and their capabilities. As we examine the teaching techniques for the physical education experience, keep in mind the ultimate goal of physical education: to create a physically educated human being who demonstrates an appreciation for movement and sport as a means to a healthy lifestyle. The following discussion of teaching techniques represents a compilation of information provided on teaching characteristics from Siedentop and Tannehill (1999), Phillips and Carlisle (1987), Wall and Murray (1994), Siedentop, Herkowitz and Rink (1984), Nichols (2001,1994), and Kirchner and Fishburne (2001, 1998, 1995).

## INSTRUCTIONAL TECHNIQUES

The first task of the teacher is to present information to children so that they may learn more about themselves, about others and about their environment. The instructional phase of teaching involves relaying and clarifying knowledge so that it is interesting and meaningful to the children. Not only does the teacher present the content, but he/she must also help the children to know both the "how" and the "why." It is necessary for the learner to understand both how to do something and why it is important. The goal of the effective physical education teacher is to have high instructional time devoted to ALT–PE. Remember that ALT–PE refers to the amount of time that children are actively involved in doing the skills that are being taught, and during which they are successful 80% of the time. Research tells us that this is the time when children learn best. Therefore, the teacher strives to have maximum class time on task with psychomotor skill work.

### *Presentation Skills*

Effective teachers provide information clearly through both demonstration and teaching cues. They draw the children's attention to relevant aspects of each skill to be learned and do not spend time talking for long periods of time about the skill. Within the presentation they tell the children why the skill is important, but they do not dwell on its virtues. They keep in mind that the child learns best visually and that "a picture is worth 1000 words," actually showing the skill themselves or with student models. Effective teachers are enthusiastic about the content and about the students. Information should be presented in an exciting as well as informative way. The teacher should demonstrate a love and true appreciation for the art of movement and should convey those feelings to his/her students.

## *Active Supervision*

While children are working on the material to be learned, the effective teacher moves systematically throughout the area offering feedback on the task to the children. She/he may provide the feedback to a child on a one-to-one basis, or she/he may work with small groups of children who may be having the same difficulties. The teacher, as active supervisor, recognizes the time to stop the class and provide feedback to the entire class in order to aid performance.

## *Feedback*

Feedback may be performance-related or it may be motivational in nature. It is very important that the play area have a positive climate for growth and therefore the feedback should be framed in a positive manner. Performance-based feedback is given to help the child to increase efficiency of the skill that is being learned. The teacher can remind the student of the teaching cues for the skill and can work with the child to make the skill approximate what was originally demonstrated. Performance-related feedback is usually corrective in nature but may be framed in a positive way. "I like the way you crouched low for your take-off, Gail. Now let's see if you can swing your arms a bit harder so that you can jump farther." Or, "Nice arm swing, Philip! Can you now work on landing softly?" It is best to find something that has been done well, praise the child, and then lead the child to build upon that success. Motivational feedback is just such praise. Encourage the child to do even better by adding praise to the corrective feedback. Motivational feedback may also be general: "Way to go!" "Super Job!" "Now you've got it!" It may also be a sign of thumbs up, a clap, a pat on the shoulder, or a smile. Children value such feedback and they learn to value the skills they learn because they can see that their success is important to the teacher.

## *Lesson Closure*

When the lesson is almost over, the effective teacher pulls the learning together in such a way that the students are able to recognize exactly what they have learned during the class period. He/she takes a few moments to review the major points that were covered. He/she may ask the students some questions to check for understanding and for overall learning. When closure is put into a lesson, the children should leave feeling as if they have accomplished something and they are not left hanging in the middle of a game or activity. It is also at this time that the teacher can emphasize working on skills at home.

# Management Techniques

Management skills reflect the teacher's ability to organize both children and equipment and to run a class smoothly with few, if any, interruptions. Management is viewed as "preventive medicine" in that the class that is running smoothly should be void of behavior disruptions. It is logical that the idle child may become the problem child whereas the busy child lacks the time to be a problem! The effective manager is able to keep the lesson flowing and keep the largest number of children active as is possible within the framework of the lesson. Maximum participation should be a priority when a teacher plans a lesson. Not only do children have more opportunities to learn, but they are more likely to stay on task.

## INITIAL ACTIVITY CONTROL

When the children are headed to the gymnasium for physical education class, the teacher should tell them exactly what they are to do when they enter the play area BEFORE they arrive. It is best to provide this information beforehand because children are usually excited about the class and are anxious to begin to move. The wise teacher will have a movement activity ready for the children to do immediately upon entrance so that energy can be released and excitement can be controlled. This is an excellent time for a fitness game or activity. Games such as Turtle Tag, as described in the Ms. Fitness' lesson, work to increase heart rate and provide a good warm-up activity for the children. The first few minutes of class is not the appropriate time to introduce a new game to the children. Use activities that they have learned throughout their physical education classes. Some teachers like to do traditional calisthenics for warm-up activities. Experience has shown that active, maximum participation games are more valuable, and truly help in motivating the children. These games are such that the children can play them at home in the neighborhood. It is not likely that children will take calisthenics home for after-school fun.

## ORGANIZATIONAL PATTERNS

There are an infinite number of organizational patterns that may be used for learning in physical education, depending on the objective of the learning experience. The teacher needs to plan how to teach the selected skills and activities in such a way as to provide for maximum participation. The teacher needs to select the appropriate pattern as well as plan how to get the children into that particular formation. Management refers to moving groups of children from one formation to the other for different activities. Much class time is often wasted on these tasks and the efficient manager strives to have a maximum amount of time devoted to ALT–PE.

### *Typical Formats For Teaching Physical Activities*

As you work in different activities with your students, you may wish to organize the class into different formations that will satisfy the goals that you have. The following formats are the most popular for working on skill development:

Partners working opposite each other on lines help the teacher to be able to see the children easily and to provide active supervision.

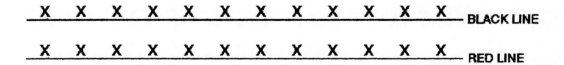

This formation allows for a "leader" to pass a ball or an object to each person in line and then the leader changes places with the next child in line.

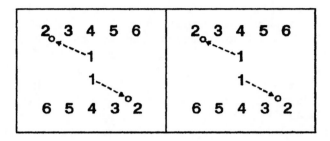

The shuttle drill formation can be used when there is limited equipment available.

X X X                    X X X
X X X                    X X X
X X X                    X X X
X X X                    X X X

For games or drills in circle formation, several small circles should be used versus a single circle in order to increase maximum participation.

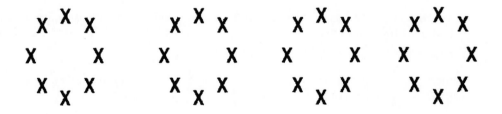

Depending on the kind of activity the teacher is presenting, he/she may want groupings to be dependent on skill level. A very unique organizational system which could be used in the classroom as well as in physical education was developed by Lambdin (1989). The students in the class are each assigned one of four to six colors, a number, and a shape. They will retain these assigned designations for the entire school year. Each child's name is listed on a chart in the classroom as a handy reminder. The teacher may have the red group work together, or the number 3s may work together that day. The teacher may have the triangles form a group, the circles another, etc.

The teacher may ask the blue group to help with the equipment. Groups may be formed by color (four groups of six children), by shape (three groups of eight children), by number

|   | BLUE | RED | GREEN | YELLOW |
|---|---|---|---|---|
| 1 | Aaron △ | Sarah □ | Doug ○ | Laura △ |
| 2 | Mindy ○ | Steve △ | Cathy □ | Jon ○ |
| 3 | Jeanine □ | David ○ | Karen △ | Ronnie □ |
| 4 | Danny □ | Linda ○ | Rob △ | Carol △ |
| 5 | Craig ○ | Susan △ | Roger □ | Sally ○ |
| 6 | Allison △ | Fred □ | Andrea ○ | Billy □ |

(six groups of 4 children), by combining numbers (two or three teams), or by combining colors (two teams). By changing the grouping strategy, children will work with different children almost every time. Look at the figure and see how many different ways you can organize your class.

Sometimes it is advantageous to have groups of equal skill for game play, or to have children grouped by high, medium or low skill levels for learning different skills. If the teacher is able to make this differentiation, you can use the following format:

| 1 | Medium (b) | Medium (g) | Medium (b) | Medium (g) |
|---|---|---|---|---|
| 2 | High (g) | High (b) | High (g) | High (b) |
| 3 | Low (g) | Low (b) | Low (g) | Low (b) |
| 4 | High (b) | High (g) | High (b) | High (g) |
| 5 | Low (b) | Low (g) | Low (b) | Low (g) |
| 6 | Medium (g) | Medium (b) | Medium (g) | Medium (b) |

This will provide the advantage of being able to teach to the skill level when working with small groups.

If children know their color, shape and number, groupings may be made efficiently and quickly. Time will not be spent on the time-honored physical education tradition of counting off by 2s, 3s, or 4s to form teams or groups. This organizational method will also avoid the stigmatizing and heartless practice of choosing teams during the class period. Anyone who has been selected last for a team will be able to identify with the feelings of rejection the child feels who is the last or close to the last to be chosen in physical education class. Nowhere but in this practice do we do more to defeat a child's rapidly forming self-concept. Therefore, Lambdin's system addresses not only the psychomotor needs of the child, but the affective needs as well.

There are other ways to divide the physical education class into squads, teams, or small groups. The purpose of doing this management activity quickly and efficiently is to use the majority of class time for activity. If the class is divided into teams a game can be readily organized or stations utilized without using a great deal of time.

***Colored Chips.*** Students can be divided into small groups or teams by having them pick a chip or small piece of colored paper out of a container as they enter the gymnasium. Various colors of construction paper can be laminated and then cut into 1/2" to 1" squares. These can be used over again many times. This method allows for teams to be changed not only quickly but also on a daily basis if desired. This would be considered a random manner for selecting groups. It also allows for the number of teams as well as the size of the teams to vary. As an example: There is a need to develop 8 different stations and the class size consists of 24 students. By placing 24 chips in a container, using 3 chips of 8 different colors, students can be quickly divided into groups of 3. Each station is assigned a color and the student drawing that color begins at the station corresponding to that color. Zip lock bags are wonderful for separating like colored chips. The students would then participate in the activity at each station for 3 minutes and then move up to the next station.

***Numbering Off.*** Students number off from 1 to eight. This time you have only 4 stations. Numbers 1 and 2 being at station 1, 3 and 4 at station 2 and so forth. Another way of dividing by numbers would be to have all the ones at station one, and so on, however this time there are 8 stations. This is also a random way of dividing students quickly.

***Electing Captains.*** Another way of dividing into groups would be to elect captains. Traditionally physical educators have had two children stand in front of the class and select children one by one, a situation that causes stress for many children. Children should have the opportunity to be a captain but there are better ways to assign this role than through the "picking format." The captain method is also more time consuming; however, it usually allows for a better division of skills and gives the students some choice regarding team selection. If a captain method must be used, the following rules for selection must be applied:

1.  Students are placed on teams in grades K–2. A captain may be assigned.
2.  Once a person has a turn as captain he/she does not get another turn until everyone in the class has had a turn.
3.  Captains are not allowed to pick teams publicly. They may use a class list privately, divide the children, and then the teacher can assign each captain to a team, not necessarily the one that captain picked! This provides for more evenly skilled teams.

***Separation by Abilities.*** Another way of dividing the class into teams would be for the teacher to assign students to a group according to abilities. As an example all of the students of higher ability may start at station 6 while those with low abilities would start at station 1.

This is somewhat difficult at times depending on how familiar the teacher is with students' physical abilities. However, it allows for a greater challenge for the better students and less frustration for students with lower skill development.

At times the teacher may specifically wish to assign students with varying abilities in each group. In many cases a student with lower skill development can help to improve their skill level by working with someone who is at a higher level of skill development. An example would be that a student could improve his/her striking skills by playing against someone who can actually return the ball over the net and inside the boundary line rather than playing against someone who always hits the ball out of bounds.

Whatever method one chooses to divide teams, team names can be put on 6'' by 8'' cards which are then placed in a small file box. The cards can be used for attendance similar to a seating chart. Rule infringements, absences, skills acquired, or skill progress can all be listed on these cards behind the student's name when appropriate. They can also be used by a substitute teacher in order to identify individual students.

***Dividing by Partners.*** In grades K through 2, partners are often used as a way to divide students into smaller groups for basic skill development as well as for certain dance skills. At times, students may be allowed to choose their own partners. Anyone who is not chosen can either be placed with a set of partners by the teacher or may choose any pair they wish to join.

# Equipment Management

Distribution of equipment is a major factor in organization for learning. The teacher must plan for a way to accomplish this efficiently. There are many ways to distribute equipment quickly. The teacher may ask the number 1's to get the equipment, such as hula hoops, for every child in their respective color groups. He/she may have the equipment, such as playground balls, placed carefully around the perimeter of the gymnasium and instruct students to get a ball and move to self-space. The equipment, such as beanbags, may be in a bin by the door and the children may pick up a beanbag as they enter the gymnasium. The teacher may call the red triangles to go to the bin to get equipment, followed by blue circles, yellow squares, etc.

Obviously you, as both the classroom teacher and the physical educator, will not be able to prepare equipment ahead of time since you will be arriving at the play space at the same time as the children. This makes planning even more important for you. You must devise a quick way to start the class as well as distribute the necessary equipment. The use of children's abilities to set up and pick up in the play area is fondly referred to as "kid power." Be sure to use "kid power" to increase your effectiveness.

# Behavior Management

The teacher should have a signal for attention. Since the play space is a very large area and children are usually excited about participation, the signal needs to be precise and easy to recognize. Usually the beginning teacher uses a whistle for a signal. Experienced teachers might use a clap, a raised hand or a teaching phrase, ". . . and now we are coming to a stop." Whatever the signal chosen, it needs to be taught to the children and the response needs to be practiced so that the children learn to stop quickly. The signal may be used to halt activity, to get attention in order to give group feedback, to teach a new skill, to signal transitions between stations, or to cause activity to halt due to safety problems or emergency. Teachers often teach the signal by playing a game with it so that the children learn to respond quickly, thus increasing the time available for learning.

We mentioned before that the busy child does not have the opportunity to be a problem to others in the class. However, there are times when disruptive behavior occurs and it may result in injury to the offending child or to others in the class. The classroom teacher should carry the classroom discipline policies into the physical education class so that rules are consistent; however, consequences for violating those rules may be different.

It is suggested that the teacher discuss appropriate behavior for the physical education setting with the class. Two rules that should be included in every classroom or play space are: 1) no child shall keep the teacher from teaching and 2) no child shall keep other children from learning. Because physical education is usually a favorite class for elementary school children, a good consequence for misbehavior is "time out." In this system, the teacher has an assigned penalty area where, depending on the severity of the infraction, the child spends a designated amount of time before returning to activity. Usually the time is designated so that the child has long enough to regain control and then re-enter the activity. This is not to suggest that the "time out" method will work for every situation, nor for every child. You, as the classroom teacher, know your children well and will be able to determine punishments, if necessary, that will be effective. If the children are interested and busy in their work, behavior problems should be nonexistent.

In order to be an effective teacher in the play environment, you will need to apply the information provided in this chapter. Effective instruction and management take practice: success does not occur overnight. Applying the principles of effective teaching will allow for high instruction time and little management time.

# Teaching Style

Choosing an appropriate teaching style is a matter of personal preference and is directly related to the selected subject matter. A teaching style represents the teacher's way of organizing and instructing children in the appropriate subject matter (Nichols, 2001, 1994; Kirchner & Fishburne, 2001, 1998, 1995). Teaching styles vary with different areas of the curriculum and the same teacher may use several different styles. Kirchner and Fishburne (1995) present the concept of three kinds of teaching styles: direct, combined and indirect. Each style represents a different degree of direction given by the teacher. In all cases the teacher directs the learning experience, but students have more choice in decision making with the combined and indirect methods of teaching.

Kirchner has developed his categories of teaching styles from the Mosston Spectrum of Teaching Styles (Mosston & Answorth, 1986) which is studied and used by those people who are preparing to be certified physical educators in the elementary school. Kirchner's styles are less detailed and are appropriate methods for use by the classroom teacher for physical education.

## DIRECT TEACHING

In this style the teacher tells the children what to do, when to do it, how to do it, and where to do it. He/she also tells the children why they are doing it. The teacher plans the lesson precisely and makes all of the decisions concerning the lesson. Beginning teachers like to use the direct method because it seems to demonstrate the most control over the class situation. A good example of the direct style would be teaching the children to hit a plastic whiffle ball off a batting tee. The children would be arranged in partners so that one child stands with bat in hand by the tee, the other child is 10–12 yards away "in the field." The teacher demonstrates the striking motion, gives auditory cues for the important points, and then asks the children to try the skill. As the children work, they hit the balls off the tees to the fielders who throw it back for the batters to hit again. The teacher walks behind the batters, helping by giving feedback to correct or enhance the quality of the swings the children are exhibiting. All children are learning the same kind of swing. The teacher's lesson plan will reflect every step taken in the lesson. The two scenarios presented at the beginning of this chapter represent the direct style of teaching. In the first situation, the tumbling class, all children are doing the same thing and working on the same goals. In the second situation, the children are working on different tasks at different stations, and, hence, are working on different skills, but all tasks are teacher designed and designated. Therefore, the direct teaching style focuses on teacher-selected learning experiences, and the children follow the directions given. This style is also characterized by expected performance characteristics in that it assumes that there is one right way and many wrong ways to perform in each area. Because of the teacher control in this style of teaching, it is often used if participation may involve danger of any kind, for example, archery.

## COMBINED STYLE

In this teaching style the teacher uses two different methods of teaching and switches between them throughout the lesson. The teacher decisions involve the organization of the learning experience and the selection of the skill concepts to be emphasized in the class period. In this format the teacher would introduce, for example, the overhand throw. She/he would then develop a series of questions or challenges to pose to the children such as "Can you throw the ball very high? Can you throw the ball very fast? Can you throw the ball straight overhead?" As the children try these different tasks they learn about various applications for the overhand throw, plus their attempts to meet the challenges are never incorrect. The children have the freedom to interpret the challenges on their own. Their trials are limited in that they must use the overhand throw.

The teacher will alternate between direct and indirect, teaching specifics and then allowing for experimentation with the skill. This method begins to allow for some creativity on the part of the children as they try to meet the different challenges that the teacher has given them. The teacher still plans her/his lesson, and thoroughly plans for the challenges to be offered to the children. She/he will still move through the teaching area and provide feedback to the children about their skills.

## INDIRECT STYLE

The indirect style of teaching changes the teacher from the <u>director</u> of the learning experience to a <u>guide</u> of the learning experience (Kirchner & Fishburne, 1995). This method of teaching works best when the objectives of the lesson are more global, such as, "the children will learn to travel in many different ways by using different body parts as support in the movement." In this lesson the children would learn about concepts such as which body parts, when combined, will provide the best base of support in traveling, how they might alternate body parts as they move (e.g., in a cartwheel children turn hand-hand-foot-foot), or which movement forms will be the most efficient. The teacher begins with broad objectives and uses movement challenges to lead the children to learn about the concepts stressed in the objective. "Can you travel in a way that both feet leave the floor at once? Can you find a way to travel so that every time you come to a corner of a mat, one hand touches the corner? Can you find a way to travel, leap into the air, and land softly?" Numerous movement challenges lead the children to discover what their bodies can do. This approach is more appealing to the creative child who finds many ways to meet the challenges. The difficulty for the teacher is in designing the challenges to keep the children interested and excited about what they are doing. This kind of teaching works best with dance and gymnastics concepts but may also be used for developing fundamental motor skills, and for teaching sport concepts. For example, "Can you and your partner find a way to travel on the court and keep the ball away from another player?" This indirect style encourages children to use their critical thinking skills.

## Class Rules And Safety Considerations

Over fifty percent (50%) of the accidents that occur at school happen in the physical education class. The closest rival area is that of the playground during recess and free playtime. The reason for the greater number of accidents in physical education is, of course, the fact that children are actively moving and are not sitting safely at desks in the classrooms.

There are many ways to "accident proof" a physical education class; however, no matter how careful you might be, an accident could still take place. There are several specific areas of which each teacher should be aware and keep actively up-to-date.

The most important area is supervision. The teacher must be with the students at all times. Beginning teachers are often told to develop "eyes in the back of the head" so that they can always see what is going on. Physical education teachers are taught to move around the learning area but to try to move at the perimeter and keep as much of the class in view as possible. Then, if an accident does occur, one can respond quickly, and, when questioned, say "Yes, I saw it happen," rather than expressing surprise that it happened in the class. There should be a defined, clear set of rules for behavior in physical education class, and the teacher should be rigorous in applying those rules. The children should understand what the rules are and why they are asked to behave in certain ways.

- Be aware of others moving around you.
- Avoid collisions at all costs.
- Be courteous to other players.
- Stay in self-space and avoid others' self-space.
- Be gentle with the equipment.
- Share equipment nicely when asked.
- Remember to put equipment away neatly and safely.
- Follow the rules of the games.
- Show respect for officials' decisions.

Just as rules are important in the classroom, physical education rules are extremely important in the gymnasium. It is very important to go over the rules to be followed in physical education on the very first day of class so that students will know what is expected of them as well as the consequences for rule infringements.

Physical education class rules should encourage children to respect others and their individual differences, to wear appropriate apparel for active participation, to listen to instructions and follow directions. Children should come into and leave the gym quietly, take care of and respect equipment, always be aware of safety precautions and use equipment properly. The teacher should help children to remember to follow the rules of good sportsmanship and to work as a team member.

Following through with safety rules is a major part of supervision. When you read about teaching behaviors, you learned about active supervision. You should recall that this means the teacher moves throughout the teaching space while observing AND giving performance-based feedback. Providing that feedback is a safety technique in itself: the children hear you and can tell that you are watching them.

Sometimes physical education classes are taught outside on the playground. Once again, the teacher must stay with the children. If a child becomes ill, have another student help him/her go in to see the nurse: the teacher does not go, as his/her responsibility is to the larger number of children. If a child takes off and leaves the group, the teacher does not go after the child. He/she sends two students in to report the incident to office personnel. Why two students? Depending on the distance the class is from the building itself, it is a good idea to send someone with a buddy. The teacher should watch them as they go to be sure that non-school personnel do not approach them in route. This is another part of supervision: protect the children from suspicious characters who might be outside the school. Unfortunately, this is necessary in today's society.

A second area of safety would be recognizing and pointing out hazardous areas in play spaces. Water on the floor, muddy areas, ditches to the side of play areas, broken glass and other debris could be dangerous for the children. A preliminary examination of the play space would help the teacher prepare for the class; some hazards could be eliminated and those that could not be eliminated could be pointed out to the children. An often-overlooked hazard in many elementary school gymnasiums is the lack of padded walls. Children should be cautioned against running into any walls, padded or not, but padding does help if a child loses control and runs into the wall.

A third area of particular importance deals with equipment. Physical education involves the use of many different pieces of equipment. It is your responsibility to check the equipment for any defects prior to use. A good example would be the use of beams or benches in educational gymnastics: are they sturdy as well as steady? Are there rough edges that may result in splintering? Individual equipment such as rackets or bats should be checked periodically. Within the equipment area comes the concept of wearing protective equipment. For example, eye guards should be worn when playing floor hockey; face and chest protectors should be worn by catchers in softball games; shin guards should be worn for soccer.

Schools have established rules for behavior as well as procedure. It is very important that you hold the students accountable to those rules. If a rule is broken and an accident occurs, you may be held liable for the occurrence. An example case tells of a child who was moving on playground equipment in the winter with mittens on his hands. The child fell and was injured. The courts ruled that the teacher in charge was liable as school rules called for "no gloves or mittens on playground equipment." Be careful about following school rules. In that same vein, be sure that children follow your gymnasium and classroom rules.

If an accident should occur in your physical education class, and a child is injured, you should do the following: treat for shock (cover to keep body temperature stable) and send two children to alert the school nurse and/or principal. If there is serious bleeding you should have rubber gloves immediately available and then you may apply direct pressure to stop the bleeding until the nurse arrives and takes over. In any case, do not move the child until the nurse or the principal assumes the responsibility for the move. Check with the school in which you are employed for specific procedures for emergency situations.

There is no excuse for ignorance of safety precautions. Every child has a right to a safe environment in which to pursue his/her education.

Effective teaching in the gymnasium does not really differ from effective teaching in the classroom. In both places it is essential that the teacher be able to manage efficiently to save time for instruction. As long as the teacher recognizes the need for slightly different techniques in a movement situation, the class will go well and run at the highest of efficiency.

# Summary

There is often a debate about which comes first, good management skills or good teaching skills. As you can see in this chapter, both are of equal importance in order to have an effective gymnasium. Good management skills allow for more teaching time, and, hopefully, more ALT–PE.

# References And Suggested Readings

Dawson–Rodriques, K., Lavay, B., Butt, K. & Lacourse, M. (1997). A plan to reduce transition time in physical education. *Journal of Physical Education, Recreation and Dance*, 68(9), 30–33.

Gallahue, D. (2005). *Developmental physical education for all children*. Human Kinetics.

Gallahue, D. (1997). *Developmental physical education for today's children*. McGraw Hill.

Gallahue, D. (1987). *Developmental physical education for today's children*. Macmillan.

Gray, G.R. (1995). Safety tips from the expert witness. *Journal of Health, Physical Education, Recreation and Dance*, 66(1), 18–21.

Grineski, S. (1992). What is a truly developmentally appropriate physical education program for children? *Journal of Physical Education, Recreation and Dance*, 63(6), 33–35.

Kirchner G. & Fishburne, G.J. (2001). *Physical education for elementary school children*. McGraw Hill.

Kirchner, G. & Fishburne, G.J. (1998). *Physical education for elementary school children*. McGraw-Hill.

Kirchner, G. & Fishburne, G.J. (1995). *Physical education for elementary school children*. Brown & Benchmark.

Lambdin, D. (1989). Shuffling the deck, a flexible system for class organization. *Journal of Physical Education, Recreation and Dance*, 60(4), 25–28.

Manross, D. & Templeton, C.L. (1997). Expertise in teaching physical education. *Journal of Physical Education, Recreation and Dance*, 68(3), 29–35.

Mosston, M. & Arnsworth, S. (2001). *Teaching physical education*. Allyn & Bacon.

Mosston, M. & Arnsworth, S. (1986). *Teaching physical education*. Merrill.

Nichols, B. (2001). *Moving and learning: The elementary school physical education experience*. McGraw Hill.

Nichols, B. (1994). *Moving and learning: The elementary school physical education experience*. Times Mirror/Mosby.

Nichols, B. (1990). *Moving and learning*. Times Mirror/Mosby.

Pangranzi, R. P. (2007). *Dynamic physical education for elementary school children*. Benjamin-Cummings.

Pangrazi, R.P. (2003). *Dynamic physical education for elementary school children*. San Francisco: Benjamin Cummings.

Pangrazi, R.P. (1998). *Dynamic physical education for elementary school children*. Needham: Allyn & Bacon.

Pangrazi, R. P. & Dauer, V. P. (1992). *Dynamic physical education for elementary school children*. New York: Macmillan.

Pangrazi, R.P. & Dauer, V.P. (1995). *Dynamic physical education for elementary school children*. Needham Heights: Allyn and Bacon.

Petersen, S.C. (1992). The sequence of instruction in games: Implications for developmental appropriateness. *Journal of Health, Physical Education, Recreation and Dance*, 63(6), 36–39.

Phillips, D.A. & Carlisle, C. (1987). *The physical education teaching assessment instrument*. Greely: University of Northern Colorado.

Ratliffe, T., Ratliffe, L. & Bie, B. (1991). Creating a learning environment: Class management strategies for elementary physical education teachers. *Journal of Physical Education, Recreation and Dance*, 62(9), 24–27.

Siedentop, D. & Tannehill, D. (2001). *Developing teaching skills in physical education* Boston: McGraw Hill.

Siedentop, D. & Tannehill, D. (1999). *Developing teaching skills in physical education*. Mountain View: Mayfield.

Siedentop, D. (1991). *Developing teaching skills in physical education*. Mountain View: Mayfield.

Siedentop, D., Herkowitz, J. & Rink, J. (1984). *Elementary physical education methods*. Englewood Cliffs: Prentice-Hall.

Siegenthaler, K.L. (1996). Supervising activities for safety. *Journal of Physical Education, Recreation and Dance*, 67(7), 29–30 and 36.

Wall, J. & Murray, N. (1993). *Children and movement*. Boston: McGraw Hill.

Wall, J. & Murray, N. (1989). *Children and movement*. Dubuque: Wm. C. Brown.

Williams, N.F. (1996). The physical education hall of shame, part III: Inappropriate teaching practices. *Journal of Physical Education, Recreation and Dance*, 67(8), 45–48.

CHAPTER

# 3

# Perceptual-Motor Development

It is commonly known that human beings function on a stimulus-response basis. Since such stimuli must be received and understood in order to elicit responses the perceptual system (efficiency of the senses) must be functioning well within the human body's central nervous system. Therefore, all movements may be described as perceptual-motor in nature. And, research has shown that perceptual-motor abilities are important to cognitive growth. It has been demonstrated that perceptual-motor abilities are definitely related to academic readiness. Hence, the relationship that stands between perceiving (cognitive) and performing (motor) is not in the least bit negligible and is extremely important for the elementary school teacher to know.

## A Definition of Perceptual-Motor Development

Perceptual-motor development refers to the increasing ability of the child to perceive sensory stimuli, transmit same to the appropriate area of the brain through the afferent nerve tracts, interpret and process the signals in the appropriate association areas, and then to initiate the correct motor response by sending information from the motor cortex via the efferent nerve tracts to the muscles needed to effect the movement. The child responds in kind to stimulation from the environment in order to function effectively and efficiently, and as he/she grows older and more experienced the child will refine this system to enhance effective and efficient movement qualities (Gallahue, 1982, 1987; Williams, 1983).

A simple example of a perceptual-motor response would be when the child touches a hot stove, the signal is received through the tactile sensory receptors (sense of touch), is sent upward through the sensory nerve tracts to the brain, is interpreted and sent to the motor cortex where a motor response is organized and sent back down the motor pathways to the muscles to cause the child to withdraw his/her hand from the stove. Since the child is a complex being, this action-reaction occurs within milliseconds and rarely is the child burned severely.

# Importance of Perceptual-Motor Development to Cognitive Learning

You have read that perceptual-motor development is directly related to cognitive growth. Such learning begins in the Sensorimotor Period as defined by Piaget, when the infant learns about the world through movement and exploration, and progresses in that learning throughout early and later childhood. All information that a child, or for that matter an adult, takes in comes via the sensory systems. This development involves primarily the tactile-kinesthetic system (touch and awareness of body position), the auditory system (hearing) and the visual system (seeing). It is important that you understand how the process begins at birth in order to see the progression in learning and where you, as the elementary teacher, will step in to the progression.

## TACTILE AND VISUAL EXPLORATION

The infant first relies on the tactile-kinesthetic sense to learn about the world, by limited movement within the environment. The child learns about texture, temperature, weight, etc. through explorations primarily with the hands. As the child moves through the early years, this reliance on tactile-kinesthetic information continues to aid him/her in movements and reactions to the environment. The child's reliance on tactile-kinesthetic information is assisted by that of visual reliance as the child develops efficiency of coordination of the visual system in order to receive and interpret information in the environment. The young child then begins to coordinate visual information in such a way as to guide movement behaviors. Since the adult human being is known to be a primarily visual animal, this early use of the visual system begins the progression to development of the highly efficient visual system that we know as adults (Williams, 1983).

## INTERSENSORY   INTEGRATION

The young child is also developing efficiency in auditory, gustatory and olfactory senses, and gradually learns to use more than one sense at a time. Intersensory integration allows the child to receive information from two or more perceptual systems at the same time (Williams, 1983). The contributions of the gustatory and olfactory senses to the basic movement repertoire of the child are quite negligible, but the auditory sense becomes very important to the child. Since the child can receive information through more than one sense at the same time, the child's learning is enriched. For example, the child as early as 6 years of age will learn to perform a task best by watching a demonstration (visual) when the demonstration is accompanied by verbal cues (auditory).

## INTRASENSORY INTEGRATION

At the same time the child is growing in the ability to use intersensory integration, he/ she is refining his/her abilities in each sensory area. Neurologically, the tactile-kinesthetic areas of the brain are most highly developed first in infancy, followed by the auditory cortex, and then, after approximately six months, the visual cortex. This is not to say that development is complete at this time, but rather is progressing as the child moves from infant to early childhood, and from early childhood on to later childhood. The systems continue to increase in efficiency. Research indicates that from 3 to 8 years of age, children rely heavily on the visual sense for the majority of information and they are considered to be in a crucial development for perceptual-motor skills. In addition, the ages from 3 to 6 are crucial in the areas of auditory and tactile-kinesthetic refinement (Williams, 1983).

# Visual-Motor Coordination

As previously noted, the child learns best visually, especially in the preschool and early childhood years. This reliance on visual information is of particular importance to the learning of skills in physical education.

## VISUAL ACUITY

Visual acuity refers to the sharpness, or detail of the visual image that the child is receiving. Since the eyeball is not at its most spheroid shape, the child will tend to be a bit farsighted. Therefore detail will be perceived better at greater distances, implying that a young child will be able to see objects better farther away and that as such objects travel toward the child some detail will be lost (DeOreo & Williams, 1980b). Visual acuity is at its height of development by ages 10–12 (Payne & Isaacs, 2001, 1995, 1991; Williams, 1983). Since most physical activities that the child will pursue will involve visual-motor coordination (the eyes guide the response), it is important to understand that the farsightedness is a normal condition at this age and will affect achievement.

## VISUAL FIGURE-GROUND PERCEPTION

This perceptual aspect refers to the child's ability to see objects as distinct from their backgrounds. This phenomenon is illustrated in the games of hidden pictures where children try to find the objects disguised within the drawings. Figure-ground perception is also an extremely important component in being able to read. The child must have the ability to see the words and letters as separate from their background pages. Visual acuity contributes to this ability as well. Children have been shown to be more ground than figure-oriented until approximately 10–13 years of age which coincides with the precise development of visual acuity (Deoreo & Williams, 1980b). In physical education, it is very important that the child be able to see a ball as separate from its background; he/ she must be able to distinguish appropriate targets; and, eventually, will need to be able to distinguish teammates from other players in the game.

## OCULOMOTOR TRACKING

The oculomotor system consists of muscles to the eyeball that are responsible for moving the eye. As the muscles work to cause the eye to follow, or track, the movement of an object, kinesthetic receptors in the muscles provide information to the brain regarding the speed, size, distance and trajectory (arc) of the object (Gabbard, 1992; Payne & Isaacs, 1995, 1991). "Keep your eye on the ball" is often heard in gymnasiums, cueing the child for tracking the object in question.

## COINCIDENCE-ANTICIPATION TIMING

As the child tracks the ball, the information given by the oculomotor muscles gives the child the cues necessary to successfully intercept the object. Coincidence-anticipation refers to the child's ability to perceive where the object will be at the appropriate time and to move or adjust body position in order to contact or catch the object (Gabbard, 1992; Payne & Isaacs, 1991, 1995, 1991). Coincidence-anticipation is the result of the visual-motor process. We more commonly refer to this ability as eye-hand or eye-foot coordination.

## AN INTEGRATED EXAMPLE

Probably the best example of visual-motor coordination would be the catching of a ball. First the child must be able to see the ball (visual acuity) and perceive it as separate from its background (figure-ground perception). Then, as the ball travels toward the child, the child tracks the ball (oculomotor muscle system) and thus receives cues regarding the flight characteristics of the ball, such as speed, trajectory and distance. Vision guides the ball into the child's hands where the ball is secured (coincidence-anticipation timing). Thus, the act of catching a ball is actually a complex perceptual-motor task. To illustrate the importance of visual-motor coordination to physical activity, consider the position of a 9-year-old Little League baseball player, standing in right field. As the batter comes to the plate, the right fielder assumes the ready position that the coach has taught, bent forward, head up, hands on knees. The batter contacts the ball. As the ball comes off the bat, our fielder detects the ball through the use of visual acuity and figure-ground perception. He/she knows that the ball is coming toward right field because his/her oculomotor system transmits cues concerning the speed, direction and trajectory of the ball. The information moves from the visual receptors to the brain for processing: decision making skills must be quick. The fielder must anticipate and predict where the ball is going and when it will arrive. Decisions must be made regarding where to go to intercept the ball, the best way to catch the ball, and what to do with the ball once the catch has been made. Catching a ball in this situation has become a sophisticated task involving decision making, and the child needs to have developed the basic skills prior to having to use them in a stressful game situation.

# Auditory Perception

Some children may be auditory learners so that hearing is the primary mode for their acquisition of knowledge and skills. There are considerably less children in the population who learn through the auditory mode. Although the auditory perceptual mechanism is not as important in the learning of physical skills as is the visual mechanism, it does have importance in providing supplementary information. Children usually have well established and efficient auditory perception by age 10 (Williams, 1983).

## AUDITORY   ACUITY

In the auditory mode, acuity refers to the ability to detect the presence of sound (Williams, 1983). Children may vary in the distance that they may hear sounds, so it is important that the teacher recognize problems in this area.

## AUDITORY FIGURE-GROUND PERCEPTION

The auditory mechanism allows the child to discriminate relevant information from background noise (Williams, 1983). For example, the child can distinguish the teacher's directions from background noise or chatter. This ability is of particular importance in a gymnasium or on a playing field where noise may be a problem.

## LOCALIZATION

Localization refers to the ability of the child to detect from where sounds are coming, linking sounds and their sources (Williams, 1983). On a playing field it is important to be able to hear and know where teammates are who are open.

## DISCRIMINATION

Auditory discrimination is important to the child in that it is essential for the understanding of speech, pitch and loudness (Williams, 1983).

## AN INTEGRATED EXAMPLE

A 7-year-old child is learning to jump a long rope. The child stands sideways to the rope, directly in the center, facing a turner. The rope should swing from the jumper's left to the right in the learning phase since the child is learning to track from left to right in reading skills and will help in transfer of skills. As the rope is overhead, the turner says "jump!" This timing allows the child to use his/her auditory acuity, figure-ground perception, and discrimination to send the signal to the motor cortex to elicit a jump at the right time.

Whenever a child is learning a physical skill it is important that the demonstration be accompanied by auditory cues. The more sensory channels employed by the user, the better the learning that will occur.

# Tactile-Kinesthetic Awareness

Tactile-kinesthetic awareness refers to the ability of the child to sense the different positions of the body and various body parts, as well as range and speed of movement. The kinesthetic system is intimately related to the tactile system; working together, the combination of both systems is referred to as haptic perception (Williams, 1983). Kinesthetic awareness is basically reflexive; the child is not directly aware of the system nor of its role in movement. This awareness is of particular importance to the learning of physical skills because the child must be aware of the positions of various body parts in the execution of a physical skill in order to coordinate the movement. Children 12 years of age are usually mature in this ability (Gabbard, 2003,1992).

## PROPRIOCEPTORS

Sensory receptors that are located in the skin, deep tissue, joints, muscles and inner ear are called proprioceptors. They send signals through afferent tracts to the brain to help the child receive information about body position in the external environment as well as information about objects within that space (DeOreo,& Williams, 1980b; Gabbard, 2003, 1992).

## BALANCE, SPEED AND POSITION

The proprioceptors in the inner ear, called the vestibular system, send signals constantly to the brain regarding the position of the head with regard to balance (Gabbard, 2003, 1992). When a signal is received that indicates the body is off balance, the motor response is primarily reflexive and draws the body quickly back to a balanced position. These same sense organs provide information about speed of movement and range of movement (Gabbard, 2003, 1992; Williams, 1983).

## AN INTEGRATED EXAMPLE

A child is having difficulty with coordination in the skill of overhand throwing. Demonstration and auditory cues have been ineffective so the teacher takes the child's arm and moves it through the correct pattern for the overhand throw. The child "feels" the movement, and repeats the movement over and over, first with assistance and then on his/her own so that he/she can consciously help direct the proprioceptors to send the appropriate signals to the brain. For some reason the child had not been receiving appropriate signals from the proprioceptors. When all perceptual systems are working efficiently, the kinesthetic system would be working to allow the child to copy a demonstrated movement. A child with good tactile-kinesthetic awareness will demonstrate sound balance, and smoothly coordinated motor skills. These three perceptual systems are of extreme importance in the growth and development of the child in all three domains. As the child interacts with his/her environment, all three major sense areas will be honed for efficiency, the quality dependent on the practice environment that is available to the child. The crucial developmental period of 3–8 years of age places accent on the preschool and primary grade years.

# Development of Perceptual-Motor Concepts

Movement plays a key role in the development of perceptual-motor concepts. Learning of these concepts contributes considerably to cognitive growth in academic areas. As children

become efficient movers in these areas, they are able to take the concepts from large spatial areas, such as a gymnasium, and reduce them to the smaller planes of pencil and paper.

## SPATIAL  AWARENESS

Children need to develop an awareness of space and of where they can fit in relation to the space available (Gabbard, 2003, 1992; Gallahue, 1987; Payne & Isaacs, 2001, 1995, 1991). At first children learn about *self-space*, the physical area that the body assumes which may be described as a bubble. Whenever the child moves, the bubble moves and that self-space travels surrounding the child. Since the space is personal, it cannot extend into others' self-spaces, and children learn to control their own movements, avoiding any possible collisions with people or equipment. Children who have poor concepts of spatial awareness may be termed "clumsy," and may constantly bump into objects in the environment. Children learn that when the self-space travels that it moves into *general space*. This space belongs to everyone and it should be respected, i.e., no collisions allowed. As children move during various games and activities, they experience the movement of self-space as well as the changing dimensions of that space. For example, an obstacle course may cause the child to move over or under objects; the child may need to crawl through a tunnel, or roll on a mat. These different roles cause the child to alter that self-space. Through experience in games such as tag or soccer that cause the child to move with and around others, he/she learns about space and his/her role within that space. Once the child learns about the spatial areas of the physical world, he/she can reduce those dimensions to apply them to writing skills. The same principles apply to placing letters and numbers in the correct spatial orientation on paper. Children learn to place letters in spaces defined by certain lines; they learn to place answers to mathematical problems in exact spaces. The child who has difficulty with spatial awareness in movement is most likely to have difficulty with writing skills.

## BODY AWARENESS

Body awareness refers to the child's knowledge of the body, its parts, and what they can do (Gabbard, 2003, 1992; Gallahue, 1987; Payne & Isaacs, 2001, 1995, 1991; Siedentop, et al, 1984). This learning begins in infancy and early childhood when we play the game of "So Big" with the child, and we teach him/her about parts such as nose, ears, eyes, etc. By 9 years of age most children can clearly identify all body parts and can state their uses (Gabbard, 2003, 1992). Inside the mind of the child is the *body schema*. This is an internal vision or picture that the child has of the body. This has been formed in the mind of the child as he/she grows and moves (DeOreo & Williams, 1980a; Williams, 1983). Of course this schema changes and alters with the child's age and is definitely related to societal influences regarding the perfect body. A child with only one arm may have a body schema with two arms; this may indicate that he/she may have difficulty accepting himself/ herself.

Whenever the child compares his/her self-perception to that of the body schema, there is an emotional reaction. This is referred to as the *body image*. The way the child feels about self is a major component in the body image (DeOreo & Williams, 1980a; Siedentop, Herkowitz & Rink, 1984). The child evaluates his/her own physical attributes and abilities, and he/she develops an attitude regarding self. This attitude appears to grow more specific as the child ages.

In order to assess body schema and body image, you should ask the child to draw a picture of himself/herself. You can then see if the child has a knowledge of what body parts should exist, although caution must be exercised in interpretation of the picture. If the child is asked to draw a picture of self, this may not be the same picture as that of what he/she would like to be. Also, often children who wear glasses draw themselves without the glasses; children in wheelchairs draw themselves standing up. The teacher should discuss the drawing with the child to determine if the child really knows what a body should look like; perhaps the emotional component of body image is impairing the child's knowledge of body awareness.

## DIRECTIONAL   AWARENESS

As the child moves the self-space bubble in general space, an understanding of directional awareness is developed. This refers to the knowledge of range of body size, location of objects and people in space in relation to self, and specific spatial relationships such as left and right dimensions (Gabbard, 2003, 1992; Gallahue, 1987; Payne & Isaacs, 2001, 1995, 1991).

### *Laterality*

Laterality refers to an inner awareness of two sides of the body. Children recognize that there are two arms, two legs, two eyes, two ears, etc. but can they acknowledge that they are on opposite sides of the body? Activities to enhance laterality teach children that arms and legs can move simultaneously or independently of each other. Coordinated movement calls for understanding of laterality (Gabbard, 2003, 1992; Gallahue, 1987; Payne & Isaacs, 2001, 1995, 1991; Williams, 1983). For example, when making Angels-in-the-Snow, the child lies on his/ her back, legs together and arms at sides. He/she then moves arms and legs out to the sides simultaneously, thus creating an image of an angel on the floor. Variations of this activity teach children about laterality. For example the child may practice moving both arms only, both legs only, left arm and leg only, right arm and leg only, left arm and right leg, right arm

and left leg. As the child works through this series of variations, he/she is developing the ability to recognize laterality as well as to cross the *midline.*

Each of us has an imaginary vertical *midline* that bisects the body into left and right halves, and an imaginary horizontal *midline* that divides the body into top and bottom halves. A child who has difficulty with laterality tasks, and with tracking tasks (such as moving the eyes from left to right to follow an object) has a midline problem. The greatest development of the ability to cross the midline seems to be 5–7 years of age when children are learning fundamental motor skills (Williams, 1983).

As the child walks and swings the arms in opposition to the legs, he/she is crossing the vertical midline. In effect this is the same action as Angels-in-the-Snow where the child moves left arm and right leg, or right arm and left leg. If a child does not swing arms in opposition to legs as he/she walks, a midline problem should be suspected. If you suspect a midline problem, you should ask the child to creep on hands and knees on the floor: the oppositional pattern should be displayed in this most basic movement pattern. Children may be taught to cross the midline through activities that stress the oppositional pattern: walking, running, throwing, kicking, etc.

Problems with the horizontal midline are less prevalent. A child may have difficulty in bending down to touch toes, or in the more complicated action of touching left hand to right toe, right hand to left toe. Horizontal midline problems are more noticeable in fine motor cognitive tasks. For example, a child may not be able to do mathematical problems if they are in the vertical format whereas problems written horizontally are no problem.

A sixth grade teacher told the story of Katie, a learning disabled child in her class. The teacher was working on basic math facts with Katie and the child was to solve the problem of 3 + 1 and in response Katie had written h. The teacher pointed to the numbers, one at a time, and said, "Katie, how much is 3 plus 1?" Katie replied, "h." The teacher then rewrote the problem as follows: 3 + 1 = and in response Katie wrote 4. There may be evidence of two problems here: the inability to cross the horizontal midline and answer a problem in a vertical format, and, "h" may be interpreted as an upside down and reversed 4. Children who do have such problems can be encouraged to do exercises and activities such as tumbling or windmills which cause them to physically cross the horizontal midline.

### Right-Left Discrimination

Right-Left Discrimination is a spatial area in which children relate to objects and other people. Usually the ability to identify left-right dimensions in self and others may not be efficient until 8–9 years of age (Williams, 1983) First the child learns left and right as they apply to his/her own body. Then the child learns to apply directional concepts into the environment, e.g., the teacher is to the left of the desk. Left and right discrimination needs to be taught and can be learned successfully only if the child is proficient in laterality.

## Directionality

Directionality refers to concepts of up/down, over/under, in front of/in back of, etc. It is an extension of left-right discrimination (Gabbard, 2003, 1992; Gallahue, 1987; Payne & Isaacs, 2001, 1995, 1991; Williams, 1983). Teachers might encourage the development of these concepts through activities in which the child must follow a series of directions: "Go UNDER the table, AROUND the cone, THROUGH the tire, jump OVER the hurdle, etc. The child might be encouraged to repeat the verbal directions, further enhancing his learning of those concepts.

Directionality also contributes to the child's ability to read and write. In our society, reading progresses from left to right. The child needs to be able to orient himself/herself on the page and to progress in this fashion. In writing, young children often make letters and numbers backwards. This is called reversal. Reversals demonstrate the child's lack of understanding of the directional concepts as designated above; or, if the understanding is present, it may be understood only on the larger body movement scale and the child may have difficulty applying the directional concepts to a writing mode. Therefore, the child with reversals may not understand the spatial concepts, or may lack the fine-motor coordination to draw letters and numbers within spatial constraints. Reversals are quite common in the five-year-old child but are matters of concern for the six-year-old. An example of a directionality exercise for a child with reversal problems would be to progress from a gross motor (large muscle) activity to a fine-motor (small muscles) activity. The teacher would have the child make the required letter or number with a long jump rope. The child would then walk on the form in the way that it would be written. The child then makes the same form with a small jump rope, then with a strip of playdoh, then with a pencil on paper. Continuing with activities such as this will help the child to learn to avoid or recognize reversals in the academic world. If the child forms the number or letter incorrectly at any stage of the above progression, the teacher should tell the child the form is backwards and should have the child correct it. Physically moving the form from backwards to forwards causes the child to remember the correct pattern.

## Summary

Traditionally perceptual-motor programs have been designated as either "concept developing" or "concept reinforcing" (Gallahue, 1982). "Concept developing" programs were designed for children who needed extra help in growth and development of perceptual-motor skills. These children may have been raised in overprotective environments where the opportunities were not prevalent for their participation in movement activities to enhance development. "Concept reinforcing" programs represent the traditional curricula of preschools and kindergartens where these perceptual-motor concepts are actively used and taught by knowledgeable teachers. Any activity that is found in this book will promote sound perceptual-motor development. Specific activities for concept developing programs may be found in Chapter Fifteen, "Activities for Perceptual-Motor Development."

Although more technical in nature, this chapter is extremely important for understanding the nature of teaching and learning. Once you can see how the brain processes the information that is perceived, you can understand your role in presenting the best information to the child.

## References and Suggested Readings

Deoreo, K. & Williams, H.G. (1980a). Characteristics of visual perception. In Corbin, C.B. (Ed.) *A textbook of motor development*. W.C. Brown.

Deoreo, K. & Williams, H.G. (1980b). Characteristics of kinesthetic perception. In Corbin, C.B. (Ed.) *A textbook of motor development*.W.C. Brown

Gabbard, C.P. (2003). *Lifelong motor development.* Benjamin-Cummings.

Gabbard, C. (1992). *Lifelong motor development.* Wm. C. Brown.

Gallahue, D. L. (2005). *Developmental physical education for all children*. Human Kinetics.

Gallahue, D. (1997). *Developmental physical education for today's children*. McCraw-Hill.

Gallahue, D.L. (1987). *Developmental physical education for today's elementary school children*. Macmillan.

Gallahue, D.L. (1982). *Understanding motor development in children*. Wiley.

Payne, V.G. & Isaacs, L.D. (2007). *Human motor development: A lifespan approach*. McGraw-Hill.

Payne, V.G. & Isaacs, L.D. (2001). *Human motor development: A lifespan approach*. Mayfield.

Payne, V.G. & Isaacs, L.D. (2001). *Human motor development: A lifespan approach.* Mayfield.

Payne, V. G. & Isaacs, L.D. (1991). *Human motor development: A lifespan approach.* Mayfield.

Siedentop, D., Herkowitz, J. & Rink, J. (1984). *Elementary physical education methods.* Prentice-Hall.

Williams, H.G. (1983). *Perceptual and motor development.* Prentice-Hall.

CHAPTER

# 4

# Fundamental Motor Skills

Have you ever watched a child run? Or throw a ball? Have you ever watched to see what motor skills children use in their day-to-day playtime? In order for children to function as efficient and effective movers in the environment, they must first achieve competence in fundamental motor skills. These skills form the movement repertoire that the child needs to play successfully with friends and classmates.

## Definition of Fundamental Motor Skills

The fundamental motor skills are the building blocks for all future movement endeavors. These seven skills provide the stepping stones to other movement forms that children commonly employ in play and sport (Gabbard, 2003, 1992; Gallahue, 1987; Payne & Isaacs, 2001, 1995, 1991; Siedentop, et al, 1984; Wickstrom, 1983). These skills are: walk, run, jump, throw, catch, strike and kick.

Each fundamental motor skill has a defined process: once a child has developed proficiency in the fundamental skill, he/she then begins to adjust and adapt it for different uses. For example, once the child learns the fundamental overhand throw, he/she may then learn to adjust the action for more distance, or for more speed. The child may learn to throw sidearm, or a curve ball. He/she may adjust the action from a softball to a football, and eventually to a flying disc! The child will be able to adapt the movement and refine it for use in different games and sports.

Most children are physically able to perform the skills efficiently by age 6, if their early environmental experiences included experience in motor skills. Efficient performance for the fundamental skill for both the child and the adult is the same: obviously the 6-year-old child will not be able to exert as much force as will an older child or an adult, but the basic pattern is the same. And, acquisition of these skills is definitely dependent on previous experiences. Since all children do not have the same environmental experiences, many do not have efficient control of the basic fundamental skills upon entering school and it is essential that the young elementary child receive instruction and movement experiences involving these skills through the physical education program. Age expectations for performance of motor skills for 3-5 year-olds can be found in the Preschool Activity Chapter.

**BASIC MOVEMENT SKILL REPERTOIRE**

| LOCOMOTOR | MANIPULATIVE | NON-LOCOMOTOR |
|-----------|--------------|---------------|
| Run | Catch | Bend-Stretch |
| Jump | Strike | Twist-Turn |
| Hop | Kick | Swing-Sway |
| Leap | Bounce | |
| Gallop | | |
| Slide | | |
| Skip | | |

# Observing The Fundamental Motor Skills

Once you become familiar with the performance points of the fundamental motor skills, you will be able to watch children move and will be able to pick out errors that may be occurring. General observation of a class moving in general space performing different movements as designated by the teacher will lead the teacher to be able to pick out those who have difficulty with selected movements.

When you have decided where the problem areas are, you would begin to intervene to help the children achieve efficient patterns of movement. To do this, you would provide a wide range of movement experiences to encourage development of proper form and execution of the skill in question. For those children who can already perform the fundamental motor skills efficiently, the wide range of movement activities would serve as a refining time for skills. A suggested evaluation form can be found at the end of the chapter.

# Importance of the Contralateral Pattern

In Chapter Three we talked about the importance of the child's ability to cross the midline. This is a crucial area of perceptual-motor development that contributes to the child's achieving sound levels of coordinated movements. The ability to smoothly cross the midline indicates that the child has good neurological development. The contralateral pattern refers to motion in which the left arm and right leg work together as do the right arm and left leg. The first stage of development of the contralateral pattern can be seen in the crawling and creeping motion of the child when hands move in opposition to knees. Then, as the child walks, arms swing in opposition to each other. Coordinated movement calls for him/her to swing the left arm forward when the right leg steps forward, and visa versa. When the child runs, the same pattern is evidenced as arm swing becomes synchronized with opposite leg action. When the child throws a ball, he/she exhibits the contralateral pattern by stepping forward with the foot opposite the throwing arm. In kicking a ball, the child swings the opposite arm through as the foot contacts the ball and follows through. Finally, in striking tasks, such as swinging a bat, the child steps sideways toward the oncoming object with the foot that is opposite the dominant striking hand (i.e., the right-handed batter steps with the left foot). The remaining fundamental motor skills, jumping and catching, do not have a contralateral pattern but rather are bilateral coordination skills, where the arms and legs work together in parallel.

The child who does not have a contralateral pattern will be awkward in movements. He/she may exhibit homolateral (arm and leg on same side synchronized) patterns, or, in some cases, no patterns at all. Some children keep hands in their pockets, or keep arms stiff at their sides when moving. This is not a normal coordination pattern and needs remediation. The contralateral pattern should be the first observation point for these five fundamental motor skills.

## Initial, Transitional and Mature Movement

In fundamental motor skills, children will display initial, transitional or mature patterns of movement (Sherrill, 1993). An initial pattern refers to one that is acceptable and appropriate for the age of the child and usually refers to movement patterns typically displayed by children under five years of age. It is one that would not be acceptable in an older child. A transitional pattern is one in which the child exhibits some deficiencies in performance and the movement is not mechanically efficient. A mature pattern follows a generally accepted form as described in this chapter. These performance points have been generally accepted by motor development specialists as being biomechanically correct (Gabbard, 2003, 1992; Gallahue, 1987, 1982; Payne & Isaacs, 2001, 1995, 1991; Wickstrom, 1983). It is important for you to remember that these skills form the base for the development of more advanced sport skills. The child will learn to build upon the base by varying the skills for different situations.

## Performance Points for Fundamental Motor Skills

Each fundamental motor skill pattern is described in the following sections. Ideas for appropriate teaching progressions and intervention are given for each skill. Whenever possible, the skill should be practiced in a <u>closed environment</u>. This means that the environment has no effect on the performance of the skill, i.e. practice striking with a bat off a tee, rather than from a pitch. Also, equipment used for these basic skills should be developmentally appropriate: yarn balls for throwing; lightweight plastic paddles or bats for striking, larger colorful non-threatening balls for catching. Once the skill is achieved in a closed situation, the child can progress to an <u>open learning environment</u>.

## *Walking*

The walk is a basic fundamental motor skill that is acquired naturally in the environment. As the child walks, the arms swing in opposition to the legs (contralateral pattern) and the weight transfers from heel to toe during the step. Because the walk is very basic and familiar to most people, an elaborate biomechanical analysis is not necessary. You should be able to observe children walking and immediately notice if problems are evident.

Example activities for teaching or exploring the walk would include:

1.  Walking forward, emphasizing the swing of the arms in opposition
2.  Walking forward, backward, sideways in general space
3.  Walking in the imitation of animals: bear, dog, etc.
4.  Walking creatively, i.e., on a windy day, an icy day, in deep snow, etc.
5.  Walking with a partner, walking in a group
6.  Walking at different levels: high, medium, low
7.  Walking at different speeds, different strides, i.e., giant steps, baby steps
8.  Walking with weight on different parts of the feet, i.e., toes, balls of feet, heels, sides

*Cues:  heel to toe, swing arms*

During each activity you should be discussing with the children how each kind of walk feels, which is easiest, etc. Exploring the different forms of walking gives the child the opportunity to understand why the fundamental pattern is most efficient.

## *Running*

The run is another skill that develops naturally as the child grows and matures, but some instruction will help to increase the efficiency of the skill. When running, the child should exhibit the contralateral pattern, carrying his/her arms close to the body, swinging in a vertical plane and in opposition to the legs. The toes should point straight ahead and contact with the ground should be on the ball of the foot, near the toe. There should be a flight phase in the run, during which the child is airborne for a minimal amount of time. The knees should be lifted close to 90 degrees and the body should be inclined forward slightly. There should be limited movement of head and trunk.

Example activities for the exploration and development of running skill would include the following:

1.  Running slowly with emphasis on swinging arms in opposition to legs
2.  Running with arms in different positions, i.e., overhead, out to sides, behind back
3.  Racing a designated distance to crash through a finish line
4.  Running in general space with all members of the class moving at the    same time
5.  Running and tag games

*Cues:  ball of foot, swing arms*

In order to teach running on a closed skill basis, the child should run in a straight line through an obstacle-free environment. The skill becomes open when the child must run at the same time as other children or when the ground surface is not smooth or straight, i.e., outside on fitness trails.

The run is a difficult skill to isolate and children will usually demonstrate their most mature patterns when speed is required. Thus, encouraging the child to run as fast as possible will elicit the dominant running pattern. Usually this will be the child's most efficient form. The use of a finish line in racing encourages continued force production by the runner. Running in alleys defined by crepe paper lines or strings would be very useful for the child who swings his/her arms out to the side when running, instead of swinging properly on the vertical plane.

## *Jumping*

The standing long jump is the form of jumping most likely to be built upon for more complex skills. It is basic in the progressive development of skills, being prerequisite to the hop. The standing long jump is the first form of jumping exhibited by the child. The child should begin with a deep crouch, arms back behind the body. The takeoff should be from two feet with arms swinging forward and carrying the inclined body into the air in a forward direction. In flight the legs should come up and forward and the child should land with weight forward, knees bending to absorb the force of the two-foot landing. Eyes should focus on the landing area.

Example activities for the development of jumping skill would include:

1. Jumping down from various heights
2. Jumping from a line for maximum distance
3. Jumping over different distances as described in "Crossing the Brook," (Chapter 8)
4. Jumping in and out (forward, sideways, backwards) of hula hoops placed on the floor
5. Jumping over obstacles of varied heights
6. Jumping in games adapted for the jumping skill, i.e., vary any running or tag games so that the children jump instead of run

*Cues: crouch, arms back, swing arms, push, land softly*

Special activities for intervention may help a child who is earthbound; this means that the child cannot take off from the ground with two feet at the same time, or he/she may not be able to leave the ground at all. These children may be helped by stepping down from various heights, bouncing on mini-trampolines, or by the use of an imaginary techniques such as "placing bubble gum between the feet to stick them together." Mini-trampolines may be set in a row and the child may jump from one to the next. Objects may be suspended over a jumping area to encourage a child to reach up and tap the object on take-off. Hoop patterns may be made on the floor to encourage jumping from one to the other.

## *Throwing*

The overhand throw is the basic throwing pattern from which other propulsion skills will emerge. Numerous childhood games incorporate the throw as a necessary skill. In the mature pattern of the overhand throw, the child holds the ball in line with the ear and shoulder, the elbow is back behind the shoulder, and the body is rotated back from the waist. The child stands with the foot opposite the throwing arm slightly ahead of the other. As the elbow begins to move forward on a horizontal plane the opposite foot steps forward, the body begins a forward rotation starting with the hips and on up to the shoulders as the arm moves forward, releasing the ball with a snap of the wrist, and following through across the body. A forceful throw may be accompanied by a step forward with the back foot as a follow-through move.

Example activities for the development or refinement of throwing may include:

1. Standing facing the target with one end of a jump rope held in the throwing hand at the shoulder and the other end of the rope on the floor behind, step with the opposite foot and swing the jump rope over the shoulder toward the target
2. Standing with the non-throwing side toward the target, then step and throw a ball to the target
3. Throwing balls at various targets
4. Throwing balls for different distances
5. Throwing balls at different levels
6. Playing games such as "Snowball," "Meteorite Blast," and "Pin Bombardment" (Chapter Eight)

    *Cues: arm back, step, throw*

 If a child is having difficulty stepping with the opposite foot, you may place footprints on the floor showing how the feet would start and then one foot steps forward with the throw. The child then stands on the footprints to throw. Also, you may ask the child to stamp the moving foot loudly to emphasize the step.

Balls that are used for learning and exploring the overhand throw should be developmentally appropriate: lightweight and small enough to be held with the fingers of the throwing hand. Yarn balls are particularly good for this learning experience.

Targets that are used should be attractive and interesting to the child, larger to begin with, progressing in difficulty to smaller ones. Targets should be stationary at first: moving targets involve complex perceptual functioning skills. The child should be encouraged to throw as hard as possible, imparting a lot of force to the ball. Targets may encourage force production rewarding the child by making noise when hit, or having lights that shine on contact.

## *Catching*

The catch is a manipulative fundamental motor skill that requires good hand-eye coordination and perceptual abilities. The catch is a visual-motor task. This is the one fundamental motor skill that cannot be taught from a closed skill perspective. Catching is the only manipulative fundamental motor skill in which the environment is always a factor since the object must travel toward the child. In the mature catching performance, the child should step toward the ball, arms spread a realistic amount apart relative to the size of the ball, palms facing, fingers outward. The ball should be contacted with the hands in a bilateral movement and the elbows should bend in to absorb the force of the ball. If the force is particularly hard, the child may step backwards as well to absorb the additional force. The catch does not have a contralateral pattern. However, the child will most likely step forward with the preferred foot.

Example activities for the development and refinement of catching ability include:

1. Rolling the ball back and forth between seated partners, emphasizing reaching out to the ball and pulling it in to the body
2. Catching the ball on a bounce from a partner
3. Catching the ball from a toss upward to self
4. Catching the ball on an easy toss from a partner
5. Catching the ball arriving at different levels
6. Catching the ball while moving

*Cues: step, reach, bring in to chest*

Balls used to learn to catch should be developmentally appropriate in size (8.5" is best) and should be non-threatening. Foam or "Nerf" balls are best in this situation. Smaller balls are harder to track visually, and larger balls are difficult to handle on contact. Research has shown that children attend better to balls of their favorite colors, or to balls of yellow or blue (Payne & Isaacs, 2002). It is important that the ball be a color in contrast to the background behind the thrower.

## *Striking*

Striking involves being able to hit an object either with the hand or with an implement and causing the object to travel forward. For our purposes, striking will be described with the plastic bat, an appropriate object for manipulation by the school-age child. The child stands sideways to the target, with the non-preferred side toward the target. Feet are parallel, shoulder-width apart. The bat is held with both hands back and tilted upward, the non-preferred hand closer to the bottom of the bat and the other hand directly above. The knuckles of the hands should be in line. The body is rotated back from the hips and both elbows are bent. Weight is on the back foot. The swing is initiated by the non-preferred foot step sideward, and followed by forward rotation of the hips, followed by shoulders, elbows and bat on a horizontal plane, contacting the ball at a point approximately waist level for the child.

Example activities for the development and refinement of striking include:

1. Standing sideways to a ball suspended by a string, hit the ball with open hand, emphasizing a step with the foot opposite the striking arm
2. Standing sideways to the ball on a string or to a batting tee, use a striking implement to contact the ball, i.e., table tennis paddle, badminton racket, plastic "fat" bat, whiffle ball bat
3. Using a plastic bat and a batting tee for the ball, hit the ball to targets at varying heights

*Cues: arms back, step, swing*

For the basic skill of striking, the ball will be stationary so that learning is a closed task. You may vary the size of the ball for success, an 8.5" foam ball would be easier to hit than a softball sized yarn ball. Targets should be large at first, becoming smaller with skill. Balls should be larger in the beginning stages. Eventually the skill will become open and the child will need to use visual-motor coordination to track and hit the oncoming ball. It is essential that the child have control of the fundamental pattern prior to practicing with an oncoming ball.

## *Kicking*

Kicking is a form of striking but involves eye-foot coordination rather than eye-hand coordination. In the fundamental motor skill of kicking, the ball should be stationary. In the mature pattern the child should take steps to approach the ball, take a back-swing with the dominant foot, kick through with toe pointed straight ahead lifting the ball into the air. As the kick is executed, the trunk is inclined back, the head is bent forward, and the arm in opposition to the kicking leg is forward, illustrating the contralateral pattern. The child follows through by stepping with the kicking leg.

Example activities for the development and refinement of kicking skill include:

1. Kicking a stationary ball placed directly in front of the child's preferred foot
2. Kicking a stationary ball placed 3–4 feet in front of the child
3. Kicking a stationary ball toward varied sizes of targets
4. Kicking a stationary ball for different distances
5. Kicking different sizes of stationary balls
6. Kicking a ball rolling toward the kicker
*Cues: run, kick, follow through*

Kicking is learned most efficiently as a closed skill. Once the ball is rolled to the child as an open skill, the task becomes more complex and success is dependent on the child's visual-motor coordination. Larger balls are easier to kick at first, progressing to smaller balls as skillfulness emerges.

These descriptions and example activities for each of the fundamental motor skills will give you an idea of how to proceed in teaching the basics. You should not assume that children older than 6 do not need instruction in these areas. In fact, some fifth and sixth grade students will still need assistance in many of these skills. Remember that motor performance is based upon the experiential background of the child: the child who grows up in a non-physically oriented family will be most likely to encounter performance deficits in motor skills.

## OTHER IMPORTANT MOTOR SKILLS

There are other motor skills that are regarded as basic for the emerging specialized skills of the movement repertoire. These would include the skills of hopping, leaping, galloping, sliding, skipping and ball bouncing.

## *Hopping*

In order to learn to hop, the child must be able to jump. This requires both leg strength and balance. To hop, the child will take off on one foot and land on the same foot. His/her control of balance must be greater than that of the jump since the supporting surface in the hop is one-half of that in the jump. Coordination and leg strength are both basic to the ability to hop repeatedly and to put the hop and the jump together into games such as Hopscotch.

Activities for the development and refinement of hopping skill include:

1. Balancing on one foot, then on the other
2. Balancing on one foot and taking off while holding a hand or other supporting surface and landing on the same foot
3. Hopping over a jump rope lying on the floor
4. Hopping in general space using the hop to move in different directions
5. Hopping from one line to the next
6. Hopping for distance and height
7. Playing in basic games where hopping is required as the locomotor movement

*Cues: balance, bend knee, up, land softly*

## *Leaping*

The leap involves a take-off on one foot, landing on the opposite foot with a period of flight time in between. The child usually goes into a leap from a run.

Example activities for the development and refinement of the leap include:

1. Leaping over lines on the floor
2. Leaping over objects of varying heights
3. Leaping with varied patterns, i.e., run-run-leap, or leap-leap-leap, etc.
4. Leaping holding the arms in various positions, i.e., out to the sides, over the head, in close to the body, etc.

*Cues: run, run, leap, bend knee to land*

## *Galloping*

The gallop combines a short leap and a step, keeping one foot constantly in front, and stepping the back leg up to a position just behind the lead leg, continuing forward with the front leg again. The knee of the lead leg is held high during the short leap. The gallop is a favorite movement in childhood, often acquired before the hop.

Example activities for the development and refinement of the gallop include:

1. Starting the leap-step pattern slowly and gradually increasing the speed
2. Moving creatively, i.e., ponies in a circus
3. Galloping with rhythmic verbal cues, "one foot always in front, face the way you are going"
4. Galloping with both arms held straight ahead, pointing to destination

*Cues: one foot always in front, face the way you are going*

## Sliding

The slide is the same movement as the gallop but action is to the side and the feet stay close to the ground. The slide is often used in musical games and dances.

Example activities for the development and refinement of the slide include:

1.  Standing with the side toward the destination point, step sideways with first foot, bring back foot up to meet it, step with first foot again
2.  Standing sideways, increase speed of travel as in #1 but side-leap off back foot, reach with front foot
3.  Sliding in a figure eight
4.  Sliding in a circle, changing from facing in to facing out
5.  Sliding with verbal cues, step-together-step

*Cues: turn gallop sideways, side, together, side, together*

## Skipping

The skip is a complex skill in that it requires the child to do step-hops in sequence. The skip is accomplished by stepping and hopping on the same foot, then stepping and hopping on the opposite foot. The arms move in a contralateral pattern as the child moves forward in the skip.

Example activities for the development and refinement of the skip include:

1.  Stepping over a jump rope, hopping, stepping over next rope and hopping, etc.
2.  Moving slowly, exaggerate the step-hop with each foot
3.  Holding hands and skipping with a partner who can skip very well
4.  Skipping in games requiring locomotor movements as the main skill

*Cue: step hop*

## Ball Bouncing

An additional skill that is basic to childhood play is ball bouncing. Bouncing represents a striking pattern. Children should cup the hand over the ball, let the fingers push the ball downward and lift the hand slightly as the ball comes back up, then giving another push. Bouncing seems to be learned most easily with an 8.5" ball.

Example activities for the development and refinement of ball bouncing include:

1.  Dropping and catching the ball from a bounce
2.  Dropping and pushing the ball with two hands
3.  Pushing the ball continuously in place with the preferred hand
4.  Pushing the ball continuously in place with the non-preferred hand
5.  Walking in general space while bouncing the ball with the preferred hand, with the non-preferred hand

*Cues: push the ball down, let hand ride back up*

# General Teaching Principles

Teaching for development of or refinement of the fundamental motor skills can be accomplished in many ways. First of all, the teacher should teach in proper progression. There is not an order to the learning of the fundamental motor skills, but some are learned more easily than others. The walk is prerequisite to the run and jump. All skills should be taught first in the closed skill format, progressing to open skill format.

Secondly, the teacher should be creative in designing tasks to encourage children to participate in activities. A lesson in running would hardly be appropriate if all the children did was to run around the gymnasium while the teacher gave feedback. As a matter of fact, it is best if each lesson includes work in many or all of the fundamental motor skills. Variety is important in learning.

A third point to keep in mind is that the equipment used and the activities selected must be developmentally appropriate. The equipment should fit the child's physical size; the activity should fit the child's cognitive as well as psychomotor functioning levels.

The teacher should know the performance points for each skill extremely well. This is necessary in order to provide appropriate feedback for skill development.

## EVALUATING THE BASIC SKILL

The easiest and most time-expedient way to evaluate children's basic locomotor skills is to ask children to cross the gymnasium area while the teacher observes and makes note of the level of performance. The teacher can have them cross the area in 2 different groups, or can create smaller groups. Observation can also be done in a game situation where different locomotor skills are involved. A form that could be used for such an evaluation appears below:

It is suggested that the teacher then take those who are exhibiting immature patterns for their age levels and evaluate again, noting the problems evidenced so that suggestions can be made to parents to help the children in their skills. Similar charts can be made for the other skills.

| Date: | Walk | | | Run | | | Jump | | | Gallop | | | Slide | | |
|---|---|---|---|---|---|---|---|---|---|---|---|---|---|---|---|
| Andrew | I | T | M | I | T | M | I | T | M | I | T | M | I | T | M |
| Jennifer | I | T | M | I | T | M | I | T | M | I | T | M | I | T | M |
| Matthew | I | T | M | I | T | M | I | T | M | I | T | M | I | T | M |
| Brian | I | T | M | I | T | M | I | T | M | I | T | M | I | T | M |
| Alison | I | T | M | I | T | M | I | T | M | I | T | M | I | T | M |
| Jeffrey | I | T | M | I | T | M | I | T | M | I | T | M | I | T | M |
| Timothy | I | T | M | I | T | M | I | T | M | I | T | M | I | T | M |
| Krista | I | T | M | I | T | M | I | T | M | I | T | M | I | T | M |
| Martha | I | T | M | I | T | M | I | T | M | I | T | M | I | T | M |

Circle the Appropriate Letter: I = Immature, T = Transitional, M = Mature

# Summary

The fundamental motor skills represent the blocks in the base of motor performance. You should not think that there are correct and incorrect ways of performing these skills but rather that there are ways that are most efficient. The older child can take the basic and adapt them for sport participation; that adaptation occurs due to the environment, the child's skill level, and the readiness to adapt and refine.

# References and Suggested Readings

Gabbard, C.P. (2003). *Lifelong motor development*. Benjamin-Cummings.

Gabbard, C.P. (1992). *Lifelong motor development*.Wm. C. Brown.

Gabbard, C., Leblanc, E., & Lowy, S. (1994). *Physical education for children, building the foundation*. Prentice-Hall.

Gabbard, C., Leblanc, E., & Lowy, S. (1987). *Physical education for children, building the foundation*. Prentice-Hall.

Gallahue, D. (2005). *Developmental physical education for all children*. Human Kinetics.

Gallahue, D. (1997). *Developmental physical education for today's children*. McGraw Hill.

Gallahue, D.L. (1987). *Developmental physical education for today's children*. Macmillan.

Gallahue, D.L. (1982). *Understanding motor development in children*. Wiley.

Kirchner G. & Fishburne, G.J. (2001). *Physical education for elementary school children*. McGraw Hill.

Kirchner G. & Fishburne, G.J. (1998). *Physical education for elementary school children*. Brown & Benchmark.

Kirchner G. & Fishburne, G.J. (1995). *Physical education for elementary school children*. Brown & Benchmark.

Nichols, B. (2001). *Moving and learning*: *The elementary school physical education experience*.McGraw Hill.

Nichols, B. (1994). *Moving and learning*: *The elementary school physical education experience*. Times Mirror/Mosby.

Nichols, B. (1990). *Moving and learning*. Times Mirror/Mosby.

Pangrazi, R.P. (2006). *Dynamic physical education for elementary school children*. Benjamin-Cummings

Pangrazi, R.P. (2003). *Dynamic physical education for elementary school children*. Benjamin Cummings.

Pangrazi, R.P. (1998). *Dynamic physical education for elementary school children*. Allyn & Bacon.

Pangrazi, R.P. & Dauer, V.P. (1995). *Dynamic physical education for elementary school children*. Allyn & Bacon.

Pangrazi, R.P. & Dauer, V.P. (1992). *Dynamic physical education for elementary school children*. Macmillan.

Payne, V.G. & Isaacs, L. D. (2007). *Human motor development: A lifespan approach*. McGraw-Hill.

Payne, V.G. & Isaacs, L.D. (2001). *Human motor development: A lifespan approach*. Mayfield.

Payne, V. G. & Isaacs, L.D. (1991). *Human motor development: A lifespan approach*. Mayfield.

Sherrill, C. (2003). *Adapted physical activity, recreation and sport*. McGraw Hill.

Sherrill, C. (1993). *Adapted physical activity, recreation and sport*. Dubuque: Brown & Benchmark.

Siedentop, D., Herkowitz, J, & Rink, J., (1984). *Elementary physical education methods.* Edgewood Cliffs: Prentice-Hall.
Wickstrom, R.L. (1985). *Fundamental motor patterns.* Lea & Febiger.

CHAPTER

# 5

# Integrating Physical Education and Academics

You certainly cannot deny that you learn better when you are studying subjects that are of interest to you. In that same vein, the children learn better when teachers allow for their innate desires to play and move to become an important part of the learning process. Learning then becomes fun and interesting. No one could deny the fact that a child will learn much better if the learning process is appealing. In the "Perceptual-Motor Development" chapter you read that helping a child progress through perceptual-motor development enhances cognitive skills. In this chapter you will learn how to use the physical education classroom to teach cognitive concepts.

With national emphasis on student achievement test performance, many school districts have chosen to reduce "specials" time, and children receive less art, music and physical education. Some school systems insist that children focus so hard on the tests that no physical education can be taught during the week's testing period. It is a fact that exercise stimulates the production of endorphins that cause children to be more alert and ready for learning and performance. Children should actually participate in a vigorous activity prior to sitting down for testing! Think of what an impact you could make if you had your children do an aerobic warm-up each morning!

## Moving and Learning

When children move in the environment, exploration results in learning in all of the sensory channels that are used. Information is gleaned through each channel: visual, auditory, tactile and kinesthetic. You have learned about inter-sensory integration, and that children learn best when they can receive information through many different ways by using as many sensory systems as possible. To say that a child learns through movement is to say that not only does the child absorb information in the cognitive domain, but also this learning is further emphasized through the psychomotor domain, particularly through tactile-kinesthetic and visual channels. Moving through learning experiences tends to solidify knowledge and tends to commit that knowledge to memory.

For example, how do children learn about force and motion? These concepts contribute heavily to the development of efficient physical skills and apply to the science curriculum as well. In the science classroom the children might learn about these concepts through experiences that depend on the written word, video demonstrations, or experimental tasks involving small objects and fine-motor control. However, most children will have a better understanding of these scientific principles if learning experiences also occur in the gymnasium where the body becomes an integral part of the experiment.

Children should learn about several basic principles of force and motion in order to be efficient movers: (a) the better the coordination of integral body parts, the greater the force that will be generated (force production); (b) the more muscles used, the greater the force exerted (force production); (c) a follow-through is important for the complete application of intended force (force production); (d) a body or object that is in motion will remain in motion until something interferes with that motion (inertia); and, (e) in order to absorb force effectively, the body must "give" with the received force (force absorption) (Kirchner & Fishburne, 2001; Nichols, 2001; Pangrazi, 2003). Depending on the age of the child, the degree of understanding of these principles will vary. It is important that you talk about these concepts as you teach so that the acquisition of such knowledge occurs naturally.

Children who develop coordination such that they can stop and start the actions of the body on signal, are utilizing principles of force production, force absorption and the principle of inertia. When directed "On the signal to go, run as fast as you can and stop when you hear the whistle," the children explode forcefully at the start, remain in motion until, hearing the whistle, they exert sufficient force absorption to stop the moving body. Should they not absorb that force at the end, the body will remain in motion. Will the child better understand the principle of inertia by reading the words of the definition, or by being that body in motion? In the latter case the children are learning through both cognitive and psychomotor domains. In the classroom, learning is often only in the cognitive domain.

Considering the principle of inertia once again there are many other ways to demonstrate the principle through physical education. Here are a few suggestions:
- rolling a ball across the floor
- performing a series of forward rolls
- pushing oneself on a scooter

Now, add the principle of force production to inertia:
- roll the ball hard across the floor
- performing a series of forward rolls as quickly as possible
- pushing oneself fast on a scooter

What is it that the child does in order to create more force? Ask the child to experiment with different degrees of force (roll the ball easily, hard, softly) and verbalize the results. In rolling the ball across the floor the child produces force in propelling the object.

Perhaps the best way for the children to understand concepts of force production is to participate in play activities involving manipulation (in this case, propelling) of objects. Throwing, striking and kicking are the primary forms of propelling. Through experimenting with objects of different weights and sizes, the child learns how to adjust the degree of force necessary to propel objects quickly, slowly, hard, softly, high, low, etc. The child learns to control the direction of the force: to emphasize the force at the right time so that the object will reach the desired target.

Force absorption enters the learning task in order to stop the action. When a ball hits a wall, what does it do? Does it rebound or stop completely? Why does it rebound? Because the wall is an inanimate object without the property to absorb force; consequently the ball rebounds. If children were to catch the balls before the balls contact the wall, they could absorb the forward momentum (force) of the ball by bringing arms and hands in toward the body on contact. Children are capable of absorbing force because they are not inanimate objects. If the child were to hold his/her hands stiffly in front of his/her body when the ball comes, what would the ball do? It would rebound, because the child chose not to absorb the force. Therefore, an understanding of this principle is truly important in the learning of skillful movements.

Let's consider the child's use of the gymnasium scooter. If children are in a prone position on the scooters and using bilateral over-arm patterns to propel their bodies forward across the room, what will happen when they want to stop? The children will overcome inertia by absorbing the force of the moving scooter with their hands on the floor in front. To develop the use of force in another way, have the children travel on the scooters, experimenting with many different ways to produce force (using arms or legs in different combinations). At the same time have the children see how many different body parts they can use to absorb the force in order to stop. In the forward roll sequence, the child exerts force by the push-off given at the beginning of the roll sequence and at subsequent critical points in the skill. As long as the body remains in the correct position (rounded and tucked), the series of rolls can continue. When the body opens, however, the force of the roll is absorbed and the rolling action stops. Through active manipulation of the body in gymnastic type activities, the children learn that greater force is created when the body is compact and the movements are coordinated, smooth and fluid.

## Learning About Stability

Concerning principles of stability (balance), children have been actively learning since they first started to lift their heads as infants. Control of stability is essential to all efficient movement and the school age child is usually capable of maintaining equilibrium in daily tasks. To develop a cognitive understanding of stability, or balance, it is necessary for the children to experiment with activities that cause them to move body parts such that the center of gravity (the point in the body around which all body parts are balanced) is shifted and the children can then reflect on what it was that they did to maintain balance.

Children need to learn and understand several basic principles: (a) the larger the base of support, the better the balance; (b) the center of gravity should be centered over the base of support to maintain balance; and, (c) the lower the center of gravity over the base of support, the better the balance (Kirchner & Fishburne, 2001,1998, 1995; Nichols, 2001, 1994, 1990; Pangrazi, 2003, 1998).

What activities can we provide for children in order for them to learn these principles first-hand? In order to cause the child to adjust the center of gravity, have the child experiment with walking in different ways: on toes, on heels, flat-footed, etc. Discuss which way is most efficient and why. Have the child place his/her hand on the center of gravity (at the umbilicus, or belly button, for children Grade 2 and under, slightly lower in the abdominal cavity for older children) and feel the adjustment that must be made for each different kind of walking pattern. Hopefully the child will recognize the height change from the floor. Do the same for running, jumping, hopping, galloping, skipping, etc.

Have the child compare the jump and the hop. You may discuss force production and force absorption as well as balance. The child will see that the jump (force production with two feet, center of gravity positioned directly above the base of support, and force absorption with two feet) is definitely more stable and controlled than the hop where one foot must create and absorb the force. Have the child continue to try the jump and the hop. Discuss the differences: was there one in the take-off stage? What was done to absorb force on landing?

Another excellent way to teach children about the principles of balance is to have the children do partner and group balances. These activities can be found in Chapter Twelve. Supporting a partner causes the child to think about his/her movements and to adjust his/her own body to compensate for the added weight and position of the partner. Also, activities with balance boards and balance beams will help the child learn to shift the center of gravity and will help to develop the understanding of the mechanical principles necessary for efficient performance.

## Learning about Levers

Levers represent another mechanical movement principle that may be taught through physical activity. After an introduction to the three kinds of levers (first, second and third class), have the children work in partners to see how many levers they can identify in the human body. The children will discover that third-class levers are the most evident, where the muscle acts as the force and rests between the fulcrum and the resistance.

Basic principles that may be learned include: (a) the purpose of a third-class lever is to gain a mechanical advantage, either for speed or trajectory; (b) the longer the arm from object to fulcrum, the more force that can be generated; and (c) the longer the arm from object to the fulcrum, the faster the object will travel.

Giving children various objects to propel (of varied weights, shapes and sizes) will encourage the development of understanding of the arm as a third class lever. The child will come to understand that the longer the lever, the faster the object will be propelled. Therefore, a ball hit with a bat or a racket should travel farther than if it were simply thrown. The child may experiment by trying different ways of propelling objects and measuring the distances that they go. As children experiment with the overhand throw, they learn that it is necessary to vary the force produced or speed of movement of the lever in order to accomplish different tasks. Adjustments are made to make a ball travel a short distance, far, high, or directly to the ground. Eventually, with practice, the child learns the fluid motion of the overhand throw and experiments with changing environmental aspects, such as participation in a baseball game, and learns how to adapt the lever's force level to accomplish different throwing tasks.

## Learning About Trajectory

Children learn through physical activity that different angles of propulsion will result in different distances of travel for objects. They learn to adjust the trajectory of the ball by varying the point of release. The major principles to be understood are: (a) the distance an object will go is determined by the angle of release; and, (b) objects should be released directly in line with the intended target.

Have the children throw overhand with partners, and step backward one step after each successful catch. This will gradually increase the distance between the thrower and the target and will cause the child to make gradual changes in the angle of release in order to get the ball to the target. Discussion with the learner should center on recognizing the changes that need to be made in the angle of release of the object to lead the child to discover that trajectory is related to distance.

Just because mechanical movement principles are utilized in physical education does not ensure that children learn these principles. Active participation with such concepts will create an efficient mover; however, without the teacher's placing stress on the cognitive concept understanding may not be attained by the child.

Consequently, actively teaching the principles of mechanical movement cognitively adds meaning and sense to basic movement. The thinking child will be able to apply these principles in other movement situations. Active teaching and active learning go hand-in-hand.

## Integrating Academic Concepts with Physical Education

There are many ways that the teacher can integrate academic concepts with the activities in the gymnasium. When you are the physical educator as well as the classroom educator, you can demonstrate to your children an appreciation for both cognitive learning and physical activity. If you have a physical educator in your building, hopefully you will work with that individual so that your children will develop an understanding that both physical activity and academics are intimately related! Some special examples follow:

For very young children, activities such as this may be used to reinforce knowledge of different shapes and letters:

> Scatter the letters in the center of the play area. Give each child a jump rope. Show the children how to make a rectangle on the floor with the jump rope. Have the children walk on the jump rope while saying the sentence "This shape is a rectangle. It is long and wide." Ask each child to go to find a letter of the alphabet, bring it back and place it in the rectangle. Go to each child and ask if he/she knows the name of the letter in his/her rectangle. If he/she does not know, tell the name of the letter. Have the children walk on the rectangle again saying "The letter ___ is in my rectangle." Have them run around their rectangles repeating the name of the letter quickly. Send them to get another letter. Repeat the above action. You may ask them to find the letters that start their names. Show them the letter "E." Ask if they know of

any animals whose names starts with "E." When they give a suggestion, such as Elephant, have them all walk around their rectangles like elephants; emphasize the long trunk, and have them make sounds like an elephant. Other answers might be Eagle, Egret, etc. Ask what other words begin with E: Eat, Enormous, etc. Ask them to try to make "E" with the jump ropes. Have them walk on the "E," jump over the "E," and jump around the "E."

Pedometers have become popular tools for encouraging active lifestyles with children. Teachers are encouraged to combine academics with walking programs so that children are stimulated both physically and academically. For example, children can pick a destination, such as Disney World, find the mileage, and use the pedometers to measure walking distances, either in physical education or in a classroom walking activity! They can add all of the students' walking totals together and mark distances on a map to Disney World. When they reach the destination, they can have a Disney movie, or party!

Similar activities can be created with difficulty according to the child's academic level. Measuring can be done of different areas, such as the school corridors; miles or portions of miles can be converted to feet, inches, and metric terms. Children can have homework assignments that include doing walking wearing pedometers and then filling out worksheets pertaining to the measurements. Depending on the quality of the pedometers, one can also track calories burned. Children can then equate the calories burned to a favorite food. This is a good way to show how much activity is needed to counteract junk food!

Gilbert (1997, 2000) wrote an excellent book for integrating movement and academics called *Teaching the Three R's through Movement Experiences*. Based on the belief that children learn better while actually moving through problems or learning experiences, Gilbert offers numerous "lesson plans" demonstrating how the following academic concepts can be taught in a fun and amusing way: language arts, mathematics, science, social studies and art. Pangrazi (2003, 1998) stresses the importance of integration of physical education with academic subject matter and gives example activities in such areas as art, geography, history, language arts, music and mathematics.

One excellent example from the Gilbert book will help to clarify integration: In a science lesson on matter, each child in the class represents a molecule. The teacher asks the "molecules" to move as they naturally would in different forms: gas, liquid or solid. The children would demonstrate their knowledge of molecule behavior by adjusting their space in relation to others and adjusting the speed of movement. The teacher asks the children to find a partner and show what a hydrogen atom would look like. The partners should become an electron and a proton and the electron should circle around the proton. In this way the children can learn about the different atoms, their make-up and their characteristics.

If you use lessons such as those from the Gilbert (1977, 2000) book, you must keep in mind that you are teaching academics through movement, you are not teaching physical education. Physical education is maximum participation, maximum activity time. That is not to say that while children are in physical activity they cannot learn about academics. The following section deals with amending game rules to stress academic concepts while playing.

# Ideas for Coordinating Games with Academic Curriculum

All of the games in the "Developmentally Appropriate Games" chapter have example cognitive applications. These were designed as examples of how to integrate academics and physical education. The teacher should know that, first of all, when selecting a game for the children to play, it is not a law that the game must be played directly as given in the textbook. Coordination of a game with the academic curriculum is limited only by the teacher's own creativity. Several examples follow.

*Title:* __*Fire Chief*__
*Skills Enhanced*: spatial awareness, locomotor movements, auditory discrimination
*Equipment Needed:* none.
*Directions:* Have the children form a circle in the center of the play area, standing and facing the inside of the circle. Choose one child to be the "Fire Chief." The fire chief walks around the outside of the circle, tapping 3 other players while saying "firefighter" to each child tapped. The fire chief then goes into the center of the circle and calls "FIRE!" At this point the three children tapped run as quickly as possible in a clockwise direction rounding the circle and back to their original spaces. The first child back, standing straight and tall, is the next Fire Chief.

First of all there are a few problems with the game: too many children standing around, some "fire chiefs" will choose only friends, and the game has the potential to be boring after a few plays. However, suppose it is the beginning of the year and you are teaching your primary grade children about shapes and colors. You develop a set of colored playing cards with a shape drawn on each card. You pass out these cards to the children at the beginning of the game. Then, you call a color, "RED", and all the children holding red cards run; you call "TRIANGLE" and all the children holding triangle cards run; you call "GREEN RECTANGLES" and only the green rectangle card children run. The children receive the same physical exercise as in the fire chief game, but the game eliminates choosing of friends and guarantees a turn for each child while reinforcing classroom concepts. You could do the same with flashcards of reading or spelling words, or of mathematics. You can call "words that start with the mmm sound," "words that end with the puh sound," "the answer to $4 + 3$," etc. Making the learning into a special game makes it more memorable. It is enough to reward the "winner" by saying "Jimmy is first this time!" and then immediately calling another color or shape. Children need to learn that winning is not everything and we should de-emphasize the glory-of-winning element of the game.

*Title:* __*Midnight*__
*Skills Enhanced*: spatial awareness, locomotor movements, auditory discrimination; balance and agility; dodging
*Equipment Needed*: none
*Directions:* The children in the class stand on an end line in the play area. One child, selected by the teacher, to be Mr./Mrs. Fox, stands approximately 10 yards in front of the group, WITH his/her back to the children. On signal the group of children begin to approach the Fox, saying "What time is it Mr./Mrs. Fox?" The Fox answers any time he/she wishes, but if he/she says "MIDNIGHT!" he/she immediately chases the children back to the line, trying to tag as many as possible. Those children who are tagged become helpers for Mr./Mrs. Fox and assist in the tagging of others on the next round of play.

This game is all right as it is. Activity time is high and children are busy. Now, perhaps you are teaching the concept of telling time. You could prepare a series of playing cards with clock faces indicating different times. Since you would know the times you put on the cards, you would call the time in answer to each query by the children. Instead of all sneaking up to Mr. Fox, the children would advance toward Mr. Fox only if their times were called. At any time, you may call "MIDNIGHT!" Of course you could also use your cards from the Fire Chief game to learn about shapes and colors as well.

These examples should show you what you can do with almost any game that you may select for your class. Of course you will be selecting it as appropriate for the content in physical education that you are stressing, but certainly you can incorporate cognitive content as a bonus learning time!

Mathematics concepts are easily included within the physical education framework. Scoring for individual accomplishments (how many sit-ups can you do today?) to team scoring (how many points did your team earn?) provides the opportunity to apply academic concepts. Children can be encouraged to add scores together, to subtract one day's score from the other, to figure averages, etc. In games that depend on the number of students being equal on each team and there is an extra child, it would be most fitting to compute average scores! If multiplication were the subject of concern, why not have the children use those principles to calculate final scores, e.g., every time a team scores, multiply it by 13.

### *Title:    Whistle Mixer*
*Skills Enhanced:* locomotor movements, auditory discrimination, spatial awareness
*Equipment Needed:* none
*Directions:* The children move independently in general space using a locomotor skill designated by the teacher. When they hear a whistle blown a certain number of times, e.g., three, they immediately get into groups of three, join hands and circle clockwise. Any leftover children come to the center area and raise their hands. On signal the children again begin to move independently, listening for the next whistle series.

Now let's use our mathematics concepts to make this game more cognitive. Instead of whistle blows, verbally call math problems to the class. The children must form groups according to the answers to the problems. For example, "2 x 3!" The children form groups of six. "2 x 3 − 5!" The children turn clockwise in space independently.

### *Title:    Bounce and Add*
*Skills Enhanced*: dribbling
*Equipment Needed*: a playground ball for each child, markers with numbers and/or equations on them
*Directions:* Scatter markers (polyspots would work well) throughout the play area that have numbers on them, appropriate to the math level of your students. Have each child take a playground ball and stand at one of the markers. On the signal to begin, the students dribble the ball the number of times indicated on the marker; they then move to the markers that come next in counting and repeat the task at the new markers.

Variations for older children: use markers that have different kinds of equations and the students must "bounce" the correct answer before moving on.

Again, cognitive adaptations for your games are only a matter of your own thoughtfulness and creativity. Capitalize on the child's innate desire to play—make learning fun!

# Creative Movement Experiences

Dancing or acting out a story through movement from a reading text gives meaning to the new vocabulary words that are encountered in the story. Actually moving through the actions of a story may help children who have difficulty remembering the new words. Play acting in this sense also lends meaning to the progression of the story, of the plot leading to a climax.

Children who are learning about punctuation may be encouraged to "Start with a capital letter" (stand tall), "say what you want to say" (move in general space), and "end it with a period" (child returns to partner and ends movement in a small ball shape on the floor). Likewise, directions can lead the child to pause in movement (comma), and end with exclamation points, or question marks.

# The Development of Learning Centers

Teachers use many forms of learning centers in the classroom. The learning centers may be used in several ways, one of which is to promote additional learning during children's free time, or time when work is done. Physical education learning centers provide an important link to content in the physical education arena, and, teaching physical education concepts may contribute directly to academic learning as well. The center may be developed by the physical educator or the classroom teacher. Each center should be attractive to the children and should incorporate fun in learning.

A physical fitness learning center may be used in the classroom in order to reinforce concepts of proper nutrition, exercise habits, caloric intake and output, body mass index, pulse rates, blood pressure, skinfold calipers, leisure activities, and many other factors which relate to proper fitness and healthy bodies. Relatively inexpensive skinfold calipers can be purchased through several different suppliers of physical education equipment. Most of these calipers include an instruction booklet, explaining how to measure Body Mass Index (BMI) using these calipers. The results of the Body Mass Index using the skinfold calipers are then compared to the height weight measurements using the BMI Chart included in the "Physical Fitness" chapter. An accurate weight scale is included in the learning center along with a tape measure, in order that students may weigh and measure themselves at various times throughout the year. Students can then look up their individual BMI results throughout the year to see how their growth, exercise, etc. affects the BMI results. Word Searches, Crossword Puzzles, and Color By Number Activities can be designed for students K through 6 relating to fitness, nutrition, exercise, and other factors.

An automated blood pressure monitor may be purchased through various pharmacies, physical education supply companies, or at a variety of other stores. Kuntzleman (1978) has written a book entitled Fitness Discovery Activities which has many activities related to taking one's pulse, blood pressure, leisure activities, as well as activities related to calories and nutrition, to name a few. This book is no longer in print, however, your local chapter of the American Heart Association may be able to assist in finding copies of these activities and others because of their affiliation with the "Feeling Good Program" which recommended the book Fitness Discovery Activities. There are many activities in this book which are excellent activities for a fitness learning center. Parlay International also has many handouts related to fitness, which would work out well in a fitness learning center. Parlay International is located in Emeryville, California (1-800-457-2752). The classroom teacher can adapt this center with activities appropriate for grades K through 6.

A stop watch and the "Take Your Pulse Activity" may also be included in the Fitness Learning Center allowing students the opportunity to take and time their own pulse rates.

The National Dairy Council, 10255 Higgins, Rosemont, Illinois 60018 (847-803-2000) has nutrition kits available which can be purchased at a reasonable cost. Calorie charts can be found at the library, or purchased at a local bookstore in order to assist the teacher with the activities entitled "Calories Taken In Through Food," and "Calories Burned Through Exercise." In the first of these activities a food is described related to the calories taken in when this particular food of a given measured serving is eaten. In the second activity, various exercises are described including how many calories are burned when performing a certain exercise for a specific amount of time. Students will choose an index card from each envelope and then compare how much exercise would be required in order to burn up the amount of food ingested. Several other activities can be included related to the body, heart, and fitness facts by using those items and activities found through the National Dairy Council, Parlay International, and Fitness Discovery Activities.

Suppose that the children are involved in a bowling unit in the gymnasium. There could be a bowling learning center with the primary objective of teaching the children about the scoring system in bowling. It would also incorporate practice in mathematics. There could be four activities involving scoring, and score sheets would be provided for the players. First, a workbook could be available for children to work on various scoring problems. In this way they can learn independently about scoring. In "Pick Your Pin" there would be 30 paper bowling pins in the pocket. The pins are selected one at a time and are recorded on the score sheet. More than one child may play, taking turns. For "Roll a Score" the children may use two dice, each side marked with a number of dots from 0 to 5. The children then mark their score sheets after each throw. Finally, "Spin a Strike" represents another way to play the scoring game. A spinner indicates what to write on the score sheet (Regimbal, 1998).

In the learning center "Meet Skel E. Ton," the objective is to teach children about the different bones in the body. Activities involve making one's own "scary skeleton;" reading "amazing facts" about bones; playing "Fish Bones" a form of concentration matching the official bone name with the layman term (e.g., coccyx - tailbone); playing "Old Skeleton," a version of Old Maid with pictures of bones to match with names of bones; labeling the bones on a skeleton worksheet; and playing "Funny Bones," a series of cards showing parts of a skeleton where the children try to collect all the parts and assemble their own skeleton. Each day the center may accent a new bone: the names placed on the center with a string going to the correct bone on the skeleton. What is the connection to physical education? Children should learn the names of the bones as they exercise in physical education class (Regimbal, 1998).

Older children may develop learning centers as projects to learn about different sports or to teach younger children about physical education. The development of learning centers further emphasizes the link between cognitive and psychomotor learning. Children will learn to value both when their teachers set the example. Centers can also be set up in the gymnasium area for children to work when unable to take part in physical education activities.

## Summary

It is truly important that physical education be valued in the classroom as well as in the gymnasium. Working at learning centers can help children to work on academic concepts in a "fun way," as well as learning academic concepts in the play arena of the gymnasium. Learning is very appealing when it is coupled with a pleasurable activity such as play or movement.

## References and Suggested Readings

Butler, J. (1997). How would Socrates teach games? A constructivist approach. *Journal of Physical Education*, Recreation and Dance, 68(9), 42–47.

Gilbert, A.G. (2000). *Teaching the three r's through movement experiences.* University of Washington.

Gilbert, A.G. (1977). *Teaching the three r's through movement experiences.* Burgess.

Kirchner G. & Fishburne, G.J. (2001). *Physical education for elementary school children.* McGraw Hill.

Kirchner G. & Fishburne, G.J. (1998). *Physical education for elementary school children.* Brown & Benchmark.

Kirchner G. & Fishburne, G.J. (1995). *Physical education for elementary school children.* Brown & Benchmark.

Kirkpatrick, B. & Buck, M.M. (1995). Heart adventures challenge course: A lifestyle education activity. *Journal of Physical Education, Recreation and Dance*, (66)2, 17–24.

Kuhrash, C. (2001). http://db.pecentral.org/lessonideas.

Kuntzelman, C. T. (1978). *Fitness discovery activities.* Arbor Press.

Nichols, B. (2001). *Moving and learning: The elementary school physical education experience.* McGraw Hill.

Nichols, B. (1994). *Moving and learning: The elementary school physical education experience.* Times Mirror/Mosby.

Nichols, B. (1990). *Moving and learning.* Times Mirror/Mosby.

Pangrazi, R. P. (2006). *Dynamic physcal education for elementary school children.* Benjamin-Cummings.

Pangrazi, R.P. (2003). *Dynamic physical education for elementary school children.* Benjamin Cummings.

Pangrazi, R.P. (1998). *Dynamic physical education for elementary school children.* Allyn & Bacon.

Regimbal, C. (1998). Personal interview, University of Toledo, Toledo, OH.

CHAPTER

# 6

# What to Teach in Physical Education

We have established the fact that physical education is a very important, integral part of the elementary school curriculum. Now you need to decide what you will teach in order to insure quality daily physical education for our students. It is essential that you work closely with your physical education teacher to coordinate your effort and to provide for systematic programming leading the children to accomplish the following by the end of the elementary experience: increased and maintained physical fitness, acquired fundamental skills progressing to sport-related skills, sound body management and control in movement, well-defined positive self-concepts, and cognitive knowledge of and appreciation for physical education and physical fitness.

## Program Emphasis

In order for children to have fun and feel successful in a physical play situation, they need to have the skills to be efficient and effective movers. The preschool and/or kindergarten teachers represent the beginning of the child's formal public schooling: It is here that learning through movement is essential. Young children need to learn about their bodies and what they can do. They need to learn about space, shapes, pathways, and movement. They need help and guidance in coordination skills and they need to have a variety of movement experiences designed to enable them to gain efficiency in movement. In Grades 1 and 2 children learn to use these skills effectively by refining and applying them in structured movement settings. It is in the beginning years, also, that physical fitness needs to be stressed and actively pursued for the entire years of schooling. Children are never too young to learn about fitness principles and all children can be taught to take a pulse. The Physical Fitness chapter presents important information regarding the implementation of fitness activities as well as ways to assess fitness and develop a cognitive understanding of wellness in students. Understand that physical fitness activities are to be an integral part of each day's lesson, and that although fitness itself does not appear in the overall content to be taught, you must be sure to include it and stress its importance to your students.

Each grade level curriculum builds from the movement foundation that is established in the grade level below. The basic skills that are learned, refined, and applied in the primary grades form the base for all major team or individual sport forms that are part of the adult lifestyle.

As the child reaches grades 3–4, he/she is entering the intermediate stage where all of these foundational skills are taken and applied into meaningful movement experiences that result in skills resembling those to be later applied to sport forms. The 5th–6th grade years represent learning about sport and activity for lifetime fitness, and should represent the time that the child consolidates and emerges with good attitudes toward sport and exercise as being critical to a healthy lifestyle. Positive beliefs regarding physical activity during the elementary years will lead to positive attitudes in the secondary school program.

## Basic Movement Skills

Referring to "Suggested Content for Elementary School Physical Education," you will note that the fundamental motor skills are taught to the children in grades K–1–2 and, along with direct skill instruction in those basic skills, comes the use of the skills in developmentally appropriate games. It is suggested that children learn and practice the skills in a closed format and then use them in carefully selected games. In this sense the game becomes a laboratory for practice and application in a structured movement setting. For example, if you are teaching the skill of jumping, you would follow the instruction and practice time with a game such as "Freeze Tag" (See "Developmentally Appropriate Games" chapter) but all players would jump instead of run. You might use a game such as "Crossing the Brook" (See "Developmentally Appropriate Games" chapter) or any games that you may adapt to use jumping as the primary means of locomotion. Therefore, for this portion of the curriculum you would rely very heavily on your knowledge of fundamental motor skills (Chapter Four) and the information in "Developmentally Appropriate Games" chapter. It is at this level of the curriculum that you will stress building a strong movement base. For children in Grades 3 and 4, it will become very important for them to refine their skills and be able to apply them in both developmentally appropriate games and in sport lead-up games. Grade 3 really represents a transition year where children are moving from games of lower organization and complexity to an understanding of higher level activities. You will note that specific sport areas have been selected for the different grade levels. These are suggested, but you may select other sport areas to teach. One of the historical problems with physical education has been the fact that teachers repeat the same sport forms year after year for short periods of time. It makes more sense to use longer periods of time (units) and to select different sport areas for grade levels for two reasons: (1) to take the time to fully develop the skills and knowledge of the activities, and (2) to prevent boredom. Think about the classroom curriculum: reading, math, social studies and science are taught every year, but the content is varied! Why should physical education be any different? This same concept applies to the children in grades 5 and 6 who are working on adapting the fundamental motor skills to become efficient sport-related skills.

You should note that lead-up games are indicated in the suggested content. In the "Sports Skills" chapter, you will find that each sport section has information on lead-up games that teach different aspects of the adult sport. Children have the opportunity to play many sports in their adult form in youth sport programs. The adult forms of sport usually involve one ball and 22 players, for example, soccer. How many opportunities do you think a child would have to contact the ball in an adult game of soccer? Not many! Therefore, lead-up games are designed for maximum participation (everyone has equal and plentiful opportunities to play), and they focus on specific skills that will be used within the adult game. Lead-up games increase in complexity and should be selected for Grades 3–4 differently than they are selected for Grades 5 and 6.

### Suggested Content For Elementary School Physical Education

| Kindergarten, Grades 1 & 2 | Grades 3 & 4 | Grades 5 & 6 |
|---|---|---|
| *Fundamental Motor Skill Development (FMS)* | *Refinement/Application & Variation of FMS* | *Sport Related Skill Development* |
| Run, Jump, Throw, Catch, Strike, Kick, Gallop, Hop, Slide in Developmentally Appropriate Games | Basic lead-up games for Soccer, Softball, Tennis, Basketball, Volleyball, Developmentally Appropriate Games | Complex lead-up games for Soccer, Softball, Tennis, Basketball, Volleyball |
| *Manipulative Skills* | *Manipulative Skills* | *Manipulative Skills* |
| Balloons, Beanbags, Balls, Hoops, Scooters, Jump Ropes, Parachute, Batons, Lummi Sticks | Balls, Scooters, Jump Ropes Batons, Flying Discs, Scoops, and Balls | Flying Discs, Juggling, Jump Ropes, Scoops and Balls |
| *Movement Exploration* | | |
| Space, Body Awareness, Movement Quality | | |
| *Rhythms* | *Rhythms* | *Rhythms* |
| Folk, Social and Square Dances, Lummi Sticks, Marching | Folk, Social and Square Dances, Intermediate Lummi Sticks | Folk, Social and Square Dances, Advanced Lummi Sticks |
| *Body Management* | *Body Management* | *Body Management* |
| Animal Walks, Individual Stunts, Basic Tumbling Skills | Individual Stunts, Partner Stunts, Intermediate Tumbling Skills | Partner Stunts, Partner Balances, Advanced Tumbling Skills |

For basic movement skills, then, think of learning on a continuum and building from step to step. The foundation must be established through instruction and practice, efficiency must be developed through refinement and application, and effectiveness must grow from adapting learned skills to efficient sport-related skills. The means to arrive at efficient and effective mover quality should vary, because the more movement opportunities a child has, the more likely he/she will be to: (1) be able to adapt to different sport forms, and (2) to find at least one sport form that is pleasurable and that will be pursued for a lifetime.

# Manipulatives

One might note that throwing, catching, kicking and striking are manipulative skills since they involve the use of an object or objects. This is very true and points out the fact that our content areas overlap and interact. It is not possible to draw distinct lines between the content areas as they are all highly related. Remember, our objective is to make a physically educated individual.

In the "Manipulative Skills" chapter, you will see that many more activities are noted for children in Grades K–1–2 than for 3–4–5–6. There is a reason for this. Remember that you learned that experience is very important in the shaping of the child's movement repertoire. The child needs to have numerous, varied experiences in which to apply his/her newly acquired skills. Exposure to the different manipulative activities contributes highly to the child's perceptual-motor development in spatial awareness, body awareness, etc. As the child learns to move and interact with each piece of equipment, basic educational movement themes are stressed. As children grow older, specially selected manipulative activities are in order. Therefore specialization in complex activities is appropriate for these children.

With manipulative activities, the child develops efficiency in eye-hand coordination but at the same time learns about space, body awareness and movement quality. Therefore, these two content areas overlap considerably. In fact, all movement incorporates these themes: space (direction, level, range, pathways), body awareness (shape, weight-bearing, execution, and body zones) and movement quality (time, force, flow and balance).

# Educational Movement Themes

Space, body awareness and movement quality need to be taught in the K–1–2 grades, and these areas are applied in the older grades. For space, children need to learn about self-space and general space; they need to learn about directions in which they may move, forward, backward sideways, up or down; they need to be able to adjust their movement to different levels, high, low, medium; they need to understand how far their movement may range in front, behind, above, below; and they need to understand that they may travel through space on different pathways, diagonal, zig-zag, straight, or combinations of those. For body awareness, children need to learn about different shapes the body may assume, short, tall, crooked, curled, symmetrical or asymmetrical; they need to experience movement in which different parts of the body take the weight-bearing responsibility as the body assumes different shapes in traveling; they need to develop efficiency in execution, moving in a bilateral (two sides), unilateral (one side) or contralateral (opposition) fashion; and they need to learn about the different body zones or planes, front, back, side, right, left. Quality of movement pertains to the efficiency of movement. Children need to learn about time, by working at different speeds and in different rhythmical patterns; they learn about force in experimenting with movements that generate force or absorb force; learning about flow causes them to be smooth in coordinated skills and they become able to sustain movement or suspend movement at appropriate times; and finally, throughout every movement activity the body experiments with balance, first losing and then recovering and maintaining a state of equilibrium that is efficient.

These areas are indicated as separate curriculum content areas for Grades K–1–2. Teachers should provide movement experiences that cause children to think about these qualities and to use them actively. As children grow older and more experienced, movement quality is incorporated into the gradual development of efficient movement.

# Rhythm

In order to be coordinated, a child must have an internal time structure. Otherwise referred to as temporal awareness, the internal time structure is developed and enhanced through participation in rhythmic activities. In the early years of K–1–2 simple dances and marching activities contribute to this development. Moving to music teaches the child to move to a certain beat and to coordinate his/her movements in rhythmic patterns. Children learn sequencing by following directions and repeating those directions as the games and dances go on. Creative dance activities may also be employed, allowing the child more freedom of choice in the movement repertoire to express himself/herself through rhythmical movement.

Rhythm activities should continue through the upper elementary grades. Content should build from year to year, just as indicated in the basic motor skill development. Dances should increase in complexity with the age of the child and the teacher should select those dance activities that are developmentally appropriate in complexity.

# Body Management

Centering on animal walks, stunts and tumbling skills, body management is a very important part of the child's movement repertoire development. The child needs to be able to control himself/herself in different movement situations. These gymnastic areas cause him/her to experience different body positions and movements from varied perspectives, such as weight-bearing on the hands versus the feet. The "Body Management" chapter provides information on content for these areas. Note that these skills also should build in complexity over the years. It is not necessary to re-learn a forward roll each year.

These areas are the basic content areas to be stressed for children in Grades K–6. The amount of time to be spent in each area is difficult to determine as so many different activities contribute to many areas at the same time.

# The Yearly Plan

The usual school year is based on approximately 40 weeks. Within those 40 weeks there are holidays, so the standard school year is actually 180 days. School districts may vary with more days allocated but never fewer than 180. The best way to form a yearly plan is to take the curriculum areas you choose to teach and designate specific times for them throughout the year. You need to take into consideration weather and seasons so that you may designate content appropriately. Also, you will need to work with your physical educator so that you are coordinating the units of instruction so that the children receive quality daily physical education.

This yearly plan is developed on the basis of five days per week of physical education, 30 minutes per day. For the most part the year is divided into 5-day units. It is the classroom

**Example Yearly Plan for 5-Day-Per-Week Physical Educaction for Grades K-2**

| Week | Kindergarten | Grade 1 | Grade 2 |
|------|--------------|---------|---------|
| 1 | General Exploration of Movement and Assessment of FMS | General Exploration of Movement and Assessment of FMS | General Exploration of Movement and Assessment of FMS |
| 2 | Walk, Run, Jump | Run, Jump, Hop, Leap | Gallop, Slide, Skip |
| 3 | Throw, Catch | Throw, Catch | Throw, Catch |
| 4 | Kick, Strike | Kick, Strike | Kick, Strike |
| 5 | Balloons, Beanbags | Ball Skills | Ball, Skills |
| 6 | Hoops, Skooters | Hoops, Skooters | Jump Ropes |
| 7 | Jump Ropes | Jump Ropes | Jump Ropes |
| 8 | Parachute, Balls | Parachute, Balls | Ball Skills |
| 9 | Simple Dances | Simple Dances | Simple Dances |
| 10 | Animal Walks | Individual Stunts | Individual Stunts |
| 11 | Stunts | Basic Tumbling | Basic Tumbling |
| 12 | Walk, Run, Jump | Run, Jump, Hop, Leap | Gallop, Slide, Skip |
| 13 | Throw, Catch | Throw, Catch | Throw, Catch |
| 14 | Kick, Strike | Kick, Strike | Kick, Strike |
| 15 | Balloons, Beanbags | Ball Skills | Ball, Skills |
| 16 | Hoops, Skooters | Hoops, Skooters | Jump Ropes |
| 17 | Jump Ropes | Jump Ropes | Jump Ropes |
| 18 | Parachute, Balls | Parachute, Balls | Ball Skills |
| 19 | Movement Exploration | Movement Exploration | Movement Exploration |
| 20 | Simple Dances | Simple Dances | Simple Dances |
| 21 | Animal Walks | Individual Stunts | Individual Stunts |
| 22 | Stunts | Basic Tumbling | Basic Tumbling |
| 23 | Walk, Run, Jump | Run, Jump, Hop, Leap | Gallop, Slide, Skip |
| 24 | Throw, Catch | Throw, Catch | Throw, Catch |
| 25 | Kick, Strike | Kick, Strike | Kick, Strike |
| 26 | Balloons, Beanbags | Ball Skills | Ball, Skills |
| 27 | Hoops, Skooters | Hoops, Skooters | Jump Ropes |
| 28 | Parachute, Balls | Parachute, Balls | Ball Skills |
| 29 | Movement Exploration | Movement Exploration | Movement Exploration |
| 30 | Simple Dances | Simple Dances | Simple Dances |
| 31 | Simple Dances | Simple Dances | Simple Dances |
| 32 | Animal Walks | Individual Stunts | Individual Stunts |
| 33 | Stunts | Basic Tumbling | Basic Tumbling |
| 34 | Reassessment of FMS and Exploration of Movement | Reassessment of FMS and Exploration of Movement | Reassessment of FMS and Exploration of Movement |
| 35 | Developmentally Appropriate Games | Developmentally Appropriate Games | Developmentally Appropriate Games |
| 36 | Field Days and Special Activities | Field Days and Special Activities | Field Days and Special Activities |

teacher's responsibility to see that his/her children have daily physical education. You will notice that it is suggested that units are kept short (one week) and that each unit appears

**Example Yearly Plan for 5-Day-Per-Week Physical Education for Grades 3-4**

| Week | Grade 3 | Grade 4 |
|------|---------|---------|
| 1 | Physical Fitness Assessment Motor Skill Evaluations | Physical Fitness Assessment Motor Skill Evaluations |
| 2 | Developmentally Appropriate Games | Developmentally Appropriate Games |
| 3 | Soccer Skills | Soccer Skills |
| 4 | Soccer Skills | Soccer Lead-Ups |
| 5 | Soccer Lead-Ups | Soccer Lead-Ups |
| 6 | Soccer Lead-Ups | Soccer Lead-Ups |
| 7 | Physical Fitness: Aerobic Activity Emphasis | Physical Fitness: Aerobic Activity Emphasis |
| 8 | Folk and Social Dance | Folk and Social Dance |
| 9 | Folk and Social Dance | Folk and Social Dance |
| 10 | Folk and Social Dance | Folk and Social Dance |
| 11 | Physical Fitness: Aerobic Activity Emphasis | Physical Fitness: Aerobic Activity Emphasis |
| 12 | Developmentally Appropriate Games | Developmentally Appropriate Games |
| 13 | Volleyball Skills | Tennis Skills |
| 14 | Volleyball Skills | Tennis Skills |
| 15 | Volleyball Lead-Ups | Tennis Lead-Ups |
| 16 | Volleyball Lead-Ups | Tennis Lead-Ups |
| 17 | Physical Fitness: Aerobic Activity Emphasis | Physical Fitness: Aerobic Activity Emphasis |
| 18 | Jump Ropes | Jump Ropes |
| 19 | Individual Stunts | Review Basic Tumbling Skills |
| 20 | Review Basic Tumbling Skills | Review Intermediate Tumbling Skills |
| 21 | Partner Stunts and Balances | Partner Stunts and Balances |
| 22 | Physical Fitness: Aerobic Activity Emphasis | Physical Fitness: Aerobic Activity Emphasis |
| 23 | Developmentally Appropriate Games | Developmentally Appropriate Games |
| 24 | Square and Social Dance | Square and Social Dance |
| 25 | Square and Social Dance | Square and Social Dance |
| 26 | Square and Social Dance | Square and Social Dance |
| 27 | Physical Fitness: Aerobic Activity Emphasis | Physical Fitness: Aerobic Activity Emphasis |
| 28 | Basketball Skills | Scoops and Balls Activities |
| 29 | Basketball Skills | Ultimate Frisbee |
| 30 | Basketball Skills | Basketball Skills |
| 31 | Basketball Lead-Ups | Basketball Lead-Ups |
| 32 | Softball Skills | Softball Skills |
| 33 | Softball Skills | Softball Lead-Ups |
| 34 | Softball Lead-Ups | Softball Lead-Ups |
| 35 | Physical Fitness Assessments | Physical Fitness Assessments |
| 36 | Field Days and Special Cooperative Activities | Field Days and Special Cooperative Activities |

**Example Yearly Plan for 5-Day-Per-Week Physical Education for Grades 5-6**

| Week | Grade 5 | Grade 6 |
|---|---|---|
| 1 | Physical Fitness Assessment Motor Skill Evaluations | Physical Fitness Assessment Motor Skill Evaluations |
| 2 | Developmentally Appropriate Games | Developmentally Appropriate Games |
| 3 | Soccer Skills | Volleyball Skills |
| 4 | Soccer Skills | Volleyball Lead-Ups |
| 5 | Soccer Lead-Ups | Volleyball Lead-Ups |
| 6 | Soccer Lead-Ups | Ultimate Frisbee |
| 7 | Physical Fitness: Aerobic Activity Emphasis | Physical Fitness: Aerobic Activity Emphasis |
| 8 | Folk and Social Dance | Folk and Social Dance |
| 9 | Folk and Social Dance | Folk and Social Dance |
| 10 | Folk and Social Dance | Folk and Social Dance |
| 11 | Physical Fitness: Aerobic Activity Emphasis | Physical Fitness: Aerobic Activity Emphasis |
| 12 | Developmentally Appropriate Games | Developmentally Appropriate Games |
| 13 | Volleyball Skills | Tennis Skills |
| 14 | Volleyball Lead-Ups | Tennis Skills |
| 15 | Volleyball Lead-Ups | Tennis Lead-Ups |
| 16 | Volleyball Lead-Ups | Tennis Lead-Ups |
| 17 | Physical Fitness: Aerobic Activity Emphasis | Physical Fitness: Aerobic Activity Emphasis |
| 18 | Jump Ropes | Jump Ropes |
| 19 | Partner Stunts and Balances | Review Intermediate Tumbling Skills |
| 20 | Review Intermediate Tumbling Skills | Advanced Tumbling Skills |
| 21 | Advanced Tumbling Skills | Group Stunts and Balances |
| 22 | Physical Fitness: Aerobic Activity Emphasis | Physical Fitness: Aerobic Activity Emphasis |
| 23 | Developmentally Appropriate Games | Developmentally Appropriate Games |
| 24 | Square and Social Dance | Square and Social Dance |
| 25 | Square and Social Dance | Square and Social Dance |
| 26 | Square and Social Dance | Square and Social Dance |
| 27 | Physical Fitness: Aerobic Activity Emphasis | Physical Fitness: Aerobic Activity Emphasis |
| 28 | Basketball Skills | Juggling |
| 29 | Basketball Skills | Basketball Lead-Ups |
| 30 | Basketball Lead-Ups | Basketball Lead-Ups |
| 31 | Basketball Lead-Ups | Basketball Lead-Ups |
| 32 | Softball Skills | Softball Lead-Ups |
| 33 | Softball Skills | Softball Lead-Ups |
| 34 | Softball Lead-Ups | Softball Lead-Ups |
| 35 | Physical Fitness Assessments | Physical Fitness Assessments |
| 36 | Field Days and Special Cooperative Activities | Field Days and Special Cooperative Activities |

three times in the school year. The units will build with natural progression from first time to second and from second to third and therefore content will be varied in each unit, but the main focus remains the same. This type of yearly plan allows for more variety from week to week. Of course when one considers that each unit represents two-and-one-half hours of activity, it becomes obvious that intended skills will not be learned, refined and applied all within that one week experience. Therefore the units are repeated with similar but varied content and with the same general objectives.

The yearly plan acts as a map of the year, directing the teacher throughout the school term. Yearly plans for Grades 3–4 and 5–6 follow. You will notice that they are similar. Most units are 3 or 4 weeks long, giving the children 7.5–10 hours of instruction for each one. Integrated at approximately every 5 weeks there is a unit on physical fitness in which the teacher would work with the students by presenting activities that they can use to develop their aerobic endurance. The "Physical Fitness" chapter gives material for this unit. You should select activities for their inherent value in increasing aerobic fitness; however, you should also consider selecting those which the children are likely to do on their own time as well. These "fitness break" mini-units actually serve as workshops to allow the children time to learn more activities for increasing and maintaining aerobic fitness. Each lesson in every unit taught should have a fitness developing component; fitness should not be ignored until time for the mini-units!

These yearly plans designate a number of weeks of sport skill development, then a number of weeks of lead-up games. The lead-up games used for grade 4 should be different from those used for Grade 6, and those for Grade 6 should be increased in complexity. The sport unit choices for the grades are somewhat arbitrary: the point of selecting them as we have is to avoid parallel repetition of units year after year. When you consider the fact that repeating each sport each year would possibly allow for 2 week units at best, or 5 hours of instruction, you can see that not much will be accomplished each year. Perhaps it is better to learn a few sports well than to experience many sports. If yearly plans were designed for in-depth units, the child, by the time he/she reaches high school physical education, should be able to participate in an elective program and select sports he/she chooses to learn more about or to increase skill in certain areas.

Each of the three yearly plans indicates that there will be an assessment period during the first week so that the teacher can familiarize himself/herself with the skill level of the class. Grade 1 and higher will take a physical fitness test as well. This assessment is repeated at the end of the year. This will indicate both growth and learning that has occurred over the year. With a 5-day-per-week program you surely will make a difference in the child's physical performance.

Each year in the spring most elementary schools hold some kind of field day event. It is usually the job of the physical educator to organize and direct such an event. Field Days are discussed further later in this text.

## The Unit Plan

The unit plan presents an outline of the weeks designated in the yearly plan. A general objective is given for the unit, and this objective should relate to all three domains: psychomotor, cognitive and affective. The first unit is an outline of Week 2 from the K–1–

2 yearly plan and is designated for Grade 1. The objectives are stated, and the equipment that is needed is indicated. The day-by-day outline is referred to as a block plan. Each block has four components: Fitness Activity (F), Instructional Focus (I), Activity (A), and Closure (C). At the end of the unit the method of evaluation is given.

The Fitness Activity should be of a vigorous nature. Gone are the days of the laborious calisthenics. Children want to be able to move and play as soon as possible when they enter the gymnasium. Therefore the fitness activity can be a maximum participation, active and vigorous game previously learned in class. The beginning fitness activity should not be something with complicated instructions but rather movement that can begin immediately. The fitness activity consists of general movement in general space and four vigorous games, one per day. This activity will last approximately 5–7 minutes.

The Instructional Focus indicates the skills to be taught and emphasized. The amount of time needed for this portion is dependent on whether or not the skills are new or previously encountered. This period of time should consist of your teaching a certain skill and then practice time by the students so that you can move around the gymnasium and provide feedback for the children.

The Activity portion of the lesson is still a practice time for students, and feedback should continue, but this is the "laboratory time" in which the children have the chance to use the new skill or skills in a specific movement activity. Developmentally appropriate games have been selected for four days of the unit; one day is a creative exploration activity (Day 1) with emphasis on speed and pathways.

Closure is an extremely important part of the lesson although it takes the least time. Since children should know what they have learned for the day, it is wise to review the class objectives with them. This time is mostly cognitively and affectively oriented; after a discussion with the teacher about the importance of the class and of their participation, the children leave with answers to the age-old question "What did you do in school today?" Closure also reinforces the importance of physical education. This part of the lesson may be as little as 1 minute in duration.

**Example Unit Plan for 5-Day-Per-Week Physical Educaction for Grades K-12**

*Fundamental Motor Skills*
*Grade 1: Run, Jump Hop Leap*

*Unit Objective:  to provide instruction and experiences tn running, jumping, hopping, and leaping so that Grade 1 children will be able to work on learning effective movement skills in order to be efficient movers.  As efficiency builds, the Grade 1 children will be able to understand when and how to use these skills in developmentally appropriate games and will feel good aboout themselves when meeting with success in participation.*

*Equipment needed:  3 yarn balls, 6 long jump ropes, 12 short jump ropes*

| | | | | | |
|---|---|---|---|---|---|
| **Day 1** | F: | FMS in general space | **Day 2** | F: | Run and Roll |
| | I: | Running, Leaping | | I: | Jumping, Hopping |
| | A: | Traveling with varied speed in different pathways | | A: | Crossing the Brook |
| | | | | C: | Review skills |
| | C: | Review skills | | | |
| **Day 3** | F: | Turtle Tag | **Day 4** | F: | Skunk Tag |
| | I: | Running, Leaping | | I: | Jumping, Hopping |
| | A: | Barnyard Upset | | A: | Jump the Shot |
| | C: | Review Activities | | C: | Review Activities |
| **Day 5** | F: | Walk, Trot, Sprint | | | |
| | I: | Review run, leap, jump, hop | | | |
| | A: | Hill Dill, Where's My Partner | | | |
| | C: | Evaluate | | | |

*Evaluation:  On the last day children will cross the gymnasium in groups of six, performing the designated motor skills.  Teacher will note those with any problems.*

Presented next is a unit plan for third grade tumbling. The structure is the same as that above. You will note that a vigorous warm-up is used. The first day is a review of some of the skills learned in the units in Grade 2. Then instruction begins on a progression and builds for 5 days. On day 7 the children will work on combining tumbling skills (such as a headstand to a forward roll). On days 8 and 9 they will develop and perform routines with combinations of tumbling skills. And, on day 10 the teacher will evaluate the skill development. The Instructional Focus identifies the skills to be taught. The Activity portion indicates "practice." It is here that the unit plan becomes unique to its content. Where the fundamental motor skill used games as laboratories for learning, tumbling has a different focus. Its main objective is body control and management. Therefore the lesson will be set up so that one skill is taught and then the children practice as the teacher moves about the room giving feedback. Then the second skill is taught; practice ensues; and the teacher provides feedback. At the end of the class period closure will consist of talking about the skills learned, perhaps what muscles were used, etc.

## Example Unit Plan for 5-Day-Per-Week Physical Education for Grades 3–4

*Intermediate Tumbling*
*Grade 3*

*Unit Objective: To provide instruction and experiences in intermediate tumbling skills so that the Grade 3 child will increase abilities in the areas of body management, coordination, balance, strength, and flexibility. Through this instruction the child will learn about force production and inertia. Through success in skills learned the child will increase self-esteem.*

*Equipment needed: 24 yarn balls, 12 (6' x 12') tumbling mats, 2 tumbling wedges*

| | | | |
|---|---|---|---|
| **Day 1** | F: Hot Tomato<br>I: Review forward roll, forward roll from stand, tip-up, stork stand<br>A: Practice<br>C: Review skills | **Day 2** | F: Run and Roll<br>I: Forward roll from jump, headstand<br>A: Practice<br>C: Review skills |
| **Day 3** | F: Greedy Tag<br>I: Headstand Variations, Back Shoulder Roll<br>A: Practice<br>C: Review skills | **Day 4** | F: Shipwreck<br>I: Thread the Needle, Cartwheel<br>A: Practice<br>C: Review skills |
| **Day 5** | F: Running Mania<br>I: Chinese Get Up, Review Cartwheel<br>A: Practice<br>C: Review skills | **Day 6** | F: Galloping Lizzie<br>I: Egg roll, Handstand<br>A: Practice<br>C: Review skills |
| **Day 7** | F: Shadows<br>I: Combinations of skills<br>A: Practice<br>C: Review skills | **Day 8** | F: Tortoise and Hare<br>I: Routines<br>A: Design and Practice<br>C: Review skills |
| **Day 9** | F: Back and Forth<br>I: Routines<br>A: Practice<br>C: Review skills | **Day 10** | F: Hexagon Havoc<br>I & A: Skill Evaluation<br>C: Review unit |

*Evaluation: On the last day children will be tested in groups of six on the skills taught in this intermediate tumbling unit. A checklist will be used to indicate if the skill level is "O" for outstanding, "S" for satisfactory, "I" for improvement needed, or "U" for unsatisfactory.*

A two week Flying Disc unit is presented below. Each day has a fitness component. Skill development progresses with both practice time and lead-up games for the children to use their skills. Remember that the Instructional Activity usually means that you teach something, the students try it and you give feedback. That feedback is also given during the Activity portion of the class. Games that are indicated are maximum participation games, and they can always be presented for small groups, perhaps 6 games of 4 children going on at once. This gives each child many more opportunities to respond. Keep in mind that the class period is usually no more than 30 minutes in length. Therefore practice time is really minimal!

**Example Unit Plan for 5-Day-Per-Week Physical Education for Grades 5–6**

*Flying Disc*
*Grade 5*

*Unit Objective: To provide instruction and experiences in refining hand-eye coordination and applying these learned skills to a novel game, one appropriate for leisure time pursuit. Physical benefits of the Flying Disc Unit include agility and aerobic endurance. The child will find participation in flying disc activities to be pleasurable.*

*Equipment needed: 12 flying discs, 12 hula hoops, 24 flags, 12 beanbags, 6 pylons*

| | | | |
|---|---|---|---|
| **Day 1** | F: Barker's Hoopla<br>I: Backhand throw, thumb up catch<br>A: Practice<br>C: Review skills | **Day 2** | F: Squad Tag<br>I: Underhand throw, thumb down catch<br>A: Practice<br>C: Review skills |
| **Day 3** | F: Flag Chase<br>I: Throwing at different levels, distances<br>A: Practice<br>C: Review skills | **Day 4** | F: Rope jumping<br>I: Throwing at different targets<br>A: Practice<br>C: Review skills |
| **Day 5** | F: Turtle Tag<br>I: Stunts and tricks<br>A: Practice<br>C: Review skills | **Day 6** | F: Fitness Go-Round<br>I: Partner Routines<br>A: Practice<br>C: Review skills |
| **Day 7** | F: Back and Forth<br>I: Small Team Keep Away<br>A: Play<br>C: Review game | **Day 8** | F: Hexagon Havoc<br>I: Small Team Keep Away<br>A: Play<br>C: Discuss strategy |
| **Day 9** | F: Rhythmic Running<br>I: Round Robin Keep Away<br>A: Play<br>C: Discuss standings | **Day 10** | F: Walk, Jog, Sprint<br>I & A: Skill Evaluation<br>C: Review unit, discuss benefits |

*Evaluation: On the last day children will be tested in groups of six on the skills taught in this Flying Disc unit. Targets will be used to measure accuracy of throws. Children will be graded "O" for outstanding, "S" for satisfactory, "I" for improvement needed, or "U" for unsatisfactory.*

# The Lesson Plan

Each day of the block plan is enlarged into a lesson plan. This plan will be extremely specific in nature and provides a means for good organization prior to its implementation. In writing a good lesson plan, you should think thoroughly through the lesson. Plan carefully what to do, when to do it and how to do it. Since physical education involves a great deal of movement, you must plan how to get students into the desired formations as well as what to teach them when they get there! The lesson plan gives basic information about the lesson, the equipment needed for the class, and the objectives for the lesson. Then the body of the lesson is divided into 4 columns: Time, Instruction, Cues and Organization. Example lesson plans are provided for three different grade levels. If you refer to the respective unit plans given previously you will see that these lesson plans are from those units.

The time column represents the estimated amount of time it will take for the activity indicated. Most fitness activities are 5–7 minutes. The instruction column tells what the children will be told to do to accomplish the objectives of the lesson. Student teachers and beginning teachers find it very helpful to write out exactly what they intend to say. This may seem somewhat laborious, but does provide for a much better lesson. The cues column refers to teaching cue words that you may use when the children are practicing the skills. This serves as a reminder to the teacher to look for specific performance points of the skills. The organization column indicates where the students will be and how they will get into certain formations. It also indicates where the equipment is and how it will be distributed and collected. All organizational information belongs in this column.

As you look at the example lesson plans, note that the organizational material and teaching cues are placed so that each part goes along with the instruction area. See how the objective is given to the children at the beginning of the lesson: they know not only what they will be doing, but also why. As you read through each lesson plan see if you can visualize what will be happening in the lesson. The plan should be written so precisely that a substitute could carry on your program in your absence.

### Example Lesson Plan for K–1–2

Unit: *FMS: Run, Jump, Hop, Leap*

Focus: *Jump, Hop*

Equipment: *24 jump ropes, six placed in each corner of gym*

Objective: *The student will have the opportunity to practice both the jump and the hop during movement instruction activities and in the game "Crossing the Brook." The game will also teach the student about varying force production to move over varying distances. Cooperation will be stressed through partner work.*

| Time | Instruction | Cues | Organization |
|------|-------------|------|--------------|
| 5 min. | *Fitness activity: Run and Roll. When the whistle blows you may run anywhere in the gym and when it blows again you do a log roll on the floor. Next whistle means to run, next roll. Ready? (whistle)* | | *Students enter gym and go immediately to squad positions. Six jump ropes are in each corner of the play area.*<br><br>*After 5 min. teacher gives signal to stop* |
| 10 min. | *Today we will work on our skills of jumping and hopping. These skills will help you to be able to play lots of games with your friends. Everyone find a space and stand still with your feet slightly apart, arms by your side, facing me. Let's swing our arms to the front and to the back. See if you can bend your knees when you do this. Now as you bend and your arms go back, crouch down low, like this. Then swing arms forward and spring into the air!* | *Swing, bend*<br><br>*Low, reach*<br>*Swing up* | *Children spread apart* |

| Time | Instruction | Cues | Organization |
|------|-------------|------|--------------|
| | *You just did a jump! You took off on two feet and you landed on two feet. Let's do it again and be sure to bend your knees again when you land. Let's do this 5 times!* | *Ready, down, swing, lift, land* | |
| | *Let's see how FAR you can jump. Remember to crouch low, swing arms and reach OUT and UP on the jump. 10x.* | *Reach! Stretch!* | |
| | *Now please stand on one foot and bend the other leg back behind you. Bend your knee. Take a little crouch, hands by your waist. Spring UP! Land on the same foot. That's a hop! See if you can hop 10x.* | *Hop*<br>*Use your arms to balance* | |
| 1 min. | *When I say "go" I want everyone to begin to jump around the room. Let's be Mexican jumping beans! Go!* | *Jump! Reach!* | |
| 1 min. | | | |
| 2 min. | *When I say "go" I want you to hop on your right foot. Go! Switch to the left foot. What do your arms do when you hop?* | | |
| 9 min. | *When I say "go" get a jump rope from the corner closest to you and take it to your self space.* | | |
| | *Place the rope on the floor like this (v shape). Stand at the point of the V. See if you can JUMP over to the other side. Now HOP to the other side. Try a different place on your rope. Can you JUMP across the widest part? Try to HOP across the widest part. Let's try to jump sideways. Is that easy to do?* | *Crouch*<br>*Reach*<br>*Land Softly*<br><br>*Hop lightly* | |
| | *Place your rope on the floor in a straight line. Place the second rope next to it. Now you have a skinny brook! JUMP over the brook. HOP over the brook. Make the brook wider. JUMP. HOP. Continue to make the brook wider and see how big a brook you and your friend can jump! Can you HOP that far? Who can tell me what you do to jump? What is the difference between a jump and a hop? What did you do to make your jump bigger? What kinds of animals jump? Do you know of any that hop?* | | *Find a friend to work with.* |
| 2 min. | | | *Put your rope back in the corner where you found it. Then walk to the door and make a quiet line.* |

You should notice several things about this lesson. The objective is given to the children at the beginning of the class period. Jump ropes were already placed in corners: this way not all children will run to the same place to pick up a piece of equipment. Spreading out the equipment allows for the children to get ready quickly. Note how the teaching of the skills was very direct; then the skills were used in a game-like challenge situation for the children. All children could be successful because of the shape of the rope in a V: each child could determine where to jump or hop across according to his/her own perception of ability. Closure of the lesson involved the cognitive learning of the day and led the children to think more about the jump and the hop.

Example Lesson Plan for 3–4

Unit: *Intermediate Tumbling*

Focus: *Forward Roll, Headstand*

Equipment: *12 tumbling mats, already in place*

Objective: *The student will have the opportunity to* practice *the forward roll from a jump takeoff, and to learn how to do a headstand. These skills will help the child in the areas of body awareness, body management and control, general motor coordination, strength, flexibility and balance. The student will work with changing the center of gravity. Cooperation skills will be used in partner work.*

| | Instruction | Cues | Organization |
|---|---|---|---|
| | | | *Students enter gym and go immediately to squad positions. Tumbling mats are on the gym floor.* |
| | *Fitness activity: Run and Roll. When the whistle blows you may run anywhere in the gym and when it blows again you do a log roll on the floor or on a mat. Next whistle means to run, next roll. Ready? (whistle)* | | *After 5 min. teacher gives signal to stop* |
| | *When I say "go" find a friend to work with and sit down by a mat.* | | xx ___ xx ___ xx___<br>xx ___ xx ___ xx___<br>xx ___ xx ___ xx___<br>xx ___ xx ___ xx___ |
| | *Today we will work some more on our tumbling skills. These activities will help you to increase your strength and flexibility. Yesterday we did the forward roll from a stand. Now I want you to learn to do it from a jump. Watch as I do this. Stand with both feet at the edge of the mat. Bend to a slight crouch, hold your arms to the front. Keep them bent and loose like this. As you take a small jump into the air, tuck your chin, reach for the mat with your hands, land on your upper back and roll to a stand. Did everyone see? Watch one more time. Crouch, jump, tuck and reach, roll and stand. Remember to keep your body round like a ball. Take turns with your friend. I will walk around to help you.* | *Tuck*<br>*Roll*<br>*Jump*<br>*Spring* | |

| Time | Instruction | Cues | Organization |
|------|-------------|------|--------------|
|  | *Stop and sit down. Now we are going to work on the headstand. Yesterday we reviewed the tip-up. This is what it looked like. Now I am going to make it into a tripod. My hands will be two points, my head goes to the mat to be the third point. I am not on top of my head but balancing just above the forehead. Can everyone see? I have my knees balanced on my elbows. Help your friend to do a tripod. Remember to spot at the side as you did for the tip-up yesterday.* | *Tip up slowly Knees on elbows* |  |
| 4 min. | *Now, if you were able to do this very well, you may try the next step. Watch me. I tip into the tripod. Very slowly I lift my legs to extend upward. Be sure to keep both your hands and your head on the mat. Your partner can help you from the side. Be sure to go back down the way you went up. Watch once more. If some of you want to work on just the tripods, that's fine. Let's begin to work.* | *Be balanced Slowly Adjust* |  |
| 1 min. | *Now take a few minutes to work with your partner as a coach. Try both the roll from a jump and the tripod and headstand. Coach your partner.* |  |  |
| 1 min. | *When I say "go" I would like you and your partner to carry your mat over to me. Then go quietly to the door to line up. Go.* |  |  |
|  | *What did you have to remember in order to roll from a jump? Why was the tripod easier than the tip-up? Was it easier than the headstand? Why? Did you center yourself over the balance point? How did you do that?* |  |  |

This lesson was very structured in that it involved risk activities. In a tumbling lesson it is very important for the teacher to supervise very closely and carefully as there is a greater potential for injury in this unit than in many others. Note that the teacher did the demonstrating. If you feel that you cannot demonstrate a skill it is very appropriate to have a child do the demonstration as you talk. Sometimes this is even better than having the teacher demonstrate because often children will react to a difficult activity by saying, "Sure you can do it. You're the teacher!" But if a peer can also do the task it may seem less ominous. This lesson truly demonstrates the meaning of progression: tip-up to tripod to headstand. Also notice that the children were asked to be spotters for each other. This is very important so that children can feel confident in trying new skills when the fear of injury is reduced. A spotter should be helpful to the performer. The teacher uses "kid power" to stack the mats at the end of class. The lesson stated the objective, developed along lines of progression, and closed with a discussion emphasizing the cognitive learning as well as the psychomotor.

## Example Lesson Plan for 5–6

Unit:     *Flying Disc*

Focus:    *Backhand throw, Thumb up catch*

*Equipment: 12 flying discs, 4 hula hoops, 24 beanbags, 24 yarn balls*

*Objective: The student will have the opportunity to learn how to throw and catch the flying disc successfully. Cooperation will be stressed in working with partners so that the throws are easy to catch*

| Time | Instruction | Cues | Organization |
|---|---|---|---|
| | | | *Students enter gym and go immediately to squad positions.* |
| 7 min. | *When I say "go" the squad leader is to get one hoop and six beanbags. The second student will get 6 yarn balls. Go. Place the hoop on the floor in a corner I designate, place the beanbags and yarn balls inside the hoop.* | | |
| 1 min. | *We will warm up today with Barker's Hoopla as our fitness activity. When I say "go" you may run to anyone's hoop and steal one object. You may take only one at a time. Take it back quickly and place it inside your squad's hoop. Then get another. Everyone is to work as quickly as possible. At the end of the game we will count to see who has the most objects. No one may act as a guard. Everyone is to be a thief! Go!* | | |
| 8 min. | *Stop. Count your loot. Let's take a ten second heart rate. Squad members 3 and 4 put the objects away and bring back 3 flying disks for your group.*<br><br>*Find a friend in your group who has a flying disc. Then stand across from your friend on the basketball key lines.* | | |

| Time | Instruction | Cues | Organization |
|------|-------------|------|--------------|
| | *Flying disc games are really fun. Lots of people like to play with the discs. You will be able to play this with your friends after school and on weekends. Have any of you ever thrown a disc? Watch and I will show you how. Hold it in your throwing hand, thumb on top. Spread your fingers underneath. See how mine are? Now I hold the disc over by my opposite hip. To throw it I step forward toward my target and extend my arm outward, snapping my wrist on release. Everyone put the discs down on the floor. Stand as if you are ready to throw the disc. Now step, swing across, snap the wrist. Good. One more time. Now when you catch the disc have your thumb DOWN and pinch the disc between your fingers and your thumb. It is very important to watch the disc at all times. Step toward it, reach, catch and pull it in to your body. Pick up the discs and let's try playing throw and catch with partners.* | *Step-snap Reach and pinch Stand sideways* | |
| 4 min. | *If you and your partner are doing really well, step back away from each other a bit. Keep working.* | | |
| 2 min. | *See how many throws and catches you can make in a row. If you miss start to count all over again.* | | |
| 2 min. | *See if you, as the catcher, can clap your hands after the disc leaves your partner's hands and still be able to catch it. What other tricks can you do?* | | |
| 7 min. | *Now let's spread out in general space and see if you can move and pass the disc on the move. Be careful to look for oncoming players so that you avoid collisions. Give yourself 2 points for every successful pass you make (your partner catches the pass). Go.* | | |
| | *Those of you who have the discs may put them away on your way to line up at the door.* | | |
| | *Why wouldn't it work to throw the disc as we do a ball? Why is the step important to your throw?* | | |

This lesson was also in the direct style. The teacher uses children to take care of the equipment. The children also decided about the distance they could be apart in order to be successful.

# Summary

Teachers should work closely with physical educators to plan content to provide for quality daily physical education. Each grade level curriculum builds upon the movement foundation that is established in the grade level below. Planning is especially important in physical education due to the many management details as well as the attention that must be paid to safety.

# References and Suggested Readings

Gabbard, C.P., LeBlanc, E., & Lowy, S. (1989). *Games, dance and gymnastics activities for children.* Prentice-Hall.

Gallahue, D. (2005). *Developmental physical education for all children.* Human Kinetics.

Gallahue, D. (1997). *Developmental physical education for today's children.* McGraw Hill.

Gallahue, D. (1987). *Developmental physical education for today's children.* McGraw Hill.

Kirchner G. & Fishburne, G.J. (2001). *Physical education for elementary school children.* McGraw Hill.

Kirchner G. & Fishburne, G.J. (1998). *Physical education for elementary school children.* Brown & Benchmark.

Kirchner G. & Fishburne, G.J. (1995). *Physical education for elementary school children.* Brown & Benchmark.

Kuntzelman, C., Kuntzelman, B., McGlynn, M. & McGlynn, G. (1984). *Aerobics with fun.* Fitness Finders.

Nichols, B. (2001). *Moving and learning*: *The elementary school physical education experience.* McGraw Hill.

Nichols, B. (1994). *Moving and learning*: *The elementary school physical education experience.* Times Mirror/Mosby.

Nichols, B. (1990). *Moving and learning.* Times Mirror/Mosby.

Pangrazi, R.P. (2006). *Dynamic physical education for elementary school children.* Benjamin Cummings.

Pangrazi, R.P. (2003). *Dynamic physical education for elementary school children.* Benjamin Cummings.

Pangrazi, R.P. (1998). *Dynamic physical education for elementary school children.* Allyn & Bacon.

Pangrazi, R.P. & Dauer, V.P. (1995). *Dynamic physical education for elementary school children.* Allyn & Bacon.

Pangrazi, R.P. & Dauer, V.P. (1992). *Dynamic physical education for elementary school children.* Macmillan.

# CHAPTER
# 7

# Preschool Physical Activity

Since research has shown that perceptual-motor abilities are directly related to academic readiness skills, we know that preschool children benefit tremendously from movement activities that focus their learning in a positive direction. Capitalizing on children's innate desires to play, preschool physical education activities help children to learn to love physical

activity as well as fostering development of academic readiness skills. There is no place for a sedentary classroom for preschoolers: movement is key to learning.

Through a preschool physical education program, children have the opportunity to participate in movement activities with developmentally appropriate equipment and movement sequences that allow for growth in the psychomotor, cognitive and affective domains. Children can refine their perceptual abilities as they move and play within environments designed specifically for them. It is very important that, at this age, children are allowed to explore different ways of moving and interacting with equipment, and are encouraged by teachers to invent movements and to imitate movements of others.

Since the time for the greatest development of perceptual abilities is ages 3 to 8, the preschool years are critical for enhancement of motor skills. When a physical education program is designed to introduce and reinforce academic skills of alphabet, numbers, shapes and colors in all activities, children receive a double bonus: an active learning environment that contributes to development in all three domains.

Weikart (2000) suggests that as children participate in positive, active exploration, movement environments, they can be encouraged by their teachers to think about their movements, pre-plan those movements, and verbalize or describe those same movements. Language acquisition is reinforced as children say what they are going to do, and then do it. They may then describe what they have done. Therefore, it is key for teachers to use appropriate verbal cues (i.e., "step and throw") so children will repeat the cues during performance and make them part of their movement vocabularies.

Since research also tells us that attitudes are formed by age 8, a positive experience in a play environment will encourage children to be life-long participants in physical activity. Therefore, it is crucial that preschool children participate in quality daily physical education that is designed specifically for their age and ability levels.

## Goals of A Preschool Physical Education Program

The following represent global goals for a preschool physical education program:

1. To capitalize on the child's innate desire to play and learn through structured movement experiences
2. To provide movement experiences that will be fun and interesting, helping the child to establish a positive attitude toward physical activity for its own value
3. To help the child to become an efficient and effective mover, one who will be valued as a playmate throughout his/her childhood
4. To begin to develop the awareness of physical fitness for life
5. To teach basic academic readiness concepts in an atmosphere of play and movement

## METHODS FOR TEACHING PRESCHOOL PHYSICAL EDUCATION

Because children's developmental levels in play stages vary, and because cooperative skills are not yet under control, the very best way to teach physical education to preschoolers is to set the stage for movement exploration. Weikart (2000) gives a complete description of "eight key experiences in movement" that underlie a child's basic movement repertoire. These experiences are:
- acting upon movement directions
- describing movement
- moving in nonlocomotor ways

- moving in locomotor ways
- moving with objects
- expressing creativity in movement
- feeling and expressing steady beat
- moving in sequences to a common beat

(Weikart, 2000, p. 12)

Where these experiences form the heart of the young mover, the child who begins kindergarten after a wholesome preschool physical education experience may be expected to be able to do the following:

- creeping and crawling
- starting and stopping without falling down
- climbing up and down stairs with a change of lead foot
- rolling and tumbling
- throwing, kicking. catching and striking balls
- identifying parts of the body and knowing how they move
- moving about without bumping into others
- imitating simple sequences of movements
- responding to simple sequences of verbal directions
- talking about what one is doing, planning what to do, and recalling correctly how one moved
- synchronizing a single motion with a single word (learner say & do)
- walking to a musical beat
- walking, running, jumping, hopping, galloping, sliding, skipping, with relative ease of movement

(Weikart, 2000, p. 13)

As a potential teacher, you probably have noted that there are many children in elementary school who do not have all of these capabilities, and yet we are suggesting that Weikart's expectations are very realistic: provided that children have quality preschool physical education experiences as well as support in movement experiences at home and in the regular classroom. It should be your goal to help each and every preschool child achieve these goals en route to being a physically educated individual!

A common mistake that appears to be prevalent in school physical education programs is that sport forms are taught to children in grades lower than third. We contend that it is essential to form a basis for participation in sports, and that parent games and skills DO NOT belong in the primary grades. Even third grade is only the barest beginning of forming specialized sport skills. Many physical educators will say that children are participating in organized sport at younger and younger ages and therefore they need to have competitive sport experiences in school. This notion is totally ridiculous; not all children are ready cognitively for organized sport, the majority of primary grade children do not have the skills necessary for playing in competitive leagues, and children need a time to play for the sake of play. It is absolutely essential that teachers provide positive, success-oriented, developmentally appropriate content to primary grade children in order to build the foundation. Therefore, for the preschool children, exploration, encouragement and reinforcement should be the mode of teaching in the movement environment. When equipment is used, each child should have his/her own object to manipulate. The teacher should move around the environment, acknowledging the different ways that the children are moving, i.e. "Whitney is kicking the ball with her toe!" The teacher may ask children to try Whitney's way and then look for another child to lead the action. No moves are wrong, and each child is encouraged to be creative.

Using background music during the physical education class is very appropriate. Moving to music will help to develop that inner sense of rhythm. Children enjoy music and this will often encourage a display of more creative movement. It is very appropriate for each class period to include a singing game or simple dance. Do not expect children to remain in a set formation, however; they should be able to move in general space during the activity.

For older preschool children (4+ years), a station approach may be set where they may go to explore with developmentally appropriate equipment. However, each station should have minimal directions and simple tasks: for example, a throwing station where "feet" are on the floor indicating the step forward in the throw. This might be called the "Step and Throw" station. This chapter will describe activities where there may be 2-6 children playing at a time as well as very simple group activities. To begin each class, it would be most appropriate to have a standard starting routine such as a follow the leader routine with fundamental motor skills. At one point during the physical education period, the children should participate in a group activity: it would be appropriate for a simple game, singing game, or dance to end the class period. Most preschool classes have aides to help with special children. Aides should be assigned to help at the stations to individualize instruction as much as possible.

Utilization of the station approach encourages the children to have a chance to work in small groups with a great deal of individual instruction. Preschool children do not yet have the cognitive understanding of working together in a group to achieve a goal, and certainly not to compete. Station work allows for successful, fun participation with a few other children.

# Content For Preschool Physical Education

## EXPECTATIONS FOR PRESCHOOL MOVEMENT PATTERNS

The pyramid of motor development tells us that children learn to move in a progression. At first a reflexive being, the infant's movements are primarily concerned with survival. At approximately age 1, the child enters the rudimentary skill period where he/she deals with stability, general manipulation and forms of locomotion. From ages 1 to 2 years, the child develops basic patterns that help him/her to cope with his/her environment. By age 2, the child is developing not only a movement repertoire, but also a movement vocabulary. It is at this point that we can begin to work with the child in developing fundamental motor skills.

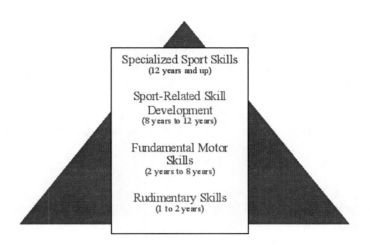

Specialized Sport Skills
(12 years and up)

Sport-Related Skill
Development
(8 years to 12 years)

Fundamental Motor
Skills
(2 years to 8 years)

Rudimentary Skills
(1 to 2 years)

## FUNDAMENTAL MOTOR SKILLS

First and foremost, preschool children need to learn to be efficient and effective movers. Previously, you learned about the fundamental motor skills as well as other basic skills of childhood play. It is in preschool that the foundation can be established for the development of those fundamental skills. By the time the children reach kindergarten, they should be ready to learn the mature pattern for the fundamental skills.

The "Fundamental Motor Skills" chapter describes the mature form for each fundamental motor skill. Since preschool children lack the coordination, strength and balance to display the mature form, it is essential that teachers understand what to expect from these children in the performance of the movement skills. Preschoolers should be encouraged to explore different ways of moving and be gradually led toward performance of the fundamental motor skill.

## *Walking*

When children first begin to walk, we see them with a wide base of support, feet often turned outward and arms bent at the elbows with hands held high. This appears to be the best way to compensate for the pull of gravity, since their centers of gravity are higher than those of adults. The majority of children typically attain most aspects of mature walking by the time they are 3 years old. Smooth coordination will come with age and activity. The "Fundamental Motor Skill" chapter describes the mature walking pattern in detail. The following section provides expectations for the young children in the fundamental motor skills followed by activities that will help them to advance in skill."

## *Running*

When children first begin to run, the base of support is wide, the period of non-support is barely present, the feet are flat, and the arms are held high. Gradually the base reduces in size, feet turn straight ahead, and arms come down to be bent at the sides. The arm swing should be in opposition to the step. Often the child will demonstrate a better pattern when asked to run "as fast as you can!" Common problems that contribute to a lack of efficient movement are: swinging arms sideways, toeing in or out, and kicking outward on the backswing. See the "Fundamental Motor Skills" chapter for a detailed description of the mature walking pattern.

## *Jumping*

Once children begin to run, they have the strength to learn to jump. There is a flight phase in the run, although it is brief, and, obviously there is a flight phase on the jump. Typically children first learn to jump by: (1) stepping down from an object such as a stair step, (2) jumping down from the same object, and (3) taking off and landing from the floor. Young children typically crouch down very low, put arms back when asked and jump forward a small distance. The direction of flight is usually more upward than outward. They often land without bending the knees to absorb force. See the "Fundamental Motor Skills" chapter for a complete description of the jump pattern that is the goal; young children will exhibit some of the characteristics at different times. With practice and instruction, they will learn to perform a mature basic jump.

## *Throwing and Catching*

The fundamental motor skill of throwing is an overhand throw. Typically young children hold the ball behind the head and fling it forward without any other body movement other than bending forward. The mature form of the throw is described in the "Fundamental Motor Skill" chapter. It is critical that young children use the oppositional pattern, stepping with the foot opposite the throwing hand. The other characteristics of the throw are also important, but will follow learning to "step and throw."

Targets for beginning throwing activities should be large and colorful. Targets that make a sound when hit with a ball also encourage children to practice their throwing skills. Balls should be small enough to be grasped easily - softball sized yarn balls are excellent for throwing practice. It is best to place markers on the floor (small footprints would be good) that encourage the child to step forward with the opposite foot when throwing.

Catching is a difficult skill to teach because it is taught in an "open" environment. This means that the object is moving when the child is expected to intercept it, and, therefore, the environment has an effect on the skill performance. The correct progression involves beginning with the child sitting on the floor and receiving a rolling ball (large ball). Young children typically extend arms out stiffly in the beginning stages of catching, resulting in "trapping the ball" to the body after it strikes the chest! The child should be cued to reach out to the ball, close hands on the ball, and bring it in to the body, absorbing force. Eventually the child should step toward the oncoming object, reach and draw it in to the chest. See the "Fundamental Motor Skills" chapter for a description of the mature form. Objects used for learning to catch should be colorful and non-threatening (foam balls).

A wide variety of items may be used to assist preschool and early childhood children with the skills relating to throwing and catching. Items should be made from a variety of materials as well as various sizes. Such items as playground balls, yarn balls, soft balls, vinyl balls, beach balls, "Gator Skin" balls, and beanbags are just some of the many items to be used to reinforce throwing and catching skills.

## *Striking (hand and arm)*

Striking skill with the upper body leads the child to be able to swing a bat or a racquet to make contact with an object. The fundamental motor striking pattern is described in the "Fundamental Motor Skill" chapter with a child swinging a bat. At the preschool level, children should be encouraged to do all sorts of activities that will help them increase their hand-eye coordination in order to be efficient in striking objects. Striking with hands also moves into the later sport-specialized skills for sports such as volleyball.

## *Kicking*

The beginning kicking action for the preschool child is simply a run into the ball. Arms are usually held in the high guard position. The action progresses to a flexion of the knee as the child stands by the ball and simply hits the ball with the foot. Children eventually move toward the mature pattern, as described in the "Fundamental Motor Skills" chapter, where they are balanced and more directed in the kick.

## COMBINATION ACTIVITIES

### *Galloping*

The gallop is a rhythmic skill that children enjoy performing. Young children often substitute the gallop for a skip. The 2-year-old is capable of performing a gallop. In this skill, one foot is always in front and the back foot comes forward when the front foot is in the air.

### *Hopping*

The skill of hopping, a one foot take-off to a same foot landing, is commonly mastered during the 3-year-old's motor skill development. Since a hop requires both leg strength and balance, it s a logical progression from the jump. When first attempting hopping, children hold arms out to the sides and high; the hop motion is usually in a vertical plane. To be able to hop forward, the child will need support to regain balance on landing.

### *Skipping*

Skipping is a combination of the step and the hop. This is a complicated skill, due to the coordination and rhythm needed for its performance. Young children usually perform a gallop or a one side skip when asked to skip. Of course some children can skip early in their lives, yet the majority will be able to coordinate the movement around 5 to 6 years of age.

## OTHER MOVEMENT SKILLS

### *Ball Bouncing*

Young children typically slap at a ball in order to make it bounce. They lack the coordination to continuously bounce a ball and probably will not begin to show any "developing" pattern until, on the average, age 4. This is, of course, largely dependent on experiences and opportunities the child has to practice the skill. Children should be encouraged to "push" the ball, rather than slap.

### *Underhand Toss*

The underhand toss involves stepping with opposition toward the target, and releasing the ball or object when the hand is approximately at waist level. Preschool children start the toss at the side of the body and "flick" the ball forward, often bending at the waist and keeping feet together and stationary.

## SPATIAL AWARENESS

You read about spatial awareness in the "Perceptual-Motor Development" chapter. Each child needs to learn to move safely and efficiently within the environment. Children need to know where they can fit, how big they are, and how to move in relation to others. Within this category comes the development of directionality: i.e., concepts of up/down, over/under, in front of/behind. In order to be an effective and efficient mover, a child must be able to participate in activities without collisions with other children.

Before moving about the play area, preschool children need to spend time learning to move into empty spaces away from other children. An activity to use to practice would be something like this: If a child is moving in Billy's direction, Billy is instructed to change direction, moving into large empty spaces and away from other children. Music can be played, and children are instructed to move into large empty spaces until the music stops, at which time they are to freeze like a statue. Distances from other children are pointed out at this time in order to reinforce looking for large empty spaces. After it is felt that the children have learned to avoid running into other children, a variety of movements may be attempted. Children may be encouraged to imitate farm animals such as dogs, cats, cows, pigs, or any other type of farm animal they can imagine. Imitating circus animals or circus acts such as clowns, tight rope walker, or any other circus act is also an exciting addition to an activity such as this that encourages development of good spatial awareness.

## BODY AWARENESS

The preschool years offer the ideal time to teach the child about his/her body parts and what they can do. Identification of those parts is involved in many games, encouraging children to develop body image as well as capabilities.

## ACTIVITIES FOR PRESCHOOL MOTOR SKILL DEVELOPMENT

It is important to remember that young children are egocentric. They are mostly concerned about themselves and are not ready for team activities, nor for competition. If games are used, rules must be extremely simple. Instruction needs to be brief. The attention spans of these youngsters are short and it is essential that your lesson move quickly. You may use a lot of repetition, and should do so. It is important that preschool children have vast opportunities to move and interact with toys and equipment in the environment. The activities described in this chapter may be used to create lesson plans that provide diverse and interesting activities to encourage children to work on increasing efficiency in motor skills and concepts.

The following activities incorporate many of the fundamental motor skills in various ways. These activities contribute to the development of basic skills, hand-eye and foot-eye coordination, body awareness, spatial awareness, laterality, directionality, rhythm and fitness in general. These descriptions will give you many different ideas about the kinds of play that you can enjoy with your children. Always feel free to be creative, change the format, change the theme, and encourage children to move freely.

***Title:*** ***Angels in the Snow***
- Level: ages 4-5
*Skills Enhanced:* body awareness, laterality
*Equipment Needed:* 8" balloon for each child
*Description:* Using the mats in a large rug-like formation instruct the children to attempt each of the following after the teacher has demonstrated the following patterns one at a time:

Children are instructed to lie flat on their back with both arms and legs spread out to the sides in a straddle position. Children are to move only the right arm and right leg bringing them in close to the body while keeping them straight, and then moving the same arm and leg away from the body while attempting to keep them straight. The terms favorite (preferred) leg and arm or arm on the same side may be used in preference to right and left. Repeat with the opposite side.

Children are to move both arms. They are to move the arms at the same time, moving them up over the head and down towards the hips while keeping them on the mat. This is known as the bilateral pattern. Repeat with legs alone.

Children are to move their right arm and their left leg only at the same time while keeping them in contact with the mat. This is known as the contralateral pattern. Repeat with opposite limbs.

### *Title:*    ***Balloon Catch***
- Level: ages 3-5

*Skills Enhanced*: hand-eye coordination, catching, body awareness

*Equipment Needed*: 8" balloon for each child

*Description:* Balloons are developmentally appropriate objects for learning to catch because they travel very slowly. An assortment of colors creates a "fun" atmosphere for the child. Give each child a round balloon; an 8" balloon is best. Have the children tap the balloon overhead and reach up, use two hands to catch and bring the balloon in to the body. Use body part commands for the activity:

a.   Catch the balloon and touch it to your nose (Children say "nose")

b.   Catch the balloon and touch it to your knee (Children say "knee")

c.   Etc. Continue with different body parts; have children name the parts as they play the game.

   Progress to : BEACH BALL CATCH
       Use the same activity using an appropriately sized beach ball.
   Progress to: BEANBAG CATCH
   Use the same activity as  using a beanbag.
   Progress to : FOAM BALL CATCH
   Use the same activity as using a foam ball.

### *Title:*    ***Balloon Frenzy***
- Level: ages 3-5

*Skills Enhanced*: hand-eye coordination, spatial awareness

*Equipment Needed*: 8" balloon for each child

*Description:*
   Have the child tap the balloon in the air overhead using two hands or one hand.
   Have the child catch the balloon by reaching up to get it and drawing it in to the body.
   Have the child tap the balloon in the air using different body parts.
   Have the child tap the balloon with the body part called by the teacher.
   Have the child travel in general space, tapping the balloon so it travels as well.
   Have the child keep the balloon in the air with an implement such as a paddle or lummi stick.

### *Title:* __Balloon Race__
- Level: ages 4-5

*Skills Enhanced*: spatial awareness, hand-eye coordination
*Equipment Needed*: 8" balloon for each child
*Description:* Have children tap balloons up in air and keep tapping them as they cross the designated play space.

### *Title:* __Base Run__
- Level: ages 3-5

*Skills Enhanced*: running, spatial awareness, stopping and starting
*Equipment Needed*: 4 bases or poly spots
*Description:* Place colored circles in a diamond form, simulating bases. Lead children from "home" to 1st, then 2nd, then 3rd, then home. Then, ask each child to run all four bases. Children may follow each other. Next, have one child run to 1st and stop, next child runs to 1st and other runs to 2nd, etc. Have children call the names of the "bases" as they run.

### *Title:* __Beach Ball Punch__
- Level: ages 4-5

*Skills Enhanced*: hand-eye coordination, striking
*Equipment Needed*: beach ball for each child
*Description:* Feed a beach ball to the child on a bounce and have him/her try to hit it back, swinging his/her arm with closed fist (sideways swing). If successful, have them do it in partners, and, if successful here, over a low net.

### *Title:* __Beanbag Balance__
- Level: ages 4-5

*Skills Enhanced:* balance, body awareness, spatial awareness, directionality
*Equipment Needed:* beanbag for each child
*Description:* Have the children place their beanbags on the floor in self space and give them the following directions:
Balance on one part of your body on the beanbag.
Can you do that with a different part?
Place the beanbag on your head; now balance on three body parts without losing the beanbag. How about four body parts? Two? One?
Can you make a bridge over the beanbag on the floor? Try to make a bridge with four body parts touching the floor. Try a bridge with two body parts on the floor.

### *Title:* __Beanbag Blast-Off__
- Level: ages 4-5

*Skills Enhanced*: hand-eye coordination, catching
*Equipment Needed:* beanbag for each child
*Directions:* In self-space have children toss and catch the beanbag; Use both hands. Have the children try tossing the beanbag at different heights.

### *Title:* __Beanbag Buddies__
- Level: ages 2-5

*Skills Enhanced*: body awareness, spatial awareness, fundamental motor skills
*Equipment Needed*: beanbags

*Description:* Have the children balance the beanbag on various body parts as they move with designated locomotor movements in general space. Have partners play follow the leader in general space carrying the beanbag on different body parts and doing different kinds of stunts. Have the children place their beanbags on the floor and see how many different ways they can find to move around or over the beanbags.

### *Title:*   *Beanbag Hoop Toss*
- Level: ages 2-5

*Skills Enhanced*: underhand toss, spatial awareness, contralateral pattern
*Equipment Needed*: nine hoops in a 3X3 format, beanbags
*Description:* Designate a space for the children to stand and place "feet" there for development of opposition.  Have children toss to different hoops designated by letter or color.

### *Title:*   *Big Bubba*
- Level: ages 3-5

*Skills Enhanced*: hand-eye coordination, directionality
*Equipment Needed*: 2-3 30" lightweight balls
*Description:* Using the big balls, have children and teachers stand in a circle and pass the balls around by rolling them in a clockwise manner around the circle.  You may need to enlarge the circle.

### *Title:*   *Bounce 'n' Catch*
- Level: ages 3-5

*Skills Enhanced*: hand-eye coordination, catching
*Equipment Needed*: 8" lightweight ball that bounces
*Description:* Use a developmentally appropriate ball that bounces well.
Have the children drop the balls and catch them from a bounce.  Have children say: "drop, catch." Have the children toss the balls with two hands high into the air, circle the arms backward and come under the bounce of the balls to catch.  Have children say "Toss, bounce, catch."
For 4-5-year-olds:

Repeat above but have the children try to catch the balls before the bounce. Have children say "Toss, catch."

Repeat, and have the children touch the body part that you call before catching the balls. Have the children say "Toss, -head- , catch."

Working against a wall space, have the children throw the balls to the wall so that they bounce on the floor on the way back for the catch, wall-floor-catch. Have children say "Wall, floor, catch."

In the same wall space, have the child throw the ball so that it hits the floor near the wall and bounces off the wall for an in-air catch, floor-wall-catch. Have child say, Floor, wall, catch."

### *Title:*   *Bouncing Kids*
- Level: ages 3-5

*Skills Enhanced:* jumping, balance

*Equipment Needed*: mini-trampoline

*Description:* If you have access to a mini-trampoline, be sure to attend to safety issues as you spot the child. Never allow children to play unsupervised on the mini-trampoline. While other children in the group jump in a circle around the mini-trampoline, have one child bouncing and verbalizing to the rhythm of the bouncing:

    a.      1-2-3-4-5-6-7-8-9-10

    b.      A-B-C-D-E-F-G-H-I-J-K-L-M-N-O-P-Q-R-S-T-U-V-W-X-Y-Z

    c.      Spelling names J-A-C-K-I-E

Children who are jumping AROUND the mini-trampoline on the floor should be verbalizing with those on the apparatus. Change children and repeat.

*Title:*    ***Bubble Bubble***

• Level: ages 3-5

*Skills Enhanced*: hand-eye coordination

*Equipment Needed*: soap bubble liquid and blower

*Description:* The teacher blows bubbles and has children track them and pop them with different body parts, i.e. pointer finger, clap hands, nose....

*Title:*    ***Catch the Cloud***

• Level: ages 3-5

*Skills Enhanced*: catching, spatial awareness

*Equipment Needed*: a plastic grocery bag or a juggling scarf for each child

*Description:* A developmentally appropriate way for children to work on catching is to use plastic grocery bags or juggling scarves. These travel very slowly in the air and can be grasped if necessary.

    1.      Toss the object up and catch it with both hands

    2.      How many times can you toss and catch the object with two hands before a miss?

    3.      Toss high, run in a circle, turn and catch with both hands

    4.      Spin around, holding object, let go and catch before it hits the ground

*Title:*    ***Follow the Leader Run***

• Level: ages 3-5

*Skills Enhanced*: running

*Equipment* Needed: none

*Description:* Children love to imitate and leading the children on a run throughout the play space can be exciting and fun. Stress swinging the arms, running slowly, running quickly, sprinting, and jogging.

*Title:*    ***Hoop Follow the Leader***

• Level: ages 3-5

*Skills Enhanced*: jumping and landing

*Equipment Needed:* hula hoops

*Description:* The "Manipulative Skills" chapter has a progression for jumping in hoops that will work well with preschool children (tasks 1-8). Have the children "follow the leader" through the hoop patterns to the best of their ability. These patterns can also be incorporated in obstacle courses.

### *Title:* *In-And-Out*
- Level: ages 3-5

*Skills Enhanced:* directionality, jumping

*Equipment Needed:* hula hoop for each child

*Description:* Each child has his/her own hula hoop. After a period of active exploration, give directions to jump in, jump out, jump sideways in, jump sideways out, jump backwards out, jump forward in, etc. Have children jump AROUND the hoop. Have the children jump repeatedly in place: BEHIND the hoop, IN FRONT OF the hoop, BESIDE the hoop. Have children verbalize the directional words as they jump. Also use sentences, "I am jumping in the hoop," or "I jumped in the hoop."

### *Title:* *Jumping from Heights*
- Level: ages 3-5

*Skills Enhanced:* jumping and landing

*Equipment Needed:* 3-4 folding tumbling mats

*Description:* Fold one tumbling mat to its smallest position. Two other mats are spread out on either side of the folded mat in order to allow for a soft landing.. The child will still use the fundamental motor skill as described in the "Fundamental Motor Skills" chapter, even though the action is downward. It is important that the child absorb force on landing by bending the knees. The concept of soft versus hard landings can be explored. A demonstration of a soft landing by the teacher or aide will assist the children in learning to land softly on their feet with the knees slightly bent to absorb the force of the landing. A demonstration of proper jumping and landing techniques should be given by the teacher, such as bending the knees and swinging the arms to assist with balance.

After a demonstration by the teacher, children are instructed to attempt the following activities:
1. With the teacher holding both of the child's hands the child will jump off the folded mat onto the stretched out mat.
2. The child will now jump off the mat without holding the teacher's hands and use a soft landing (knees slightly bent).
3. Another mat is added to make the platform higher. This time the child will jump down off the mat with the teacher holding both of his/her hands for balance.
4. Children may then attempt to jump down without holding the teacher's hands.

The words "up, down, on, off, jump and land" may be used in order to reinforce vocabulary words. Pictures of animals that jump as a means of moving from place to place may help to visually reinforce some of these concepts.

### *Title:* *Jumping the Brook*
- Level: ages 3-5

*Skills Enhanced:* jumping and landing

*Equipment Needed:* two long jumpropes

*Description:* Using two long jumpropes, lay out a "brook" on the floor.

Children stand on one side of the "brook" and jump over to the other side. Increase the distance between the ropes. You may have the ropes laid in a triangular fashion so the "brook " is narrow at one end and wider at the opposite end. Then children can work at their own ability levels. With this format you can also play the game "In the Creek, On the Bank."

Children stand with toes next to the line and follow your directions to jump in the creek or on the bank. Be sure to call "in the creek" or "on the bank" several times in a row so they do not just jump in and out, but they listen to directions!

*Title:* ***Jumping Shapes***
- Level: ages 3-5

*Skills Enhanced*: directionality, jumping

*Equipment Needed:* colored shapes

*Description:* Spread colored shapes on the playing surface. Have the children jump ON the red square, ON the green square, ON the green circle, ON the yellow star, etc. Continue to give directions involving colors and shapes. Change task to jump BETWEEN the shapes and OVER different colored shapes. Children should verbalize the colors, the directions and the shapes.

*Title:* ***Keep It Quiet***
- Level: ages 4-5

*Skills Enhanced*: hand-eye coordination, catching

*Equipment Needed*: 8.5 "beach ball, vinyl ball or playground ball.

*Description:* Working in self space with tossing the ball high, have the toss go on signal "1-2-3-toss" and see if all balls can be caught without a bounce, meaning there will not be a sound in the play area.

*Title:* ***Kick and Stop***
- Level: ages 4-5

*Skills Enhanced:* foot-eye coordination, kicking, hand-eye coordination

*Equipment Needed:* 8.5 " beach ball, vinyl ball or playground ball.

*Description:* Using a wall space, standing approximately 3 yards from the wall, have the child place the ball at his/her feet and kick the ball to the wall with the preferred foot. The child should bend over and stop the return of the ball with the opposite hand. Kicks should not be forceful.

*Title:* ***Kick Away***
- Level: ages 3-5

*Skills Enhanced:* foot-eye coordination, kicking

*Equipment Needed:* 8.5 " beach ball, vinyl ball or playground ball.

*Directions:* Have each child find a self-space on the sideline of the play area, facing a far wall. Each child will then perform a stationary kick, trying to propel the ball to the wall. The child runs to retrieve the ball after all have kicked.

*Title:* ***Leader Toss and Catch***
- Level: ages 3-5

*Skills Enhanced:* hand-eye coordination, catching

*Equipment Needed*: 8" foam balls

*Description:* Use a developmentally appropriate object for the group that you are teaching. Have the children stand in a line facing you and toss the ball gently underhand to each child in succession, emphasizing their step toward the object, reaching out with two hands, and pulling the object in to their bodies. Be sure that you are standing close to the line of children. Have the children count as each catch is made. Depending on the age and the skill of the group, you may do this with rolling when they are seated (for very young), progressing to sitting, kneeling, standing. Have the child verbalize, "I am rolling the ball," or work on directionality: "I am kneeling," "I am standing."

Child   Child   Child   Child

"Teacher"

### Title:   *Mirror Me*
- Level: ages 2-5

*Skills Enhanced*: body awareness, fundamental motor skills

*Equipment Needed*: none

*Description:* Have the children stand facing the teacher and pretend that they are looking into a mirror. The teacher then touches different body parts and says "I am touching my _____ " while the children touch the same parts and say the name, such as "Shoulders." Then the teacher strikes different poses to see if the children can imitate the positions. Difficulty may increase by adding movements such as running in place, jumping in place, or hopping on one foot. The teacher should encourage the children to vocalize by making statements such as "I am standing on one foot."

### Title:   *Out and Over*
- Level: ages 3-5

*Skills Enhanced*: jumping, landing, balance

*Equipment Needed*: markers or poly spots

*Description:* Using markers, have the children jump from a starting line, land and place markers in front of their toes. Continue to do this until he/she has crossed the designated space (about 5 yards). Be sure to emphasize bending knees, arms back, swing through on take-off, bend knees on landing and fall forward.

### Title:   *Partner Bounce 'n' Catch*
- Level: ages 4-5

*Skills Enhanced:* hand-eye coordination, catching

*Equipment Needed*: 8.5 " beach ball, vinyl ball or playground ball.

*Description:* Have the children sit on the floor and roll the ball back and forth with their partners.. Have the children sit on the floor and send the ball to the partners with one bounce in the middle.
Have the partners play throw and catch on a bounce from a standing position.

Have one partner try to roll the ball through the facing partner's legs in stride position. The target partner lets the ball go through, turns and runs after the ball brings it back and rolls it under the opposite partner's legs. Continue this pattern.

Have the first partner turn around, bend over and roll the ball back through his/her own legs to his/her partner. The partner catches the ball facing front, then turns and rolls the ball back between his/her own legs. Continue this pattern.

### Title:   *Cheer!*
- Level: ages 4-5

*Skills Enhanced*: hand-eye coordination, body awareness

*Equipment Needed*: two pom poms for each child.

*Description:* There are several activities that can be performed using pom poms to assist preschool children with such concepts as mirroring, movement patterns, and laterality. The leader will  touch the pom pom to the various body parts as follows:
1.  Right pom pom to right shoulder
2.  Right pom pom to left shoulder
3.  Left pom pom to left shoulder
4.  Left pom pom to right shoulder
5.  Both pom poms to both shoulders
6.  Repeat #1 using toes, knees, ankles, waist, etc.
7.  Cross pom poms and touch each of the above mentioned in #6.

The teacher will perform the activity and each preschooler will imitate the teacher's movements as if looking in a mirror.  The teacher may make up cheers for preschool children to say while moving with the pom poms again mirroring the teacher.  Example, "we've got the spirit, yes we do, we've got the spirit, say howdy do."  Preschoolers may echo the cheers.  Use one arm, cross arms in front of each other, lunge with arms together straight overhead.  One can use any movements resembling cheers.

Pom poms  may also be used for body awareness.  Again following the teacher's lead, touch the various body parts with the pom poms (head, shoulders, knees, feet, etc).

Pom poms may also be used for spatial awareness.  Shake pom poms in front of, behind, to one side, to the other side, up, down, all around, over, under, in and out.

### *Title:*     *Push It Down*
*   Level: ages 4-5
*Skills Enhanced:* hand-eye coordination, bouncing
*Equipment Needed:* 8.5 " beach ball, vinyl ball or playground ball.
*Description:* Have the child bounce the ball in front using two hands.  Emphasize pushing the ball down (fingers push) and allowing the cupped hands to ride upward (give) with the ball on the rise, then push down..

Have the child work on bouncing the ball in place with the preferred hand.  Emphasize the push and the give.

Have the child start to walk into general space while bouncing the ball with the preferred hand.

### *Title:*     *Rocket Blast-Off*
*   Level: ages 3-5
*Skills Enhanced:* jumping, landing, balance
*Equipment Needed:* none
*Description:* Have children in small crouching position while they count down 10-9-8-7-6-5-4-3-2-1-BLASTOFF! Then they jump as high in the air as they can.

### *Title:*     *Scooter Fun*
*   Level: ages 4-5
*Skills Enhanced:* laterality, body awareness, fitness
*Equipment Needed*: a scooter for each child

*Description:* As the children explore movement with the scooters, encourage them to try the following:

Sit on the scooter and use legs to travel forward and then backward.

Kneel on the scooter and move using arms only.

Lie on the scooter on tummy, and move with arms only, with legs only, with a homo-lateral pattern, and with a contralateral pattern.

Place hands on the sides of the scooter and run, holding and pushing the scooter throughout the play area.

### *Title:*    *Speedy Shoes*
- Level: ages 3-5

*Skills Enhanced*: running

*Equipment Needed*: finish line

*Description:* Have children show you how fast their "shoes can run." Create a finish line between two standards for them to "crash through." Crepe paper is an excellent finish line.

### *Title:*    *Toss Jump Pick*
- Level: ages 3-5

*Skills Enhanced*: jumping, spatial awareness

*Equipment Needed*: a beanbag for each child

*Description:* Have children stand on sideline of the play area with their beanbags. On the signal they toss the beanbag and then jump over it, pick it up, and toss again

## GROUP ACTIVITIES

### *Title:*    *Back to Back*
- Level: ages 4-5

*Skills Enhanced:* spatial awareness, fundamental locomotor skills

*Equipment Needed:* none

*Description:* Children move in general space while the leader calls for different kinds of movements. When the leader calls "back to back" children hurry to stand back to back with a partner. The leader also finds someone to stand with. Left over player calls the next movements.

### *Title:*    *Beanbag City*
- Level: ages 4-5

*Skills Enhanced:* spatial awareness, fundamental locomotor skills, directionality

*Equipment Needed:* Beanbags are of varying colors with a symbol on each beanbag such as a letter, shape, or number, perhaps a picture. The beanbags are scattered throughout the gymnasium.

*Description:* Give the following directions: "On the signal to go, run in general space and whenever you come to a beanbag, run in a circle around it and then move on to another."

"When I say go, run in general space and leap high over each beanbag that you come to."

"On the signal to go, begin to move in general space. Each time you come to a beanbag, step on it and change your movement (level, speed, direction, etc.)"

*Title:*   ***Beanbag Tales***
- Level: ages 4-5

*Skills Enhanced:* spatial awareness, fundamental locomotor skills, directionality
*Equipment Needed:* Beanbags are of varying colors with a symbol on each beanbag such as a letter, shape, or number, perhaps a picture.
*Description:* All children will sit in a circle on the floor. Several beanbags will be passed around the circle while the music plays. When the music stops, one at a time the children will name the symbol on the beanbag they are holding when the music stops.

*Title:*   ***Hot Potato***
- Level: ages 3-5

*Skills Enhanced:* hand-eye coordination, catching, tossing
*Equipment Needed:* beanbags, yarnballs
*Description:* Have the children in the group sit in a circle. Use several different shaped objects to pass around the circle as quickly as possible. Challenge the children to pass quickly and directly into the hands of the next child. For older children, gradually increase the size of the circle by having children move backwards and having the pass become a toss. Be sure to use developmentally appropriate objects and use only one when the game moves to tossing. Have the children recite the alphabet as they pass the objects. You may also teach them the rhyme:

    One potato, two potato, three potato, four
    Five potato, six potato, seven potatoes, MORE!
    On "MORE" any child holding an object carries it and runs quickly around the outside of the circle and back to his/her place.

*Title:*   ***Fragile Rock***
- Level: ages 4-5

*Skills Enhanced:* spatial awareness, fundamental locomotor skills
*Equipment Needed:* none
*Description:* Children scatter into general space and place their beanbags on the floor. On signal the children run anywhere in general space while the rock collector, the teacher, picks up 3-4 beanbags and then calls "To a rock!" The children run to place one finger on a beanbag. There can be more than one child on a beanbag. Continue to play, varying the locomotor movements, until only 3-4 beanbags remain on the floor.

*Title:*   ***Freeze like A….***
- Level: ages 4-5

*Skills Enhanced:* body awareness
*Equipment Needed:* none
*Description:* Children move in a designated space with different locomotor movements as called by the teacher. The teacher calls "Freeze like a _____!" and the children stop in space and imitate whatever the teacher has called (elephant, car, airplane, cat…..etc.)

*Title:*   ***Hideaway***
- Level: ages 3-5

*Skills Enhanced:* spatial awareness, fundamental locomotor skills
*Equipment Needed*: a tumbling mat for each child
*Description:* Stand the tumbling mats on end and bring around to form "houses." Have the children hide in the houses and on the signal to go, have them move to a new house quickly.

Variation: Have a ball inside each house and when the signal to run comes, they must throw the ball up and out of the house, run to get a new ball and take it into another house.

*Title:*    ___Hoop Adventure___
- Level: ages 4-5

*Skills Enhanced:* spatial awareness, fundamental locomotor skills

*Equipment Needed:* hula hoop for each child

*Description:*  Give the following directions:

"When I say go, run and put your foot inside a yellow hoop."

"When I say go, skip to a blue hoop and put your elbow inside. When I say go, slide to a red hoop and put your knee inside."

"When I say go, gallop to a green hoop and put your hand inside."

Continue to give directions for different locomotor movements and different body parts.

The teacher gives the following directions:

a.    "When I say go, roar like a lion to a blue hoop."
b.    "When I say go, leap like a deer to a red hoop."
c.    "When I say go, slide like a snake to a yellow hoop."
d.    "When I say go, gallop like a horse to a green hoop."
e.    "When I say go, skip like a lamb to a blue hoop."
f.    "When I say go, lumber like an elephant to a red hoop, then jump like a rabbit to a green hoop.  When I say go, jump like a frog to three different green hoops."
g.    "When I say go, ride on a motorcycle to a blue hoop, fly an airplane to a yellow hoop, and chug to a red hoop on a train."

Continue to give directions that allow the children to be creative and, at the same time, work on spatial awareness moving within general space.

*Title:*    ___Hoop Mania___
- Level: ages 3-5

*Skills Enhanced:* spatial awareness, directionality, body awareness

*Equipment Needed:* a hula hoop for each child

*Description:*
1.    Children stand in front of their hoops
2.    In back of
3.    Under
4.    Around
5.    On one side
6.    On the other side
7.    Move the hoop high
8.    Move the hoop low
9.    Stand inside the hoop
10.    Stand outside the hoop
11.    Stand under the hoop
12.    Hold the hoop below their knees
13.    Put various body parts called out by the teacher through the hoop

14. Children perform a variety of movements inside the hoop such as hopping on 1 foot, jumping, etc.
15. Children step forward over the hoop
16. Children step backwards over the hoop
17. Children jump forward over the hoop
18. Children jump backwards over the hoop

### *Title:*    *Hoops of Fun*
• Level: ages 4-5

*Skills Enhanced:* spatial awareness, directionality, body awareness

*Equipment Needed:* a hula hoop for each child

*Description:* After allowing some time for exploration with the hoops, give the following directions.

"Bend down and pick up the hoop with arms extended out to sides. Try to lift the hoop all the way overhead without touching your body. On the count of three, clap your hands and let the hoop fall around you. 1-2-3. Did the hoop touch your body when it fell? Try again and see if you can do it so that the hoop does not touch your body."

"Try to spin the hoop like this (an eggbeater) on the floor in front of you. Can you run around the hoop and back to your place before it stops spinning? See if you can stop the hoop by putting one of your feet inside the eggbeater!"

Can you balance on two body parts inside your hoop? Find two different body parts. How about two others?

Balance on two body parts, one inside and one outside of the hoop.

Balance on three body parts, two outside and one inside the hoop.

Balance on three body parts, two inside the hoop and one outside.

Continue to give balance challenges to the children.

### *Title:*    *Hoop Travel*
• Level: ages 4-5

*Skills Enhanced:* spatial awareness, directionality

*Equipment Needed:* a hula hoop for each child

*Description:* Using music, have half of the group of children stand still and hold their hoops on the ground vertically and perpendicular to themselves. The other children drop their hoops and travel in and out of the still hoops while the music plays. When the music stops, they change roles.

With the same musical and hoop format as in #5, have one group sit on the floor and hold the hoop horizontally about 5" off the floor (have the sitting children rest the held hoop on top of their shoes for proper height). The traveling group will run and step, hop or jump (whichever direction you choose) into each hoop while the music plays.

### *Title:*    *Jumping Jacks*
• Level: ages 4-5

*Skills Enhanced:* general coordination

*Equipment Needed:* none

*Description:* Help children with coordination in jumping jacks. Go slowly and use cues, OUT, TOGETHER, OUT, TOGETHER for the feet. Do not add the arms until the footwork has been mastered.

*Title:*    ***Magic Turn***
- Level: ages 3-5

*Skills Enhanced:* body awareness

*Equipment Needed:* one hula hoop per child

*Description:* Have children stand in hoops facing the teacher. When the teacher says "Abracadabra" the children spin slowly in their hoops; the teacher calls a body part (e.g. "Nose!") and the children stop with hands on nose. The game continues with different parts of the body being called.

*Title:*    ***Oscar's Garbage Can***
- Level: ages 3-5

*Skills Enhanced:* spatial awareness, directionality, cooperation

*Equipment Needed:* tumbling mats, beach balls

*Description:* Take two 6X12 mats, stand them on their sides and hook together in a CIRCLE. Allow one child to be inside as Oscar. Spread 10-12 beach balls around the play area. On the signal to go, the other children run to get the balls and "shoot" them into the GARBAGE CAN. "Oscar" shoots the balls out again as they come in. After two minutes, switch "Oscars." Play game until every child has had a chance to be OSCAR.

*Title:*    ***Parachute Activities***
- Level: ages 3-5

*Skills Enhanced*: spatial awareness, directionality, cooperation

*Equipment Needed*: small parachute

*Description:* Parachute activities are described in Chapter 10, Manipulative Activities. Preschool children love to work with the parachute — it is colorful and exciting!

*Title:*    ***Tumble Rumble***
- Level: ages 3-5

*Skills Enhanced*: spatial awareness, fundamental locomotor skills aerobic fitness

*Equipment Needed*: 8-10 tumbling mats

*Description:* Gather all the tumbling mats available and spread them out, then push them together to form a large rug like area. Children perform the locomotor skill the teacher calls, but on a special signal they drop to the mat and roll. On another special signal they jump up and travel. Teacher continues to change signals. Children should be instructed to watch out for other children, being careful not to roll into someone else's space or touch any other child.

*Title:*    ***Turtle Tag***
- Level: ages 4-5

*Skills Enhanced*: aerobic fitness

*Equipment Needed*: two yarn balls

*Description:* Choose two children to be taggers and give each a yarn ball to use to tag. If a child is tagged, he/she goes down on the floor in a pushup position. Other players may "free" the turtle by crawling underneath him/her.

*Title:*    ***Who's in My Garage?***
- Level: ages 3-5

*Skills Enhanced*: spatial awareness, fundamental locomotor skills

*Equipment Needed*: a hula hoop for each one
*Description:* Using hula hoops on the floor in the play area, have each child stand in one; when you say "Who's in my garage?" they leave their garages and "drive" to new ones. You, as the teacher go to a garage also. The child left out gets to say "Who's in my garage?" Game continues. Increase difficulty by spreading "garages" out more.

## BODY MANAGEMENT ACTIVITIES

The "Body Management Skills" chapter provides many activities for helping children with general coordination and tumbling. It is essential to remember that very young children will not be able to sustain long periods of instruction. Therefore some techniques are suggested here for working in the body management area. Exact descriptions of the skills and activities can be found in the "Body Management" chapter.

### *Let's Be a Parade!*

Have the children spread out and find their own spaces. Tell them it is time to practice for the "Animal Parade!" ("Circus Parade!" "Barnyard Parade!"). Give them the name of an animal and have them move like that animal in their own space, to practice. Pick a good one and have them all try to move just like that child. Then show them your interpretation, which would match the one in the "Body Management" chapter. Those animal walks that would be particularly good for preschool children to do would be: bear walk, crab walk, crocodile walk, dog walk, rabbit jump, frog jump, and seal walk. All of these skills contribute to flexibility and strength.

After practicing for the parade, make a line, put on some music, call out animal names and have the children move as if in a parade through the play space.

### *Tricks! Tricks! Tricks!*

The following stunts are renamed in order to appeal to the young child. The teaching format should be such that every child has a mat space , and the teacher says: "I can do a trick! Watch and see if you can do it too!"

### *Wheels on the Bus*

The child assumes a side-lying position with one arm positioned with the hand on the floor. The child lifts himself/herself so that the arm takes the body weight and is fully extended and the side of the bottom foot rests on the floor. The child then, keeping the body as straight as possible walks the feet so that the body moves around the pivot arm (which stays in place). This skill contributes to arm strength.

### *Hot Dog Roll*

The child lies down on the floor or the mat with his/her arms extended directly by the ears and overhead. He/she then rolls sideward, keeping the arms extended and rolling in a straight line. This skill contributes to flexibility, coordination and balance.

## Barney Sit-Stand

The child begins in a standing position, arms folded across chest, and feet crossed on the floor. He/she then lowers his/her buttocks to the ground to a sitting position. Next he/she will, keeping the body in the same position, stand up in the same place. This skill contributes to leg strength and balance.

## Clown Ball

Sometimes incorrectly referred to as the somersault, the forward roll is just that: a roll on a mat in a forward direction. The child begins in a squatting position with knees together, hands on the mat just in front of and outside the knees. He/she tucks the chin to the chest and pushes with the legs up and over forward, keeping the body in a round, tucked position, and contacting the mat on the top of the upper back. The child should hold the tucked and rounded position to keep momentum going so he/she rolls directly back to the feet and comes to a stand from the roll. Children often display one of the following problems: putting the top of the head on the mat and trying to roll (cue: "tuck your chin; miss the mat with your head"), opening from the tucked and rounded position too soon and landing in a sitting position, legs extended (cue: "stay in a ball until you roll to your feet"), or bending one arm more than the other and rolling over sideways (cue: "keep strong arms"). If there are children with problems, use the spotting technique described at the end of this section. Once the child gains a kinesthetic sense of what he/she is supposed to be doing, skill will be enhanced.

Spotting: Squat down to the side of the tumbler. Place the inside hand at the back of the tumbler's neck to keep the head tucked. Place the other hand or arm under the tumbler's bottom. This way you can safely guide the child through the skill.

## Circus Performers

The teacher or aide should demonstrate the balancing activities before the children attempt them. These same balancing activities may be attempted directly on the floor first, by either using a straight line painted on the floor or a long jump rope stretched out straight also on the floor. Then children may start on the beams which are directly on the floor (painted 2'x4' wood works well) and then move to the higher beams. The child may need to have assistance, such as a hand, to maintain balance. Have the child walk first by keeping one foot always in front. Progress to the normal walking pattern. Be sure the child moves either slowly or at a normal walking pace, not running on the beams. The child who runs is simply avoiding balance. Vary the task by having the child move sideways and, eventually, backwards.

After the teacher or aide demonstrates each of the following activities, one at a time the children are to attempt to imitate the teacher.

1. The child stands on the beam moving forward
2. with one foot in front of the other, in a heel to toe manner.
3. The child walks forward on the beam moving with one foot in front of the other, turns (up on the toes) to face the other direction and moves back to the starting place.
4. The child walks backwards with one foot behind the other.

5.  The child walks backwards with one foot then the other, turns and walks backwards to the starting position.
6.  The child walks forward, stops, then walks backwards to the starting position.
7.  The child balances a beanbag on his/her head while attempting 1 through 5
8.  The child balances a beanbag on various body parts while attempting 1 through 5 (hand, arm, elbow, neck, shoulder, etc.)
9.  The child stands on one foot on the balance beam
10. The child stands on the other foot on the balance beam
11. The child stands on one foot while touching the opposite hand to the head while balancing on the balance beam.
12. The child stands on the other foot while touching the opposite hand to various body parts while balancing on the beam (elbow, wrist, shoulder, etc.
13. The child attempts to move the arms in various patterns while standing on the balance beam (example – homo-lateral, bilateral, contralateral). Assistance and demonstrations are required for all activities.
14. The child attempts a standing scale while standing on the balance beam.
15. The child is asked to balance the beanbag on one of the higher body parts.
16. The child is asked to balance the beanbag on one of the lower body parts.
17. Progression is dependent on child's age and abilities.

## Silly Statues

Using the mats in a large rug formation children are instructed to try each of the following, one at a time, after a demonstration by the teacher or aide:
1.  Lie on one side of the body
2.  Lie on the other side of the body
3.  Lie on one side of the body and raise the opposite arm
4.  Lie on the other side of the body and raise the other arm
5.  Balance on two knees
6.  Balance on one knee
7.  Balance on one knee and lean the body forward
8.  Balance on the other knee and lean the body forward
9.  Balance on one knee and put both hands on the mat
10. Balance on the other knee and put both hands on the mat
11. Repeat 9 and 10 and add putting the head on the mat
12. Stand on two feet and place both hands on the mat bending at the waist while also bending the knees slightly
13. Repeat 12 and place the head on the mat also
14. Stand up straight and balance on one foot
15. Repeat 14 balancing on the other foot
16. Repeat 15 and bring both arms out to the side at shoulder height
17. Children lie on one side and attempt to lift body parallel to the mat while balancing on one hand and one foot
18. Repeat 17 only on the other side of the body
19. Modified push up
20. Push up
21. Modified curl up
22. Curl up
23. Using the mat instruct children to see how many or few body parts they can balance themselves upon (1,2,3,4, etc.)

## *Obstacle Course*

Obstacle courses are excellent ways to have children use their movement skills and spatial awareness to navigate and travel.

Tumbling mats may be folded in such a way that they form tunnels. Several tunnel mats may be spread throughout the gymnasium for the children to crawl through. Tunnel mats can be made into an obstacle course in order that children may move in various ways through the course moving through the tunnels when they appear in the obstacle course. Several tunnel mats may be set up end to end in order that children may move through one long tunnel. Hula hoops may be inserted into styrofoam holders in order to make them stand in an upright position. There are also tunnels which are made out of soft material using covered plastic or wire coils to keep the material rigid, which can be purchased through equipment catalogues in order to practice tunneling activities.

Balance beams, alphabet letter squares, climbing apparatus, hurdles, cones, and other equipment may be used to create obstacle courses that give children the opportunity to go under, over, around, between, etc.

## *Keep the Beat*

It is important that preschool children be given the opportunity to learn how to feel and move to an even beat. Young children enjoy listening and moving to music. Perhaps it will be necessary to seek assistance from the music teacher in order to teach preschool children the difference between the beat and rhythm. Simple instruments can be helpful when teaching children about the rhythm and beat. Rhythm sticks, lummi sticks, drums, and other percussion instruments can be beneficial to this process. The beat of a song remains even and is the same throughout the song, whereas the rhythm is uneven and would be the word syllables

into which the song has been divided. When introducing rhythmic activities to preschool children it is wise to use a variety of exercises to help them master the skill of keeping time to an even beat. You may wish to use your own creativity in inventing helpful exercises. The following exercises are suggestions progressing from simple to more complex activities. The following activities can be helpful in teaching preschool children beat versus rhythm.

While seated:

1.  The teacher lets the children look and listen while the teacher claps his/her own hands together, while keeping an even beat.
2.  The teacher will move the child's hands for him/her keeping an even beat.
3.  The teacher will clap both of the child's hands for him/her on various body parts (knees, legs, etc.) while keeping an even beat.
4.  The teacher will help the child by clapping the child's lummi sticks together while keeping an even beat.
5.  Repeat all of the above, only this time the child will work his/her own hands without the teacher moving hands for them.
6.  The child will now clap his/her own hands together.
7.  The child will clap his/her hands against the teacher's hand.
8.  The child will clap his/her own lummi sticks together.
9.  The child will clap his/her lummi sticks against the teacher's lummi sticks.
10. The child will clap both of his/her hands on various body parts (arms, legs, etc.
11. The child will clap one hand on one knee, and the other hand on the other knee, while keeping and even beat.
12. The children will move to the beat. As the teacher claps the beat, the children will march to the beat, keeping time with the beat.
13. The children will all attempt to move together while keeping time to the beat.
14. Children will clap their hands to the rhythm of the music instead of the beat while singing a simple song such as "Skip to my Lou".

## SPECIAL MUSIC TRAVELS

### *"Parading Kids"*

Children are asked to name the different kinds of people, animals and objects that they might see in a parade. With circus music playing, and the children in follow-the-leader formation, the teacher leads the group, calling out different roles for the children to imitate: clowns, horses, trumpets, trombones. drummers, acrobats, tightrope walkers, cars, fire engines, baton twirlers, flag carriers, etc.

### *"Ice Capades"*

Using any kind of waltz music, the teacher gives each child two paper plates and asks the children to skate (one plate under each foot) to the music. Encourage them to jump off their skates and turn in the air!

### *"Kool-Aid to Popsicle"*

Each child stands straight and tall in a hoop that is on the floor; children are frozen (the popsicles). Play different kinds of music with definite beats and ask the children to move to the beat of the music until it stops (moving children represent kool-aid). When the music stops, children freeze into popsicles in hoops.

## *Singing Games*

### *Title: "ABC" (The Alphabet Song)*
- Level: 3-5 years

*Music:* 2/4 time.

*Formation*: Children form a circle or scattered formation. Teacher leads.

*Instructions:* Cards with letters on them may be distributed to children. Teacher may point to the child who has that letter as sung and that child holds up the letter. All children may march about the room holding up their letter as it is mentioned in the song. The number of letters used will depend on the number of children.

| F | | Bb | F Bb | F | C7 | | F | C7 F | C |

A   B   C   D   E   F   G   H   I   J   K   L   M   N   O   P   Q   R   S   T   U   V

F     C7 F

W   X   Y   Z

Now I know my ABC's, tell me what you think of me.

### *Title: "Did You Ever See A Lassie?"*
- Level: 4 to 5 years.

*Music*: 3/4 time.

*Formation*: Children form a circle. The teacher begins as the leader in the center.

Instructions: During the first part of the song the entire group may skip, gallop, slide, or circle to the left or right while the person in the center is trying to think of an activity to perform. The center child may be given a subject in order to help them think of an activity or motion, such as farm animals, personal daily care, chores around the house, etc. The teacher/ child in the center performs an action of choice at the part of the song which states "Go this way and that way." The other children on the outer circle imitate the actions of the center person. At the end of the song the center child picks a new leader and the entire song is repeated with a new leader in the center. The words "go, this, that, and way" may be written on erasure boards to reinforce vocabulary words.

> Did you ever see a lassie, a lassie a lassie?
> Did you ever see a lassie go this way and that?
> Go this way and that way, go this way and that way.
> Did you ever see a lassie go this way and that?

### *Title: "Eensy Weensy Spider"*
- Level: 3 to 5 years

*Music:* 6/8 time.

*Formation*: Children may form a circle or start in a scattered formation. Teacher leads.

*Instructions:* Children will act out the motions of the song using hands only. As the actions of the spider are described in the song the children will move their fingers and hands in a climbing motion, raining motion, shaking motion, and again climbing motion. Illustrations of spiders and other insects may be helpful to reinforce learning about spiders and other creatures. The words spider, web, crawl, and climb may be written on erasure boards in order to help reinforce these concepts as well as the movements in the song.

| D | | A7 | D |

The eensy weensy spider went up the water spout.

                            A7                    D
Down came the rain and washed the spider out.
                        Bm   Em    A7    D
Out came the sun and dried up all the rain
A7     D    A7    D  G    A7                 D
So the eensy weensy spider went up the spout again.

### *Title: "The Farmer In The Dell"*

- Level:  4 to 5 years

*Music:* 2/4 time.

*Formation*:  Children form a circle with the teacher standing in the center acting as the farmer.

*Instructions:*  The children all join hands and face the center of the circle moving in a counterclockwise direction.  The children on the outer circle may walk, gallop, slide, or follow the appointed leader.  The person in the center acts as the farmer.  When the song states that the farmer is to take a wife, the center person chooses a child from the circle to represent the wife.  The new child moves to the center of the circle and at the appropriate time picks a child from the outer circle to represent the child.  All children join in singing the song "The Farmer in the Dell."  During the portion of the song that a child is being chosen from the outer circle, the teacher holds up a card with an activity drawn on it and the children perform that activity (toe touches).  When a cheese is chosen all those in the center (farmer, wife, etc.) join back in the circle.  The circle moves to the center and everyone claps hands above the their heads.  The cheese may become the new farmer.  After the last verse children jump up and down and clap while a new farmer is being chosen.  The words "arm, toe, tap, knee, dog, cat, rat, cheese, child, wife, farmer, and nurse" may be written on an erasure board in order to the reinforce vocabulary as well as other concepts related to the song.

 A list of possible activities to perform while the children are being selected from the outer circle is listed here:

1.  toe touches knees bent
2.  arm circles forward
3.  arm circles backwards
4.  clap hands together
5.  trunk twist
6.  jump in place
7.  tap toe in place
8.  raise both hands above head
9.  any creative activity the leader can think of

F                  C7   F
The farmer in the dell, the farmer in the dell
   Bb   F        Gm7  F   C7    F
Heigh ho the derry oh, the farmer in the dell

Additional verses:
      The farmer takes a wife
      The wife takes a child
      The child takes a nurse

The nurse takes a dog
The dog takes a cat
The cat takes a rat
The rat takes the cheese
The cheese stands alone

### Title: "Head, Shoulders, Knees And Toes"

- Level: 3 to 5 years.

*Music:* 2/4 time.

*Formation*: Children form a scattered pattern formation. Teacher leads.

*Instructions:* Children are to touch each body part with the fingers of both hands as that part is named in the song. The song may be repeated several times, increasing the speed each time. This song can be used for the reinforcement of body awareness. The words "head, shoulder, knee, and toe" may be written on erasure boards in order to reinforce the concepts in today's lesson.

  C
Head, shoulders, knees and toes, knees and toes.
                      G7
Head, shoulders, knees and toes, knees and toes.
 C            F
Eyes and ears and mouth and nose
 G7
Head, shoulders, knees and toes, knees and toes.

### Title: "I'm A Little Teapot"

- Level: 3-5 years

*Music:* 2/4 time

*Formation*: Children form a circle or scattered formation. A leader is suggested.

*Instructions:* Children are to act out the motions of the teapot using arms and body. One hand is at the waist with the elbow bent and the other arm is straight out but bent at the elbow to represent a teapot. As the teapot pours out the liquid, the children will lean their bodies in the appropriate direction. If a leader is chosen, the children will follow the movements of the leader. The words "teapot, water, in, out, and bend" are all written on erasure boards in order to reinforce these vocabulary words as well as the movements associated with this song.

Bb          Eb    Bb
I'm a little teapot, short and stout
F7        Bb Gm7 F7   Bb
Here is my handle, here   is my spout.
            Eb   Bb
When I get all steamed up then I shout.
Cm7    F7    Bb
Tip me over and pour me out

    I'm a clever teapot, that is true
    Just take a look what I can do
    I can change my handle and my spout

Tip me over and pour me out.

### Title: "London Bridge"

- Level: 4 to 5 years.

*Music:* 2/4 time.

*Formation:* Two children form an arch while remainder of children form a line.

*Description:* Two children will face each other joining both hands to form the bridge. Other children form either a single file line or a line of partners. Children in line will march in place while singing the song. The children making the bridge hold their arms up making an arch for other children to pass under. During the verse "My Fair Lady" the bridge is lowered capturing whomever is under the arch. The child who is caught under the arches changes places with one of the bridge children. The children in line going under the bridge move under the arch and around the room, back to the end of the line. Children in line march in place until it is their turn. Galloping, sliding, etc., may be used. The words "down, fall, build, and up" may all be written on erasure boards in order to reinforce the concepts in today's lesson.

```
    F                            C7         F
```
London bridge is falling down, falling down, falling down.
```
    F                            C7   F
```
London Bridge is falling down, my fair lady.


Additional Verses:

    Build it up with iron bars
    Iron Bars will bend and break
    Build it up with solid gold
    Suppose someone should steal the gold?
    Get a man to watch all night
    Suppose the man should fall asleep?
    Get a dog to bark all night
    Suppose the dog should run away?
    You can watch the bridge yourself


### Title: "The Muffin Man"

- Level: 5 years

*Music:* 2/4 time

*Formation:* Children form a circle facing center around a leader who stands in the middle or this may also be performed in a scattered formation.

*Instructions:* The song begins with one leader (the muffin man) preferably the teacher, in the center. The center person chooses one person. The two join hands and skip around the outside of the circle as the children in the circle move (skipping, sliding, galloping, etc.) clockwise as they sing. The two children then each choose another child and skip with their new partners. This continues until all children have a partner. Children skip with their partners during the verse "Have you seen the muffin man?" and choose a new partner during the verse " Oh yes, I've seen the muffin man." As a variation, once a new partner has been chosen, the next partner will join the two and the three will skip together, etc. The children in the circle may perform a different activity while the muffin men are skipping. With each verse change the activity such as arm circles, toe touches, raising one's hand and touching one's nose, etc. The words "you, man, skip, and march" can be written on erasure boards in order to reinforce these vocabulary words.

> Oh, have you seen the muffin man?
> The muffin man, the muffin man
> Oh, have you seen the muffin man?
> Who lives on Drury Lane.
> Oh, yes we've seen the muffin man
> The muffin man, the muffin man
> Oh, yes we've seen the muffin man
> Who lives on Drury Lane.

### Title: "The Mulberry Bush"
- Level:  3 to 5 years.

*Music:* 6/8 time.

*Formation*: Children form a single circle facing center. Teacher leads.

*Instructions:*  Children form a circle with hands joined.  During the chorus children will skip or walk, gallop or march around the circle counterclockwise.  During the verses children will act out the activity mentioned in the song.  Children will follow the movements of the leader. A subject category may be used to reinforce particular activities such as health habits, chores, or holiday ideas.  The words "wash, comb, brush, teeth, and clothes" may be written on erasure boards in order to reinforce these concepts.

> Here we go round the mulberry bush.
> The mulberry bush, the mulberry bush
> Here we go round the mulberry bush
> So early in the morning

*Additional verses:*

> This is the way we wash our clothes
> Wash our clothes, wash our clothes
> This is the way we wash our clothes
> So early Monday morning.

| | |
|---|---|
| Iron our clothes | Tues. |
| Scrub the floor | Wed. |
| Mend the clothes | Thurs. |
| Sweep the floor | Fri. |
| Bake some pies | Sat. |
| Say our prayers | Sun. |

the above verses are merely suggestions taken from the old folk tune.  Any activities may be substituted for the above if felt to be appropriate.  For example, various types of transportation, holiday activities, personal care activities, or school activities may be used, to name a few.

### Title:  "Old MacDonald Had a Farm"
- Level:  3 to 5 years

*Music:* 2/4 time

*Formation*: Children may be in a circle or scattered formation.  Teacher leads.

*Instructions:* Children will make the sounds of the animal mentioned by the leader during the song. As an example when the song states that on his farm he had some pigs, everyone makes oinking noises. Children will also attempt to move in the manner the animal mentioned would move. If an animal is mentioned for which a sound is unknown, then the leader or each child may make up a sound. As new animals are mentioned, the old sounds should be repeated or added after the new sounds, while keeping the same order. Pictures of various farm animals can be used as illustrations in order to assist in learning about farm animals. The words pig, cow, horse, sheep, dog, and cat can be written on erasure boards to reinforce these vocabulary words as well as the movements and sounds relating to the various farm animals.

F    Bb F
Old MacDonald had a farm
 C7
E I E I O
And on this farm he had some pigs
E I E I O
With an oink oink here
And an oink oink there
Here an oink, there an oink
 C7
Everywhere an oink oink
F    Bb F
Old MacDonald had a farm
 G7
E I E I O

*Other Verses*:
Repeat above using cows this time. After repeating the entire song using cows and their sounds, add oink, oink here, oink, oink there, here an oink, there an oink, everywhere an oink, oink. A moo moo here, a moo moo there, here a moo, there a moo, everywhere a moo moo. Old MacDonald had a farm, E I E I O.
Other animals that may be added: Ducks, chickens, horses, sheep, etc. and any other appropriate farm animals.

### *Title: "Paw Paw Patch"*
- Level: 3 to 5 years

*Music:* 2/4 time.

*Formation*: scatter

*Instructions:* Children will imitate the movements described in the song. When searching for Nelly, children may choose a way to move around the room (such as, skipping, walking, galloping, running, or marching) while pretending to search for Nelly. Children will follow the movements of the leader. Children will pretend to pick something up and put it in their pretend pockets. The words "find, look, and go" may be written on the erasure boards in order to reinforce these vocabulary words.

 D
Where oh where, is dear little Nelly?
 A
Where oh where, is dear little Nelly?
 D
Where oh where, is dear little Nelly?

A                    D
Way down yonder in the paw paw patch.

Come on kids let's go find her
Come on kids let's go find her
Come on kids let's go find her
Way down yonder in the pawpaw patch

Picking up pawpaws, put 'em in her pocket
Picking up pawpaws put 'em in her pocket
Picking up pawpaws put 'em in her pocket
Way down yonder in the pawpaw patch.

### Title: "Pease Porridge Hot"
- Level: 4 to 5 years

*Music:* 2/4 time

*Formation*: Children form a circle or scattered formation. Teacher leads.

*Instructions:* Children are instructed to clap their own hands together in time to the music. After they appear to be able to keep the beat themselves they will find a partner and clap their hands against their partners' hands. Partners may use whatever hand patterns they wish as long as they are in time with the beat of the song. An example of a clapping pattern would be: "clap your own hands, clap both of your hands against both of partner's hands, clap one of partner's hands against one of your hands, clap the other hand of your partner against your other hand, clap own knees, clap own thighs." The words "hot, cold, and porridge" may all be written on erasure boards in order to reinforce these vocabulary words. This sequence may be very difficult for many of the children so it may need to be reduced to only two moves.

D              G          D
Pease porridge hot, pease porridge cold
A7        D   Bm  Em  A    d
Pease porridge in the pot, nine days old
D              G          D
Some like it hot, some like it cold.
A7        D         A        D
Some like it in the pot, nine days old.

### Title:"Ring Around The Rosie"
- Level: 3 to 5 years.

*Music:* 2/4 time.

*Formation:* Children form a circle with everyone facing center. Teacher leads.

Instruction: The children circle to the right (walking, galloping, skipping, etc.), on the words "Ring around the Rosie." On "we all fall down," they all fall to the ground. On the words thunder and lightning they jump up and down and make a lot of noise. They may clap their hands or use rhythm instruments to symbolize the noise of thunder. In general the children are to imitate or act out the words in the song. The words "rain, sun, jump, circle, and fall" may all be written on erasure boards in order to reinforce these vocabulary words.

C

Ring around the rosie, pocket full of posies
          G      C
Ashes, ashes, we all fall down.

The cows are in the meadow
Lying down and sleeping
Thunder! Lightning!
We all jump up

### Title: "Round And Round The Village"
- Level:  5 years

*Music:*  2/4 time.

*Formation*:  Children form a single circle facing center with hands joined.  One or two leaders are chosen to be outside the circle.  If the group is rather large, more than one circle may be necessary in order to insure maximum participation.

*Instructions:*  Children join hands forming a single circle facing center.  The two children chosen are outside the circle.  The outside children join hands and skip, gallop, slide, or march clockwise around the circle.  The circle represents the village.  The children forming the circle join hands also, walking or skipping clockwise.  The children that are part of the circle raise their arms, and stand still, when the song states "go in and out the windows."  At this point the two children on the outside go under the arches moving inside, then outside of the circle, in a weaving pattern.  It might be wise to have the teacher demonstrate how to weave in and out of the windows or perhaps even be one of the two children on the outside of the circle.  Everyone both in and outside the circle will choose a partner and honor that partner when the song states "stand and face your partner."  To honor one's partner, boys bow and girls curtsey while facing their partners.  All partners now face counterclockwise and skip around the circle when the song states "now follow me to London."  All partners will shake their partners' hands when the song states "shake hands before you leave me."  When the song begins from the start, all children form a single circle facing center and two new children are chosen to start on the outside of the circle.  The entire song is repeated including all of the movements.  The words "stand, go, round, stand, shake, in and out" may all be written on erasure boards in order to reinforce these vocabulary words.  During the song the child's hometown may be substituted for the word London in the song.  The child's hometown may also be written on an erasure board.

    Go round and round the village
    Go round and round the village
    Go round and round the village
    As we have done before.

Additional verses:
    Go in and out the windows
    Now stand and face your partner
    Now follow me to London
    Shake hands before you leave me

### Title: "The Shoemaker's Dance"
- Level:  4 to 5 years.

*Music:*  4/4 time.

*Formation*:  Children may form a circle or scattered pattern formation.  Teacher leads.

*Instructions*: Children will imitate the motions mentioned in the song. When winding the bobbin, children will fold their arms in front of their chests and make a winding motion with their arms. 3 times forward. For the pulling motion, children will again fold their arms in front of their chests, however this time they will point their elbows, pulling elbows away from the body while keeping the elbows lifted up at chest level. Clap three times. The tapping motion is represented by making two fists, again held at chest level and pounding one fist on top of the other. During the verse children will walk or march for 16 counts. Each child may be given 2 lummi sticks or rhythm sticks and all of the above activities may be performed using the lummi or rhythm sticks. The sticks may be clapped together keeping the beat of the song as children are moving around the circle. The sticks may also be tapped as if pounding nails, one stick pounding the other down during the tapping part of the song. The words "wind, pull, and tap" may be written on erasure boards in order to reinforce movement and vocabulary.

F
Wind, wind, wind the bobbin  (forward)
F
Wind, wind, wind the bobbin   (backward)
Bb      F      C7
Pull and pull and clap,. Clap, clap
C7      F   C7
Tra la la la la la la
C7          F   C7
Tra la la la la la la
F
Wind, wind, wind the bobbin
F
Wind, wind, wind, the bobbin
Bb             C7      F
Pull and pull  and tap, tap, tap

### *Title: "Skip to My Lou"*

• Level: 5 years.

*Music*: 2/4 time.

*Formation*: Children are in a scattered or a circle formation.

*Instructions:* When the song begins children will move about the room and singing along. During the verse "lost my partner" children will skip about as individuals or with partner, inside hands joined. During the verse "I'll find another one prettier than you" children will find a new partner and link elbows with that new partner, now forming a set of two. All children are facing the same direction and skip with elbows joined. As the song continues couples or sets separate on the verse "Lost my partner" and find a new partner or set during the verse "I'll find another one." For "chicken in the haystack," put hula hoops around the room and have children skip with a partner through the hoops. For "cows in the barnyard," have children gallop by themselves moving through the hula hoops. For "train is a coming," all children form a line one behind the other making a train and moving together in one long line. The words "I, my, and skip" may be written on erasure boards in order to reinforce those vocabulary words.

     F          F
Lost my partner, what'll I do?
C7             C7

Lost my partner, what'll I do?
F                    F
Lost my partner, what'll I do?
G7                    F
Skip to my Lou my darling
F                    F
Skip, skip, skip to my Lou
C7          C7
Skip, skip, skip to my Lou
F                    F
Skip, skip, skip to my Lou
C7                    F
Skip to my Lou my darling

> *Additional verses:*
> I'll find another one prettier than you
> Flies in the buttermilk, shoo fly shoo
> Chicken in the haystack
> Cows in the barnyard
> Train is a coming choo choo choo

### Title: "Ten Little Indians"

- Level: 4 to 5 years.

*Music:* 2/4 time.

*Formation:* Children may form a circle or scattered pattern formation.

*Instructions:* Children are numbered off from 1 to 10. Each child is given a card with his/her assigned number written on the card, as well as that number of Indians on the card. Example, if the number is 5 there are 5 Indians on that card. If there are more than 10, children start numbering another circle or give more than one child the same number. Children will sing along with the verses of the song. When a child who has that number is called the child with that number will hold up his/her card. At the end of the song, children may be instructed to go over to a hula hoop and pick up the number of items on their card and bring them back to the large circle. Yarn balls, beanbags, or some other items are placed in a hula hoop ahead of time. The teacher and aide will have to assist the children in choosing the right number of items. When all arrive back at the circle, one at a time they hold up their card and count out their appropriate number of yarn balls, etc. After all the children have a turn to count out their number of items, all items are returned to the hula hoop so the activity may be repeated. The numbers one to ten are written on erasure boards in order to reinforce the concepts of today's lesson.

F
One, little, two little, three little Indians
C7
Four, little, five little, six little Indians
F
Seven little, eight little, nine little Indians.
C7                    F
Ten little Indian boys.
Ten little, nine little, eight little, Indians.

Seven little, six little, five little Indians.
Four little, three little, two little Indians.
One little Indian boy/girl.

### Title: "This is the Way"
- Level: ages 3 to 5 years

*Music*: 6/8 time.
*Formation*: Children may be in a circle or in a scattered formation. Teacher leads.
*Instructions*: Children are instructed to act out the motions in the song along with the teacher. As an example, when the song states this is the way we brush our teeth, the children act out putting toothpaste on a toothbrush and the motions involved in brushing the teeth.

This song may be used to reinforce proper health principles. The verses may state such things as brushing or combing one's hair, washing clothes, etc. The words "wash, brush, comb and toothbrush" may be written on erasure boards in order to reinforce these vocabulary words, as well as the movement activities in the song.

F
This is the way we wash our hands,
C7
Wash our hands, wash our hands.
F
This is the way we wash our hands,
   C7
So early in the morning.

Other verses may include the following or other activities
Brush our teeth
Comb our hair
Put on our coats
Wash our clothes
Hang up our clothes
Wash our hair
Create your own activities such as climb the stairs, ride our bikes, etc.

### Title: "A Tisket A Tasket"
- Level: 3 to 5 years

*Music*: 4/4 time.
*Formation*: Children form a single circle facing center. One child is chosen to be outside the circle.
*Instructions*: The children in the circle all join hands. The child on the outside of the circle is given a handkerchief. The child on the outside of the circle walks slowly counterclockwise around the circle while all sing "A tisket a tasket." The child drops the handkerchief behind one of the children in the circle. That child then chases the child on the outside attempting to catch him/her before he/she reaches the chaser's empty spot in the circle. If the child is caught before reaching the empty space the original child continues as "it." If not caught, the chaser becomes "it." In order to achieve maximum participation, the children in the circle will perform activities demonstrated by the teacher as the chase goes on. Such activities may include arm circles, touching one's nose, touching one's toes, etc. The "it" and the

chaser may skip, hop, gallop, slide, or march instead of running. The words "run, 'it,' chase, tag, and drop" may be written on erasure boards in order to reinforce vocabulary.

> A tisket, a tasket, a green and yellow basket
> I wrote a letter to my love and on the way I dropped it
> I dropped it, I dropped it and on the way I dropped it
> I wrote a letter to my love and on the way I dropped it

### Title: "Where is Thumbkin"

- Level: 3 to 5 years.

*Music:* 2/4 time

*Formation*: Children may be in a circle or scattered formation. Teacher leads.

*Instructions:* Children will stand in a circle or scattered formation, facing the leader. The leader will instruct the children regarding the four fingers and a thumb on one hand. An illustration of an outline of a hand would make an excellent visual. All four fingers and the thumb are able to move together or individually. The class will attempt to name each finger. They may wish to assign each digit a number, letter, or color, starting with the thumb. They may wish to choose names such as thumb, index finger, middle or center finger, ring finger, and little finger or pinkie.

Children are instructed to start with both hands at their sides. As Thumbkin is mentioned they will bring one hand out in front at about chest level making a fist with the thumb being the only digit pointing upwards. As Thumbkin is mentioned a second time they will bring the second hand to the front in the same manner. On the words "Here I am, Here I am" they will wiggle the first thumb and then the second. They will wiggle both thumbs during the words "How are you this morning?, Very well I thank you." On the last phrase they will move the hands one at a time behind their backs. The song is repeated 4 more times substituting the names chosen for each finger, using the previous movements with each new finger as it is mentioned in the song.

```
C                    G7      C
Where is Thumbklin? Where is Thumbkin?
C   Dm  C       Dm   C
Here I   am. Here I    am.
D7              C
How are you this morning?
G       C
Very well I thank you.
G7  C     G7  C
Run away,    Run away.
```

### Title: "The Wheels On The Bus"

- Level: 3 to 5 years

*Music:* 2/4 time.

*Formation*: Children may form a circle, be in scattered formation, or in a line behind the leader. Teacher leads.

*Instructions:* The children will imitate the motions mentioned in the song. Each child is given a hula hoop to begin. When the song states "The wheels on the bus go round and round" the children will roll their hula hoops around the gymnasium. Also the children may pretend that the hula hoop is a steering wheel and pretend they are driving the bus around the gymnasium. On the verse, "The people on the bus go up and down " the children will bend at their knees and move up and down. During the verse "The driver on the bus says move on back," the children in a line behind the teacher will move backwards while staying in their line. The teacher may then pass out flying discs and let the children pretend to drive and beep the horn (flying disc) on the verse "the horn on the bus goes, beep, beep, beep." The children may then drive using the flying disc as a steering wheel, however, they must stay on the lines in the gymnasium, which are the roads. If another car is coming on their roads or lines, they must switch roads or back up. Also ask the children if they can identify the various colors of flying discs as well as the various colors of hula hoops.

> The wheels on the bus go round and round
> Round and round, round and round
> The wheels on the bus go round and round
> All through the town.

*Additional verses:*
> The people on the bus go up and down
> The driver on the bus says "move on back"
> The babies on the bus go wa wa wa
> Mommies on the bus say sh sh sh
> The horn on the bus goes beep, beep, beep

# DANCES

### Title:  "The Chicken Dance"
*Music:* 4/4 time.
- Level : 3-5 years

*Formation*: A single circle with everyone facing the center of the circle. Can be performed with or without partners. This dance can also be performed in a random scattered pattern around the room. The teacher should lead the children in dong the dance.

*Instructions and Cues:* Using the fingers and thumbs on both hands, children make movements imitating a chicken opening and closing its beak by moving the fingers and thumbs together. Next children put their hands under their arms to form wings and flap their arms to resemble a chicken flapping its wings. Children then put their arms at their sides and shake their hips while moving downwards toward the floor while bending at the knees, then returning to standing. This movement is to resemble a chicken shaking its body. Next the children clap their hands four times. As the music changes, children will then swing their partners with an elbow swing (age 5). As a variation to this last movement ,children may move around the circle swinging several people one at a time and turning them each around once.

*Cues*:  Beak movement four times
>      Wing movement four times
>      Shake hips down and up for four beats
>      Clap hands four times
>      Swing partner two times in one direction then

twice in the other direction

### Title: "The Hokey Pokey"

*Music:* 4/4 time.

- Level: 3 to 5 years

*Formation*: Children form a single circle facing center or dance can be performed in a random pattern of children scattered throughout the room. The directions for the Hokey Pokey are usually verbally stated on the record itself. The teacher leads.

*Instructions and Cues*: Following the directions in the song, children will place their right hands forward towards the center of the circle, then place their right hands behind them, away from the center of the circle. They again place their right hands forward towards the center of the circle, this time shaking their right hands. The instructions state that children are to do the Hokey Pokey and turn themselves around. Children are given the opportunity to be creative by making up their own movements as they turn around followed by clapping their hands four times. The song continues with the same basic idea of putting a certain body part towards the center of the circle, putting it outside the circle, putting it again inside the circle and shaking it. The order of body parts are the right arm, left arm, right foot, left foot, right elbow, left elbow, right hip, left hip, head, backside, and whole self. During the chorus the children are again given the opportunity to be creative by creating their own movements to keep time with the music. Shaking one's hands over their head or making shapes using one's arms can often be seen. One child may be chosen to stand in the center of the circle to lead the other children. Creativity is encouraged while doing the chorus and verse related to the Hokey Pokey.

### Title: "Loobie Lou"

- Level 3 to 5 years

*Formation*: Children form a single circle facing center or dance can be performed in a random pattern of children scattered throughout the room. Very similar to the Hokey Pokey but danced to a different song. The directions for Loobie Lou are stated on the record itself. The teacher will act as the leader and children will model the teacher.

*Instructions*: The children first put one hand towards the center of the circle and the move the same hand away from the center. Children then shake that hand followed by turning around in place. These same movements are used only substituting various body parts. First one hand, then the other hand, next one foot, then the other foot, lastly the whole self and the song ends. The chorus is sung between each verse.

> Here we go Loobie Lou
> Here we go Loobie Lie
> Here we go Loobie Lou
> All on a Saturday night
> I put my right hand in
> I put my right hand out
> I give my hand a shake, shake, shake and turn myself about

### Title: "Chicken Fat"

- Level: 3 to 9 years of age

*Formation*: Children may stand in a circle, in lines or in a scattered formation.

*Instructions*: Children may stand next to a desk if performed in the classroom. Students will follow the same movements demonstrated by the teacher or leader

Toe Touches - Touch toes with fingers while bending at the waist and also attempting to keep knees straight. Perform 10 times

Push Ups - Drop to the floor and attempt to do push-ups or modified push- ups. Perform 10 times.

Knee to Elow - Put hands behind head, standing with feet next to each other and bend the left knee while lifting this same knee upwards. At the same time bring the right elbow downward touchig it to the left knee. Perform 10 times

Arm Flings with Bent Elbows - Stand with feet apart and elbows at shoulder level and hands at chest level, with palms down. Quickly move the elbows backwards and then bring elows back to starting position. Throw the arms out to the sides and bring arms back to starting position. Perform 6 times.

Run and Jump - run in place 16 counts. Jump with feet apart and then bring feet together. Perform 3 times.

| | |
|---|---|
| Toe Touches | 10 times |
| Push Ups | 10 times |
| Knee to Elbow | 10 times |
| Arm flings with bent elbows | 6 times |
| Run in place | 16 counts |
| Jump apart and together | 3 times |

## STORY PLAY

Young children love to pretend. The teacher can read stories for the children to act out, but it is difficult to find many stories that use a lot of movement. Therefore, story play in physical education works much better if the story is preplanned around the movement challenges. One excellent source for story play is *My Neighborhood Movement Challenges* by Clements (1995). The teacher is limited only by his/her own creativity.

An example follows:

## *The Lion Hunt*

We were all sleeping in our beds when, suddenly, very early, the alarm went off!

We JUMPED out of BED and we RAN to the bathroom where we WASHED OUR FACES and BRUSHED OUR TEETH.

Then we RAN back to our rooms and we PULLED ON our pants, PUT ON our shirts, FOUND our shoes, TIED them and SKIPPED to the kitchen for breakfast. We ATE a big pile of pancakes and DRANK our juice and milk. Then we GRABBED our coats, PUT them on, and OPENED the closet door to get a big net. We RAN out the door, LOOKED BOTH WAYS and CROSSED the street. We RAN into the jungle! We PUSHED aside the tall grass, we SWAM across a wide river, we JUMPED over logs, and suddenly we SAW a lion! We LOOKED UP into a tree and there he was!

He was a big lion! We DROPPED the net, we TURNED and ran. We JUMPED over logs, we SWAM across a wide river, we PUSHED aside the tall grass. We RAN out of the jungle! We LOOKED BOTH WAYS and CROSSED the street. We RAN through the door of the house, SKIPPED to our bedrooms, and JUMPED into bed! And we fell asleep....

## FITNESS PLAY

### *Muscle Kid*

Have 2, 3 or 4 children working together to carry one of the lighter big balls (36+") overhead a specified distance and then throw it into a goal. Challenge with heavier big balls. With the light ones, see if individual children can carry it overhead!

### *Push 'n' Kick*

Using ONE of the big balls, have children play in a circle pushing the ball around the circle to each other. If the children are strong enough, have them sit in the circle and travel with crabwalk to kick the ball to others in the circle. Talk about PUSHING the ball.

### *Big Ball Roll*

Using the three large balls, have children stand behind the balls, facing the goal. On the signal to "Go," have them run and push the ball all the way to the goal. Then repeat back to the starting line.

## SPECIAL HOLIDAY ACTIVITIES

### *Which Witch? (Which Elf? Which Cupid? Which Bunny? Which Turkey?)*

Place hula hoops in a defined area. Each child stands in a hoop, one child (or teacher) is without a hoop. The one without a hoop says "Which witch is in my house?" On that signal everyone flies on a broom (have them use the hockey sticks to simulate brooms) to a new hoop while the caller jumps into one. Game proceeds with new caller.

### *Haunted House Obstacle Course: Play the "Monster Mash" song (Trip to the North Pole, Where the Easter Eggs Hide)*

Using tunnels, small beams, vertically set hoops, ladders and mats on end covered by parachute to make a house, set an obstacle course. If you do not have the music, make up a Halloween story for the children as you go through the course, i.e. walking on the beam high above the witch's house, sneaking through the tunnel without touching the slimy sides, etc. Have children make scary noises as they go through the course.

### *Pumpkin Bash (Cupid's Arrow to the Heart, Snowball Squash)*

Children use yarn balls and teacher taps orange balloons in air for children to throw balls trying to hit the balloons.

### GhostlyTag (Reindeer Tag, Turkey Tag, Bunny Tag)

If tagged a child has to stay in place, wave arms and howl like a ghost until a "Ghostbuster" (a free player) tags him/her to set him/her free.

### Kick a Pumpkin (Kick the Snowball)

Roll beachballs to children in turn, having them kick toward the "pumpkin" as far as possible.

### Big Fat Pumpkin (Big Fat Snowman, Big Fat Rabbit)

Teacher starts game as leader with children on a line about 15 yards away. Teacher turns and hides eyes while children sneak up; teacher turns and chases children back to line and if he/she tags one, the child helps the Big Fat Pumpkin in the next round. Remember to specify your boundaries.

## Summary

Preschool aged children present a unique challenge in physical education. Eager to move and play, their enthusiasm often supersedes their ability to listen and to follow directions. You will need to recognize this and keep directions quick, clear and simple. Many activities must be planned for even the shortest amount of active time. Always remember that you are helping children to establish their movement skill base; a good, firm base will set the stage for an enjoyable lifetime of physical activity.

## References And Selected Readings

Clements, R.L. (1995). *My neighborhood movement challenges: Narratives, games and stunts for ages three through eight years.* NASPE.

Gabbard, C.P., LeBlanc, E., & Lowy, S. (1989). *Game. dance, and gymnastic activities for children.* Prentice-Hall.

Gabbard, C., Leblanc, E., & Lowy, S. (1987). *Physical education for children, building the foundation.* Prentice-Hall.

Gallahue, D.L. (2005). *Developmental physical education for all children.* Human Kinetics.

Gallahue, D.L. (1997). *Developmental physical education for today's children.* McGraw-Hill.

Gallahue, D.L. (1996). *Developmental physical education for today's children.* Macmillan.

Hammett, C.T., 2001, PE Central http://db.pecentral.org/lesson ideas

Kirchner, G.& Fishburne, G.J.(1996). *Physical education for elementary school children.* Brown & Benchmark.

Kuntzelman, C., Kuntzelman, B., McGlynn, M. & McGlynn, G. (1984*). Aerobics with fun.* Fitness Fi.nders.

Nichols, B. (1994). *Moving and learning.* Times Mirror/Mosby.

Orlick, T. (1996). *Cooperative games and sports* . Human Kinetics.

Orlick, T. (1978). *The cooperative sports and game-book.* Pantheon.

Pangrazi, R. P. (2006). *Dynamic physical education for elementary school children.* Benjamin Cummings.

Pangrazi, R. P. & Dauer, V. P. (1998). *Dynamic physical education for elementary school children.* Allyn & Bacon.

Pica, R. (2001). *Wiggle, Giggle and Shake.* Gryphon House, Inc.

Plimpton, C.E. & Sweeney, V.J. (2003). *Physical education methods for the elementary classroom teacher.* Huron Valley.

Plimpton, C.E. & Sweeney, V.J. (2001). *Physical education methods for the elementary classroom teacher.* Huron Valley.

Siedentop, D., Herkowitz, J. & Rink, J. (1984). *Elementary phyilcal education methods.* Prentice-Hall.

Weinberg, K. (2001). Grocery Bag Fun. http://db.pecentral.org/lessonideas.

Weikart, P.S. (2004). *Round the circle: Key experiences in movement for young children.* High/Scope Press.

Weikart, P.S. (2003). *Round the circle: Key experiences in movement for young children.* High/Scope Press.

Weikart, P.S. (2000). *Round the circle: Key experiences in movement for young children.* High/Scope Press.

CHAPTER

# 8

# Physical Fitness

In 1956 President Eisenhower established the President's Council on Youth Fitness. This organization is currently known as The President's Council on Physical Fitness and Sports. This council was established as a result of the review of the findings of the 1953 Kraus and Weber study which divulged that American youth were not as fit as European youth, and, in fact were out of shape and overweight. Many professionals and physical educators feel that the situation has not only deteriorated but is getting even worse in today's society. You have read about the current trends regarding fitness in Chapter 1.

Probably the most popular definition of physical fitness is given by Pangrazi and Dauer (1992) who state that physical fitness is "the ability to carry out daily tasks with vigor and alertness, without undue fatigue, and with ample energy to enjoy leisure pursuits and to meet unforeseen emergencies" (p. 209). Our goal for children, therefore, would be to have sufficient energy to study and play, and to make it through each day as happy and contented human beings. Physically fit children should feel good about themselves, both physically and psychologically.

A review of our derived definition of physical education reminds us that the physically educated person will develop "a level of fitness necessary to maintain a healthy lifestyle . . ." (Chapter One). To many people the terms "physical education" and "physical fitness" are synonymous; we know better, however, and we acknowledge that a sound degree of physical fitness is necessary to be an efficient and effective mover. Physical education is much broader in scope than physical fitness.

We would hope that the outcomes of our physical fitness emphasis would be three-fold: (1) that the children would participate regularly in physical activities; (2) that the children would gain sufficient knowledge about fitness to value the need for such participation; and, (3) that the children would be able to recognize and evaluate their own levels of fitness and be able to change those levels if necessary (Allsbrook, 1992). It is to these ends that we apply teaching of and about physical fitness; and we will do just that within the framework of developmentally appropriate physical education.

# Definition of Health-Related Physical Fitness

Sound health-related physical fitness refers to the efficiency of the body systems to maintain appropriate levels of cardiorespiratory (aerobic) endurance, body composition, flexibility and muscular strength (anaerobic) and endurance (aerobic). Therefore, health-related physical fitness is physiological (Payne & Isaacs, 1991).

## CARDIORESPIRATORY ENDURANCE

Cardiorespiratory endurance refers to the ability of the heart, lungs and vascular system to deliver oxygen to the working cells of the body and to remove waste products. Because its main function is to supply oxygen for the muscles to be able to work efficiently, cardiorespiratory endurance is aerobic in nature (Payne & Isaacs, 1991).

The child who is aerobically fit will be able to maintain levels of continuous activity (i.e., cycling, swimming, jumping rope, aerobic dance) for a long duration and at a high level of intensity without fatigue. Aerobic activities are rhythmical and repetitive and should be a part of the child's everyday lifestyle (Gallahue, 1987). Children develop aerobic fitness by participating in activities that cause the heart rate to rise and maintain the high working rate for a minimum of 20 minutes, at least three non-consecutive days per week. This high working rate is referred to as the target zone and it is between 70% and 85% of the child's maximum heart rate. The typical maximum heart rate for a child who is working at a high intensity activity will be approximately 220. Therefore, the activity level should be sustained for a minimum of twenty minutes at a heart rate of 160–180 beats per minute (Kirchner & Fishburne, 1995).

It is easy to see that the physical education program cannot make significant impact on the aerobic fitness of the child as well as teach all of the content areas when physical education times are limited to 30 minutes per day, and usually meeting only two to three times per week. The best approach is for the teacher to present fun aerobic games at the beginning of class that the children will like and will play on their own time during recess or after school hours. Also, the teacher can design skill practice sessions that are vigorous in nature and cause the child to be working at a high level of intensity while learning and refining skills. For example, when learning the dribble for soccer, each child would have a ball and travel in general space with the ball at varying speeds as designated by the teacher. Maintaining such a jogging and dribbling pattern would be a good aerobic activity as well as having the child practice dribbling skills and acquainting himself/herself with aspects of spatial awareness in working with and around other players (Allsbrook, 1992).

## FLEXIBILITY

Flexibility refers to the ability of the joints to move easily throughout their potential range of motion (Payne & Isaacs, 1991). Levels of good flexibility allow the child to move efficiently. Children seem to be naturally flexible but this flexibility declines with age as well as with lack of overall activity. Since flexibility is joint-specific (flexible shoulders will not affect the flexibility of the hips), children should be encouraged to participate in a variety of activities that cause use of all of the body joints. Climbing, tumbling, dancing and stretching activities contribute to the maintenance of good flexibility levels. If stretching activities are used, they should be done at the conclusion of the class, perhaps during closure. Stretching is appropriate only for warm muscles; therefore it makes sense to lead the class in stretching activities while having the lesson's closure discussion (Allsbrook, 1992).

## MUSCULAR STRENGTH AND ENDURANCE

Muscular strength refers to the ability to make muscles contract (Payne & Isaacs, 1991). It is anaerobic in that it usually refers to one maximum effort. For example, performing a standing long jump uses the muscular strength of the legs. Muscular endurance refers to the ability to repeat muscle contractions for a period of time (Gallahue, 1987). Here the child may be performing a series of jumps, perhaps with a jump rope. His/her muscular endurance represents the ability to continue to jump over a certain period of time.

Most adults work on muscular strength and endurance through weight training programs. Research has questioned the use of such programs for young children (Payne & Isaacs, 1991, 1996). It is currently believed that such programs are not developmentally appropriate for children unless the equipment has been designed to fit the child. At any rate, working in such programs tends to become tedious and children are easily bored. It is necessary to keep the "fun" in fitness in order to encourage children to continue to participate in muscle strengthening activities. Allsbrook (1992) suggests that children will develop muscular strength and endurance in activities that cause them to be moving their body weight in locomotor skills and supporting their body weight in various ways in non-locomotor movements, such as tripods or head and handstands. Traveling in general space and taking weight on hands at the signal incorporates both aerobic endurance and muscular strength moves.

## BODY COMPOSITION

Body composition refers to the amounts of fat and lean body mass in the child's physical makeup (Gabbard, 1992). A child who is overweight will have difficulty participating in many physical activities. Many of these children are embarrassed by their sizes, and they tend to withdraw from activities in which they may not succeed. Other children often tease the overweight child, causing him/her to be extremely self-conscious. Participation in physical activity is just what the child needs, but psychologically the child is not ready to participate.

All movement activities contribute to body composition. Children need to learn to equate caloric intake to exercise output. When they understand the balance between calories and exercise they will be more likely to work on maintaining a good body composition.

# Definition of Motor Fitness

Motor fitness refers to a state of competency in movement abilities such that the child is perceived as an efficient and effective mover. The motor fitness areas are: agility, balance, coordination, power, and speed (Pangrazi & Dauer, 1992).

## AGILITY

Agility refers to the ability to change directions quickly and with minimum effort. Children use agility for dodging in tag games or in sport situations to avoid a tackle.

## BALANCE

Balance refers to one's ability to maintain equilibrium while still or moving. The ability to balance is key to the effective mover, and allows him/her to move without falling or stumbling.

## COORDINATION

Coordination refers to the ability to move in a synchronized, fluid manner to accomplish a task. Both eye-hand and eye-foot coordination are important to physical education tasks. The coordinated child moves with a minimum of extraneous movement.

## POWER

Power refers to the ability to exert one maximal effort. It is definitely related to strength. The child uses power to jump high or far, to throw hard and fast. Power represents the ability to summon the muscles to produce a quick forceful response.

## SPEED

Speed refers to the ability to travel from one place to another quickly. Aerobic endurance contributes to speed as does the degree of power the child can summon for the start of the activity.

# Relationship between Health-Related and Motor Fitness

The health-related fitness components refer directly to body systems in that they are physiological components. If a child chooses to train within the guidelines for improving and maintaining fitness in these areas, he/she will be able to achieve the goal. Of course success will be individual, as children come in many different shapes and sizes. The obese child will have a more difficult time achieving a level of physiological fitness than will the normal weight peer. However, both children may be successful with individual progress in the direction of fitness.

The motor fitness components are performance based. They may be viewed as movement skills. These components can be taught through physical activity; the more varied the movement experiences the children have, the more likely they will be to be competent in these movement skills. However, just as shown for the health-related components, children are different. Due to genetic variables such as size, children will be different in the quality of their motor fitness components. Some will acquire the abilities easily; others will struggle.

Do children need to be competent in the motor fitness skills in order to work on the health-related components? Or, must children have developed a state of fitness in the health-related components in order to be able to learn the motor fitness components? Are the two phases of fitness related? And, is a child viewed as physically fit only if he/she displays efficiency in both health-related and motor fitness areas?

There seem to be no direct answers to these questions. Perhaps the best reply would be that both areas of fitness develop somewhat concurrently. It seems logical that the child who has good motor fitness abilities would be able to work more successfully at the health-related components because he/she would have developed competency in the means to pursue the health-related fitness. It also seems logical that in order to develop motor fitness the child has to have a certain level of health-related fitness to participate successfully in the activities needed to develop competency in motor fitness. One thing is certain: the child definitely can improve his/her physiological health-related fitness level; he/she may improve his/her motor fitness level.

## Assessment of Physical Fitness Levels

Standardized physical fitness tests are available for use in the physical education program. Standardized tests are those which have been used with thousands of children at each age level and normative data have been established so that the physical educator can compare the performance of his/her children to the rest of the nation's children. Ideally children's fitness levels should be assessed twice annually, once at the beginning of the school year and once at the end. Changes in fitness levels will reflect the growth and maturation process as well as differences due to physical education learning.

Parents should receive reports on their child's fitness level and they should be given an idea of activities that they could do with their children in order to help them improve if necessary. This assessment should be performed by your physical educator. Comparison to the national norms should not be as meaningful as detection of improvement in the child's fitness development. The child who has shown improvement should be encouraged to feel proud of that accomplishment, hopefully causing him/her to strive even harder in the future. Physical fitness is a state of well-being and is important to each and every individual.

## Target Heart Rate

In order to improve cardiorespiratory fitness, the target heart rate must be maintained for at least 20 minutes during exercise for at least 3 to 4 times per week, not occurring on consecutive days. Children need to learn about target heart rate: what it is, how to reach it, and how long to maintain activity that keeps the heart rate in the target zone.

The first recommended activity is one dealing with target heart rates. Kirchner & Fishburne (1998) indicate that children in elementary school should have a maximum pulse rate of 220+ beats per minute. This number is simply an indicator of the desired beats per minute during or directly after exercise. This means that if a child's heart rate reaches the 200–200+ range they are working too hard and should slow down. The target heart rate for elementary school age children is between 154 and 187 beats per minute. This number was achieved by multiplying the maximum heart rate (220) by 70% and again by 85%. This gives the target heart rate as a range of 70%–85% of the maximum heart rate. If the child's heart rate during and right after exercise is below 154, this indicates that the child needs to work harder in order to reach the target rate.

In order to assist children in discovering what exercises and activities will have an effect on cardiorespiratory fitness, you should teach them to take their own pulse rates. Students need to sit quietly for 5 minutes in order to get their resting heart rate. You can use this time to explain fitness, target heart rates, and how to take one's pulse. After the 5 minute period, students should practice taking their own pulses by placing the three middle fingers of one hand on the inside of the opposite wrist. They need to turn the palm of one hand upward and place the three middle fingers of the other hand on the inside of the wrist just below the thumb.

Another way of taking the pulse is to place the three middle fingers on either side of the neck just below the jaw and midway between the nose and ear. Care should be taken not to press too hard. Students may need to move the fingers around this area slowly until they are able to locate the pulse. Students should feel a pulsating or beating sensation. One count is taken for each beat or pulsation. Once everyone has located their pulses, using a stopwatch, you can instruct the students to "BEGIN" counting. After 15 seconds have elapsed on the stopwatch you will instruct the students to "STOP" counting, and remember the number of beats. This number will then be multiplied by four in order to calculate the resting beats per minute. A chart on the wall which multiplies the 15 second pulse rate by 4 is extremely helpful, especially for very young children Students should be taking their pulse rates after various activities and exercise. The more practice they have in taking their pulse rates, the more proficient they will become.

The 15 second target heart rate range for elementary children is approximately 39–47 beats. In order to reach this point, children should participate in a somewhat strenuous activity such as a vigorous maximum participation tag game for about 5–7 minutes and then as they are doing their cool down or walking, they can take their pulse rates to see if they reached their target heart rates. You can instruct them to begin counting when all children are walking and have located their pulses. This will help them to understand what the target heart rate feels like and what they must do in order to reach it.

Any children whose heart rate is 39–49 beats for the 15 second interval will have reached their target heart rates. Students should be given the opportunity to take their pulses often during the school year after a variety of activities and exercise: this will teach them what exertion level and which activities are best for them to increase or maintain cardiorespiratory fitness.

You just read that it is necessary for children to work at the target heart rate for a minimum of 20 minutes three–four non-consecutive days a week. Due to the limited amount of time afforded the class of physical education it is not practical to expect this to happen. This is because there is too much in the curriculum that needs to be taught, including physical fitness, and not enough time to do it all well. Therefore the students should learn about the target heart rate, how to raise their heart rates, and how to take their heart rates. They should be encouraged to do activities outside of school for the prescribed amount of time.

## Fitness Testing

In Chapter 18, evaluation for physical education is discussed. The authors advocate assessment of fitness as an important element of evaluation, and in fact, this may be the only true measurement that the classroom teacher will feel comfortable doing for the students. Physical fitness tests are standardized tests that are objective rather than subjective. These tests also allow students to see how they compare in fitness performance to other students of comparable ages throughout the United States. It is important to assist students early on, regarding the discovery of health and fitness concerns, while it is still possible to change habits and evaluate necessary and possible changes in living styles, nutrition, leisure activities, exercise, and time management. Students can always improve their fitness levels at any age; however, it is easier to break bad habits earlier in life than to change them after years of reinforcement. Periodic testing will help to increase this awareness.

There are many fitness tests available many of which contain the same items and are easy to administer with a minimal amount of time and equipment. The President's Challenge from the President's Council on Physical Fitness and Sports is the physical fitness test which has been included in this text due to its ease in administration and the fact that it is available free of charge. A booklet explaining the test is available from The President's Challenge, Poplars Research Center, 400 E. 7th Street, Bloomington, IN 47405, (1-800-258-8146).

There are some optional test items which are explained in the test booklet; however, due to ease of administration, the items selected for this text are: partial curl-ups, shuttle run, 1/4, 1/2 or one mile run/walk, pull-ups, and sit and reach. Normative data for these tests have also been included in this text. It is further recommended that students be weighed and measured in order to determine their body mass index (BMI) as an additional indicator of fitness and obesity. A chart indicating BMI has also been included in this text.

## President's Challenge

The President's Challenge can be easily administered by the classroom teacher and or parent volunteers. 4 of the 5 events in the President's Challenge and The Body Mass Index can all be completed in a 30 minute class period with proper planning. The last event, the 1/4, 1/2, or the 1 mile run can be completed during another class period. Parent volunteers or university students can be recruited to assist with fitness testing.

The gymnasium can be set up with 4 stations. The teacher and 3 parent volunteers or university students are needed for this approach. Each of the test items would be done at a separate station: Station One—Curl Ups, Station 2—Pull Ups, Station 3—Sit and Reach and Body Mass Index, Station 4—Shuttle Run. The students would be divided into 4 equal groups with each group being assigned to start at a different station. When the students have completed an event and their scores have been recorded, they would move to the next station. The rotation schedule needs to be explained before testing begins. Class lists are necessary at each station so scores can be recorded at the station. Student scorecards could be carried with the student, allowing the students to record their own scores on their individual score sheets. A sample score sheet has been provided for you (Figure 7.1).

The run/walk needs to be administered outside and will probably take between 15 to 30 minutes depending on whether or not parent volunteers are used. This test can be administered by one person, but it is better if a parent volunteer is available to supervise the activities planned for the half of the class that is not being tested.

**FIGURE 7.1**

Physical Fitness Testing Scorecard

## PRESIDENT'S CHALLENGE

Name _____ Grade/Teacher _____ Date _____

| TEST | FALL | NORM | SPRING | NORM |
|------|------|------|--------|------|
| PARTIAL CURL-UPS | | | | |
| PULL-UP | | | | |
| SIT AND REACH | | | | |
| SHUTTLE RUN | | | | |
| BMI | | | | |
| 1/4, 1/2 or ONE MILE RUN | | | | |

There are several ways to mark off an area for this test. Probably the easiest would be to measure the area with your car's odometer. Most playground areas also serve as a parking facility when school is not in session. A flat, smooth, dry, blacktop area is needed to serve as a track for the mile run. A circular blacktop area such as the school bus turn around, may also be used. Traffic cones, tape measure, spray paint, and/or car are needed to measure the area. If you are using your automobile you would start by placing 4 cones on the rectangular area of the playground. 3 to 4 feet are needed for a passing lane on the outside and around the entire track if possible. Start at one cone which would be the starting line. Mark this corner with spray paint. You would then drive your car, staying outside the cones if possible until your car's odometer registers 1/4 mile, being sure to count the laps. You would then put a small line 2 to 3 feet, on the blacktop to mark 1/4 mile. Get back into your car and drive around the outside to the cones until the odometer registers 1/2 mile. Mark this point on the blacktop with a small line of spray paint for the 1/2 mile marker. Continue in this manner until the 1 mile marker is completed. You will need to be sure to count the laps or times around the cones for each marker, so that students will know how many laps they need to complete for each run.

If your area is circular, such as a bus turn-around, you would place a cone and mark a starting line on the blacktop with spray paint. Drive around the track counting 1 lap for each time you pass the cone. When your odometer reads 1/4 mile you would mark a line on the blacktop, repeating the above description for marking 1/4, 1/2, and 1 mile distances. You need to exert care that you can distinguish the lines marking the various distances as well as keeping track of the laps necessary for each run. Perhaps using a different colored paint for each distance would help distinguish them from one another. Also when marking the lines with spray paint one might spray the numbers 1/4, 1/2 or 1 next to the line. If you are unable to drive on the track area, a measuring tape may be used to measure 1 mile on a square or rectangular track.

Most high schools have a wheel measuring device used for several different varsity sports. This device is used for marking fields, and distances in general. This device if available can be borrowed from the high school in order to assist you in marking your track. Only a few small lines are needed in order to mark the track. Once your markings are in place, it will be necessary to spray them once or twice a year so they do not have to be measured again. Permanent spray paint will eventually wear off due to weather conditions. If you have to measure your track area with a large tape measure, figuring out the distance for 1/4, 1/2, and 1 mile distances would be an excellent math story problem for 5th and 6th grade students.

# Body Mass Index

The BMI is an indicator of the amount of body fat. One of the better ways of measuring body fat would be to use underwater weighing, which of course is impractical in a school situation. Another method of measuring would be to use skinfold calipers. However, skinfold calipers can be difficult to use and are sometimes considered as intrusive. An easier way to determine body fat, which is less accurate than skinfold calipers, yet still a good indicator, would be to weigh and measure students. BMI-for-Age charts for boys and girls, ages 2-20, have been included in this text, allowing students and teachers the opportunity to look up BMI based on one's height and weight. These charts have been established by the National Center for Health Statistics (NCHS). Students should be weighed on an accurate bathroom scale or nurse's scale if available. A tape measure taped to the wall, allows for height measurements to the nearest inch. Students should be measured without shoes. Since the charts are metric, it may be helpful to know that 1 kg = 2.2 lbs. and 1 m = 39.37".

Children and adolescents who are in the high range for BMI or fatness need to be aware of the possibilities of developing adult obesity and therefore the health concerns related to overweight and obesity, such as heart disease, diabetes, and certain types of cancer. Also boys and girls who fall into the low range for BMI should be encouraged to return to the average rate as growth and tissues can be damaged when body fat is at a lower rate than optimal. When using BMI, care must be taken to make students aware that this is just an indicator of body fat. Koop, former Surgeon General of the United States, has questioned the appropriateness of the BMI as a truly accurate indicator for athletes or growing children and states that other factors also need to be considered when using the BMI scale such as muscle mass and growing factors. The President's Challenge Test, sponsored by the President's

Council for Physical Fitness and Sports, and The Prudential Fitnessgram, endorsed by The American Alliance for Health, Physical Education, Recreation, and Dance, both include a discussion and portion of the BMI in their testing materials. Therefore, we choose to identify BMI as a close indicator of body composition.

| Height (in.) | 40 | 45 | 50 | 55 | 60 | 65 | 70 | 75 | 80 | 85 | 90 | 95 | 100 | 105 | 110 | 115 | 120 | 125 | 130 | 135 | 140 | 145 | 150 |
|---|---|---|---|---|---|---|---|---|---|---|---|---|---|---|---|---|---|---|---|---|---|---|---|
| 42 | 16 | 18 | 20 | 22 | 24 | 26 | 28 | 30 | 32 | 34 | 36 | 38 | 40 | 42 | 44 | 46 | 48 | 50 | 52 | 54 | 56 | 58 | 60 |
| 43 | 15 | 17 | 19 | 21 | 23 | 25 | 27 | 29 | 30 | 32 | 34 | 36 | 38 | 40 | 42 | 44 | 46 | 48 | 50 | 51 | 53 | 55 | 57 |
| 44 | 15 | 16 | 18 | 20 | 22 | 24 | 25 | 27 | 29 | 31 | 33 | 35 | 36 | 38 | 40 | 42 | 44 | 45 | 47 | 49 | 51 | 53 | 55 |
| 45 | 14 | 16 | 17 | 19 | 21 | 23 | 24 | 26 | 28 | 30 | 31 | 33 | 35 | 37 | 38 | 40 | 42 | 43 | 45 | 47 | 490 | 50 | 52 |
| 46 | 13 | 15 | 17 | 18 | 20 | 22 | 23 | 25 | 27 | 28 | 30 | 32 | 33 | 35 | 37 | 38 | 40 | 42 | 43 | 45 | 47 | 48 | 50 |
| 47 | 13 | 14 | 16 | 18 | 19 | 21 | 22 | 24 | 26 | 27 | 29 | 30 | 32 | 33 | 35 | 37 | 38 | 40 | 41 | 43 | 45 | 46 | 48 |
| 48 | 12 | 14 | 15 | 17 | 18 | 20 | 21 | 23 | 24 | 26 | 28 | 29 | 31 | 32 | 34 | 35 | 37 | 38 | 40 | 41 | 43 | 44 | 46 |
| 49 | 12 | 13 | 15 | 16 | 18 | 19 | 21 | 22 | 23 | 25 | 26 | 28 | 29 | 31 | 32 | 34 | 35 | 37 | 38 | 40 | 41 | 43 | 44 |
| 50 | 11 | 13 | 14 | 15 | 17 | 18 | 20 | 21 | 23 | 24 | 25 | 27 | 28 | 30 | 31 | 32 | 34 | 35 | 37 | 38 | 39 | 41 | 42 |
| 51 | 11 | 12 | 14 | 15 | 16 | 18 | 19 | 20 | 22 | 23 | 24 | 26 | 27 | 28 | 30 | 31 | 33 | 34 | 35 | 37 | 38 | 39 | 41 |
| 52 | 10 | 12 | 13 | 14 | 16 | 17 | 18 | 20 | 21 | 22 | 23 | 25 | 26 | 27 | 29 | 30 | 31 | 33 | 34 | 35 | 36 | 38 | 39 |
| 53 | 10 | 11 | 13 | 14 | 15 | 16 | 18 | 19 | 20 | 21 | 23 | 24 | 25 | 26 | 28 | 29 | 30 | 31 | 33 | 34 | 35 | 36 | 38 |
| 54 | 10 | 11 | 12 | 13 | 14 | 16 | 17 | 18 | 19 | 21 | 22 | 23 | 24 | 25 | 27 | 28 | 29 | 30 | 31 | 33 | 34 | 35 | 36 |
| 55 | 9 | 10 | 12 | 13 | 14 | 15 | 16 | 17 | 19 | 20 | 21 | 22 | 23 | 24 | 26 | 27 | 28 | 29 | 30 | 31 | 33 | 34 | 35 |
| 56 | 9 | 10 | 11 | 12 | 13 | 15 | 16 | 17 | 18 | 19 | 20 | 21 | 22 | 24 | 25 | 26 | 27 | 28 | 29 | 30 | 31 | 33 | 34 |
| 57 | 9 | 10 | 11 | 12 | 13 | 14 | 15 | 16 | 17 | 18 | 20 | 21 | 22 | 23 | 24 | 25 | 26 | 27 | 28 | 29 | 30 | 31 | 33 |
| 58 | 8 | 9 | 10 | 12 | 13 | 14 | 15 | 16 | 17 | 18 | 19 | 20 | 21 | 22 | 23 | 24 | 25 | 26 | 27 | 28 | 29 | 30 | 31 |
| 59 | 8 | 9 | 10 | 11 | 12 | 13 | 14 | 15 | 16 | 17 | 18 | 19 | 20 | 21 | 22 | 23 | 24 | 25 | 67 | 27 | 28 | 29 | 30 |
| 60 | 8 | 9 | 10 | 11 | 12 | 13 | 14 | 15 | 16 | 17 | 18 | 19 | 20 | 21 | 22 | 23 | 23 | 24 | 25 | 26 | 27 | 28 | 29 |
| 61 | 8 | 9 | 9 | 10 | 11 | 12 | 13 | 14 | 15 | 16 | 17 | 18 | 19 | 20 | 21 | 22 | 23 | 24 | 25 | 26 | 27 | 27 | 28 |
| 62 | 7 | 8 | 9 | 10 | 11 | 12 | 13 | 14 | 15 | 16 | 16 | 17 | 18 | 19 | 20 | 21 | 22 | 23 | 24 | 25 | 26 | 27 | 27 |
| 63 | 7 | 8 | 9 | 10 | 11 | 12 | 12 | 13 | 14 | 15 | 16 | 17 | 18 | 19 | 20 | 20 | 21 | 22 | 23 | 24 | 25 | 26 | 27 |
| 64 | 7 | 8 | 9 | 9 | 10 | 11 | 12 | 13 | 14 | 15 | 15 | 16 | 17 | 18 | 19 | 20 | 21 | 22 | 22 | 23 | 24 | 25 | 26 |
| 65 | 7 | 8 | 8 | 9 | 10 | 11 | 12 | 13 | 13 | 14 | 15 | 16 | 17 | 18 | 18 | 19 | 20 | 21 | 22 | 23 | 23 | 24 | 25 |
| 66 | 6 | 7 | 8 | 9 | 10 | 11 | 11 | 12 | 13 | 14 | 15 | 15 | 16 | 17 | 18 | 19 | 19 | 20 | 21 | 22 | 23 | 23 | 24 |
| 67 | 6 | 7 | 8 | 9 | 9 | 10 | 11 | 12 | 13 | 13 | 14 | 15 | 16 | 16 | 17 | 18 | 19 | 20 | 20 | 21 | 22 | 23 | 24 |
| 68 | 6 | 7 | 8 | 8 | 9 | 10 | 11 | 11 | 12 | 13 | 14 | 14 | 15 | 16 | 17 | 18 | 18 | 19 | 20 | 21 | 21 | 22 | 23 |
| 69 | 6 | 7 | 7 | 8 | 9 | 10 | 10 | 11 | 12 | 13 | 13 | 14 | 15 | 16 | 16 | 17 | 18 | 18 | 19 | 20 | 21 | 21 | 22 |
| 70 | 6 | 6 | 7 | 8 | 9 | 9 | 10 | 11 | 12 | 12 | 13 | 14 | 14 | 15 | 16 | 17 | 17 | 18 | 19 | 19 | 20 | 21 | 22 |
| 71 | 6 | 6 | 7 | 8 | 8 | 9 | 10 | 10 | 11 | 12 | 13 | 13 | 14 | 15 | 15 | 16 | 17 | 17 | 18 | 19 | 20 | 20 | 21 |
| 72 | 5 | 6 | 7 | 7 | 8 | 9 | 10 | 10 | 11 | 12 | 12 | 13 | 14 | 14 | 15 | 16 | 16 | 17 | 18 | 18 | 19 | 20 | 20 |

**Body Mass Index Calculation**
**Weight (lb.)**

## CDC Growth Charts: United States

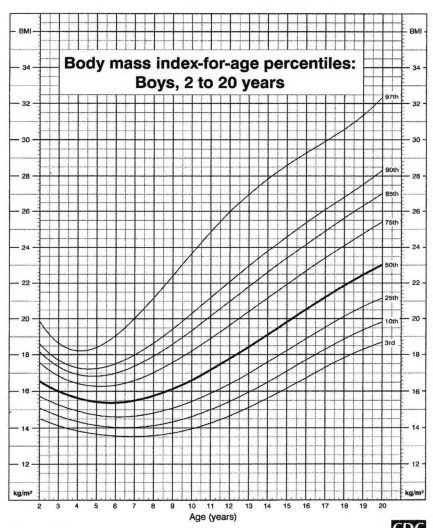

**Body mass index-for-age percentiles: Boys, 2 to 20 years**

Age (years)

Published May 30, 2000.
SOURCE: Developed by the National Center for Health Statistics in collaboration with
the National Center for Chronic Disease Prevention and Health Promotion (2000).

CDC
SAFER · HEALTHIER · PEOPLE™

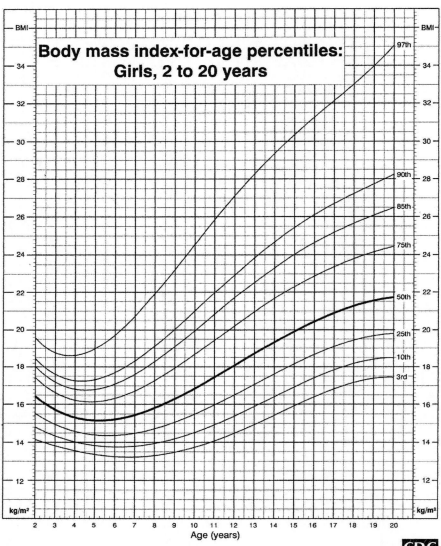

Body mass index-for-age percentiles: Girls, 2 to 20 years

Published May 30, 2000.
SOURCE: Developed by the National Center for Health Statistics in collaboration with
the National Center for Chronic Disease Prevention and Health Promotion (2000).

## ONE MILE RUN/WALK

This test is used to measure aerobic endurance. The President's Challenge Test has a 1/4 mile option for 6–7 year olds, and a 1/2 mile option for 8 to 9 year olds. For the one mile run/walk test, the class is divided in half. If several volunteers are available, students can be divided into groups and can begin at staggered times with one volunteer assigned to each group, where they are responsible for keeping track of laps and recording scores. Using this approach can cut down on the amount of time needed. 4 traffic cones, 2 stopwatches, a clipboard, class list, and a pen are needed when administering this test. Half of the class may perform the test while the other half participates in another activity, close to the track. Students are instructed to walk if they become too tired, have a problem breathing, get a cramp, or have some other problem. Students are to do their best; however, they also need to be safe. They need to be told that it is all right to walk when they feel it is necessary.

Half of the class will line up behind the first cone which is at the starting line. On the signal "GO," the teacher starts the stopwatches and students begin to run laps around the 4 cones. Each time the student passes the first cone, the teacher places a slash mark next to the student's name. It is helpful to choose a student to call off the students' last names as they cross the starting line. This is especially helpful when there are many students passing the first cone at the same time. When the individual student has only one lap to go the teacher or scorer tells that student that he/she has only one lap left until he/she is finished. When that same individual student crosses the finish line, the teacher records the time behind the student's name on the class list. The teacher keeps the stopwatches running. 2 stopwatches are started at the beginning of the test and left running throughout the test. 2 stopwatches are used in case the batteries fail or if one is inadvertently stopped by mistake. Children are instructed to keep running until the teacher tells them they are finished.

## PULL-UPS

Pull ups measure upper body strength. A chinning bar and a class list and score sheet are needed as equipment for this event.

Students may choose the use of either the overhand or underhand grip on the bar but may not change grips in the middle of the test. Students' feet may not touch the floor between pull ups. Students will pull themselves up until the chin is above the bar. They must lower themselves between each pull up and may not push off the wall. Kicking is not permitted. Their score is the number of correct, completed pull ups.

## CURL-UPS

Curl ups measure abdominal strength. This test is simple to administer and score. Students are divided into partners. One partner performs curl ups while the other partner holds the feet and counts the correct number of curl ups. Two or three tumbling mats, a stopwatch, a class list and score cards are the necessary equipment for administering curl ups.

The students are to lie flat on their backs on the tumbling mats with their feet flat on the mat and knees bent. There should be approximately 12 inches between the feet and buttocks, once the student is in proper position. Students are to cross their arms at the chest placing one hand on each of the opposite shoulders. On the signal "GO" students curl up touching their elbows to their thighs, returning their shoulder blades to the mat after each curl up. Students do as many curl ups as possible for one minute. When the teacher says stop, scores are recorded.

## PARTIAL CURL UPS

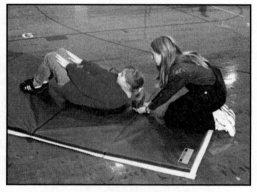

Partial curl-ups measure abdominal strength and endurance. This test is simple to administer and score. Students are divided into partners. One partner performs the partial curl-ups while the other partner kneels behind the head of the student performing the curl-ups and places cupped hands under the head of the performer and counts the correct number of curl-ups. The student performing the partial curl-ups lies on a mat with the knees bent and feet flat on the mat and the feet are about 12 inches from the buttocks. The student performing the curl ups slowly slides the fingers up the thighs until the fingertips touch the knees and then move back down towards the mat until the head touches the partner's hands. Partial curl-ups are to be done to an audio tape or metronome with 1 curl up being completed every three seconds. Curl ups are continued until the student cannot do any more in time to the tape, has not done the last three in rhythm, or has reached the target number.

## SHUTTLE RUN

The shuttle run tests agility or the ability to change direction quickly. Two students can be tested at the same time by one tester. Masking tape, 2 stop watches, 4 blocks of wood or chalkboard erasers which measure 2" x 2" x 4" are needed as the equipment for this test.

2 lines of masking tape are placed on the gym floor 30' apart. 2 sets of erasers or blocks of wood are placed about 4 to 6 inches apart on the other side of the line. 2 students begin behind the line and opposite the erasers. On the signal "GO" students run down, each pick up one eraser and brings it back to the starting line, placing it on the other side of the line. They run back, get the other eraser and run across the line with the eraser. They may not throw the first eraser but must place it on the other side of the line. They may not slide across the line, but must run across it. The time elapsed on the stopwatch is recorded behind the appropriate names on the class list as well as on the student's individual scorecard.

## SIT AND REACH

The sit and reach measures flexibility. A sit and reach box, and score sheet or class list are necessary for the administration of this test. A plastic orange crate, which has been weighted down, and a meter stick can be adapted as a sit and reach box. When students come to this station they need to take off their shoes.. Students sit on the floor, with legs outstretched and the bottom of both feet flat against the box. Each student is allowed 3 attempts to see how far they can stretch along the top of

the box. Students are instructed to place one hand on top of the other keeping the fingertips even with one another. They are to stretch as far as they can and then place their hands flat, on top of the box. Students may not bend their knees. One student may be appointed to hold the knees slightly in order to help remind them not to bend their knees. 3 attempts are allowed, only the best score is recorded. If using a station approach, this would be the place to weigh and measure students due to the fact that they already have their shoes off. An accurate scale placed in a corner which affords some privacy, and a measuring tape taped to the wall are the only equipment besides the class list which are necessary for assessing the Body Mass Index.

Once the testing is complete, student scores are compared to the following charts of normative data. You can compare the fitness levels of your students to those of children across the United States. The awards for The President's Challenge program are also based on scores as compared to these charts. The charts are reprinted with the permission of The President's Challenge, Bloomington, Indiana.

# The Health Fitness Award

| | Age | Partial Curl-Ups (#) | One-Mile Run (min:sec) | OR Distance (min:sec) 1/4 mile | Option (min:sec) 1/2 mile | OR V-Sit Reach (inches) | Sit and Reach (centimeters) | OR Rt.Angle Push-Ups (#) | Pull-Ups | BMIO (range) |
|---|---|---|---|---|---|---|---|---|---|---|
| **Boys** | 6 | 12 | 13:00 | 2:30 | | 1 | 21 | 3 | 1 | 13.3–19.5 |
| | 7 | 12 | 12:00 | 2:20 | | 1 | 21 | 4 | 1 | 13.3–19.5 |
| | 8 | 15 | 11:00 | | 4:45 | 1 | 21 | 5 | 1 | 13.4–20.5 |
| | 9 | 15 | 10:00 | | 4:35 | 1 | 21 | 6 | 1 | 13.7–21.4 |
| | 10 | 20 | 9:30 | | | 1 | 21 | 7 | 1 | 14.0–22.5 |
| | 11 | 20 | 9:00 | | | 1 | 21 | 8 | 2 | 14.0–23.7 |
| | 12 | 20 | 9:00 | | | 1 | 21 | 9 | 2 | 14.8–24.1 |
| | 13 | 25 | 8:00 | | | 1 | 21 | 10 | 2 | 15.4–24.7 |
| | 14 | 25 | 8:00 | | | 1 | 21 | 12 | 3 | 16.1–25.4 |
| | 15 | 30 | 7:30 | | | 1 | 21 | 14 | 4 | 16.6–26.4 |
| | 16 | 30 | 7:30 | | | 1 | 21 | 16 | 5 | 17.2–26.8 |
| | 17 | 30 | 7:30 | | | 1 | 21 | 18 | 6 | 17.7–27.5 |
| **Girls** | 6 | 12 | 13:00 | 2:50 | | 2 | 23 | 3 | 1 | 13.1–19.6 |
| | 7 | 12 | 12:00 | 2:40 | | 2 | 23 | 4 | 1 | 13.1–19.6 |
| | 8 | 15 | 11:00 | | 5:35 | 2 | 23 | 5 | 1 | 13.2–20.7 |
| | 9 | 15 | 10:00 | | 5:25 | 2 | 23 | 6 | 1 | 13.5–21.4 |
| | 10 | 20 | 10:00 | | | 2 | 23 | 7 | 1 | 13.8–22.5 |
| | 11 | 20 | 10:00 | | | 2 | 23 | 7 | 1 | 14.1–23.2 |
| | 12 | 20 | 10:30 | | | 2 | 23 | 8 | 1 | 14.7–24.2 |
| | 13 | 25 | 10:30 | | | 3 | 25 | 7 | 1 | 15.5–25.3 |
| | 14 | 25 | 10:30 | | | 3 | 25 | 7 | 1 | 16.2–25.3 |
| | 15 | 30 | 10:00 | | | 3 | 23 | 7 | 1 | 16.6–26.5 |
| | 16 | 30 | 10:00 | | | 3 | 23 | 7 | 1 | 16.8–26.5 |
| | 17 | 30 | 10:00 | | | 3 | 25 | 7 | 1 | 17.1–26.9 |

Criterion standards listed above adapted from Amateur Athletic Union Physical Fitness Program; AAHPERD Physical Best;

Cooper Institute for Aerobic Research, Fitnessgram; Corbin, C. & Lindsey, R., *Fitness for Life*, 4th edition; and YMCA youth.

# The National Physical Fitness Award

| | Age | Curl-Ups (# one minute) | Partial* Curl-Ups (#) | Shuttle Run (sec) | V-Sit and Reach (inches) | Sit and Reach (cm) | One-Mile Run (min:sec) | Distance (min:sec) | Option** (min:sec) 1/2 mile | Pull-Ups (#) | Rt Angle Push-Ups (#) | Flexed-Arm Hang (sec) |
|---|---|---|---|---|---|---|---|---|---|---|---|---|
| **Boys** | 6 | 22 | 10 | 13.3 | +1.0 | 26 | 12:36 | 2:21 | | 1 | 7 | 6 |
| | 7 | 28 | 13 | 12.8 | +1.0 | 25 | 11:40 | 2:10 | | 1 | 8 | 8 |
| | 8 | 31 | 17 | 12.2 | +0.5 | 25 | 11:05 | | 4:22 | 1 | 9 | 10 |
| | 9 | 32 | 20 | 11.9 | +1.0 | 25 | 10:30 | | 4:14 | 2 | 12 | 10 |
| | 10 | 35 | 24 | 11.5 | +1.0 | 25 | 9:48 | | | 2 | 14 | 12 |
| | 11 | 37 | 26 | 11.1 | +1.0 | 25 | 9:20 | | | 2 | 15 | 11 |
| | 12 | 40 | 32 | 10.6 | +1.0 | 26 | 8:40 | | | 2 | 18 | 12 |
| | 13 | 42 | 39 | 10.2 | +0.5 | 26 | 8:06 | | | 3 | 24 | 14 |
| | 14 | 45 | 40 | 9.9 | +1.0 | 28 | 7:44 | | | 5 | 24 | 20 |
| | 15 | 45 | 45 | 9.7 | +2.0 | 30 | 7:30 | | | 6 | 30 | 30 |
| | 16 | 45 | 37 | 9.4 | +3.0 | 30 | 7:10 | | | 7 | 30 | 28 |
| | 17 | 44 | 42 | 9.4 | +3.0 | 34 | 7:04 | | | 8 | 37 | 30 |
| **Girls** | 6 | 23 | 10 | 13.8 | +2.5 | 27 | 13.12 | 2:26 | | 1 | 6 | 5 |
| | 7 | 25 | 13 | 13.2 | +2.0 | 27 | 12.56 | 2:21 | | 1 | 8 | 6 |
| | 8 | 29 | 17 | 12.9 | +2.0 | 28 | 12:30 | | 4:56 | 1 | 9 | 8 |
| | 9 | 30 | 20 | 12.5 | +2.0 | 28 | 11:52 | | 4:50 | 1 | 12 | 8 |
| | 10 | 30 | 24 | 12.1 | +3.0 | 28 | 11:22 | | | 1 | 13 | 8 |
| | 11 | 32 | 27 | 11.5 | +3.0 | 29 | 11:17 | | | 1 | 11 | 7 |
| | 12 | 35 | 30 | 11.3 | +3.5 | 30 | 11:05 | | | 1 | 10 | 7 |
| | 13 | 37 | 40 | 11.1 | +3.5 | 31 | 10:23 | | | 1 | 11 | 8 |
| | 14 | 37 | 30 | 11.2 | +4.5 | 33 | 10:06 | | | 1 | 10 | 9 |
| | 15 | 36 | 26 | 11.0 | +5.0 | 36 | 9:58 | | | 1 | 15 | 7 |
| | 16 | 35 | 26 | 10.9 | +5.5 | 34 | 10:31 | | | 1 | 12 | 7 |
| | 17 | 34 | 40 | 11.0 | +4.5 | 35 | 10:22 | | | 1 | 16 | 7 |

\* Norms from Canada Fitness Award Program, Health Canada, Government of Canada with permission

\*\* 1/4 and 1/2 mile norms from Amateur Athletic Union Physical fitness Program with permission.

# The Presidential Physical Fitness Award

| | Age | Curl-Ups (# one minute) | Partial* Curl-Ups (#) | Shuttle Run (sec) | V-Sit and Reach (inches) | Sit and Reach (cm) | One-Mile Run (min:sec) | Distance (min:sec) | Option** (min:sec) 1/2 mile | Pull-Ups (#) | Rt Angle Push-Ups (#) |
|---|---|---|---|---|---|---|---|---|---|---|---|
| | | OR | | | OR | | OR | | | OR | |
| **Boys** | 6 | 33 | 22 | 12.1 | +3.5 | 31 | 10:15 | 1:55 | | 2 | 9 |
| | 7 | 36 | 24 | 11.5 | +3.5 | 30 | 9:22 | 1:48 | | 4 | 14 |
| | 8 | 40 | 30 | 11.1 | +3.0 | 31 | 8:48 | | 3:30 | 5 | 17 |
| | 9 | 41 | 37 | 10.9 | +3.0 | 31 | 8:31 | | 3:30 | 5 | 18 |
| | 10 | 45 | 35 | 10.3 | +4.0 | 30 | 7:57 | | | 6 | 20 |
| | 11 | 47 | 43 | 10.0 | +4.0 | 31 | 7:32 | | | 6 | 19 |
| | 12 | 50 | 64 | 9.8 | +4.0 | 31 | 7:11 | | | 7 | 20 |
| | 13 | 53 | 59 | 9.5 | +3.5 | 33 | 6:50 | | | 7 | 21 |
| | 14 | 56 | 62 | 9.1 | +4.5 | 36 | 6:26 | | | 10 | 20 |
| | 15 | 57 | 75 | 9.0 | +5.0 | 37 | 6:20 | | | 11 | 20 |
| | 16 | 56 | 73 | 8.7 | +6.0 | 38 | 6:08 | | | 11 | 24 |
| | 17 | 55 | 66 | 8.7 | +7.0 | 41 | 6:06 | | | 13 | 25 |
| **Girls** | 6 | 32 | 22 | 12.4 | +5.5 | 32 | 11:20 | 2:00 | | 2 | 9 |
| | 7 | 34 | 24 | 12.1 | +5.0 | 32 | 10:36 | 1:55 | | 2 | 14 |
| | 8 | 38 | 30 | 11.8 | +4.5 | 33 | 10:02 | | 3:58 | 2 | 17 |
| | 9 | 39 | 37 | 11.1 | +5.5 | 33 | 9:30 | | 3:53 | 2 | 18 |
| | 10 | 40 | 33 | 10.8 | +6.0 | 33 | 9:19 | | | 3 | 20 |
| | 11 | 42 | 43 | 10.5 | +6.5 | 34 | 9:02 | | | 3 | 19 |
| | 12 | 45 | 50 | 10.4 | +7.0 | 36 | 8:23 | | | 2 | 20 |
| | 13 | 46 | 59 | 10.2 | +7.0 | 38 | 8:13 | | | 2 | 21 |
| | 14 | 47 | 48 | 10.1 | +8.0 | 40 | 7:59 | | | 2 | 20 |
| | 15 | 48 | 38 | 10.0 | +8.0 | 43 | 8:08 | | | 2 | 20 |
| | 16 | 45 | 49 | 10.1 | +9.0 | 42 | 8:23 | | | 1 | 24 |
| | 17 | 44 | 58 | 10.0 | +8.0 | 42 | 8:15 | | | 1 | 25 |

* Norms from Canada Fitness Award Program, Health Canada, government of Canada with permission.

** 1/4 and 1/2 mile norms from Amateur Athletic Union Physical Fitness Program with permission.

# Fitness Center Circuit

This activity has been specifically designed to assist students to improve in fitness areas related to those in which they have been tested. There are 5 stations: Station 1—Upper Body Strength, Station 2—Abdominal Strength, Station 3—Flexibility, Station 4—Agility, and Station 5—Cardiovascular Endurance. Individual eraser boards are at each station listing the activities to be performed at that station. Students will be divided into groups of 5 to 6 students, with each group starting at a different station. Students will rotate at the signal to the next station. Station 1 will move to station 2, 2 to 3, 3 to 4, 4 to 5, and 5 to 1. There will be at least 5 different activities at each station. One student will be at each activity, spending between 30 seconds to one minute at that activity and then moving to the next. Activities are also numbered so students may rotate from one activity to the next using the same rotation; however, the rotation will be within the station. A whistle may be used to indicate that it is time to move to the next activity within the station. A loud buzzer may be used to indicate that it is time to move to the next station. Music may be played in the background while performing activities, and when the music stops, this is the signal to rotate to a new station.

## STATION ONE—UPPER BODY STRENGTH

At this station a chinning bar, a modified chinning bar, 1 tumbling mat, a wall located close to the station, and an erasure board are needed as equipment. The activities to be performed follow. Using a chinning bar, either the overhand or underhand grip may be used when performing Pull Ups. Pull Ups are described in the testing portion of this chapter. Modified Pull Ups are performed using the apparatus designed for this purpose (shown here), if one is available.

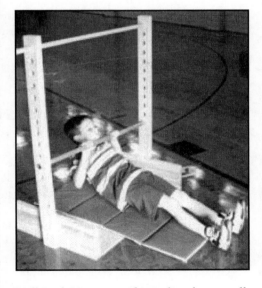

Modified Pull-Ups are performed while lying on one's back. Begin with the arms extended and using an overhand grip on the bar. Heels remain touching the floor with arms and legs extended. While bending the elbows, the student pulls upwards towards the bar. The chin should reach a height of 7 to 8 inches below the bar to complete 1 modified chin up. Wall Push Ups are performed against a wall. Wall push ups are simple to perform and can be accomplished regardless of upper body strength. The students stand facing the wall about 3 feet away from the wall, with arms fully extended and palms flat against the wall. The student bends at the elbow and leans into the wall while keeping the body straight. The student then pushes away from the wall until the arms are again straight. Push Ups are performed in the normal manner on a tumbling mat. Modified Push Ups are similar to regular push ups, however they are performed while kneeling on the mat. The activities for rotational purposes are in this order (1.) Pull Ups, (2) Modified Pull Ups, (3) Wall Push Ups, (4) Regular Push Ups, and (5) Modified Push Ups.

## STATION TWO—ABDOMINAL STRENGTH

At this station 2 tumbling mats and a eraser board are needed as equipment. The activities performed are: Curl Ups, V Sit Balance, Bicycle Sit Ups, Scissors Kicks, and Partner Push Down. Curl Ups are performed on the tumbling mats and are described in the testing portion of this chapter. The V Sit is also performed on the tumbling mat and is simply balancing on one's seat or buttocks with legs and arms straight out in front of the student at a 45 degree angle from the mat. Students are to balance on their seat and not lean back too far or they will end up on their back. Bicycle Sit Ups are also performed while lying on one's back, with the hands clasped behind the neck. The student bends at the hips, while lying on the mat, bringing the knee towards the chest and touching the opposite elbow to the knee. The student continues this exercise actually touching the right elbow to the left knee, and the left elbow to the right knee. The feet never completely touch the floor while performing bicycle sit ups. Scissors Kicks are performed while lying on one's back on the mat, with the hands under one's buttocks in order to support the lower back. The toes are pointed towards the ceiling. Both feet are raised from the floor while alternately kicking, and keeping the legs as straight as possible. This activity gives the appearance of scissors therefore are called scissors kicks. Partner Push Down is performed with a partner. One partner lies on the floor with feet elevated and soles of feet towards the ceiling. The standing partner is standing by the other partner's head with one foot next to each ear of the person lying on the mat. The person lying on the mat grasps the ankles of the standing partner. The standing partner pushes the lying partner's feet down towards the floor pushing both feet together. The partner lying on the mat offers some resistance and controls the push in order that the feet do not go all the way down to the mat. The activities for rotational purposes are in this order: (1) Curl Ups, (2) V Sit Balance, (3) Bicycle Sit Ups, (4) Scissors Kick, and (5) Partner Push Down.

## STATION THREE—FLEXIBILITY

At this station a sit and reach box, plastic orange crates with rulers (adapted sit and reach boxes), masking tape to mark a line on the floor, short ropes 3 to 4 feet in length, and an eraser board are needed as equipment. Sit and Reach is performed using the sit and reach box, or orange crates with rulers which have been adapted as sit and reach boxes. The sit and reach is described in the fitness testing portion of this chapter. Hurdler's Stretch is performed while sitting on the floor with one leg straight out in front and the other knee bent inward with the toe of the bent leg touching the knee of the straightened leg. Both legs remain flat on the floor. Repeat this stretch 5 times with each leg. Knee to Chest Stretch is performed while lying on one's back and bringing one knee to the chest and then extending that same leg straight up towards the ceiling. This should be repeated at least 5 times with each leg. Quad Stretch is performed with the student standing upright. The student bends one knee, bringing the foot of that same leg towards one's back and grasping the ankle. Hold this position for 5 to 10 seconds, then alternate legs. Calf Stretch Using The Wall is performed by finding a place next to the wall. The student uses the wall for balance. One foot is about 10 to 12 inches in front of the other foot. The student bends the front knee, keeping both feet flat on the floor while keeping the back leg straight, and stretching towards the wall. This stretch is held for about 5 to 10 seconds, then alternating legs. Rope Stretches are performed with the student lying on their back. They raise one foot placing a 3 to 4 foot rope around the sole of the foot so that the rope is held with one end in each hand. The rope is wrapped around the students hands if the length is too long. The students then stretch the leg with the rope, trying to straighten the leg completely while the rope offers resistance. This stretch can be performed with the leg straight up towards the ceiling or off to either side. V Sit Reach is performed while the student is sitting on the floor, with the heels just behind a baseline which has been taped to the floor. This first line is about 2 feet in length. A measuring tape is taped perpendicular to the first line. The student sits in a straddle position with legs about 8 to 12 inches apart with the heels of the feet just touching the line. Students, while keeping the knees straight, are attempting to slowly reach forward across the baseline as far as possible. The baseline is 2 feet long and has been made with masking tape. Legs are about 8 to 12 inches apart with the heels of the feet just touching the line. The score is the number of inches measured on the tape. The activities for rotational purposes are in this order: (1) Hurdler's Stretch, (2) Knee to Chest Stretch, (3) Quad Stretch, (4) Calf Stretch Using the Wall, (5) Rope Stretches, (6) V-Sit Reach and the Sit and Reach.

## STATION FOUR—AGILITY

At this station 10 to 12 cones, 12 hula hoops, lines 30 feet apart, a line that is about 4 foot long, 2 erasers, and one eraser board are needed as equipment for this station. The activities to be performed are: The Shuttle Run, which has been described in the testing portion of this chapter. Line Jumping is performed by having students stand on one side of the 4 foot line and jump while landing on both feet at the same time. Students are to alternate jumping on one side of the line and then the other, moving sideways. Jumping Through An Obstacle Course of Hula Hoops is performed by lining up 12 hula hoops in two lines with the hula hoops touching each other. The student will jump through the line of hoops with one foot touching inside of each hoop as they jump down the line. Zig Zagging Through Traffic Cones is performed by running through a line of 8 to 10 traffic cones alternating the sides of the cones or zig zagging. Jumping Over a Line of Traffic Cones is performed by hurdling over the cones and back, or double leg jumping over the cones and back. The activities for rotational purposes are in this order: (1) The Shuttle Run, (2) Line Jumping, (3) Jumping Through An Obstacle Course of Hula Hoops (4) Zig Zagging Through Traffic Cones and (5) Jumping Over a Line of Traffic Cones.

## STATION FIVE—CARDIOVASCULAR ENDURANCE

At this station 2 long jump ropes, 3 short jump ropes, and an eraser board are needed as equipment. The activities to be performed are: Short Jump Ropes which are performed individually by students choosing various ways of jumping such as forwards, backwards, sideways, 1 foot, 2 feet, crossing one's rope, jumping in a circle, or any other way of jumping the student can create. Long Jump Ropes which are performed with 2 students each taking an end of the rope while a third student jumps in the center. After a short turn in the middle students trade places until each of the three students have a turn at jumping in the middle. Back and Forth is performed by the student starting at one end line of the gymnasium. The student runs from the end line to the foul line, touches the foul line, turns and returns to the end line, touching the end line. The student then turns and runs to the center line, touches the center line, turns and returns to the end line. After touching the end line, the student turns and runs to the second foul line, touches it and turns, running to the end line. The student touches the end line, turns, runs to the opposite end line, touches it, and returns to the starting end line, and touches that line (Finished). Fitness Games can be performed by all the members of this group. Fitness games have been described in the fitness activities portion of this chapter. The activities for rotational purposes are in this order. (1) Short Jump Ropes, (2) Long Jump Ropes, (3) Back and Forth, and (4) Fitness Games.

# Learning About Fitness

As children progress through the elementary school years, they should understand more and more about the value of being physically fit. This means that the teacher needs to teach about the health-related and motor fitness categories so that the children understand why they are in need of vigorous physical activity periods. The children need to have an understanding of the heart as a muscle, and how to increase the strength and endurance of that muscle. As each activity is presented, children should be told which aspect(s) of physical fitness is involved.

Children should be taught to take their own heart rates, as described in the preceding section. In the 1980s Kuntzelman developed The "Feelin' Good" Program, designed to teach about physical fitness in a classroom setting. There were workbooks available for children to learn about fitness and to accent the cognitive aspect of physical fitness. Many of the activities taught about fitness while providing maximum vigorous participation. The program contained the activity book, Aerobics With Fun, the source of many of the activities given in this chapter. This program is currently out of print.

# Examples of Vigorous Games That Teach Concepts as Well

### Title:    Cigarette Chain Tag
- Level: 1–6

*Skills Enhanced:* aerobic endurance, agility, cognitive understanding of health risks of smoking
*Equipment Needed:* None
*Description:* The following activity emphasizes the point that the more one smokes, the harder it is for one to move. Also it makes the point that cigarette smokers "get hooked." "It" is the cigarette. When "It" tags someone, "It" must link elbows with the person tagged and they must travel together to tag others. The game continues until almost all children are linked together.

### Title:    Heart Attack
- Level: 3–6

*Skills Enhanced:* aerobic endurance, agility, cognitive understanding of risk factors
*Equipment Needed:* None
*Description:* The activity "Heart Attack" causes children to think about the risk factors for heart disease and shows them that exercise can be beneficial to a healthy heart. Choose three children to be "It." When an "It" tags a person, the person must stand still until another player comes to him/her and does three jumping jacks. The tagged player is then free to go again. Each time that a player is tagged he/she is given another risk factor (smoking, inactivity, poor nutrition, stress or overweight). When a person has been tagged 5 times, he/she has all five risk factors and has a heart attack and becomes an "It."

### Title:    Raymond Risk Factor
- Level: 3–6

*Skills Enhanced:* aerobic endurance, agility, cognitive understanding of risk factors
*Equipment Needed:* None

*Description:* To further emphasize the point that exercise is good for the heart, the following activity has been designed: Players line up on the end line of the play area and two-three "Its" are in the center of the area. When the teacher calls "Go!" all the children run to the other end of the area and try to avoid being tagged by a Raymond Risk Factor. If tagged, the player must stop and do mountain climbers on the spot. The players who have reached the end of the play area come back to revive the ones that were tagged by doing jumping jacks so they may play again. The teacher asks "What is bad about Raymond?" The children answer by reciting heart risk factors.

### *Title:*    *Television Tag*
- *Level: 2–6*

*Skills Enhanced:* aerobic endurance, agility, cognitive understanding concerning sedentary activity
*Equipment Needed:* None
*Description:* "Television Tag" tries to emphasize the fact that sedentary activity is not good for the heart.
Several children are designated as the "TV Bugs." Two opposite corners of the play area are designated as the TV rooms. The players move in any way they wish in the play area but if tagged, they are led to one of the TV rooms and must stay there, running in place with eyes closed, until another player dashes in to tag and free them.

### *Title:*    *Veins and Arteries*
- *Level: K–6*

*Skills Enhanced:* aerobic endurance, agility, cognitive understanding of roles of veins and arteries
*Equipment Needed:* None
*Description:* "Veins and Arteries" helps children understand the basic workings of the heart.
An area in the center of the play area is defined as the heart. Children begin spread out in general space and two–three children are designated as "Its" and must each hold one hand high overhead. When the teacher calls "Veins!" the children must run to the heart and try to avoid being tagged. When the teacher says "Arteries!" the children must run away from the heart and avoid the tag. If tagged, a child must run in place until all others are caught.

In designing games such as these you are limited only by your own creativity. Remember that children love to play; the more that we can teach through play, the more learning that will occur. In these instances the children can work on fitness while learning about it as well.

# Activities for the Development and Maintenance of Physical Fitness

Allsbrook (1992) states that "fitness should fit children." He refers to the fact that instruction in fitness should be developmentally appropriate and should follow the guidelines developed by Corbin (1986) under the acronym "FIT." First of all fitness work should be FUN (F). Children like to play and to participate in activities that give enjoyment to them. Improving physical fitness should never appear to be more like work than play: having fun while getting fit will give the child a good attitude toward developing and maintaining a good state of fitness. Secondly, fitness development should be INTRINSICALLY MOTIVATED (I).

Children should be taught to understand exactly what "feeling good" is all about. Then, children should feel good about feeling good. Activity will become rewarding for the feelings of a healthful outcome. Third, children should acquire the TWO (T) C's: COMPETENCE and CONFIDENCE. Young children learn about themselves and their abilities by the way in which others react to them. Teachers need to tell and assure children that they are competent. Improvement in fitness is a competency. The more competent the child feels, the more confidence he/she will have in his/her abilities. Allsbrook (1992) extends Corbin's acronym by adding "NESS." The N refers to NOW; the teacher needs to consider fitness development when planning any kind of physical education lesson. This means that although the objective may be for the children to learn to dribble a basketball, the activity selected might be a game such as "Dribblemania" (Chapter 11) which is a vigorous activity that will cause heart rates to rise. The E refers to EXTENDING the idea of fitness beyond the scope of the physical education class and to send the message home to involve the children's families as well. The first S is for SUCCEEDING in incorporating physical fitness into the instructional program; the last S is for devising a SYSTEMATIC and SEQUENTIAL plan regarding physical fitness outcomes for the elementary school program.

Keeping in mind that fitness should be FUN, the teacher should refrain from prescribing all exercises and no play. If fitness is to fit the child, activities and exercises should be selected that will encourage active participation. Each lesson should have an introductory, maximum participation, vigorous activity that is fitness oriented. Then, each component of the lesson should have a second goal: contribution to physical fitness.

The following developmental activities have been chosen from numerous sources and have been selected for their inherent value in the development of physical fitness for the elementary school child. They are designed for large group participation. Approximate appropriate grade levels have been designated.

## VIGOROUS MAXIMUM PARTICIPATION GAMES

Largely aerobic in nature, these games may be used effectively for lesson warm-up activities. They are designed with fun in mind and will be, hopefully, taken home to play with neighborhood children and families.

### _Title:_     ___Back and Forth___
*   _Level:_ 2–6
_Skills Enhanced:_ aerobic endurance, agility, speed
_Equipment Needed:_ none
_Description:_ Using the lines on the basketball floor, start from the baseline (#1). The key line is #2, the center line #3, the opposite key line is #4 and the far baseline is #5. Children start on line #1, run to line #2 and touch it with a hand; run back to line #1 and touch it with a hand; run to line #3 and touch, back to line #1; run to line #4 and touch, back to line #1; finally to line #5 and touch and back to line #1. Depending on the

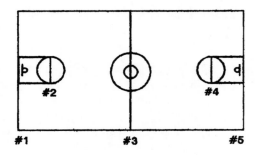

number of children playing, you may wish to send them off in groups. As soon as Group #1 heads for line #3, start the next group, etc.

### Title:    Ball Thief
- *Level:* 3–6

*Skills Enhanced:* aerobic endurance, coordination, agility
*Equipment Needed:* one 8.5'' playground ball for every set of partners
*Description:* One player starts dribbling the ball in the play area while the partner tries to take it away. Keep switching leader and thief roles as the ball is exchanged.

### Title:    Ball Toss
- *Level:* 5–6

*Skills Enhanced:* aerobic fitness, hand-eye coordination
*Equipment Needed:* six yarn balls
*Description:* Have the children standing in concentric circles, one inside the other. Designate the inside circle to jog clockwise and the outer circle to jog counterclockwise. Hand the yarn balls in to the outer circle as it moves. Players are to pass the ball to the first persons in the second circle who pass them; these players return the ball to the next passers in the outside circle. The passing continues. If a ball is dropped, the person who dropped it must take the ball, run around the perimeter of the gymnasium and back into the same circle to resume play.

### Title:    Barker's Hoopla
- *Level:* 3–6

*Skills Enhanced:* aerobic endurance, agility
*Equipment Needed:* one beanbag and one yarnball per player, six hula hoops

*Description:* Divide class into 6 teams. Each team has a hula hoop and teams are spaced equidistantly in the gymnasium space.

Each player places his/her beanbag and yarn ball inside the hula hoop on the floor. On the signal to go, all players run to another team's hoop and "steal" only one object apiece and take it back to their own team's hoop. Then they continue to run and steal from any hoop other than their own. There are no guards. Play continues for a designated amount of time. On the signal to stop the objects are counted and the team with the most is The Barker's Champ!

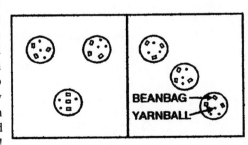

*Variation*: Beanbags represent muscle cells and yarn balls represent fat cells. Children are to give away the fat cells and steal the muscle cells!

### Title:    Bee Sting
- *Level:* K–6

*Skills Enhanced:* aerobic endurance, agility
*Equipment Needed:* a flag for each child
*Description:* Each child places the flag on his/her backside so that it hangs from a back pocket or waistband. On the signal to go, all of the children try to take the flags from

someone else. After a designated amount of time stop the game and see who has the most flags. Let that person take a victory lap while the others jog in place.

### *Title:* ***Exercise Hustle***
- *Level:* 3–6

*Skills Enhanced:* aerobic endurance, strength, flexibility
*Equipment Needed:* none
*Description:* Arrange class as in the diagram below. The leader starts an exercise and all join in except the player in position A. He/she takes off and runs around the perimeter of the gym, returns to the leader's spot and starts a new exercise. The first leader steps to position B, all players shift and do the new exercise shown while the new player in position A takes off and runs around the play area.

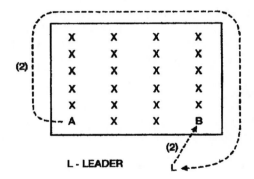

### *Title:* ***Fitness Go Round***
- *Level:* 4–6

*Skills Enhanced:* aerobic endurance, muscular strength, flexibility
*Equipment Needed:* none
*Description:* Divide class into groups of 8–10 and have them stand in a circle. Designate one leader per group. All players will be jogging in place. Each player demonstrates an exercise that he/she has selected, and all players try the exercise. The leader then calls out "What's the name of the game?" The children respond, while jogging in place, "Fitness!"
The leader then does his/her own exercise and someone else's. As the group continues to jog in place, each player who has been identified by exercise does his/her own and then another person's. The game continues until all exercises have been done. If a child cannot remember someone's exercise, he/she runs a lap of the gymnasium.

### *Title:* ***Hexagon Havoc***
- *Level:* 3–6

*Skills Enhanced:* aerobic endurance, leg strength, agility
*Equipment Needed:* six pylons
*Description:* Define the gymnasium area into a hexagon shape with the pylons. Divide the class into 6 groups and place one group in a single file line at each cone. The class will be moving around the perimeter of the hexagon, and each time a group passes a pylon, the

members must change the locomotor movement that they are using. The teacher designates the order of the activities: jog, slide, jump, hop, gallop, skip. As variations, the teacher may allow the children to switch moves independently; each pylon may designate a different movement so the entire class is not doing the same thing at the same time; or, different kinds of locomotor movements may be used.

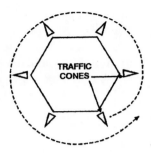

### Title:  *Hit the Deck*
* *Level:* 4–6

*Skills Enhanced:* aerobic endurance, agility, coordination
*Equipment Needed:* none
*Description:* Children are in general space facing the leader and running in place. The leader makes the calls and the children respond: "Run in slow motion," "Double time," "Hit the deck!" (prone position on floor, still running), "on your back!", "on your feet!", and "Slap your thighs!" (lift knees high and slap the thighs when up).

### Title:  *Hot Tomato*
* *Level:* 4–6

*Skills Enhanced:* aerobic endurance, agility, speed, power
*Equipment Needed:* a yarnball for every two players
*Description*: Partners move anywhere in general space in the gymnasium tossing the ball back and forth as they travel. On the whistle, the child who is holding the yarn ball must chase the partner and tag him/her as many times as possible before the whistle blows again. At this point the partners resume tossing and catching the ball as they travel in general space.

### Title:  *Indianapolis 500*
* *Level:* K–3

*Skills Enhanced:* aerobic endurance, agility, coordination
*Equipment Needed:* green flag, yellow flag, red flag, blue flag, black flag, checkered flag, hula hoop for each child, 6 pylons
*Description:* Children group at the starting line and warm-up their "engines." Each child has a hula hoop as a steering wheel. When the green flag is waving they go, racing around the track designated by the pylons. The teacher keeps changing the waving flag and the children have to watch and respond accordingly: GREEN = go; RED = Stop; YELLOW = proceed slowly; BLUE = out of gas, must shuffle step to a corner for a refill; BLACK = flat tire, must hop on one foot to a corner for repair; and CHECKERED = End of the Race.
*Variation:* Have children seated with partners just inside the track. Designate a series of exercises: sit-ups, push-ups, mountain climbers, jumping jacks, etc. On the signal to go, the first partner runs around the track while the other does sit-ups. Upon arrival the runner does sit-ups while the partner goes around the track. When the partner arrives, he/she begins doing push-ups while the first partner runs, etc.

### Title:  *Loose Caboose*
* *Level:* 4–6

*Skills Enhanced:* aerobic endurance, agility
*Equipment Needed: none*
*Description:* Children are in groups of three, single file with hands on the waist of the child in front. 3 or 4 children are designated as loose cabooses and try to hook on to the back of a "train" of three children. As soon as one hooks on, the first child in the "train" breaks off and becomes a loose caboose.

*Title:*    **Lottery Tag**
- *Level:* 4–6

*Skills Enhanced:* aerobic endurance, agility, speed, power
*Equipment Needed:* poker chips numbered from 1–6
*Description:* Each child is given a poker chip. When the teacher calls a number from 1–6, all those children having that number immediately become taggers. They chase all of the other children in the class. If tagged, a child must jog in place until another child runs by and trades poker chips with him/her. After the trade the child is allowed to run free once again. When the teacher calls a new number the taggers become runners and the new taggers chase the children.

*Title:*    **Monkey in the Middle**
- *Level:* 3–6

*Skills Enhanced:* aerobic endurance, throwing, catching
*Equipment Needed:* yarn ball for every set of three children
*Description:* Two children move in general space passing the ball back and forth while the third child tries to intercept the ball and catch it. When intercepted, the last person to touch the ball becomes the monkey in the middle.

*Title:*    **Phyllis or Phil Fit**
- *Level:* K–6

*Skills Enhanced:* aerobic endurance, agility
*Equipment Needed:* none
*Description:* All children are jogging in self space. The teacher calls out the names of two to three children. All of the other children must tag these children and return to jogging in self-space. The named children must try to avoid the tags.

*Title:*    **Run and Roll**
- *Level:* K–6

*Skills Enhanced:* aerobic endurance, agility
*Equipment Needed:* none
*Description:* All children run in general space. When the whistle blows they drop to the floor and perform log rolls; on the next whistle they jump up and resume running; the next whistle, log roll, etc.

*Title:*    **Running Grand March**
- *Level:* 4–6

*Skills Enhanced:* aerobic endurance
*Equipment Needed:* none
*Description:* All class members start to jog in a single file line to the center of the gymnasium end line where they turn and jog toward the teacher at the opposite end of the gym. As each runner comes to the teacher he/she points left or right, sending runners alternately in those

directions. They run back down the length of the gym, turn and meet a runner coming from the opposite direction and run down the center of the gym with that runner. Now the teacher sends them alternately left or right in pairs. Each pair meets another and comes to the teacher in fours. Each four meets another and comes in eight's. Eight's then come in sixteen's. At this point they split back to eighties, then to fours, to two's and to single file.

**Title:** *Running Mania*
- *Level:* 2–6

*Skills Enhanced:* aerobic endurance
*Equipment Needed:* none
*Description:* All class members start to jog in a circle formation around the play space. On signal the back runner speeds up and runs forward weaving in and out of the runners ahead of him/her until he/she gets to the front of the line. The new back runner does the same when the first one is about 3 people ahead.

**Title:** *Run Squad Run*
- Level: 4–6

*Skills Enhanced:* aerobic endurance, speed
*Equipment Needed:* none
*Description*: Divide the class into 4–6 teams or squads. Squads will jog in general space. On the signal, the last person must sprint to the front of the line and become the leader. Continue for a certain amount of time or until everyone has had a chance to sprint at least two times.

**Title: *Serpentine Jog***
- *Level:* K–6

*Skills Enhanced:* aerobic endurance
*Equipment Needed:* none
*Description:* Class members run in a single file line, keeping an eye on the persons immediately in front of them. The leader begins to wind the circle tighter; when he/she arrives at the center part of the circle, he/she then leads back out.

**Title:** *Shadows*
- *Level:* 2–6

*Skills Enhanced:* aerobic endurance, agility, speed, coordination
*Equipment Needed:* none
*Description:* Children select a partner. On the signal to go, one partner is the leader, the other is the shadow and must move everywhere the leader goes. On signal, leader and shadow change roles.

**Title:** *Shipwreck*
- *Level:* 3–6

*Skills Enhanced:* aerobic endurance, agility, speed,
*Equipment Needed:* none
*Description:* The gymnasium area is designated as bow, starboard, stern and port. As the teacher calls off the parts of the ship the children run to that area. Calls should be made quickly to keep players moving at all times.

*Title:*    **Snatch the Flag**
- *Level:* 4–6

*Skills Enhanced:* aerobic endurance, arm strength and endurance, agility, speed
*Equipment Needed:* one flag football belt per player
*Description:* Class is divided into two teams, each wearing a team color flag football belt. On the signal to go, players try to take the flags from the opponents. Once a flag is taken it is put in the designated home base (end of the court) for the capturing team. The child who lost the flag must do a seal crawl from the center gymnasium line to the opposing home base to retrieve his/her flag. During the seal crawl and the running return with the flag the player retrieving the flag is safe. One he/she crosses the midcourt line he/she is in play once again. Players whose flags have been snatched may not snatch other flags until they have retrieved their own flags.

*Title:*    **Steal the Ball**
- *Level:* 3–6

*Skills Enhanced:* aerobic endurance, coordination dribbling, agility, speed
*Equipment Needed:* 20 8.5'' playground balls
*Description:* Twenty of the players are dribbling their balls with their hands in general space. The other children try to take a ball away by reaching in and dribbling it away. Once a player loses a ball, he/she goes to take another ball away.
Variation: If the balls are not needed for the next class activity, have the players take the ball and put it away in the bin. Play until only a few players are left with balls.

*Title:*    **Tag**
- *Level:* K–6

*Skills Enhanced:* aerobic endurance, agility, (balance, speed, coordination, and power depending on the form of tag played)
*Equipment Needed:* none
*Description:* Any form of tag will contribute to fitness qualities if played vigorously. Use two to three "its," never just one. See Chapter 9 for all of the different forms of tag games from which to choose.

*Title:*    **Tortoise and Hare**
- *Level:* K–6

*Skills Enhanced:* aerobic endurance
*Equipment Needed:* none
*Description:* One child is designated as the leader. He/she faces the class as they all run in place and calls "Tortoise" (all run slowly in place) or "Hare" (all run quickly in place).

*Title:*    **Walk, Trot, Sprint**
- *Level:* 3–6

*Skills Enhanced:* aerobic endurance, leg strength, power, speed
*Equipment Needed:* none
*Description:* Children start in a circle formation around the outside of the gymnasium perimeter, facing in one direction. When the whistle blows the children start walking; when the whistle blows again the children change the pace to a trot; and, on the third whistle they break into a sprint. The fourth whistle starts the sequence again and they change from sprint to walk.

*Variation*: Children could be taught to go immediately into this activity on signal at any time during a class period. For example, if they were working on tumbling skills and they heard the signal they would go to the perimeter and immediately begin to walk. A double whistle could be the indicator to go back to the tumbling work.

# Circuit Training

Another good method for working on physical fitness components is the use of a circuit. A typical circuit for a class of 24 children would have six stations plus a water station at a drinking fountain.

Circuits can be used as the warm-up activity for a class, or may be used as the main instructional portion of the class to introduce different activities that will enhance fitness. If stretching is to be done at any of the stations, however, a cardiorespiratory warm-up is a good idea prior to working the circuit. Muscles should always be warmed aerobically before being stretched. The goal of the circuit may be: (1) for warm-up purposes or (2) to introduce new fitness activities. Children enjoy circuits that are fun and challenging. Tasks assigned at the different stations should be adaptable so that the circuit is individualized to the different capabilities of the children involved. Each station should be designed so that each child leaves with a feeling of success. Each station should influence a different area of health-related or motor fitness. Circuits are most successful when done with children in Grades 4–6. Those activities designated for stations may be done with large group instruction with younger children.

A water station is suggested in lieu of having the class take a water break and losing precious class time. As the children rotate to that station they will be allowed to rest and get drinks if needed. In this way you are assured that the child is getting enough water while working at a relatively high level of intensity at a circuit.

Typically a circuit would be run at one to one-and-a-half minutes per station for the first time around, 45 seconds for the second time around. Of course these times are dependent on whether the circuit is a warm-up activity or a main lesson focus. Whistles may be used to signal the change of stations; music makes a better working atmosphere, however. When the music stops, the children switch stations and start to work when the music begins again.

Suggested activities for the circuit stations follow. The number of repetitions of each is dependent on the abilities of the individuals at the stations as well as the time allowed at each station. When designing the circuit be sure that you space the different activities so that upper body tasks and lower body tasks are divided: do not have both stations #3 and #4 work on lower leg strength!

## UPPER BODY STRENGTH/ENDURANCE

1.   Sawing Wood: Partners face each other, palms to palms. Alternately press one arm straight then the other with the partner providing resistance.
2.   Coffee Grinder: Lie on floor on one side. Lift weight up onto one arm and walk the feet around while keeping legs straight. When back to original position repeat with opposite arm and walk the feet around while keeping legs straight. When back to original position repeat with opposite arm as support.

3.    Modified Push-Ups: On floor on hands and knees, hands directly beneath the shoulders. Keep body straight while bending the arms to allow the body to move down to the floor, extend arms to return to push-up position.

4.    Push-Outs on Wall: Stand facing wall, arms extended and palms on wall. Body is straight, feet are together and about 2–3' out from the wall. Flex arms to bring body into wall, extend arms to push out from wall.

5.    Caterpillar Crawl: Children sit on the floor, one behind the other. Wrap legs around the waist of the person in front of you. On signal, all lift with arms (front person uses feet as well) and try to walk forward on the hands.

6.    Bug Tug: Stand back to back, bend over and grasp right hands. Try to pull the partner over a designated line while he/she tries to pull in the opposite way.

7.    Scoot: Lying in prone position on scooter, using arms only, push self backwards 5 yards, then pull self forward 5 yards. Repeat.

8.    Seal Walk: Supporting self in a push-up position, "walk" forward dragging legs behind.

9.    Crab Walk: Sitting on floor with hands back by hips, knees bent and feet flat on floor, lift body up and "walk" forward, backward, or sideways.

10.   Basketball Pass: With partner within 5 yards, throw a direct chest pass back and forth with a junior basketball.

## LOWER BODY STRENGTH/ENDURANCE

1.    Crunch: Lying supine, hands behind head, knees bent, feet flat on floor. Contract abdominal muscles and lift head and shoulders off the floor.

2.    Fire Hydrant: On floor on hands and knees, lift and extend leg to the side, return to starting position and lift opposite leg.

3.    Mountain Climbers: Hold a push-up position on the floor with one leg forward. Switch leg positions rapidly.

4.    Chinese Get-Up: Partners stand back to back and hook elbows. Move feet forward until partners are leaning on each other, bend knees and move to sitting position. Return to standing position.

5.    Chinese Stand-Up: Sit facing partner with knees bent and toes touching partner's. Join hands. On signal pull and move to standing position. Lower down to sitting.

6.    Partner Bicycle Pumps: Sit on the floor facing the partner with soles of feet touching. Support self with hands to side and back. Move legs in bicycle pumping action.

7.    Scooter Push-Me-Pull-Me: Sitting on scooter and using legs only, push self forward back to start. Repeat.

8.    Chair: Stand with back flat against the wall, feet out about 1–2' from wall. Slide down until knees are bent at ninety degrees. Hold and repeat.

9.    Bear Dance: Squat down and extend left leg straight ahead. Jump forward and switch leg positions.

10.   Leg Wrestling: Supine on floor beside partner, heads at opposite ends, hips touching. Lift inside leg and cross knees with partner. Work with leg to force partner's leg to mat. Switch sides and repeat.

## UPPER BODY FLEXIBILITY

Each stretch should be held from 6 to 10 seconds.

1. Reachers: Lying on back, knees bent, feet flat on the floor, extend one arm above head on the floor with palm up, other arm down by side, palm down. Reach upward and hold; change arm positions and repeat.
2. Macaronis: Stand with fingers laced behind the head. Pull elbows back as far as possible and hold; bring elbows forward to touch in front of face and hold.
3. Hug: Cross arms in front of body and hug shoulders. "Walk" fingers as far onto back as possible.
4. Wings: Sit Indian style and stretch arms out to the side, palms forward. Push arms back at shoulder height and hold.
5. Ostrich Pecks: Kneeling position, sitting on heels with hands clasped behind back. Take forehead to the ground while lifting arms as high as possible. Hold and repeat.
6. Shoulder Squeezes: Standing position with hands clasped behind back. Bend forward and raise the arms over the head. Hold and repeat.
7. Turn The Key: Kneeling with seat resting on heels, fingers laced behind head. Bend left elbow to touch right knee; hold and repeat other side.
8. Captain Hook: Standing position, reach left arm back over left shoulder and right arm behind back. Clasp hands and hold. Change sides and repeat.
9. Isolations: Standing position, cross left arm over chest, bring right arm under, bend at elbow and pull arm in. Hold and repeat other side.
10. Dips: Kneeling with both forearms on the floor, palms grab the right shoulder. Turn head toward the right shoulder and slowly push opposite shoulder toward ground. Hold, change sides and repeat.

## LOWER BODY FLEXIBILITY

1. Rolling Ball: Sit on floor and tuck knees into chest. Put head down to knees and roll back and forth on the back in this position.
2. Sidewinders: Kneel on the floor, back straight. Extend arms overhead and lean to right and hold. Lean to left and hold.
3. Twisters: Lie on back, feet flat on floor, fingers laced behind head, elbows on floor. Twist both knees to the side and hold. Repeat to other side.
4. Runner's Stretch: Stand with one leg forward, other back. Bend forward leg and keep back leg straight. Lean forward and keep heel of back leg on floor. Hold, change legs, repeat.
5. Pretzel: Lying in a prone position on the floor, bend left leg up and grasp the foot with your right hand. Hold and repeat with other side.
6. Palm Tree: Stand with feet shoulder width apart, left hand on hip, right extended overhead. Bend sideways to left, hold. Repeat other side.
7. Reach and Hold: Sitting position, left leg extended, right leg tucked so right foot is at groin. Bend at waist to reach for left ankle and hold. Repeat with other side.
8. Yoga: Sitting on floor place soles of feet together in front. Hold ankles and press legs to floor with elbows. Hold and repeat.

## AEROBIC ENDURANCE

1. Jogging in place
2. Jogging the perimeter of the circuit
3. Jumping Jacks
4. Jumping in Place
5. Jumping Rope
6. Back to Back Glide: Stand back to back with partner and side slide around the perimeter of the circuit
7. Hop Kicks: Face partner and hold hands. Jump and then kick right legs out, jump, left legs out, etc.
8. Jump side to side over a line on the floor
9. Stepping up onto bench and down
10. Skipping around the perimeter of the circuit

## CLASSROOM EXERCISE ROUTINES

The classroom may also serve as an excellent place for physical fitness development. Ideally, a 20–30 minute routine workout each morning should start the day. Exercise gives children energy and a morning workout can contribute to readiness for academic work. It may not be feasible to spend 20–30 minutes each morning; however, simple routines can be established that the children know so that you may use the routines at any time as needed during the school day.

## CHAIRS

Chair exercises have been designed for aerobic exercise for people with special mobility problems. However, they may be used quite effectively for the healthy child in a classroom setting. The following is a sample "Peak Chair Routine" developed by Kuntzelman, Kuntzelman, McGlynn and McGlynn (1984, pp. 147–148).

This routine is done most effectively with all chairs in a large circle.
- Sit Down and Get Up—Alternately sitting and standing 3 times
- Run Around The Chair—clockwise 3 times, then reverse three times
- Step Up, Step Down—step onto seat and down 3 times
- Push-Ups—Place hands on sides of seat and do push-ups 3 times
- V-Seat—Sit on chair and lift legs together so body is held in a v-position, hands hold sides of chair
- Bicycle Pumps—sitting on chair, holding sides of seat, pump legs alternately
- Alternate Foot Taps—Sitting on edge of chair, hands on sides, toes together in front of chair. Tap left then right toes alternately for 10 taps.
- Sitting Jumping Jacks—Sitting jumping jacks 10 times
- Chair Push-Ups—right hand on chair back, left on chair seat, chest over seat; bend elbows until chest touches right hand. Repeat. Change hands and repeat.
- Body Twists—Sitting in chair, twist body back and forth.
- Steps—Standing behind the chair with hands on chair back, lift left foot to touch chair seat, down, right foot, down. Repeat.

- Switch Leaders—Sitting, walking in place. Designate one leader to choose and lead a chair exercise. On the command "Switch" the next person to the left is the leader, etc. While sitting, run in place.
- Switch Chairs—On signal stand up and change with someone across the circle.
- Stand behind chair and walk in place: lift chair with both hands to waist height; lower and lift again.

According to Kuntzelman, et al (1984), almost any regular exercise can be adapted for a chair. Have children create chair routines and take turns leading them.

Children can participate in other aerobic activities within the classroom. One idea would be to use an exercise video and have the children "aerobicize." In addition, some games are easily adaptable to the classroom:

## MACHO MOVER

Children run in place quickly, fists clenched. Teacher points to left, to right, to back of room, to front of room. At each point children turn, yell "Ho!" and continue to run in place.

## MUSICAL CHAIRS

Children walk around the room and when the music stops they sit. The one child left without a chair leads them in an exercise. The game continues.

## PRINCIPAL'S COMING

When the teacher says "Principal's Coming!" children sit and fold hands; "Recess!" children stand and run in place: "Bed Time!" children lie on floor; "Teacher's Coming!" children sit, keep feet running in place and raise one hand, etc.

# Fitness Journals

You should encourage your children to keep a fitness journal in which they would write down the kinds of exercise that they do each day, at school or at home. In the journal, the child should identify the particular exercise as aerobic or anaerobic, and should be able to tell what area of fitness was stressed. In addition, the children should write down how they feel just before exercising and then after exercising. You may wish to ask them to write down what they have eaten that day as well! Children who maintain regular journals should be rewarded. You may place their names on a "Fitness Fanatics" chart and place a star next to the name for each week of journal writing.

## FITNESS PROGRESS CHARTS

If children keep track of miles run, walked, or covered by bicycling you could have a bulletin board with a map. Each week you can mark off the total number of miles the class has gone en route to Disney World! Or to Alaska!

Children may keep individual progress charts for results of self-testing. You may have one specific time each month that you will have the children re-test their skills if they choose. Children who make individual progress should be praised and may receive stars or stickers in recognition of their achievement.

Parents should be aware of the physical fitness status of their children. Have the children take their progress charts home for parents to initial. Encourage the parents to exercise with the child!

## Summary

You now know that we cannot develop good fitness levels and maintain them unless appropriate exercise is provided for the right amount of time and on the correct number of days. With all of the content that the child needs to learn in physical education, it is literally impossible to actually change fitness levels based on physical education alone. However, it is possible to stress the importance of fitness, to give the child the content necessary to be knowledgeable about fitness and to encourage the child to take that knowledge and content home to work on his/her own fitness level. In fact, children should be encouraged to make fitness a family project!

If all of the children in the United States were provided with 5 days per week of physical education with an effective physical education teacher, it would be possible to create a "fit citizenry" within several years. Health problems would decrease significantly and the United States would be known as a fit and well nation. Physical education schedules could be developed on a curriculum such that every other day was strictly a fitness day, alternating with skill development days. Until it is recognized by our legislators that a "fit nation" is an essential goal for the United States, teachers must resign themselves to providing the knowledge and the competencies for children to develop good levels of personal fitness during leisure time.

## References and Suggested Readings

Allsbrook, L. (1992). Fitness should fit children. *Journal of Physical Education, Recreation and Dance*, 63(6), 47–49.

Anderson, A. & Weber, E. (1997). A multiple intelligence approach to healthy active living in high school. *Journal of Physical Education, Recreation and Dance*, 68(4), 57–62.

Bennett, J.G. & Murphy, D.J. (1995). Sit-ups and push-ups only—Are we heading for muscular imbalance? *Journal of Physical Education, Recreation and Dance*, 66(1), 67–72.

Brzycki, M. (1996). *Youth strength and conditioning for parents and players.* McGraw-Hill.

Brzycki, M. (1995). *Youth strength and conditioning for parents and players.* Masters Press.

Cooper Institute for Aerobics Research Staff. (2006). *FITNESS/Activitygram test administration manual.* Human Kinetics.

Cooper Institute for Aerobics Research. (1992). *The Prudential FITNESSGRAM.* Cooper Institute.

Corbin, C.B. (1987). Physical fitness in the K–12 curriculum. *Journal of Physical Education, Recreation and Dance*, 15(7), 49–54.

Deal, T.B. & Deal, L.O. (1995). Heart to heart: Using heart rate telemetry to meet physical education outcomes. *Journal of Physical Education, Recreation and Dance*, 66(3), 30–35.

Gabbard, C.P. (2003). *Lifelong motor development*. Benjamin-Cummings.

Gabbard, C.P. (1992). *Lifelong motor development*. Brown & Benchmark.

Gallahue, D. (2005*). Developmental physical education for all children*. Human Kinetics.

Gallahue, D. (1997*). Developmental physical education for today's children*. McGraw-Hill.

Gallahue, D. (1996*). Developmental physical education for today's children*. Brown and Benchmark.

Kirchner G. & Fishburne, G.J. (2001). *Physical education for elementary school children*. McGraw Hill Higher Ed.

Kirchner G. & Fishburne, G.J. (1998). *Physical education for elementary school children*. McGraw Hill

Kirchner G. & Fishburne, G.J. (1995). *Physical education for elementary school children*. Brown and Benchmark.

Kuntzelman, C. T., Kuntzelman, B., McGlynn, M. & McGlynn, G. (1984). *Aerobics with fun*. Fitness Finders.

Kuntzelman, C. T. (1978). *Fitness discovery activities*. Arbor Press.

McSwegin, P., Pemberton, C., Petray, C. & Going, S. (1989). *Physical best*. AAHPERD.

Mitchell, M. (1996). Stretching the content of your warm-up. *Journal of Physical Education, Recreation and Dance*, 67(7), 24–28.

Nichols, B. (2001). *Moving and learning. The elementary school physical education experience*. McGraw Hill.

Nichols, B. (1994). *Moving and learning. The elementary school physical education experience*. Times Mirror/Mosby.

Nichols, B. (1990). *Moving and learning. The elementary school physical education experience*. Times Mirror/Mosby

Pangrazi, R. P. (2006). *Dynamic physical education for elementary school children*. Benjamin Cummings.

Pangrazi, R. P. (1998). *Dynamic physical education for elementary school children*. Allyn and Bacon.

Pangrazi, R. P. & Dauer, V. P. (1992). *Dynamic physical education for elementary school children*. Macmillan.

Payne, V.G. & Isaacs, L.D. (2007). *Human motor development. A lifespan approach*. McGraw-Hill.

Payne, V.G. & Isaacs, L.D. (2001). *Human motor development. A lifespan approach*. Mayfield.

Payne, V.G. & Isaacs, L.D. (1995). *Human motor development: A lifespan approach*. Mayfield.

Payne, V.G. & Isaacs, L.D. (1991). *Human motor development: A lifespan approach*. Mayfield.

President's Council on Physical Fitness and Sports. (1997). *The president's challenge physical fitness program packet*. The President's Challenge.

# Internet Resources

http://www.cdc.gov/nchs

http://wwwshapeup.org/sua/dated/071196.htm

http://www.shapeup.org/sua/bmi/how.htm

CHAPTER

# 9

# Developmentally Appropriate Games

In the past it was believed that physical education was all fun and games and little or no real instruction took place. Now it is understood that games serve as vehicles for application and practice of learned skills: games are used in physical education as laboratory experiences in which children may practice and apply the movement skills they have learned. There is little use for games simply as time-fillers: it is necessary to teach children how to use psychomotor skills efficiently. Perhaps a second use for different kinds of games would be on special days that separate units, on school-wide field days, or during a regular classroom day when the children need a break from the intensity of academics.

This chapter is entitled "Developmentally Appropriate Games." You will recall from Chapter One that the term "developmentally appropriate" refers to the fact that activities are selected that match the psychomotor and cognitive needs of the child. Games of low organization represent those with little complexity (few rules, little strategy), and they involve only a few skills. Games of low organization do not fall into the team category and children play as individuals rather than as teams. As games increase in rules and strategy they move upward on the continuum of complexity and become games of higher organization. As children grow and develop, they become capable of doing and understanding more. Of course skill development is still a factor, and the selection of an appropriate game should consider the physical demands as well as the cognitive ones.

## Principles of Game Selection

When you select games for a class, you need to consider several important aspects. Each of these areas should be examined carefully to assure quality participation time for students.

## OBJECTIVE OF THE GAME

What is the objective of the game? Is it related to the skills to be enhanced? Is it cooperative or competitive?

## MAXIMUM PARTICIPATION

How many children can play at one time? Is there a lot of waiting in the game or are most children active the majority of the time? And, if active, is that participation of such a vigorous nature that it will contribute to the development of sound fitness levels as well? Are players ever eliminated in the game? What do they do if they are eliminated?

## COGNITIVE DIFFICULTY

How many rules and how much strategy is involved in the game? Will the children be able to understand and apply the rules?

## PSYCHOMOTOR DIFFICULTY

Do the students have the skills that are required to play the game successfully?

## EQUIPMENT

What equipment is necessary and is it available in an appropriate size for the children involved?

## SAFETY

What measures must be taken to assure safe participation in this activity? E.g., are shin guards necessary for the soccer lead-up games?

# Games

The authors have tried to identify games that are appropriate for each grade level. Of course selection of a game will be based on the above factors and only the teachers know the capabilities of their children. There may be games listed for first grade that can be played successfully with a kindergarten group, or they may be appropriate for a third grade class. The grade levels given are only guidelines. Please note that the complexity of the game increases with the grade level of the child.

The games in this chapter have been author-created or selected from the sources noted at the end of the chapter and are divided into several categories: tag games, games of low organization, games of higher organization, cooperative games, and relays. Care has been taken to select games that involve maximum participation and avoid sedentary elimination. When teaching a game, the teacher should put the children in the game formation and

THEN tell them how to play. Children have trouble visualizing when given conditions and rules without context.

The cognitive applications that follow each game are ideas developed by the authors or by university students, demonstrating the logical coordination of academic and physical education content.

Care has also been taken to eliminate any games that may be interpreted as violent. Professional discourse has ensued for several years regarding the inappropriate choice of games that use humans as targets; thus, the old practice of dodgeball has been eliminated. You may recall your days of physical education as fun-filled with the time-old dodgeball tradition. Give it a thought: did EVERYONE enjoy these games or were there less skilled children who withdrew from the activity? And, now that you know the purpose and worth of a good physical education experience, can you see what a waste of time it was to play such games? Dodgeball "turned off" many non-athletes from pursuing lifelong physical activity; today that would truly undermine our goals for physically educated individuals.

## TAG GAMES

Tag games usually involve locomotor movements combined with the skill of tagging (touching) other children. The tag should be taught to be gentle and never a push or a tackle. Good teaching tips for tag games are:

1. Have the "its" each carry a yarn ball and tag others by touching them with the yarn ball.
2. Choose 2–3 "its" per game to maximize the participation of those children being chased. The last children caught can be "its" for the next round of play or for the next game.
3. Establish boundaries to run to, such as the far sideline in a gymnasium, and emphasize that players are safe only if they are standing ON the line. Children need to learn to stop on the line so they do not run into the wall. NEVER have children run to a wall to be safe!

Tag games are extremely useful as warm-up activities since they usually involve constant movement, causing the activity to be aerobic in nature. Cognitive benefits to all tag games involve spatial awareness, whereby the children have to dodge and move in relation to many others and while doing this to avoid collisions. Ideas for emphasizing academic concepts within the tag game are given at the end of each game description.

***Title:*** ***Tag***
- *Level:* K–6

*Skills Enhanced:* agility, aerobic endurance, locomotor movements
*Equipment Needed:* none
*Description:* The general format for a tag game is that 2–3 children selected as "its" try to tag the rest of the class members in general space. There are numerous kinds of this form of tag, and each of these games is an appropriate aerobic fitness warm-up activity if all players keep moving at all times (some forms of tag require players to remain in one place until freed; these players should maintain activity by running in place).

1. Back to Back Tag—Players are safe from "it" if they are standing back to back with other players.
2. Freeze Tag—A tagged player becomes frozen in place but may be freed by a touch from another active player.
3. Hat Tag—The "it" players wear hats. The hat is given to any player that is tagged and the original "it" becomes a regular player.
4. Hip Tunnel Tag—When an "it" tags active players those player must run in place with hands on hips and legs in a stride position. Fellow active players may set them free by going under and passing between their legs.
5. Hospital Tag—Tagged player becomes "its" but must keep a hand on the spot where they were tagged (the "injured spot").
6. Imitation Tag—The "its" decide which way to move and all players must use the same form of locomotion. "Its" may change the form of locomotion any time they wish.
7. Line Tag—"Its" and the players must travel on the lines painted on the play area floor and may not step off. When players are tagged they do three jumping jacks, yell their names and then take the role of "it."
8. Shadow Tag—If "it" touches a player's shadow, the player becomes "it."
9. Skunk Tag—Players can avoid the tag if they put one arm under one leg and pinch their noses!
10. Stoop Tag—If players stoop down they are safe from being tagged.
11. Turtle Tag—A tagged player must drop down into a pushup position and may be freed by any player who passes under the pushup.

### *Title:*    *Barnyard Upset*

* *Level:* K–2

*Skills Enhanced:* locomotor movements, agility, aerobic endurance, spatial awareness
*Equipment Needed:* none
*Description:* Children are divided into four groups and sent to a corner of the play area. Each group has the name of a farm animal: pigs, cows, horses, chickens, etc. Two children are selected to be the farmers and they stand in the center of the area. When they call "Pigs!" all of the children in that group move in general space while the farmers try to tag them. If tagged, the "animal" goes to pace back and forth in the corral, an area designated at the side of the game. Animals not caught in a 30 second limit return to their home area and jog or "keep their feet moving" until they are called in the "Barnyard Upset!" When this is called, all children are loose except for those in the corral and the farmers try to tag as many as they can in 30 seconds. Then all animals return home and two new farmers are selected.

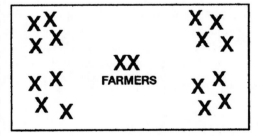

*Cognitive Applications*: Children may make the noise of their animal or may move the way their animal moves.

### Title:     Beanbag Tag

• *Level:* 4–6

*Skills Enhanced:* agility, aerobic endurance

*Equipment Needed:* three beanbags

*Description*: Three children carry beanbags and three others are designated "its." The "its" try to tag a player carrying a beanbag; if successful the two change roles. The children carrying the beanbags may pass them off to other children at any time. All players must be moving all of the time.

*Cognitive Application:* This game requires quick thinking and strategy to know when to pass the beanbag away. Other players also must be cognizant of the possibility of beanbags coming their way. Depending on the math skills students have, require the taggers to call out a math problem (e.g., 3 x 4) for each student tagged. If the players tagged give the right answer, they are safe.

### Title:     Bronco Tag

• *Level:* 3–6

*Skills Enhanced:* agility, speed, spatial awareness, aerobic endurance.

*Equipment Needed:* none

*Description:* Three players stand in a line with their hands on the shoulders of the person in front and represent the head, body and tail of a bronco. They move in general space in this formation. A "Cowboy/Cowgirl" is chased by a "Sheriff" who tries to tag the Cowperson. The Cowperson can stop behind any Bronco and attach to the rear end. The head of the bronco immediately leaves and becomes the Cowperson ( grades 3–4 version). In the grades 5–6 version, the Sheriff may attach as well and the head of that bronco would become the Sheriff. If the Sheriff catches the Cowperson they change roles. Broncos must continue to move throughout the game. The difficulty is increased in the second version since students will have to pay attention to determine the role they must assume if either the Sheriff or the Cowperson attaches.

*Cognitive Application*: This game teaches children to pay attention to roles played in order to assume the correct role when released from the bronco. The theme of the game may be adjusted for a science lesson concerning fat cells attaching and the release of fat cells for energy.

### Title:     Blob

• *Level:* 3–6

*Skills Enhanced:* agility, speed, aerobic endurance

*Equipment Needed:* none

*Description:* "It" tags an active player and they join hands. Both players then tag other players who join the line. Only the ends of the line may tag. The game continues until the entire class is a big blob!

*Cognitive Application*: When the first two join, they must keep calling "2! 2! etc." until another is attached when all three chant "3! 3! etc." This continues as students join onto each end of the chain.

***Title:***    ***Circle Run***
- *Level:* 3–4

*Skills Enhanced:* speed, agility

*Equipment Needed:* none

*Description:* Children stand in a large circle formation. Each child is assigned a number from 1 to 3. When the teacher calls their number, the children with that number run clockwise around the outside of the circle and try to tag as many people ahead of them as possible before they reach their original spot on the circle.

*Cognitive Applications:* The teacher may call numbers that are multiples of the number, math facts that have 1, 2, or 3 as an answer, etc.

***Title:***    ***Color Tag***
- *Level:* 3–4

*Skills Enhanced:* speed, agility, spatial awareness

*Equipment Needed:* 5 red hula hoops, 5 blue hula hoops, 5 yellow hula hoops, 5 green hula hoops.

*Description:* Spread the hoops out in random color order in general space. Assign children to color teams: red, blue, yellow or green. There should be one less hoop than child on each color team. One child from each group is designated "it." The other children begin by standing in a hoop of the team color. When the game begins, children try to get to different hoops of the team color without being tagged by "it." If "it" tags someone, that person becomes the new "it" and the old "it" becomes a player. "Its" may tag only those players in their own color group.

*Cognitive Application: Children work on color identification.*

***Title:***    ***Crows and Cranes***
- *Level:* K–3

*Skills Enhanced:* agility, speed, auditory discrimination

*Equipment Needed:* none

*Description:* Divide class into two teams, standing one yard apart in two facing lines across the width of the playing area. One team is named the Crows, one the Cranes. When the teacher calls "Cr...ows!" the crows chase the cranes to the endline immediately behind the cranes. Anyone tagged who is not on the endline becomes a crow. If the teacher calls "Cr...anes!" the cranes chase the crows with identical results. To increase difficulty: 1) change so that the team called is chased instead of being the chasers; 2) have the teams start standing back to back; 3) vary the calls so that other "Cr..." words are used, such as "crackers," "crunches," etc.

*Cognitive Application:* Use this game to work with beginning sounds that the children are learning. E.g., for "Ch" the game could be "Cherries" and "Chickens!" This game format would also work nicely for basic mathematics. Call the teams Even or Odd, give a problem such as 3 + 1. The Evens would then be the chasers because the answer would be 4.

***Title:***    ***Dodge and Dart***
- *Level:* 3–6

*Skills Enhanced:* running, agility

*Equipment Needed:* a yarn ball for every two players

*Description:* The taggers chase the runners and try to touch them with a yarn ball. If successful, the players change roles; if not successful, the taggers keep trying. Taggers may touch only their own runners.

*Cognitive Application*: Use the game to represent an environmental clean-up concept: a magnet collecting pieces of scrap. As the partner is touched, he/she immediately runs behind the thrower and they jog in the play area. The tagger may then tag pairs of people and if caught, the pairs must go behind and jog in the line.

### *Title:* **Double Tag**

- *Level:* 3–6

*Skills Enhanced:* agility, spatial awareness, speed, aerobic endurance

*Equipment Needed:* none

*Description:* One person is selected to be "it." "It" chases the other players and joins hands with the first one tagged. The pair then chases to find a third; the three travel to find a fourth. At this point they split in half and the two pairs are "its." The game continues until everyone is "it."

*Cognitive Application:* This game may be used to illustrate division of whole numbers so that every time a group is divisible by two they must split.

### *Title:* **Elbow Tag**

- *Level:* 4–6

*Skills Enhanced:* agility, speed, spatial awareness, aerobic endurance

*Equipment Needed*: none

*Description:* Select an "It" and a "Chaser." The other players are jogging in general space, elbows linked with a partner. The chaser chases "it" and if "it" is caught the roles reverse and the chaser becomes "it" and "it" becomes the chaser. "It" can avoid being caught by linking elbows with a couple; the player on the opposite side from "it" then calls "I'm it!" and takes off. The chaser may also stop by linking elbows. The opposite player calls "I'm chaser!" and goes after "it."

*Cognitive Application*: When the "It" or the chaser links on, he/she must say a three-letter word indicating that there are three people in the line. The opposite player who is released must call out a two letter word in order to release himself/herself. To make the play more difficult, groups could be bigger than 2.

### *Title:* **Jack Frost and Jane Thaw**

- *Level:* 1–3

*Skills Enhanced:* agility, aerobic endurance, locomotor skills

*Equipment Needed:* two blue flags, two yellow flags

*Description:* Two children are selected to be Jack Frost (blue flags) and two to be Jane Thaw (yellow flags). If a player is touched by a Jack Frost the player must jog in place until a Jane Thaw comes by to free him/her with a touch.

*Cognitive Application:* This game may be used when teaching about the principles of freezing and thawing, temperature changes and their effects in science.

***Title:***    ***Nine Lives***
- *Level:* 4–6

*Skills Enhanced:* running, agility, aerobic endurance
*Equipment Needed:* as many yarn balls as possible
*Description:* Yarn balls are distributed around the play area. On the signal, the players pick up a yarn ball and try to touch someone else with the ball. After players have been touched nine times, they become frozen in place balancing on one foot. If the frozen players are tagged by a "free" player, they may begin to play again.

*Cognitive Application:* Frozen players may be required to say the 9s multiplication table while balancing on one foot. When completed, they may again play.

***Title:***    ***Partner Posture Tag***
- *Level:* 4–6

*Skills Enhanced:* balance, agility, speed
*Equipment Needed:* a beanbag for each student
*Description:* Partners place beanbags on their heads. One is the runner and one is the chaser. When the chaser catches the runner, they switch roles. The beanbags may not be held by hands on the heads.

*Cognitive Application:* If the beanbag falls off the runner's head while the runner is moving, the tagger gives the runner a spelling word to spell. If correct, the runner can put the beanbag back on his/her head and get a 10-count advanced start; if incorrect, the runner becomes the chaser.

***Title:***    ***Protect-Me Tag***
- *Level:* 4–6

*Skills Enhanced:* agility, aerobic endurance
*Equipment Needed:* none
*Description:* Players work in groups of four. Three players form a circle by placing hands on each others shoulders. One person in the circle is identified to be tagged. The fourth person tries to tag the appointed person while the teammates keep shifting and moving the circle to protect the circle player from the tag. If tagged the player changes place with the tagger.

*Cognitive Application:* This game requires strategy to protect the identified player. It could be used for problem-solving work or strategy building.

***Title:***    ***Sharks and Barracudas***
- *Level:* K–2

*Skills Enhanced:* locomotor skills, agility, aerobic endurance
*Equipment Needed:* none
*Description:* Half the class is designated as Sharks, the other half as Barracudas, and they stand at opposite ends of the play area. The sharks turn their backs to the barracudas and the barracudas move forward toward the sharks. The head shark stays facing the approaching barracudas and, when ready, calls "Here come the barracudas!" At this signal the sharks turn around and chase the barracudas back to their home line. Any barracudas that are tagged become sharks and join the shark line. The barracudas then turn their backs and the

head barracuda determines when to chase the approaching sharks. The game continues. Head shark and barracuda should be changed several times.

*Cognitive Application:* This game could be used to enhance a science lesson concerning fish and predators. The children would learn that these kinds of fish are not safe swimming companions at a beach.

*Title:* **Sharks and Minnows**
- *Level:* 2–4

*Skills Enhanced:* running, agility, spatial awareness
*Equipment Needed:* none
*Description:* The children line up on the endline of the play area and are the Minnows. Two "sharks" are chosen to stand in the middle of the area. One shark dares the minnows to "Cross our sea." The minnows then run and try to get to the opposite end of the play area before being tagged by a shark. If tagged, minnows turn into seaweed and must stay at the spot where they were tagged. The seaweed can reach out and tag other minnows who go by.

*Cognitive Application*: The teacher may use this game to teach children about the sea, some of its characteristic components, and about survival of the fittest.

*Title:* **Trains and Tunnels**
- *Level:* 3–6

*Skills Enhanced:* speed, agility, aerobic endurance
*Equipment Needed:* none
*Description:* Two to three "its" are chosen and the rest of the players must hold hands with a partner. "Its" try to tag sets of partners. If a couple is tagged they must walk in place with arms raised overhead until another couple runs under their arms. Then they are free to run again. After the teacher's whistle blow the "its" change roles with new taggers.

*Cognitive Application:* As the "its" tag each couple they must loudly count to keep a record of the number of partner sets tagged. When the whistle blows, they must immediately call out the number of people who were frozen by the tag, causing them to think quickly and multiply the number counted by 2.

*Title:* **Rainbow Tag**
- *Level:* K–2

*Skills Enhanced:* agility, speed
*Equipment Needed:* none
*Description:* Children stand on the endline of the playing area. A child designated as the leprechaun stands in the center. The children ask "Lucky Leprechaun, may we cross your field?" Lucky Leprechaun answers, "Yes, if you are wearing _____ (a color)." Then all children wearing that color try to run to the opposite side without being tagged by Lucky Leprechaun. If tagged, they become helpers as taggers with Lucky Leprechaun.

*Cognitive Application:* As the game is designed, children may work on color recognition. Substitutions could be made in Lucky Leprechaun's response such as "If your first name begins with C; if you are wearing a sweater; if you have a birthday in May; if you can spell cat, etc."

Title: ***Two Deep***
- *Level: 3–6*

*Skills Enhanced:* agility, aerobic endurance, spatial awareness

*Equipment Needed: none*

*Description:* Children jog in place with a partner, one behind the other spread out in general space. Two players are chosen to be "its" and two players are chosen to be "Chasers." Chaser #1 chases it #1, chaser #2 chases it #2. If a chaser tags an it, they change roles. Either chaser or it may stop at any time in front of a jogging couple and begin jogging in place. If this happens, the jogger in the back takes the role of the player who stopped in front. Children must be very attentive so that they can tell if they are to become an it or a chaser!

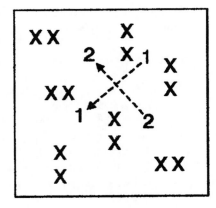

*Cognitive Application:* Besides the need to be attentive and recognize the roles they must play if a chaser stops in front of the couple, the chasers must develop strategies that let them know when it would be good to stop and send off another player. This could also be used in a science lesson where atoms are roaming, looking for a home and suddenly attach to a molecule. The back of the "molecule" has the same charge as the attaching atom and must explode away!

## GAMES OF LOW ORGANIZATION

Games of low organization involve few rules and stress simple concepts. Young children enjoy participation in such games as many use imaginative and creative themes. These games work on relatively few skills at one time so that the children have the opportunity to refine psychomotor skills in a fun atmosphere. Each game has a cognitive application that may be used to enhance academic concepts that you may wish to stress. These cognitive applications should give you ideas on how to modify games to suit your objectives. Remember that the cognitive application of the game may be more oriented to the cognitive learning and vigorous activity time may be sacrificed.

***Title:     Animal Corral***
- *Level:* K–3

*Skills Enhanced:* locomotor movements, agility

*Equipment Needed:* three yarnballs

*Description:* Children stand on the endline of the play area. Choose three children to be the taggers: they will each take a ball and stand in the center area. Children standing on the line will secretly decide if they will be a lion, a tiger, or a bear. This is an individual, secret decision. The animal hunters will take turns calling animals. If the "Bears" are called, all children who chose to be bears try to run to the end of the play area and back without being touched by a tagger. If tagged, an animal must go to the Veterinary Hospital on the side of the play area and do jumping jacks for the duration of the game to get well again. The game continues until only three children are left. They then become the taggers and begin the game again.

*Cognitive Application:* Color identification and recognition: Choose several colors instead of animal names. Hunters will flash a colored card; children who have chosen that color will run. If caught, a child would go to the "art store" and identify 5 color flashcards shown by the "artist" (a student). If correct, the artist goes out to play the game and the child becomes the artist for the next child caught.

### *Title:* __Back to Back__
• *Level:* K–2
*Skills Enhanced:* locomotor movements, auditory discrimination
*Equipment Needed:* none
*Description:* Children move in general space as the leader calls for different movements such as run, slide, walk backwards, skip, etc. When the leader calls "back to back!" children hurry to stand back to back with a partner. The leader finds someone to stand with. The child who is left without a partner is the new leader.

*Cognitive Application:* Body awareness: as children stand back to back call out other positions in which they may be together; i.e., toe to toe, shoulder to shoulder, etc.

### *Title:* __Blue and Red__
• *Level:* K–3
*Skills Enhanced:* agility, speed, color recognition, reaction time
*Equipment Needed:* cardboard disk that is red on one side and blue on the other.
*Description:* Divide class into two teams, one is Blue, the other Red.
Have teams line up at the center of the play area, facing each other, width-wise. The leader tosses the disk into the air between the two teams. The color landing up

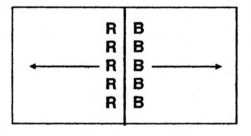

designates the running team, i.e., red lands up so the blue team chases the red team to its end line. If a red player is tagged while off the end line, he/she returns to be a member of the blue team. The game continues for a time limit.

*Cognitive Application:* Mathematics: Use a disk that has an even number of dots on one side and an odd number of dots on the other. Teams are assigned to be odd or even instead of blue or red. Proceed as indicated above. Or, instead of using a disk, have the teacher call out a math problem. If the answer is odd, the odd team chases the even team. If the answer is even, the even team chases the odd team.

### *Title:* __Busy Bee__
• *Level: K–2*
*Skills Enhanced: spatial awareness, body awareness*
*Equipment Needed: none*
*Description:* Children stand back to back with a partner in general space. The teacher or leader calls off various tasks for the children to do with different body parts such as:
Stand knee to knee
Sit back to back
Stand toes to toes

When the leader calls "Busy Bee!" the children run to find another partner and stand back to back. The commands continue. If there is an extra child, the child may be the "Loose Bee" and could be the leader. Usually the teacher can give the commands very quickly so it is better to have the teacher in the vocal leader role.

*Cognitive Applications:* Each pair of children has a long rope. The leader calls out "2 + 6." The two children make an "8" with their rope and skip around the number until all pairs have found the correct answer. On "Busy Bee" the children run to find a new partner and rope.

### *Title:*    *Circle Stride Ball*
- *Level:* K–3

*Skills Enhanced:* hand-eye coordination, simple strategy building
*Equipment Needed:* one 8.5" playground ball per group
*Description:* Divide class into groups of 10 or 12 players. Groups form circles in wide stride position with feet touching those of players next to them. The ball is rolled anywhere in the circle in an attempt to get the ball to pass under the legs of a player. If it passes through the legs of student A, A must retrieve the ball, and sit down in place until another player is caught. Then A may stand up again and resume play. Players try to catch the rolling ball to prevent it from going under their legs. They may not move their feet.

*Cognitive Application:* While a player is retrieving the ball, the rest of the children in the circle quickly change places and the retriever must tell the names of the two children he/she was between originally. If correct the child may rejoin the game; otherwise he/she sits in place until another player is caught and may then rejoin the game.

### *Title:*    *Come Along*
- *Level:* K–2

*Skills Enhanced:* locomotor skills, spatial awareness
*Equipment Needed:* none
*Description:* Children stand in a circle formation while one child moves as designated by the teacher around the outside of the circle. He/she taps another child on the shoulder and says "Come along" and the two children continue around the circle. The second child taps a third and the third child a fourth. While the four children are moving around the circle the teacher says "Go!" At this point the four children hurry to find an empty space. One child will be left to start the game again.

*Cognitive Application: Language Arts:* The students will be working on sentence development. The first child thinks of a word (Harry) to start a silly sentence. The first child says "come along Harry," to the next child who follows and says "come along Harry ate"; the next child says "come along Harry ate muffins"; this continues until the teacher decides that the silly sentence is complete. He/she then calls "Silly Sentence!" and all children run to find a spot on the circle. The last child begins the new sentence. Have the caller give each child in the circle the name of an animal. When he/she says "come along" all children will move around the circle imitating the walking pattern of the animal.

### *Title:*    *Crossing the Brook*
- *Level:* K–2

*Skills Enhanced:* jumping, leaping

*Equipment Needed:* one long jump rope per group
*Description:* Divide class into groups of 5. Children place rope on floor in a sideways V shape, then proceed to jump over the banks of the "creek" they have formed. They should follow the leader and begin with the narrowest part, progressing to the widest part.

*Cognitive Application:* When the children jump over the different areas of the brook they should use rulers to measure how far they jumped. They should then think of an object that would approximate that distance; for example, "I jumped one cereal box!"

### *Title:*   *Cut the Pie*
- *Level:* 1–3

*Skills Enhanced:* speed, agility
*Equipment Needed:* none
*Description:* Have the children divided into groups of 8–10. Each group stands in a circle that is approximately 10 yards in diameter. One child is in the center of each circle. The center child moves to two children, claps his/her hands between them and says "Cut the pie!" The two children then take off, running in opposite directions around the circle, back through their places, and stop beside the pie cutter child. The first one back becomes the new pie cutter.

*Cognitive Application:* Instead of saying "cut the pie," the child says a math problem such as "2 + 1" and the two people he/she claps between must answer the problem and then run.

### *Title:*   *Fire Engine*
- *Level:* 2–3

*Skills Enhanced:* running, agility, auditory discrimination
*Equipment Needed:* none
*Description:* One child is the fire chief and stands halfway between the children and the opposite end line of the play area. Children count off by 5s. The Fire Chief calls out any numbers from 1 to 5 and at some point yells "Fire!" The children with the number called just before "Fire!" run across the play area, trying not to be tagged by the Fire Chief. If tagged, a player becomes a helper for the Fire Chief.

*Cognitive Application:* When the number is called, players run to the fire chief. The first child there has the first chance to spell a word given by the teacher; if correct, he/she becomes the new fire chief and all others return to the starting line. If incorrect, the next child tries. If no one is correct, the same fire chief remains for another round. Instead of using numbers 1–5, the children could each be one of the pyramid food groups (vegetable, fruit, grain, meat, dairy). The fire chief than gives an example of a food and those children with that category run.

### *Title:*   *Fly Trap*
- *Level:* K–2

*Skills Enhanced:* spatial awareness, agility
*Equipment Needed:* none
*Description:* One half of the class sits Indian-style and spread out in the play area. The other half travels using the designated locomotor movements until the teacher calls "Freeze!" At this point the "flies" stop and the children who are the "trappers" reach out to try to touch the flies. Any children touched change places with the trapper and the game continues.

*Cognitive Application:* When "freeze" is called, any trapper who can reach a fly stands up and spells a word given by the teacher. If the spelling is correct, the trapper becomes a fly.

### Title:    *Frog in the Pond*
- *Level:* K–2

*Skills Enhanced:* running, agility, rhythm
*Equipment Needed:* none
*Description:* The class forms a circle with one child, the frog, in the middle. The children walk around the circle chanting:
Once there was a little frog
He went around and around
He jumped up once, he jumped up twice
     And caught a great big FLY!
On the word "fly," players scatter in the play area and the frog tries to tag them. After 30 seconds time is called and those tagged go into the center of the circle to help the frog. Play begins again.

*Cognitive Application:* This game may be used when studying about amphibians and feeding styles.

### Title:    *Hook On*
- *Level:* 2–4

*Skills Enhanced:* agility, spatial awareness
*Equipment Needed:* none
*Description*: Four children are designated as "Its." The object of the game is to hook on to the waist of another child to form a chain. The two who are attached then attempt to hook on to another couple. The chains must be started by each of the 4 "its." The object of the game is to eventually form one long chain.

*Cognitive Application:* Each "it" is given several flashcards with math problems. As he/she tags another child, the child must correctly answer in order to hook on. If incorrect the child continues to run in general space until another "it" approaches and shows another flashcard. Each child has a number. After the 4 chains are complete, the groups must add up the numbers of the children in the chain. The chain with the biggest total gets to be the lead chain, and the smallest sum is the end chain.

### Title:    *In the Creek*
- *Level:* K–2

*Skills Enhanced:* jumping, balancing, auditory discrimination
*Equipment Needed:* two long jump ropes
*Description:* The children line up side by side on a line facing a parallel line made of jump ropes 2–3 feet away. These lines are the banks of the creek. The leader gives directions "in the creek" (players jump into the middle) or "on the bank" (players jump over to other bank and turn around). Commands should be given quickly

*Cognitive Application:* Give each child in the game a color card. The leader calls "COLOR in the creek" or "COLOR on the bank" and the children follow directions according to the color of the card each is holding. The leader may call out math problems. An even answer means "in the creek" and an odd answer means "on the bank."

*Title:*    ***Jet Pilot***
- *Level:* K–2

*Skills Enhanced:* locomotor movements, agility, aerobic endurance, spatial awareness
*Equipment Needed:* none
*Description*: Children stand on the end line of the play area. A child or teacher may be the leader who stands to the side of the area and calls "Control tower to pilots! Control tower to pilots! All planes wearing _____, TAKE OFF!" Each time the leader calls a different color. The children spread their arms like airplane wings and "fly" to the designated line and back. The first child back may become the leader.

*Cognitive Applications:* Instead of calling colors, the leader could call "All planes which start with C!" Children whose names start with C can fly at that time. Or, the leader may use phonetic sounds: "All planes which start with Cuh!"

*Title:*    ***Jump the Shot***
- *Level:* 2–4

*Skills Enhanced:* jumping, timing, reaction time
*Equipment Needed:* one long jump rope per group with a ball or beanbag tied to the end
*Description:* Each group of 6 to 8 children makes a circle around one child who will be the spinner. The spinner twirls the rope around in a circle so the other players can jump it as it goes by. When someone misses, he/she takes the position of spinner.

*Cognitive Application:* The spinner selects a letter and/or a category. As each child jumps he/she must say a word that starts with the designated letter and/or fits the desired category. If a child does not give a correct answer, he/she becomes the spinner.

*Title:*    ***Kick the Pin***
- *Level:* K–2

*Skills Enhanced*: eye-foot coordination
*Equipment Needed:* one 8.5" playground ball and one bowling pin per group
*Description:* Children form circles of eight to ten players. A bowling pin is placed in the center of the circle. The players try to knock over the pin by kicking the ball at it. Each time it is knocked down, one point is scored and the pin is reset. The first circle to get 10 points is the winner.

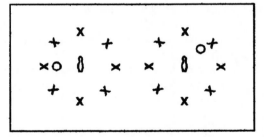

*Cognitive Application:* When the first child kicks the ball, he/she calls out a word that begins with a; next child to kick calls a word that begins with b, etc. Once the pin is knocked down the next child to kick begins again with a. Each circle begins with 10 points. For each time the pin is knocked down the circle children subtract one point. The first circle to 0 wins the game.

*Title:*    ***Magic Wand***
- *Level:* K–3

*Skills Enhanced:* agility, reaction time, eye-hand coordination

*Equipment Needed:* one 3' wand per group

*Description:* Divide class into groups of 6 to 7 children. One child is the magician and stands in the center of the circle. He/she taps the wand on the floor three times and lets go of it while calling the name of a child on the circle. The child tries to catch the wand before it falls to the ground. If successful, he/she becomes the new magician. If unsuccessful, the former magician remains.

*Cognitive Application:* With eyes closed, the magician calls out a spelling word instead of a name. The child he/she is facing must spell the word correctly and catch the wand to become the next magician. Instead of calling out the child's name to catch the wand, give each child a number and the magician will call out a math problem. The child who "is" the answer will catch the wand.

### *Title:*    ***Man from Mars***
* *Level:* K–2

*Skills Enhanced:* agility, running

*Equipment Needed:* none

*Description:* One child is chosen to be the Man from Mars. This child stands in the center of the play area. The rest of the children are on an end line. The children call, "Man from Mars, may we chase you to the stars?" and the martian replies, "Yes if you are wearing (color)." All players who are wearing the color may chase the martian and the first to tag the martian becomes the new martian. Variation: have several martians.

*Cognitive Application:* Give the children cards that have colors, shapes and numbers on them. The martians reply will then be "Yes if you have a red circle" or "Yes if your number is 2 + 3." The martian could also use categories such as the number of syllables in a child's name, etc.

### *Title:*    ***Marching Ponies***
* *Level:* K–2

*Skills Enhanced:* locomotor skills, agility, rhythm

*Equipment Needed: none*

*Description:* One child is chosen to be the ringmaster and to crouch down in the center of the circle of children. The players are the ponies and they march (or do other designated locomotor movements) around the circle, counting and stepping, 1-2-3-etc. On a signal from the teacher the ringmaster leaps up and chases the ponies. Any ponies tagged before reaching the endlines of the play area help the ringmaster.

*Cognitive Application:* One child is the zookeeper and stands in the center. He/she calls the name of an animal and all children imitate the animal as they move around the circle. He/she then imitates the sound of an animal: if the sound is correct for the animal that is being imitated, the children all make the sound. If it is incorrect the zookeeper chases the animals and tags as many as possible.

### *Title:*    ***Mousetrap***
* *Level:* K–2

*Skills Enhanced:* agility, spatial awareness

*Equipment Needed:* none

*Description:* Have children count off by 5s. Place the number 1s in the center and form a circle around them. Have the children take hands and raise the hands up high. The ones in the center are the mice and they are to scurry in and out of the trap. The teacher calls "Snap!" and the hands come down. Any mice caught in the middle become part of the trap. When there is only one mouse left, have the #2s join it and play begins again.

*Cognitive Application:* When the "mice" are caught in the center, if they can say a word that rhymes with one given by the teacher they can remain mice.

### *Title:*     *Old Man/Old Lady*
- *Level:* K–2

*Skills Enhanced:* locomotor movements, spatial awareness
*Equipment Needed:* none
*Description:* Divide the class into two teams, one with an extra person, and have them scatter in each half of the play area. The teacher designates a locomotor movement for the children to perform in their half, and on the whistle they must run to the center line and take the hand of someone across from them on the opposite team. The extra player is called the "Old Man" or "Old Lady" and must join the opposite team. Variation: play music as the children move and stop the music for them to run to take hands.

*Cognitive Application:* After they join hands they skip around in a figure eight or in whichever pattern the old man or old lady calls.

### *Title:*     *Old Mother Witch*
- *Level:* K–2

*Skills Enhanced:* speed, agility
*Equipment Needed:* none
*Description:* One child is selected to be the witch and paces in an area at the end of the play area designated as the witch's house. The other children move around the house and through the house chanting:
"Old Mother Witch
Fell in a ditch
Picked up a penny
And thought she was rich!"
The witch says, "Whose children are you?" The children may answer any name but when someone says "Yours!" the witch chases the children back to the line at the other end of the play area. Any children tagged become the witch's helpers.

*Cognitive Application:* Instead of saying "whose children are you?" the witch says a math problem such as 4 + 1. The children call out the answer but if a wrong answer is heard, the witch chases the children.

### *Title:*     *One Step*
- *Level:* K–3

*Skills Enhanced:* throwing, catching
*Equipment Needed:* one ball for every set of partners
*Description*: Partners face each other, standing on parallel lines in the play area. The partners toss and catch the ball. The ball must be thrown so that the partner moves only one foot to catch. If the catch is successful, the catcher moves back one step and throws to the partner.

Each successful catch earns one step back. Variations: designate what hand must be used to catch or throw; designate the kind of throw or toss.

*Cognitive Application:* The tosser calls a math problem. The catcher may step back one if he/she answers correctly AND catches the ball. All children toss the ball at the same time as the teacher shouts a spelling word or math problem. The catchers must yell out the correct spelling or the answer to the problem. As the ball is caught the catcher must add or subtract a number designated by the teacher to the number of catches he/she and the partner have made.

### *Title:*     *Red Light, Green Light*
- *Level:* K–2

*Skills Enhanced:* stopping and starting, locomotor movements
*Equipment Needed:* none
*Description:* Children start on the baseline of the play area. The leader stands at the opposite end of the area, turns his/her back to the children and says "Green Light! 1-2-3 . . . 10-Red Light!" While the green light is on, the children try to move as far forward as they can without being caught. When the leader says "Red Light," he/she turns around and points to any players that are still moving. Those players must return to the starting line. Play continues in this way until a child reaches the leader without being caught. That child becomes the new leader and the game begins again.

*Cognitive Application:* The children can count the number of people who were caught, each time adding the number to the time before.

### *Title:*     *Run, Baby, Run*
- *Level:* 4–6

*Skills Enhanced:* agility, leg strength, spatial awareness
*Equipment Needed:* none
*Description:* Partners stand back to back with elbows hooked, one partner facing to the inside of the circle, the other partner facing to the outside. All pairs stand on a large circle formation. Partners sit down with elbows linked, legs straight out in front. On the signal "Run, Baby, Run!" they must run to the right around the circle. This means the inner circle will go counterclockwise and the outer circle clockwise. At "Stop, baby, stop!" each player finds his/her partner, links elbows and sits. The last couple to sit gets one penalty point.

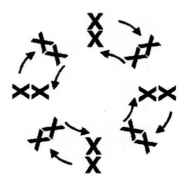

*Cognitive Application:* As the children sit back to back in the circle, they count consecutively around the circle. On the number 7, one that contains 7, or one that is a multiple of 7, that pair must stand and run as above.

### *Title:*     *Seven Dwarfs*
- *Level:* K–2

*Skills Enhanced:* speed, agility, auditory discrimination

*Equipment Needed:* none
*Description:* Choose one child to be Snow White, and seven others to be the seven dwarfs. They stand at the end of the play area. The rest of the children approach the area and ask "Who's at home?" Snow White responds that "Sneezy is home" or any of the other dwarf names, but if she says "The old witch is here," she and the dwarfs chase the children back to the other end of the play area. Any children who are tagged go back with the dwarfs to help tag others.

*Cognitive Application:* This game could be used with any story the children have read or heard and if the leader gives a name of someone or something NOT in the story the children are chased.

### *Title:* **Snowball**
• *Level:* K–2
*Skills Enhanced:* throwing, agility
*Equipment Needed:* 20–30 yarn balls
*Description:* Divide the class into two teams, each spread out on half of the play area. Toss the balls out into general space. On the signal to go, the children throw the balls to the opposite side of the play area. Play continues for a time limit. The team with the fewest balls on its side at the end is the winner.

*Cognitive Application:* By using differently colored balls, the game could teach colors and combinations thereof. For example, using red, yellow and blue balls: the side with the most yellow balls is the winner; the side with the fewest pairs of balls that would make green is the winner. Pick one child from each side to count the balls (different children each time). If the number is correct, the game continues and if the number is wrong, have the child recount.

### *Title:* **Squirrels in Trees**
• *Level:* K–2
*Skills Enhanced:* locomotor movements, spatial awareness
*Equipment Needed:* none
*Description:* Children begin the game in groups of three: two children hold both hands with the third child standing between the joined arms of the two children. This creates a squirrel in a tree. Any extra children are loose squirrels. When the leader calls "Find a new tree!" all squirrels leave their trees and dart into a different tree. The loose squirrels try to get a tree as well. Play 5–6 times, then have the squirrel in the tree take the place of one of the tree children. Continue to play. Then change so the third child has a chance to be a squirrel. The object of the game is to have a tree as many times as possible.

*Cognitive Application:* Tell the children a story about squirrels and how they go out to look for nuts and berries. Have the squirrels act out the story and have them scurry for a tree when they hear that the Red Fox is coming near!

### *Title:* **Steal the Bacon**
• *Level:* 3–6
*Skills Enhanced:* agility, speed, hand-eye coordination
*Equipment Needed:* one beanbag or yarn ball for each set of partners

*Description:* Children stand in 2 lines the width of the playing area, partners facing. Partners should be 5 yards apart with the beanbag resting between them on the center line. On the signal to go, each child tries to steal the beanbag and take it quickly to the end line behind him/her to score 2 points. The child who does not steal the beanbag tries to tag the partner who did. If the child is tagged, the tagger earns one point. Children keep track of their own scores. After each round of play, one team rotates one position so there is a new opponent.

*Cognitive Application:* Children each have 5 cards with numbers on them. When they go to the center each child puts down a card, face down. The stealing child, if successful, adds the two numbers together and that is his/her score. If the stealer is tagged, the tagger adds the two together and gets the points.

### Title:    *What to Play*

• *Level:* K–2

*Skills Enhanced:* visual matching, psychomotor skills dependent on choice of activities

*Equipment Needed:* none

*Description:* Children form a circle around the leader and walk clockwise around singing:

"Mary show us what to play

What to play, what to play

Mary show us what to play

Show us what to play."

The leader says, "play this!" and pantomimes an action. The children imitate the action until the leader steps to the circle and changes places with a new leader.

*Cognitive Application:* Teacher holds clock face made from paper plate. The child selected to be the new leader must be able to tell the time by the hour in order to become the leader.

### Title:    *Wild Horse Round-Up*

• *Level:* 1–2

*Skills Enhanced:* agility, running

*Equipment Needed:* none

*Description:* Both ends of the play area are designated as the mountains, the center of the play area the range. An area to the side is designated as the corral. 3 boys and 3 girls are the cowboys and cowgirls. When the leader calls "Wild Horses!" the other children all run in the range space and try to avoid the tag. If tagged a horse must go to the corral and jog in place. The last six children to be caught become the next cow people.

*Cognitive Application:* The children in the corral must name an animal that lives in a cold mountainous region in order to rejoin the game.

## GAMES OF HIGHER ORGANIZATION

Games of higher organization involve more skills, a higher level of skills, more rules, more complicated concepts, and the use of strategy on increasingly higher levels. The majority of higher organization games are designated for grade 3 and above, although some are applicable to younger children. These games may be used for special day activities, or for their cognitive value in working on the academic concepts. Whenever possible, the class should be divided into 4 groups so that two games can be played at the same time for maximum participation. Children should never be standing around inactively.

*Title:*   ***Alaska Baseball***
- *Level:* 3–6

*Skills Enhance:* running, agility, spatial awareness, directionality
*Equipment Needed:* one volleyball per game
*Description:* Divide the class into two teams per game. The batter uses his/her fist to hit a volleyball out to the fielding team and then runs around his/her team (who are standing in a single file line) as many times as possible before the fielding team calls "STOP." The first fielder who catches the ball stops and holds the ball overhead. The rest of the fielding team gets in line behind #1 and receives the ball overhead, continuing to pass the ball to each player overhead until the last player gets the ball and calls "STOP." After half the team has batted, teams change roles. The second inning the fielders should pass the ball under their legs to each other; the third inning they should pass the ball alternately overhead, under legs, etc.

*Cognitive Application*: Have the scoring counted in fractions, such as 3 and one-half times around, 4 and one-quarter, etc. After each runner, the batting team must add on the new score to the former score. At the end of the game have the teams find the average running score for the team.

*Title:*   ***Basket Baseball***
- *Level:* 4–6

*Skills Enhanced:* eye hand coordination, throwing, fielding, passing, base running, agility, speed
*Equipment Needed:* a junior sized or dense foam basketball and 4 bases for each game.
*Description:* Divide the group into two teams. The batting team stands along the first base line; home plate is set on the free throw line. The batter throws the ball into the field and runs all the way around the bases to home. The fielders must get the ball to the catcher who tries to make a basket for 2 points before the runner gets home. Arrival home before the basket gives the runner the two points. Rotate to a new catcher with each batter. It is helpful to have team members number off so each knows when it would be his/her turn to catch. Teams change places after all batters have run.

*Cognitive Application:* Using categories, the fielders must throw the ball to different fielders, each of whom must name something within the category. The category should be announced by the batter. It would be helpful to have cards printed with logical categories from which the batter may draw. When the category is finished, the ball may be thrown to the catcher who shoots for a basket. Categories must have a reasonable number of components. For example, the United States would be a poor choice because the team would have to toss the ball fifty times. Good choices might be planets, Great Lakes, primary colors, vowels, etc. Using spelling words, the fielders could toss the ball around while each child says the next letter in a word.

### *Title:*   *Beatball*
- *Level:* 3–6

*Skills Enhanced:* eye-hand coordination through throwing and catching, speed, spatial awareness

*Equipment Needed:* 4 bases, one dense foam ball per game

*Description:* Set up the bases in diamond formation with home, lst, 2nd and 3rd bases. Divide the class into 2 teams for each game. The batter throws the ball into the outfield and then tries to run all of the bases and home before the ball gets back to the catcher at home plate. Outfielders must retrieve the ball and pass it to lst base, 2nd base, to 3rd base, and then to home. Base players must touch the base with a foot while holding the ball. Teams change after everyone has a turn to throw. Variations: the players kick or bat to make the game different.

*Cognitive Application:* Using the names of the 50 states, the fielder throws the ball to first base and calls out a state name. The first baseman must say a state that is adjacent to it before passing the ball to 2nd base; the 2nd baseman calls the name of a state adjacent to the lst baseman's state, etc. Fielders should rotate positions for each batter so that all have a chance to name the states.

### *Title:*   *Bombardment*
- *Level:* 3–6

*Skills Enhanced:* hand-eye coordination, agility

*Equipment Needed:* 6 (8.5'') dense foam balls and 12 bowling pins per game

*Description:* Divide the class into two teams per game. Each team sets six bowling pins out on its end line of the playing area. On the signal to go, players throw the balls, trying to knock down the opponents' bowling pins. If a pin falls down at any time, it must be left

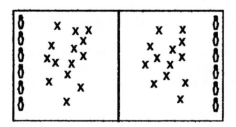

down. The game continues until one team's pins are all down. Variation: to make the game easier, move the pins in from the end line.

*Cognitive Application:* This game poses some problems for which the children will need to devise some strategy. They will eventually develop the idea of guards for the pins and designated throwing players. They also may learn that a throw to the wall will cause a ball to bounce back off to hit a pin. Arrival at this knowledge will be dependent on knowledge of scientific principles of motion and stability.

### *Title:* ___Boundary Ball___
* *Level:* 3–6

*Skills Enhanced:* hand-eye coordination, agility
*Equipment Needed:* 10 (8.5") dense foam balls per game
*Description:* Divide the class into two teams per game, each spread out in one half of the playing area. Each team starts with 5 balls. On the signal to go, team members try to throw the balls past the opponents' end line. Each ball that crosses the line scores one point. Players continue to catch and throw balls until the signal to stop. The team with the highest score is the winner.

*Cognitive Application:* Each time a ball crosses the end line, a child retrieves it and goes to a math worksheet to the side of the game, completes one problem and comes back into the game. The score for the team will be the number of correct answers on its sheet as well as the number of throws past the line at the end of the game. Thus, if a person gets a math problem right it negates the point that the opposing team earns by throwing the ball past the line.

### *Title:* ___California Kickball___
* *Level:* 4–6

*Skills Enhanced:* running, agility, passing and fielding
*Equipment Needed:* one 8.5 playground ball and four bases per game
*Description:* Batting and fielding teams are set on a kickball diamond. The pitcher rolls the ball to the first kicker: any kick is legal, there are no fouls in this game. First base is the only one where the fielding team may touch base to get the player out; at all other bases the player must be touched with the ball. Kickers may stay on a base as long as they wish and any number of kickers may occupy the same base. If the fielders throw the ball to the pitcher, any runners caught between bases must go back one base. If a fly ball is caught with runners between bases, the runners are out. Teams switch roles after each player on the team has had a turn to kick.

*Cognitive Application:* The kicker calls out a word to the fielders when he/she kicks the ball. The first fielder to touch the ball must call out a rhyming word. The fielders must pass the ball to three different players. Each fielder must call a rhyming word. Once the rhyming is completed, the ball is in play.

### *Title:* ___Call A Guard___
* *Level:* 3–6

*Skills Enhanced:* hand-eye coordination, agility
*Equipment Needed:* 1 dense foam ball and 1 bowling pin per team
*Description:* Divide class into 3–4 teams and have team members number off consecutively. Each team makes a circle around a bowling pin which is set in the center. Circle players should be at least 5 yards from the pin. The leader calls a number and the person having that number goes to the circle to his/her right to guard the pin. On the signal to go, players pass the ball around and try to knock down the pin. The first team to knock down its pin earns a point. If the center player knocks the pin down it is a point for the passing team. Center players return to their teams and another number is called.

*Cognitive Application:* Instead of having the leader call out a number, have him/her call out a math problem. The answer to the problem would be the player to become the guard.

### *Title:*    *Capture the Flag*
- *Level:* 4–6

*Skills Enhanced:* agility, speed, spatial awareness
*Equipment Needed:* two flags, 8 pylons
*Description:* Place the flags on the end lines of the play area in the center of the line. Use the pylons to designate the back right corners as "jails." The object of the game is for one team to get a player across to the opposite end to hold the flag overhead for a point. Teams spread out in their respective halves of the area. Whenever a player crosses the center line he/she is eligible to be tagged. If tagged, a player must report to jail. Players in jail may be freed by teammates who get successfully to the jail and then lead the freed player by hand

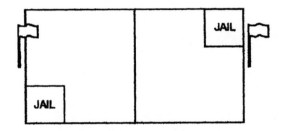

back to the opposite side (free trip back for both prisoner and rescuer). Prisoners should be freed in the order that they were captured.

*Cognitive Application:* If a player is tagged and must go to jail, there is a worksheet there for them to answer questions. The child who frees the jailed person must check the work; freedom comes only to those with correct answers.

### *Title:*    *Crab Soccer*
- *Level:* 3–6

*Skills Enhanced:* leg and arm strength, eye-foot coordination
*Equipment Needed:* nerf or junior soccer ball, or a cageball for each game
*Description:* Divide class into 2 teams per game. Players set up on their own side of the floor and assume the crab position (supported by hands and feet, seat toward the floor) The teacher rolls the ball into the game and play begins. Players try to kick the ball so that it hits the wall at the opponents' end line. Players may move while in a crab position anywhere in the play area. A goal counts one point, and play is resumed by a kickoff at the center by the non-scoring team.

*Cognitive Application:* If someone from the opposite team commits a foul (touches the ball with a hand), the first child on the opposite team who can name one of the Great Lakes may take the free kick. The teacher may choose other categories depending on the subjects being studied in the classroom.

### Title: Keep Away

- *Level:* 3–6

*Skills Enhanced:* hand-eye coordination in throwing and catching, agility, spatial awareness
*Equipment Needed:* one 8.5'' playground ball per game
*Description:* Divide class into teams of 6–7 players. The ball starts with an inbounds pass from the sideline by one team. Teammates try to complete passes to each other without the other team's intercepting the ball. Teams should count their passes out loud to see how many they can make before losing the ball. If the ball goes out of bounds, it is given to the team who did not last have possession.

*Cognitive Application:* In counting the passes children can practice their math facts by counting by 2s, 3s, 4s, etc.

### Title:     Novelty Ball

- *Level:* 3–6

*Skills Enhanced:* agility, speed, throwing, catching, running, striking
*Equipment Needed:* 4 short jump ropes, 4 basketballs, 4 Indian clubs, 8 bases, 2 whiffle balls and 2 plastic bats, 2 basketball hoops
*Description:* Divide class into four teams. Two teams play against each other on each side of the basketball court. The game goes as follows: One team is in the outfield. The batter hits the whiffle ball (tossed by pitcher) and runs to first base where the batter jumps rope 5 times. The batter continues to second base and shoots until making a basket. The batter continues to third base, knocks over the Indian club and sets it back up using only the feet and continues home. If the runner reaches home before the ball, a run is scored. There is no stopping on bases. In order to get the batter out, the outfield team must do the following: the fielder throws the ball to first base where the first baseperson must touch the base and then jump rope 5 times; then the first baseperson must throw the ball to second base where the second baseperson touches the base and shoots for a basket until successful; the second baseperson throws the ball to third base where the third baseman must touch the base, knock over the Indian club and sets it up using only feet; the third baseperson then throws the ball to the catcher who touches home plate. If the ball reaches home before the batter, the batter is out. In order for either a run or an out to count, all players on the team must be running in place.

*Cognitive Application:* Children who are waiting for a turn at bat are given a category and must give (as a team) as many correct answers as possible that apply, e.g., Great Lakes, Oceans, Continents. For every correct answer, one run is scored.

### Title:     Place Football

- *Level:* 4–6

*Skills Enhanced:* kicking, running, agility
*Equipment Needed:* one soft football and 4 bases per game, kicking tee
*Description:* Divide the class into two teams per game. The fielding team spreads out in the diamond, the batting team lines up behind home plate. The football is stationary at the plate. The kicker kicks the ball into the field and then runs: to 1) first base and back (1 point), 2) to first base, second base and back (2 points), or 3) all the way around the bases

and back (3 points). The fielder who catches the ball tries to beat the runner back by holding the ball and running to touch home plate. If the fielders get the ball there first, the runner is out. The runner must judge which bases to run based on his/her kick. After three outs the teams switch roles.

*Cognitive Application:* For runners to score a run, they must also be able to name and spell correctly one of the continents. If incorrect, no run is scored. The fielder must also be able to answer the same question in order to get the runner out. If the fielder is incorrect the runner is safe. Both players must cross the plate before the questions are asked. If both are correct or incorrect there is neither score nor out.

### Title:    Poison Ball
- *Level:* 3–6

*Skills Enhanced:* hand-eye coordination in throwing and catching, agility
*Equipment Needed:* 8 (8.5')' playground balls, 2 (12") playground balls per game.
*Description:* Divide each group into 4 teams and designate one side of a square formation for each to stand. In the center of the square place the 2 (12") balls (Poison Balls). The 8.5" balls are given to the teams. On the signal to go, the teams try to throw the 8.5" balls to hit the poison balls and make them cross an opponents' team goal line. The teacher puts the poison ball back in the center after a score. Only the 8.5" balls may be used to force the poison balls one way or another. Players may not cross the center line of the play area nor may they obstruct a ball which is about to cross the end line unless they have the 8.5" balls to throw to prevent the score.

*Cognitive Application*: Instead of accumulating points each time the ball goes over a goal line, a letter is scored for each one. Teams will be named according to their positions, North, South, East or West. In order for a team to win, it would have had to score 4 times on the East (E-A-S-T), 4 on the West, 5 on the South, etc.

### Title:    Scooter Hoops
- *Level:* 3 –6

*Skills Enhanced:* leg strength, spatial awareness, eye-hand coordination
*Equipment Needed:* a gymnasium scooter for each player, 2 hula hoops and 2 playground balls per game
*Description:* Divide the class into 4 teams, 2 for each game. Set the hoops out at each end of the play areas as goals. This game begins when the teacher rolls the ball into the center of the play area. Players may move only on scooters and must roll the ball to other players in an attempt to get the ball to someone who can throw the ball in the hoop on a bounce to score. Following a score, the defensive team takes possession at the goal.

*Cognitive Application:* Each scorer must spell a word given by the teacher. If incorrect, the other team has a chance to steal the point by spelling the word correctly.

### Title:    Shipwreck
- *Level:* 2–4

*Skills Enhanced:* auditory perception, agility
*Equipment Needed:* none

*Description:* Players stand in self space, looking forward to the "captain" of the ship. The play area represents the ship. The Captain calls out commands and the players follow the directions. The commands are:

Name the part of the ship (bow, stern, port, starboard) and players run to that area

    Hit the Deck—players lie on the floor

    Roll Call—players form one long line and salute

    To the Crow's Nest—players pretend to climb a ladder

    Anchors Away—players do a V-sit and do a bicycle with their legs

    Swab the Deck—players sway back and forth, swinging arms

    Bring in the Anchor—players pretend to pull in an anchor

    Sharks!—players get in a circle and hide their heads

    Abandon Ship—players pair up and pretend to row

    Man Overboard—one player on all fours, other stands with one foot on the first players
        back, hand to the brow to look for the lost person

    Mates in the Galley—sit in groups of threes and hold hands

    Inspection—players form lines of three or four

    Man the Pumps—players do push-ups

    Signal in the Tower—players wave arms as flag

*Cognitive Application*: This game could be adapted for most any category that students are learning about in the classroom.

### *Title:*    *Star Wars*

- *Level:* 3–6

*Skills Enhanced:* agility, arm strength, leg strength, spatial awareness

*Equipment Needed:* 4 bowling pins per game

*Description:* Divide the class into 4 teams and have each team sit side-by-side in a square formation: The bowling pins are set in the center of the square, one designated for each team. Children are numbered off consecutively. The teacher calls a number and the child with that number gets up and runs through his/her own space, clockwise around the outside

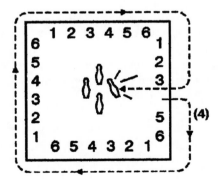

of the square, back in through his/her own space, and knocks the pin down. The first team back gets "ST" and second team back gets "S." The first team to spell "STAR WARS" gets a point. For each round of play, vary what the team players left behind are to do while the runners are running: push-ups, sit-ups, squat thrusts, jog in place, windmills, etc.

*Cognitive Application:* Instead of having numbers, the students will have the names of states. The teacher will then call a capitol, or a characteristic of the state and the children with that state will run. Instead of spelling "Star Wars" the children could spell something else related to astronomy, i.e., telescope, Galileo.

*Title:*    ***Touchdown***
- *Level:* 3–6

*Skills Enhanced:* agility, strategy building

*Equipment Needed:* one small object, such as a table tennis ball per game

*Description:* This game is best played in groups of five or six per team. The offensive team decides who will carry the ball. The offensive team tries to carry the ball past the end line of their playing area to score 6 points. They will have 2 tries to get it there. The carrier conceals the ball in his/her hands, and all players hold their hands as if they have the ball. On the signal to go, the offensive team tries to get past the defensive players who try to tag the offensive players. Any player tagged must stop in place. When all offensive players are tagged (or if all are over the end line), they open their hands. If the ball is in the hands of one across the end line, 6 points are scored and the ball goes to the other team at the center of the play area. If the ball is in the hands of a tagged player, play begins again from the line on which the tagged player is standing. If the ball does not get across the line on the second play, it is turned over to the opposite team on the spot.

*Cognitive Application:* Tagged players may be set free if they can answer multiplication facts posed by the teacher.

# Cooperative Games

The elementary years represent an excellent time for children to learn about sharing as well as cooperative activity. Cooperative games have been designed to encourage working together toward a goal, and the stress and pressure of competition is minimized, if not eliminated. If children are taught to cooperate first, when they are ready to understand competition they will be able to cooperate within a team in order to be successful in competition. These games invite problem solving as well as active participation in physical activity. Since they do not teach specific motor skills, but rather teach cooperative strategy, these games are not a good choice for high level activity. They can be used successfully at recess times, as closing activities in a lesson, as activities for special days, as stations in field day events, and as activities in a non-competitive intramural program. Field days and intramural programs will be discussed later in the text.

According to Kirchner and Fishburne (2001) cooperative games provide for equality, participation, success, and trust. Each player has an equal role in the game, meaning that he/she will have the same number of opportunities to play as any other player in the game. Each game involves maximum participation so that all players are active the majority of the time. There are no losers in cooperative games, so children experience success. And, many of the games call for players to trust other players, teaching players to rely on teammates.

*Title:*    ***Caterpillar Mania***
- *Level:* 5–6

*Skills Enhanced:* flexibility, arm strength, spatial awareness

*Equipment Needed:* none
*Description:* First player bends over and places weight on hands and feet on the floor in front of the partner. The partner stands behind, bends over forward and grasps the ankles of the first player. The partners move in this manner in the play area. The leader calls for "fours" and two caterpillars must link together; "eights" and two groups of 4 join together, etc.

*Cognitive Application:* When linking arms together the players must name something related to the transformation of a caterpillar to a butterfly (e.g., chrysalis, cocoon). If unable to name an appropriate term, they must continue to search for a new caterpillar.

### *Title:*   ***Cross-Over Blanket Ball***
- *Level:* 4–6

*Skills Enhanced:* teamwork, spatial awareness
*Equipment Needed:* a blanket for each group of 6–7 players, a volleyball for each game
*Description:* The members of each team hold a blanket. Have the players count off so each has a number. One team tosses a ball from its blanket over a net or a rope to the opposite team who catches it on their blanket. As soon as the ball is tossed, the number one player from the tossing team runs under the net and joins the other team. Once the ball is caught it is then tossed back to the first team to catch; the number one player from this group runs under the net to join the 1st team. This procedure continues as the players see how many times they can pass the ball successfully to the other group. Number two players go under the net, then threes, etc. Variation: use a long rope as the net and have several teams playing at the same time. Balls must be passed on a whistle blow.

*Cognitive Application:* The teacher gives a developmentally appropriate spelling word. As the children toss the ball they all say the correct letters of the word: one letter for each ball toss. When the word is finished the next person in order runs under the net to join the other team.

### *Title:*   ***Fish Gobbler***
- *Level:* 2–6

*Skills Enhanced:* running, agility, auditory discrimination
*Equipment Needed:* none
*Description:* The "Fish Gobbler" stands in the center of the play area and calls "Ship!" and all players run toward the designated wall. When he/she yells "Shore!" they run immediately to the opposite side. At any point he/she may call "Fish Gobbler!" and at this point he/she attempts to tag as many fish as possible. When the children hear "Fish Gobbler" they drop down on their bellies and link together with a group of friends: they may link together with arms or legs—the bodies need to be touching. If everyone is safe, the Fish Gobbler calls "Rescue!" and all jump up, raise a fist in the air and shout "Yeah!" The fish gobbler also may call "Sardines" and players must sit on partners' knees, "Crabs" and players back up to a partner, bend over and grasp hands between legs, or "Fishnet" and the players must all join hands to form the big net. Fish who do not do as called can be tagged and make swimming arm movements as they run one lap around the play space, then re-enter the game.

*Cognitive Application:* The fish, after running one lap, must name one type of fish before they re-enter the game.

## RELAYS

The relay race is thought to be a favorite of children in the elementary grades. *In fact, it is one of the worst activities that may be selected as far as self-esteem and self-concept development are concerned.* In the traditional form of the relay race, five children perform some sort of a skill while traveling to a pylon and back while 20 others watch them do it. This is a social evaluation situation where the children are being observed by peers and if they do not do well, their peers will tell them so, often with unkind words or treatment. Young children do not understand the concept that a relay race is a team effort and they do not grasp the idea that a loss is not necessarily the fault of one slow person. For these reasons the relays given in this section revolve around the principle of maximum participation. They are designed to have as many people active as possible, and to provide little time for social evaluation.

There are several key points to remember in order to make relay races safe and effective:
Specify starting lines and turning points precisely;
Designate the proper way to tag the next person or group of persons;
Always use a turning or stopping point that is well away from the walls;
Reduce the emphasis on winning by rotating children to different teams after each race. For example, after the first race have all the leaders move to the rear of the team to their left. After the second race have the second persons shift to the team on the right, etc.

*Title:*    *Attention Relay*
- *Level:* 3–6

*Skills Enhanced:* auditory discrimination, speed, agility, spatial awareness
*Equipment Needed:* none
*Description:* Divide class into 4–5 teams of 6 people. Assign numbers to children, 1–6. The leader calls "Attention number 4!" The child whose number is 4 leaves his/her place and runs clockwise around his/her team and back to his/her place. The first one back gets a point for the team. The game continues as the leader calls numbers at random. Variation: the teacher calls two consecutive numbers; those players face each other and form an arch

```
    ┌ - - - - - →  ┌ - - - →
  ┌ 1  2  3  4  5  6 ┐
  └ - - - - - - - ← - - - - ┘
    1  2  3  4  5  6

    1  2  3  4   5   6

    1  2  3   4   5   6
```

with their arms. The players in front of the arch run to a front marker, around it and back through the arch ending in their original places. The players behind the arch run first through the arch and then around a back marker and back to their places. When all have returned, the arms are dropped and the team stands at attention.

### Title:   *Box Ball Relay*

- *Level:* 3–6

*Skills Enhanced:* eye-hand coordination, spatial awareness, agility

*Equipment Needed:* one large cardboard box with four dense foam balls inside per game

*Description:* Divide the group into four teams. Each child has a number. When the teacher calls "2" #2 runs to the box, takes a ball, and runs back to the place of #1. As soon as #2 left, #1 should move to the vacant spot. #2 then passes the ball to #1, #1 to #3, #3 to #4, #4 to #5, #5 to #6 who runs to the box, puts the ball in the box and runs back to his/her line. First team to finish earns one point. The relay continues as the teacher calls different numbers. The numbers will soon be out of order on the line but that is all right: the first number called

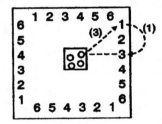

will always run back to position #1 and the person who happens to be in position #6 will always return the ball to the box.

### Title:   *Caterpillar Relay*

- *Level:* 3–6

*Skills Enhanced:* arm and leg strength, flexibility, coordination

*Equipment Needed:* none

*Description*: Team players stand in a single file line, bend over and hold the ankles of the player in front; the first player may use his/her hands any way he/she wishes. On the signal to go, the team moves forward to the finish line. When the tail of the caterpillar crosses the finish line the team is done.

### Title:   *Choo-Choo Relay*

- *Level:* 3–6

*Skills Enhanced:* spatial awareness

**1 1 1 1 1 1 1 1 ⟶ 2 2 2 2 2 2 2 2**

**3 3 3 3 3 3 3 3 ⟶ 4 4 4 4 4 4 4 4**

*Equipment Needed:* none

*Description:* Divide the class into four equal teams. On the signal, teams 1 and 3 place hands on the waist of the child in front and weave their way in and out of the members of teams 2 and 4. The first team to complete the weave and remain joined together wins a point. Teams 2 and 4 repeat. Variation: Teams 1 and 2 could be working together so that the last person on team 1 is on the end line; the #1 train weaves through the #2s and stops; the #2s weave through the 1s in their new position and stop, etc. until one train reaches the far side of the play area. 3s and 4s would do the same.

### *Title:* __Cyclone__
- *Level:* 4–6

*Skills Enhanced:* agility, spatial awareness

*Equipment Needed:* none

*Description:* Team members lie on their backs in a circle, heads in toward center of circle, legs stretched outward. On the signal to go, player 1 gets up and steps over player 2, who then gets up and follows. Each player stands after the last player has gone over him/her. As each player returns to his/her place, he/she lies down again and the "cyclone" of children finish over them. The team is finished when everyone is back in the original position.

### *Title:* __Hurdle Relay__
- *Level:* 4–6

*Skills Enhanced:* leg power, coordination

*Equipment Needed:* a jump rope for each group

*Description:* Divide class into teams of 8–10 players. Set them in parallel lines: #1 and #2 hold the ends of a jump rope and, holding it about 6'' from the floor, they move back down the line with the teammates between them, jumping the rope as it comes to them. #1 stays at the end, #2 runs with the rope back to the front and hands the end to #3. The #2 and #3 move back down the line of teammates as they jump. This pattern continues until #8 and #1

```
1 2 3 4 5 6
1 2 3 4 5 6
1 2 3 4 5 6
```

have carried the rope. Then all are returned to their original places and #1 runs to the front of the line to finish.

### *Title:* __Jack Rabbit Relay__
- *Level:* 5–6

*Skills Enhanced:* aerobic endurance, leg power, leg strength

*Equipment Needed:* one jump rope and one pylon per team

*Description:* Divide class into teams of 5 or 6. #1 and #2 hold the ends of the jump rope and run to the pylon. They yell "Go!" and #3 leads the entire team to run down and around the pylon and back to the starting line. At the same time that #3 is leading the team down, #1

and #2 are running back to the start with the rope held approximately 6" off the ground. As team members meet #1 and #2 they must jump over the rope. When the entire team returns

```
6 5 4 3 2 1          Δ
6 5 4 3 2 1          Δ
6 5 4 3 2 1          Δ
6 5 4 3 2 1          Δ
```

to the start, #2 and #3 run down with the rope and call "Go!" #1 is now at the end of the line and #4 is leading the group. This continues until #8 and #1 have carried the rope.

### *Title:* **Over and Over**
- *Level:* 4–6

*Skills Enhanced:* eye-hand coordination, memory
*Equipment Needed:* one ball per group
*Description:* Team members stand in single file line, arm's length apart. First person passes the ball overhead to #2. #1 immediately turns around and slaps five with #2 who balances the ball in one hand. #1 runs to the end of the line, #2 passes the ball overhead and turns, slaps five with #3, and runs to the end of the line, etc. This procedure continues until the line has moved a designated distance across the play area.

### *Title:* **Over and Under Relay**
- *Level:* 1–6

*Skills Enhanced*: directionality, eye-hand coordination
*Equipment Needed:* one dense foam ball per team
*Description:* Team members stand single file, the ball is in the first player's hands. On the signal to go, the ball is passed overhead to each player in line, the last person takes the ball, runs to the front of the line and passes the ball back. The team that is finished first gets a point. Repeat with the task of passing the ball under the legs. Repeat with passing the ball alternately overhead and under legs. Variation: For older children you may add the variation of passing backwards on the right side, back on left side, back on right side, etc.

### *Title:* **Pass and Duck**
- *Level:* 3–6

*Skills Enhanced:* throwing and catching, spatial awareness
*Equipment Needed:* one dense foam ball for each team
*Description:* Divide the class into teams of 6: #1 starts with the ball and tosses it to #2; #2 tosses it back and squats down; #1 passes to #3 who tosses back and squats down; this continues until the ball is tossed to #6. At this point #1 runs to squat down in front of #2 and #6 carries the ball, straddles the team as he/she moves forward to take the place of #1. The

```
1          °2 3 4 5 6
1           2 3 4 5 6
1           2 3 4 5 6
1           2 3 4 5 6
```

entire team moves back one space and play continues in the same fashion as #6 throws to #1. The activity is over when #1 is back in his/her original place.

*Title:*     ***Race the Bases***
- *Level:* 4–6

*Skills Enhanced:* running, agility, spatial awareness
*Equipment Needed:* 4 bases
*Description:* Divide the class into 4 teams. Each team lines up at a different base, with bases set up as if in a baseball diamond. Running the bases in sequence, runners make the circuit and tag the next player on their teams. When all players on a team have completed the circuit, the team is finished.

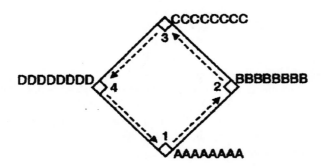

*Title:*     ***Skin the Snake Relay***
- *Level:* 3–6

*Skills Enhanced:* team cooperation, agility, spatial awareness
*Equipment Needed:* none
*Description:* Teams stand in single line formation. Players bend over and extend right arm and hand through legs to player behind. On the signal to go, #6 lies down on his/her back and the team members move backwards, still holding hands. When #5 is past #6, #5 lies down, then #4, #3, #2, and finally #1. #1 then stands up and walks forward, straddling the players, pulling up #2, then #3 comes up, #4, #5 and finally #6. Hands must be held throughout the stunt.

1 2 3 4 5 6

1 2 3 4 5 6

1 2 3 4 5 6

*Title:*    ***Tadpole Relay***
- *Level:* 3–6

*Skills Enhanced:* eye-hand coordination, agility, running
*Equipment Needed:* one dense foam ball
*Description:* Team A forms a circle (approximately 7–10 yards in diameter) in the center of the play area. The other teams are placed like spokes of a wheel. On the signal to go, the first player (closest to the circle) in each spoke runs counterclockwise around the outside of the circle, but in front of the teams, and tags his/her next team member who repeats the task. He/she then goes to the end of the line and sits down. This continues until all players have run around the circle and are back in their original positions. In the meantime, the circle team is passing the ball around the circle and counting each catch, trying to catch the ball as many times as possible before all running team members are back in their original positions. Then Team A takes Team B's place and Team B does the passing and catching, etc.

*Title:*    ***Supine Relay***
- *Level:* 3–6

*Skills Enhanced:* agility, running, spatial awareness
*Equipment Needed:* none
*Description:* Team members lie on their backs in a circle formation with heads in toward the center and legs stretched outward. Each child has a number. When the number is called the child gets up and runs around the circle leaping over the players and back to his/her spot and lies down. First child back earns a point for his/her team.

## Summary

Numerous developmentally appropriate games have been presented that will provide enjoyment for children as well as provide maximal physical activity. Teachers should be sure to use the principles of game selection to determine which games will be appropriate for children's needs and to meet objectives. Remember that play is learning and that when the emphasis is placed in the correct direction, children will learn valuable skills and values for participation in carefully selected activities.

## References and Suggested Readings

Gabbard, C.P., LeBlanc, E., & Lowy, S. (1989). *Games, dance and gymnastics activities for children.* Prentice-Hall.

Gabbard, C., LeBlanc, E., & Lowy, S. (1994) *Physical education for children, building the foundation.* Prentice-Hall.

Gallahue, D. (2005). *Developmental physical education for all children.* Human Kinetics.

Gallahue, D. (1997). *Developmental physical education for today's children.* McGraw Hill.

Kirchner G. & Fishburne, G.J. (2001). *Physical education for elementary school children.* McGraw Hill.

Kirchner G. & Fishburne, G.J. (1998). *Physical education for elementary school children.* Brown & Benchmark.

216     Physical Education for the Elementary Classroom Teacher

Kirchner G. & Fishburne, G.J. (1995). *Physical education for elementary school children.* Brown & Benchmark.

Kuntzelman, C., Kuntzelman, B., McGlynn, M. & McGlynn, G. (1984). *Aerobics with fun.* Fitness Finders.

Nichols, B. (2001). *Moving and learning*: *The elementary school physical education experience.* McGraw Hill.

Nichols, B. (1994). *Moving and learning*: *The elementary school physical education experience.* Times Mirror/Mosby.

Nichols, B. (1990). *Moving and learning.*Times Mirror/Mosby.

Pangrazi, R. P. (2006). *Dynamic physical education for elementary school children.* Benjamin Cummings.

Pangrazi, R.P. (2003). *Dynamic physical education for elementary school children.* Benjamin Cummings.

Pangrazi, R.P. (1998). *Dynamic physical education for elementary school children.* Allyn & Bacon.

Pangrazi, R.P. & Dauer, V.P. (1995). *Dynamic physical education for elementary school children.* Allyn & Bacon.

Pangrazi, R.P. & Dauer, V.P. (1992). *Dynamic physical education for elementary school children.* Macmillan.

Siedentop, D., Herkowitz, J. & Rink, J. (1984). *Elementary physical education methods.* Prentice-Hall.

Wall, J. & Murray, N. (1990). *Children and movement.* Wm. C. Brown.

CHAPTER

# 10

# Manipulative Activities

Whenever children use any body parts to interact with an object or objects, they are using manipulative skills. Probably the most familiar term associated with manipulation would be hand-eye coordination. You read in the perceptual-motor development chapter about the perceptual processes involved in visual-motor coordination which usually involves the eyes and hands. You know that vision guides the hands to accomplish the designated task. The same is true for eye-foot coordination.

In order for children to develop smooth coordination patterns in either area, they need to have many varied experiences, allowing them to experiment with their capabilities. In physical education there are many pieces of equipment that allow them to do just that. Children enjoy interacting with the novel kinds of toys that are traditionally used to encourage the development of manipulative skills.

In the early grades these activities become components of manipulative skill units. You may wish to concentrate on one type of equipment for a week, e.g., playground balls, or you may wish to use different types of equipment each day of the unit. Whatever the choice, the activities contribute to the development of eye-hand and eye-foot coordination, depending on the choice.

Some of these activities are more difficult and are designed to challenge the upper elementary child, such as juggling. In this case the child would already possess good eye-hand coordination skills, a prerequisite to leaning a skill such as juggling.

You will find that there are many other activities that you may try with the manipulative equipment in addition to those listed. You are limited only by your own creativity!

## Balloons

Balloons are excellent in order to learn beginning catching skills because they travel slowly through the air and children have time to react. They are also excellent for teaching volleyball skills where children need to learn certain skills for striking the object. Children enjoy using balloons for simply working on hand-eye coordination and often balloons are selected as a favorite play medium for young children.

### Individual Skills

1.  Have the child tap the balloon up into the air overhead using two hands, one hand and emphasize the catch by reaching up with two hands and pulling the balloon in to the chest.
2.  Have the child tap the balloon, keeping it in the air by using different body parts.
3.  Have the child tap the balloon according to the body part that the teacher calls.
4.  Have the child travel in general space, tapping the balloon so that it travels too.
5.  Have the child keep the balloon in the air with an implement such as a lummi stick.

### Partner Skills

1.  Have partners tap the balloon back and forth in the air.
2.  Have the partners travel, taking turns at striking the balloon and trying to cover a specified distance.
3.  Have one partner hold a hoop vertically in the air while the other partner taps the balloon through and runs to the other side to tap it back. Change roles after ten tries.
4.  Have partners tap a balloon across a net to each other, using two hands, one hand.
5.  Each set of partners has one balloon and one yarnball. The partners with the yarn balls form a large circle around those partners with balloons. The children in the center tap the balloons high overhead and the children with yarn balls throw and try to hit the balloons. The throwers may pick up any thrown yarnball and throw again. Children should keep track of the number of balloons they hit. Change roles and play again.

## Ball Skills

The first set of individual, partner and group ball skill activities is designed for learning with the typical playground ball. These balls come in many sizes, but the best one for learning is the 8.5''. This ball fits the cupped hand well and is of an appropriate weight for the children to lift easily. The ultimate goal of effective ball handling skills is to make the ball perform as if it were actually a part of the body. The child should become so skillful that he/she can control the ball at all times whether in a stationary or a traveling mode. Mini-units in ball handling skills should be repeated throughout the year in the primary grades. Developing efficiency in ball skills contributes greatly to eye-hand coordination, eye-foot coordination, spatial awareness, and agility. Skills should be done in progression:

first the child learns to handle a ball alone, then with a partner and finally in cooperation with a group. Most lessons devoted to ball handling skills will do some work in each area (individual, partner, and group) but the skills will relate to one another and will not be vastly different. For example, members of a class may work on bouncing skills individually in place, then walking in general space, then walking and sharing the bouncing with a partner, and finally playing a game such as "Ball Thief."

## *Individual Ball Skills*

1.  Have the child drop the ball and catch it from a bounce.
2.  Have the child bounce the ball in front using two hands. Emphasize pushing the ball down (fingers push) and allowing the cupped hands to ride upward (give) with the ball on the rise, then push down.
3.  Have the child work on bouncing the ball in place with the preferred hand. Emphasize the push and the give.
4.  Repeat #3 using the other hand.
5.  Have the child start to walk into general space while bouncing the ball with the preferred hand.
6.  Repeat #5 using the other hand.
7.  In self space, have the child alternately bounce the ball with left-right-left-right-etc.
8.  Have the child move in general space, bouncing the ball with alternate hands.
9.  Using flat circular markers which have been scattered throughout the play area, have the children bounce the ball, using the preferred hand, while zig zagging around and between the circular markers.
10. Repeat #9 using the other hand.
11. Repeat #9 alternating hands.
12. Have the child toss the ball with two hands high into the air, circle the arms backward and come under the bounce of the ball to catch.
13. Repeat #12 but have the child try to catch the ball before the bounce.
14. Repeat #12 but have the child touch the body part that you call before catching the ball
15. Working against a wall space, have the child throw the ball to the wall so that it bounces on the floor on the way back for the catch, wall-floor-catch.
16. In the same wall space, have the child throw the ball so that it hits the floor near the wall and bounces off the wall for an in-air catch, floor-wall-catch.
17. Have the child stand sideways to the wall, drop the ball with one hand and "bat" the ball to the wall with the preferred hand. Have the child face the wall and catch the ball on the return. Stress having the arm extended when striking the ball.
18. Have the child stand in self-space and pass the ball quickly around his/her waist; do the same around each leg and then attempt a figure eight pass around the lower legs.
19. Have the child bounce the ball and lift the opposite leg up and over the ball on each fourth bounce, 1-2-3-lift.
20. As skill develops with #17, vary the task to pass the ball on a bounce under the right leg, then under the left, alternating.
21. Have the child place the ball by his/her feet and travel in general space, giving the ball tiny taps with the toes; change to insteps.
22. Moving to a wall space and approximately 3 yards from the wall, have the child place the ball at his/her feet and kick the ball to the wall with the preferred foot. The child

should bend over and stop the return of the ball with the opposite hand. Kicks should not be forceful.

23. Repeat #22 but have the child use his/her foot to stop the ball by trapping the ball on its return by placing his/her foot lightly on top of the ball.

24. Have each child find a self-space on the sideline of the play area, facing a far wall. Each child will then perform a stationary kick, trying to propel the ball to the wall. The child runs to retrieve the ball after all have kicked.

25. From the same position as in #24, have the child face the far wall, hold the ball in front at waist level with two hands. The child drops the ball and when it bounces, kicks from beneath and lifts the ball high toward the far wall. Retrieve after all have kicked.

26. Using the same drill as in #25, have those children who have been successful with the bounce kick now work on the drop kick: holding the ball in front at waist height, drop the ball and kick as it is dropped toward the foot. Retrieve after all have kicked.

27. Have the children lie down on their backs in self space, placing the ball between their feet. Have them lift their feet straight up, tossing the balls to their hands, catching, and sitting up to replace ball. Continue this sequence.

## Partner Ball Skills

1. Have partners approximately five yards apart. Distance may be altered with increased skill.

2. Have the children sit on the floor and roll the ball back and forth with their partners.

3. Have the children sit on the floor and send the ball to the partner with one bounce in the middle.

4. Have the partners play throw and catch on a bounce from a standing position.

5. Have one partner try to roll the ball over a 5 yard distance through the facing partner's legs in stride position. The target partner lets the ball go through, turns and runs after the ball, brings it back and rolls it under the opposite partner's legs. Continue this pattern.

6. Have the first partner turn around, bend over and roll the ball back through his/her own legs to his/her partner. The partner catches the ball facing front, then turns and rolls the ball back between his/her own legs. Continue this pattern.

7. Repeating the pattern from #5, have the partners "hike" the ball to the opposite partner; toss the ball up to the partner's hands.

8. Have partner #1 roll the ball to #2; #2 tosses the ball back on a bounce. Continue this pattern and then change roles.

9. Have partner #1 roll the ball to #2, #2 throws the ball in a bounce to #1, #1 throws the ball to #2's chest, #2 rolls, #1 bounces, #2 throws to #l's chest, etc.

10. Have the children stand facing each other and one partner bounces the ball with two hands, moving around the partner and back to his/her spot.

11. Have the partners play catch by sending the ball with one bounce, back with two bounces, back with three bounces, etc. Partners will need to gradually increase the distance between them for this skill.

12. Have partners move in general space passing the ball to each other on a bounce.

13. Have the partners move in general space passing the ball to each other in the air.

14. Have partner #1 dribble the ball with his/her feet across, around #2 and back to place. Have #2 repeat.

15. Have the partners pass the ball back and forth in stationary positions with their feet.

16. Have the partners travel in general space and try to keep the ball under control while passing it back and forth with their feet.
17. Have the partners place a hula hoop between them on the floor and toss the ball so that it goes into the hoop and back up to the opposite partner. Keep changing the position of the hoop.
18. Have partner #2 hold a hula hoop horizontally to the side and have #1 toss the ball into the hoop. Vary the height of the hoop. Change roles.
19. Have partner #2 hold the hoop high and against the wall. Partner #1 tosses the ball so that it hits inside the hoop and comes back off the wall. Repeat several times and change roles.
20. Have partner #1 toss the hoop out with a reverse spin and have #2 throw the ball through the hoop. Have #1 retrieve the ball and #2 catch the hoop. Continue in this pattern.
21. Have the partners try to keep the ball going between them on a bounce by striking the ball with an extended arm and fist.

## *Group Activities*

There are numerous games that may be played with playground balls and you will find them in Chapter 8. Those activities selected for use here are ones that have maximal time with the ball for each individual. A game that involves one ball and numerous players does not contribute highly to the efficient development of ball handling skills.

1. Have the children stay in self-space and keep the balls bouncing while you call "both hands," "left hand, or "right hand." If the ball gets away from the child he/she must stand in place and march until the signal for lost balls to be retrieved.
2. Working in self space with tossing the ball high, have the toss go on signal "1-2-3-toss" and see if all balls can be caught without a bounce, meaning there will not be a sound in the play area.
3. "Ball Thief": Each child has a ball and bounces it while traveling in general space. The teacher takes one ball away from a child and sends the child to steal another's ball. The balls must be kept bouncing and the player may not try to take his/her own ball after losing his/hers to the ball thief. Every time someone loses a ball to the thief, that person becomes the thief and takes another. Variation: if this is the last ball activity for the day have the ball thieves put each stolen ball away in the ball bin. Then there will be many thieves and the management task of putting the balls away is completed for you.
4. In groups of three, each with one ball, have the children play "Monkey in the Middle." One child stands between the two others and tries to intercept the ball as it is tossed back and forth. If the monkey gets the ball, he/she trades places with the person who last threw the ball. This may be played with the ball on a bounce or in the air.
5. In groups of four, each with one ball, have the children play 2-on-2 "Keepaway". Partners try to complete as many passes as possible before the ball is intercepted by the other set of partners who want to complete as many passes as they can as well.
6. Have the children play the game, "Shipwreck" (See "Developmentally Appropriate Games" chapter) while bouncing the ball.

When working on throwing or tossing skills with children, it is best to use a smaller ball so that it is easily grasped properly in the hand. There is a great number of balls made of varying materials such as yarn balls, "gator skin balls," "super bounce foam balls," and "whiffle balls," to name a few. Yarn balls are especially good for the learning stage. They come in varied sizes, but probably the softball sized ones are the best for most activities. Stuffed footballs which are about 5 in. or less in diameter are excellent for learning overhand throwing skills. They are of such a size and weight that young students can grasp them properly as well as being able to throw them long distances (a detailed description of the overhand throwing skill can be found in Chapter Four). Children can do many of the activities listed above with yarn balls, and a variety of the other balls. Stuffed footballs and yarn balls are not meant for bouncing and kicking activities. Additional activities for yarn balls, stuffed footballs and a variety of other balls are listed here:

## *Individual Activities*

1. Have children work in self-space at a wall, at least 3 yards back, and throw forcefully overhand to the wall. Tell the children that you want to hear their feet stomp on the step forward.
2. Have the children move gradually away from the wall and continue to throw forcefully at the wall.
3. Have children vary their throws against the wall. Sometimes using an underhand throw and sometimes and overhand throw.
4. Tape a piece of paper or a paper plate to the wall to use as a target, and have children attempt to hit the target while varying their throws.
5. After 5 underhand throws and 5 overhand throws have the children exchange the ball they are currently using for a different variety of ball.

## *Partner Activities*

Have partner #1 throw the ball to partner #2. Partner #2 attempts to catch the ball and throw it back to #1. Emphasize using correct overhand or underhand throwing skill.

1. Have partners attempt to increase the distance of the throw, gradually moving away from one another.
2. Have partners attempt to increase the height and arc of the throw.
3. Have partners try to make the ball spiral on the throw, when using stuffed footballs.
4. Have partners attempt to visualize their partners as being target.
5. Have partners pass the ball to each other as they are moving in the play space.
6. Have partners change the levels of the throws (high, low, and medium).
7. Have one partner hold a hula hoop vertically in front of him/her. Have the throwing partner try to send the football, yarn ball, etc. through the hoop. Change roles after 5 tries.
8. Have the partners pass slightly ahead of a partner (a lead pass) so the other player needs to catch the ball on the move.
9. On the teacher's signal have children change partners so children will be able to have the opportunity to work with students of varying skill levels.
10. Repeat #10 several times.
11. On the teacher's signal have children exchange the ball they are currently using for a different type of ball.
12. Repeat #11 often so children have an opportunity to use a variety of balls.

13. Have the pairs of children join another pair so there are four in the group with two balls. Have them play catch to the child diagonally across the group. They should keep both balls going at the same time.
14. In groups of four, use one football and try to pass the ball around a triangle of three while the fourth person tries to intercept the balls. If he/she does intercept it, he/she takes the place of the thrower on the triangle.
15. In groups of four, play team "Keepaway" with the ball. Partners should count the number of passes they complete before the ball is intercepted When this game seems successful play 4 on 4, then 8 on 8.
16. "One Step," "Developmentally Appropriate Games" chapter

## *Beanbags*

Beanbags are excellent for learning throwing and catching skills. Children can also do many games and stunts with the beanbags. They are easier to grasp than a ball and their weight is appropriate for their uses. The creative teacher will find that activities with beanbags contribute to spatial awareness, body awareness, flexibility, agility, and balance, as well as to eye-hand coordination.

## *Individual Activities*

1. In self-space have children toss and catch the beanbag; Use both hands, just right hand, just left hand. Have the children try tossing the beanbag at different heights.
3. Have children try tossing the beanbag high and to the rear so they can turn around and catch it.
4. Have the children toss, clap once and catch; toss, clap twice and catch; toss, clap three times and catch, etc. Challenge them to clap as many times as possible before catching the beanbags.
5. Have the children toss the beanbags, touch designated body parts and catch. Increase the difficulty by calling several body parts: toss-shoulders-knees-catch, etc.
6. Have the children toss the beanbags slightly ahead so they have to move to catch. Have the children travel in general space while tossing and catching the beanbags.
7. Have the children balance the beanbag on various body parts as they move with designated locomotor movements in general space.

8.  Have the children place their beanbags on the floor and see how many different ways they can find to move around or over the beanbags.

## *Partner Activities*

1.  Have partners toss and catch the beanbag from various distances and heights.
2.  Have partners play follow the leader in general space carrying the beanbag on different body parts and doing different kinds of stunts.
3.  Have the children stand back-to-back with the partner and pass the two beanbags from hand to hand around both bodies as quickly as possible.
4.  Have partners toss two beanbags back and forth.
5.  'Beanbag Horseshoes": Children stand approximately five yards apart with the hoops on the floor at their feet. #1 tosses the beanbag: he/she wins 2 points if the bag lands in the hoop, 1 point if the bag lands on the hoop. Then #2 tries. The game continues until 10 points; then switch partners. Different target formations can be made with the hoops.

## *Group Activities*

1.  "Fragile Rock": Children scatter into general space and place their beanbags on the floor. On signal the children run anywhere in general space while the rock collector, the teacher, picks up 3–4 beanbags and then calls "To a rock!" The children run to place one finger on a beanbag. There can be more than one child on a beanbag. Continue to play, varying the locomotor movements, until only 3–4 beanbags remain on the floor.
2.  "Enchanted Castle": Each prince or princess has a crown (beanbag) on his/her head. He/she moves around as designated in the castle area but if the beanbag falls off, he/she must stand still on one foot, arms out to sides. Another child may pick up the beanbag and put it back on the child's head; the child may then resume playing.
3.  "Toss-Jump-Pick": Have children stand on sideline of the play area with their beanbags. On the signal they toss the beanbag and then jump over it, pick it up, and toss again. This procedure continues until the entire class has crossed the play area.
4.  "Beanbag Relay": Teams of 5–6 stand in single file lines. On the signal to begin the first player passes the beanbag overhead to #2, and the beanbag is passed to each person overhead to the last one who runs to the front of the line, stands in front of #1 and passes the beanbag overhead. The team is finished when they are all back to their original places. Repeat by passing the beanbag under the legs, then alternately over the head and under the legs. Repeat by passing the beanbag on the right side only, the left side only, and alternately left and right.
5.  In groups of 4–5 players in circle formations, have the children toss the beanbags around the circle clockwise, seeing how many beanbags they can keep tossing.
6.  "Hot Potato"—With the entire class seated in a circle, pass the beanbags quickly in a clockwise direction. Designate one beanbag to be "baked" and the child who is holding the "baked potato" on the teacher's signal must stand up and do jumping jacks until the next person is caught.
7.  Have the children place their beanbags on the floor in self space and give the following directions:

- Balance on one part of your body on the beanbag. Can you do that with a different part?
- Place the beanbag on your head; now balance on three body parts without losing the beanbag. How about four body parts? Two? One?
- Can you make a bridge over the beanbag on the floor? Try to make a bridge with four body parts touching the floor. Try a bridge with two body parts on the floor.

8. Have the children work in general space with the beanbags scattered in the play area. Give the following directions:
- On the signal to go, run in general space and whenever you come to a beanbag, run in a circle around it and then move on to another.
- When I say go, run in general space and leap high over each beanbag that you come to.
- On the signal to go, begin to skip in general space. Each time you come to a beanbag, step on it and change your locomotor movement (level, speed, direction, etc.)

# Flying Discs

Flying discs have grown to be very popular in the recreational aspects of play. They are relatively inexpensive, can be acquired at local toy stores, and can be used by individuals, small groups, and large groups. The flying disc requires a unique sidearm throwing motion, and catching a flying disc is a complex eye-hand coordination task due to the flight pattern. Children need to be able to perceptually employ their tracking skills and combine these with logical anticipation of where the flying disc will be and when it will be easiest to catch. The unique shape of the flying disc makes it more difficult to catch as well.

Introduction to the flying disc may be in the primary grade years but it is probably more appropriate to save this skill until grades 3–6. At this time the majority of children should be able to acquire the skills much easier than would the majority of children in grades K–2.

When throwing a flying disc, the player should hold the disc with the thumb on top, the index finger along the side, and the rest of the fingers beneath the disc. The player should, while holding the flying disc, stand sideways to the target, reach across his/her body with the flying disc, take a step toward the target while bringing the flying disc hand forward and releasing the disc horizontally, ending the throw with a flick of the wrist. The throwing hand should stop the motion when pointed toward the target.

As mentioned before, catching the flying disc is more difficult. Players may catch either with a thumb-down or thumb-up position. The flying disc is to be caught with one hand, thumb-up if it is below waist level, thumb-down if higher. The rest of the fingers grip the flying disc on the opposite side from the thumb. Trick catches will be developed as the player becomes more and more competent in play with the flying disc.

## Partner Activities

1.  Have the children play throw and catch with their partners; change levels of throws; change distances between partners.
2.  Have the children try to catch the flying disc by catching it flat between both hands.
3.  Have one partner hold a hula hoop vertically in front of him/her. Have the throwing partner try to send the flying disc through the hoop. Change roles after every 5 tries.
4.  Have the children place the hoop on the ground and try to make the thrown flying disc land in the hoop. Change roles.
5.  Have the partners pass to each other as they are moving in the play space.
6.  Have the partners pass slightly ahead of the partner (a lead pass) so the player needs to catch the flying disc on the move.
7.  Have the children try releasing the flying disc on an angle instead of parallel to the ground. The partner will have to move to intercept the disc.
8.  Have the children join another pair so there are four in the group with two flying discs. Have them play catch to the child diagonally across the group. They should keep both flying discs going at the same time.
9.  In groups of four, use one flying disc and try to pass the disc around the triangle of three while the fourth person tries to intercept the disc. If he/she does intercept it, he/she takes the place of the thrower on the triangle.
10. In groups of four, play team "Keepaway" with the flying disc. Partners should count the number of passes they complete before the disc is intercepted. When this game seems successful, play 4 on 4, then 8 on 8.

## Games

"Ultimate Flying Disc"—This game is played between two teams, and the point is to score a goal in the opponents' half of the play area. There should be no more than 8 players per team (4 on offense and 4 on defense).

The only players who may cross the center line are the offensive players. Goal areas should be three yards in width, and no higher than 5 feet. The game begins with a toss-up of the flying disc by the teacher in the center of the play area. The team who gains possession (catches the flying disc) tries to pass the disc in such a way that it will arrive at the goal and go in for a score. Players may not: run or walk with the flying disc in hand, pull the flying disc out of another's hand, or make physical contact with another player. If there are any infractions as indicated above, the opposing team gains control of the flying disc on the spot and has a free pass. If an infraction by Team A occurs within 5 yards of the goal, a free pass is called for one of the defensive B players. If the infraction within 5 yards of the goal is by a Team B member, a player from Team A has a free, unobstructed shot at the goal from a spot marked exactly 5 yards into the field from the center of the goal. If the flying disc goes out of bounds, it is passed in at the spot it left, by a player from the team who did not have possession of the flying disc prior to its going out of play. After a goal is scored by Team A, one of the defensive players from Team B has a free pass from the 5 yard marker in front of the goal.

It is best to have two games going at once, but remember that this would involve having the students officiate. This is a good idea, but the students must know the game extremely well to do the officiating. If the teacher feels more comfortable with one game, have the waiting players practicing their throwing and catching off to the side, or have them stand on the sideline of their team and allow the play to go to these sideline players as well. They may not come onto the field but they may throw and receive passes.

"Flying Disc Golf"—This will involve the teacher in setting up nine different targets, representing nine holes of golf. If space allows, the teacher may set an eighteen hole course. The students are divided into as many groups as there are targets and each is assigned to one of the "holes" to begin play. Play begins for the next hole from the previous hole, so ideally the nine holes should complete a circuit. Each player has a flying disc. The first player in each group stands at the target and throws for the next target. Each player takes a turn. They continue to toss the flying discs in turn, starting from the furthest one back. Each child carries a pencil and a card to record the number of tosses it takes to hit the next target.

## HOOPS

Hoops are colorful, fun objects for children to use in games and activities. Not only do they serve well as targets for many games, but they are great for their own intrinsic value.

### Individual Hoop Activities

1.  Place hoop on floor and jump in, out, sideways in, sideways out, backwards out, forward in, etc.

2.  Have children jump in front of the hoop, behind the hoop, on the right side of the hoop, and on the left side of the hoop.

3.  Have children jump forward over the hoop, jump backwards over the hoop, and jump sideways over the hoop.

4.  Have the children step forwards over the hoop, step backwards over the hoop, and step sideways over the hoop.

5.  Have the children walk, run, gallop, leap, hop, skip, and slide around the outside of the hoop.

6.  Have children think of how many different ways they can move around the hoop, (speed, level, direction, etc.) and then perform these.

7.  Have children attempt to straddle the hoop.

8.  Have children attempt to throw the hoop vertically in the air and catch it as it comes down.

9.  Repeat #8 attempting to get the hoop higher each time.

10. Have the children hold the hoop higher than their heads, below their waists, and at their ankles.

11. Have children put various body parts through the middle of the hoop. Such as arm, head, foot, elbow, etc.

12. Bend down and pick up the hoop with arms extended out to sides. Try to lift the hoop all the way overhead without touching your body. On the count of three, clap your hands and let the hoop fall around you. 1-2-3. Did the hoop touch your body when it fell? Try again and see if you can do it so that the hoop does not touch your body.

13. Have the students one at a time, join right hands (handshake) with the teacher while the hula hoop is on the wrist of the student. The teacher will start spinning the hoop, moving the child's hand so it keeps spinning around the child's wrist. Once it is spinning successfully, the teacher will let go of the child's hand and move onto the next child. This helps those children who are having difficulty getting started.

14. Repeat #13, only have children who can spin the hoop successfully pair up with a child who is having difficulty.

15. Have the children work in self space and try to swing or spin the hoop on various body parts: arm, wrist, neck, waist, knees, ankles.

16. Have the students attempt to switch the hoop from one hand, or wrist to the other while spinning the hoop and without interrupting the spin.

17. Tell the younger children that sometimes hoops are magic. Show them that you can throw your hoop away and have it return all by itself (throw the hoop out vertically with a reverse spin by snapping your wrist back on release). Have the children try to throw a magic hoop. Teach children how to grasp the hoop in an overhand grip and snap wrist on release: a good progression is to have the children work in partners and toss the hoop to each other so that it goes in the air on the way to the partner; then toss the hoop toward the partner but snap the wrist back on release. Eventually the child will learn to release low with a good snap. Once the reversal is accomplished, have the children try to stop the hoop on return by stepping inside and making it fall. They can then jump inside the returning hoop to make it fall.

18. Have the children spin the hoop like an eggbeater on the floor in front of them. Challenge them to run around and back to their places before it stops

spinning. See if they can stop the hoop by putting a foot inside the eggbeater.

19. Have the children hold the hoop at waist height, hands in front in an overhand grip. Show them how to rotate the hoop in their hands so that it comes forward over their heads, and they can jump in it as it goes backwards under their feet. Challenge the children to develop a jumping rhythm with this skill.

20. Working in self space with the hoop, the children follow the teacher's directions.

21. Balance on two body parts inside your hoop. Find two different body parts. How about two others?

22. Balance on two body parts, one inside and one outside of the hoop.

23. Balance on three body parts, two outside and one inside the hoop.

24. Balance on three body parts, two inside the hoop and one outside. Continue to give balance challenges to the children.

25. Have the children stand inside the hoop to begin. Have them recite the alphabet and jump out on vowels, stay in jumping on consonants. Have children spell their names, following the same jumping rules.

### *Individual Eye-Foot Coordination Activities*

1. Divide class into groups of 4–5 players. Hoops are placed side by side in a straight line. The first player jumps in the first hoop and says "one," into the second, jumps again and says "two," into the third, jumps two more times and says "three," etc. Each child follows in turn.

2. Same hoop formation, have children alternately hop and jump in each hoop to travel to the end.

3. Same hoop formation, have children jump backwards into each hoop in succession.

4. Teacher changes one group's hoops to look like this:

The other groups then change theirs to look like the teacher's pattern. Have the children start with feet apart and jump through the hoops so that the feet stay apart-apart-apart-etc. until the ninth hoop when they jump feet together and out of the hoop.

5. Same hoop formation, have the children run through the hoops, keeping the left foot in the left hoops, the right in the right side hoops, and bringing both feet together into the last hoop.
6. Same hoop formation, have children jump forward into the left hoop, sideways to the right, forward to the next right hoop, sideways to the left, etc.

7. The teacher should change another group's hoops to the following pattern (other groups make theirs to match):
8. Have the children, in turn, jump together-together-together-apart-together-apart-together and out of the last hoop.
9. Same hoop formation, have children jump: together front, together front, together front, together forward and right, together left, together forward to center, together forward to right, together to left, together forward center and out.
10. Same hoop formation, have the children in turn: hop-hop-hop-jump with feet apart-hop-jump-hop and out.
11. Same hoop formation, have children run: right, left, right, left, right, left, right, left, right and out on the left, keeping right foot to the right hoops and left foot to the left hoops.

## *Partner Hoop Activities*

1. Have the children play catch with their partners with the hoop. Challenge them to find out how many different ways they can toss the hoop (horizontally, vertically). Have them try to catch the hoop on different body parts, such as the arm, or even the neck.
2. Have the children run through the hoop as the partner tosses it with a reverse spin. The hoops should be momentarily still on the spin moment; the non-throwing partner can time it and run through the hoop, while crouched down low, before the hoop starts to spin away.
3. Have the partners hold hands, one standing inside the hoop, one on the outside. Have them try to jump so that one is jumping backwards out of the hoop while the other is jumping forward into the hoop. Challenge them to increase the number of times that they can do this repetitively.
4. Have the children move with partners and hoops in general space with the hoop rolling vertically between them. They should take turns controlling the roll of the hoop.
5. Have the partners toss and catch two hoops, the hoops passing in the air. Change the activity to rolling the two hoops to each other.

## *Group Hoop Activities*

All children stand in general space inside their hoops.

1.  Choose a child to be the first tagger. When this child leaves his/her hoop, all of the others must leave their hoops. The tagger tries to touch a player who is outside a hoop. Players must move to at least three different hoops before they can go back to their own. Any child tagged becomes an additional tagger. Taggers can count the number of children they tag.

2.  The teacher gives the following directions:
    * When I say go, run and put your right foot inside a yellow hoop.
    * When I say go, skip to a blue hoop and put your left elbow inside.
    * When I say go, slide to a red hoop and put your right knee inside.
    * When I say go, gallop to a green hoop and put your left index finger inside.

3.  Continue to give directions for different locomotor movements and different body parts.

4.  The teacher gives the following directions:
    * When I say go, roar like a lion to a blue hoop.
    * When I say go, leap like a deer to a red hoop.
    * When I say go, slide like a snake to a yellow hoop.
    * When I say go, gallop like a horse to a green hoop.
    * When I say go, skip like a lamb to a blue hoop.
    * When I say go, lumber like an elephant to a red hoop, then jump like a rabbit to a green hoop. When I say go, jump like a frog to three different green hoops.
    * When I say go, ride on a motorcycle to a blue hoop, fly an airplane to a yellow hoop, and chug to a red hoop on a train.

5.  Continue to give directions that allow the children to be creative and at the same time work on spatial awareness moving within general space.

6.  Using music, with two songs, one designated for children who have red and yellow hoops and another for children who have blue and green hoops, have the children with red and yellow stand still and hold their hoops on the ground vertically and perpendicular to themselves. Play the "blue-green" music. On this signal the blue-green hoop children are to drop their hoops in place and travel throughout the play area, passing through without touching hoops that are held by the red-yellow players. When the music changes, the red-yellow players drop their hoops, the blue-green players pick theirs up and the red-yellow players move through the hoops without touching. Continue to change the music back and forth at different time intervals.

7.  With the same musical and hoop format as in #5, have one group sit Indian style on the floor and hold the hoop horizontally about 5'' off the floor (have the sitting children rest the held hoop on top of their shoes for proper height). The traveling group will run and step, hop or jump (whichever direction you choose) into each hoop while the music plays. Change music to change groups.

8.  Give each child a balloon and a hoop. Have the children place the hoops on the floor. As the children move around the play space with the balloon, they are to bat the balloon and, at the same time, pick up a hoop and pass it around the batted balloon, then drop the hoop to the floor. Challenge them to see how many hoops they can pick up without having the balloon touch the floor.

## JUGGLING

Juggling is an excellent activity to enhance the development of eye-hand coordination. It is a difficult skill to learn and should be taught to older children. Since it is an individual activity it is difficult to teach a large class. An excellent approach would be to teach it in a station to a small group which will then rotate on to other tasks. In this case the teacher would stay at the juggling station. Do not expect all children to be able to move easily through the sequence. It would be helpful to have a classroom learning center for practice in juggling.

### *Cascade Juggling*

1. Begin with scarves. Each child should have three lightweight scarves of different colors. Traditionally the scarves for juggling come in the colors of green, orange, and pink. Have the child use only the pink scarf to start.
2. Using an overhand grip with the right hand on the end of the scarf, toss the scarf vertically and diagonally to the left. Catch the scarf in the left hand using a downward motion. Repeat with the left hand. The beginning cue is toss-catch-toss-catch. Practice this skill until it seems to be rhythmical.

3. Place one scarf in each hand. Begin with a toss vertically to the left, then a toss vertically to the right; immediately catch with the left, then catch with the right. Cue: toss-toss-catch-catch. Practice.
4. Hold the green and orange scarves in the right hand, the pink scarf in the left hand. Hold the green scarf between thumb and forefinger, the orange between last three fingers and palm. Toss green, toss pink, toss orange, catch green, catch pink, catch orange. Start with the green from left hand and repeat the sequence the other way. Cue: toss-toss-toss-catch-catch-catch. Practice.
5. Finally, begin as in step #4. Toss green, toss pink, toss orange, catch green, catch pink, toss green, catch orange, toss pink, catch green, toss orange, catch pink. Continue to alternate tossing and catching. One scarf will always be in the air. Practice.

6.   Once this pattern can be maintained for a reasonable period of time, introduce cascade juggling with tennis balls or small yarn balls. The main difference from using scarves is that the hands will always be palm up for tossing, and or catching. The pattern remains the same, as do the cues.

## PARACHUTE

The parachute represents a manipulative team activity in which cooperation is very important to success. Working with the parachute helps children to understand the idea of working together, or teamwork. Its contribution to the psychomotor domain is in upper body strength development. Children enjoy working with the parachute, and it provides for a maximum participation activity.

Children should roll the parachute inward two times and then grip the parachute with an overhand grasp with both hands. All players should be equally distributed around the perimeter of the parachute. Have the children pull backward so that the parachute is tightly stretched, and have them bend their knees and take the parachute to a position on the floor. The basic skill needed for most of the parachute activities is this: the leader calls 1-2-3-lift, and on "lift" the children come to a stand while extending their arms overhead and holding the parachute high. Children should do this at a moderate pace with a strong pull. It works well to tell the children to pretend they are lifting something very heavy.

## *Activities*

1.   "Umbrella"—1-2-3-lift overhead and hold arms there.
2.   "Under the Umbrella"—Have the children count off by 5s. 1-2-3-lift, Number 1s!" The number 1s run under the parachute and change places with people across from them. Repeat for other numbers.
3.   "Marshmallow"—1-2-3-lift and then snap back down to the ground in front of the players. A dome will form on the floor in front of the children.
4.   "Crossing the Marshmallow"—1-2-3-lift, snap, Number 1s!" This time the children, in turn, crawl on top of the parachute to a new place.

5.  "Merry-Go-Round"—Children hold the parachute with right hand only and walk, jump, gallop, skip, or jog in a clockwise direction, turning the parachute as they move. Have them switch locomotor movements, switch directions, and switch speeds.
6.  "Tent"—1-2-3-lift, in, down. Have the children lift on command, take two steps inward, pull the parachute down behind them and sit on their pieces of parachute. All children will be in the tent.
    i. Variation: one child maybe designated as the tent pole to stand in the center and keep the parachute up while the children inside play a game. Also, exercises may be done such as bicycling which will ripple the parachute.
7.  "Flower"—1-2-3-lift, let go! Have the children lift and release the parachute (simply open their hands and leave their arms extended overhead) on command. The parachute should hover for a moment overhead.
8.  "Waves"—Have children hold the parachute at waist level and begin to shake it with small movements. Gradually increase the size of the arm movement until children are reaching far overhead and down below the knees. Stop the waves and have the #1s go and sit on the parachute. Make waves around them while they "swim" in the ocean. Give the other children turns in the middle.
9.  "Mushroom"—1-2-3-lift, walk in to center, and out. Have the children lift and walk inward with arms held high, then walk backwards to place as arms come down. The parachute will cluster overhead, similar to the top of a mushroom.
10. "Pizza Crawl"—Children lie down in prone positions, arms fully extended and parachute spread and held tightly on ground. When their number is called, the children crawl under the parachute to new places.
11. "The Floating Cloud"—1-2-3 lift, walk in to the center, 1-2-3, let go. If the children all let go at the same time the parachute will float across the room resembling a cloud floating across the sky. If they let go at varying times the parachute will fall to the ground like a dishrag. Be sure to tell the children not to run and jump on the parachute, rather remain stationary and watch what the parachute does.
12. "Hot Pancake Pass"—Students pass the parachute to the person on their right. Change directions and speed. Students should grasp the parachute with one hand and then the other.

## Games

1.  "Popcorn"—Place yarn balls and whiffle balls on the parachute. Have the children start to "heat" the pan with little waves, getting hotter and hotter as the waves grow bigger and bigger. Continue play until all of the "popcorn" is "popped" off the parachute.
2.  "Color First"—Place two yarn balls under the parachute, one yellow and one blue. Divide the class into two teams; each team is spread out holding one half of the parachute. Have each team count off consecutively so that each player has a number. One team is designated as yellow, one as blue. When a number is called by the teacher, the two children from opposite teams that have that number will go under the parachute, pick up their team's ball and stuff it out through the hole in the center of the parachute. The first one out gets the point. The command for this game would be 1-2-3-lift-FIVES!" In this case the children whose number is 5 would go under the parachute, which will settle down upon the players in the center. Variation: use 4 different colored balls and four teams instead of two, but caution the children about bumping into each other under the parachute.

3. Using the same team format as in #2, have two different colored foam or nerf balls on the top of the parachute. The object for the yellow team is to get the blue ball to pop off, the object for the blue team is to get the yellow ball to pop off. Players would use the wave technique to pop the balls. VARIATION: "Roly-Poly" have the teams try to roll their ball off on the opposite team's side while preventing the same happening to them.
4. "Run and Pass"—Have the children count off by 4s so that each has a number from one to four. Holding the parachute in the right hand the children jog slowly in a circle formation, turning the parachute around. When a number is called, those children drop their piece of parachute and run ahead to the next vacant spot where they take hold of the parachute once again.
5. "Shark Attack"—Have the children sit, holding their pieces of parachute drawn tightly to their waists. Send one child under to crawl around as the shark. When the shark touches someone's leg that child must go under and be a shark as well. Continue until there are six to eight sharks moving under the parachute.
6. "Litterbugs"—Under the parachute place numerous objects such as yarn balls and beanbags. Divide the class into four teams and have the teams count off so each child has a number. When the signal is given 1-2-3-lift-THREES!" the children with number three go under the parachute and collect as many objects as they can before the parachute touches them. They must get out before being touched in order for their objects to count. Replace the objects before the next lift.
7. "Space Missiles"—Divide the class into two teams, one is spread around the parachute, the other is spread around the outside of the team that has the parachute. Place numerous yarn balls and whiffle balls on the parachute. On the signal to go, the team holding the parachute tries to get the balls off by making waves; the outside team tries to catch the balls and throw them back on. When time is up the number of balls on the parachute is the score for the throwing team. Change roles and repeat.
8. "Spelling Bee"—Divide the class into 4 groups, each numbered consecutively. Using the class' spelling words for the day or week, call 1-2-3-lift-ONES!" In the blank insert one of the spelling words. The number ls have to run under the parachute to the center, spell the word loudly and run back to their spots.
9. "Math Mania"—Same format as #8 but call out mathematical problems so that the children must call the answer before coming back out.
10. "Follow the Director"—One child is chosen to be the director. The director will call out various stunts to be performed with the parachute; example: Mushroom, Merry Go Round, Pass the Parachute, etc. The director calls out one activity, all students participate. The director then calls out another activity. After two or three activities, the teacher picks a new director.
11. "Stunts Under The Big Top"—1-2-3-lift, the children will make an umbrella. The students have been numbered off from 1 to 6. When the teacher calls a number, example 6, all students with that number come to the middle of the parachute an perform a stunt. Children need to be cautioned that they may not do gymnastic stunts for safety purposes. Such stunts as jumping jacks, toe touches, push-ups etc. may be given as examples. Children are given an opportunity to use their creative abilities. Children also need to be informed that they must do their stunts quickly as the parachute will soon descend.
12. "Goblins" - 1-2-3 lift, the children lift the parachute and on the signal, all will release the parachute, while keeping their arms straight overhead and remaining stationary. The parachute will land covering part of the group who will resemble goblins. The

children who have not been covered by the parachute will attempt to guess who the goblins are.

13. "Scrambled Body Parts"—The children have been numbered off from 1 to 6. 1,2,3 lift, on the signal given by the teacher all children lift the parachute high. The teacher calls a number and a body part, for example "3s shoulder to shoulder." All of the number 3s move to the center of the parachute and attempt to touch shoulders with each of the other number 3s before the parachute descends. Some examples of appropriate body parts are elbows, wrists, hands, thumbs, ankles, hips, ears, toes, heads, knees, and any other appropriate command.

14. "Who Is In The Middle?"—The children have been numbered off from 1 to 6. The teacher selects one number, example 4. All of the 4s blind their eyes. The rest of the class lifts the parachute and the teacher calls another number, example 2. All of the children with number 2 move to the middle of the parachute and sit down. Everyone else sits down on the parachute. Those students whose eyes were blinded may now look. The number 4s attempt to guess who are the children (number 2s) who are sitting under the parachute.

# Scoops and Balls

The use of scoops and balls contributes to the child's development in eye-hand coordination. The scoop serves as an extension of the child's hand and therefore increases the difficulty of the throwing and catching tasks. Skill work with the scoops and balls is best done in partners, and, once the skills are reasonably well refined, the scoops and balls may be used in game situations. Many of the games in the "Developmentally Appropriate Games" chapter that require a ball may be done with the scoops and balls as well.

## *Partner Activities*

Since throwing with the scoop is difficult, you should begin with the rolls, tosses and throws coming from the hand alone. The emphasis at first is on catching with the scoop. The children should learn to reach out to the oncoming ball and "give" or bring the arm back with the ball when it is in the scoop. The "give" will prevent the ball from bouncing out. A good suggestion might be to use yarn balls instead of whiffle balls as is traditional.

1.  Have partner #1 roll the ball with the hand to partner #2 who tries to catch the ball in the scoop. #2 then puts the scoop down and rolls it with the hand to #1. The children will learn to tip the scoop so that its front edge is flat with the floor. Increase the distances between those partners who meet with success.

2.  Repeat #1 but have the partner throw the ball with the hand on a bounce toward the partner with the scoop. Continue as in #1.

3.  Have partner #1 do an underhand toss with the hand to partner #2 who tries to catch the ball in the scoop. #2 then puts the scoop down and tosses it with the hand to #1. Continue to practice the task and increase distance with success.

4.  With partners across the play area from each other, have #1 roll the ball toward #2 who must run to the ball and scoop it up. From this point have #2 throw the ball back to #1 out of the scoop (encourage the children to use the overhand throwing motion and release with a snap of the wrist, scoop held vertically at this point). Continue with #1 rolling and #2 throwing for ten tries, then change roles.

5.  Repeat #4 but have the ball thrown on a bounce to #2 (yarn balls will not work in this task).

6.  Have partners move closer together and try to toss (underhand) the ball from scoop to scoop. In this case the catch will be an underhand catch. The toss will require that the child release the ball with the scoop tipped slightly downward. Gradually increase the distance between partners.

7.  Standing farther apart, have the children throw the ball out of the scoop overhand to the partner. The catch in this instance should be made with the scoop held vertically in the air, turning and giving with the ball when it hits the scoop. This task will be more difficult than the underhand catch.

8.  Have partners work together, trying different throws and catches; introduce the sidearm throw to produce a bouncing ball for the partner to catch.

9.  Have the children see how many throws and catches they can complete in a row before dropping the ball.

10. Have the children take a second ball and each partner works in self-space on different "tricks" he/she can do alone with the scoop and ball.

11. Have the children practice throwing to the wall and catching the returns.

12. Have the partners work together to see if they can throw and catch with two balls at the same time.

13. On the signal from the teacher have children change partners so they are able to work with students of varying abilities.

14. Repeat #13 several times so students are able to work with a variety of students.

15. On the signal from the teacher children will exchange the balls they are using for a different variety.

16. Repeat #15 several times in order to give students an opportunity to work with a number of different types of balls.

## *Games*

1.  "Keep Away"—Divide the class into four teams so that two games can go on at once. Each child has a scoop and wears an identifying pinnie to show which team he/she is on. The game begins with a toss in from the sideline by one of the teams (the one that "wins the toss of a coin"). From then on each team sees how many passes they can make successfully within their team before an interception by the opposing team. When the opposing team makes an interception, the team members count the number of passes

that they can complete before another interception occurs. Remind players that this is a non-contact game and interceptions or chasing and scooping up of a missed ball are the only ways a team may gain control of the ball. After a designated time limit rotate teams so that they can play against someone different. Have them keep track of their best passing score.

2.  "Scoop LaCrosse"—This game is played the same as in "Keepaway" but there are goals set at either end of the play area and the idea is to throw the ball into the goal to score for the team. The game begins with the teacher tossing the ball high between the two center players. Ideally there should be only six players per team, three on offense and three on defense. You may have more players depending on the size of the class and the play area available. Players may take only three steps with the ball in the scoop before passing it or shooting for a goal. No physical contact is permitted and the ball must be either intercepted or picked up from a miss for a turnover to the other team. If the ball goes out of bounds, either over an end line or over a sideline, the team that did not touch it last gets a throw-in. Depending on the skill level of the players involved, the teacher may wish to call fouls whenever a hand touches the ball. All plays should be made with the scoop. Variation: have players on scooters.

As mentioned previously, other games may be adapted for the use of scoops and balls. For example, traditional kickball could be changed so that the batter throws the ball from a scoop and the fielders all use scoops to play the game. Using these implements increases the difficulty of the game.

# Scooters

Gymnasium scooters are developmentally appropriate for fostering growth in arm and leg strength and endurance. They also contribute to the development of laterality, especially bilateral coordination.

## *Individual Activities*

1.  Have the child sit on the scooter and use legs to travel forward and then backward.
2.  Have the child kneel on the scooter and propel himself/herself with arms only.

3.  Have the child lie on the scooter in a prone position, scooter located under the abdomen, and propel himself/herself with arms only, with legs only, with a homolateral pattern, and with a contralateral pattern.
4.  Have the child place his/her hands on the sides of the scooter and run, holding and pushing the scooter throughout the play area.
5.  Using the skill from #4, have the child run and then jump on his/her knees onto the moving scooter for a ride. Then have him/her try jumping onto the scooter on his/her stomach; arch the back for the ride.

## *Partner Activities*

1.  Have partner #1 sit on the scooter Indian style while #2 pushes him/her around the play area, pushing hands should be on the lower back. Change roles on signal.
2.  Have partner #1 lie down in a prone position on the scooter with knees bent, lower legs up. Partner #2 holds the feet and pushes #1 around the play area. Change roles on signal.
3.  Have partner #1 sit on the scooter Indian style, holding the end of a jump rope. Partner #2 holds the opposite end and pulls #1 around the play area. Change roles on signal.
4.  Repeat #3 with the rider in a prone position.
5.  "Wheelbarrow": Partner #1 holds scooter on the sides and supports self in a pushup position. Partner #2: Lifts #1s legs to either side of him/her and pushes the child as if he/she were a wheelbarrow. Change roles on signal.

## *Group Activities*

1.  "Scooter Cageball": Divide class into two teams. All members are sitting on scooters and may not get up from the scooter throughout the game. Each team tries to get the cageball, by kicking, throwing, or pushing to hit the wall of the play area opposite that of the team. Each time the ball hits the wall is one point. After a score, play begins again in the center of the play area when all players are back "on sides" and the teacher tosses the ball in.
2.  "Scooter Soccer": Divide class into four teams so there can be two games. Players must be on scooters at all times. The game is played the same as Scooter Cageball, but the children may not use their hands to propel the ball, and may use feet only. A nerf soccer ball would be appropriate for this game.
3.  "Scooter Lacrosse": Divide the class into four teams so that two games may be played at once. Each player has a scooter and a scoop. The object is to throw the ball into the hula hoop goal on the wall behind the opposing team. Players should pass the ball with the scoop from teammate to teammate to get the ball to the goal. When one team is on offense, the other should be on defense and try to intercept the passes. Once the ball is intercepted, play goes in the opposite direction. There are no goalies so defensive players must help to guard the goal.
    - Note: If there are not enough scooters available for every child to have one, the games may be played in the following way: The four teams are placed in the play area and six scooters are placed in the center of each game. The players are numbered off consecutively and they play in teams of three on three. After #s 1, 2, and 3 either score a goal or have been playing for two minutes without a score,

they return to the side and the next three, 4, 5, and 6 begin the game again. If there are 7 on a team, the next group to play would be 7, 1 and 2. An alternative to this is for the teacher to call numbers and the players run out, jump onto the scooters and play until a goal is scored or until two minutes is up. Players on the side should be able to move up and down the sidelines and help by receiving passes and sending the ball back into play.

4.  "Partner Scooter Relay Race" A team consists of two children. Each team has 1 scooter. Partners #1 all start at one end of the gymnasium where the scooters are already positioned, and where the race will begin. On the signal to go all #1s will propel themselves on their scooters to the opposite end of the gymnasium to their awaiting partners. Partners #2 may not cross the line at their end of the gymnasium and may not leave until #1 has crossed the line with the scooter. Partners #2 then propel themselves on the scooter back to the starting line. The first team finished is the winner. The race may be repeated several times using a different method to propel the scooter each time. On the signal from the teacher all of the 1s will move to the next person on their right in order to change teams.

## Summary

It is absolutely essential that children in the elementary school program, and especially those in grades K–2, have a constant exposure to manipulative skill activities. The establishment of eye-hand and eye-foot coordination is crucial in the development of an efficient and effective mover, and experiences with play objects contributes directly to growth in those areas. Too many teachers assume that K–2 physical education consists of merely playing games and do not realize that the children need the proper skills in order to play well and successfully. Games certainly are important and should be part of any lesson; however, you must keep in mind that physical education is a learning experience and therefore you must find a way to have learning occur through that play. Remember that you read earlier that games serve as laboratories to practice the skills learned. Use those laboratories to apply the skills and activities that you have just read about in this chapter.

## References and Suggested Readings

Gabbard, C.P., LeBlanc, E., & Lowy, S. (1989). *Game, dance, and gymnastic activities for children.*   Prentice-Hall.

Gabbard, C., Leblanc, E., & Lowy, S. (1994). *Physical education for children, building the foundation.* Prentice-Hall.

Gallahue, D.L. (2005). *Developmental physical education for all children.* Human Kinetics.

Gallahue, D.L. (1997). *Developmental physical education for today's children.* McGraw-Hill.

Gallahue, D.L. (1996). *Developmental physical education for today's children.* Macmillan.

Kirchner G. & Fishburne, G.J. (2001). *Physical education for elementary school children.*   McGraw Hill.

Kirchner G. & Fishburne, G.J. (1998). *Physical education for elementary school children.* Brown & Benchmark.

Kirchner G. & Fishburne, G.J. (1995). *Physical education for elementary school children.* Brown & Benchmark.

Kuntzelman, C., Kuntzelman, B., McGlynn, M. & McGlynn, G. (1984). *Aerobics with fun.* Fitness Finders.

Nichols, B. (2001). *Moving and learning: The elementary school physical education experience.*McGraw Hill.

Nichols, B. (1994). *Moving and learning: The elementary school physical education experience.* Times Mirror/Mosby.

Nichols, B. (1990). *Moving and learning.*Times Mirror/Mosby.

Orlick, T. (1996). *Cooperative sports and games.* Human Kinetics.

Orlick, T. (1996). *The cooperative sports and game-book.* Kendall/Hunt

Orlick, T. (1978). *The cooperative sports and game-book.* Pantheon.

Pangrazi, R.P. (2006). *Dynamic physical education for elementary school children.* Benjamin Cummings.

Pangrazi, R.P. (2003). *Dynamic physical education for elementary school children.* Benjamin Cummings.

Pangrazi, R.P. (1998). *Dynamic physical education for elementary school children.* Allyn & Bacon.

Pangrazi, R.P. & Dauer, V.P. (1995). *Dynamic physical education for elementary school children.* Allyn & Bacon.

Pangrazi, R.P. & Dauer, V.P. (1992). *Dynamic physical education for elementary school children.* Macmillan.

Siedentop, D., Herkowitz, J. & Rink, J. (1984). *Elementary physical education methods.* Prentice-Hall.

CHAPTER

# 11

# Sport Skill Development

Children should be applying learned skills to sport forms beginning in the third to fourth grade years and they should be selected so that children will learn skills for a lifetime of participation. Hopefully, the physical education program has been strong and children have had an adequate foundation established in manipulative and motor skills in order to move forward to these specialized sport skills. As indicated previously, a minimal number of sports should be taught each year to increase the likelihood of sound skill development and understanding.

First, basic skills should be introduced and practiced with developmentally appropriate equipment for games of a sport nature. The skills necessary for successful elementary school participation in sports as well as suggested equipment have been identified for each sport section. Drills are selected that will be challenging and fun for the children so that they may practice these skills in a positive environment.

Lead-up games have been given that teach different aspects of the sport. Elementary children should play 2–3 of these games per unit, and should play them several times in order to learn to develop strategy and skill in their execution. Just as one skill is not learned after only one attempt, a game does not provide learning in only one attempt.

Children should not play the parent game in the elementary school physical education program. The parent game does not provide for maximum participation, and children need to actively manipulate the sport object (e.g., ball, racquet, etc.) in order to develop sound skills. Playing the parent game would be suitable for play in the intramural program.

Since children need to participate in lead-up games to learn skills and strategies for play, children should be told that the way the games are played in physical education class are not the way the games are played in youth sport or in high school. This will help to eliminate confusion caused by well-meaning parents and siblings who tell the child that he/she is incorrect in the way he/she plays the game.

Sport is an integral part of our society. Our goal is to find at least one sport that a child will like and will be successful so that participation during leisure time becomes a part of his/

her life forever. The authors of your text have selected 5 sports that would be appropriate for elementary school physical education programs. There are many more sports, but with physical education scheduled only twice per week, and in some cases, less, it makes sense to concentrate on learning a few sports well rather than becoming acquainted with many. Also, we believe that doing the same sports every year for the entire physical education program, grades 3-12, result in too little time to establish any proficiency as well as creating boredom!

# Basketball

Basketball is a sport that is very popular in the United States. It was invented in 1891–92 by James Naismith in Springfield, Massachusetts, where the goals were old peach baskets! For children, learning of basketball skills helps in the development of hand-eye coordination, speed and agility. The usual pace of a good basketball drill or lead-up game will contribute significantly to aerobic fitness. Due to the popularity of basketball in society, it is an excellent sport to learn in a young child's sport education.

Most play areas in schools have basketball courts painted on the floor's surface. And, most play areas have baskets in place, usually at the regulation height of 10 feet. As the concept of developmentally appropriate physical education grows toward prominence, some schools are recognizing the need to have adjustable height baskets so that they may be lowered to accommodate the size of the elementary school child. Elementary school children should not be expected to become proficient at shooting at the 10' rim, and the creative teacher will find an alternative target that will allow the child to be successful and still learn the basic skills of basketball. For example, a hula hoop might be suspended from the basket frame to represent the basket for younger children. Due to the physical limitations of the child, it is not possible for him/her to learn skills that are biomechanically correct if targets are too

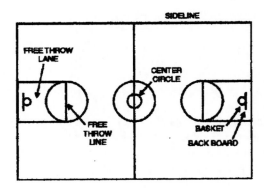

high, or if the basketballs are too large and heavy. Therefore, the height of the baskets should be adjusted and junior basketballs should be used.

## BASKETBALL SKILLS

There are many different skills that are used in the game of basketball at the varsity and intercollegiate levels. It is very important that the groundwork be laid for the potential to develop the highly specialized skills, and, therefore, there are certain basic skills that need to be developed in order to play basketball-type games successfully at the elementary school level. These skills are: dribbling, passing, catching, shooting and guarding.

*Dribbling*.  Dribbling refers to a method of moving the ball in the court. Players may not walk with the ball in the parent game, so they must dribble the ball if they are going to move their feet. Children should have mastered basic bouncing skills in grades K–2, and should be able to transfer this knowledge to dribbling. The dribble is executed by pushing the ball downward off the fingertips to the floor where it will rebound to the hand; the cupped hand lifts slightly with the rebound force of the ball and then pushes the ball down again. The player continues this sequence as he/she moves in the court. The ball should be slightly ahead of the player and slightly to the preferred side, for basic dribbling technique. The head of the dribbler should be up so that he/she can move efficiently in the space allowed and can keep teammates and opponents in view. Players should learn to dribble with both left and right hands.

*Passing*.  Passing is a method of sending the ball from one player to another. Players may learn to pass from a stationary stance and then from a moving position. There are three types of basic passes important to the game of basketball. Players use the chest pass, for short distance passes. The player holds the ball at chest level. The hands are held basically behind the ball with fingers spread to the sides and thumbs close to each other on the back of the ball. Elbows are held down by the sides. To pass the ball, the player steps toward his/her target and extends arms forward, releasing the ball toward the target.

The bounce pass is used to get the ball from one player to another when opponents are guarding on a high level, arms up. The player holds the ball with two hands at waist level, hands behind the ball, fingers spread to the sides. He/she then steps forward at the same time extending the arms and releasing the ball so that it contacts the floor approximately 2/3 of the way to the target player. The ball will then rise to the waist level of the catcher.

The overhead pass is the last basic pass needed by the beginning player. This pass is often used for in-bounding a ball from the sideline so that it goes over the heads of the opponents. The player stands with feet in a slight stride position with the ball held overhead. Hands are beneath the ball and fingers are spread upward on the sides. The player steps forward and releases the ball above and slightly in front of his/her head. The wrists snap on the release.

*Catching*.  Catching the ball involves use of the basic catching motion, but caution needs to be exercised in that the junior basketball is a harder ball than most children have experienced. Children should be taught to hold the hands in front with thumbs close and fingers spread out to the sides, not straight ahead. The ball should be caught with the fingers, and elbows bend to bring the ball in to the body, absorbing the force of the pass.

*Shooting*.  Shooting the ball is a favorite activity of children. As mentioned in the beginning, the basket should be at a height appropriate to the size of the child. It has been recommended that the height be between 7 and 9 feet. If the height requirements are met, and if the junior basketball is used, there is no reason that the grade 3 child cannot learn the basic set and jump shots that are used in basketball play. The player performs the set shot by facing the target, bending the knees slightly, holding the ball in the preferred hand just above and beside the ear, non-preferred hand resting behind the ball for support. The player holds eyes on the target, bends the knees, lifts, and extends the arms, flexing the wrist and putting spin onto the ball on release. The ball should follow an arc to the basket., The jump shot is the same basic action, but the player jumps into the air just prior to the arm extension. The set shot is used when the player is stationary; the jump shot is used mostly when the player is on the move.

*Guarding*.  Part of the game of basketball is defending the goal and attempting to intercept opponents' passes. The player learns to try to keep his/her body between the goal and the guarded player; in doing so, the player assumes a guarding stance. With knees bent, and upper body tilted slightly forward, the guard holds hands approximately shoulder height and toward the opponent. The player uses a shuffle step to move with the player being guarded.

It is not recommended that the "real" game of basketball be played in the elementary physical education class. However, it may be played in an after-school intramural program or in youth sport programs. The reasons include the facts that only ten children can play at one time, that unless skills are efficient and effective the game will not progress, and that the majority of students in the physical education classes will not possess these efficient skill levels. For those programs outside of the physical education class, the parent game is described as follows.

### *Title:*     *Basketball*
• *Level:* 5–6 Intramural Activity
*Skills Enhanced:* hand-eye coordination, speed, agility, spatial awareness, aerobic fitness
*Equipment Needed:* pinnies, one junior basketball
*Description:* Five players are on the floor at one time from each team. The object of the game is to score the most points through baskets. A basket made from the field is worth two points, from a free throw, one point. The game begins with a jump ball in the center circle between two players. Each tries to tap the ball to a member of his/her own team. The ball is then in play. During play the players may not walk with the ball without dribbling; dribble the ball, stop, and dribble again; step out of bounds with the ball; or stay more than three seconds in the offensive key without the ball. As a penalty for the above infractions, the opposing team takes a throw-in from the sideline. Also, the players may not have any physical contact. If physical contact occurs, a foul is called and the non-offender takes a free throw at the foul line. If the non-offender was in the act of shooting, he/she takes two free throws. Whenever the ball goes out of play, the opposing team takes a throw-in where the ball went out of bounds. After a basket, the non-scoring team takes the ball and throws it in from under the basket.

## TEACHING BASKETBALL SKILLS

Following the basic principles for teaching psychomotor skills, the skill should be demonstrated with auditory cues, and should be practiced through to refinement. Once the skill works well in a closed environment, it should be applied in drills that incorporate moving. Drills may be used for different aspects of practice but the teacher should take care to make the drills both meaningful and fun. Only after the players have become relatively skillful should the skills be used in many lead-up games. Lack of skill will provide for frustration in playing.

## *Skill/Drill Activities for Fun and Success*

The following drill activities are designed for maximum participation. All children will be working at the same time, which will contribute significantly to spatial awareness and ball and body control.

*Title:*     ***Dribble My Way***
- *Level:* 3–6

*Skills Enhanced:* dribbling, ball control
*Equipment Needed:* junior basketball per student
*Description:* Each child has a ball and the children stand in scatter formation in the gymnasium facing the teacher. The teacher dribbles the ball while moving left, right, forward and backward, using left and right hands and alternating same. The children imitate the teacher and dribble the same way going in the same directions.

*Title:*     ***Hoop Around***
- *Level:* 3–6

*Skills Enhanced:* dribbling, ball control
*Equipment Needed:* a hula hoop and a junior basketball for every student
*Description:* Each player has his/her own hoop and ball. The player moves around the hoop while dribbling the ball in the hoop, dribbles by alternating left and right hands with the ball bouncing inside the hoop, and stands inside the hoop and dribbles the ball around the outside.

*Title:*     ***Dribble and Split***
- *Level:* 3–6

*Skills Enhanced:* dribbling, agility
*Equipment Needed:* a junior basketball for every student
*Description:* Players follow each other in lines of four, dribbling the basketballs. On a signal from the teacher they break away from their group and dribble throughout general space, returning quickly to follow in 4s on the next signal. Continue to give the signals at different intervals of time.

*Title:*     ***Knock It Off***
- *Level:* 3–6

*Skills Enhanced:* dribbling, ball control
*Equipment Needed:* junior basketballs for half of the class.
*Description:* Players are in scattered formation throughout the basketball court. One half of the players have basketballs, half do not. Players dribble the balls anywhere in the court while stationary players try to knock the balls away from the dribblers. Non-dribblers may move only one foot in the attempt to knock a ball away.
*Variation*: All dribble except for three children who can move in the area and try to tap the balls away from the dribblers. Any child losing a ball becomes a tagger, taggers become dribblers.

**Title:** _One on One_
- _Level:_ 3–6

_Skills Enhanced:_ dribbling, guarding, agility
_Equipment Needed:_ junior basketballs for half of the class
_Description:_ One player dribbles while the other assumes a defensive guarding stance and travels the court facing the dribbler as he/she moves around the court. On the signal from the teacher, roles are reversed.
_Variation_: Signals can be given to indicate when to speed up or slow down.

**Title:** _Pass Me By_
- _Level:_ 3–6

_Skills Enhanced:_ passing, moving to open space
_Equipment Needed:_ junior basketballs for one-third of the class
_Description:_ Players form groups of three. One is to pass the ball in from the sideline to the intended receiver. The third player is the guard and tries to intercept the pass. After each five passes change roles.
_Variation:_ The passing players are now moving on the basketball court, the guards are trying to intercept.

**Title:** _Snatch_
- _Level:_ 3–6

_Skills Enhanced:_ passing, moving to open spaces, guarding
_Equipment Needed:_ 6–8 junior basketballs
_Description:_ Playing two on two, each two-person team tries to complete as many passes as possible without being intercepted. When an interception occurs, the intercepting team then completes as many passes as possible.

**Title:** _Stay Out_
- _Level:_ 3–6

_Skills Enhanced:_ dribbling, guarding, agility
_Equipment Needed:_ junior basketballs for half of the class
_Description:_ Tape boxes 6' x 6' on the floor. The guard is inside the box; the dribbler tries to pass through the box. The guard's goal is to keep the dribbler out by shuffling in the defensive position and deterring the dribbler. The goal of the dribbler is to pass through the box as many times as possible without losing the ball.

**Title:** _Guard Ball_
- _Level:_ 3–6

_Skills Enhanced:_ passing, guarding
_Equipment Needed:_ 4–6 junior basketballs
_Description:_ Players form teams of three and three teams work together in this format:

    **A A A**
    **B B B**
    **C C C**

Each member of Team A has a ball. Team A tries to pass the ball to Team C without interception by Team B. Teams A and C should count the number of completed passes in the time allowed. Then rotate team positions.

*Title:*     ***Set and Shoot***
- *Level:* 5–6

*Skills Enhanced:* passing, set shot

*Equipment Needed: 6 junior basketballs*

*Description*: With players in groups of five or six at each basket, the leader stands under the basket with a ball. The others stand in a semi-circle facing the basket. The leader throws to the first player who does a set shot; the leader rebounds the ball and passes to the second person. After the last person shoots, he/she rebounds his/her own ball and passes immediately to the leader who is now in the position of the first player on the semi-circle (others have shifted one position to the left).

*Variation:* players take a jump shot from the pass; after the rebounder passes the ball he/she immediately goes to the shooting player and assumes a guarding stance, trying to divert the shot.

## LEAD-UP GAMES

The following games have been selected to reinforce practice of basic basketball skills. They progress in difficulty and should be used in the basketball unit as the actual games that are played. Whenever possible teams should have a minimal number of players and several games should be played, depending on the facilities available. Remember, the parent game of basketball should not be played as a part of the elementary physical education program but may be played in intramural programs or in after-school sports.

*Title:*     ***Dribble Mania***
- *Level:* 3–6

*Skills Enhanced:* dribbling, spatial awareness

*Equipment Needed:* one junior basketball per player

*Description*: Students are in scattered formation in the play area, each dribbling a ball. On signal all children move and dribble the balls within the play area. If any two children touch each other, both must dribble around the entire perimeter of the area and then return to the game. The teacher should gradually reduce the size of the play area increasing the difficulty of controlling the body and the ball. Variation: As children are dribbling, they also try to tap other players' balls away. If a player does lose control, he/she must take the ball and dribble around the perimeter before rejoining the game.

*Title:*     ***Four and Out***
- *Level:* 3–6

*Skills Enhanced:* passing, catching, moving to open spaces, guarding

*Equipment Needed:* pinnies to designate teams, one junior-sized basketball per game

*Description:* Two teams, four players per team, spread out within the play area. Play begins with one team taking the ball out of bounds and passing it in to a teammate. The object of the game is for a team to complete four passes without interception by a member of the opposite team. On the completion of four consecutive passes, the scoring team gets one point and the ball is taken out on the side by the opposing team. If an interception occurs, the intercepting team immediately tries to complete four consecutive passes. It is illegal for two players to pass the ball back and forth between only themselves; at least a third player must be involved; it is illegal for any physical contact to occur. Players may not move when in possession of the ball but must pass it. Penalty for any of these infractions is a turnover of the ball to the opposing team.

Variation: To increase the difficulty of the game the teacher may designate the kind of pass that the students must use; dribbling may be allowed in between passes; additional players may be on the sidelines and may receive and throw the ball but may not move from their positions.

### Title:    *Rapid Repeaters*
- *Level:* 5–6

*Skills Enhanced:* shooting and dribbling

*Equipment Needed:* 24 junior basketballs

*Description*: A team consists of 12 players. There are 2 teams. 24 balls are placed on the center line with spacing in between. Teams line up on the end line at opposite ends of the court. One team is designated as the shooting team while the other is the dribbling team. When the whistle blows both teams run to the center line and pick up a ball. The shooting team players dribble on their own half of the court to one of the hoops and shoot, making as many baskets as possible. At the same time all the players on the dribbling team will dribble three times around the large rectangle on their half of the court, staying on the line formed by the sidelines and end line. Any player committing a dribbling violation

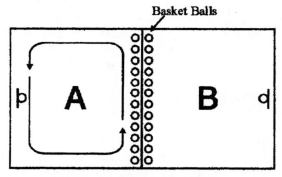

**Bs shoot at basket on their half**
**As dribble around a rectangle on their half**

must make an extra trip around the rectangle. All baskets are counted as points. Shooting stops when the last person on the dribbling team has made it around three times. At this point scores are reported and teams switch activities. The dribblers then become shooters and play begins again on the whistle.

### Title:    *Five Star Challenge*
- *Level:* 5–6

*Skills Enhanced:* chest pass

*Equipment Needed:* 10 junior basketballs

*Description:* A team consists of 5 players. There are 5 teams. Each team forms its own circle. The diameter of the circle is approximately 15 feet. Players 1 and 2 start out with the basketballs. Players number off consecutively from one to five counterclockwise. Players are given a specific star pattern in which to pass the ball. The object is to see how many times the pattern can be repeated successfully. Both basketballs are being passed at the same time. If the ball is dropped or the pattern is incorrect, the team starts over. Player 2

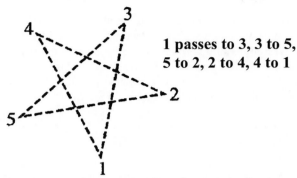

**1 passes to 3, 3 to 5,
5 to 2, 2 to 4, 4 to 1**

passes his/her ball as player 1 is passing his/her ball. The pattern is: 1 passes to 3, 3 to 5, 5 to 2, 2 to 4, and 4 to 1. A chest pass is used in order to pass the ball.

***Title:*** ***Pass and Trot***
• *Level:* 5–6
*Skills Enhanced:* passing, catching
*Equipment Needed:* one junior basketball per team
*Description:* A team consists of no more than 6 players. There are 4 teams. On opposite sides of the court each team forms a large circle. Players are reminded to keep the diameter of the circle constant. Team members number off consecutively. At the sound of the whistle both teams jog counterclockwise with one person standing in the center with a basketball. The person in the center passes the ball in order to each person on the circle. The chest pass is used when throwing the ball. When the last player receives the ball he/she throws it back to the center and yells "stop". Player 2 and the center person trade places. The first person in the center is number one. If a pass is missed or dropped it must be repeated until done correctly. The circle may move in the opposite direction on alternate rotations. Players may also move in different ways each rotation such as skipping, galloping, etc.

***Title:*** ***Dribble and Shoot***
• *Level:* 5–6
*Skills Enhanced:* dribbling, passing, and shooting
*Equipment Needed:* 20 bowling pins, 12 junior basketballs
*Description:* A team consists of 6 players. There are 4 teams. Two games are going on at the same time, one on each half of the court. Each team has 5 bowling pins placed on the end line, at the corner closest to their own team. Teams line up equidistantly under the basket on the end line. The first two players on each team have basketballs. On the signal to

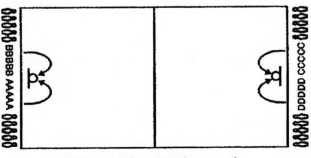

**2 Games going on at the same time**

go, the first player on each team dribbles to the closest end basket and shoots once. Both players are shooting at the same basket. If the player makes the shot he/she takes one of the other team's bowling pins and carries it back to the half court line, while dribbling the basketball. When the dribbler reaches half court he/she passes the ball to the next person in line. The bowling pin is then carried and placed with his/her team's pins. If the player fails to dribble while carrying the pin he/she has to put the pin

back. If the player misses the basket he/she dribbles back to half court and passes the ball to the next player. The second player may leave as soon as the first player has taken one shot at the basket.

### Title:    *Basketball Snatch Ball*
*Level:* 4–6
*Skills Enhanced:* dribbling, shooting
*Equipment Needed:* 4 hula hoops and 4 junior basketballs
*Description:* There are four teams of 6 players. Two teams play on each half court and stand side by side on the sideline of the court, across from each other. Each child has an assigned number. The hula hoops are placed in the center of the play area, a ball in each hoop. The teacher calls a number and the children with that number run to their team's ball, pick it up and dribble to the basket where they shoot until they make the basket, dribble back and place the ball in the hoop. The first one to replace the ball in the hoop earns one point for his /her team. At this point the other shooters return their basketballs to the respective hoops.
*Variation*: For 5th and 6th grade only, call two numbers. The first number called gets the ball and is the shooter, the second number called guards the opponent as he/she tries to dribble in and shoot a basket. The guard tries to get the ball and dribble back to the hoop for

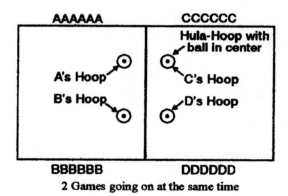

2 Games going on at the same time

a point; the shooter gets two points if a basket is made. For further complexity the teacher may call four numbers, the first two being guards and the second two being shooters.

### Title:    *Touch and Score*
•    *Level:* 5–6
*Skills Enhanced:* passing, agility
*Equipment Needed:* four junior basketballs

*Description:* Four teams, each in circle formation, with players numbered off consecutively so that each player has a number. When the player's number is called, he/she goes to an opponents' circle and stands in the middle. On the signal to go, the team members pass the ball quickly to players on the circle (it must go across the circle) while the opposing player tries to touch the ball. The first player to touch the ball wins a point for his/her team. The center players then go back to their own teams and another number is called.

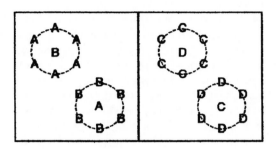

### Title:     *Flag Dribble*
- *Level:* 5–6

*Skills Enhanced:* dribbling, ball control

*Equipment Needed:* a flag football belt and a ball for each player

*Description:* Children are in scattered formation in the play area, wearing flags. All children move throughout the play area dribbling balls. At the same time, they try to take the flags off the belts of others. If a child's flag is removed, he/she must stay in place with his/her ball and, with legs spread, pass the ball in a figure eight around his/her legs until there is only one dribbler left. Then the game begins again.

### Title:     *4 Zone Basketball*
- *Level:* 5–6

*Skills Enhanced:* passing, dribbling, shooting, spacing

*Equipment Needed:* one junior basketball, pinnies

*Description:* Divide each half of the basketball court into 4 equal areas, one player from each team stands in each quadrant on each side. Players may move only in their assigned areas. They may pass to other active teammates or to players on the sidelines. They may dribble a maximum of three times before passing or shooting the ball. The game begins with a throw-in from a designated sideline player. The goal is to score a basket (two points).

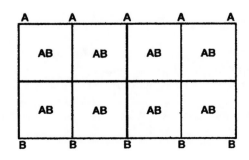

After a score, the sideline players become the active players and vice versa. The non-scoring team throws the ball in from the sideline. Children should rotate between end zone and mid-court zones at each switch.

### *Title:*    *Partner Basketball*
* *Level:* 4–6

*Skills Enhanced:* Guarding and Shooting

*Equipment Needed:* 4 junior basketballs and three sets of colored pinnies

*Description:* A team consists of two players. There are 12 teams. Players are matched by their abilities if possible. Four basketball hoops are needed for this game. Each basketball hoop is assigned a number, 1 through 4. Teams 1 & 2 play against each other at hoop number one and team 3 is also assigned to hoop one and is the waiting team. The waiting team comes in when a basket is scored or an infraction occurs. The waiting team always comes into the game as the defensive team. One of the two starting teams plays offense and the other team plays defense. If the offensive team scores the waiting team comes in as defense, and the defensive team goes out and becomes the waiting team. If the defensive team during play, gains possession of the ball they become the offensive team, and the waiting team comes in as defense. If a player is fouled while shooting, the basket will count and the waiting team comes in as defense. Only the side lines are considered out of bounds. Offensive players continue shooting without having to take the ball back to the half court. Any team having 2 non-shooting fouls must change places with the waiting team. At the end of a 5 minute period, the winning team stays at the present hoop and the other 2 teams rotate to a different hoop.

### *Title:*    *Sideline Basketball*
* *Level:* 5–6

*Skills Enhanced:* passing, catching, dribbling, shooting

*Equipment Needed:* one junior sized basketball

*Description:* Divide the class into two teams, half on the court and half spread out along the sideline. The teacher tosses a jump ball in the center between two opponents. The players jump and tap the ball toward a team member. Once the ball is in play the following rules apply:
* A player must dribble the ball in order to move;
* A player may not dribble, stop and dribble again; ·
* A player may not make physical contact with another;
* Sideline players may not shoot for the basket;

Players use their passing skills in the game and may pass to the players on the sideline as well at to those on the court. The goal is to score a basket, receiving two points. After a basket is scored, or two minutes are up (whichever comes first), the teams change between sideline and court players. A jump ball again begins the play.

### *Title:*    *Halfcourt Basketball*
* *Level:* 5–6

*Skills Enhanced:* dribbling, passing, shooting, spatial awareness

*Equipment Needed:* pinnies, one ball per game

*Description:* Two teams will be playing on 1/2 court with two teams on the other 1/2 court while the 3rd team or teams stand on sideline. In teams of five, the children play basketball on the 1/2 court, following the rules of basketball with the exception of dribbling which is

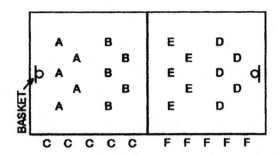

limited to two dribbles. As soon as a basket is scored, the third team takes the losing team's place. Play begins with a pass in from the sideline by the non-scoring team.

# Racquet and Paddle Games:  Pickleball, Badminton and Tennis

The development of racquet and paddle skills can enhance agility, striking, endurance, and eye-hand coordination. Pickleball, badminton and tennis are complex perceptual-motor skill sports that require the player to predict the flight of the object and subsequently position oneself to be able to return the object in such a manner that the opponent is unable to hit it back over the net. Most children will not be able to be highly successful in tennis or badminton at this stage, but they will be able to develop hand-eye coordination through striking-like activities.

Most elementary schools have volleyball nets and poles that can be adapted for tennis, badminton or pickleball. Most schools also have a playground area that could be utilized for this purpose. It is not necessary for tennis courts to be provided. Striking skills for these individual sports need to be taught from a developmentally appropriate perspective.  Skills should first be taught with a paddle and then progress to shortened versions of the different racquets. Regulation wooden racquets can be shortened by cutting off part of the handle and using the gripping material to re-grip the shortened handle. The shortening of the racquet allows for greater success when learning the striking skills. There is a number of super bounce foam balls, as well as a variety of other balls which may be used that will be easy to strike. Students need to be instructed to watch out for others when swinging racquets as well as when moving into someone else's area to retrieve a ball.

In some cases it will be appropriate to play the parent game with these individual sports if your facilities allow.  Logical progression would involve pickleball, badminton and then tennis. Therefore, we have given the basic rules for the three activities below. Following those descriptions are skill/drills and lead-up games that you may use to help children develop skills in hand-eye coordination so that they may move toward success in paddle and racquet sports.

### *Title: Pickleball*
* *Level:* Late Grade 3 through Grade 6
*Skills Enhanced:*  hand-eye coordination, timing, spatial awareness, teamwork
*Equipment Needed:* wooden paddle for each player, one whiffle ball per game
*Description:*  The game is played in a doubles format, although it may be adapted for singles play. The serve starts with the player in the right-hand court and goes diagonally across the net to the opponent. The sever must have one foot behind the back line and serves

underhand. The opponent MUST allow the ball to bounce once before hitting it back, and the opponents must let it bounce once before hitting it. From then on the ball may bounce once or not as play continues. Points are scored only for the serving team. When the game begins the serving team is allowed to have only the right-hand court player serve. He/she continues to serve, alternating sides of the court for the serve, until the receiving team wins the serve. From then on, each team member serves until the receiving team stops him/her. Then the serve goes to the two members of the other team.

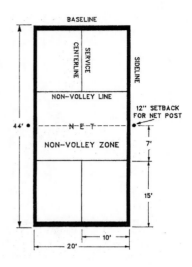

"Faults" in the game are: hitting the ball out of bounds, not clearing the net with the ball, volleying in the no-volley zone, or not having one foot behind the back line on the serve. When a fault occurs, the serve goes to the next person in order. A game is played to 11 points and a team must win by two.

## BADMINTON

Often regarded as a backyard recreational game, badminton is actually a high speed/ fast-paced game that is played indoors and is an Olympic sport. If teaching tennis, it is best to use the outdoor shuttlecocks (rubber bases) for young children. At the elementary stage, we suggest developing the backyard form of badminton and saving the fast-paced competitive form for high school.

### Title: Badminton

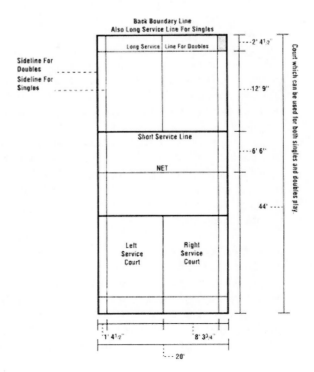

- *Level:* The parent game is not recommended for elementary school students. Modified game play is suggested for children in grades 4-6.

*Skills Enhanced:* hand-eye coordination, timing, spatial awareness, teamwork

*Equipment Needed:* badminton racquet for each player, one shuttlecock per game

*Description*: There are two versions of badminton, singles and doubles.

**Singles.** In the singles games, a player is responsible for the entire side of the court minus the side alleys. One player serves until he/she loses the point, and the serve then goes to the opponent. The serve must go across the net to the court diagonally from the server. To begin the game, the server serves from the deuce court. He/she then serves alternately from the ad court, then the deuce court, depending on the score. During the game, when a player first receives the serve, he/she serves from the deuce court if his/her score is even and from the ad court if his/her score is odd. Once the shuttlecock has been served, it is in play and may be hit by the opponent. The object is to return the shuttlecock so that the opponent misses or hits it out of play. Scoring is one point per turn; males play to a score of 15 and females to a score of 11 in singles. Special rules apply in badminton if scores are tied at different points; it is beyond the scope of this book to go into minute technicalities. Suffice it to say that a player must win by two points. Faults occur if: a server does not have two feet in contact with the ground on the serve, a player does not serve underhand, or if the shuttlecock is caught on the racquet and "flung" over the net (this is called a "carry"). Also, a player may not touch the net on a play, nor reach over the net to hit the shuttlecock.

**Doubles.** Doubles partners are identified as "deuce" or "ad." This is important to remember because partners switch sides for each serve of their own team and remain on the appropriate side to receive serves from the opponents. So, the "deuce" player is always in the "deuce" court when the score is even and in the "ad" court when the score is odd. The "ad" player is always on the "ad" side when the score is even and on the "deuce" side when the score is odd. When a doubles game first begins, the serving side has the "deuce" player serve until losing the point. At that time the serve goes to the "deuce" player on the opposing team. He or she serves until losing the point, and then his/her partner serves until the point is lost. At that point, serve switches to the opponents and the player standing in the "deuce" court serves, continuing until losing the point. His/her partner then serves. Only on the first service of the game does the partner not have a chance to serve. Both males and females play until 15 points in doubles and must win by two points. The same faults apply as in singles. If interested, you may find the more intricate rules to badminton on the internet.

## TENNIS

Tennis is an individual racquet sport which is popular all over the world and is played on both indoor and outdoor courts. Tennis originated from a game comparable to handball which was played by the ancient Greeks and Romans.

It is definitely not recommended that the parent game of tennis be played at the elementary school level. Although some children are very skilled at this age, the majority are not. Tennis skills are very difficult to learn; the purpose of including tennis here is to have a sport unit that involves racquet skills stressing hand-eye coordination with an implement. The basic rules for tennis follow only for informational purposes. If students do learn how the "real game" is played, it will contribute to cognitive knowledge for appreciation of the sport.

*Title:*     *Tennis*
- *Level:* The parent game is not recommended for elementary school students.
*Skills Enhanced:* hand-eye coordination, spatial awareness, working with a partner, strategy building
*Equipment Needed:* tennis racquet for each player, three tennis balls per court.

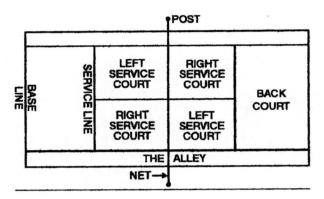

*Description*: There are two versions of tennis, singles and doubles.

***Singles.*** In the singles games, a player is responsible for the entire side of the court minus the side alleys. One player serves the entire game and points are scored after each serve and rally episode either for the player or the opponent. The serve must go into the serving box diagonally across the net from the server. The serve must bounce before the opponent may hit it back. It may bounce only once before being returned. The server serves first from the deuce court (the server's right hand court). The server has two chances to make a good serve. A serve that hits the net and does not go into the service area afterwards is a fault; a serve that hits the net and does go into the service area afterwards is called a "let" and the server may take that serve over. There is no limit to the number of "lets" a server may make. Once the ball has been served it is in play and it may be hit in the air or after one bounce on a side. The object is to return the ball so that the opponent misses or hits the ball out of play. Scoring is 15 for the first point, 30 for the second, 40 for the third and Game for the fourth. If a score is tied at 40–40 it is called deuce, and the next serve will yield either "advantage in" (if the server wins the point) or "advantage out" (if the opponent wins the point). The next serve comes from the "ad" court (left court for the server) and depending on who wins the point will go back to deuce or to "Game." The player who wins after an original deuce must win by two points. A "set" is finished when one player has won 6 games. A "match" is usually when one player has won 2 out of 3 sets. If a set is tied at 6–6, a tie-breaker is played. It is beyond the scope of this book to teach a tie-breaker procedure. Players may not reach over the net to play a ball, run into the net, or hit the ball after more than one bounce.
***Doubles.*** Doubles players follow the same rules as for singles and scoring is the same, but the alleys are now in play. One server serves the entire game, the next game is served by the opponent in the deuce court. At the third game the serve comes to the first team to the player in the ad court, and then the fourth to the player on the opponents' side in the ad court. This sequence continues for the duration of a set. Servers always begin games by serving from the deuce court; when a doubles team is receiving the serve one player always starts in the deuce court and one in the ad court. They must receive in these positions for every game in the set. If they wish to change sides for a second set, they may, but they must remain in those receiving positions for serves. After a serve has been received, players may move anywhere on the court.

# Skill Progression for Paddle and Racquet Games

When children learn to use striking skills, they should begin with the hand as an implement, progressing to a lightweight paddle, on to a bigger paddle, shortened racquets, and, finally, junior size racquets. If the physical education program has been developmentally appropriate, the children in preK-Grade 2 have had lots of experience with manipulative skills in progression. By the latter part of third grade the children should be ready to work with paddles and possibly shortened racquets. As in the other sports in this chapter, we have identified the skills that children will need to develop in order to be successful in paddle and racquet games. We acknowledge that skills will be expanded and refined in secondary school years and these are only the basics. To ask for more would not be developmentally appropriate. Progression calls for the child to use equipment that is appropriate for his/her size and skill level; eventually, with proficiency, the child can move on to more specialized equipment.

## FOREHAND STRIKING

The child should stand sideways to the target with preferred side away from the target. He/she should drop the ball for a bounce, and bring the preferred hand and arm backward, swing through, coming from below the waist and contact the ball at just below waist level, extending toward the target. The child should step forward with the opposite foot. Once the underhand form is achieved, the child may add the sidearm strike to his/her repertoire. The striking implement will still swing from low to high, but will come from the side rather than from below the waist.

### *Forehand Return*

Here the child is now encountering an open environment and must intercept and return an object that is coming toward him/her. The child gauges where the ball will bounce, moves to it, positions him/herself sideways, and swings underhand, contacting the ball as above, extending toward the opponent. This will also progress to add a sidearm swing.

## BACKHAND STRIKING

Backhand is an extremely difficult skill in any striking game or activity. Backhand is done with the non-preferred side toward the target and is similar to the above forehand skills. Children should work on backhand skills only after developing competency in forehand.

### *Volley*

The volley refers to a hit that occurs before the ball bounces. In games with shuttlecocks, all of the game consists of volleying. The volley may be forehand or backhand and takes more accurate coincidence-anticipation timing than intercepting from a bounce.

## TEACHING RACQUET/PADDLE SKILLS

Skills should be introduced through demonstrations with auditory cues. The children will need to have many opportunities to practice developmentally appropriate racquet skills. Drill activities as well as lead-up games should be presented.

# Skill/Drill Activities for Fun and Success

*Title:*    ***Racquet/Paddle Dribble***
- *Level:* 3–6

*Skills Enhanced:* ball control

*Equipment Needed:* one shortened racquet/paddle and one appropriate ball for each student.

*Description:* Students are spread out throughout the play area. The racquet face is held parallel to the floor. Each student tries to dribble the ball on the face of the racquet by hitting the ball upwards. Students count the number of times they are able to dribble the ball without missing. This is performed in a stationary position. Students then try to bounce the ball on the floor with the racquet/paddle as many times as possible without losing control.

*Title:*    ***Rally Wall-Forehand Swing***
- *Level:* 3–6

*Skills Enhanced:* forehand swing as well as ball control.

*Equipment Needed:* one shortened racquet/paddle and one appropriate ball for each student.

*Description:* Each student is assigned his/her own space approximately 10 feet from the wall. Using the forehand swing, students practice rallying the ball against the wall allowing it to bounce only once between swings. All left handed players are placed at one end of the gymnasium in order to avoid collisions.

*Title:*    ***Rally Wall-Backhand Swing***
- *Level:* 5–6

*Skills Enhanced:* backhand swing as well as ball control

*Equipment Needed:* one shortened racquet/paddle and one appropriate ball for each student

*Description:* Each student is assigned a space about 10 feet from the wall. Using the backhand swing, students practice rallying the ball against the wall allowing it to bounce only one time with each swing. All left handed players are placed at one end of the gymnasium in order to avoid collisions.

*Title:*    ***Flip It Over***
- *Level:* 5–6

*Skills Enhanced:* ball control

*Equipment Needed:* one shortened racquet/paddle and one appropriate ball for each student.

*Description:* Each student is given a racquet/paddle and ball. The ball is dribbled against the face of the racquet/paddle first on one side of the racquet/paddle face then on the other. This is accomplished by turning the wrist in such a way that the racquet face turns completely over. This is performed in a stationary position.

*Title:*    ***Partner Rally***
- *Level:* 3–6

*Skills Enhanced:* ball control, forehand

*Equipment Needed:*  2 shortened racquet/paddles and appropriate ball

*Description:* Using a volleyball net which has been lowered to tennis position (by using a sliding ring on the volleyball pole) students will practice rallying the ball with a partner. The court has been divided into 6 rectangles (see diagram). There are 3 rectangular areas on

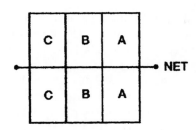

each side of the net. Students must stay in their own area (rectangle). Students practice rallying the balls to their partners using forehand swings and allowing the balls to bounce only one time. Students are to count the number of successful hits made without missing the ball.

### *Title:*  *Backhand Partner Rally*
- *Level:* 5–6

*Skills Enhanced:* backhand stroke, and rallying

*Equipment Needed:* 2 shortened racquet/paddles and one appropriate ball

*Description:* Using a volleyball net which has been lowered to tennis position (by using a sliding ring on a volleyball pole) students will practice rallying using their backhand swing whenever possible. The court has been divided into 6 rectangles. There are 3 rectangular areas on each side of the net. Students must stay in their own area (rectangle). Students should also watch out for other students and their racquets, especially those playing in adjacent rectangles. Students are to count the number of successful backhand rallies made without missing the ball.

### *Title:*  *Forehand and Backhand Partner Rally*
- *Level:* 6

*Skills Enhanced:* forehand and backhand rallies

*Equipment Needed:* 2 shortened racquet/paddles and one appropriate ball

*Description:* Using a tennis net and the court which has been divided into 6 rectangles, students will alternate using the forehand and backhand rallies with their partners. Students will count the number of successful rallies made without missing..

## *LEAD-UP GAMES*

The following games have been selected to reinforce practice of basic racquet/paddle skills. They progress in difficulty and should be used in the unit as the actual games that are played. Whenever possible teams should have a minimal number of players and several games should be played, depending on the facilities available. The parent game of tennis should not be played as a part of the elementary physical education program. The point is to work on a sport that involves a great deal of concentration and hand-eye coordination.

### *Title:*  *Four Square Tennis*
- *Level:* 3–6

*Skills Enhanced:* striking, and positioning oneself

*Equipment Needed:* one shortened racquet/paddle for each player, one appropriate ball and a court for each game

*Description:* There is a court consisting of a large square that has been divided into 4 smaller squares. Each square is eight feet by eight feet. The squares are numbered one through four. This game is played with four players, each player occupying one square. This game can be played either inside or outside, on a dry flat surface. The game begins with player number one bouncing the ball and hitting it with the racquet/paddle into one of the other squares. The player in the square in which the ball bounces hits the ball with the racquet after one bounce, into one of the other three squares. The game continues until a fault occurs. A fault occurs when the receiving player is unable to play the ball, the ball hits the line, or the ball goes out of bounds. The player causing the error moves to square four and each of the other players move up to the next level. The idea is to see how long a player can remain in square one.

### *Title:* ___*Oriental Racquet Ball*___
- *Level:* 5–6

*Skills Enhanced:* striking

*Equipment Needed:* one shortened racquet/paddle for each player and one appropriate ball

*Description:* Three players stand in a single file line, facing a wall space 10 feet away. Player number one bounces the ball then hitting it with the racquet on the rebound in such a way that the ball passes the service line on the court. The second player hits the ball with

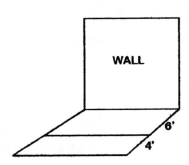

the racquet after one bounce. If the ball is hit successfully, player one continues. If the ball is missed player three replaces player one or 2, whichever player missed the ball. The ball may also be played directly off the wall, without a bounce on the floor. If the ball is not struck after one bounce from the floor, if the ball is not hit so it bounces from the floor to the wall, or if the ball is not hit so that it bounces past the six foot line, a fault is called. A fault results in the next player taking the place of the player committing the fault.

### *Title:* ___*Hit the Wall*___
- *Level:* 5–6

*Skills Enhanced:* forehand and backhand

*Equipment Needed:* one racquet/paddle for each player and one appropriate ball per game

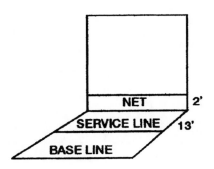

*Description:* There are two teams consisting of two players on each team. In this game, only the serving team may score. The same team continues serving until one of them commits a fault. Each time the opponent commits a fault, the serving team receives one point. If the serving team commits the fault the opposing team wins the serve. The first team to score 15 points is the winner. Team members alternate playing the ball as well as serving. Play begins with a serve, executed by bouncing the ball against the floor and hitting it with the racquet/paddle from the rebound in such a way that it hits the wall above the net line and rebounds in-bounds past the service line. A player from the opposing team hits the ball with the racquet in such a way that it hits above the net line. The ball may be played directly from the wall without a bounce. Play continues alternating players until a fault occurs.

Faults include:
- the ball is not served or returned above the net line
- the ball is hit out of bounds
- the ball does not hit the wall before hitting the floor
- the ball does not bounce beyond the service line on the serve.

### *Title:*    *Hit and Run*
- *Level:* 5–6

*Skills Enhanced:* running, striking

*Equipment Needed:* one shortened racquet/paddle for each player and one appropriate ball

*Description:* A team consists of 6 players. There are 2 teams, one on each side of the net. Teams form a single file line back by the service line. The first player hits the ball over the net and then runs to the opposite side of the court going to the end of the opposing team's line. The first player of the opponent's team hits the ball back and runs around the net to the other side's team, going to the end of that line. Play continues to see how many from each team are able to switch sides while keeping the ball in play.

### *Title:*    *Boss of the Court*
- *Level:* 5–6

*Skills Enhanced:* forehand, backhand

*Equipment Needed:* a shortened racquet/paddle for each player, one appropriate ball per game

*Description:* A team consists of 6 players. Two players play tennis singles on opposite sides of the net. As soon as the point is scored the winner (boss) remains and a new challenger from the other side enters the court. Teams line up on opposite sides of the net. Challengers

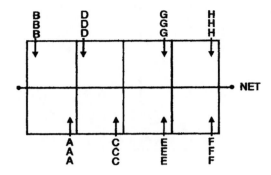

enter from the front of their own line. While team members are waiting their turn to be challenger or after coming out of the game, they will practice dribbling the ball against the floor using their racquet/paddles.

### *Title:* ***Sharp Shooter***

- *Level:* 3–6

*Skills Enhanced:* striking at a target

*Equipment Needed:* one shortened racquet/paddle for each player, one appropriate ball
One traffic cone or 3 plastic bowling pins for each team.

*Description:* A team consists of 4 members. A target is set up at the corner of the service area. One team will serve at the target on the other side of the net, while the opposing team will shoot at the target on the first team's side of the net. The target will be either a traffic cone or 3 plastic bowling pins. The first player will serve the ball 5 times attempting to hit the target. The last player on the other side of the net will set up the target when the target is hit. Players who are waiting their turn to serve at the target will practice dribbling the ball against the racquet, by hitting the ball upwards. After the server has 5 attempts at hitting the target, he/she will go to the end of his/her team's line, becoming the target setter for the opposing team. Players should keep track of how many targets they hit. The player with the highest score at the end of the activity is the winner.

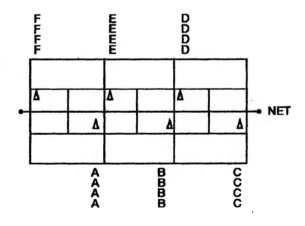

### *Title:*    *Rally Ball*

- *Level:* 5–6

*Skills Enhanced:* striking for accuracy, rallying, and serving

*Equipment Needed:* one shortened racquet/paddle for each player, one appropriate ball for each game.

*Description:* A team consists of 4 players. The court is divided in half. Two team members playing play against two team members on the other side. When a point is lost the next two players come into the game. The idea of this activity is to keep the rally going. A point is lost if a player hits the ball in such a way that the opponent is unable to return the ball. The play starts with a serve.

### *Title:*    *Volleying the Ball*

- *Level:* 5–6

*Skills Enhanced:* striking for accuracy, volleying.

*Equipment Needed:* one shortened racquet/paddle for each player, one appropriate ball for each game.

*Description:* A team consists of 4 players. Two team members play while 2 wait, dribbling the ball on alternate sides of the racquet while waiting. In this game no serves are allowed and the court is smaller. The ball is volleyed back and forth without hitting the ground. The team with the most volleys wins. When the point is lost, the two team members waiting replace the two that were playing. The idea in this game is to keep the volley going. A point is lost if a player hits the ball in such a way that the opponent is unable to return the ball.

### *Title:*    *Balance Ball*

- *Level:* 5–6

*Skills Enhanced:* striking for accuracy, playing close to the net, rallying

*Equipment Needed:* one shortened racquet/paddle for each player, one appropriate ball for each game.

*Description:* A team consists of 4 players. 2 players participate while the other two wait. While two players are waiting they will practice assorted dribbling skills of their choice. All four of the players in the game start at the net. Play begins by balancing the ball on the net. Whatever side the ball falls on, those players must return the ball. Play then continues as usual. When the point is scored, players return to the net and begin with a new balance on the net. When a point is lost the two players waiting take the place of those losing the point.

### *Title:*    *Three's A Crowd*

- *Level:* 5–6

*Skills Enhanced:* basic striking skills

*Equipment Needed:* one shortened racquet/paddle for each player, one appropriate ball for each game.

*Description:* There are three players on a side instead of two as in doubles. Two players play up at the net, while one player covers the baseline or backcourt. Instruct students that they must be sure to call out for the ball as well as to watch out for other players' racquets to avoid collisions. The backcourt player is the server and players rotate after each point.

# Soccer

The origin of soccer has been credited to Ireland, Greece, England and Italy where it is known as "football." It is credited as being the national sport of at least 53 countries. Of all the team sports, soccer is probably the easiest one for children to learn the basics and to play. Advantages for the child include refinement of eye-foot coordination, enhancement of agility, and development and maintenance of aerobic fitness.

Many youth sport programs have children as young as 5 years of age competing in soccer contests. Remembering that 11 on 11 play restricts the playing opportunities for children, it is still recommended that children in elementary physical education classes participate in soccer lead-up games with small teams versus participation in the parent game. Soccer as such may be played during intramural time and during youth sport programs.

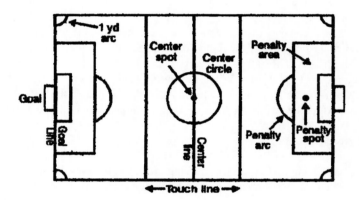

## SOCCER SKILLS

The skills basic to fundamental success at the elementary level in soccer are: dribbling, trapping, passing, and shooting. The throw-in and the punt may also be introduced. Goalkeeping skills involve the ability to catch the ball or to block an oncoming shot.

***Dribbling.*** Dribbling is a method for the individual player to use to carry the ball alone. Children should learn to tap the ball gently with the inside of the foot, alternating feet as they move with the ball. The taps should be short, keeping the ball relatively close to the player, making it difficult for other players to take it away.

***Trapping.*** Trapping is a ball control move, used to stop the ball from a pass or after an interception, where the player gains control over the ball. Children may learn to trap the ball with the inside of the foot, with the sole of the foot, or with the thigh or chest. When using the inside of the foot trap, the foot is turned outward and the ball force is absorbed by the surface of the foot; the sole of the foot trap involves placing the foot gently toward the top of the ball to stop the ball motion completely; and the thigh or chest traps involve "giving" with the ball force, or absorbing force with these body parts, causing the ball to drop and be played.

***Passing***.  Passing is used in the game of soccer to get the ball to teammates. The easiest pass is executed by contacting the ball with the inside of the foot and following through in the direction of the pass. Players may also pass with the outside of the foot for short distances; and, players may use a long pass kick when a lofted ball is desired. When performing the long pass the player contacts the ball with the top of the kicking foot, toe pointed down, so contact is on the laces of the shoe.

***Shooting***.  Players may use any of the passing skills to shoot for a goal. Taking a shot at the goal is essentially the same as passing.

***Throw-ins***.  Throw-ins occur when the ball passes out of the field of play over a sideline. The player from the opposing team holds the ball back with two hands behind the head and brings the ball forward and out, keeping both feet in contact with the ground.

***Punting***.  Punting is a skill used by the goalkeeper to clear the ball in a lofting manner. The player holds the ball approximately waist high in front of his/her body. The player steps forward with his/her kicking foot, then stepping on the non-kicking foot, bends the knee, extends the toe and swings forward with the kicking foot as the ball is dropped by the hands. Contact is made on the top of the foot, on the shoelaces, and the ball is lofted upward and outward.

It is strongly suggested that the official form of basic soccer, as described here, not be used in physical education classes but may be played in intramural programs. Lead-up games with small sized teams should be used to maximize participation and skill practice opportunities for children in physical education classes.

### *Title:*     *Soccer*
*   *Level:* 3–6 Intramural Activity
*Skills Enhanced:* dribbling, ball control, spatial awareness, agility, passing
*Equipment Needed:* a foam or junior soccer ball for every game
*Description*: Each team has eleven active players: one goalie, two fullbacks, three halfbacks, and five forward line players. The game begins with a kick-off by the designated -team; all players but the kicker must be outside of the center circle for the kick-off. After a goal is scored, the non-scoring team is awarded the kick-off. Players may not touch the ball with their hands, with the exception of the goalie. If a player touches the ball with his/her hands, a free kick is awarded on the spot to the opposing team. Usually the defensive players take the free kicks. Free kicks are also awarded for violations such as pushing, tripping, or any other physical contact between players. If the ball goes out of bounds over the sideline, the opposing team takes a throw-in. Again, usually the defensive players take the throw-ins so the forward line players (offensive) can move down the field. If the ball goes over the end line off the foot of the defending team, not in the goal, a corner kick is awarded to the offensive team. If the offensive team sends the ball over the end line, not in the goal, a goal kick is taken by either the goalie or a defensive fullback, 12 feet out from the goal. Direct kicks (goals may be scored) are awarded for all personal fouls; a penalty kick (with only the goalie to defend) is taken at the 12 foot mark toward the goal whenever a personal foul occurs within the penalty area by a defender; and an indirect free kick (a goal may not be scored) is given when a player taking the free kick touches the ball again before another player does or for dangerous plays.

## TEACHING SOCCER SKILLS

As with all sport-related skills, soccer skills should be taught in a progression from a closed skill to open skill. Since many of the soccer skills may have been developed through basic ball-handling practice, the closed format may represent practice of skills without opposition, and the open format may have opposing players to work against. Drills that are designed for development and refinement of these skills should be fun and interesting to the players.

Developmentally appropriate junior soccer balls should be used; dense foam soccer balls are even better. Since soccer does not allow players to catch the ball (other than the goalkeeper), players use their bodies to block the flight of the ball and subsequently to trap it. Removing the fear of injury from a hard soccer ball should ensure better quality of practice and play time.

# Skill/Drill Activities for Fun and Success

The following drill activities are designed for maximum participation. The more opportunities the child has to contact the ball, the better his/her skill will become.

*Title:*    *Dribble This Way, Dribble That*
- *Level:* 3–6

*Skills Enhanced:* dribbling, ball control, spatial awareness, agility
*Equipment Needed:* a junior soccer ball for every student
*Description*: Each child has a ball and the children are in scatter formation, facing the teacher. Have the children dribble the ball in various directions, at differing speeds, and changing directions and speeds on signal. Children should learn to trap the ball quickly on the whistle and proceed immediately upon the signal to go. They should learn to avoid collisions with others in the play area and to keep their own soccer balls under control at all times.

*Title:*    *Dribble and Pass*
- *Level:* 3–6

*Skills Enhanced:* dribbling, passing and spatial awareness
*Equipment Needed:* junior soccer balls for half of the class
*Description:* The children work with partners in the open space of the soccer play area, traveling together but maintaining a spacing of approximately 5–10 feet. One partner dribbles and on the signal passes immediately to the partner, who then dribbles the ball. On signal he/she passes the ball back.

*Title:* ___Pass and Go___

● *Level:* 3–6

*Skills Enhanced:* passing, spatial awareness and agility

*Equipment Needed:* 8–10 junior soccer balls

*Description:* Children work in threes and position themselves in a triangle position, approximately 5 yards apart. As player A passes the ball to B, he/she immediately runs around the triangle in the direction of the pass and back to his /her position. Player B immediately passes to C and runs. C passes to A, etc.

Variation: increase distance between players.

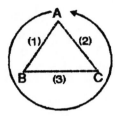

*Title:* ___Four Pass___

● *Level:* 3–6

*Skills Enhanced:* passing

*Equipment Needed:* 6–8 junior soccer balls

*Description:* "A" passes the ball to one player and immediately follows his/her pass to the new position. The ball is trapped by the receiving player and passed to another player, the passer then moves to follow the ball, following the pass.

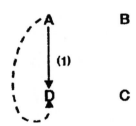

**Player passes ball and then
follows the ball**

*Title:* ___Pass Call Ball___

● *Level:* 3–6

*Skills Enhanced:* passing

*Equipment Needed:* 8–10 junior soccer balls

*Description:* Players work in groups of three, players are at three corners of the square formation. The player with the ball passes to the open corner while calling the name of one of the other players. The player whose name is called runs to intercept and trap the ball at the open space. He/she immediately passes the ball to the new open space and calls a name. Play continues in this fashion.

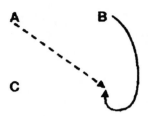

### Title:    *Single File*
- *Level:* 3–6

*Skills Enhanced:* dribbling, ball control, spatial awareness
*Equipment Needed:* junior soccer ball for every student
*Description:* Players each have soccer balls and dribble in single file lines of three. The first player leads the line as all three dribble throughout the play area. On signal, each player traps the ball, the first player leaves his/her ball and moves to the last ball, the other two players move to the ball ahead. The new leader resumes the dribbling lead.

### Title:    *Soccer Thief*
- *Level:* 3–6

*Skills Enhanced:* dribbling, ball control, tackling
*Equipment Needed:* 20 to 25 junior soccer balls
*Description:* All but five children dribble the soccer balls in general space. The five without the balls use their feet to try to take away other players' soccer balls. If the ball is taken away, the player who lost it goes to another player to steal his/her ball.

### Title:    *Pass and Tackle*
- *Level:* 3–6

*Skills Enhanced:* passing, defending
*Equipment Needed:* 10 junior soccer balls
*Description:* In threes, Player A passes the ball to Player B and immediately moves after the pass to try to regain possession of the ball as Player B passes to Player C. If A intercepts the pass he/she takes the ball back to the starting point and starts again, this time passing to

player C. B and C try to pass the ball back and forth as many times as possible without having it intercepted by Player A. After five turns, A changes places with B; five turns and B changes places with C.

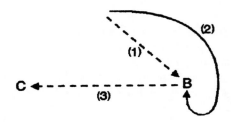

### Title: *Quick Pass*
- *Level:* 3–6

*Skills Enhanced:* passing, trapping, intercepting the ball

*Equipment Needed:* 6–8 junior soccer balls

*Description:* Four players stand in the corners of a square, 10 yards apart. A defender stands in the middle and tries to intercept the passes between the players. If he/she intercepts the ball he/she takes the place of the one who just passed the ball.

### Title: *Six Spot Keepaway*
- *Level:* 3–6

*Skills Enhanced:* passing, intercepting

*Equipment Needed:* 1 junior soccer ball per game

*Description:* Divide class into groups of three; three groups per game. To begin, teams A and B are working together. The ball starts with the center player and the A and B players try to make as many good passes as they can without having the ball intercepted by a C player. Members of teams A and B stay in their positions while C players may move to try to intercept. A and B players may pass to anyone but may not pass the ball directly back to the player from which it came. Each team should have a 2 minute time limit as defenders.

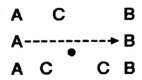

### Title: *Lead On*
- *Level:* 3–6

*Skills Enhanced:* passing, intercepting and dribbling

*Equipment Needed:* 10–15 junior soccer balls

*Description:* Arrange the children in partners with one ball per set of partners. Have the children dribble and pass the ball as they move in the play space. Emphasize passing the ball a little ahead of the partner so that the player has to move ahead to intercept.

**_Title:_     _Shoot  on Goal_**
- *Level:* 3–6

*Skills Enhanced:* shooting

*Equipment Needed:* 12 junior soccer balls and 6 pylons

*Description:* Divide class into groups of six, each with two pylons to form a goal and three balls per group. Goals should be set so they are 5 yards wide. Player A dribbles the ball to a point 12' out from the center of the goal, stops the ball and then runs to the end of the B line. B runs forward and kicks for a goal. B retrieves the ball and gets in the back of the A line.

*Variation:* A passes the ball out to the shooting point where B is waiting, B stops the ball and shoots; A passes the ball to the 12' mark and B then moves in to intercept the ball, control it and shoot; have players take turns being the goalie and trying to prevent the scoring as B shoots, having the same goalie stay for a minimum of five shots.

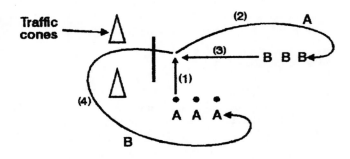

**_Title:_     _Kick for Distance_**
- *Level:* 3–6

*Skills Enhanced:* free kicking and clearing the ball

*Equipment Needed:* 10–15 junior soccer balls

*Description:* Players work in partners, directly across from each other on designated lines. Beginning at approximately 5 yards apart, have the partners kick the ball from a stationary position to the partner across the way. After each successful trap, players take one giant step back before the next kick. Encourage the players to take a running start to the ball when distance is far.

## LEAD-UP GAMES

The following games have been selected to reinforce practice of basic soccer skills. They progress in difficulty and should be used in the soccer unit as the actual games that are played. Whenever possible teams should have a minimal number of players and several games should be played, depending on the facilities available. The parent game of soccer should not be played as a part of the elementary physical education program but may be played in intramural programs or in after-school sports.

***Title:*** ***Circle Kickball***
- *Level:* 3–4

*Skills Enhanced:* passing, spatial awareness, ball control

*Equipment Needed:* junior soccer ball per group

*Description:* Divide class into groups of five or six players. Children pass the ball around to other members of the circle as quickly and as controlled as possible. Count the number of passes made in a certain time period.

Variations: change the distance of the passes by increasing the size of the circle.

***Title:*** ***Circle Soccer***
- *Level:* 3–4

*Skills Enhanced:* trapping, blocking, passing

*Equipment Needed:* one junior soccer ball per group

*Description*: Divide class into groups of 10–15 players. Players join hands forming a circle. The ball is passed around the inside of the circle, using passing, trapping, and blocking skills. If the ball gets out of the circle, the two players between whom it passed must turn around and continue to play facing out of the circle. Play continues until only five players are left facing inside the circle.

***Title:*** ***Double the Goals***
- *Level:* 5–6

*Skills Enhanced:* kicking, dribbling, general soccer skill

*Equipment Needed:* 16 pylons, pinnies for everyone, 6–8 junior soccer balls.

*Description:* A team consists of 6 players. There are 4 teams with two games going on at the same time. Therefore the gymnasium needs to be set up for two playing areas. Instead of two goals there are three goals. One goal at each end as usual and one goal at each sideline making three goals. Pylons will be used instead of goal nets. Teams use basic soccer rules, except they may shoot at any goal, side or end, defense or offense. When a goal is scored that goal is closed until the next goal is scored, then the new score's goal is closed. Only one goal is closed at a time. Players can shoot for any goal they wish, either side, either end. There are no goalkeepers. Two or three balls can be added, all being played at the same time.

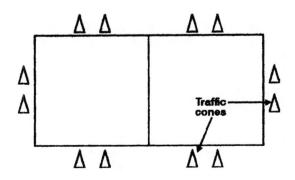

### Title:    *Invaders from Mars*

- *Level:* 5–6

*Skills Enhanced:* dribbling and maneuvering

*Equipment Needed:* 16 pylons, pinnies for everyone, 6 to 8 foam balls.

*Description:* There are four teams consisting of 6 to 8 players on each team. The playing area is divided into two large rectangles with two teams playing at each rectangle. One team is lined up along the sideline of each rectangle facing opponents who are lined up on the opposite side of the rectangle. 6 to 8 cones are lined up in the center of the rectangle. Several balls are given to each team on the sideline. One player is chosen from each team to dribble the ball through the cones down and back through the center of the rectangle. While the player in the center is dribbling sideline players attempt to kick the ball and hit the center player's ball. If successful, the sideline player takes the place of the center player. The center player attempts to not only control the ball he/she is dribbling but also to maneuver in such a way as to avoid the ball's being hit by the sideline players. Only foam balls are used for safety reasons.

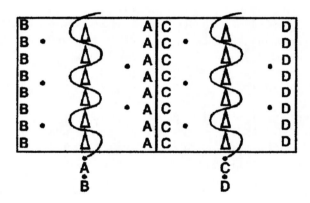

### Title:    *Moon Soccer*

- *Level:* 3–4

*Skills Enhanced:* passing, trapping

*Equipment Needed:* one foam soccer ball per game

*Description:* Two teams of six players form a large circle, each team spreads out in its respective half. The circle represents the moon. The leader rolls the ball, "green cheese," into the center of the moon and the opposite teams of moonies try to kick the ball out of the circle on the opponent's side of the circle to score a point. The circle should be large so that

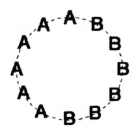

players have room to move. Play resumes after a goal with the teacher again rolling the ball into the center.

### *Title:* *Opposites*

* *Level:* 3–6

*Skills Enhanced:* kicking and trapping

*Equipment Needed:* one foam or junior soccer ball per game

*Description*: A team consists of 6–8 players. Players form a circle around a leader who is in the center. The leader passes the ball to someone in the circle calling out either "kick" or "trap." The person on the circle performs the opposite of what is called. If the person on the circle misses the ball or does the wrong activity, they change places with the person in the center. Play continues until everyone has had several chances to kick or trap the ball.

### *Title:* *Soccer Goal Kick*

* *Level:* 3–4

*Skills Enhanced:* trapping, kicking, agility

*Equipment Needed:* one ball per game, one base

*Description:* One team (5–6) players) lines up single file at the corner of the soccer goal, this is the kicking team. The other team (5–6 players) spreads out in the area in front of the goal. The base is set at a point approximately 15–20 yards from the kicking team and away from the goal area. After the kicker kicks the ball, he/she runs to the base and back, trying to get back before the fielding team receives the ball and kicks it through the goal. A point is scored if the runner returns before the goal is scored. Teams change roles after everyone on one team has kicked.

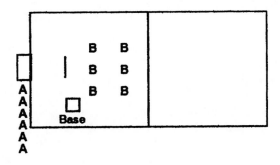

### *Title:* *Throw and Cross*

* *Level:* 3–4

*Skills Enhanced:* arm strength, throw-in skill

*Equipment Needed:* one foam or junior soccer ball per team

*Description:* Divide class into teams of 5 to 6 players. Players stand in single file lines facing a goal line 10 yards away. On the signal to go, the first player carries the ball to the goal line, turns and throws the ball with two hands overhead to the second player in line. The second player throws the ball back to #1 and then runs to the line, takes the ball from #1 and throws to #3; #3 catches the ball and throws back to #2, then runs, takes the ball from #2 and throws it to #4, etc. When all players are across the goal line, the team is finished.

Variation: adjust goal line distances according to the players' abilities to throw; have the team continue the drill and return to the original starting line in the same manner.

*Title:* **Soccer Trap Ball**
- *Level:* 3–4

*Skills Enhanced:* passing, intercepting, trapping
*Equipment Needed:* one ball per group of 8 children
*Description:* Six children form a circle around the other two players. The six players on the circle pass the ball back and forth across the circle to different players and the two players in the middle try to trap the ball. If the ball is trapped, the most recent passer changes places with the trapper. The ball may be held only three seconds.

*Title:* **Diagonal Soccer**
- *Level:* 3–4

*Skills Enhanced:* dribbling, passing, shooting, defending
*Equipment Needed:* one ball per game
*Description:* Players from respective teams spread out on two sides of a large square play area. Pylons are placed in opposite corners at a width of 10 feet from each other, representing non-play areas. Players are numbered off consecutively and three players go into the center of the square to play against the first three players from the opposing team. Players on the sidelines spread out to cover all spaces. The active players try to score a goal by kicking the ball below shoulder height and through the sideline players of the opposing team. Active players may go anywhere they wish in the play square. Players on the sidelines may intercept and kick balls that come to them but they may not shoot to score. Players may not touch the ball with their hands and may play the ball with only their feet. A point is awarded when a goal is scored or when the opposing team touches the ball illegally; a point is awarded to the non-shooting team if a shot travels above the shoulders of the non-shooting team. Play begins when the ball is given to one team, determined by a flip of a coin. After a score, the next three players come into the square and the ball is given to the non-scoring team to begin.

*Title:* **Dribble Dribble**
- *Level:* 3–4, variation 5–6

*Skills Enhanced:* dribbling, ball control, spatial awareness
*Equipment Needed:* one ball for each child
*Description:* All children dribble the ball in general space; if a collision occurs, both players must dribble their soccer balls out of the play area and must dribble around the perimeter of the play area before returning to the game.
*Variation:* As the children are dribbling, they must also try to kick other children's soccer balls out of the play boundaries. Then any players who have to retrieve their soccer balls must dribble around the play area perimeter before returning to the game.

*Title:* **Bullseye**
- *Level:* 3–4

*Skills Enhanced:* dribbling, ball control, spatial awareness
*Equipment Needed:* one ball per player
*Description:* In groups of 6–8 children, one child holds the ball in his/her hands and watches the others dribbling in the play area boundaries. He/she tries to throw the ball so that it hits

a ball that is being controlled by another player. If successful with the throw, the thrower becomes a dribbler and the ball hit becomes the bullseye.

### *Title:* ***Kick Pin Soccer***
- *Level:* 3–6

*Skills Enhanced:* shooting, trapping

*Equipment Needed:* 4–6 dense foam soccer balls per game

*Description:* Divide the group into two teams, players standing side by side on the sidelines of the play area. In the middle of the area place 10 bowling pins or Indian clubs, equidistantly spread down the center. Each team begins with half of the balls. The object of the game is to knock over as many pins as possible. Players continue to kick and trap the soccer balls until all pins are down. Score is kept and play begins again after the pins are reset.

### *Title:* ***Sideline Soccer***
- *Level:* 5–6

*Skills Enhanced:* dribbling, passing, shooting

*Equipment Needed:* one ball per game

*Description:* Divide the class into two teams and have each team stand on a sideline of the play area. Children should count off so each child has a number. Goals are set at each end of the play area and should be 5–10 yards in width, depending on the level of skill of the players (small goal = better accuracy). There are no goalies in this game. The first three players from each team come onto the play area, facing the goal where they are to score. One team is awarded the kick-off, therefore the first possession of the ball. The game is

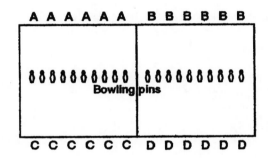

played three-on-three until a goal is scored or 2 minutes has elapsed. The next three players come in and a kick-off is awarded to the non-scoring team, or, if no goal was scored, to the team that did not have the kick-off first. A goal scores one point. Players on the sidelines can receive passes and can pass to other sideline players or to the active players on the field. Throw-ins are awarded when the ball goes out of bounds over the sideline, and are taken by the sideline players. If the ball goes over the end line, not through the goal, it is put into play by a free kick in front of the goal by a defending active player. The active players can move anywhere within the play area but must be on-sides for the kick-off. Sideline players must stay in their assigned areas. If a player touches the ball with his/her hands, the opposing team is given a free kick (ball is stationary and the team is given time to take the kick) on the spot. Similarly free kicks are awarded for pushing, holding, or tripping, and if play is especially rough a point will be awarded to the non-offending team.

*Variations:* The number of active players may be increased in relation to the size of the class or the size of the play area. It is best to keep the area smaller than the usual 100 yard field and to play two games at once so that opportunities to play the ball are increased.

### Title:     Manyball Soccer
- *Level:* 5–6

*Skills Enhanced:* dribbling, passing, shooting, defending

*Equipment Needed:* six dense foam soccer balls per game

*Description:* Divide the class into two teams and have the entire team set up in its own defensive end of the play area. Goals are set 5–10 yards in width and one or two players are goalies at each goal (number of goalies depends on the width of the goal). Set the six soccer balls on the center line, assigning the kickoff of three balls to each team. The object of the game is to score goals and all six balls will be in play at the same time. Rules as in Sideline Soccer apply for balls that leave the boundaries (throw-ins or free kicks) and for penalties (free kicks). This game is non-stop; after a goal is scored the ball is retrieved by the scorer and taken to the center line where it is given to an opposite team player for a kick-off. Since this game is very difficult to officiate, it should be played with classes who have learned to call their own fouls, and who can behave responsibly in that direction.

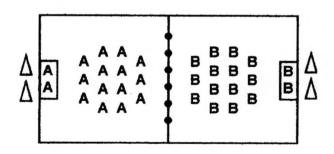

***Title:*** ***Addition Soccer***

*Level:* 5–6

*Skills Enhanced:* dribbling, ball handling

*Equipment Needed:* a ball for each player except one

*Description:* Each player dribbles a ball within the play area while one child, as defender, tries to touch a ball with his/her foot. If the ball is touched, the ball is taken away and given to the teacher who serves as the collection agent for seized soccer balls. The player who lost the ball joins hands with the defender and the two travel together to try to touch another soccer ball. When another ball is touched, the player takes the ball to the collection site and waits for another player to be eliminated. These two then join hands and enter the play area, moving about and trying to touch another ball. Play continues until all but one ball has been taken, that player becomes the first defender for a second round of play.

***Title:*** ***Zone Keep Away***

* *Level:* 4–6

*Skills Enhanced:* dribbling, tackling, spatial awareness

*Equipment Needed:* a ball for every offensive team member

*Description:* The play area is divided into three zones and the children are divided into teams of 6. It would be appropriate to have at least two games going. The offensive team members line up on the end line with their soccer balls. The offense tries to dribble their soccer balls to the opposite end of the play area, thus scoring one point for each successful dribbler. After each successful player crosses the end line with the ball, he/she picks up the ball and runs back to the side of the play area to immediately start to dribble again. The goal of the offensive team is to make as many points as possible in a 5 minute time limit. Two defenders are waiting in each of the three zones that the dribblers must cross. They try to take the ball away from the dribbler, and if successful, the dribbler immediately picks up the ball and returns to the first end line, immediately starting to dribble again. The defensive team does not score points by taking the ball away, but does prevent a point from being scored on that play. After five minutes the teams change roles. Continue to play in five minute intervals.

**2 games going on at the same time**

### *Title:* *Lane Soccer*

- *Level:* 4–6

*Skills Enhanced:* dribbling, passing, shooting, tackling

*Equipment Needed:* one ball per game

*Description:* Divide the class into two teams per game, depending on the play space available. The space is to be divided into eight zones in the center portion of the field and one goalie is assigned to each goal. A player from each team is assigned to each zone and may play only within that space; therefore there will be a defender and an offensive player in each zone. Extra players may stand on the sideline. The same rules apply as in Sideline Soccer for out-of-bounds plays and fouls. Also free kicks are awarded to the non-offending team if a player crosses out of his/her zone. Goalies may use their hands to save goals. Players should rotate zones after every score or after a designated time limit with no score. Extra players should rotate in, and all players should have chances to play in each zone. Rotate goalies as well.

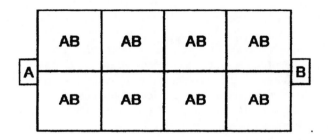

### *Title:* *Line Soccer*

- *Level:* 3–6

*Skills Enhanced:* dribbling, passing, shooting, tackling, goalkeeper skills

*Equipment Needed:* one ball per game

*Description:* Divide class into two teams, standing on the opposite play area end lines. Designate a restraining line 15 feet in front of each end line. Have players count off until each player has a number. The ball is placed in the center of the area and the teacher calls three numbers. Those players are the active players and run out to immediately play the ball. The object of the game is to kick the ball past the team members who are on the end lines. All players on the end lines may use their hands to prevent scoring as well as their

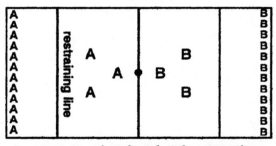

**2 games may be played at the same time**

feet; they must drop the ball immediately, however, and kick it back into play. No punting is allowed. They must stay between the restraining line and the end line. The active players may move anywhere in the play area except behind the restraining line. If, during play, a player commits a foul, the opposing team is awarded a free kick taken 12 feet out from the restraining line. Only the goalies may block the kick. If the ball goes out of bounds over the sideline it is put back into play by the opposing team's active player with a throw-in. After a goal is scored, or two minutes have elapsed, the active players return to their respective lines, the ball is replaced in the center and three new numbers are called.

***Title:    Mini-Soccer***
* *Level:* 5–6

*Skills Enhanced:* dribbling, passing, shooting, tackling, goalkeeper skills, knowledge of corner kicks

*Equipment Needed:* one ball per game

*Description:* Divide the class into teams of seven active players; there will be one goalie, three defensive and three offensive players per team. The game begins with the above set up: The goal area is to be three yards in width. Play begins with a kick-off by the designated team; after a goal, play is resumed with a kick-off by the non-scoring team. Rules are followed as in Sideline Soccer with the exception of the addition of the corner kick. If the defensive team kicks the ball out over the end line, the offensive team places the ball on the corner of the field and has a free kick. A goal may be scored from this kick so it is called a direct kick. Position play is encouraged in this form of soccer. Both offensive and defensive players may cross the center line, but defense should not pass offensive players. The teacher should stress the responsibility of each defensive player for one of the offensive players, introducing the concept of a person-to-person defense.

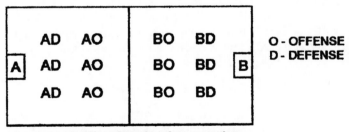

**2 games may be played at the same time**

# Softball

Softball is a very popular sport in America. It evolved from baseball. Students in the elementary school may develop speed, agility, eye-hand coordination, striking skills, throwing skills and catching skills through learning softball. Softball drills and lead up games can also contribute to aerobic fitness when such drills and games are designed in maximum participation format. Playing traditional softball, one game, is inappropriate in the elementary school.

Most elementary schools have outside playing fields or playgrounds which can be adapted for learning softball skills. Many skills can be learned in the gymnasium setting when equipment is adapted for indoor use.

In order to be developmentally appropriate, lightweight plastic bats, padded bats, as well as an assortment of balls, should be made available. Batting helmets, catcher's masks, fielder's gloves, and a variety of other equipment may be used when playing softball outdoors. Plastic bats and super bounce balls or plastic balls are appropriate for indoor softball skills.

## SOFTBALL SKILLS

In order for a child to participate successfully in games of softball, competency should be achieved in the following skills: throwing, running, fielding, and batting. Older students may also work on pitching skills.

***Throwing.*** The overhand throw is the fastest and most accurate of the throws used in softball. The player holds the ball in the dominant hand with the index finger and the second finger on top of the ball and the other two fingers and the thumb spread comfortably to the side and under the ball. The feet are spread comfortably apart with the foot opposite the dominant hand being forward and the non-dominant shoulder pointing towards the target. The elbow is bent with the wrist being behind and above the head, with the upper arm being parallel to the ground. The arm is brought forward, the elbow straightens as the arm extends and the ball rolls off of the fingers. As the ball is being released the forward leg moves in the direction of the target at the same time the body rotates to face the target.

***Fielding.*** Catching is the main skill used in fielding. The fielder watches the ball in flight anticipating where it will land and moves to intercept the ball. If the ball is bouncing, the catch will be made as the ball ascends from the ground. If the ball is rolling on the ground, the fielder will scoop the ball with the wrist and fingers. Fly balls should be caught while standing still and at shoulder level when possible. This assists in preventing the fielder from

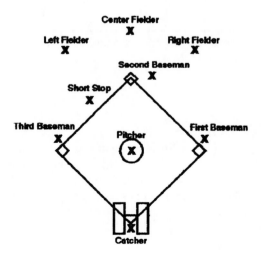

being off balance as well as allowing for an unobstructed view when throwing the ball. Players should use both hands when catching any type of ball.

***Batting.*** The grip, stance, stride, and swing are all important in developing appropriate batting skills. A player grips the bat with the non-dominant hand several inches above the end of the bat. The other hand is placed above and touching the first. The joints of the fingers and the knuckles are aligned on both hands. The stance consists of moving the feet comfortably apart with the knees slightly bent. The upper trunk is facing home plate. The bat is held up and behind the head with the non-dominant arm almost straight. The batter's head is turned towards the pitcher. Just before the pitched ball reaches the plate, the batter steps toward the pitcher with the forward leg and swings the bat to meet the ball. During the swing the bat moves forward and is kept level while meeting the ball. The hips rotate as the batter turns towards the pitcher. The arms are extended as the bat meets the ball and a follow through is executed.

***Pitching.*** The ball is held with the tips of the thumb, index and middle fingers. Only one step is allowed which is taken at the time of delivery while moving towards the batter. The dominant arm swings forward while the player steps forward on the opposite foot. The ball is thrown underhand and released below the hip. This skill should be taught to children in grade 5 and up.

***Running the Bases.*** As the child runs to first base the choice must be made, based on the hit, to either round first base, tagging the inside corner, or to run through first base. If the child chooses to run through the base, he/she is deemed safe if the ball arrives at the base after the child has tagged it and run through. This would be when the hit was fielded quickly and the defense has a good chance of getting the ball to the first baseperson before the runner arrives. The child should decide to round the base if the hit is strong and long and he/she feels the possibility of making it to more than one base.

For developmentally appropriate as well as safety reasons there are no sliding, stealing bases, lead-offs, or bunts allowed. These should be saved for competitive softball. Balls should not be called; the student must swing and miss in order for a strike to be called. Any student throwing the bat is automatically out for safety reasons.

The parent game of softball is given below so that students may be familiar with rules. It is not recommended that this official game be played except in intramural participation due to the inactivity levels of children waiting for turns. If the official rules are applied, it is recommended that students play in mini teams of 6 on 6.

***Title:*** ***Softball***
- *Level:* 4–6 Intramural Activity

*Skills Enhanced:* batting and fielding, base running

*Equipment Needed:* a bat, ball, and fielder's gloves for each team.

*Description:* A softball team consists of nine players: catcher, pitcher, first baseperson, second baseperson, short stop, third baseperson, left fielder, center fielder and right fielder. A game consists of seven innings; an inning consists of the time period in which both teams have had their turns at bat. A batting order is established and maintained for the duration of the game. A team stays at bat until three players have been called "out." A player may be called "out" after three strikes (misses at pitches, or a foul hit on either of the first two strikes), if tagged with the ball while running between bases, if "forced out" when the ball arrives to the baseperson who steps on the base before the runner arrives (if the runner has no choice but to run to that base), or if a fly ball is caught by a fielding team player. If a player rounds a base and heads for a second base, or third base, he/she must be tagged out. If a fly ball is caught, a runner must return to the original base, tag up, and may make the choice to run to the next base. If the runner does not "tag up." the ball may be thrown directly to the original baseperson and the player will be out. When making any outs, the fielding players must be in control of the ball at all times. A run is scored when a runner successfully crosses home plate without being called out. Fielding players must stay clear of the baselines and may not impede a runner's progress unless they have control of the ball. Runners may not go outside of the baselines more than 3 feet.

## *TEACHING SOFTBALL SKILLS*

Skills should be introduced through demonstrations using auditory cues. The students will need to have several and various opportunities to practice softball skills which are developmentally appropriate. Lead-up games and drill activities should be presented. The softball equipment used needs to be developmentally appropriate.

# Skill/Drill Activities for Fun and Success

### *Title:*     *Grip 'n' Swing*
- *Level:* 3–6

*Skills Enhanced:* batting grip

*Equipment Needed:* a developmentally appropriate bat for each student

*Description:* Students are shown the correct way to grip the bat. Each student is given his/ her own bat. Students practice swinging the bat using the proper grip. The teacher checks each student's grip to make sure he/she is performing the grip correctly. Students need to be spaced in such a manner that no one is in danger of being hit by a bat. It is suggested that plastic bats be used. If there are not enough bats for each student to have his/her own, this activity can be used in station formations.

### *Title:*     *Swing 'n' Step*
- *Level:* 3–6

*Skills Enhanced:* swinging the bat, stance formation

*Equipment Needed:* a plastic bat and a base for each student (a paper plate can be used to represent home plate).

*Description:* Students are shown the correct way to swing the bat, as well as the proper stance. Students practice swinging the bat using correct grip, swing, and stance. The teacher will check each student to be sure he/she is using the proper grip, swing, and stance. Students should be spaced out in such a manner that there is no danger of hitting other students with the bat. If there is not enough equipment for each student to have his/her own bat, this activity may also be performed in station formation.

### Title:     *Pitch and Score*

- *Level:* 5–6

*Skills Enhanced:* throwing for accuracy, and pitching.

*Equipment Needed:* a yarn ball or other appropriate ball for every student, and several targets marked with tape on the wall.

*Description:* Students are shown the correct way to pitch the ball. Targets are drawn on the wall and a line is placed on the floor about 38 feet from the wall. Students attempt to throw the ball underhand and hit the target on the wall. The target is drawn to represent the strike zone in softball, with particular attention to the size and shape of the strike zone. Several students may attempt to pitch at the strike zones at the same time. Colored tape may be used to form targets.

### Title:     *Fun with Fielder's Gloves*

- *Level:* 3–6

*Skills Enhanced:* throwing and catching

*Equipment Needed:* a fielder's glove for each student, and appropriate balls for each set of partners.

*Description:* Each student is given a fielder's glove. Students are then asked to divide into partners. Each set of partners is given a super bounce foam ball. Partners will practice throwing and catching using the gloves. Students will practice both the overhand and the underhand throws..

### Title:     *Tee Bat*

- *Level:* 3–6

*Skills Enhanced:* batting

*Equipment Needed:* as many batting tees as are available, cones may sometimes work for batting tees, appropriate balls for every tee, and a plastic bat for each student.

*Description:* Batting tees are set up at varying heights. Students practice hitting the ball off the tee, into the wall. Students need to be spaced in such a manner that they will not hit another student with the bat or ball.

### Title:     *Field and Score*

- *Level:* 5–6

*Skills Enhanced:* fielding and throwing

*Equipment Needed:* 5 plastic bats, 5 appropriate balls, 20–25 fielder's gloves.

*Description:* There will be 5 students on a team. There will be 5 to 6 teams. One player will act as the batter, while the other 4 students take positions in the field. The batter will hit the ball in a variety of ways, sometimes so that the ball will be a fly ball and other times so that it will be a ground ball. Students are spread out either in the field outside or around the gymnasium. Students will field the ball and throw it back to the batter. Students earn 3 points for a grounder caught, and 2 points for a fly ball. After the batter has hit the ball 5 times, students will rotate positions. Everyone will have an opportunity to be the batter. The batter will throw the ball up in the air, hitting it into the field on the descent.

### Title:     *Propel*

- *Level:* 3–6

*Skills Enhanced:* catching and throwing

*Equipment Needed:* a ball for each team and fielder's gloves for everyone.

*Description:* Divide the class into four groups. Form 4 large circles with players about 8 to 12 feet away from each other. This game may be played either indoors or outdoors. One ball for the team and a fielder's glove for each player is required. Players are to propel or toss the ball as quickly as possible around the circle. Players toss the ball to the person next to them who catches it and throws it to the next person. The ball starts out moving in a clockwise direction. When the ball reaches the person who started the first toss, that person changes the direction to a counterclockwise one.

## *LEAD-UP GAMES*

The following games have been selected to reinforce practice of basic softball skills. They progress in difficulty and should be used in the softball unit as the actual games that are played. Whenever possible, teams should have a minimal number of players and several games should be played, depending on the facilities available. The parent game of softball should not be played as a part of the elementary physical education program but may be played in intramural programs or in after-school sports.

### *Title:*    *How Far Can You Go*
- *Level:* 5–6

*Skills Enhanced:* batting, running, and fielding.

*Equipment Needed:* one ball, 4 bases, and bat for each team

*Description*: Create four teams so two games may be played. Bases are arranged in a straight line. The first player hits the pitched ball and runs the bases. The runner receives one point for each base touched. The runner has to make it back home before the ball. The batter decides what base they can make it to and back depending on where the ball travels. Fielders must retrieve the ball and throw it from the spot where it was picked up. If a fielder runs with the ball he/she must return to the spot where he/she retrieved the ball and throw it over again from that spot. A batter is out if a fly ball is caught, the catcher gets the ball before the runner gets back home, or if the runner goes out of bounds. If anyone on the outfield team interferes with the runner, the runner is awarded 2 extra runs. If the infield team interferes with the catcher, the runner is out.

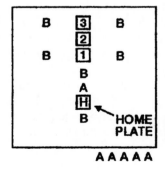

### Title:     *Batter Battery*

- *Level:* 5–6

*Skills Enhanced:* batting and fielding

*Equipment Needed:* one bat, ball, and 4 fielder's gloves for each team.

*Description:* A team consists of 5 players. There are 5 teams. One player is the batter and the rest are fielders. One of the fielders throws an easy pitch to the batter who hits the ball. The batter tries to hit the ball in different ways to allow the fielders an assortment of fielding practice. Grounders, fly balls, and pop ups are all hit by the batter. After 10 hits everyone rotates positions. The batter earns points for each ball caught: fly ball 5 points, grounder 3 points.

### Title:     *Field and Toss*

- *Level:* 5–6

*Skills Enhanced:* running and tagging

*Equipment Needed:* one ball, 2 bases, and 3 fielder's gloves for each team

*Description:* A team consists of 4 players. There are 6 teams. A runner, pitcher, first, and second basemen are required. The runner starts off on first base. When the runner leaves the base, the pitcher throws to the first baseman who chases the runner trying to tag him. The first baseman will limit the number of throws to the second baseman trying instead to tag the runner without throwing the ball. A throw to the second baseman is permitted; however, it is not a good idea to throw the ball back and forth. When the runner is tagged out, everyone rotates positions. If the runner makes it safely to second base one point is scored and everyone rotates positions.

### Title:     *300 Points*

- *Level:* 5–6

*Skills Enhanced:* batting and fielding

*Equipment Needed:* one bat, ball, and several fielder's gloves

*Description:* A team consists of 5 players. One player is the batter and the rest are fielders. The batter tosses up the ball and hits it to the fielders. A pop fly, when caught, is worth 100 points. A ball caught on one bounce is worth 75 points. A ball caught after 2 bounces is worth 50 points. A ball caught after 3 or more bounces is worth 25 points. Fielders call for the catch and when this is done other fielders stay clear. When one of the fielders accumulates 300 points, that person becomes the new batter. Each time 300 points is accumulated, players rotate positions so that each player has a turn to be the new batter.

### Title:     *First 'n' Back*

- *Level:* 5–6

*Skills Enhanced:* batting, running, and fielding.

*Equipment Needed:* one ball, bat, fielder's gloves, and 2 bases for each team.

*Description:* A team consists of 5 players. A batter, catcher, pitcher, and 2 fielders are needed. The batter hits the pitched ball and begins running. The batter attempts to run from home to lst base and back to home. If he achieves his goal he gets another turn, if not, all players rotate positions.

### Title:     *Hit the Wall*

- *Level:* 5–6

*Skills Enhanced:* throwing and catching

*Equipment Needed:* 2 cones and 1 playground ball for each team.

*Description:* A team consists of 3 players. The teams will line up in single file formation to the right of the cone. The first cone is approximately 10 feet from the wall and the 2nd cone is 15 feet from the first cone. When the whistle blows the first player runs to the second cone and throws the ball so it rebounds off the wall. The second player starts to run when the first player passes the first cone. The second player attempts to catch the ball and throws it against the wall for the third player. The team receives a point each time a teammate catches the ball. Players must throw and catch at the cone, not past it. Passing the cone on the throw results in that player having to retrieve the ball and going back to the cone and running around it twice before trying again. If the ball passes the cone on an attempted catch the player must retrieve the ball and go back to the cone before throwing it. The player will not receive a point when the player or ball passes a cone when throwing or catching.

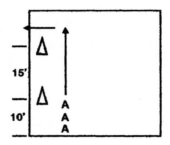

### Title:    *Face Off*

- *Level:* 5–6

*Skills Enhanced:* fielding

*Equipment Needed:* one ball and tape to mark the two lines.

*Description:* Two players face each other about 15 to 20 feet apart. A line is drawn in front of each player on the floor using masking tape. The line is about 6 to 8 feet long. The idea is to get the ball past the line. It may be thrown hard on the line, bounced hard off the floor in between, or by throwing a fly that is difficult to catch. If the ball gets past the other player's line a point is scored for the thrower.

### Title:    *Eighteen*

- *Level:* 3–6

*Skills Enhanced:* throwing and catching

*Equipment Needed:* fielders' gloves or plastic scoops for each player and a ball for each team.

*Description:* Partners face each other approximately 30 to 40 feet apart or more. All players will be facing in the same direction in order not to run into each other. A team consists of two players. Partners practice throwing and catching using fielders' gloves and appropriate balls. If the ball is thrown to the chest area and caught, 3 points are awarded. If a throw is able to be caught but forces one's partner to stop, twist, turn, or move his/her feet, 2 points are awarded. If a ball is thrown so it cannot be caught, 1 point is subtracted. Players are encouraged to catch using both hands. The first team scoring 18 points wins. Players then rotate so partners are new and the game begins again.

*Title:*     ***Target Ball***
- *Level:* 3–6

*Skills Enhanced:* throwing for accuracy

*Equipment Needed:* several hula hoops, and several appropriate balls.

*Description:* 6 hula hoops set up in various parts of the gymnasium. A team consists of 4 players.. A small hula hoop is suspended from the ceiling, a bar or whatever may be available. Each team is assigned a hula hoop. Students form a line with the first player attempting to throw the ball through the hoop. After 5 throws he/ she goes to the end of the line and the next player attempts 5 throws. If the ball goes through the center, 15 points are awarded. If the ball hits the hoop but still goes through, 8 points are awarded. A player gets 3 points if the ball hits the hoop. The player with the most points at the end of the activity is the winner.

*Title:*     ***In a Pickle***
- *Level:* 3–6

*Skills Enhanced:* running bases and tagging

*Equipment Needed:* 2 fielders' gloves, a ball and 2 bases for each team.

*Description:* Teams are set up in lanes which are parallel to each other in order to avoid running into players on other teams. A team consists of 3 players. Two bases are set up approximately 15 feet apart. One player is the runner and the other two players are basemen. The runner runs from one base to the other, trying not to get tagged. When the runner is tagged, one of the basemen will trade places with the runner. This activity will work well as one station in a station formation activity. Round flat plastic discs, or rubber backed carpet squares work well as indoor bases. A softball, super bounce foam ball, or tennis ball may be used, as well as any other appropriate ball.

*Title:*     ***A Swing and A Miss***
- *Level:* 5–6

*Skills Enhanced:* pitching and batting

*Equipment Needed:* one ball, bat and fielder's glove are needed for each team.

*Description:* All of the batters are set up at one end of the gymnasium in order to avoid collisions. A team consists of 3 players. There is no running in this game. One player is the batter, one the pitcher, and the other the umpire who fields the ball. The object is to strike the batter out. The batter gets 10 pitches. He/she must actually swing and miss in order to get a strike. After 10 pitches the batter must remember how many hits he/she made. One point is awarded for each successful hit. If he/she gets 3 strikes, he/she is out. After 10 pitches, players will rotate positions. At the end of the activity, the team member with the highest score is the winner.

*Title:*     ***On Down the Line***
- *Level:* 3–6

*Skills Enhanced:* throwing from a short distance

*Equipment Needed:* a ball for each team

*Description:* Players form single file lines on their own teams. Two teams stand parallel to each other in order to see how the other team is performing while their own team is participating in the activity. A team consists of 4 players. Players form a single file line formation about 10 to 15 feet apart from each other. The first player picks the ball up off of the ground in front of him and throws it to the next person in line who throws it to the next and so on. When the ball reaches the other end of the line the last player starts the ball back down the line. The idea is for players to catch the ball, turn and throw it to the next player. The object is to see which team can finish first without making errors.

### Title:     _Running On Time_
* Level: 5–6

*Skills Enhanced:* running bases, pitching, and batting

*Equipment Needed:* one ball, appropriate bat, 4 bases, and a stopwatch are needed for each team.

*Description:* A team consists of 4 players. The batter attempts to hit the ball thrown by the pitcher. Upon hitting the ball, the runner runs the bases, no matter where the ball goes. The run is timed to see how long it takes the runner to make it around all the bases back to home. All 4 team members are timed when it is their turn to bat. The 4 times are added together in order to determine how long it took the team to run the bases.

### Title:     _Round the Bases_
* Level: 3–6

*Skills Enhanced:* running bases, and fielding

*Equipment Needed:* one ball, bat, bases, and fielder's gloves are needed for each team.

*Description:* All batters are set up at one end of the gymnasium in order to avoid collisions. A team consists of 4 players: a catcher, 1st, 2nd, and 3rd basemen. The teacher or other designated hitter, hits the ball to 3rd base, then to 2nd base, and finally to first base, in that order. The basemen field the ball and throw it to home plate. This is an excellent game for allowing practice in fielding grounders. This can be played indoors or outdoors. After 3 successful circuits, players rotate positions.

### Title:     _Speedy_
* Level: 3–6

*Skills Enhanced:* running and throwing

*Equipment Needed:* one ball, and 4 bases are needed for each team.

*Description:* Teams should be arranged in lanes in order to avoid collisions. A team consists of 4 players. The catcher starts the game by picking up the ball which is on the ground in front of home plate. The runner begins to run the bases as soon as the catcher picks up the ball. The catcher throws to the first baseman who must catch the ball and throw it to second base, etc. If the ball is missed, it must be retrieved before it can be thrown to the next base. If the runner beats the ball home, a run is scored. If the ball reaches home first, it is an out. The baseman must throw the ball from the base.

### Title:     _Weird Ball_
* Level: 5–6

*Skills Enhanced:* running, batting, pitching, fielding and throwing

*Equipment Needed:* one ball, bat, fielders' gloves and 4 bases are needed for each team.

*Description:* Two fields with the home plates next to each other but outfields in opposite directions. A team consists of 6 players. Two games are going on at the same time. After hitting the pitched ball, the runner may run to any base he/she wishes. Runners may run the bases in any sequence as long as contact is made with each base and none of the bases are touched twice. Home plate must be the last touched. Two runners are allowed on the same base. If the ball gets to the base before the runner, more than two runners are standing on the same base, or if the runner goes to the same base twice, the runner is out. There are no force outs. Otherwise the game is played according to the basic softball rules.

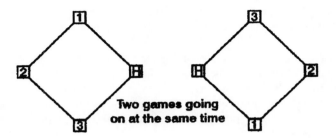

**Two games going on at the same time**

# Volleyball

Volleyball was originated by William Morgan, a YMCA director in Holyoke, Massachusetts in 1895. Volleyball has long been a popular sport in the physical education programs of junior and senior high schools, and success is highly dependent on the player's ability to use refined eye-hand coordination to strike the ball in the appropriate ways. Since striking is a fundamental motor skill, one can understand that the ability to play good volleyball comes only after a sound basic foundation has been established in striking. Additionally, volleyball necessitates working with coincidence-anticipation timing in that the player must be able to track the flight of the ball and move to assume an appropriate position from which to contact the moving ball. Therefore, volleyball is a complex perceptual-motor skill sport.

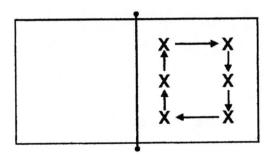

Developmentally appropriate practices tell us that we should not begin to develop volleyball skills with a regulation ball. Although small and relatively light, the ball is inappropriate for elementary school children because it is hard and contact often hurts. Children will fear the ball due to the potential for pain and teachers who insist on using regulation balls at the elementary level will succeed in turning a great percentage of children off to the sport. Beach balls, foam balls and gator balls, balloons, or vinyl play balls are most appropriate for the elementary level drills and games. There is also a larger ball, called a volleyball trainer, that is very appropriate for the elementary school-aged child. Due to the expense, not that many schools provide trainers for the elementary volleyball program.

## VOLLEYBALL SKILLS

In order to play the true game of volleyball, the player needs to know how to perform the serve, the overhead set, and the forearm pass. Skills such as spiking, blocking, and digging may be better left to the secondary physical education program. The first three skills mentioned will allow the child to play efficiently at the elementary level.

*Serving.* It is recommended that children learn to perform the underhand serve in volleyball. The student places the ball in his/her non-dominant hand, extending the arm so that the ball is held out in front of the dominant side. To serve the ball, the player steps forward with the opposite foot at the same time swinging the dominant arm forward. The ball is dropped at the appropriate time when the dominant hand contacts the ball and the follow-through is toward the net and slightly upward. The contact point may be the inside of the wrist, the heel of the hand, or the surface of a fist, whichever seems easiest for the player. The serve is used to begin play in volleyball games.

*Overhead Set.* The overhead set involves the student receiving the ball overhead and returning the ball to that overhead position, for a teammate to send over the net to the opposing team. The purpose of the set is to get the ball high in the air to clear the net or for a teammate to spike. Since spiking is not a recommended skill at this level of play, children should be taught that the overhead set and pass is for receiving a high ball and passing it on. For the overhead set, the student holds his/her hands just above the forehead as he/she looks up to the ball. Both elbows and knees should be bent, hands should be held with fingers toward the ceiling, palms out, fingers extended with forefingers and thumbs forming a triangle above the forehead. As the ball contacts the fingertips, the elbows and knees give slightly to absorb the force and then both extend forcefully upward to send the ball high off the fingertips in the desired direction. At no time should the palms contact the ball.

*Forearm Pass.* The forearm pass is a skill used to receive the ball when it comes to the student lower than shoulder level. The child stands in a ready position, feet shoulder width apart, knees bent, arms extended in front of the body with forearms facing upward and next to each other. One hand sits in the palm of the other hand and contact with the ball is made on the forearms near the wrist. The legs extend on contact and the arms lift the ball and follow through in the direction desired.

It is not recommended that the official game of volleyball be played in the elementary school as it restricts players to six per side which does not allow for maximum participation

### Title: Volleyball
• *Level:* 5–6 Intramural Activity
*Skills Enhanced:* overhead set, serve, forearm pass
*Equipment Needed:* gator ball and volleyball net.
*Description:* There are six players on a regulation volleyball team. They are set as indicated in the rotation formation. It is recommended that, for this age level, the net be set at 7 feet. Points are scored only by the serving team, when the ball hits the floor on the serving team's side or a member of the serving team hits the ball out of bounds a "side out" is called and the receiving team becomes the serving team but does not get a point. Only three hits are allowed per side, and a player may not hit the ball two times in a row. The ball may be played off the net, meaning that if it hits the net during play, play may continue. If the ball

hits the net on a serve, a side out is called and the receiving team becomes the serving team. Players may not touch the net nor cross the center line. If they do, either a point is awarded (if the violating player is on the receiving team) or a side out is called (if the player is on the serving team).

### TEACHING VOLLEYBALL SKILLS

Skills should be introduced through demonstration with auditory cues. The children should then have numerous opportunities to practice the skills in meaningful, fun drill activities and in volleyball lead-up games. Equipment used should be developmentally appropriate.

## Skill/Drill Activities for Fun and Success

The following activities are designed for maximum involvement and participation by the children. Since most play spaces will have room for only one or possibly two nets, it is suggested that the teacher select several different drills to be done in station format; students can then rotate through the stations.

*Title:* ***Bumpity, Bump***
• *Level:* 3–6
*Skills Enhanced:* volleying, bumping
*Equipment Needed:* vinyl balls or other appropriate balls for 1/2 of the class
*Description:* The class is divided into partners. One of the partners throws the ball to the other partner, who bumps it back to the first person. After 10 bumps partners switch positions. When both partners are proficient at bumping, the throw may be eliminated and they simply see how many times they can bump the ball back and forth without missing.

*Title:* ***Circle Bump***
• Level: 3–6
*Skills Enhanced:* bumping and volleying
*Equipment Needed:* 4 vinyl balls or other appropriate balls
*Description:* There are 8 players on a team. There are 4 teams. Players form a circle around a player in the center. The center player sets up the ball to each player on the circle, giving each player a turn to bump it back to the center player. The team will count the number of times the ball can make it around the circle without the ball touching the floor. Each time the bump is supposed to come back to the center player.

*Title:* ***Bump on the Run***
• *Level:* 3–6
*Skills Enhanced:* volleying, bumping and running
*Equipment Needed:* 4 vinyl balls or other appropriate balls
*Description:* A team consists of 6 to 8 players. There are 4 teams. Two games are going on at the same time. The teams line up in single file lines about 4 feet apart and facing each other, teams one and two face each other and 3 and 4 face each other. The first student in line one bumps the ball to the first player in line 2. At the same time the first player in line three bumps the ball to the first player in line four. After bumping the ball, the student runs to the end of the other teams' line. Play continues until each player has had several turns to

bump the ball. Line one and two line up next to each other. Lines three and four line up next to each other. Everyone should eventually end up across from where they started.

### *Title:*     *Three Against Three*
• *Level:* 3–6
*Skills Enhanced:* bumping, passing, and general volleyball skills
*Equipment Needed:* 5 vinyl balls or other appropriate balls, and 2 volleyball nets.
*Description:* There are three players on each team. There are 8 to 10 teams. One team is on each side of the net across from the opposing team. The teacher throws the ball into the court to start the game. Players may bump, pass, and whatever is needed to hit the ball over the net and keep it from touching the ground. The ball must be volleyed at least twice on a side before sending it over the net, and three times is even better. A point is scored each time the ball is hit successfully, whether or not it crosses the net.

### *Title:*     *Volley Follies*
• *Level:* 3–6
*Equipment Needed:* one vinyl ball or other appropriate ball for every student.
*Description:* Each child has a ball and is in his/her own self-space with the ball. For each of the following challenges, the child throws the ball vertically into the air and then applies the principles learned about the overhead pass and set. Give the children numerous opportunities to practice in this manner.
1. Throw the ball high, let it bounce, and then catch it in the semi-crouched body position for the set, hands forming a triangle over the head.
2. Throw the ball high, let it bounce, set it high overhead, set it once more, catch in the semi-crouched position.
3. Repeat.
4. Repeat #2 but continue to set the ball as many times as possible while staying within self-space.
5. Have the children move to a space facing a wall, (a) Throw ball to wall, set, catch; (b) Throw ball to wall, set, set continuously.
6. Repeat activities 1–3 with the forearm pass.

### *Title:*     *Partner Setting*
• *Level:* 3–6
*Skills Enhanced:* bumping,
*Equipment Needed:* one vinyl ball for each set of partners
*Description:*
1. Standing approximately ten feet away from a partner, students toss the ball overhead back and forth. Tosses should be high and received overhead. On each catch the student should contact the ball with hands in the triangle position and on fingertips, bending and giving with the catch, then extending up to toss the ball back.
2. Repeat #1 but, after tossing, the tosser moves to a new spot. The partner must receive the ball and then send it to the new position.
3. Repeat #1 and #2 with the players using the overhead set, partner #1 tossing and partner #2 setting it back to the tosser. Change roles after 10 tries.
4. Have the partners move to a wall. Partner #1 throws the ball to the wall, partner #2 sets the ball back to partner #1. 10 tries and change roles.
5. Partners stand across from each other at a net. Partner #1 tosses high over the net to partner #2 who sets the ball back to #1 to catch. 10 trials. Change roles.

6.   Partners set the ball back and forth over the net.

### *Title:    Partner Passing*

- *Level:* 3–6

*Skills Enhanced:* forearm pass

*Equipment Needed:* one vinyl ball for each set of partners

*Description:*

1.   Standing about ten feet apart, partner #1 tosses the ball to partner #2 low so that partner #2 can pass the ball back to #1 who catches it. 10 trials and switch roles.
2.   Partner #1 tosses the ball alternately to the left and right of partner #2 so he/she has to move in order to receive the ball and pass it back to #1. 10 trials and change roles.
3.   Partner #1 passes the ball on a bounce so #2 has to get in position underneath and pass the ball back to #1. 10 trials, change roles.
4.   Partner #1 tosses the ball to #2 who passes the ball back to #1 who passes the ball to #2, etc. Play "Keep It Up" as a partner team and see how many passes can be completed before losing control of the ball.

### *Title:    Partner Serving*

- *Level:* 3–6

*Skills Enhanced:* underhand serve

*Equipment Needed:* one vinyl ball for each set of partners, and 2 volleyball nets.

*Description:* Partners serve back and forth to each other over the net. Have partners adjust their position in relation to the net according to the level of success (closer to the net if necessary). Then have the receiving partner attempt to pass the ball back to the server using either the overhead set or the forearm pass.

### *Title:    Triangle Passing*

- *Level:* 3–6

*Skills Enhanced:* passing and setting, moving to open space

*Equipment Needed:* 8 to 10 vinyl balls

*Description:*

1.   Students are grouped in three's with one ball per group. To begin, players set the ball to each other around the triangle. Players should be 10–15 feet away from each other.
2.   In the same formation, after #1 sets to #2 he/she moves to #2's place, #2 sets to #3 and moves to #3's place. Continue.
3.   Repeat the activities with the forearm pass.

### *Title:    Shoot the Hoop*

- *Level:* 3–6

*Skills Enhanced:* overhead set

*Equipment Needed:* 10 hula hoops and 10 vinyl balls or other appropriate balls.

*Description:* Players are arranged in sets of three with one hula hoop on the floor by leader #1:

#1 tosses high to #2 who sets the ball high, trying to have it come down and land in the hoop. #2 is approximately 8–10 feet back from the hoop. #2 then goes behind #3. Leader #1 holds his/her position until #2 and #3 have each had 10 trials, then switch.

***Title:*** **_Set and Over_**
- *Level:* 3–6

*Skills Enhanced:* overhead set

*Equipment Needed:* 6 to 8 vinyl balls, and 2 volleyball nets

*Description:* Player #1 tosses the ball high to #2 at the net who sets the ball high to #3 who sets the ball over the net to #4 who catches the ball.

*Variation:* #4 attempts to set the ball back to #1.

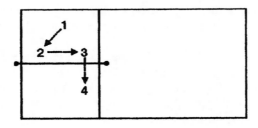

***Title:*** **_Shuttle Set_**
- *Level:* 3–6

*Skills Enhanced:* overhead set

*Equipment Needed:* 5 vinyl balls or other appropriate balls

*Description:* C sets the ball to D and immediately runs to a position behind F. D receives the ball and sets it to B, immediately running to a position behind A, etc. Have groups see how many sets they can do before losing control of the ball.

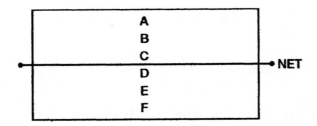

***Title:*** **_Partner Serving_**
- *Level:* 3–6

*Skills Enhanced:* overhand, underarm, and sidearm serve

*Equipment Needed:* vinyl balls for 1/2 of the class and 2 volleyball nets

*Description:* The class is divided into partners. Each pair is given a vinyl ball. After the teacher demonstrates the overhand, underarm, and sidearm serves, the partners stand across the net from each other behind the service line. The service line may be brought up closer to the net for younger students. Partners take turns serving the ball in the correct manner over the net. One partner serves the ball over the net, while the other partner then retrieves the ball and serves it back. Students will practice all three serves. The teacher will help those having difficulty.

## Title:    *Setting Up The Ball*
- *Level:* 3–6

*Skills Enhanced:* team strategy and positioning the ball

*Equipment Needed:* 6 to 8 vinyl balls or other appropriate balls and 2 volleyball nets.

*Description:* The class is divided into groups of four. Each group is given a vinyl ball. Two players are on one side of the net with the other two players across from them on the other side of the net. One player is close to the net, while the other player is eight to twelve feet or more directly behind the net player. The player in the back sets the ball up to the net player who hits it over the net. After five hits on one side players trade places. The players on the same team on the other side of the net do the same skills after retrieving the ball on their side of the net. After practicing several times setting the ball from the back position to the net position, players will stand side by side next to the net and continue to set up the ball to each other.

## Title:    *Team Rotation*
- *Level:* 3–6

*Skills Enhanced:* rotation

*Equipment Needed:* 2 volleyball nets

*Description:* Students are divided into groups of six. They stand in the correct positions for a volleyball game. After a demonstration and explanation of correct rotation, the team rotates positions when the teacher blows the whistle. All teams will rotate at the same time. This drill can also be helpful in assisting students to understand rotation for station formations.

## Title:    *Across and Back*
- *Level:* 3–6

*Skills Enhanced:* volleying

*Equipment Needed:* 6 to 8 vinyl balls or other appropriate balls, and 2 volleyball nets.

*Description:* Students are divided into groups of four. Each group is given a vinyl ball. Two students from each group are on one side of the net across from the other two students in their group. Students will practice volleying the ball across the net to the other two students in their group. Groups are to count the number of times they are able to volley the ball without missing.

## Title:    *Hold Your Place!*
- *Level:* 3–6

*Skills Enhanced:* throwing and catching, playing one's position

*Equipment Needed:* 2 deck tennis rings, and 2 volleyball nets

*Description:* The class is divided into four teams with six players on each team. One deck tennis ring is given to each court. Teams are to use basic volleyball rules using the deck tennis ring rather than a volleyball. Students will throw and catch the deck tennis ring. Players must stay in their own position while throwing and catching the ring. If a player moves into someone else's space the opposing team receives one point. If the ring is on the line, players must call for the ring and the first player to call for it, is responsible for catching it. The boxes are taped on the floor with masking tape to mark off spaces. After students have become proficient with this skill, teams will be divided in half with only three players on each team. The station formation would work well when using only three players on a team due to equipment limitations.

## *LEAD-UP GAMES*

The following games have been selected to reinforce practice of basic volleyball skills. They progress in difficulty and should be used in the volleyball unit as the actual games that are played. Whenever possible teams should have a minimal number of players and several games should be played, depending on the facilities available. The parent game of volleyball should not be played as a part of the elementary physical education program but may be played in intramural programs or in after-school sports. In order to maximize

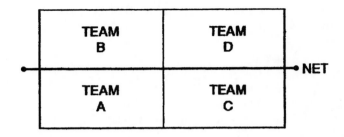

participation, team games should be played with: 4 teams, net or rope between each two teams:

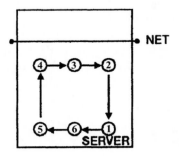

Two games will be going on simultaneously for maximum participation. Team playing space may be small. Scatter formation will be adequate for most games for grades 3–4 but 5–6 graders should use serving formation:

After #1 completes his/her serving responsibility and the ball is turned over to the other team, players remain in this position. When the ball is again turned over and this team becomes the serving team, #2 moves back to the #1 position and becomes the server. Numbers 3 and 4 move one position to their right sides, #5 moves one space forward, and #s 1 and 6 move one space to the left. There may be more players than six on a team and the teacher may place those players in the rotation as well.

### Title:    *Sand Volleyball*

- *Level:* 5–6

*Skills Enhanced:* general volleyball skills

*Equipment Needed:* a beach with sand volleyball set up, or a sandy area on the playground with a volleyball net set up.

*Description:* Sand volleyball is played on the sand with general rules of volleyball applying. Sand volleyball is usually played as doubles, however more can play if desired. The sand creates an interesting composition to play on.

### Title:    *Add On Volleyball*

- *Level:* 3–6

*Skills Enhanced:* serving, volleying, and scoring

*Equipment Needed:* 2 vinyl balls or other appropriate balls, and 2 volleyball nets.

*Description:* Divide into teams with 6 to 8 players on each team. There are 4 teams. Regular volleyball rules apply with the following exceptions. One re-serve is allowed for each serve which may be taken from anywhere in the court. Any time the serve or volley goes over the net the team serving or volleying it successfully gets one point. A successful bump is worth 3 points. Points are added on an ongoing basis as the ball successfully crosses the net. When the ball is successfully passed to a teammate 1 point is also scored. There may be a variation for the various grade levels. The number of volleys for third graders is unlimited on their own side of the net, whereas fourth graders are allowed 8 hits or volleys on one side. Fifth and sixth graders are to stick to the regular volleys allowed in regular volleyball which would be 3. The idea is to keep adding up the score.

### Title:    *Switch Sides*

- *Level:* 3–6

*Skills Enhanced:* running, bumping, and serving

*Equipment Needed:* 2 vinyl balls or other appropriate balls and 2 volleyball nets.

*Description*: There are four members to each team. Teams will position themselves in regular volleyball formation with only 4 players instead of 6. The right back player serves the ball over the net. The receiving team returns the ball back over the net. If successful the server and the player who bumped the ball switch sides. If the ball is missed by the receiving team the server rotates so there is a new server. Play continues until both teams have all member on the other side of the net. Regardless of what side of the net team members are on, they must play their best. After changing sides players will bump the ball to other players on their side of the net so play can continue. When everyone is on the opposite side of the net from where they started, players may begin to switch back. If either player misses the ball, players remain on their own side of the net.

### Title:    *Shooting Stars*

- *Level:* 3–6

*Skills Enhanced:* throwing and catching

*Equipment Needed:* 15 vinyl balls per game and 2 volleyball nets

*Description:* Teams consist of 6 to 8 players. There are 4 teams. When the teacher blows the whistle play begins. The vinyl balls are showered over the net as fast as possible. If a ball hits the floor, goes out of bounds, or goes under the net, that ball is taken out of the game. Players are not allowed to walk with the ball. After 5 minutes play stops and the team with the fewest number of balls is the winner. Play begins again with the whistle. Teams rotate courts after each game.

### *Title:* **_Comet Ball_**
- *Level:* 3–6

*Skills Enhanced:* setting the ball and bumping

*Equipment Needed:* 4 to 6 vinyl balls or other appropriate balls

*Description:* A team consist of six players. There are 4 teams. Players divide into letter order from A to F. The first player bumps the ball and calls "A". In alphabetical order each player on the team attempt to hit the ball to keep it from hitting the floor. Each time the ball is hit the next player calls out their own letter. If the ball is caught, hits the ground, or is touched by an incorrect player the game is halted and the score is called out. A net is not needed for this game and is played only among the team members themselves. The score is the number of times the ball is successfully hit without a fault. The idea is to keep the ball in the air, hitting it in alphabetical order, therefore getting 1 point for each successful hit.

### *Title:* **_One Bounce_**
- *Level:* 3–6

*Skills Enhanced:* forearm pass, overhead set, serve

*Equipment Needed:* beach ball, foam or gator ball

*Description:* Team members are arranged in scatter formation for grades 3–4, in rotation formation for grades 5–6. This game may be played either with or without a net. The server hits the ball to the opposing team. The ball must bounce before being returned or hit by any of the receiving team players. The ball may bounce up to three times before it is considered dead, and the serving team receives a point. Then a second server starts the ball. Players should try to return the ball after the bounce using the forearm pass, or the overhead set if the bounce is high enough. Teams may have as many hits on a side as necessary. If the receiving team returns the ball to the serving team, the serving team has a maximum of three bounces before hitting it again. If the serving team fails to return the ball, the receiving team gains possession of the ball and becomes the serving team. A point is not scored but the ball is turned over. Only serving teams can earn points.

### *Title:* **_Nebraska Ball_**
- *Level:* 3–6

*Skills Enhanced:* serving, overhead set, forearm pass

*Equipment Needed:* beach ball, foam or gator ball

*Description:* Players are in scatter formation in their respective spaces for grades 3–4; rotation formation for 5–6. Any player serves the ball across the net from any position on the floor; team members receiving the ball may use the overhead set and forearm passing skills to return the ball and the ball may be hit by as many players as is necessary to get the ball back over the net. When the ball hits the floor on one side of the net, the nearest player starts the ball going again with a serve.

*Variation:* only three players from one side may contact the ball, but they may hit the ball as many times as necessary to return it over the net.

### *Title:* **_Shower Service Volleyball_**
- *Level:* 3–4

*Skills Enhanced:* serving

*Equipment Needed:* at least 12 foam or gator balls

*Description:* Two teams are each in scatter formation (on their own sides of the net). Each team has six or more balls to begin. On the signal to go, players serve the balls simultaneously across the net from a designated serving line (distance dependent on skill of children).

Players without balls try to catch the serves as they come over the net. If a serve hits the floor, a point is scored for the server. The catchers take the balls immediately to the serving line and serves them over the net. Players keep track of their own points (balls that hit the floor on the opposite side without being caught).

***Title:*** ***Modified Volleyball***
* *Level:* 5–6

*Skills Enhanced:* forearm pass, overhead set, serve

*Equipment Needed:* foam ball or gator ball

*Description:* Teams in rotation positions. The server serves from a position behind the end line. If the serve does not appear to be going over, other players may help it over. The receiving team tries to hit the ball back and may have an unlimited number of hits on the side before passing the ball over the net, but the ball may not touch the floor. If it does, a point is awarded to the serving team and the same server serves again. A player may hit the ball more than one time in a row. Play continues until the ball hits the floor on either side of the net. If the ball hits the floor on the server's side, the ball is turned over to the opposing team who becomes the serving team. Players should rotate at this point.

Variations: Restrict the number of hits on one side to three; do not allow players to hit the ball twice in succession.

## Summary

This sports chapter is designed so that you will understand how to present skill learning in a fun way. Rather than relying on traditional drills of the past, each activity should have a game-like climate so that children are enjoying their learning. You should always maximize participation and be sure to have as many games or activities going at a time as is possible so children have many opportunities to play and interact with the equipment. Never should there be one game of 11 on 11 soccer, for example, in elementary physical education. Save those games for the intramural program.

## References and Suggested Readings

Dieden, B. (1995). *Games to keep kids moving*. Benjamin Cummings.

Dieden, B. (1995). *Games to keep kids moving*. Parker.

Gabbard, C.P., LeBlanc, E. & Lowy, S. (1989). *Games, dance and gymnastics activities*. Prentice-Hall.

Kirchner G. & Fishburne, G.J. (2001). *Physical education for elementary school children*. McGraw Hill.

Kirchner G. & Fishburne, G.J. (1998). *Physical education for elementary school children*. Brown & Benchmark.

Kirchner G. & Fishburne, G.J. (1995). *Physical education for elementary school children*. Brown & Benchmark.

Langley, D.J. & Woods, A. M. (1997). Developing progressions in motor skills: A systematic approach. *Journal of Physical Education, Recreation and Dance*, 68(7), 41–45.

Nelson, K. (1994). *Pickle, pepper and tip-in too*. Simon & Schuster.

Nichols, B. (2001). *Moving and learning: The elementary school physical education experience.* McGraw Hill.

Nichols, B. (1994). *Moving and learning: The elementary school physical education experience.* Times Mirror/Mosby.

Nichols, B. (1990). *Moving and learning.* Times Mirror/Mosby.

Pangrazi, R.P. (2006). *Dynamic physical education for elementary school children.* Benjamin Cummings.

Pangrazi, R.P. (2003). *Dynamic physical education for elementary school children.* Benjamin Cummings.

Pangrazi, R.P. (1998). *Dynamic physical education for elementary school children.* Allyn & Bacon.

Pangrazi, R.P. & Dauer, V.P. (1995). *Dynamic physical education for elementary school children.* Allyn & Bacon.

Pangrazi, R.P. & Dauer, V.P. (1992). *Dynamic physical education for elementary school children.* Macmillan.

Vannier, M. & Poindexter, H.B. (1968). *Individual and team sports for girls and women.* Saunders.

## Website Sources

http://www.douglas-sports.com/FieldDiagrams.htm
http://www.pickleball.com/Rules.asp
http://www.usapa.org/court.htm

CHAPTER

# 12

# Dance and Rhythmic Activities

Coordinated movement has a rhythmic base. Because of our inherent sense of rhythm (temporal awareness) we become efficient movers. Children develop a sense of timing in movement through their interactions with the environment during play. Activities specifically involving rhythmic activities help them to refine their coordination as well as to move rhythmically to patterns and to music. It is important that children in grades K to 3 experience numerous dance and rhythmic activity units. Children in grades 4 to 6 also benefit from dance and rhythmic units, probably in the form of folk, square, and social dance.

## Teaching Dance and Rhythmic Movement Activities

Depending on the complexity of the activity, logical teaching progression may vary from a whole teaching approach to a part-whole teaching approach. For simple dances, routines to the music are elementary and the teacher can actually teach the dance by having the children walk through the motions with the help of auditory cues. In each case the children should be placed into the formation for the dance or activity and then given instructions.

Once the children are in the formation, you may lead them to walk through the activity or dance. If it is simple, one walk-through may be sufficient, then the music may be added. If the complexity of the parts is increased, you may teach part 1, perform part 1 to the music; teach part 2, perform part 1 and part 2 to the music, etc. Some teachers prefer to teach the entire activity in this part-whole sequence completely through without the music; others prefer to introduce the music early in the teaching sequence. Practically speaking, if tapes are used it will be easier to teach without the music, for rewinding will take time and will be imprecise. Working with records or CDs is much easier. If tapes are the only option having one dance on one tape makes the use of time more efficient.

Once the game or dance has been learned, it should not be put away. It should be reviewed and used again later in the unit. The learning process is often slow and the children do not get adequate practice time in rhythms. The practice time comes in actually doing the dance or activity. Many dances are of such a pace as to contribute highly to aerobic endurance. This is especially true in square dance. Therefore, learned dances would make excellent warm-ups for classes that are not even part of dance units.

## Organization of Dance and Rhythmic Activities

One of the first considerations in organizing a dance and rhythmic activities unit would be to consider the equipment and facilities needed. An interesting consideration regarding the teaching of dance and rhythmic activities is that this can be accomplished in a large room or even on a playground or parking lot, providing the weather cooperates and the surface is dry. The gymnasium would be the ideal location; however the cafeteria or other large room could be utilized. Some rhythmic activities are well suited to the classroom.

The equipment needed would be a record player (preferably with a microphone hookup), a cassette recorder/player, a heavy duty outdoor extension chord, a cart with wheels for storing and the moving record player, recorder, etc. (with outlets built into the cart), several appropriate dance records, CDs and tapes. It is wise to have back up tapes for dances to be taught from records in case of damage or breakage. Included at the end of this chapter is a list of suggested records, CDs, and tapes as well as some possible sources for their purchase.

Dance is very adaptable towards teaching large groups especially when using a team teaching approach. Because review is an important factor in teaching dance, appropriate grade levels can be combined. For example fifth and sixth grades can be brought together in order to teach square, folk, or social dance. Using a team teaching approach one teacher may actually teach the steps or parts of the dance while the other teachers walk around and assist individual squares or students. The teachers who are assisting can also attend to any discipline problems, should this be necessary.

The next consideration in beginning the dance unit would be in moving classes into the proper formations. There are many different dance formations including lines, single circle, semi circle, double circle, squares, individuals, partners, and threesomes. Flexibility in moving from one formation to the next with the least amount of chaos is necessary. If a large permanent circle has been painted on the floor this can be very helpful in getting younger children into circular formations. If there is not a circle on the floor, then having the children hold hands to form a circle will usually work well. From this position children can be told to drop hands and take 2 or 3 giant steps backwards, being sure to keep in a circle formation. A double circle can be formed by having boys on the inside of the circle and girls on the outside either by facing each other, or in a side by side formation. It is often easier to pick boy-girl partners randomly when partners are required. At times choosing a higher functioning student to be with a lower functioning student can be very helpful. Telling students that several mixers will be used in the dance unit in order to have the opportunity to change partners may help alleviate student concerns relating to being with the same partner throughout the unit. Students seem to enjoy changing partners.

By starting out with the same partner at the beginning of each class period, time spent on dividing into partner groups can be saved. However, it is possible to change partners each class period if so desired. If there is an uneven number of boys and girls, those not already divided into boy-girl partner groups can be divided into same gender partners. If the overall class has an uneven number of students the left-over student can sometimes be included in a group of three, dance with one of the teachers, or dance alone until the class changes partners as in a mixer. It appears most beneficial to have boy-girl partners because many dances have specific steps or sequences for boys and a different sequence for girls. All students should be involved whenever possible. Hats or pinnies may be used to distinguish boys who are dancing the girls'part or vice versa. However, even primary students are capable of performing the appropriate steps when a boy is dancing the part of a girl if given specific directions. Rules for proper dance etiquette set up at the beginning of the dance unit help alleviate discipline problems. Respect for others and their feelings needs to be discussed. Students must realize that misbehavior and improper etiquette will not be tolerated; this concept must be established before the dance unit begins.

It has been discovered that although some boys at first complain regarding the fact that they will dance with girls, many of these same students voluntarily confess they actually enjoy the dance experience. The same has been true for girls. This is especially significant in grades 5 and up. The attitude of the teacher concerning the dance unit is reflected through the students. Dance is a very important part of the physical education curriculum and needs to be covered adequately in order to assist students to refine their coordination as well as to develop rhythmic movement patterns. Dance can and has been an enjoyable experience for numerous students and teachers throughout the world.

There are several ways to divide students into squares when teaching a square dance unit. Dividing the number of students in the class by eight will determine the number of squares in that particular class. Many times there will be students left over. Children left over can sit at the sidelines and be placed into the squares at the end of each dance. Every student should eventually dance every dance. Therefore, many dances will have to be repeated when there are students left over. Often there will be occasions when there will be an uneven number of boys or girls. When this occurs the girls may take the boys' part or visa versa. When selecting squares the teacher may randomly pick the four couples for each square. Numbers or colored chips may by used much the same as explained in Chapter Two regarding dividing into squads or teams. Another way of selecting squares would be to ask for volunteers to be the head lady and the head gent for each square. The head gent would then pick the boys in his square and the head lady would pick the girls in her square. The students on the sideline waiting their turn to dance might be allowed to choose the person whose position they wish to replace.

## SPECIFIC DANCE INFORMATION

Each dance has been broken down into six parts in order to assist the novice teacher to teach an assortment of folk, social, and square dances. The dances selected in this chapter have been selected for their popularity as well as for variety. They have been successfully taught at the level suggested for many years to a wide variety of students of varying skill levels. The categories included are music, level and difficulty, history, instructions, and cues.

## MUSIC

When teaching dance, one of the most difficult tasks is to find the appropriate music. Therefore, 3 music CDs have been included with this book, which contain almost all of the music necessary to teach the dances found in the preschool and dance chapters. Most of the Folk Dances have musical arrangements by Michael Herman. The square dance music has a square dance caller which assists the teacher, when attempting to teach a square dance unit. Many popular social dance songs are also on the CD, as well as appropriate music to accompany the four ballroom dances found in the book. The music CDs were obtained from The Kentucky Dance Foundation. The Kentucky Dance Foundation is affiliated with the Folk Dancer Record Center at 6290 Olin Road Brandenburg, Kentucky 40108.

The music used as accompaniment for dance is extremely important to the success of teaching dance. Not only is the beat important in helping to execute the proper steps at the appropriate time, but the tempo also assists the dancer to perform the dance at the appropriate speed. The music gives the student a feel for the culture of the various countries from which the dances originated. There are several records available for the same dance; however the music which closely resembles that used when the dance was created appears to add to the interest and appeal of the students. For example, there are several varied arrangements of The Twist; however, Chubby Checker's version seems to appeal the most to students.

There are a variety of records available for an assortment of folk dances; however, whenever possible, obtaining Michael Herman's arrangements seem to be closer to the original versions. Michael Herman uses a variety of instruments which assist in closely relating the music to the country from which the particular dance originated.

## LEVEL AND DIFFICULTY

The dances in this chapter have each been classified as to the appropriate grade level as well as a rating regarding the difficulty of each dance. All dances have been successfully taught at the grade level specified.

## HISTORY

To integrate history, geography and other classroom subjects into the dance unit, a short history for many of the dances has been included whenever the history is known. It is helpful to teach a dance from a specific country while studying that country in the classroom, whenever possible. When listening to the music, and dancing a specific country's dance, students are able to experience a feeling of the culture of that country. During a program when dances from a variety of countries or from various eras are performed, a brief history presented to the audience appears to add interest and appreciation for those dances as well as for the performance itself.

## FORMATION

Dances are performed in semicircles, circles, double circles, lines, double lines, squares, partners, and individuals. They may be performed in specific patterns or in a scattered random pattern. The formation portion of each dance deals with the specific dance and its pattern or formation.

## INSTRUCTIONS

The instructions portion for a specific dance describes in detail the steps and footwork for each dance. The instructions are meant to be very detailed and specific. It is suggested that the instructions be carefully read and then put together with the music before actually teaching the dance. A demonstration of each part of the dance with specific footwork has been found to be extremely significant to student learning. The instructions have been broken down in a step by step fashion in order to assist teachers in understanding the dance.

## CUES

Cues are the words used to assist the student verbally in order to keep the beat and remind students what comes next. Calling out the words as stated in the cue section seems to help both teacher and student to fit the appropriate steps in time with the music.

# Lesson Plans

It is extremely important to organize and structure the physical education class in such a way that students are actively participating for the majority of the class period. Physical education is a physical movement class therefore it is important to direct the physical movement. Dance lends itself to keeping every student active for the majority of the class period. Dividing into partners, getting into formations, organizing dances, and management of equipment all need to be done in an efficient and timely manner. This can be accomplished by organizing the dance unit ahead of time and using efficient lesson plans. In order to assist the teacher with directions for each dance, the pages of actual cues and instructions can either be copied from this book, or written on large index cards. Instructions and cues should be written in such a way that they may be read from the cards or sheets directly to the class. The teacher of course, will need to review the instructions and cues before each class. This chapter has been written for the novice teacher who has had little or no actual dance background. With a positive attitude, the instructions and cues included in this book, and a desire to share the wonderful world of dance with one's students, a comprehensive dance unit can be successfully taught to grades K through 6.

# Suggested Dances per Grade Level

## *Kindergarten*

"Get Ready to Square Dance" Album Side 1
Chicken Dance
Bunny Hop
YMCA

Patty Cake Polka
Hokey Pokey
The Shoemaker Dance
Macarena
Bingo
All of Singing Games from the Preschool Chapter

## Grade One

All of the Above Dances
Ve' David
The Chimes of Dunkirk
Twist
Seven Jumps
Bingo
Kinderpolka
Twist
Mayim Mayim

## Grade Two

All of Grade One Dances
The Waltz
Mayim Mayim
Kinderpolka
Basic Swing Dance
Greensleeves
Electric Slide
Swing Dance Basics

## Grade Three

The Waltz
The Virginia Reel
La Raspa
The Electric Slide
The Twist
YMCA
Milonovo Kolo
Chicken Dance
Bunny Hop
Macarena
Swing Dance
Cha Cha
Fox Trot

## Grade Four

All of Grade 3 Dances

The Hora
The Fireman
The Montgomery County Cha Cha Cha
Fox Trot
The Stroll
Troika
Korobushka
Limbo
Tinikling

## *Grade Five*

All of Grade 4 Dances
The Electric Slide
Macarena
"Get Ready to Square Dance" Side 2
Around the Outside and Swing
Do-sa-do and Swing
Solomon Levi
Marching through Georgia
Life on the Ocean Wave (Head Two Ladies Cross Over)
Red River Valley
Make an Arch
Yankee Doodle
Hinkey Dinkey Parlez Vous
Divide the Ring
Hot Time in the Old Town (Girls to the Center)
Take A Little Peek
Form An Arch
Push Her Away
Cha Cha
Fox Trot
Swing

## *Grade Six*

All of Grade 5 Dances
Pass the Left Hand Lady Under
Tinikling
Troika
Foxt Trot
Cha Cha
Swing

# Folk Dance

Folk dances represent several different traditions and cultures. Folk dance originated from a great number of different sources including celebrations, rituals, weddings, occupations, harvesting crops, and a variety of other events that were significant in the lives of the people and society at the time they originated or were celebrated. Folk dances offer a rich variety of patterns, styles, and movements. They are a reflection of the culture and history of the people they represent.

## SOME OF THE OBJECTIVES TO TEACHING FOLK DANCE

A positive regard for a variety of cultures and nations may be developed through experiencing folk music and dances. Folk dance when performed properly can be of cardiorespiratory benefit as with all dance. New patterns, styles and steps are learned through the performance of folk dance. Both physical and mental alertness as well as endurance can be improved by participating in complicated and demanding dance steps and patterns.

Folk dancing can assist in integrating history and geography through the physical education class. Students can get a feel for a particular culture by actually performing a specific country's folk dances. When studying a specific country, students' appreciation of that country's culture may be enhanced by giving students the opportunity to learn a folk dance which originated in that particular region. An appreciation of the music which accompanies that particular dance may also be acquired.

Some of the well known popular folk dances have been included in this chapter. Many of these dances may have been observed by students who have attended weddings or celebrations of a particular ethnic culture.

_**Title:**_    _**Chimes of Dunkirk**_
_Music:_ The music to accompany this dance can be found on volume 1, band 1, on the music CD included with this book. 4/4 time.
_Level and Difficulty:_ Grades K–3. Moderate.
_History:_ This dance originated in France and is a simplified version of the French mixer performed in a circle formation and known as "Carillon de Dunkirque" which, in French, means "Chimes of Dunkirk." The stamping of feet and clapping of hands is believed to represent the chimes of the church bells in the town of Dunkirk.

_Formation:_ A double circle with the boys on the inside of the circle, girls are on the outside and partners are facing each other.
_Instructions:_ Partners begin with the boys folding their arms at chest level and girls placing their hands on their hips. All dancers stamp alternating feet 3 times in place, followed by clapping their hands 3 times. Next, partners will join both hands and circle in place moving clockwise around each other until dancers are back to their starting positions. With hands still joined couples take 4 steps to the boys' right. Boys start with their right feet and girls with their left feet. The boys parts necessitates stepping with the right feet and bringing the left feet up to the right, then stepping with the right feet again and bringing the left feet up to the right feet again. The girls move in the same direction as the boy only using the opposite feet. The entire action is repeated to the boys left. The boys start with the left feet stepping to the left and bringing the right feet up to the left and again stepping with the left feet bringing the right feet up to the left. The whole sequence is repeated starting with the right feet. Refer to the cues section of this dance. At this point the entire sequence from the beginning is repeated throughout the dance.

      *Cues:*     Stamp L, stamp R, stamp L (the cues reflect the boy's part, girls use opposite
              feet)
              Clap, clap, clap
              Turn the lady once around (clockwise)
              Right together left, right together left
              Left together right, left together right
              Right together left, right together left
              Left together right, left together right
              Repeat entire sequence throughout dance

## *Title: Greensleeves*

*Music*: The music to accompany this dance can be found on volume 1, band 2, on the music CD included with this book.

*Level and Difficulty*: Grades 3-6. Moderate.

*History*: Greensleeves originated in England. During the dance as dancers are moving forward and backwards through the arches. This is believed to represent turning the sleeves inside out.

*Formation*: Greensleeves is performed in sets of 2 couples. The dance begins by having students form a double circle with boys on the inside and girls on the outside. Dancers will move in a counterclockwise direction. Once the double circle has been formed, students will be divided into sets of two couples remaining in a double circle moving counterclockwise.

*Instructions*: All couples begin by marching forward sixteen steps. The front couples turn to face the other couples (the back couples). All dancers put their right hands into the center and perform a right hand star, walking forward in a circular pattern for eight counts. All four dancers then turn the other way putting their left hands in the center and again walk forward in a circular pattern for eight counts. This movement is known as a right hand star followed by a left hand star. All dancers now return to their original positions. The back or rear couples form an arch by raising their inside arms only, keeping hands joined. At the same time the rear couples move forward four steps as the front couples walk backwards four steps under the arch. The new front couples now move under the arch as the new back couples move forward. This action is repeated again until both couples are back to their original positions. The action of moving through the arches four times is known as "turning the sleeves inside out." Dancers will repeat the entire sequence throughout the dance.

      Cues:     March 2,3,4,5,6,7,8,9,10,11,12,13,14,15,16
              Right hand star 2,3,4,5,6,7,8
              Left hand star 2,3,4,5,6,7,8
              Arches 2,3,4 (back couple forward)
              Arches 2,3,4
              Arches 2,3,4
              Arches 2,3,4

## *Title:*   *The Hora*

*Music:* The music to accompany this dance can be found on volume 1, band 3, on the music CD included with this book. 4/4 time.

*Level and Difficulty:* Grades 4–6. Moderate.

*History:* The Hora originated in the Balkans and was later brought to Israel where it is now considered to be a national dance of Israel. The Hora is often performed to the Israeli folk song, "Hava Nagila." The Hora can be performed to many traditional songs and is often performed at a variety of celebrations, weddings, etc. The Hora is credited as being an Israeli symbol of spirit and strength.

*Formation:* A single circle with students facing center, with hands joined or arms around the waist of the other dancers. The circle may change to a line with the leader weaving the line through arches formed by students in the circle raising arms with the person next to them.

*Instructions:* Dancers begin by stepping to the right with the right feet, then stepping with the left feet, behind the right feet. Next dancers step with the right feet followed by kicking the left legs diagonally in front of the right legs. Then dancers step with the left feet in place and kick with the right legs in front of the left legs. This whole sequence takes place while always moving in a counterclockwise direction.  Dancers will repeat the entire sequence until the end of the song. Meanwhile the speed of the music becomes faster and faster as the dance continues. As the speed accelerates hops may be substituted for the steps.

> *Cues:*    Step right, back left, step right, kick left, step left, kick right
> Repeat entire sequence moving to the right or counterclockwise

### *Title:*    *Kinderpolka*

*Music:* The music to accompany this dance can be found on volume 1, band 4, on the music CD included with this book. 4/4 time.

*Level and Difficulty:* Grades K–3. Moderate.

*History:* Kinder is the German word for "children." The Kinderpolka does not have a polka step in the dance. Children seem to especially enjoy the finger shaking, scolding action in this dance. The Kinderpolka originated in Germany.

*Formation:* A partner dance in circle formation, with girls on the boys' right. Start with partners facing each other and moving sideways together towards the center of the circle. While moving sideways children bring their arms up to shoulder level, joining hands with arms extended out to the sides. (Arm position is known as the butterfly).

*Instructions:* Boys will start with their left feet, girls with right both moving towards the center of the circle with arms extended in butterfly position.  Both dancers move at the same time starting with opposite feet, boys start with the left feet, girls with the right feet.  The boys step sideways on the left feet then bringing the right feet next to the left. The same step is repeated again still moving towards the center of the circle. All dancers will then stamp in place three times.  The girls move with the boys doing the same steps but with the opposite feet.  The same steps are repeated only moving away from the center of the circle and using the opposite feet.  Therefore the boys' part would be to step on the right and bring the left feet next to the right, repeat this movement, followed by stamping three times. This entire sequence is repeated. While facing their partners, dancers slap their hands against their own thighs, once. Dancers clap their own hands together once and then clap their own hands against their partners hands 3 times (pat). Dancers will repeat this movement of clapping thighs, clapping hands, and patting partners hands.  Dancers now hop once on the left feet extending the right heels forward to touch the floor and at the same time shake their index fingers at their partners, 3 times. Dancers will repeat this action with left heels touching floor. Each dancer now turns completely around once and stamps 3 times. Dancers will repeat this entire sequence throughout the dance.

> *Cues:*    Step left together right (towards the center)
> Step left together right
> Stamp, stamp, stamp

Step right together left (away from the center)
Step right together left
Stamp, stamp, stamp
Repeat entire sequence from beginning
Thighs
Clap
Pat 2, 3
Thighs
Clap
Pat 2, 3
Hop shake 2, 3
Hop shake 2, 3
Turn around
Stamp, stamp, stamp

*Title:* **_Korobushka_**

*Music:* . The music to accompany this dance can be found on volume 1, band 5, on the music CD included with this book. 4/4 time.

*Level and Difficulty:* Grade 5–6. Difficult.

*History:* It is believed that the dance Korobushka, meaning "little basket" in Russian originated in the United States by Russian immigrants after World War II. This dance is performed to a popular Russian folk song describing a peddler's pack.

*Formation:* Korobushka is performed in a double circle with couples facing each other. Boys have their backs towards the center of the circle, and girls towards the outside of the circle. Partners join both hands.

*Instructions:* The boys start with their left feet and the ladies begin with their right feet. Boys take three steps forward and then hop on their left feet. This pattern is known as the schottische step and is performed by stepping on the left feet, then stepping with the right feet bringing them next to the left feet, stepping on the left feet followed by hopping on the left feet (while the boys are moving forward). The girl moves backwards performing the same steps on the opposite feet. Dancers repeat this sequence, only the boys move backwards on the opposite feet, which would be starting with their right feet, while the ladies moves forward, beginning with their left feet. The step is repeated again with the boy moving forward and the girl moving backwards. For the next sequence both boys and the girls hop on the left feet and at the same

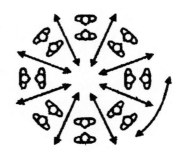

**Double circle with partners facing each other, moving into the center and away from the center or clockwise, counterclockwise**

time point their right toes touching them to the floor in front of the left feet. Partners both hop again on the left feet, this time pointing the right toes, touching them to the floor to the right side. All dancers hop again on the left feet, this time bringing the feet together. On the third hop dancers may jump in place and click heels together after a great deal of experience. Dancers will now pause and release hands. Both boys and girls will move at the same time to their own right performing one schottische step away from each other. Dancers perform the schottische step by stepping forward on the right feet, followed by stepping on the left feet bringing them next to the right feet, stepping again on the right feet and hopping on the right feet. Partners will turn towards each other and perform another schottische step, starting with the left feet this time. Partners will now join right hands, both the boys and the girls step on the right feet, leaning towards each other and then stepping on the left feet leaning away from each other. This is known as "balancing towards your partner" and "balancing away from your partner." With four running steps partners exchange places and all dancers release hands. Partners will repeat one schottische step to the right away from each other, followed by one schottische step towards each other. "Balance towards your partner," "balance away from your partner" and "change places" are the cues used to help dancers to execute the proper steps. Dancers will repeat the entire sequence from the beginning throughout the entire song.

    *Cues:*    Both hands joined, boys move forward with right foot while girls move backward with left foot
Right, left, right, hop (boys forward, girls backwards)
Left, right, left, hop (boys backwards, girls forward)
Right, left, right, hop (boys forward, girls backwards)
Forward, side, together
Drop hands, move away from partner
Right, left, right, hop
Move toward your partner
Left, right, left, hop
Join right hands. Balance right
Balance left. Change places
Drop hands, move away from partner
Right, left, right, hop
Move towards your partner
Left, right, left, ho
Join right hands. Balance right
Balance left. Change places
Repeat whole sequence from the beginning throughout the dance.

### Title:    La Raspa

*Music:* The music to accompany this dance can be found on volume 1, band 6 on the music CD included with this book. 4/4 time.

*Level and Difficulty:* Grade 3–6. Easy.

*History:* La Raspa is a simple dance that originated in Mexico. It has been confused with the complicated Mexican Hat Dance. In Spanish La Raspa has been translated as the "rasp" or the "file." The shuffling steps in La Raspa are believed to symbolize the rasp or file.

*Formation:* A double circle with partners facing each other. Boys are on the inside of the circle and girls are on the outside. This dance may also be performed in a random scattering of partners.

*Instructions:* Students stand with hands on hips. Starting with the right heel on the floor change from the right heel to the left heel, then back to the right heel by hopping from one foot to the other. Then couples face each other and join inside elbows, swing four counts and clap twice. Reverse and swing partner the other way. Repeat the swing and clap as before. Repeat the whole dance from the beginning.

*Variation:* A variation from the elbow swing in La Raspa would be to do the grand right and left around the large circle with boys moving counterclockwise and girls moving clockwise.

> *Cues:*    Right, left, right, clap, clap
> Left, right, left, clap, clap
> Right, left, right, clap, clap
> Left, right, left, clap, clap
> Repeat whole sequence
> Swing 4, clap, clap, swing 4, clap, clap
> Swing 4, clap, clap, swing 4, clap, clap
> Repeat whole sequence from the beginning throughout dance

### Title:    *Mayim Mayim*

*Music:* The music to accompany this dance can e found on volume 1, band 7, of the music CD included with this book.

*Level and Difficulty:* Grades K–3. Easy.

*History:* It is believed that the dance Mayim, Mayim originated in a Kibbutz, which is an Israeli settlement along the shores of the Sea of Galilee. Mayim, Mayim is associated with the waves of the sea as well as the discovery of water in the desert. The word Mayim is Hebrew for "water." Mayim Mayim is thought to signify joy and thankfulness and was performed at celebrations and rituals.

*Formation:* A single circle facing center without partners and hands joined.

*Instructions:* This is a simple version of Mayim Mayim. There are some versions of Mayim Mayim that are more complicated than the one presented here. Moving counterclockwise all dancers walk 16 steps, next everyone face the center of the circle. Dancers will take four steps forward to the center of the circle and four steps backward to their own places. Everyone clap their own hands together for four count, followed by pausing for four counts. Dancers now point the left toes in front of the right feet and tap the toes forward on the floor for eight counts. Next everyone will point the right toes forward in front of the left feet and tap them on the floor for eight counts. Dancers will repeat the entire sequence from the beginning throughout the song.

> *Cues:*    Walk 16 counts in a circle counterclockwise
> Forward 2, 3, 4 (toward center of circle)
> Back 2,3,4 (away from the center of the circle)
> Clap 2, 3, 4
> Pause 2, 3, 4
> Tap left 2, 3, 4, 5, 6, 7, 8
> Pause for 4 quick counts
> Tap right 2, 3, 4, 5, 6, 7, 8
> Repeat whole sequence from the beginning throughout dance

### Title:    *Milanovo Kolo*

*Music:* The music to accompany this dance can be found on volume 1, band 8, on the music CD included with this book. 4/4 time.

*Level and Difficulty:* Grades 3–6. Easy to Moderate.

*History:* The dance Milanovo Kolo originated in Yugoslavia, and contains steps and patterns that are representative of Slavic dances. This dance was named after a man named Milan, with the word kolo meaning circle hence we have the circle dance entitled The Milanovo Kolo.

*Formation:* A single circle facing center, without partners and with hands joined.

*Instructions:* All dancers turn to the right counterclockwise and take two step hops (right, hop, left, hop), then facing center step on right feet, crossing left feet behind right, then take three lively steps (right, left, right) in place. Dancers will repeat this entire sequence moving clockwise. Everyone will now take two step hops to the left (left, hop, right, hop) then facing center step on the left feet, crossing the right feet behind the left take three lively steps (left, right, left) in place. Facing center with hands joined all dancers move forward towards the center of the circle while moving arms slowly upward. At the same time dancers take three steps followed by holding for 1 count (right, left right, pause) and continue forward again (left, right, left, pause). Dancers will continue with the dance moving backwards as arms are slowly lowered in time to the music (right, left, right, pause, left, right, left, pause).

   *Cues:*   Step, hop, step, hop
             Step, back, 1, 2, 3
             Step, hop, step, hop
             Step, back, 1, 2, 3
             Moving forward
             Right, left, right, hold
             Left, right, left, hold
             Moving backwards
             Right, left, right, hold
             Left, right, left, hold
             Repeat whole sequence through the entire dance.

### *Title:*   *Seven Jumps*

*Music:* The music to accompany this dance can be found on volume 1, band 9, on the music CD included with this book. 4/4 time.

*Level and Difficulty:* Grades K–2. Easy.

*History:* This dance originated in Denmark and is performed by men and boys. Today this dance is also performed by girls and women and contains a follow the leader style by adding new actions to each verse.

*Formation:* A single circle facing counterclockwise without partners.

*Instructions:* All dancers are in one large circle with all hands joined and facing counterclockwise. Everyone will walk or skip 16 steps to the right, then turn and walk 16 steps to the left. Everyone then turns to face the center of the circle and on the first long note lift the right knees, and on the next long note put the right knees down. All dancers take 16 steps to the right and 16 steps to the left. On the next long note, the dancers will lift theirs right knees, put them down, then lifting the left knees putting them down. Everyone again takes 16 steps to the right, followed by 16 steps to the left. Dancers will lift their right knees, putting them down, then lifting their left knees, put them down, followed by kneeling on the right knees and then standing up. Continue with this pattern adding left knees, right elbows, left elbows and finally heads.

   *Cues:*   16 steps (or skips) to the right, 16 steps to the left
             Lift right knee, put it down, pause (Skip to the right and to the left 16 counts
             between each addition)
             Add one at a time
             Lift left knee
             Kneel on right knee
             Kneel on left knee
             Right elbow down on floor
             Left elbow down on floor
             Head

*Title:*     ***The Shoemaker's Dance***

*Music:* The music to accompany this dance can be found on volume 1, band 10, on the music CD included with this book. 4/4 time.

*Level:* Grades K–2. Easy.

*History:* The Shoemaker's Dance originated in Denmark. In Europe skilled workers belonged to a guild or organization representing their occupation. The guild performed dances that represented their craft on holidays or special celebrations. The Shoemaker Dance is an example of such a dance.

*Formation:* The Shoemaker's Dance is performed in a double circle with partners facing each other. Boys are on the inside of the circle and girls are on the outside. All dancers place their hands on their hips.

*Instructions:* With the arms bent at the elbow and in front of the chest, dancers perform a rolling motion forward with the fists tightened and parallel to each other. This represents a winding motion, to symbolize the winding of thread. This winding motion is performed three times in a forward motion and three times in a backward motion. With the elbows still bent dancers point and draw elbows backwards tightly two times. This is believed to represent the tightening of the thread. Dancers clap their own hands together three times. Everyone repeat the winding motion forward (circling the forearms in a circular motion around each other) three times, then backwards three times. Dancers pull their elbows backwards again twice. This time instead of clapping their hands together, dancers will tap their own fists on top of their other fist three times. This represents pounding the nails. Dancers join inside hands with their partners, skipping forward around the circle in a counter clockwise direction for sixteen counts. The dancers free hands are placed on their hips.

      *Cues:*    Wind forward 3 times
                 Wind backward 3 times
                 Pull backward 2 times
                 Clap, clap, clap
                 Wind forward 3 times
                 Wind backward 3 times
                 Pull backward 2 times
                 Pound fists 3 times
                 Skip 16 counts counter clockwise
                 Repeat entire sequence throughout the dance

*Title:*     ***Tinikling***

*Music:* The music to accompany this dance can be found on volume 1, band 11, on the music CD included with this book. 3/4 time.

*Level and Difficulty:* Grades 4–6. Moderate to Difficult.

*History:* Tinikling originated in the Philippines. This dance is believed to represent the actions of the long necked bird the Tinikling. The poles symbolize an attempt to catch the Tinikling's legs between the poles.

*Formation:* Two bamboo poles, two blocks of wood, and two people working the set of poles are needed when performing Tinikling. Bamboo poles are best, however there are plastic poles available that would also work well. The poles should be roughly nine feet long and of equal length. Shorter or longer poles may be used. Two by fours cut to approximately two and a half to three feet work well for the blocks of wood.

Two blocks of wood are needed for each set of poles. At least four sets of poles and blocks are needed in order to teach Tinikling to an average size class. If only one set is available this dance could be taught in stations with one station using the set of poles and three other stations practicing various steps.

*Instructions:* Two students sit on the floor with legs folded, one at each end of the set of poles. These students need to be sure they sit far enough back so that their knees are not in the way of the poles. These students will strike the poles apart and against the blocks of wood twice and then strike the poles together once. The cue for the strikers would be "down, down, together." Students working the poles need to synchronize the poles.

One or two dancers may dance between the poles while the poles are apart and down. The cues for the dancers would be "in, in, out." The dancer will do two steps between the poles when the poles are apart and must be outside the poles when the poles are struck together.

There are several variations of the dance steps performed in the middle of the poles. The dancers start on one side of the poles and jump, landing on both feet between the poles twice, then outside landing on one side with both feet. Dancers may either land on the side they started on or on the opposite side. Dancers should experiment and try various ways of jumping between the poles and landing outside the poles. Dancers may start with feet astride the poles, one foot on each side and jump with both feet inside and then jump astride outside the poles. As dancers jump out of and astride the poles, they can also turn to face the opposite direction. Dancers may start on one side and hop in on one foot, lift that foot and hop on the other foot and then jump out astride the poles. Many times dancers will jump on one foot only and simply keep the foot they are not using lifted in the air. The important point to remember is that both feet must be out of the center of the poles when the poles are struck together. Students may experiment and try to figure out a variety of different ways to dance between the poles.

When two dancers are dancing between the poles at the same time dancers often face each other and hold hands as both jump twice in the center and then outside the poles. Dancers may also wish to be in a back to back position, or in a line facing the same direction, one behind the other.
If there are several sets of poles available the poles may be lined up so the class can move down the line of parallel poles jumping from set to set, keeping in time to the music as they perform "Tinikling."

The more advanced students may wish to try two sets of poles that are crossed much like a "tic tac toe" board formation. The dance may be performed either diagonally through the middle square or landing in one of the four corner spots. Again experimentation is helpful. There are many, variations and patterns that can be performed when dancing Tinikling.

    *Cues:*    Pole Strikers: Down, Down, Together
                   Repeated throughout entire dance.
                   Dancers: In, In, Out
                   Repeated throughout entire dance.

### *Title:*   *Troika*
*Music:* The music to accompany this dance can be found on volume 1, band 12, on the music CD included with this book. 4/4 time.
*Level and Difficulty:* Grades 4–6. Easy to Moderate.

*History:* The word Troika means "three horses" in Russian. This dance is believed to represent 3 horses running side by side as in pulling a wagon or sleigh. At holiday programs the Troika may be performed to the song "Jingle Bells". Running or leaping steps are used in the Troika to represent the movements of the 3 horses. The Troika can be a mixer by having the middle dancers move up to the next set after each completed sequence.
*Formation:* Groups of three facing counterclockwise. The middle person joins hands with the person on each side. Those on the outside of the threesome can either place their free hand on their hips or raise it to shoulder height. This dance can be performed with any

gender combination. It can be performed in a random pattern, in scattered threesomes or in a big circle of threesomes all facing counterclockwise.

*Instructions:* All three dancers move together using running or leaping steps throughout the dance. Therefore, all steps mentioned are to be performed while running or leaping. All three dancers begin with the right feet and move diagonally to the right for 4 steps. Dancers will repeat these 4 steps while moving to the left in a diagonal direction. Next all dancers will move 8 steps forward and straight ahead.

At this point dancers stop and the dancer on the right will use 8 running steps to move under the arch formed by the center and left side dancer raising their inside arms with hands still joined. The middle dancer will follow the dancer on the right under the arch, turning while moving under the arch. The dancer on the left will repeat the same eight steps while moving under the arch with the middle dancer following the dancer on the left.

Each group now forms a small circle and runs while circling twelve steps counterclockwise, then stamping three times. This action is repeated circling twelve steps clockwise, then stamping again three times. The entire sequence is repeated from the beginning throughout the entire song.

> *Cues:*    4 steps to the right (diagonally)
> 4 steps to the left (diagonally)
> 8 steps forward
> Person on the right under the arch (8 steps)
> Person on the left under the arch (8 steps)
> Circle right, (12 steps) stamp, stamp, stamp
> Circle left, (12 steps) stamp, stamp, stamp
> Repeat entire sequence throughout the dance

### Title:    *Ve' David*

*Music:* The music to accompany this dance can be found on volume 1, band 13, of the music CD included with this book. 4/4 time.

*Level and Difficulty:* K–2. Easy

*History:* In 1956 Rivkah Sturman, an expert on Israeli folk dancing, created Ve' David. Ve' David is a popular Israel mixer with dancers changing partners often. Ve' David is performed to the song entitled " Ve' David Y' Fey Enayim" which means "And David of the Beautiful Eyes".

*Formation:* Double circle with the boys on the inside and the girls on the outside, with couples moving counter clockwise in a circle.

*Instructions:* Dancers join inside hands and couples will walk forward eight steps in a counterclockwise direction. Dancers then turn towards the center of the circle and walk, as a couple with hands still joined, forward 4 steps and then walk 4 steps backwards. Just the girls then walk four steps forward towards the center and four steps back to place as the boys clap 4 times. The boy then walks 4 steps forward and as they are backing up, they move on to the next girl to the right and swing this girl with an elbow swing. The boys each have a new partner. This dance is considered to be a mixer. The entire sequence is repeated from the beginning throughout the entire song.

> *Cues:*    Walk 8 counts (counterclockwise)

Forward 4 and back 4 (couple)
Forward 4 and back 4 (girls)
Forward 4 (boys) and onto the next and swing
Repeat the entire sequence throughout the dance

### *Title:* **_The Virginia Reel_**

*Music:* The music to accompany this dance can be found on volume 1, band 14, on the music CD included with this book. 4/4 time.

*Level and Difficulty:* Grades 3–6. Moderate.

*History:* The Virginia Reel was derived from an English dance entitled "Sir Roger de Coverly" which was popular with English Royalty and was often the last dance at the ball. The Virginia Reel was considered one of the favorites of the nineteenth century American Country Dances.

*Formation:* The Virginia Reel is considered to be a contra or longways dance. It consists of two parallel lines facing each other. Boys are in one line and their girl partners are in the line across from them. There are six couples in each set. However this dance can be adapted for a set of less than 6 couples if necessary.

*Instructions:* All dancers take four steps towards the center of the set and four steps back to place. Partners walk forward joining right hands and walk around each other clockwise and then back to their original place. Partners walk forward this time joining left hands and again walk around each other then back to place. Next partners walk forward and join both hands, walk around each other then back to place. Now partners walk forward passing right shoulders, moving sideways back to back, and return to place passing left shoulders and backing up to their home position. This is known as a "do-sa-do." The head couple is the couple at the beginning of the set and also the couple that is closest to the music. The head couples walk forward towards each other joining both hands and using sliding steps move sideways down the set to the other end and back to place. This is known as a "sashay." The head couple then join right elbows and turn each other one and a half turns around and then go to the opposite line (boy to girls' line and girl to boys' line) and turn the next person half way around with left elbows joined. The head couple returns to the middle and turn each other again half way around and then back to the next person in the opposite line and turn that person half way around. The head couple continues down the line until each person in the opposite line has been turned, always being sure to return to the middle in between to turn their own partner. This is called "reeling the set." When reeling the set has been completed the head couple sashays back to the head of the set. The head couple then cast off which means the boys turn to their own right and the girls turn to their own left. All of the boys line will follow the head gent, in order, until the end of the set while the girls line follows them. At the end of the set the head couple form an arch and the rest of the couples go through the arch, in order, towards the head of the set. Now couples two are the new head couples. The dance continues until each couple has a turn to be the head couple. The entire sequence from the beginning is repeated throughout the song.

    *Cues:*    Forward and Back
                Right hand round
                Left hand round
                Both hands round
                Do-sa-do
                Head Couple Down and Back—Sashay
                Reel the Set (right elbow to your partner and left elbow to the next)
                 Sashay back

Cast off
Form an arch
Repeat entire sequence throughout the dance

# Social Dance

When teaching social dance teachers should pay particularly close attention to progression, purpose, and continuity. Social dance is just that, a social activity. The main purpose of social dance is to bring about physical enjoyment through the use of rhythm and movement. Social dance can be an aesthetically as well as a satisfying movement experience. Many social and folk dances may be performed at evening or holiday programs in order that parents and others may enjoy observing them.

## SOME OF THE OBJECTIVES TO TEACHING SOCIAL DANCE

The main objective of social dance is to provide social and physical pleasure in an enjoyable manner through the use of rhythm and active movement. When teaching social dance or any other dance, the objective, sequence, continuity, and flow are all important to consider.
Social dancing, especially slow dances like the waltz, can help students to develop the ability to lead and follow successfully when performing dance movements. Social skills are encouraged by helping students to feel comfortable during social situations involving the opposite sex. Social dance also contributes to the student's awareness of moving to a specific rhythm or beat. Good posture is encouraged. Creativity is promoted by adding ones own style to patterns, steps, and movement in general. When teaching social dance, as with all dance, the teacher needs to be mindful that the dance progression follows a continuity and purpose.

*Title:* ***Bingo***
*Music:* The music to accompany this dance can be found on volume 1, band 15, on the music CD included with this book. 4/4 time.
*Level and Difficulty:* Grades K–2. Easy.
*History:* Bingo is believed to have originated from a Welch-English folk song. There are several variations of Bingo and this dance is one of the simpler versions. Bingo was once popular in the Appalachian Mountain regions.
*Formation:* Single circle of partners all facing center with boys on the left, girls on the right.
*Instructions:* All dancers join hands and circle counterclockwise by walking 7 steps in a circle formation then turning towards the opposite direction. Everyone

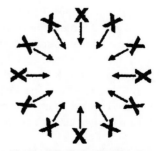

**Single Circle facing Center**

then walk seven steps, circling in a clockwise direction. All dancers drop hands. Only the girls will walk four steps forward towards the center of the circle and 4 steps backwards, while the boys clap in time to the music. Then boys will move 4 steps forward and 4 steps backwards while the girls clap. Partners will then face each other slapping their right hands together on B, and slapping their left hands together on I. Dancer will then slap both hands together on N, followed by slapping their own knees on G. Dancers will then turn their own partner around once with an elbow swing on O. The entire sequence is repeated from the beginning throughout the entire song.

> *Cues:*  Circle right, circle left
> Girls center and back
> Boys center and back
> B - right hand, I - left hand,
> N - both hands, G - knees
> O - swing her around once

### Title:    *Bunny Hop*

*Music:* The music to accompany this dance can be found on volume 1, band 16, on the music CD included with this book. 4/4 time.

*Level and Difficulty:* Grades K–2. Very Easy.

*Formation:* One long single file line with students placing hands on the waist of the student in front of them.

*Instructions:* Dancers will move their right heels out away from the left feet touching the right heels to the floor, then stepping with the right feet next to the left feet. This movement is repeated. Next all dancers will move the left heels out away from the right feet touching the left heels to the floor, then stepping with the left feet next to the right feet. This movement is repeated. All dancers will perform these movements while standing in one place. All dancers then hop forward with both feet together once, followed by hopping backwards with both feet together once, followed by everyone hopping forward with both feet together three times. This entire sequence is repeated from the beginning until the dance is completed.

> *Cues:*  Out in out in (right foot
> Out in out in (left foot)
> Hop forward
> Hop backward
> Hop, hop, hop forward

### Title:    *The Chicken Dance*

*Music:* The music to accompany this dance can be found on volume 1, band 17, on the music CD included with this book. 4/4 time.

*Level and Difficulty:* Grades K–2. Easy.

*Formation:* A single circle with everyone facing the center of the circle. Can be performed with or without partners. This dance can also be performed in a random scattered pattern around the room.

*Instructions:* Using the fingers and thumbs on both hands dancers make movements imitating a chicken opening and closing its beak by moving the fingers and thumbs apart and together. Dancers will put their hands under their arms to form wings and flap their arms to resemble a chicken flapping its wings. Everyone then puts their arms at their sides and shakes their hips while moving downwards toward the floor while bending at the knees, then returning to standing position. This movement is to symbolize a chicken shaking its body. Next the dancers will clap their own hands four times. As the music changes dancers will swing their partners with an elbow swing. As a variation to this last movement dancers may move around the circle swinging several different dancers one at a time and turning them each around once.

*Cues:*    Beak movement four times
Wing movement four times
Shake hips down and up for four beats
Clap hands four times
Repeat this sequence 3 more times
Swing partner in one direction then twice in the other direction, repeat sequence
Repeat entire sequence throughout dance

### *Title:*    *The Electric Slide*

*Music:* Appropriate music to accompany this dance can be found on volume 1, band 25, on the music CD included with this book. Also the songs entitled "The Electric Side", "Achy Breaky Heart", and other assorted country western songs are appropriate to accompany this dance. 4/4 time.

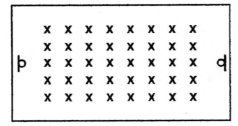

**Class as one large block, all turning
in the same direction at one time**

*Level and Difficulty:* Grades 2–6. Moderately Easy.

*Formation:* A very large space is needed for this dance as it is performed in several lines with dancers spread an arm's length apart.

*Instructions:* All dancers will be in lines facing forward and at an arms length apart. The dance begins with the grapevine step to the right. Dancers start with the right foot, by stepping to the right with the right feet, stepping behind the right feet with the left feet, stepping again to the right with the right feet and bringing the left feet next to the right touching the left toes to the floor without putting weight on the left feet. This same grapevine step is repeated only this time to the left and starting with the left feet. Then the dancers take three steps backwards starting with the right feet, step right, left, right and touching with the left feet. Next dancers will step forward with the left feet, touching with the right feet. Then they will step backwards with the right feet and touch with the left feet. The last part of this sequence is performed by stepping forward with the left feet and at the same time turning a quarter of a turn on those same left feet while kicking the right feet and touching that right toes next to the left feet. The whole dance sequence is repeated as above throughout the dance each time turning a quarter turn counterclockwise Each time the sequence is started with the right feet and is performed by moving first to the right.

The quarter turn appears to be difficult for primary children; however, it can be taught if broken down to simple terms. By having the class all face in the same direction while spread out in lines an arm's length apart, pick something on the wall to focus on such as the windows, door, clock, or whatever. Assign a focal point to each of the four walls in the gymnasium, cafeteria, or whatever room is being used. Instruct the class to practice turning a quarter turn, always turning counterclockwise while referring to the focal point on the wall. This seems to assist very young children in being able to perfect the quarter turn.

Cues:    Right, Left, Right, Touch
               Left, Right, Left, Touch
               Back Right, 2, 3, Touch
               Front (Left), Touch
               Back (Right), Touch
               Step (Left), Turn, Kick (Right), Touch

### Title:  The Fireman

*Music:*  The song entitled "The Bop" and other assorted country western songs are appropriate for accompaniment to The Fireman Dance. A local record store may be helpful in locating a copy of "The Bop" on CD or cassette tape.

*Level and Difficulty:*  Grades 3-6. Moderate.

*History:*  The Fireman is a country western line dance.

*Formation:*  Performed in lines with all dancers facing forward.

*Instructions:*  The Fireman begins by standing in place and moving the right toe only. Right toes are moved to the right side, right toes to the front, right toes again to the right side, right toes again to the front. Next dancers will tap the right heels forward twice, followed by tapping right toes backwards twice. Dancers will step forward with the right feet touching left toes next to right feet. Everyone will then step backwards with the left feet touching the right toes next to the left feet. Dancers will repeat this movement by stepping forward with the right feet, and touch, then stepping backwards with the left feet, and touch. Dancers will step with the right foot to the right, stepping then with the left foot behind the right, step to the right again with the right foot, this is known as the grapevine step. Dancers will now stamp with their left feet. Dancers will repeat the grapevine but this time moving to the left. Dancers will step with the left feet to the left, then step with the right feet behind the left, and step to the left with the left feet. All dancers will now stamp with their right feet. This movement is known as grapevine right and grapevine left. On the grapevine left, dancers will turn a quarter turn to the left on the stamp. Dancers will now scuff two steps forward beginning on the left feet. Dancers will scuff left, scuff right and stamp the right feet next to the left feet. The entire sequence is repeated from the beginning throughout the entire dance. Teaching a quarter turn to elementary students is explained in the previous dance "The Electric Slide". The quarter turn in this dance "The Fireman" is always performed in a counterclockwise direction.

Cues:    Tap, side (right toe)
               Tap front
               Tap side
               Tap front
               Right heel tap twice forward
               Right toe tap twice backwards
               Step forward, touch (left foot)
               Step backwards touch (right foot)
               Step forward, touch (left foot)
               Step backwards touch (right foot)
               Step right, behind, right stamp
               Step left, behind, left, stamp
               Quarter turn counterclockwise
               Scuff two steps forward, stamp

### Title:    The Hokey Pokey

*Music:* The music to accompany this dance can e found on volume 1, band 18, on the music CD included with this book. 4/4 time.

*Level and Difficulty:* Grades K–2. Very Easy.

*Formation:* Students form a single circle with all dancers facing center. The Hokey Pokey could also be performed in a random pattern of students scattered throughout the room or in the classroom next to the students' desks. The directions for the Hokey Pokey are usually verbally stated on the record itself,

*Instructions:* Following the directions in the song dancers will place their right hands forward towards the center of the circle, then placing their right hands behind them, away from the center of the circle. Dancers again place their right hands forward towards the center of the circle, this time shaking their right hands. The instructions state that dancers are to do the Hokey Pokey, and turn themselves around. Dancers are given the opportunity to be creative by making up their own movements as they turn around followed by clapping their own hands together four times while keeping time with the music. The song continues with the same basic idea of putting a certain body part towards the center of the circle, putting it outside the circle, putting it again inside the circle and shaking it. The order of body parts are the right arm, left arm, right foot, left foot, right elbow, left elbow, right hip, left hip, head, backside, and whole self. Shaking one's hands over their head or making shapes using ones arms can often be seen. One child may be chosen to stand in the center of the circle to lead the other children. Creativity is encouraged while doing the chorus and verse related to the Hokey Pokey.

Cues:       Right hand in, right hand out, right hand in and shake
            Left hand in, left hand out, left hand in and shake
            Do Hokey Pokey turn around clap 4 times
            Chorus - Be Creative!
            Same sequence as above with right foot, left foot,
            Chorus right elbow, left elbow
            Chorus, left hip, chorus, head,
            Back side, whole self, chorus

### Title:     The Limbo

*Music:* The music to accompany this dance can be found on volume 1, band 19, on the music CD included with this book. 4/4 time.

*Level and Difficulty:* Grades K–6. Easy.

*Formation:* A single line with dancers taking turns, one person going under the stick at a time. Two students hold the limbo stick. When a student is finished going under the stick, that student goes to the end of the line.

*Instructions:* Using a plastic baton, broomstick, pole, or bamboo pole two dancers hold the stick parallel to the floor. Dancers lean backwards while moving under the limbo stick. Dancers are not allowed to touch the pole or the floor with their hands. Dancers also may not bend their knees in order to duck under the stick. When dancers are eliminated they may walk around the outside parameter of the gymnasium or do sit ups, push-ups, jumping jacks etc. while the dance continues. After each dancer moves under the stick he/she returns to the end of the line. Dancers are to move under the stick one at a time. When everyone in the line has had a turn to move under the limbo stick at the current level, the stick is slightly lowered and the dance continues until one person remains.

### Title:    *Macarena*

*Music:* The music to accompany this dance can be found on volume 1, band 20, on the music CD included with this book. It is important to be sure that the words set to the music of some popular songs like the Macarena are not offensive. 4/4 time.

*Level and Difficulty:* Grades K–6. Easy.

*Formation:* The Macarena is often seen performed as a line dance; however, it can be performed in a single circle with everyone facing center with someone in the center acting as the leader. It may also be performed in a random scattered pattern.

*Instructions:* During the Macarena all of the movements are performed while keeping time with the music. Dancers will raise their right arms to shoulder level with their palms down. Dancers will then raise their left arms to shoulder level with the palms down. Everyone then turn right hands over with the palms up, followed by turning the left hands over with the palms up. Dancers then place their right hands on their left shoulders, followed by placing their left hands on their right shoulders (arms will be crossed in front of the chest). Dancers will then place their left hands on back of left sides of their heads, followed by placing their right hands on the back of their right sides of their heads. Dancers now place their left hands on the right front of their hips, followed by placing their right hands on the left front of their hips (hands will be crossed in front at about waist level or lower). Dancers now place their right hands on their right lower backs, followed by placing their left hands on their left lower backs. Dancers swing their hips back and forth to the music for three counts. Everyone now turns a quarter turn counterclockwise. Repeat entire sequence through the dance.

*Cues:*

| | |
|---|---|
| Palms down, right | Left hand on right hip |
| Palms down, left | Right hand on left hip |
| Palms up, right | Lower Back, right |
| Palms up left | Lower Back, left |
| Right hand on left shoulder | Swing Hips (three counts) |
| Left hand on right shoulder | Turn 1/4 left |
| Head, back left | Repeat entire sequence |
| Head, back right | |

### Title: *Montgomery County Cha Cha Cha*

*Music:* Any contemporary music appropriate for the Cha Cha. "The San Antonio Stroll" and "Darlene" are just two country western songs that can be used as accompaniment for The Montgomery County Cha Cha Cha.

*Level and Difficulty:* Grades 3-6. Moderate to Difficult.

*History:* Originated in the United States.

*Formation:* Performed in lines with all dancers facing forward.

*Instructions:* All dancers will place their weight on their left feet while moving their right heels forward touching them to the floor in front of themselves. Dancers will touch their right toes next to the left feet. Dancers will perform three cha cha steps in place by stepping on the right feet, stepping on the left feet, and again stepping on the right feet. Dancers now step forward on the left feet, stepping in place on the right feet and perform three cha cha steps by stepping on the left feet while bringing them back next to the right feet, then stepping on the right feet and again stepping on the left feet. The dancers will now step backwards on the right feet, step in place on the left feet and perform three cha cha steps by stepping in place right, left, right. Everyone will now step forward on the left feet and pivot one half turn clockwise, to face the opposite direction. To pivot, dancers will rise up on their toes and turn on the toes to face the opposite direction. Dancers will bring their left feet up to their right feet and perform three cha cha steps in place, stepping left, stepping right and stepping left. Everyone will now step forward with the right feet and pivot ½ turn counterclockwise to face the opposite direction. All dancers will now bring their right feet up to their left feet and perform three cha cha steps in place, stepping right, left, right. All dancers will pause for two counts. Dancers will step to the right by crossing their left feet in front of the right feet and stepping on their left feet, then stepping on their right feet in place. Three cha cha steps are performed by stepping on the left feet while bringing them back next to the right feet, stepping on right feet, then stepping on the left feet (cha, cha cha). Dancers will step to the left by crossing the right feet in front of the left feet while stepping on the right feet, then stepping on the left foot in place. Perform three cha cha steps by stepping on the right feet while bringing them back next to the left feet, stepping on the left feet, and then stepping on the right feet (cha, cha, cha). While standing in place dancers swing their hips to the right and to the left, then pausing for two counts. Dancers will repeat the entire sequence from the beginning throughout the whole dance.

| | |
|---|---|
| *Cues*:  Heel, Toe | Turn |
| Cha Cha Cha (right, left, right) | Cha Cha Cha (right, left, right) |
| Forward left | Pause 1,2 |
| Step on right | Step on left foot crossing in front of right |
| Cha Cha Cha (left, right, left) | Step on right foot (in place) |
| Back right | Cha Cha Cha (left, right, left) |
| Step on left | Step on right foot crossing in front of left |
| Cha Cha Cha (right, left, right) | Step on left foot (in place) |
| Forward left | Cha Cha Cha (right, left, right) |
| Turn | Swing hips right, Swing hips left |
| Cha cha cha (left, right, left) | Pause 1,2 |
| Forward right | Repeat entire sequence throughout dance |

### Title:    *Patty Cake Polka*

*Music:* The music to accompany this dance can be found on volume 1, band 21, on the music CD included with this book.  4/4 time.

*Level and Difficulty:* Grades K–2. Easy

*History:* The Patty Cake Polka was created in Colorado Springs in 1947 and has been a popular mixer since it originated. It has been discovered that the steps will also fit to the Christmas song "Jingle Bells" and can therefore be performed at holiday programs if so desired.

*Formation:* A double circle with girls on the outside and boys on the inside facing each other with hands joined.

*Instructions:* Girls will begin with their right feet and boys with their left feet. Dancers place the heels of the appropriate feet on the floor then place the toes of the same feet on the floor, twice. Next the couples will perform three sliding steps counterclockwise. Using the other foot (boys right feet, girls left feet) dancers again perform the heel toe heel toe movements followed by three sliding steps clockwise. Couples will now clap their right hands together twice, left hands together twice, both hands together twice and then slap their own knees once. Partners will swing with an elbow swing. This dance can be turned into a mixer by having all of the girls move up one boy to the right after turning their own partners one time around with an elbow swing.

*Cues:*

   Heel toe, heel toe, slide, slide, slide (counterclockwise)
   Heel toe, heel toe, slide, slide, slide (clockwise)
   Right hands clap (2 times), left hands clap (2 times), both hands clap (2 times)
   Slap knees (once)
   Swing around once, and onto the next

### *Title:* ***The Stroll***

*Music:* The music to accompany this dance can be found on volume 1, band 22, on the music CD included with this book. The music is in 4/4 time; however, the dance is in 3/4 time.

*Level and Difficulty:* Grades 3–6. Moderate.

*Formation:* Partners form two lines facing each other. Boys are in one line facing girls who are in a line across from the boys. Students should be spread out in order to give themselves room to move.

*History:* The Stroll was performed on Dick Clark's American Bandstand in the 1950s to 1960s era. Whenever an episode of the American Bandstand Anniversary Show is seen on television you will probably see the stroll performed.

*Instructions:* Boys will begin with their right feet, girls will begin with their left feet, both lines will be moving together in the same direction. Boys point the right feet forward and in front of the left feet, then point the right feet to the right side, and point the right feet forward again. Boys will step with their right feet to the right side, stepping with the left feet behind the right, then stepping to the right with the right feet. This same sequence is repeated only starting with the left feet and moving to the left. Girls will do the same steps only starting with the opposite feet while moving in the same direction as the boys' line. Both lines should be moving together in the same direction. While the lines continue to perform the basic step, the first couple will move down the line together keeping in time with the music while creating their own style and steps. Dancers may wish to do a grapevine type step, cartwheels, etc. However if dancers choose to do cartwheels care needs to be taken not to kick other dancers that are dancing in their lines. As soon as the couple moving down the center gets to the end of the line, the next couple at the head of the line begins down the middle.

Cues:         Point front, point side, point front
              Step right, step back left, step right
              Repeat moving in opposite direction

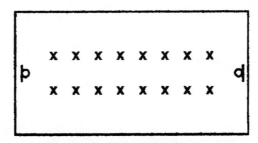

**2 Long Lines, Partners Facing Each Other**

*Title:*    ***The Twist***

*Music:* The music to accompany this dance can be found on volume 1, band 23, on the music CD included with this book. 4/4 time.

*Level and Difficulty:* Grades K–3. Very Easy.

*History:* The twist became popular in the 1950s & 1960s by Chubby Checker.

*Formation:* Varied formations are possible. Students form a single circle with all dancers facing center. One student may volunteer to be the leader in the middle of the circle. Other children follow the lead of the student in the center who is given the opportunity to be creative. When the leaders run out of ideas or are getting tired, they may pick someone whose hand is raised to take their place in the center. Dancers can also do the twist while scattered randomly around the room, next to their desk as an aerobic activity in the classroom, or with a partner.

*Instructions:* The twist can be performed standing in one spot while the hips, knees, and ankles are moving back and forth in a twisting motion. The dance can be performed at various levels, twisting high and twisting low close to the ground, etc. Dancers are encouraged to use circular motions with their hands, arms, and fingers as well as to use twisting movements with their feet while moving up on their toes. This is a creative type dance whereby children are given the opportunity to express their impression of twisting movements. Even primary children can interpret the twist. In fact younger children seem to be less inhibited about being creative in their movement than are some 5th graders and older level students.

*Title:*    ***YMCA***

*Music:* The music to accompany this dance can be found on volume 1, band 24, of the music CD included with this book. 4/4 time.

*Level and Difficulty:* Grades K–3. Very Easy.

*Formation:* Varied formations are possible. Dancers may form a single circle with all dancers facing the center or one student may volunteer to be the leader and stand in the middle of the circle. Other dancers follow the lead of the center person. Disco movements or steps can fit into the dance YMCA. Student leaders can express their creativeness when performing the YMCA. When the leader runs out of ideas they may choose another student to take their place. The YMCA can also be performed in a random scattered formation, beside the students' desks in the classroom, with a partner or in a small group.

*Instructions:* The only constant part of the dance is during the verse of the song in which dancers use arm movements to spell out the letters YMCA. The dancers will raise both arms straight over their heads and apart to form a Y. Dancers bend both arms at the elbows and over their heads with fingers pointing to the center and top of their heads to form an M. Students curve their arms one over their heads the other at waist level to form a large semi circle to indicate the letter C. Lastly dancers raise both arms above their heads keeping arms straight and bringing finger tips together to form an A. Other than the verse students can be creative when dancing the YMCA.

## BALLROOM DANCE

In elementary school, children are able to perform the basic steps for many ballroom dances beginning as early as second grade. During the dance unit students in grades two through 6 can be taught the basic steps for the Cha Cha, Foxtrot, Swing, and Waltz. A few other variations may be added to these dances such as the underarm turn, etc. Elementary students seem to enjoy performing ballroom dances especially the Cha Cha and Swing when these dances are accompanied by popular music from the present time. An excellent source of appropriate music for ballroom dance is Dance Trax International. The address for Dance Trax International is 2217 N. Woodbridge Street, Saginaw, Michigan 48602 (1-800-513-2623). Their E-Mail address is MAGNUMRP@aol.com. If requested Dance Trax will list on the back of the CD which songs are appropriate for each type of dance.

The rhythm for teaching ballroom dance is generally divided into "slows" and "quicks". A slow is given two counts with dancers stepping on the first count and pausing on the second count. A quick is given one count with dancers take a step for one count.

### *Cha Cha*

*Music*: Music to accompany the Cha Cha can be found on volume 2, band 16, on the music CD included with this book.
*Level and Difficulty:* Grades 3 – 6. Moderate.
*Formation*: The Cha Cha is a partner dance performed in many different dance positions. In elementary school partners will face each other with both hands joined.
*Instructions*: Students will begin all facing in the same direction without partners and in lines so that students can see the instructor. All dancers begin by taking one step forward with the left feet, pausing for one count (slow). Dancers step in place with the right feet pausing for one count (slow). Dancers then bring the left feet back next to the right feet, while stepping on the left feet (quick). Dancers step on the right feet (quick) and then step on the left feet in place for one count (quick). On the last step dancers keep their weight on the left feet and get ready to step back with the right feet. The rhythm would be considered slow, slow, quick, quick, quick. The second half of the cha cha is performed exactly the same as above only moving backwards and starting with the right feet. Dancers will step back with the right feet and pause, step on the left feet in place and pause, step on the right feet bringing it next to the left feet, step on the left feet and step on the right feet. After dancers have time to practice and the teacher is sure everyone knows the basic step, dancers can be divided into partners facing each other, joining both hands. The boys move forward with their left feet as the girls move backwards with their right feet. Both dancers are performing the exact same steps only as the boys move forward the girls move backwards and as the girls move forward the boys move backwards. After all students have mastered the basic step, students may then practice some variations, turns, etc.

> Cues:   Forward left
>         Step in place right foot
>         Step left, right, left
>         Backwards right
>         Step in place left foot
>         Step right, left, right

### *Cha Cha  Half Turn*

Only the dancer moving forward may turn. Both dancers do not turn at the same time. As dancers step forward with their left feet, the dancers then shift their weight up onto their toes and pivot a half turn clockwise then bringing the left feet, stepping next to the right feet and finishing with a, cha cha cha. Partners are now in a line with one of the partners in front of the other. The dancers who turned can perform a half turn back by stepping forward again with the left feet, moving up on their toes, and pivoting clockwise another half turn to end up at their original position.   However, as an alternative for the second part of the turn or to return to the original position, the dancers can turn back the way they came by stepping forward with their right feet, and pivoting on their toes while turning counterclockwise one half turn.

Cues:    Step turn cha cha cha   or   Forward turn, left, right, left

### Cha Cha Complete Turn

A full turn is also executed when the dancers step forward with the left feet.  The dancers after stepping forward with the left feet, move up on their toes pivoting clockwise all the way around making a full turn, then step on the left feet placing them next to the right feet, after the turn.  Stepping on the left feet in place is the first part of the cha cha cha step, which is completed by stepping on the right feet followed by stepping on the left feet.

Cues:    Step left, turn, cha cha cha

### Cha Cha Cross Over Step

Partners will begin with both hands joined while facing each other. Dancers will perform several basic steps.  Partners will drop both hands when beginning the cross over step. Both dancers will move in a sideways direction, moving together in the same direction. As partners move sideways dancers bring inside hands together touching the palms of the hands together.  If the boys are moving to their left they drop their left hands and the girls will be moving to their right and will drop their right hands.   The boys start with their right feet and cross their right feet in front of the left feet, stepping on the right feet, at the same time turning to face the right.

Boys then pick up their left feet and step in place with their left feet.  Next the boys bring their right feet back to the original position while turning back to face their partners stepping on their right feet next to their left feet (cha).  They then step on their left feet (cha), then step on their right feet (cha).  The girls do the same steps as the boys only using opposite feet.  As dancers come back to their original positions, partners join both hands.  When moving to the opposite direction dancers again drop one hand and when returning again to original position join both hands.

Cues:    Cross, step, cha cha cha.

### **Fox Trot**
*Music*: Music to accompany the Fox Trot can be found on volume 2, band 17, on the music CD included with this book.
*Level and Difficulty*: Grades 3 – 6.  Moderate

*Formation*: The Fox Trot is performed in the closed position.  The closed position can be found and is described in detail under the formation section of the Waltz.

*Instructions*: Dancers will begin by all facing in the same direction without partners and in lines in order to see the instructor.  Although both boys and girls dance parts will be explained all dancers will begin and continue to do the boys part moving forwards until the

basic step has been mastered. Dancers begin by stepping forward with the left feet and pausing for one count (slow). Dancers then step forward with the right feet bringing it slightly ahead of the left and pausing for one count (slow). Dancers then step to the left sideways with the left feet (quick) and then bring the right feet next to the left feet (quick). The rhythm would be slow, slow, quick, quick. This is the boys' part. Once all dancers have mastered the boys' part, all dancers will practice the girls' part moving backwards. The girls' part is the same except moving backwards and starting with the right feet. Therefore, step back with the right feet and pause. Step back with the left feet bringing it slightly behind the right feet and pause. Step sideways to the right with the right feet and bring the left feet next to the right. Dancers repeat the same steps moving in the same direction. The next sequence will begin with the same feet. The foxtrot is a slow, graceful dance sometimes compared to a walking step. After dancers have mastered both the boys and the girls parts dancers will be divided into partners and get into the closed position. Boys continue to move forward and girls continue to move backwards. The boys part would be forward left, forward right, side together, forward left, forward right, side together, etc. The girls part would be backwards right, backwards right, side together, backwards right, backwards right, side together. Once the basic step has been mastered dancers may try some variations, turns, etc.
Cues: Forward, forward, side together

### Foxtrot Conversation Step

Dancers begin in open position turning in such a manner that partners are both facing the same direction with hands joined as in the closed position, and inside shoulders are next to each other. Boys begin with their left feet, girls with right feet. Dancers step forward and pause, and using the opposite foot step forward again and pause. Partners then turn to face each other in a closed position and take two side steps moving in the same direction. Boys step forward with their left feet, then forward with the right feet, followed by a side together. Girls step forward with the right feet, then forward with the left feet followed by a side together.

Cues:    Forward, forward, side together.
         Forward, forward side together

### Foxtrot Roll Turn:

Dancers begin in open position turning in such a way that both partners are facing the same direction with inside shoulders next to each other. Dancers are both moving forward beginning with outside feet. Boys will start with their left feet, while girls begin with their right feet. Partners take two steps forward at the same time, then both dancers will turn back to the closed position facing each other. The boys take two steps sideways to the left starting with their left feet and bringing their right feet next to their left. As the boys takes their first side step, they raise their left arms and the girls move forward clockwise and under the boys left arms, performing an underarm turn as the boys complete the second step of the side steps. Both dancers are now ready to perform a basic step, moving forward in the conversation position.

### Foxtrot Magic Turn:

Dancers in closed position perform the basic step described earlier, boys moving forward, girls moving backwards. When dancers wish to turn and move in another direction a magic turn is executed. The boys step forward with their left feet and transfer their weight to the rear feet as they turn, followed by a side together. The girls step backwards with their right feet and transfer their weight to the left feet as they turn with the boys, followed by a side together. Dancers perform as many turns as it takes to get them moving in the right direction. The turn is similar to a rock step in that the weight is simply shifted forward and back followed by a side together step. On the side together the boys step to the left side with their left feet then bringing their right feet next to the left. The girls follow the boys lead by stepping sideways to the right with their right feet then bringing the left feet next to the right moving in the same direction as their partners.

Cues:    Forward, back turn side together

### Swing

*Music*: Music to accompany swing dance can be found on volume 2, band 18, on the music CD included with this book.
*Level and Difficulty:* Grades 2 – 6. Moderate to difficult.
*Formation:* Two hands joined with partners facing or open position.
*Instructions:* Elementary students are able to successfully perform swing dance especially if modifications are made. Swing is in an uneven rhythm of slow, slow, quick, quick. The main dance steps beginning with the boys' part are to, step left, step right, rock step. The rock step appears to be very difficult for elementary students, therefore a march, march or step, step has been substituted to enable elementary students to perform swing and stay in time to the music. Dancers will begin by forming two lines facing each other. Boys are in one line and girls across from their partners in another line. The teacher may stand between the two lines to act as a model in order that dancers may see a demonstration of the proper steps. Boys will begin with their left feet and girls with their right feet. Boys take one step with their left feet to the side and apart from the right feet and pause for one count (slow), then take one step with the right feet keeping them apart from the left feet and pause for one count (slow). Instead of the rock step, boys will step on the left feet again, bringing it next to the right feet (quick) and then step on the right feet in place (quick). Girls do the exact same step as the boys only starting with their right feet. Swing dance is very fast therefore a great deal of practice is needed to be sure all students can perform the basic step correctly and in time to the music. Boys will step apart on the left feet, pause, step on the right feet, pause, step left, step right. Repeat throughout entire dance. Girls will step apart on the right feet, pause, step on the left feet, pause, step right, step left. The rock step may be taught to older students. The rock step is used in place of the march, march or together, together. Boys when performing the rock step, will step back with the left feet (stepping behind the right feet), pick the right feet up and put them down in place. The rock step is followed by stepping on the left feet apart from the right feet in the original position followed by stepping on the right feet. The girls perform the same exact step only stepping back with the right feet. The cues for the boys would be step left, step right, rock step. The cues for the girls would be step right, step left, rock step. The terms march, march have been substituted for the rock step. Once all students are able to correctly perform the basic swing step, partners can move forward and join both hands while continuing to perform the basic swing step. Dancers may try some variations, turns, etc., once the basic swing step has been mastered.

Cues:    Step, step, march, march or  apart, apart, together, together.

### Over Under and Back Turn

After partners have executed several basic steps, the boys will continue with the basic step and switches the girls' right hands to their right hands from their left hands. On the first step the boys raise their right arms and lead the girls forward turning them clockwise under the boys raised arms. The girls are now standing behind and to the side of the boys, with right hands still joined. The boys now bring the ladies back under their raised right arms, bringing them back the way they came, to their original positions. The boys continue with the basic step as the girls are moving back and under their raised arms.

> *Cues*:    Over, under and back.
>             Over, under and back

## *Wrapping the Lady*

After partners have executed several basic steps, the boys continue with the basic step and switch the girls' right hands to their right hands from their left hands. The boys raise their right arms while turning the girls clockwise, bringing the girls' right arms in front of the girls and over their heads in such a manner that the girls' arms are crossed in front of them. The girls are to the right side of the boys. Hands remain joined throughout the turn. Partners continue performing the basic step while in a side by side position. The boys then reverse the wrap by raising their right arms and turning the ladies backwards and counterclockwise, returning them to their original positions.

> *Cues*:    Wrap the lady, unwrap her.

## *Put Her Hand Behind Her Head*

Dancers seem to enjoy this variation of a swing dance movement that is very simple if directions are followed. Dancers face each other performing the basic step. Partners keep hands joined. The boys put the girls left hands behind their heads keeping their own right arms and elbows straight. The boys then slide their hands down the ladies outstretched right arms catching their right hands in the boys' right hands. The boys now have the ladies right hands in their right hands and execute and over under and back turn. The boys lead the ladies under their right arms by turning the ladies forward and counterclockwise. The girls are now to the right sides and behind the boys. The boys continue to do the basic swing step while returning the ladies to their original positions by turning them backwards and clockwise under the boys' right arms.

> *Cues:*    Put your hand behind her head.
>             Slide your arm and catch her hand.
>             Over under and back.
>             Over under and back.

*Wring the dishrag*

Dancers will continue to perform the basic swing step. The dishrag is executed with both hands joined. Partners while facing each other with hands joined turn together in the same direction all the way around turning one complete turn, without releasing hands.

*Underarm Turn*

Partners continue performing the basic swing step. The boys have the girls' right hands in their left hands and the other hands are free. The boys raise their left arms turning the girls clockwise under the boys raised arms. Partners trade places as the girls turn under the boys' arms taking the boys places while the boys walk forward and around the ladies taking their places. The boys need to allow their fingers to move freely in their hands so that the ladies wrist can move freely during the turn.

    *Cues*:    Trade places

### Title  The Waltz

*Music:* Music appropriate for the Waltz can be found on volume 2, band 19, on the music CD included with this book. An impressive song that may be used during the winter holidays and in particular for a school performance program would be The Carpenters' version of "The Christmas Waltz."    3/4 time.

*Level and Difficulty:* Grades 2–6. Moderate.

*History:* The Waltz originated in Austria in the seventeenth century. In the 18th century the Waltz was brought from Austria to France and England where it became popular. The waltz consists of 3 walking steps performed in 3/4 time. The continuously flowing turning steps contribute to the elegance of the Waltz.

*Formation:* The waltz is performed with a partner in the correct closed dance position. Students can be arranged in a double circle with the boys on the inside and the girls on the outside. The girl places her left hand on the boy's right shoulder while the boy places his right hand on the girl's waist. Partners join their other hands at shoulder level, with the elbows bent. By using a double circle the waltz can become a mixer in the class situation by having the girls, on signal, move to the next boy on their right or in a counterclockwise direction. This gives students an opportunity to dance with a variety of partners. The waltz can also be performed with partners in a random scattered pattern. It is best to have boy-girl partners whenever possible. However, if there is an uneven number of boys related to girls or visa versa then same gender students may be partners. When same gender partners are dancing together, the closed dance position is not required; instead, partners join both hands while facing each other. Using only boy-girl partners is suggested when dancing the waltz in a school program. If in the class situation there is one student left over, that student can practice the steps alone and when the girls move to the right he/she will have a partner and someone else will take a turn practicing the steps alone.

*Instructions:* Boys will start with their left feet and girls with their right feet. Whatever the gender the dance pattern is the same. Dancers will start with both feet together, stepping forward with the left feet, bring the right feet to the front side position, then bring the left feet next to the right. This pattern forms a box and has often been referred to as the box step. The step is repeated only this time moving backwards. Again dancers starting with both feet together, step backwards with the right feet, bring the left feet to the back side position, then bring the right feet next to the left feet. The entire sequence is repeated from the beginning throughout the entire song. Continue doing the same step in time to the music. Boys and girls are partners and face each other. As the boys move forward with their left feet, the girls move backwards with their right feet. After they are able to not only keep in time with each other but also to the music, encourage dancers to turn as they are dancing making sure to keep the same step sequence, not adding or subtracting steps. Dancers are also encouraged

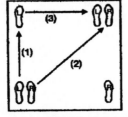
Forward (L), Side (R), Together (L)

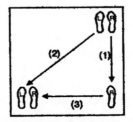
Back (R), Side (L), Together (R)

to talk to their partners while dancing, as the waltz is a form of social dance. When teaching the waltz, demonstrations, visuals, and lots of practice are necessary. Many special needs students have been able to master the waltz at an early age when given specific instructions as well as adequate practice time. Sometimes using feet cut out of construction paper and taped to the floor assists dancers that are having difficulty with the step sequence. The left feet cut outs that are marked with an L are made from one color of construction paper while the right foot cut outs marked with an R are made from another color. Many seven year old dancers have successfully mastered the waltz. The following diagrams have been helpful in assisting both teachers and students to understand the waltz pattern or box step.

> *Cues:* Forward Left, side (right) together (left)
> Forward, side, together
> Backward Right, side (left) together (right)
> Back, side, together

# Square Dance

Settlers in colonial times gathered for a social outing after the work of crop harvesting, quilting and husking bees, sheep shearing, and barn raising were complete. The social times often consisted of square dancing. Square dancing began in rural areas and eventually spread to the cities. Square dancing grew in popularity during and after World War II.

## SOME OF THE OBJECTIVES OF TEACHING SQUARE DANCING

Square dancing, when performed properly, can be an excellent cardiovascular activity. It can also assist students in learning to appreciate some of the culture and history of the United States. Students are given the opportunity to experience firsthand how colonial Americans socialized and celebrated through dance and song. Socially, square dance gives students the opportunity to work together as a group or square using a variety of movements and patterns. It can assist students in the development of proper social interaction with others.

## GENERAL SQUARE DANCE INSTRUCTIONS

When teaching square dance the sequence in which the dances are taught is important. In the primary grades side 1 of the record "Getting Ready to Square Dance" teaches the elementary patterns and basics of square dancing. Such terms as promenade, swing your partner, honor your partner, circle, and into the center and back will become familiar to the primary student. The actual patterns, formation, and calls will be taught in the intermediate grades. Actually dividing into squares can be dealt with in grades three through six.

When teaching square dance, once the squares are formed it is essential to explain the basics of square dancing that can be found on the pages included in this chapter under the section entitled Square Dance Basics. The dances on side 2 of "Get Ready to Square Dance" reinforce these basics in dance form. Once "Get Ready to Square Dance" side 2 has been completed, dances are chosen for their pattern variety. The next set of dances utilizes the grand right and left. Finally the most complicated of the square dances selected apply the allemande left, followed by the grand right and left.

## THE SUGGESTED ORDER FOR TEACHING SQUARE DANCE

Grades K–3
Honor Your Partner—"Get Ready to Square Dance"
Side 1
Circle Left/Right and Into the Center and Back—"Get
Ready to Square Dance" Side 1
Swing Your Partner and Circle—"Get Ready to Square
Dance" Side 1
Into the Center and Back and Swing Your Partner—
"Get Ready to Square Dance" Side 1
Promenade and Square Your Set—"Get Ready to
Square Dance" Side 1
Grades 4–6
Introduction to Basics
Forward and Back and Swing Your Partner—"Get Ready to Square Dance" Side 2
Do-Sa-Do and Promenade—"Get Ready to Square Dance" Side 2
Allemande Left, Allemande Right and Star—"Get Ready to Square Dance" Side 2
Introduction to Patterns
Hoedown—"Get Ready to Square Dance" Side 2
Tie a Yellow Ribbon—"Get Ready to Square Dance" Side 2
Around the Outside and Swing
Do-Sa-Do and Swing
Solomon Levi
Marching through Georgia
Life on the Ocean Wave (Head Two Ladies Cross Over)
Make and Arch
Introduction to Grand Right and Left
Red River Valley
Yankee Doodle

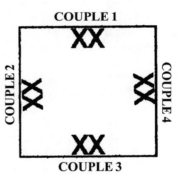

Hinkey Dinkey Parlez Vous
Divide the Ring
Hot Time in the Old Town (Girls to the Center)
Take A Little Peek
Allemande Left with Grand Right and Left
Form an Arch
Push Her Away
Pass the Left Hand Lady Under

## SQUARE DANCE BASICS

The girl is on the boy's right. The boy will raise his right hand in order to be sure the girl is in the right place.

• *Couple number one* is the couple with their backs to the music. The music may originate from a caller, a band, or a record, cassette, or CD player.

• *Couple number two* is the couple to the right of couple number one.

• *Couple number three* is the couple to the right of couple number two.

• *Couple number four* is the couple to the right of couple number three.
• S*et* is the term that refers to each individual square.

• *Home position* is the term used in referring to everyone's original position. When all four couples are in their original positions the couples form a square with all dancers facing the center of the square.

• *Square your set* is the term used to refer to all couples being in their correct places, thereby forming a square with everyone in that square facing the center of the square.

• C*orner* is the person next to the dancer who is not their partner. The boy's corner is on his left and the girl's corner is on her right.

• *Honor* is the term used in referring to a boy bowing to his partner or corner and a girl curtsying to her partner or corner.

• *Swing your partner* is the term used in reference to partners facing each other and joining inside bent elbows. Partners then turn each other around in a circle while staying in place.

• *Promenade* is the term used in reference to partners joining inside hands with each other, boys are on the inside of the square and girls are on the outside. All couples face counterclockwise. Dancers walk forward all the way around the square until everyone is back to home positions. *All promenade.*

• *Allemande Left* is the term used in reference to corners facing each other joining their left hands. Dancers walk forward around each other back to home positions.

• *Allemande Right* is the term used in reference to partners facing each other joining their right hands. Dancers walk forward around each other back to home positions.

• *Grand Right and Left* is the term used in reference to partners facing each other joining right hands. Partners walk past each other. Pass right shoulders. Partners drop hands joining left hands with the next person who should be of the opposite gender or a person taking the part of the opposite gender. Continue walking forward and this time pass left shoulders. Drop that person's hand and join right hands with the next person. Continue alternately joining right and left hands until partners meet. When partners meet the boy turns the lady around so she is walking in the same direction that he is which will be counterclockwise. Keep walking forward until everyone returns to home position. Girls will follow the girl in front of them and boys will be following the boy in front of them as they are performing the Grand Right and Left. Boys will be walking in a counterclockwise direction and girls will be walking in a clockwise direction.

• *Allemande Left followed by a Grand Right and Left* is the term used in reference to corners facing each other joining left hands. Corners walk forward around each other returning to home position. Next partners face each other joining right hands. Partners walk past each other giving the left hand to the next person, right to the next and alternating hands until partners meet. When partners meet the boy turns the girl around so she is walking in the same direction that he is which will be counterclockwise. Partners continue walking forward until everyone returns to home position.

• *Circling* can be performed with one, two, three, or all four couples.

• *Circle Right* is the term used in reference to everyone in the square joining hands while facing the center of the square. All walk to the right or counterclockwise and back to the home position. Circle *Left* is the term used to refer to everyone in the square joining hands while facing the center of the square. All walk to the left or clockwise and back to the home position.

• *Do-Sa-Do* is the term used to refer to two of the dancers facing each other, walking forward passing right shoulders. Side step to the right, back to back without turning and then back up into their own places passing left shoulders. The caller will give directions regarding which two or more dancers will do-sa-do. A do-sa-do is performed with the arms folded in front of the chest.

• *Forward and Back* is the term used in reference to two or more dancers walking four steps towards the center of the square and then taking four steps backwards to their original positions

• *Into the Center* is the term used in reference to everyone joining hands and walking forward towards the center of the square and then back to their original place while continuing to keep their hands joined.

• *Right Hand Star* is the term used in reference to having the participants walk to the center of the square and placing their right hands on top of each other. The hands are kept at shoulder level as dancers walk forward in a circle, walking clockwise. The caller will give directions regarding which dancers will participate in the star.

• *Left Hand Star* is the term used in reference to having the participants walk to the center of the square and placing their left hands on top of each other. The dancers walk forward in a counterclockwise direction.

• *Form an Arch* is the term used in reference to having dancers face their partners or another dancer with whom they have been instructed to form an arch. The two dancers face each other and join hands holding their arms straight above their heads, which forms the shape of an arch. Others will be instructed by the caller to go under the arch. Sometimes the arch is made by joining only inside hands when standing next to your partner, instead of joining both hands.

• *Couple One Separate* is the term used in reference to couple number one moving away from each other. Starting in their home position the girl moves to her own right outside the square walking in a counterclockwise direction. At the same time boy one moves to his own left outside the square moving in a clockwise direction. They pass each other behind couple number three and keep going in the same direction until arriving at their home positions. The caller will give instructions as to which couples will separate and at what time.

• *Outside the Ring* is the term used in reference to dancers moving around the outside of the square.

• *Inside the Ring* is the term used in reference to dancers moving around the inside of the square.

### *"Get Ready to Square Dance"*

This entire CD is great for teaching the basics of square dancing. This CD is available through Educational Record Center. Side one is appropriate for grades K through 3. It illustrates the basic concepts of circle right, circle left, promenade, forward and back, swing your partner, honor your partner. Part one is such that the class does not have to be divided into squares but rather partners in a circle formation works well.
Side two is excellent for teaching square dance for grades 4 through 6. Part 2 illustrates the basic concepts of the right hand star, left hand star, do-sa-do, allemande right, allemande left, promenade, swing, forward and back, honor your partner, and circle. The entire second side of the album is appropriate for reviewing as well as teaching general square dance basics and is performed in a square formation.

Side 1
*Title:*   **Honor Your Partner**
*Music:* "Get Ready to Square Dance" Band 1. 4/4 time.
*Formation:* Partners form a double circle with the boys on the inside and the girls on the outside with all dancers facing counterclockwise joining inside hands.
*Instructions:* Dancers are divided into partners and will form a double circle facing counterclockwise, with boys on the inside of the circle and girls on the outside. Partners will join inside hands and walk counterclockwise for 16 counts. Partners will now join both hands and circle around each other. Dancers now drop hands and honor each other (boys bow, girls curtesy). Continue with the entire sequence throughout the whole dance.

*Title:*   **Circle Left, Circle Right, Into the Center and Back**
*Music:* "Get Ready to Square Dance" Band 2. 4/4 time.
*Formation:* A single circle with all dancers facing center without partners.

*Instructions*: Dancers will all join hands and circle clockwise. Everyone will take four very, small steps towards the center of the circle, followed by four steps, back to place. Dancers will repeat the four very small steps into the center followed by four steps back to place. The entire sequence is repeated from the beginning of the dance, however, this time the dancers will circle counterclockwise followed by four small steps into the center and four steps back to place. It is necessary to remind the students not to pull on other students' arms and not to run into the center but rather take small steps.

> *Cues:*    Circle Left (clockwise)
> Into the center (4 small steps)
> Back to Place
> Into the center (4 small steps)
> Back to Place
> Circle Right (clockwise)
> Into the center (4 small steps)
> Back to Place
> Into the center (4 small steps)
> Back to place
> Repeat entire sequence until the end of the song.

### Title:    *Swing Your Partner and Circle*
*Music:* "Get Ready to Square Dance" Band 3. 4/4 time.
*Formation:* A large circle with partners all facing center with the girls on the boys' right.
*Instructions:* All dancers will face the center of the circle and alternately stamp their feet and clap their own hands together approximately 8 times. Joining right elbows, partners will swing each other for 16 counts. Everyone will join hands making one large circle with all facing the center and circle clockwise for 16 counts. Dancers will now circle counterclockwise for 16 counts. The entire sequence is repeated from the beginning throughout the whole dance.

> *Cues:*    Stomp, clap, stomp, clap, stomp, clap, stomp, clap, stomp, clap, stomp, clap, stomp, clap, stomp, clap. Swing your partner with the right elbow. All circle left, circle right.

### Title:    *Into the Center and Back and Swing Your Partner*
*Music:* "Get Ready to Square Dance" Band 4. 4/4 time.
*Formation:* One large single circle with all facing the center, girls are on the boys' right. Partners are required.
*Instructions:* Dancers all join hands and walk four steps into the center of the circle and four steps back to place. Again, dancers will walk four steps forward and four steps back to place. Partners will now join right elbows and swing each other. During the song on the word "so" all dancers will stop until the next verse starts. The entire sequence is repeated from the beginning throughout the whole song.

> *Cues:*    Forward and Back
> Forward and Back
> Swing
> Pause (on the word "So")
> Repeat entire sequence

*Title:*    ***Promenade and Square Your Set***

*Music:* "Get Ready to Square Dance" Band 5. 4/4 time.

*Formation:* Double circle with boys on the inside, girls on the outside. Begin by all facing the center of the circle.

*Instructions:* Dancers will stamp in place four times, followed by clapping their hands together four times. This movement is repeated four times. Partners will then join inside hands and walk counterclockwise. The caller will tell dancers when to honor their partners. At this point, dancers stop and honor their partners: boys bow and girls curtsey. This entire sequence is repeated from beginning throughout the entire song.

> *Cues:*     Stomp, 2, 3, 4
> Clap, 2, 3, 4
> Stomp, 2, 3, 4
> Clap, 2, 3, 4
> Stomp, 2, 3, 4
> Clap, 2, 3, 4
> Stomp, 2, 3, 4
> Clap, 2, 3, 4
> Promenade
> Honor Your Partner
> Repeat sequence

Side 2

*Title:*    ***Forward and Back and Swing Your Partner***

*Music:* "Get Ready to Square Dance" Band 6. 4/4 time.

*Formation:* Squares

*Instructions:* The head two couples (1 and 3) walk four steps forward towards the center of the square and four steps back to place. The side two couples (2 and 4) walk forward towards the center of the square and back to place. Corners will swing each other followed by partners swinging each other.

> Cues:     Heads forward and back
> Sides forward and back
> Swing corner
> Swing partner

*Title:*    ***Do-Sa-Do and Promenade***

*Music:* "Get Ready to Square Dance" Band 7. 4/4 time.

*Formation:* Squares

*Instructions:* The head two couples (1 and 3) walk four steps forward towards the center of the square and four steps back to place. The same two couples do-sa-do each other. Dancers will promenade with their own partners. The side two couples (2 and 4) walk forward and back to place. The same two couples will do-sa-do. Dancers will promenade with their own partners. This entire sequence is repeated until the end of the song.

> Cues:     Heads forward and back
> Heads do-sa-do
> Sides forward and back
> Sides do-sa-do
> Promenade

*Title*:     ***Allemande Left, Allemande Right and Star***
*Music:* "Get Ready to Square Dance" Band 8. 4/4 time.
*Formation:* Squares
*Instructions:* Dancers will honor their partners. Dancers will honor their corners. Dancers will do-sa-do with their own corners. Dancers will do-sa-do with their own partners. Dancers will now allemande left with their corners. Dancers will allemande right with their partners. All four boys walk to the center and make a right hand star by putting their right hands on top of each other and walking clockwise in a circle. Boys turn and make a left hand star. Boys will walk back to their places. Girls will move to the center and make a right hand star. Girls turn and make a left hand star. Girls walk back to their own places. The entire sequence from the beginning is repeated throughout the entire song.

       Cues:     Honor partner
                   Honor corner
                   Do-sa-do corner
                   Do-sa-do partner
                   Allemande left corner
                   Allemande right partner
                   Boys right hand star, left hand star
                   Girls right hand star, left hand star

*Title:* ***Hoedown***
*Music:* "Get Ready to Square Dance" Band 9. 4/4 time.
*Formation:* Squares
*Instructions:* All dancers will honor their partners. All dancers will honor their corners. Everyone joins hands and circle left (clockwise), then circle to the right (counterclockwise). Dancers will square their sets. The two head couples walk forward and back (1 and 3). The head two couples circle left and circle right. Dancers will do-sa-do with their own corner. Dancers will swing with their own partner. All dancers will promenade. Dancers will follow the calls on the record. If all dancers have performed all of the dances up to this point on side 2 of "Get Ready to Square Dance" they should now be familiar with all of the calls.

*Title:* ***Tie a Yellow Ribbon***
*Music:* "Get Ready to Square Dance" Band 10. 4/4 time.
*Formation:* Squares
*Instructions:* Everyone join hands and circle left (clockwise). All swing partners. Do-sa-do corners. All promenade. Allemande left with corners. Follow the directions of the caller. The calls are varied, however, dancers should be familiar with all calls.

*Title:* ***Around the Outside and Swing***
*Music:* The music with calls to accompany this dance can be found on volume 2, and 1, on the music CD included with this book. 4/4 time
*Level of Difficulty:* Grades 4–6. Moderate.
*Formation:* This dance is performed in a square formation.
*Instructions:* Refer to the square dance basics portion of this text for specific instructions regarding how to perform the calls of honoring, swinging, promenading, do-sa-doing, and moving into the center and back. For the pattern portion of this dance, couple one separate, the boys walk clockwise (left), and the girls counterclockwise (right) around the outside of the square. Dancers meet behind couple three and swing there. Couple one separates again

continuing in the same direction previously walking, until dancers reach their home positions. Everyone swings their corner ladies and promenades their corner ladies home. The girls follow the boys to their home positions. The girls are always on the boys right (on the outside of the square as they are promenading). Boy 1 again separates from his new partner meeting her behind couple three where dancers swing. New couple one separates again continuing towards the boy's home position. Everyone again swing their corner girls and boys promenade the corner girls to their home positions. At this point everyone joins hands and circle left, and circle right. All move into the center and back, and again into the center and back. Boy 2 now separates from his partner meeting her behind couple four where couple two swings. Dancers separate again and meet at home. Everyone swings their corner girls and boys promenade their corner girls to the boys' home position. Boy 2 will repeat this pattern again. Dancers will do-sa-do with their corners. Dancers will do-sa-do with their partners. All dancers will promenade. The record is played again so that couples three and four have an opportunity to complete the pattern. The entire sequence is repeated from the beginning throughout the entire song.

> *Cues:*   Honor your partner
> Honor your corner
> Swing your corner
> Swing your partner
> Promenade
> First couple separate
> Couple one swings behind couple 3
> Separate
> All corners swing
> Promenade corner
> Couple 1, again separate
> Meet behind 3 and swing
> Separate again
> Swing corner
> Promenade corner
> All join hands and circle left
> Circle right
> All into the center and back

### *Title:*   *Do-Sa-Do and Swing*

*Music:* The music with calls to accompany this dance can be found on volume 2, band 2, on the music CD included with this book. 4/4 time.

*Level and Difficulty:* Grades 4–6. Moderate.

*Formation:* This dance is performed in a square formation.

*Instructions:* Refer to the square dance basics portion of this text for specific instructions regarding how to perform the calls for honoring, circling, do-sa-doing, swing, walking into the center and back, and promenading. For the pattern portion of this dance, couple one walks over to couple two and the four of them join hands and circle to the left, once around. All four dancers drop hands. Dancers will do-sa-do with their opposites and then will swing their opposites. Boy 1 do-sa-do with girl 2, at the same time girl 1 do-sa-do with boy 2. Boy 1 swings girl 2, while girl 1 swings boy 2. Couple one moves to the center and swings. Couple one moves on to couple three where the pattern is repeated. After again swinging in the center couple one moves on to couple number four. After the pattern is repeated with couple four, all four couples swing. At this point everyone joins hands and circles left and circles right, all dancers move into the center and back and again move into the center and back. Couple two then repeats the entire sequence, starting to the right with couple three. When couple two has finished the entire sequence the record is played again so that couples three and four have an opportunity to complete the pattern with each couple in the square.

*Cues:*     Honor partner
            Honor corner
            Promenade
            First couple to the right
            Couples 1 and 2 circle left
            Do-sa-do opposite
            Swing opposite
            Couple 1 (only) swings in the center
            Onto the next couple (couple 3)
            Repeat the pattern 2 more times
            Everyone swing
            Promenade
            All join hands and circle left
            Circle right
            All into the center and back
            Again into the center and back
            Couple 2 to the right and repeat pattern with couple 3
            Do-sa-do your corner
            Do-sa-do your partner
            Promenade
            Play the song through one more time so that couples 3 and 4 have the opportunity to complete the pattern.

*Title*:    ***Solomon Levi***

*Music*: The music with calls for this dance can be found on volume 2, band 14 on the music CD included with this book.

*Level and Difficulty*: Grades 4-6. Easy.

*Formation*: This dance is performed in a square formation.

*Instructions*: Refer to the square dance basics portion of this text for specific instructions regarding how dancers will honor circle, swing, promenade, and separate. For the pattern portion of the dance couple one separates at home. Girl 1 walks outside the square to the right and at the same time boy 1 walks outside the square to the left. When the couple meets behind couple 3, the dancers pass each other and continue walking in the same direction he/she had been walking. When couple 1 reaches home the couple pass each other again and both face his/her corner, giving a military salute to his/her corner. Couples 2,3, and 4 repeat the same pattern as couple 1. Next the head 2 couples 1 and 3 repeat the pattern. Then the side 2 couples, 2 and 4 repeat the pattern. Finally all 4 couples repeat the pattern at the same time. All dancers swing their partner, followed by a promenade.

     Cues:     Honor partner
               Honor corner
               Circle left

            Circle right
            Couple 1 separate
            Salute corner
            Swing partner
            Promenade partner
            Couples 2, 3, and 4 repeat pattern
            Head 2 couples repeat pattern
            Side 2 couples repeat pattern.
            All 4 couples repeat pattern

*Title*:    ***Marching Through Georgia***
*Music*: The music with calls for this dance can be found on volume 2, band 15, on the music CD included with this book.
*Level and Difficulty*: Grades 4-6. Easy.
*Formation*: This dance is performed in a square formation.
*Instructions*: Refer to the square dance basics portion of this text for specific instructions regarding how dancers will honor, circle, swing, and promenade. For the pattern portion of this dance, girl 1 marches around the inside of the square moving in a counterclockwise direction. When she reaches her partner she swings him. Everyone then turns to the right and places his/her inside hand on the shoulder of the person in front of him/her. Everyone then swings his/her own partner. Girls 2, 3, and 4 repeat the pattern. Boy 1 marches around the outside of the square moving in a clockwise direction. When he reaches his partner he swings her. Everyone then turns to the left and places his/her inside hand on the shoulder of the person in front of him/her. Next everyone swings his/her partner.

    Cues:    Honor partner
               Honor corner
               Circle left
               Circle right
               Swing partner
               Promenade twice
               All swing
               Girl 1 march around inside
               Swing partner
               Everyone turn to right
               Hand on shoulder of person in front
               All swing
               Girls 2, 3, and 4 repeat pattern
               Boy 1 marches around outside
               Swing partner
               All turn to left and put hand on shoulder of person in front
               All swing
               Boys 2, 3, and 4 repeat pattern

*Title*:    ***Life on the Ocean Wave***
*Music:* The music with calls for this dance can be found on volume 2, band 3 on the music CD included with this book. 4/4 time.
*Level and Difficulty:* Grades 4–6. Moderate.
*Formation:* This dance is performed in a square formation.

*Instructions:* Refer to the square dance basics portion of this text for specific instructions regarding how dancers will honor, circle, swing, and promenade. For the pattern portion of this dance, the head two girls cross over (girls 1 and 3 change places). Next the side two girls then cross over (girls 2 and 4 change places). All dancers then join hands and move towards the center of the square. Dancers will honor their partners, and swing their corners. Their corners now become their new partners. Dancers will promenade with their new partners. Girls will follow the boys counterclockwise to the boys' home positions. Dancers repeat this pattern three more times. The whole sequence is repeated until each dancer ends up with their original partner. All dancers will then promenade with their own partners. The entire sequence is repeated from the beginning throughout the whole song.

> *Cues*:   Honor your partner
> Honor your corner
> Swing your corner
> Swing your partner
> Promenade your partner
> Head two ladies cross over
> Side two ladies cross over
> All join hands and move towards the center of the square
> Honor your partner
> Swing your corner
> Promenade your corner (who becomes your new partner)
> Repeat pattern 3 more times until you end up with your original partner
> Promenade
> All join hands and circle left
> Circle right
> Into the center and back
> Do-sa-do your corner
> Do-sa-do your partner
> Promenade your partner

### *Title*:        *Make An Arch*

*Music*: The music with calls for this dance can be found on volume 2, band 11 on the music CD included with this book.

*Level and Difficulty*: Grades 4-.6. Moderate.

*Formation*: This dance is performed in a square formation.

*Instructions*: Do not confuse this dance with the dance "Form an Arch", which is described later in this chapter. Refer to the square dance basics portion of this text for specific instructions regarding how dancers will honor, circle, swing, separate and promenade. For the pattern portion of this dance couple number one walks four steps forward and four steps back to place. Couple 1 again walks forward and continues moving forward while separating couple 3. Girl 1 walks to the right outside the circle while boy 1 walks to the left outside the circle. When couple 1 arrives at home, dancers pass each other moving onto the next couple. Boy 1 is now with couple 2 and girl 1 is with couple 4. Each group of 3 circles right and then circles left. Both groups drop 1 persons hand keeping the other hands joined so that dancers are now forming 2 lines of three with lines facing each other. If there are 2 boys and 1 girl in a group the girls should be in the middle and if there are 2 girls and 1 boy, the boy should be in the middle. Both groups walk forward and back towards each other and away from each other. This is known as forward six and back. The same groups move forward again and stretch arms high while joining hands with the dancers directly across from each other. This is known as making an arch. Couple 3 is the lonesome couple and will swing and tunnel through the arches. Couple 3 swings at the other end and tunnels back. Everyone finds his/her own partner and partners swing. All promenade. Couples 2, 3, and 4 repeat the patter.

      Cues:     Honor partner
                Honor corner
                Circle left
                Circle right
                Swing partner
                Promenade
                Couple 1 forward and back
                Couple 1 forward again and split couple 3
                Pass each other at home
                Onto the next couple
                Circle with them
                Break to a line
                Forward and back
                Forward again and make an arch
                Lonesome couple swing and tunnel through
                Swing at the foot and tunnel back
                All swing your own partner
                Promenade
                Repeat pattern with couples 2, 3, and 4

### *Title:*   *Red River Valley*

*Music:* The music with calls to accompany this dance can be found on volume 2, band 4 on the music CD included with this book. 4/4 time

*Level and Difficulty:* Grades 4–6. Easy.

*Formation:* This dance is performed in a square formation.

*Instructions:* Refer to the square dance basic portion of this text for specific instructions regarding how dancers will honor, swing, circle, and promenade. During the pattern portion of this dance, couple number one walks over to couple number two. Both couples join hands and circle to the left and circle to the right. The boys will swing the other girls, then boys will swing their own partners. Couple one moves on to couple three and repeats the pattern. Couples one and three then circle left, followed by a circle right. The boys will swing the opposite girls, the boys then swing their own partners. Couple one moves on to couple four and repeats the same pattern with couple four. Everyone will swing their own partners and all will promenade. Couples two, three, and four will all take a turn repeating the pattern with each couple. The calls for the dance are on the music CD included with this book.. The teacher may call out the cues over the microphone after the caller in order to reinforce the directions for the students. The entire sequence is repeated from the beginning throughout the entire song.

      *Cues*:     Honor your partner
                Honor your corner
                Circle left
                Circle right
                 Swing partner
                Promenade
                Swing your partner

Couple one walk over to couple two
Circle left
Circle right
Swing the opposite lady
Swing your own partner
Couple one moves onto couple three
Repeat pattern with couple three
Repeat pattern with couple four
All swing your own
Promenade
Couple 2, 3, and 4 will repeat entire sequence

### Title:    *Yankee Doodle*

*Music:* The music with calls to accompany this dance can be found on volume 2, band 5 on the music CD included with this book. 4/4 time.
*Level and Difficulty:* Grades 4–6. Moderate.
*Formation:* This dance is performed in a square formation.
*Instructions:* Refer to the square dance basics portion of this text for specific instructions regarding how dancers will honor, circle, swing, promenade, and grand right and left. For the pattern portion of this dance, couple one walks over to couple two. Couples one and two place their right hands to the center, with hands on top of one another forming a star formation. All four dancers walk forward in a circular movement. Dancers will change hands and walk in the other direction, performing a left hand star. Couples one and two swing their opposites, and then swing their own partners. Couple one then moves onto couple number three. Both couples form a star pattern, again with the right hand in the center and circle walking forward. All four dancers turn, placing left hand in the center and circle walking forward. Again couples one and three swing their opposites and then swing their own partners. Couple one moves onto couple four repeating the previous pattern. All dancers swing their own partners and all promenade. Dancers will then perform the grand right and left followed by the promenade. Couple two will repeat the entire sequence. The record is played again so that couples three and four have an opportunity to complete the pattern with each couple in the square. The entire sequence is repeated from the beginning throughout the entire song.

*Cues*:    Honor your partner
Honor your corner
Grand right and left
Promenade
1st couple walk over to couple 2
Right hand star
Left hand star
Swing your opposite
Swing your own
Couple 1 repeat with 3 & 4
Everybody swing
Promenade
Grand right and left
Promenade
Couple 2 repeats entire sequence
Play the song through one more time so that couples 3 and 4 have an opportunity to complete the pattern.

### Title:     ***Hinkey Dinkey Parlez Vous***

*Music:* The music with calls to accompany this dance can be found on volume 2, band 6, on he music CD included with this book... 4/4 time.

*Level and Difficulty:* Grades 5–6. Moderate.

*Formation:* This dance is performed in square formation.

*Instructions:* Refer to the square dance basics portion of this text for specific instructions regarding how the dancers will honor, swing, circle, promenade, grand right and left, do-sa-do, and forward and back. During the pattern portion of this dance, girls 1 and 3 (head girls) move forward and back to the center of the square and back to their original positions. The same 2 girls move forward again and this time do-sa-do with each other. All dancers will do-sa-do their corners. All dancers will now do-sa-do their partners. Partners swing each other and all will promenade. The side 2 girls, the head 2 boys, and finally the side 2 boys will all repeat the pattern. All dancers will have the opportunity to repeat the pattern. The entire sequence is repeated from the beginning throughout the entire song.

> *Cues:*     Circle left
> Circle right
> Grand right and left
> Promenade
> Head two girls forward and back
> Same two girls do-sa-do
> All do-sa-do your corner
> All do-sa-do your partner
> Swing your partner
> Promenade
> Side two girls repeat the pattern
> Grand right and left
> Promenade
> Head two gents repeat the pattern
> Side two gents repeat the pattern
> All join hands and circle left
> Circle right
> Grand right and left
> Promenade

### Title:     ***Push Her Away***

*Music:* The music with calls, to accompany this dance can be found on volume 2, band 7, on the music CD included with this book. 4/4 time.

*Level and Difficulty:* Grades 4–6. Moderate.

*Formation:* This dance is performed in a square formation.

*Instructions:* Refer to the square dance basics portion of this text for specific instructions regarding how dancers will honor, swing, promenade, allemande left, and grand right and left. For the pattern portion of this dance, all four boys move to the right. Boy 1 moves to girl 2, boy 2 moves to girl 3, boy 3 moves to girl 4, and boy 4 moves to girl 1. All dancers will perform a balance. To balance, the boys take the girls right hands in their right hands and at the same time both girl and boy step on their right feet and swing their left feet across and in front of their right feet. Dancers repeat this action stepping on the left feet and swinging the right feet. Boys bow to the girls, kneel to the girls, and swing the girls. Boys take the girls right hands and step back away from the girls, next the boys will step up to the girls and swing them. Again boys step away from the girls, then step up to the girls and swing again. This action is referred to as "push her away." All 4 boys move to the right and repeat the sequence. This is repeated two more times until the boys end up with their own partners. The entire sequence from the beginning is repeated throughout the whole song.

> *Cues:*   Honor your partner
> Honor your corner
> Swing your partner
> Promenade
> All 4 gents lead to the right
> Balance with the lady
> Bow to the lady
> Kneel to the lady
> Swing the lady
> Push her away
> Swing the lady
> Push her away again
> Swing her again
> All 4 gents move to the right
> Repeat the entire sequence 3 more times
> Promenade
> Allemande left
> Grand right and left
> Promenade

### Title:    *Divide the Ring*

*Music:* The music with calls to accompany this dance can be found on volume 2, band 8, on the music CD included with this book. 4/4 time

*Level and Difficulty:* Grades 5–6. Moderate.

*Formation:* This dance is performed in square formation.

*Instructions:* Refer to the square dance basics portion of this text for specific instructions regarding how dancers will honor, swing, promenade, grand right and left, and do-sa-do with the other dancers. For the pattern portion of this dance, couple one bow and swing. Couple one walks down the center of the square and between couple three, the couple right across from couple one. This is called "dividing the ring" (cut off 6). Girl 1 walks to the right outside of the square and boy 1 walks to the left outside the square. Couple one meet at their original position, and swing. Couple one continues down the center of the square this time, girl 1 walks between girl 2 and boy 3, while boy 1 walks between girl 3 and boy 4 (cutting off four). Again dancers meet at home and swing. Couple one continues to walk down the center of the square this time girl 1 walks between couple two, while boy 1 walks between couple four (cutting off 2). When couple one reaches home everyone swing. Each couple will have a turn to complete the pattern. The entire sequence is repeated from the beginning throughout the whole dance.

> *Cues:*   Honor your partner
> Honor your corner
> Grand right and left
> Promenade
> Couple 1 bow and swing

Go down the center divide the ring (cut off 6)
Swing
Cut off 4
Swing
Cut off 2
Everybody swing
Promenade
Couple 2 complete pattern
Do-sa-do corner
Do-sa-do partner
Grand right and left
Promenade
Couples 2, 3 and 4 complete pattern

### *Title:*     *Hot Time in the Old Town (Girls to the Center)*

*Music:* The music with calls to accompany this dance can be found on volume 2, band 9, on the music CD included with this book. 4/4 time.

*Level and Difficulty:* Grades 5–6. Moderate.

*Formation:* This dance is performed in square formation.

*Instructions:* Refer to the square dance basics portion of this text for specific instructions regarding how dancers will honor, circle, swing, grand right and left, and promenade with their partners. For the pattern portion of this dance, all four girls walk to the center of the square, in a back to back position. All four girls now have their backs to each other. The boys will walk counterclockwise around the girls. When the boys reach their own partners, after circling the group of girls one time, the boys will move to the next lady to their right and swing this lady. Again the girls move to the center back to back. Boys will move around the outside of the circle and stop at the girl they just finished swinging and swing the next girl. Again the boys walk around the outside and swing the next girls. Boys continue this pattern until ending up with their own partners. The boys will also repeat the pattern by moving to the center with the girls moving around the outside. Each of the girls will also swing each of the boys. The entire sequence is repeated from the beginning until the entire song is finished.

    *Cues:*    Circle left
Circle right
Grand right and left
Promenade
Swing your partner
All four girls to the center back to back
All four boys walk around the outside of the girls
Pass your partner and swing the next girl
Repeat this pattern 3 more times until all end up with their own partners
Circle left
Circle right
Grand right and left
Promenade
Swing your partner
All four boys to the center
All four girls walk around the outside

Pass your partner and swing the next boy
Repeat this 3 times until all end up with their partners

*Title:*    ***Take a Little Peek***
*Music:* The music with calls to accompany this dance can be found on volume 2, band 10, on the music CD included with this book.  4/4 time.
*Level and Difficulty:* Grades 5–6. Moderate.
*Formation:* This dance is performed in square formation.
*Instructions:* Refer to the square dance basics portion of this text for specific instructions regarding how dancers will honor, swing, grand right and left, and promenade with their partners. During the pattern portion of this dance couple one walks over to couple two. Couple one separates and peeks around couple two by taking a step so that girl 1 is facing and to the side of boy 2 while boy 1 is facing and to the side of girl 2. Couple one then peeks at each other by moving their heads around couple two's back so that couple one can see each other. Couples one then swing in the center of the square and again separate and peek around couple two again. This time both couples swing. The pattern is repeated with couples three and four. All 4 couples take their turn at repeating the pattern. The entire sequence is repeated from the beginning throughout the entire dance.

      *Cues:*    Bow to your partner
               Swing
               Promenade
               Couple 1 walks over to couple 2 and peeks around couple 2
               Couple one walks to the center and swings
               Couple 1 again peeks around couple two and this time both couples swing
               Couple one moves on to couples 3 and 4 repeating the pattern with each couple
               Everyone swings
               Promenade
               Couples 2, 3, and 4 all repeat the pattern with each couple
               Everyone swing
               Promenade
               Grand right and left
               Promenade

*Title:*    ***Form An Arch***
*Music:* The music with calls to accompany this dance can be found on volume 2, band 12, on the music CD included with this book.  4/4 time.
*Level and Difficulty:* Grades 4–6. Moderate.
*Formation:* This dance is performed in a square formation.
*Instructions:* Do not confuse this dance with "Make an Arch", which is described earlier in this chapter. Refer to the square dance basics portion of this text for specific instructions regarding how the dancers honor, circle, swing, promenade, grand right and left, and allemande left with their partners.  For the pattern portion of this dance, the head two couples walk forward and back. Dancers walk forward again and join outside hands with the person across from them. Girl 1 joins her right hand with gent 3's left hand, while gent 1 joins his left hand with girl 3's right hand. These two couples raise the joined hands  (the outside hands) to form an arch. The two side girls, 2 and 4 will walk under the arch to the opposite gent. Girl 4 walks over to boy 2, and girl 2 walks over to boy 4. All 4 boys swing the opposite girls. Boy 1 swings girl 3, and boy 3 swings girl 1. All dancers promenade the set with their new

partners. The entire sequence is repeated with the head two couples again moving forward and back.  Dancers move forward again forming an arch and the two side girls will move under the arch to the opposite boys. The pattern is repeated two more times, this time with the side two couples performing the pattern.  The entire sequence is repeated from the beginning throughout the entire song.

          *Cues:*     Honor your partner
                       Honor your corner
                       Circle to the left
                       Circle to the right
                       Allemande left
                       Grand right and left
                       Promenade
                       Head two couples forward and back
                       Same two couples forward again
                        Same two couples form an arc
                       Side two ladies move through the arch
                       Everyone swing your opposite
                       Promenade your opposite
                       Head two couples repeat previous sequence
                       Allemande left
                       Grand right and left
                       Promenade
                        Side two couples repeat sequence twice

### *Title:*     ***Pass the Left Hand Lady Under***

*Music:*  The music with calls for this dance can be found on volume 2, band 13, on the music CD included with this book. 4/4 time.

*Level and Difficulty:* Grades 5–6. Difficult.

*Formation:* This dance is performed in a square formation.

*Instructions:*  Refer to the square dance basics portion of this text for specific instructions regarding how dancers will honor, swing, circle do-sa-do, promenade, allemande left, and grand, right and left, with their partners.  Couple one will lead to the right and circles clockwise with couple two. Boy 1 leaves his girl there and goes on to the third couple. The three dancers then circle left. Boy 1 takes girl 3 with him onto couple four. The four dancers will circle clockwise. Boy 1 leaves girl 3 with couple four and goes home alone. The side two boys each have an extra girl. These two groups of three face each other and walk forward and back. The two single boys do-sa-do. The side two boys cross the two girls in front of themselves, passing the left hand girls under the arch onto the next boys and the right hand ladies then move in front of the boys they are with onto the next boys. The girls on the right of boy 2 will end up with boy 1, and the girls on the left of boy 2 will end up with boy 3. The girls on the right of boy 4 will end up being with boy 3 and the girls on the left of boy 4 will end up with boy 1. If both girls and boys remember that the girls will cross in front of the boys they are with, walking forward and onto the next boy, it will make the pattern work out correctly. Now the head two boys have an extra girl. Again the two lines of three move forward and back. The single boys will do-sa-do. The boys with the extra girls will pass the left hand girls under and the right hand girls moves in front of the boys they are with onto the next boys. This pattern is repeated two more times. All dancers will swing their own partners and promenade. Couple two leads to the right and circles left. The boy leaves the girl with couple three and goes on to couple four alone. Boy 2 will circle with couple four and take girl 4 along to couple one. They circle with couple one and boy 2 leaves both girls there and goes home alone. This pattern repeats until each couple has a turn to complete the entire pattern. In order to pass the left hand girl under, the boy who is in the middle of the two girls, while in the two groups of three facing each other, raises his right hand. With hands joined this forms an arch with the girl on the right. The girl on the left moves under the arch and onto the next boy, as described earlier. As soon as the girl on the left crosses under the arch the girl on the right crosses in front of the middle boy over to the next boy. This is the pattern entitled "pass the left hand lady under."

*Cues*:  Honor partner
            Honor corner
            Do-sa-do corner
            Do-sa-do partner
            Promenade
            Couple one moves to couple two and circles
            Gent one leave lady one with couple two
            Gent one goes over to couple three and circles
            Gent one takes lady 3 and moves over to couple 4
            Gent l, lady 3, and couple 4 circle
            Gent l leaves lady 3 with couple 4 and goes
            home alone
            Two lines of 3, forward and back
            Head two gents do-sa-do
            Pass the left hand lady under (both side
            gents)
            Pass the left hand lady under 3 more times
            with the forward and back pattern
            Everyone swing own partner
            Promenade
            Allemande Left
            Grand right and left
            Promenade

# Rhythm Activities

Jump ropes, batons, and lummi sticks are only a few of the many rhythm activities that are appropriate for the physical education class. These four have been included due to their popularity or ease in teaching.

## BATON ACTIVITIES

The batons used for this activity are plastic and are therefore relatively safe. The primary safety concern, besides someone getting hit with a baton, might be if someone were to be accidentally hit in the eye. It is recommended that students wear safety goggles in order to protect students' eyes from injuries.

Each student is given a baton. A CD or other recording with marches can then be used as background music as well as to keep the proper marching rhythm. Students can be organized

in a variety of formations; however a very large circle with everyone marching in the same
direction seems to work out well. Included is a list of various activities that can be performed
with batons for the purpose of general coordination, eye hand coordination, dexterity, upper
body coordination, and general fitness. Students will march in circle formation keeping in
time to the music while performing various activities and patterns with the baton.

Suggested Activities:
Carry baton on the shoulder like a rifle
Inside the circle - right shoulder
Outside the circle - left shoulder
Tap left shoulder with the baton while marching
Tap right shoulder with baton while marching
Tap left foot with the baton while marching
Tap right foot with the baton while marching
Tap left knee with the baton while marching
Tap right knee with the baton while marching
Move the baton up and down like a drum major leading the band
Move the baton to the left, out in front, then to the right
Tap the floor to the left, lift up to shoulder
Tap the floor to the right, lift up to shoulder
Hold the baton in the center pushing it away and bringing it back
Hold the baton in the center making motions like rowing a boat
Balance the end of the baton on the hand see how long one can keep it balanced there
Make a figure 8 in front of one's body
Make a figure 8 in front then under one leg
Make a figure 8 in front then pass it in back of oneself
Twist the baton back and forth as if leading up to a twirl
Twirl it under the arm vertically
Twirl it in front of the body horizontally
Twirl it in one hand moving it between each of the fingers
Twist or twirl it from one hand to the other and back
Stop Marching - Balance the baton on different body parts. Examples: Head, back of
     neck, knee, nose, foot, stomach, etc.
Toss baton from one hand to the other
Hold one end of the baton and toss from end to end
Toss to yourself
Toss away from yourself
Toss in the air & catch (horizontally so one can catch it)
Create you own patterns
Grand March Formations (with batons)
Weave single file into and out of a circle
Single file in a straight line
In twos or pairs
In fours
In eights
Divide back into fours
Divide further back into twos
Make an arch, the first couple moves all the way through the arch to the end and make
     a new arch.
Staying in the arches, couples will go over then under the arches all the way to the end.

## JUMP ROPE ACTIVITIES

Jumping rope is an excellent form of aerobic exercise for children. It is inexpensive and can be performed outside as well as inside. A spool of rope may be ordered from the physical education supply company and then cut to lengths for both individual as well as long jump rope activities. A variety of music can be played in the background as an accompaniment for jump rope activities. Students enjoy bringing in their own tapes for jump rope background music. It is suggested that individual jump ropes all be cut the same length for the elementary school; therefore students do not argue over jump ropes. If the length needs to be adjusted for shorter students ropes can be wrapped around the hand once or twice if necessary. However, in most cases this is found to be unnecessary. A rope of approximately 9 feet in length is found to be appropriate for students from 5 through 14 years of age..

There are many traditional long jump rope rhymes found in several books on jump rope activities in the public library. An example of traditional rhymes is Edwin Adams' book entitled "Jump Rope Rhymes." Long jump rope activities appear to be easier for young children to learn before individual rope skills, because students can concentrate on jumping while two other students turn the rope.
The basic safety rules are:

      1.  Children should never put the rope around their own or anyone's necks.
      2.  Spacing should be such that no one will be hit by a swinging rope.
      3.  The rope should never be swung in such a way as to result in hitting someone in the face or eye with the rope.

### *Long (Two-Turner) Jump Ropes*

The most difficult task for the child who is learning to jump rope is the turning of the rope rhythmically and smoothly. Therefore it makes more sense to teach children to jump the long rope first; once the jumping rhythm has been established, the child is ready to learn to turn the individual rope.

Long jump rope turners should stand on marked spots on the floor where there is also a mark on the floor midway between them. The jumper stands on the midway mark facing one of the jumpers. In the initial learning stages it is best to have the jumper's left side to the rope. This will cause the rope to be turned in a tracking pattern for the jumper from left to right. The child should be encouraged to jump up and down on the mark to prevent "traveling" while jumping.

The turners should be able to coordinate the turning of the rope with a slow, steady pace. As the rope reaches over the head of the child, the cue "jump" should be given. This should give the child enough reaction time to jump for the rope to pass beneath the feet.
The child should learn to jump in two different ways. One would be the single jump each time the rope turns. The second way is called a jump-bounce and is done when the child jumps rhythmically with a high jump for the rope to pass under and then a small bouncing jump when the rope is overhead.

Once the child is able to jump rhythmically for 10–15 jumps in a row, it will be time to teach the individual rope skills.

As children get older they can learn to time the long rope swing so that children can "run in" and immediately begin to jump. The easiest approach is through the "front door" and this means that the child waits on the side where the rope is turning toward him/her. The cue is given as the rope slaps the floor, "Now-now-now-now" until the child takes the cue, runs to the center mark and immediately begins to jump. Children who are talented in this area may also enter by the "back door," cues being the same for this more difficult side.

## *Individual Ropes*

The individual jump rope activity for young children would begin by teaching students how to turn the rope. Have children hold both ends of the rope in one hand and practice swinging it forward; then switch the rope to the other side. Stress smaller movements of hands and wrists; negate large arm swings. Students can practice turning the rope over their heads and jumping over the rope either as it lies by the feet, or as it swings through. After students have learned to successfully swing the rope they may begin to practice jumping over the rope. Instruct them to listen for the rope to hit the floor and then jump over it. A cue that may be used is to "swing tap and jump." Learning the coordination of timing the jump with the swinging of the rope takes practice. Students that have an opportunity to have many short practice periods over several days have been found to become proficient in jumping rope. Patience is required with small children.

There are a wide variety of ways to jump rope some are listed here.

1. Jump forward landing on two feet at the same time.
2. Jump backward landing on two feet at the same time.
3. Jump forward landing on one foot at a time (skipping rope).
4. Jump backward landing on one foot at a time (skipping rope).
5. Jump forward landing on only one foot.
6. Jump forward landing on the other foot.
7. Jump backward landing on one foot.
8. Jump backward landing on the other foot.
9. Jump sideways.

10.      Jump sideways on the other side.
11.      Jump in a circle.
12.      Jump backwards in a circle.
13.      Jump in a circle going the other direction.
14.      Jump backwards in a circle going in the other direction.
15.      Cross your rope and uncross your rope (this is done by crossing your arms, while crossing your rope, and uncrossing your rope and jumping through it).
16.      Cross and uncross your feet while jumping rope.
17.      Try crossing your feet and crossing your rope at the same time.
18.      Cross your rope backwards.

Students can create different ways of jumping rope. Students enjoy having contests to see who can jump a certain way the longest. Students who stop or miss must put their rope down and jog in place while the other students continue jumping until they stop or miss.

Jump ropes may also be used during play or recess. Both long jump ropes and individual jump ropes are excellent recess activities.

# Parachute Routines

Parachute routines can be created to fit with a specific song. These routines give the students an opportunity to be creative. They are also impressive when used in school programs or performances. Counting the beats and measures of a song and then adding parachute activities to fit that beat is one way of developing parachute routines. An example of such a routine follows.

This routine was designed to fit the song "The Duke of Earl." Music for "The Duke of Earl" can be found on albums that contain songs from the 1950s and 60s. As a class, students will take a place around the parachute. Students are then numbered off by 2s. They are told to remember their positions as well as their numbers. The routine is taught all the way through without the music. Students are given written instructions of the parachute routine to take home and memorize. The class is assisted in the memorizing of the routine by talking through the routine and asking which patterns are next. The routine is rehearsed without the parachute or music. When it is felt that the class has memorized the routine, the parachute is then added and practice continues. When the pattern appears to have been learned correctly, the music is added. Parachute routines require a great deal of practice and review. The parachute is a group activity and the class must learn to work together. Student leaders are chosen from students who seem to understand what comes next. Other class members are told to watch the student leaders especially if they are unsure which pattern is next in the routine. Many students, especially special needs students, who have difficulty in memorizing sequences can still perform well by following the lead of other students.

## A PARACHUTE ROUTINE TO "THE DUKE OF EARL" 4/4 TIME

*Umbrella:* Dancers begin with the parachute at waist level. Dancers will take 8 counts to get the parachute up and 8 counts to bring it back to waist level. This movement will take a total of 16 counts.

*Grapevine:* Dancers will take 4 steps counterclockwise while facing the center of the parachute. Dancers will step with the right feet to the right, followed by stepping with the left feet behind the right feet, stepping again to the right side with the right feet and then bringing the left feet next to the right. The grapevine is repeated only this time moving clockwise. This movement should take a total of 8 counts

*Umbrella:* Dancers will take 4 counts to get the parachute up, followed by 4 counts for the 1s to let go of chute and turn around behind the 2s, the 1's then grab hold of the parachute. The 2s will have 4 counts to do the same movement as 1s by letting go of chute and turn around behind 1s. All dancers will now bring the parachute back to waist level. This movement will take a total of 16 counts.

*Inside the Mountain:* Dancers will have 4 counts to get the parachute up, 4 counts to go inside the chute, 4 counts to turn around inside the chute and pull the parachute down and hold, and 4 counts to get out of the mountain. This movement should take a total of 16 counts.

Repeat this whole sequence from the beginning. (Umbrella, Grapevine, Umbrella (1s and 2s change), and Inside the Mountain).

*Merry Go Round:* Dancers perform the merry go round for 8 counts counterclockwise, and again perform the merry go found for 8 counts clockwise. This movement will take a total of 16 counts.

*Umbrella:* Dancers will have 4 counts to get the parachute up, 4 counts for the 1s go to the center, 4 counts for the 1s to make a right hand star, 4 counts for the 1's to come back out of the center backing up while the 2s are holding the chute up during the entire time. This movement will take a total of 16 counts.

*Merry Go Round:* Dancers will perform the merry go round for 8 counts counterclockwise and then perform the merry go round for 8 counts clockwise. This movement should take a total of 16 counts.

*Mushroom*: Dancers will have 4 counts to get the parachute up, and 4 counts to walk into the center. Dancers will hold the chute up for 4 counts, and will have 4 counts to bring the parachute back down. This movement should take a total of 16 counts.

*Outside the Mountain*: Dancers will have 4 counts to get the parachute up, 4 counts to get the parachute down and kneel on it. Dancers will hold the parachute down for 8 counts with their heads lowered and their arms back. This is the ending of the parachute routine. This movement should take 16 counts.

## Lummi Sticks

There are many excellent record albums that come with detailed instructions for the use of lummi sticks. Lummi sticks can either be homemade or purchased. These rhythm sticks are an excellent form of rhythmic activity which can be performed in the classroom or other limited space. Lummi sticks assist students in the development of rhythm, motor skills, and coordination.

Instructions for lummi sticks have not been included in this chapter because the instruction booklets that come with the record albums are well done and also come with illustrations included.

The following two albums have activities appropriate for grades K through 6. "Simplified Rhythm Stick Activities" is appropriate for grades K through 2. "Lively Music for Rhythm Stick Fun" is appropriate for grades 3 through 6. These two albums are available through Educational Record Center, as well as many other sources. There are a number of albums that have been designed to accompany lummi stick activities.

## Ribbon Streamers

There are some excellent CDs that come with detailed instructions for the use of ribbon streamers. Ribbon streamers can either be homemade or purchased. Ribbon streamers are an excellent form of rhythmic activity. The primary safety concern while using ribbon streamers would be if a child might be accidentally poked in the eye. Therefore it is strongly recommended that children wear safety goggles when using ribbon streamers. There are two types of ribbon streamers that may be purchased through physical education supply companies. One type has a shorter handle that is approximately 1 ½ to 2 inches in diameter with a very long plastic streamer attached. The other type is a long wooden handle slightly larger than a pencil in diameter with a very long plastic streamer attached.

Instructions for ribbon streamers have not been included in this chapter because an excellent instruction booklet comes with the ribbon streamer CD and includes illustrations.

## Summary

It is extremely important to organize and structure the physical education class in such a way that students are actively participating for the majority of the class period. Dance and rhythmic activities lend themselves to keeping every student active for the majority of the class period. Dividing into partners, getting into formations, organizing dances, getting out and putting away equipment all need to be done in an efficient and timely manner. This can be accomplished by organizing the dance and rhythmic activities unit ahead of time and by using efficient lesson plans. This chapter has been written for the novice teacher who has had little or no actual dance background. With a positive attitude, the instructions and cues included in this book, and a desire to share the wonderful world of dance and rhythmic activities with one's students, novice teachers can successfully teach a comprehensive dance and rhythmic activities unit to grades K through 6.

## References and Suggested Readings

Capon, J. & Hallum, R. (1977). *Teachers guide: Get ready to square dance.* Educational Activities, Inc.

Harris, J., Pittman, A. & Waller, M. (1994). *Dance a while: Handbook of folk, square, contra & social dance.* Allyn & Bacon.

Hayes, E. (1980). *An introduction to the teaching of dance.* Krieger Publishing Company.

Hayes, E. (1964). *An introduction to the teaching of dance.* The Ronald Press Co.

Hipps, R. & Chappell, W. (1970). *World of fun.* Melody House Publishing Co.

Jackson, S. (1965). *All time favorite folk dances for children.* Dance Records, Inc.

Kraus, R. (1964). *Folk dancing.* MacMillan Co.

Kraus, R. (1950). *Square dances of today and how to teach and call them.* Ronald Press.

Kulbitsky O. & Kaltman, R. (1959). *Teachers' dance handbook: number one: kindergarten to sixth year.* Bluebird Publishing Co.

Pittman, Anne M., & Waller, M. (2004). *Dance a while: Handbook for folk, square, contra & social dance.* Benjamin Cummings.

Ray, O. (1997). *Encyclopedia of line dances country-western volume 1.* Siddall and Ray Research Publications for Dance.

Sorensen, J. (1990). *Aerobic dancing.* Universal Home Video.

Sorensen, J. (1981). *Aerobic dancing.* Macmillan.

Sorensen, J.. (1979). *Aerobic Dancing.* Rawson, Wade, Inc.

Weikart, P. (2003). *Teaching movement & dance: A sequential approach to rhythmic movement.* High/Scope Press.

Weikart, P.. (1998). *Teaching movement & dance: A sequential approach to rhythmic movement.* High/Scope Press

**Specific CD and Available Sources**
The three music CDs included with this book were obtained through Folk Dancer Record Center.

*CD Catalogues:*

Educational Record Center. 1-800-438-1637. 3233 Burnt Mill Drive, Suite 100, Wilmington, North Carolina 28403-2698.

Kimbo Records. 1-800-631-2187. Dept. X, P.O. Box 477, Long Branch, NJ 07740-0477.

Palos Sports. 1-800-233-5484. 12235 South Harlem Ave., Palos Heights, IL 60463.

CHAPTER

# 13

# Body Management Skills

One of the most important phases in the motor development of the child is the acquisition of BODY MANAGEMENT SKILLS. This term refers to those movements that are executed by the child as he/she interacts with the environment. To move with grace and coordination, with minimal extraneous movement of body parts, represents the concept behind the development of body management skills. Such skills would be balance, agility, fluidity of movement, and general overall coordination.

You are already familiar with many of these movement qualities and about ways to teach children to be efficient in these areas. You have read previously that one of the major objectives of a good physical education program is to teach the child to be an *efficient and effective* mover. Through practice and refinement of motor skills, the child will develop such qualities. Let us consider the child who is labeled "clumsy." We have all seen this child who often stumbles, falls frequently, and has difficulty moving to avoid objects in his/her path. You might say that a lack of spatial awareness is the cause for this child's problems. You are correct indeed, for spatial awareness is an important component of body management skills. However, spatial awareness is an outward projection of knowledge, whereas body management skills are internal and are under muscular control. Can you see how the lack of body management skills may affect the clumsy child?

Now, how might we work on body management skills all together, at the same time? Traditionally this has been accomplished through children's participation in physical education units of gymnastics. Some programs teach stunts and tumbling within the gymnastics unit, others teach it as a separate unit. Whichever way it has been taught makes little difference. Both units are very important to the child's physical education. However, due to liability concerns and reserved budgets, schools have been eliminating the course of study in traditional gymnastics. Equipment such as the pommel horse and the uneven parallel bars have been sent to storage. This is truly unfortunate because participation in gymnastics was the one area where children could develop upper arm and shoulder girdle strength. There are few activities that do contribute to this area of strength. Anyone who teaches traditional gymnastics should be someone well trained in the sport; if you, as the classroom teacher, do not have a strong, personal level of traditional gymnastics skill and training, **do not teach it**. This text is not designed to prepare you to teach traditional gymnastics; it will prepare you to provide basic essential experiences in body management skills for your students.

# Educational Gymnastics

One form of gymnastics, called *Educational Gymnastics*, has become quite popular with physical educators and is a good alternative to the more rigorous traditional gymnastics. You, as the classroom teacher, may find it to be an excellent, creative and safe way to teach body management. Educational gymnastics is based on the theory that all children can be successful in learning gymnastic-type movements. The teacher may use equipment or not, and he/she develops a series of questions to lead the class through selected movement experiences involving body management skills.

Picture in your mind a gymnasium setting with mats placed randomly about the floor, several balance beams set near the mats, and perhaps some wooden benches to serve as wider balance beams (most schools do not have numerous balance beams). The children are spread out in the gymnasium space either working alone or with a partner. The teacher moves throughout the learning environment asking pre-planned movement questions, and the children answer with movement responses to solve the problems posed by the teacher. For example, the teacher may select a theme for the day's lesson. It may be something like FLIGHT. The teacher may ask: "Can you find a way to leave the ground and stay in the air as long as possible?" Then, "Can you find a way to stay longer? Could you now try to take off on one foot? Is there a different way for you to land than on your feet?" The teacher uses planned sequences but also looks around the room and responds to the students' own responses. He/she may ask "Can you find a way to take off from the floor and fly over an object?" And then, "Can you now start on top of an object and fly to a low landing?" This is a very difficult method of teaching and requires significant planning.

Educational gymnastics allows children to roll, to twist, to turn, and to travel in various ways. Questions may be designed to lead most children to the accomplishment of a cartwheel or a handstand, for example. Rather than telling the children that they will learn to do handstands in class, the teacher leads them through the skills without ever mentioning the word. Then, some children may accomplish the handstand, another may learn to do the tip-up or tripod, others may learn the headstand: what is significant about educational gymnastics is that everyone has the same opportunities, they may all work at their own levels, and they will all be successful in their own ways. This eliminates the pain some children experience when they find that they cannot do some skills that others can. Traditional gymnastics and gymnastic tumbling skills in general work best with a certain body type. All children were not cut out to be gymnasts: however, they can all learn body management skills to be efficient and effective movers. Further examples of questions used in an educational gymnastics plan are:

## *THEME:* BALANCE AND MOTION

"As you travel to the open spaces of the play area, see if you can move very quietly, yet quickly." "Now, as you move, see if you can take just 10 steps and then freeze in some kind of balanced position. Hold the balance for at least 3 seconds and then move again." "This time when you balance, see if you can use a base that has three points in contact with the floor." "How about four points? Two points? One point?" "Now see if you can do your one point balance on a very HIGH level." "How about a very LOW level?" "Travel quickly and quietly, and after every ten steps, stop and hold a one-point balance. When you do this, change the level of the balance each time."

## *THEME:* PATHWAYS

"Think about the different kinds of pathways that we use (straight, curved, zigzag). See if you can travel in the open spaces and use each of the three kinds of pathways to cross the play area." "This time, every time you come to a mat, change your pathway to get to the next one. Be sure to visit all of the mats." "Now we will use the mats. Each time you come to a mat, use a straight pathway to roll down the mat." "After you roll, be sure to change the pathway to travel to the next mat." "This time see if you can use a zigzag pathway when moving in the open spaces, and a straight pathway on the mats." "See if you can travel your pathways using a sideward locomotor movement. How about backwards?"

## *THEME:* INVERSION

"Today we are going to work on some skills that allow us to be upside down. First, you should travel the open spaces, and each time you come to a corner of a mat you should leap across to the other side." "Now each time that you come to a mat, I want you to stop, put your hands on the mat and kick high in the air. Then travel on." "See if you can travel on your hands when you kick high." "This time kick high but land on the other side of the mat." "Everyone find a partner and a mat. The two of you are going to work together to find an upside-down position for each of you. Take turns practicing your positions." "As you practice, see if there is a way to have one body part higher than all the other parts when you are upside-down."

# Stunts and Tumbling

Stunts and tumbling is an area in which it is important that the teacher feel able and competent. That is not to say that you should be able to DO all of the skills, but rather that you need to know how to teach them properly and how to "spot" as well. Spotting refers to preventing the child from injury while he/she is practicing a skill. You may be the spotter yourself, or you may teach children to "spot" each other. Your choice depends on the difficulty of the skill. The stunts and tumbling curriculum is broken down into animal walks, balances, individual stunts, partner stunts, partner balances, group stunts and tumbling skills. When planning a lesson, you should take some skills from several different categories. Variety makes the lessons much more interesting and challenging.

## ANIMAL WALKS

One of the ways to work on general body management skills with children is through the teaching of various animal walks. Children love to be creative and give their interpretations of the ways that different animals move. However, traditionally animal walks have been defined to capture the particularities of each animal. For example, the *bear walk* is don with the child on hands and feet, moving the right arm and right leg forward at the s?

time, the left arm and leg move together at the same time. This causes the child to move with a homolateral pattern rather than with the contralateral pattern that is so easy for him/her to do. And, this is how bears walk! Descriptions of the following animal walks are presented along with the psychomotor objectives for each:. Each skill contributes greatly to the child's flexibility levels.

## *Cat Walk*

The child begins on the floor on all fours (hands and feet). Using a contralateral pattern, the child will place the right hand and the toe of the left foot on the floor, while lifting the left hand and right foot off of the floor. The cat walk continues with the left hand and the toe of the right foot placed on the floor while lifting the right hand and the left foot. The cat walk is a graceful one.

## *Crab Walk*

The child begins in a sitting position, knees bent, feet flat on the floor, hands on floor just behind hips. The child then lifts the hips off the floor and raises the back and stomach to be parallel to the floor, then moving forward, backward, or sideward. This contributes to upper arm and shoulder girdle strength and leg strength.

## *Crocodile Walk*

The child begins in a prone position on the floor. Then, by placing forearms flat on floor, the child pulls the body forward with alternating arms reaching and pulling. As the child reaches and pulls with the right arm, the same should happen with the right leg, bending the knee and sliding the knee and leg forward.

The pattern is repeated on the left side. The child uses a homolateral pattern in this skill which contributes to arm and leg strength.

### *Duck Walk*

The child begins by squatting down with the knees and elbows bent., while balancing on the balls of the feet. The arms are to resemble wings as the child walks on one foot at a time, while flapping his/her wings. Deep knee bends are not a good position for the child to be in for an extended period of time. Therefore, the child should be in this position for only a short period.

### *Elephant Walk*

The child may bend forward with arms straight, hanging in front of the body with the hands clasped together to resemble an elephant's trunk. The elephant usually takes big slow steps because of its weight. However, when upset, the elephant can run quickly with trunk held high. Slow lumbering movements describe the elephant walk, with trunk swinging. Small children enjoy imitating an elephant's walk, as well as its run.

### *Inch Worm*

The child begins on the floor in an "up" push-up position and shuffles the feet with little tiny steps (keeping feet together and legs straight) bringing the feet as close to the hands as possible. Next the hands "walk" forward until the child is back in the push-up position. The feet then begin again. This skill helps in upper arm strength as well as in coordination. It is very difficult for children to keep the feet still while the arms move and vice versa.

### *Frog Jump*

The child begins by squatting down on the floor, knees turned outward and hands on the floor in front of the body. He/she then pushes off the floor with both hands and feet at the same time, extending arms and legs in flight and landing a bit ahead in the starting position. This skill contributes most to the development of power and leg strength as well as to general coordination.

## *Giraffe Walk*

The child walks on tip toes, with arms extended straight overhead, stepping on one foot at a time. Do not bend the knees while doing the giraffe walk. The giraffe can reach up high to eat leaves from a tree, and bends down low to get a drink from a stream.

## *Lame Puppy*

The child assumes a push-up position on the floor and bends one knee to lift one leg in the air. He / she then travels using only three appendages, hopping the back leg along after the arms move. In this skill one arm then the other move, then the back leg hops. This skill contributes to upper arm and shoulder girdle strength, leg strength, and coordination.

## *Rabbit Jump*

The child begins in a squatting position, knees together, and hands on floor slightly ahead and to the sides of the knees. He/she then reaches forward and places the hands on the floor ahead, then, taking weight on his/her hands, jumps the feet up to met the hands. The coordination key is to move hands, then feet. They do not move together. This skill contributes to upper arm and shoulder girdle strength, leg strength and coordination.

## *Seal Walk*

The child begins in a push-up position. Relaxing the feet, he/she then walks forward using the arms and dragging the legs behind. The arms should be straight so that the chest is held high off the floor. This skill contributes to arm and shoulder girdle strength.

# BALANCES

All physical activities require balance, whether it be static or dynamic. When children are encouraged to adjust their centers of gravity in order to assume a certain pose, they must also use their cognitive knowledge of balance. The use of the kinesthetic sense is paramount to these tasks.

## *Knee Scale*

The child assumes a position on hands and knees on the floor or mat. The child is then asked to lift one hand and hold it out to the front, keeping his/her head up. The task might be further complicated by asking the child to also lift one leg and extend it. Many other combinations of knee balances are possible. For the most part this is a safe balance in that it keeps the performer close to the floor and fear of falling is not a factor.

## *Front Scale*

The child begins in a standing position and bends forward at the waist, lifting one leg to the back. The back is then arched and both arms are extended out to the sides, head up.

## *Single Leg Squat*

The child stands on one leg only. Bending the knee, bring the other leg straight out in front of the body while lowering the body towards the floor and bending the knee deeply. Both arms should be straight out to the sides and parallel to the floor. A spotter is needed in order to assist the student in maintaining balance.

## *Stork Stand*

Standing still, the child lifts one foot placing that foot on the knee of the opposite leg. The arms are extended straight out to the sides, parallel to the floor. The balance should be held for 10 seconds. Have the child close both eyes and try to hold this balance for another 10 seconds.

## *Supine or Bridge*

The child lies supine on the mat. The knees bend and the feet are placed flat on the mat. Placing the hands flat on the mat next to each ear with the fingers pointed toward the body, and keeping the hands and feet flat on the mat, the child pushes up so the back is arched and the head is off of the mat, while looking down at the mat. When the balance is completed, the elbows bend slightly, the neck bends forward, and the child slowly lowers the body back to the mat. Children with low back problems should avoid performing this activity.

## *Thread the Needle*

While standing still, the child puts hands together in front of the body with the fingers laced together. One foot is lifted and moved through the loop formed by the hands and arms. Next the other foot goes through the loop, and the child stands straight up with the hands still joined but now behind the back. Then the whole stunt is reversed by backing through the loop formed by the hands and arms one foot at a time. A spotter is needed in order to help children maintain balance and avoid falling.

## *V Sit*

Sitting on the mat, the child balances on the buttocks while bringing the arms and legs up straight and together into the shape of the letter V. Most children have a tendency to lean back too far ending up on the back instead of the seat. Have children try to touch their fingers to their toes while balancing on their seats.

## *Tripod*

The lead-up skill to the headstand, the tripod is an extremely important skill to master. Most children can do tripods, regardless of their sizes or skill levels, so it is a skill that has a great deal of success. The child squats down, facing the mat, knees out, hands on mat inside knees. Leaning forward while bending the elbows, the head, just above the forehead, is placed on the mat. The knees should automatically roll right up onto the elbows. This three-point-stance is a tripod. To come down from the tripod, the

child should tip back from the elbows and come to a stand and should not roll over forward. Rolling forward may cause injury to the neck. Spotting: squat down to the side of the tumbler and support the tumbler's back— prevent the child from curling and rolling over

## *Tip-Up*

The tip up is more difficult than the tripod because it asks for balance on two points instead of three. It is done in exactly the same way as the tripod except that the head does not touch the mat.

## *Headstand*

Once in the tripod position, the child slowly extends the legs upward. There will have to be some experimentation with balance points to see what feels best. The spotter can help in this case by standing at the side and gently supporting the legs until the tumbler finds a point of balance. The child should come down from the headstand by bringing the legs, one at a time, back to the floor. The child should not roll out of the headstand until the skill has been refined and there is sufficient arm strength to push the body up, tuck the chin, round the back and roll. Note: It is extremely important that the child not roll out until physically ready. Coming out of a headstand the wrong way can cause injury to the neck.

## *Handstand*

The teaching of the handstand often begins with a stunt: the mule kick. For the mule kick, the child places both hands on the mat, bending over from the waist. Keeping arms straight, both feet and legs are then kicked up and back. After the kick, the feet snap to the floor to recover. This stunt shows the child what it is like to balance on the hands for a few seconds. For the handstand itself, it is best learned with a competent spotter. The child tips forward from the waist, places the hands (arms straight, elbows locked) on the mat and lifts one leg straight in the air. The other leg is then lifted to meet the first. The spotter should be to the side of the tumbler, and should catch the first leg and then the second to hold them in position. Then the tumbler moves to adjust the position to balance. Usually an arch in the back will help. The spotter holds on less and less as the tumbler adjusts. The tumbler then comes back down by dropping the feet and standing. A more advanced tumbler might tuck the chin and roll out of the handstand.

## PARTNER BALANCES

Children should pick partners of as equal height as possible. Heavier or stronger children should assume the roles of base. For each balance, children should learn to tighten muscles and hold positions once a balance point has been reached. The accomplishment of the balances strongly contributes to the positive self-concept of the child and contributes to the ability to cooperate and coordinate movement with others. A very important element of partner balances is that each child can experience success: even those heavy children who have difficulty with some of the stunts and tumbling activities. In partner balances these children have very important roles as the bases. All partner stunts need at least one spotter and two would be even better in order to assist students in maintaining balance and avoiding falls.

## *Angel Balance*

The base takes off his/her shoes and lies down on the mat, knees bent, feet flat on the floor. The top stands by the knees, facing the base. The base lifts his/her legs and places the feet in a toed out position at the top's hips. The base reaches up and takes the top's hands. The base then extends the legs upward, at approximately a 45-degree angle, lifting the top. The top arches his/her back, extending and straightening legs, lifts the head, and extends his/her arms to the side as the base releases the hands. With muscles tight, the top holds the balance. To come down, the base and top rejoin hands, the base bends his/her knees and brings the top safely to the mat. A spotter or two would be useful to support the top at the shoulder and prevent him/her from falling forward.

## Box Balance

A favorite of many children, the box balance requires a great deal of strength in both the arms and legs of both top and bottom. The base lies on his/her back, knees bent, feet flat on the floor, and hands by ears, palms up. Both the base and the top should have shoes off. The top straddles the head of the base, facing toward the base's feet. The top gently places one foot in each of the base's hands, keeping initial weight on the heel that is still on the floor. The base extends his/her legs directly upward and the top places his/her hand on the soles of the base's feet. The base gives the signal "1-2-3" and on 3 the top jumps and bends at the waist, extending the arms directly downward. On 3 the base extends the arms directly upward and holds the pose. The top has the responsibility of adjusting himself/herself to match the "box" position of the base. To come down the base slowly lowers the arms to the mat by his/her head and the top steps off. Spotters can help the children to achieve a good balance point.

## Midriff Stand

The base kneels on the mat placing the hands shoulder's width apart, directly under the shoulders, and flat on the mat. The top person stands close to the base placing his/her hands under the base, grasping the base's midriff area. The top person leans forward over the base's back while kicking both feet straight up and together. A spotter is needed to help the top person avoid flipping over the base, Two spotters would work out even better

## Doublemint

The base kneels on the mat, placing the hands shoulder's width apart and flat on the mat. The top person places one knee on each of the base's hip areas. The top person should not kneel in the small of the back. The top person places one hand on each of the base's shoulder blades.

## *Horizontal Stand*

The base lies on the back, with knees bent and feet flat on floor. The top stands with one foot next to each ear of the base facing the base's knees. The top leans forward placing the hands on the base's knees, one hand on each knee. The base grasps the top's ankles and pushes the top's legs straight up over the base's head with arms straight. When balance is complete, the base bends elbows and places the top's feet back on the floor next to the base's ears..

## *Knee Shoulder Balance*

The base lies on the back with knees bent and feet flat on the floor. The top person stands facing the base with one foot next to each of the base's ankles. The top person leans forward and places both hands on the base's lower knees, with fingers pointing downwards towards the mat. At the same time the base places one hand on each of the top person's shoulders (not around the neck). The top person, with the help of a spotter, kicks up to an upside down inverted position. The spotter keeps the top person from flipping over the base.

## *Back Lay Out*

The base lies on his/her back with feet and knees bent with the tops buttocks on the soles of the bases feet, the top facing away from the base. The top actually sits on the base's feet with arms out to the sides and parallel to the base. As the top bends backward to a layout position the base reaches upward to grasp the wrists of the top. Spotters are needed to assist in maintaining balance and avoiding falls.

## *Sitting Balance*

Using the same procedure as for the base in the angel balance, the top starts with his/her back to the base and the base places his/her feet in a toed out position at the top's buttocks. To lift, the base reaches up for the top's hands, then extends the legs. The top extends the legs forward and the arms out to the sides, and holds the balance. To come down, the base reaches up to take the top's hands, bends

the knees and brings the top slowly and safely to the mat. The spotter should be to the side of the balance and again spot at the shoulder.

## *Thigh Stand*

The base partner stands with feet shoulder's width apart, keeping the feet flat and the knees bent. The top partner stands with back to the base, and close to the base, placing the right foot on the base's right thigh. The base places the right hand on the top person's right knee to support the top person. The same procedure is used for the left thigh and left knee. The top person leans forward arching the back, with the arms straight out to the sides. The base leans slightly backwards for balance. A spotter assists partners in maintaining balance.

## *Triangle Balance*

The base lies on the back with knees bent and feet flat on the mat, elbows bent and one hand next to each ear. The top stands with one foot next to each of the base's ears. The top person places one foot in each of the base's hands and leans forward placing hands on the base's knees. The base then pushes the top person's feet straight up over the base's head.

## *Reverse Triangle Balance*

As a variation the top person stands with one foot next to each of the base's hips. The top person stands with one foot on each of the base's knees and joins hands with the base. Both base and top person keep their arms straight. The spotter should again be to the side and at the shoulder.

## INDIVIDUAL STUNTS

Individual stunts are activities that children like to do as challenges. Sometimes referred to as "tricks," children of all ages enjoy these activities. As with the animal walks, the individual stunts contribute significantly to the child's flexibility level.

## Coffee Grinder

The child assumes a side-lying position with one arm positioned with the hand on the floor. The child lifts upward on the one arm so that the arm takes the body weight and is fully extended and the side of the bottom foot rests on the floor. The child then, keeping the body as straight as possible walks the feet so that the body moves around the pivot arm (which stays in place). This skill contributes to arm strength and agility.

## Heel Click

The child jumps high in the air, bending the knees, and bringing the heels together while in the air. Feet are placed quickly back on the mat when descending in order to maintain balance.

## Heel Slap

The child begins by standing on the mat, jumps high bending the knees, and slaps the hands against the heels of the feet while in the air. Feet are placed quickly back on the mat when descending in order to maintain balance.

## Toe Slap

The child jumps high bringing the feet in front of the body while attempting to touch the toes with the fingertips. Feet are placed quickly back on the mat when descending in order to maintain balance.

## Human Ball

The child lies on the floor on ones side. While bending the knees, the child grasps them, hugging them close to the body with both arms. The child then rolls both from side to side and back and forth while keeping the knees grasped.

## Human Rocker

The child starts in a prone position on the floor. He/she then bends the knees, lifts the chest, and reaches back to grasp the ankles. This should cause the thighs to come slightly off the floor. The child then rocks forward and back on his abdomen. This skill contributes to flexibility.

## *Log Roll*

The child lies down on the floor or the mat with his/her arms extended directly by the ears and overhead. He/she then rolls sideward, keeping the arms extended and rolling in a straight line. This skill contributes to flexibility, coordination and balance.

## *Over the Head*

The child lies on the back with arms at sides and palms on the floor. The child then brings the legs up over the head touching the toes behind the head, while keeping the legs straight

## *Seal Slap*

The child begins in an "up" push-up position, hands flat on floor, arms extended under shoulders, toes on floor. The child then pushes upward with the arms and tries to clap his/her hands together before catching himself/ herself back in the push-up position. This skill contributes to arm strength and power.

## *Straddle Seat*

The child sits with the legs apart in a straddle position, leaning forward and gently stretching to touch the fingertips as close as possible to the toes.

## *Swing Up from Knees*

The child kneels on the mat with the body straight over the knees. Leaning backwards and swinging the arms forward and back, the child springs upwards jumping onto both feet at the same time. Remind the children that they must spring up from the knees not just stand up.

## *Turk Sit-Stand*

The child begins in a standing position, arms folded across chest, and feet crossed on the floor. The body bends at the waist and the buttocks lower to the ground to a sitting position. Next, keeping the body in the same position, the child stands up in the same place. This skill contributes to leg strength and balance.

## PARTNER STUNTS

### *Chinese Get-Up*

Two children sit down on the floor and sit back-to-back with elbows linked. Knees should be bent, feet should be flat on the floor. They then counterbalance each other by pushing backs against each other to come to a standing position with ease.

### *Churn the Butter*

Two children stand back to back and link elbows. One child leans forward while the other child leans backwards and at the same time lifts his/her feet off of the mat. Partners rock back and forth repeating the previous activity. Children are not to flip all the way over their partner's back.

### *Double Rolling*

The base lies on his/her back on the mat with elbows bent, arms and back of hands flat on the mat, and legs straight up. The top person stands with one foot next to each of the base's ears. The base grasps the top person's ankles and the top person grasps the base's ankles. The top person places the base's feet apart and flat on the mat. The top person does a forward roll between the base's feet, keeping the base's ankles grasped. As the top person is rolling the base comes to a standing position being sure to keep his/her grasp on the top person's ankles. The base then places the top person's feet apart and flat on the mat then rolling between the feet, etc. The important thing to remember is that it is important to keep chins tucked and to place the feet apart and flat before rolling.

### *Row Your Boat*

Partners sit across from each other, legs straight and feet flat against each other. Partners join hands, keeping arms and legs straight. One partner will gently lean forward as the other partner gently leans backwards.

## *Rocking Horse*

Partners sit facing each other, knees together and feet together on the floor. Each partner moves forward and sits on the other partners feet. Partners extend arms and hold shoulders. As one partner rocks back, he/she lifts his/her feet and the other partner rocks forward.

## *Wheelbarrow*

 Child A lies on the floor in a prone position, arms bent and hands directly by shoulders, legs extended and slightly apart. The second child (B) stands between A's legs, bends over and places his/her hands just above child A's knees and lifts the legs as child A pushes upward with his/her arms. Child A then begins to walk forward on his/her hands as child B "pushes" the wheelbarrow. Children should be cautioned to put the legs down easily when the stunt is finished. This stunt contributes to arm strength.

## *Wring the Dishrag*

Children A and B stand facing each other and join hands overhead to form a bridge. While continuing to hold hands, child A turns to the right, B to the left, and on around until they are facing each other again. This can be repeated several times in succession. This skill contributes to coordination and balance.

## GROUP STUNTS

## *Pyramids*

Pyramids can be built with as few as three children or as many as is deemed safe for the situation. Children will enhance the sense of balance as they cooperate with others to build a "structure" of people. The creation of a pyramid calls for both cognitive and affective aspects of development: cognitive to understand correct placement for balance and counterbalance, and affective for cooperation with others to be successful in the task. Of course the psychomotor development contributions would be in the areas of strength, balance, and ability to assume different body positions. When children are assigned the task of building a pyramid, they should be told to consider the size of each child involved. Heavier and stronger children should be the base, or near the bottom, and lighter, more agile children should be near or on the top. Children should be working on mats and in stocking feet or barefoot to form pyramids. The most simple pyramid is formed with three children, A and B as the base and C as the top. In the first pyramid, A and B are next to each other on hands and knees, arms extended directly under shoulders, and knees placed directly under hips. Child C approaches from the back of the pyramid and gently places one knee, then the other on the coccyx area of each base child, being careful not to place weight in the sway of the lower back. Hands should be placed on the inside shoulders of the base children. All three children lift their heads and strike a balanced pose. They should be encouraged to be strong. This is the most simple form of pyramid. The simplest pyramid may become more challenging: Child C may lift chest and extend arms overhead, changing the height of the pyramid. Very carefully, C may step up to a stand on the coccyx area of the base children, and extend arms out or up. The three-person base is limited only by the creativity of the children involved. Using the basic three-person pyramid, larger pyramids can be formed by combining groups. It is important, and even more so the larger the group, to teach children how to come back down from a pyramid. The teacher should tell the children their limit for height (how many rows) and should stress safety at every opportunity. It is a good idea to teach children how to "collapse" the pyramid and they should practice this skill from a simple hands and knees position on the mat. On the count of three, "1-2-3," the children extend arms and legs at the same time and "flop" to the mat. Of course it is safer to take the pyramid back down, tier by tier, than to collapse. If children lose balance, it is best to have a safety call (1-2-3 may be sufficient) so the group collapses instead of falling. Children should be encouraged to design different configurations, perhaps in a drawing, and then direct other children in the formation. The teacher should check the designs for safety and discuss this with the designers.

## *Bridge*

This pyramid is performed using 5 children. One child stands in the center of the pyramid facing forward. Two children position themselves on hands and knees on the floor, one facing to the right side wall, and the other facing the left side wall. Two other children will form the bridge, connecting the pyramid. The one child will place
the hands on the back of the child kneeling and facing left, and at the same time, with help from the center child, will place feet on the left shoulder of the center child. The other child will place hands on the back of the child kneeling and facing right, and at the same time, with

help, will place feet on the right shoulder of the same standing child in the center. A spotter is need for this activity and two spotters would be better.

## *Headstand Archway*

This is a three person pyramid, although this pyramid can be added as a part to a larger pyramid, therefore using a greater number of children. All three children face forward. The children on each end perform a headstand. The person in the center extends both arms and grasps the ankles of each child performing the headstands, thereby assisting with the balance and forming an arch. As a variation, the children on the end will each face the opposite direction, the one child faces the wall on the right, and the other faces the wall on the left. Both children perform headstands, thereby again forming an arch.

## *Handstand Archway*

This is a three person pyramid, although this pyramid can be added as a part to a larger pyramid, therefore using a greater number of children. The three students begin by facing forward. The students on each end perform a handstand. The center student extends both arms and grasps the ankles of the students performing the handstands, thereby assisting with their balance and forming an arch.

## *Thigh Mounts and Headstands*

This pyramid calls for an even number of students, four would be ideal. One student, the base, bends knees slightly. At the same time the top student places the left foot on the left thigh of the base. The base grasps the left knee of the top child with the base's left hand. The same holds true for the right knee and thigh. After the center children have formed a thigh mount the two side children perform headstands. The top person then grasps the feet of the two children performing headstands. A spotter is necessary for assisting in maintaining balance and in order to help avoid falls.

## *Merry-Go-Round*

An even number of children, at least 8, no more than 12, children stand in a circle, facing in, and count off by 2s. The #2s sit down on the floor. The #1s reach down and take the hands of the #2s on each side. The #1s should hold arms with palms facing forward and out, the #2s should grasp the #1s arms just below the elbow. On the count of 3, the #1s then lift and step back as the #2s arch their backs, leaving their feet together in the center. The #1s now begin to move in a clockwise direction and the #2s take tiny shuffles with the feet to "turn the merry-go-round." No spotters are necessary for this skill.

## Skin the Snake

Children are to stand in a single file line. Each child bends over and puts the right hand back between the knees, joining right hands with the left hands of the people behind them. Everyone takes a step or two backwards with the last person in line lying on the floor. After passing over the person lying on the floor the second to the last person, lies on the floor and so on, until everyone is lying down. At this point the last person to lie down now gets up taking the next person in lines hand and walks forwards. Each person in turn stands up and follows the lead of the person in front of him/her. Children should attempt to keep hands joined if possible, throughout the activity.

## Walking Chair

Children are to stand in a single file line. Three or more children are needed for this stunt. The more children involved the more difficult the stunt becomes. Children are to bend their knees and squat as if sitting in a chair, while placing their arms around the waist of the child in front of them. They are to attempt to walk forward while staying in this position.

## TUMBLING SKILLS

Probably most easily identified with free exercise in traditional gymnastics, tumbling skills have specific performance points to be learned and refined. Because the skills involve inverting the body, or twisting and turning its parts, it is very important that skills be learned and practiced correctly in order to prevent injury. The learning of tumbling skills helps the child in the development of flexibility, strength, balance, and body management. You should not expect every child to be able to learn every skill; also, you should never force a child to try a skill if true fear is evident. The tumbling skills should be demonstrated for everyone, and each child should have the opportunity to try the skills. Some children will need a great deal of help in the execution of these skills.

## *Forward Roll*

Sometimes incorrectly referred to as the somersault, the forward roll is just that: a roll on a mat in a forward direction. The child begins in a squatting position with knees together, hands on the mat just in front of and outside the knees. The chin is tucked to the chest and the child pushes with the legs, up and over forward, keeping the body in a round, tucked position, and contacting the mat on the top of the upper back. The child should hold the tucked and rounded position to keep momentum going to roll directly back to the feet and come to a stand from the roll. Children often display one of the following problems: putting the top of the head on the mat and trying to roll (cue: "tuck your chin; miss the mat with your head"), opening from the tucked and rounded position too soon and landing in a sitting position, legs extended (cue: "stay in a ball until you roll to your feet"), or bending one arm more than the other and rolling over sideways (cue: "keep strong arms"). If there are children with problems, use the spotting technique described at the end of this section. Once the child gains a kinesthetic sense of what he/ she is supposed to be doing, skill will be enhanced. Once the forward roll is mastered it is not correct to then teach the backward roll. We do not advise teaching the backward roll. For some reason this is exactly what physical education teachers do. In the first place, the backward roll is a very difficult skill requiring great flexibility as well as strength. In the second place, most children will not be successful in the achievement and refinement of this skill. The correct progression, therefore is to introduce variations of the forward roll. Variations include: beginning the roll from a standing position or straddling the legs from beginning to end. Spotting: Squat down to the side of the tumbler. Place the inside hand at the back of the tumbler's neck to keep the head tucked. This way you can safely guide the child through the skill.

## *Cartwheel*

Every child wants to be able to do a cartwheel. Unfortunately, not every child has the strength or skill to be successful. In order to perform a cartwheel, a child should first be able to kick up into and hold a handstand (see Balances). Some may be able to learn the cartwheel without having mastered the handstand because in the cartwheel balance is not static as in the handstand. The cartwheel requires dynamic balance. The child begins facing the mat, in a standing position. Arms are usually extended overhead. A rocking step is taken (shift weight to back foot and step out with front foot), and the child bends forward to take the weight on hands and arms. One hand goes down, the second hand goes to the mat, as the first is coming back up the first leg is coming down, and the second leg comes down. The cartwheel causes the child to travel a certain distance. Arms and legs are held straight throughout the skill. The verbal cue for the cartwheel is "hand-hand-foot-foot." The cartwheel should be done slowly and with control. Once a good cartwheel is achieved, with control and precision, variations may be learned. One might be to run on the approach to the cartwheel; another might be bringing the feet together in the air and snapping them down to a landing. This becomes a roundoff. Spotting: Stand at the side of the mat so that the tumbler's back is to you during the skill. Place hands on the tumbler's hips as he/she goes into the inverted phase: have your arms crossed so that your right hand is on the tumbler's left hip and vice versa.

# Summary

There are numerous tumbling skills that children enjoy learning. The stunts and tumbling skills presented here will give you the basic skills that children should experience. Elementary physical education methods books have many more skills listed and defined. It is beyond the scope of this text to teach you more of these skills. And, since you are not a physical education major who has the knowledge of biomechanics, it would be to your advantage to stay with the simple activities.

# References and Suggested Readings

Gabbard, C.P., LeBlanc, E., & Lowy, S. (1989). *Games, dance and gymnastics activities.* Prentice-Hall.

Gallahue, D. (2005). *Developmental physical education for all children.* Human Kinetics.

Gallahue, D. (1997). *Developmental physical education for today's children.* MgGraw-Hill.

Gallahue, D. (1996). *Developmental physical education for today's children.* Brown and Benchmark.

Kirchner G. & Fishburne, G.J. (1998). *Physical education for elementary school children* McGraw Hill.

Nilges, L.M. (1997). Educational gymnastics stages of content development. *Journal of Physical Education, Recreation, and Dance,* 68(3), 50–55.

Pangrazi, R. P. (2006). *Dynamic physical education for elementary school children.* Benjamin Cummings.

Pangrazi, R. P. (1998). *Dynamic physical education for elementary school children.* Allyn and Bacon.

Siedentop, D., Herkowitz, J. & Rink, J. (1984). *Elementary physical education methods.* Prentice-Hall.

CHAPTER

# 14

# Inclusion for the Exceptional Child

Today's educational system calls for inclusion in schools. This means that physically and mentally challenged children are included in the regular classroom setting whereas previously many were based in special education classrooms. In addition, this means that they will be involved with your other children in the physical education setting. For the physically challenged children, this is often very difficult.

PL 94-142 (Education for All Handicapped Children) and PL 104-476 (Individuals with Disabilities Education Act) state that each child has a right to an educational experience in the "least restrictive environment" possible within the child's capabilities. These laws are of particular importance to us because they are the ONLY federal laws that specifically mention physical education. It should be noted that physical education is mentioned because physical activity is very important to the challenged child. Special educators are strong proponents of the connection between physical education and growth and development.

Physical education is defined within the law as including fitness, motor skill development, games, dance, swimming and sports (Kalakian, 2003). Therefore, these students should have the same opportunities as children without special needs. Children who are overweight or obese, who have difficulty with coordination, or who have temporary impairments or illnesses are not included for special services under this law, and yet, they will need adaptation of activities as well.

Usually, if there are several challenged students who have been tested and classified within a particular school building, there will be an adapted physical education class that is provided for them. The adapted physical educator meets with these groups separately from the remainder of students in the class. The number of meetings with the adapted physical educator is based on time available and on the needs of the children involved. This does not preclude their participation in your physical education class, however. It is the responsibility of the adapted physical education teacher in your district to evaluate any challenged students and to write an individualized education plan (IEP) for each student. Should the district not have an adapted physical education teacher, the regular physical education instructor should assume the responsibility. If, for some reason, you find that this has not been done, you have every right to ask for it, especially since you could be the person who implements the plan.

The very first thing that you should do, when you find there will be a challenged student in your class, is to do research on the particular disabling condition that the child has. Include in your research the permanent file of the student, and set up an opportunity to meet with the parents and the child, if feasible. You need to familiarize yourself with the child's needs as well as characteristics. A doctor may send you a list of activities that would be either appropriate or inappropriate for the child in physical education. Remember that it is the law that the child receive the physical education experience; it is the school's responsibility to find appropriate activities for the student. You should also note that many physicians are unfamiliar with the wonderful kinds of activities that children do now in physical education. It may be necessary for you to talk directly with the physician about your physical education program.

Within the framework of your class, you need to include the challenged student in the activities to the extent that he/she is able to participate. It is again beyond the scope of this text to discuss each disabling condition and to give specific activities that would be beneficial for each. However, teaching methods for challenged versus non-challenged children are still the same: demonstrate, try, feedback, practice, refine. Some general rules for inclusion in physical education follow:

1.  Be sure that the children in the class know about and understand the challenged child's disability. It is important that children learn to help each other and to respect individual differences

2.  Each child should have a physical fitness plan; when the challenged child is unable to participate in the general planned activity of the class, he/she can be working on the side of the area on fitness exercises. Ideas for these activities can be found in the "Physical Fitness" chapter.

3.  Each day, assign a helper to the challenged child. The helper can assist with the physical fitness work, and can also serve as a partner or guide for the child when he/she can be involved in the group activity. Note: do not have the same child be the helper the majority of the time. This would restrict the non-challenged child's own physical education time. Do choose helpers on the basis of reward, however, and be sure they will be both helpful and responsible.

4.  Always include the child in at least part of the lesson. Be sure to plan for an activity in which the child is capable. For example, if a child cannot walk, but can crawl, everyone in the class could play a game while crawling.

5.  Include the child in the parts of the activity that he/she can do. Perhaps he/she can strike a ball with a bat and the helper can be the runner. It's easy to have a wheelchair partner in square dance! A non-locomotor child could serve in volleyball. As you examine each lesson you plan, see what adaptations you can make to the activity to include the challenged child.

6.  The child can help by coaching, by refereeing, or by keeping score. It is very important that the child feel he/she is an essential part of the class.

Too often physical educators in the past sent such children to sit on the side of the play area because they thought "they can't do anything anyway." Some of these teachers even expressed that thought in front of the children; a despicable act, to be sure. Today's educators deal much better with educational diversity and demonstrate respect for individual differences. Yes, it makes teaching harder, and a little more work, to adapt activities, yet to see the smile on the face of a child after a major accomplishment is reward in itself.

Mentally challenged children, depending on the severity of the impairment, are usually able to participate in physical education without much adaptation. Just as you recognize the individual differences of the non-challenged students, you would recognize the mentally challenged in such a way that directions may be repeated more often, you may need to speak a bit slower in explanations, and you may place the child in game positions that require less decision making (outfield area instead of second base, e.g.). Once the child has done the drill or played the game and is familiar with it, he/she may move into a position of more responsibility. Experience shows that the mentally challenged child usually enjoys physical activity. In many cases such children may excel in sport: this may be the only area of education in which they feel confident and competent. Often children who suffer from learning disabilities, such as dyslexia, are really quite athletic and talented. Physical education becomes their favorite time of day, and they look forward to it with great anticipation.

In some cases, however, the mental challenge is so severe that interaction with group activities is meaningless to the child. In these cases it is still very important that the child participate in some form of physical activity, and you need to be able to motivate the child. Most children, mentally challenged or not, love to work to music. This has been found to be very true for the severely mentally challenged children. Background music helps the child by relaxing him/her and also contributes to the development of coordination through definite rhythm or beat. Should you have a severely mentally challenged child, probably the best idea would be to have a peer work on the side with him/her on fitness activities.

Upon occasion the child can participate with the group, as long as the class understands the need to support the child. In relay activity, for example, as long as the challenged child "doesn't count" in the outcome of win-loss, the entire class may be found cheering the child on. This is a wonderful opportunity for the non-challenged children to learn the affective aspect of support and ego-building, along with principles of fair play.

## Summary

Inclusion in schools has become a reality.  It seems that most of its difficulty is in the physical education arena. However, to adapt activity for the challenged child should be no different than adapting for the non-challenged child: teaching physical education is about adapting activity for all individuals. Always remember to be developmentally appropriate!

## References and Suggested Readings

Block, M.E. & Etz, K. (1995). The pocket reference A tool for fostering inclusion. *Journal of Physical Education, Recreation and Dance*, 66(3), 47–51.
Grosse, S.J. (1995). Danger ahead for students with disabilities: Beware of the swinging pendulum. *Journal of Physical Education, Recreation and Dance*, 66(1), 4–5.
Kalakian, L. (2003). Adapted physical education advocacy page. http://www.mankato.msus.edu/dept/colahn/APE/APEpage.html#anchor450311

Murata, N.M. & Hodge, S.R. (1997). Training support personnel for inclusive physical education. *Journal of Physical Education, Recreation and Dance*, 68(9), 21–25.

Sherrill, C. (2003). *Adapted physical activity, recreation and sport*. Boston: McGraw Hill.

Sherrill, C. (1993). *Adapted physical activity, recreation and sport*. Dubuque: Brown & Benchmark.

CHAPTER

# 15

# Linking Your Classroom to Healthy Kids

As the classroom teacher, you have a responsibility to your students to provide the best environment possible for them to grow and develop. Although many school districts cause you to believe that academics is the most critical part of a child's education, you now know that achievement in academics comes easier for children who are healthy It is a fact that physical exercise stimulates the release of endorphins, and that this process provides energy for learning. As the teacher of elementary aged children, you will need to keep in mind that periodic physical activity is key to keeping children on task and attentive in the classroom. A physical education program that is less than five days per week cannot provide the essential moderate-to-vigorous daily activity to which all children have a right. Many educators assume that children participate in out-of-school play at a vigorous level daily, and they assume that the school does not need to provide for such a program. Granted, *some* children actually do have a full activity schedule outside of school. The sad truth is that the majority do not. Most children will not exercise at all outside of physical education. Thus, it becomes your responsibility to see that your children are given the best of opportunities to be successful. That is just what this chapter is all about.

## Classroom Management and Time for Physical Activity

The classroom teacher is expected to teach all academic subjects and, sometimes, needs to teach art, music and physical education as well. A school day is only so long, and it is very important that everything fits into a neat and tidy schedule. As the teacher, you often wonder if there are enough minutes in the day to fit everything in. The answer, of course, lies in being a good classroom manager. In Chapter 2 you read about effective teaching in the gymnasium and you learned techniques to manage the class so that you could maximize your time for instruction. The same principle holds true for your own classroom: be highly organized and you will be able to have enough time in the day for everything you want to fit in. Just as in the gymnasium, you need a signal for attention that is consistent. You need to have routines established for passing out and collecting materials. Other routines you need to create would involve bathroom breaks, drink breaks, attendance procedures, systems for collecting money such as for lunch, transitions to other areas of the school, etc. You need to organize your room so that the children know where to go to get what they need, and where to replace things when they are finished. You need an established behavior management system that is consistent and fair, one that takes little time to implement. And, if you can be that highly organized classroom manager, you can have time to "Link Your Classroom to Healthy Kids!"

## The Influence of Physical Education on Learning

With national emphasis on student achievement test performance, many school districts have chosen to reduce or eliminate time spent on "specials," and children receive less art, music and physical education than in the past. Some schools actually insist that children focus so hard on these test sessions that no physical education can be taught during the week of testing! In December 2002, the public education officials of the state of California announced that a comprehensive study had shown that physically fit children had higher scores on standard achievement tests in reading and math than those who were not deemed to be physically fit. The study examined the nationally recognized Fitnessgram test results and the Standard Achievement Test, Ninth edition (SAT-9) of fifth, seventh and ninth grade children. This study has been significant in establishing the relationship between academic achievement and health-related fitness (http://www.cde.ca.gov/nr/ne/yr02/yr02rel37.asp). We have known for a long time that perceptual-motor development is related to academic readiness; this study has given further strength to the premise that physical activity in schools is essential. While we are discussing academic achievement tests, what should happen, in actuality, is that children should exercise prior to the test. A brisk walk with the teacher, a vigorous fitness game (see Chapter 8), or an aerobic routine will get students ready to settle down and work.

## Physical Education versus Physical Activity

Physical activity and physical education are NOT synonymous terms. There are many definitions of each, and you have studied the definition of physical education. Physical activity relates to movement and play that is not necessarily directed by a leader. It could encompass youth sport activities that are directed by coaches and intramural programs that are directed by teachers. It could involve riding bicycles, climbing trees, and walking in the neighborhood. The basic distinction that we choose to draw here is that, whereas physical education has as its goal to provide the skills, knowledge and values for children to become intelligent consumers of physically active lifestyles, physical activity is the resultant participation and, often, application of those concepts and skills. It is critical that we make this distinction because educational institutions feel that they provide adequate physical ACTIVITY time to children through recess. And, many also believe that children are physically active at home. Unfortunately, this could not be farther from the truth!

It is obviously essential that children experience quality physical education; this is a responsibility of the school to the health and wellness of its students. Unless physical education is required, many children will not experience any form of activity. Since the reality is that a very limited number of school systems have quality daily physical education, we are stressing the need for you to supplement the program and ensure daily activity times for your students.

This chapter will give you ideas for implementing daily exercise into your classroom routines.

## The Morning Routine

There are many tasks for you, as the classroom teacher, to perform each morning as you prepare to start the day. This is a critical time for children to participate in some form of activity so that they can get ready to concentrate on the day's schoolwork. It will be best for you to establish a routine whereby the students enter the classroom, put away their personal belongings, and, at a designated starting time, begin an exercise program. During this routine, you can participate as a role model, or you can do your required duties such as taking attendance. We suggest that the morning activity be 15-20 minutes of moderate-to-vigorous movement after which students will settle down to work. The routine that you use should be varied by the day of the week, and also should be varied by the grade level that you teach. In this morning routine, we suggest focusing on aerobic activity.

Here are suggested activities for the "Morning Routine."

1. Aerobic Dances led by videotape and/or DVD programs (e.g. MONDAYS)

Many CD and DVD production companies have aerobics recordings that are designed to lead children through moderate-to-vigorous workouts. In some cases you will need to review the routine yourself and then teach the various moves to the children. After that initial introduction, the children should be able to perform the routine with the recording in the lead. Children will need to learn 3-4 of these designated dances to make the workout last 15-20 minutes.

2. Station Activities within the classroom (e.g. TUESDAYS)

Children will know that on Tuesdays, for example, they will go to a certain area of the classroom to start the circuit. Station 1 could be "Tortoise and Hare" (see Chapter 7), with a child designated as the leader; Station 2 could be jumping side to side over a rope that is stretched on the floor; Station 3 could be "Head, Shoulders, Knees and Toes" (see Chapter 7); Station 4 could be jumping rope; Station 5 could be arm circles; and Station 5 could be curl-ups. The children would rotate every minute and continue for 15-20 minutes.

3. Walk/Jog (e.g. WEDNESDAYS)

Children are in a follow the-leader pattern through the classroom, through the school or out of doors. Children change between walk and jog as needed as they continue for 15-20 minutes.

4. Aerobic Dances led by videotape and/or DVD programs (e.g. THURSDAYS)

5. Chair Fitness Routines (e.g. FRIDAYS)

See the Physical Fitness chapter.

The morning routine will be excellent for you and for your children in many ways. The children will be familiar with the standard routine and, since it involves physical activity, will look forward to participating. You will either have your own little workout with the students, or be able to complete your record keeping work while they are involved. The children will be enhancing their aerobic fitness as well as stimulating the release of those endorphins which will help them get ready to learn. You may, of course, select other activities. Just remember that you will need to take time to teach the activities at first and, if you introduce new ones, there will be additional time required.

## Fitness Breaks

Just like coffee breaks may "reinvigorate" the tiring teacher, fitness breaks serve to reenergize elementary school students. These breaks may be as simple as 3-5 minutes of movement activity in the classroom. As the teacher, you could develop a code word that would be fun for the class and would indicate it is a movement break time. As you finish a lesson in reading, you might turn to the class and say something like "It's Fitness Frolic Time! 5-4-3-2-1 Let's Go!" You would need to establish a routine so that when you give the signal, the students stand, put chairs safely under desks or tables, and begin to move as designated. Games from Chapter 8, such as "Hit the Deck" or "Tortoise and Hare" could be implemented quickly. A series of exercises could be called out: "Jumping jacks, windmills, arm circles, jog in place," etc. Children could create and lead routines for "Fitness Frolic Time."

During periods of good weather you can certainly take your students outside for a brisk walk or jog. Research has shown that children do not get adequate exercise during recess periods, so please do not simply take them out to "play." You need to have some goals for them to achieve. You could order pedometers for your classroom and have children track the distances covered when they are moving. Teachers have used these in conjunction with geography (crossing the United States), math (calculating average distances covered), and meeting fitness goals of a minimum of 5000 steps a day.

## Physical Activities for the Classroom

There are activities that may be done within the confines of a classroom as breaks, special awards for work done well, and for the pleasure of participating in movement activity. You cannot deny that you learn best while having fun; children are no different. Many of these activities can also be adapted to meet academic needs, utilizing spelling words, math concepts, and other areas. This option is utilized easily by the creative teacher.

### Dances That Can be Performed in the Classroom
The Hokey Pokey, Loobie Lou, Chicken Fat, Limbo, Twist, YMCA, and Macarena are all dances that can if necessary, be performed in the classroom. These particular dances can be performed without requiring a great deal of space. The music for these dances is provided on the CDs that are included with this text. Directions can be found in either the Preschool Physical Activity chapter or in the Dance and Rhythmic Activities chapter.

### Scarf Juggling
Scarf Juggling is an activity that can be performed in the classroom. It reinforces concentration, problem solving, and coordination. Since scarves are so light and do not take up much space, it would be appropriate to teach scarf juggling in a classroom setting. There are videos available, which teach juggling in general and could be shown as an accompaniment to a scarf-juggling lesson in the classroom. The student may follow the video while standing in one spot and attempting to juggle scarves next to the desk. Juggling instructions are included in the Manipulative Activities chapter of this book.

*Lummi Stick Activities*
   Lummi Sticks is an excellent activity to do in a limited space such as the classroom.
There are two records mentioned in the Dance and Rhythmic Activities chapter, one
entitled "Simplified Rhythm Stick Activities" which is appropriate for Grades K-2, and the
other "Lively Music for Rhythm Stick Fun" which is appropriate for Grades 3-6. These 2
records are available through Educational Record Center. There are a number of other
albums also designed for Lummi Stick activities, which can be found in various music and
CD catalogues.
Three songs provided on the music CDs that have been included in this book for Lummi
Stick activities are "The Shoemaker," "Chicken Fat," and "Pease Porridge Hot." Simply
put on the CD and have the student perform the actions on the record or use the
accompanying directions in the book while hitting the sticks together.
 The following are some suggested Lummi Stick activities, which are appropriate for
grades K-3; however, they may also be used in grades 4-6 when in the classroom setting.
You can play any instrumental music and have the students imitate the teacher's or
leader's movements while performing the following tasks. The teacher or leader may vary
the number of repetitions for each activity while keeping time with the music.


Reach high and tap sticks together, then reach low while tapping sticks together.
Bending arms at the elbows, tap both sticks in front of the body, behind the back, to one
      side and then to the other side all while tapping the sticks together.
Attempt to keep legs straight and bend forward and tap sticks to floor.
Bend at the knees and tap sticks to floor.
Perform jumping jacks and tap sticks above the head.
Touch both sticks very gently to the following body parts: Head, forehead, eyes, cheeks,
      ears, nose, chin, neck, and shoulders.
 Using only one stick touch stick to 1 elbow at a time, 1 arm, 1 wrist, 1 hand, and one set
      of fingers.
 Again using both sticks touch stomach, waist, back, thighs, knees, shins,calves, ankles,
      feet, and toes.
March in place while hitting sticks together in time to music.
Jump on both feet at same time as high as possible and tap sticks together over the head.
Bend elbows and tap the ends of sticks together in front of body
Tap sticks behind knees
Lift 1 leg while bending knee and tap sticks behind that knee.
Do the same movement with the other knee.
Kick one leg out in front, keeping it as straight as possible and touch 1 stick to toes.
Do the same with other leg.
While performing sit ups touch sticks to both sets of toes.
Perform arm circles with sticks out to sides
Touch right stick to left toe while kicking leg forward and keeping the leg as straight as
      possible.
Do the same activity with the opposite arm and leg.
Making a fist, hold one stick perpendicular to the floor while using the other stick to
      pound the first stick in a downward motion to represent "pounding a nail."

Repeat the above motion using opposite sticks.


Divide students into partners and have everyone sit on the floor.

Have both students bounce one stick on its end on the floor and catch it as it rebounds
    from the floor.
Repeat this activity using the opposite stick.
Have them gently touch the body parts mentioned previously while the leader calls each
    body part out loud
Hit the floor with both sticks.
Tap one stick to the floor on one side
Tap the other stick to the floor on the opposite side.
Cross the sticks and tap them on the floor in front.
Flip the stick by throwing it in the air so it makes **only** one complete turn and then catch it
    using one hand.
Do the same motion using the opposite stick and hand.

Flip both sticks at the same time, catching both at the same time.

Partners face each other and hit both of each other's sticks at the same time.
Partners hit each other's right sticks together then hit left sticks together.
Partners hit opposite sticks together, right to left, and left to right.


**Grades 3 and up**
 Both partners hold right stick in his/her own right hand keeping the
   stick perpendicular to the floor. At the same time both students throw
    right sticks to his/her partner and both attempt to catch partner's stick
    in his/her own right hand.
Repeat above movement several times.
Repeat using left stick
Both students throw both sticks at the same time and attempt to catch both of
    partner's sticks at the same time.


**Title**:  **Straddle Ball Relay**
  *Level*: K-6
*Skills Enhanced*:  speed, throwing, and spatial awareness.
*Equipment Needed*:  Parallel rows of desks, four 6-8" foam sponge balls
*Description*: Arrange desks evenly into parallel rows. Students are to stand next to their
desks keeping their legs as straight as possible and feet apart in a straddle position. The
first person in each line (or team) is the captain. Each captain is given a sponge foam ball.
The captain rolls the ball through all straddled legs of his/her team to the last student in
the line. The last student stops the ball, picks it up and carries it while running to the
front of the line and repeats the activity. Everyone else moves back one place. Each
person in turn completes the activity until the captain is back at the head of the row.
Once the captain is again at the head of the line, the entire team sits down. The first team
finished and seated is declared the winner.
*Safety*: Students need to be careful not to run into other students, furniture, or walls.


**Title**:  **Desk Relay**
  *Level*: K-6
*Skills Enhanced*:  agility, speed, spatial awareness
*Equipment Needed*: parallel rows of desks
*Description*: Arrange desks evenly in parallel lines. Instruct the first student in each row
to run around his/her line of desks. When the student is back at his/he own desk he/she
is to sit down and touch the hand of the next student in their line. The second person

runs around the line of desks and this continues until the whole line has had a turn and the entire row is seated. The first row to finish and be seated is declared the winner.
*Safety:* Students need to be careful not to run into other students, furniture, or walls.

**Title**:   **Math Club Relay**
   *Level*: K-6
*Skills Enhanced*: speed, concentration, agility
*Equipment Needed*: Parallel rows of desks, blackboard, and 4 pieces of chalk, and four erasers.
*Description*: This game will need to be adapted according to the particular curriculum at that grade level. Arrange desks evenly in parallel lines. Be sure each row has a piece of chalk, an eraser, and a specific area of the blackboard assigned. The first person in each row will go up to the blackboard and write a math problem representative of the class math homework. The second student will run up to the board, solve the problem, and circle his/her answer. The third student writes a problem, the fourth student answers the problem and circles his/her answer, etc. As soon as a student at the board is finished with his/her part, he/she returns to his/her, row, sits down and, at the same time, touches the hand of the next person in line. The first team finished, seated, and with the most correct answers is declared the winner.
   This game can be adapted for spelling words, geography, history etc.
*Safety*: Students need to be careful not to run into other students, furniture, or walls.

**Title**:   **Shower Ball**
   *Level*: K-3
*Skills Enhanced*:  Coordination, speed, throwing, agility, catching
*Equipment Needed*:  eleven 6-8" sponge foam balls, desks moved back toward the walls as far as possible, a line dividing room in half. A long piece of yarn could be used to make the center dividing line.
*Description*:  Push the desks back towards the walls and put down a dividing line to divide the play area in half. Divide class into two teams. Each team is instructed to stay on his/her own half of the room. Anyone crossing the line will have to sit out. Balls are placed in the middle of the room. Students are instructed to throw the balls back and forth across the dividing line high enough for the other side to catch them. Students attempt to catch the thrown balls. If a ball is touched and dropped whoever touched it must move to the side and run in place. Use a 4-5 minute limit and then stop the game. Have students count the number of players on both teams that are still left in the game. The team with the most students remaining is declared the winner. Play several rounds of short games. Reorganizing teams helps to play down competition. The first game rows 1 & 2 are together. Second game rows 1 & 3 are together, etc.
*Safety*: Students may not cross the center line. Students may not throw the ball at anyone. When the teacher gives the signal to stop, everyone must freeze. Students need to be careful they do not run into other students, furniture, or walls.

**Who's Right, Quick?**
   *Level*: 1-6
Skills Enhanced:  Following directions, listening, agility, speed, and coordination.
*Equipment Needed*:  Flash cards, blackboard, 4 pieces of chalk, 4 erasers, rows of parallel desks, score card and pencil.

*Description*: Desks are arranged in 4 even parallel rows. Each team is given a specific space on the blackboard, a piece of chalk and an eraser. The teacher or leader has a large set of flashcards representing material they have been working on in the classroom. As an example, the teacher may use spelling words for the year or month written on index cards. These cards may also represent math flashcards, geography, history etc. The first student in each line runs to the blackboard. When all students have arrived at the board, the teacher reads a spelling word, a math problem, a question, or whatever is written on one of the flashcards. Each student writes the correct answer in his/her particular area on the blackboard and then runs back to his/her desk and sits in his/her seat. Each student must write an answer on the board before returning to his/her seat. Each student answering the question correctly gets one point for his/her team. The first student who has written the correct answer gets two points, and the first student answering correctly, back to their desk and seated gets 3 points. The teacher has one of the students not at the board help to keep track of points. At the end of the game, the team with the highest score is declared the winner.

*Safety*: Students need to be careful not to run into other students, furniture, or walls.

### Classroom Exercises and Activities

There are several exercises and exercise records that can be used in the classroom or other limited spaces. In the Fitness Chapter of this book Classroom Exercise Routines, Chair Routines and other games and activities to be performed with students sitting at desks or next to them are discussed.

There is a CD entitled "Get Fit While You Sit" that can be purchased through music and CD catalogues which covers, in detail, exercises that can be performed while sitting. The songs "Head and Shoulders, Knees, and Toes" and "Chicken Fat," which are on the music CDs included with this book may also be performed in the classroom. An aerobic video may be used if it contains exercises that can be performed in a limited space.

There are some run/walk programs that have been established in order to stress running and walking as either an entire school or classroom activity that can be tied into the geography curriculum. These programs are set up to motivate students to spend some of their free time working on their fitness through walking and/or running. One such program is called "Run/Walk Across America," and still another entitled "Walk Across the Country." These programs promote school children keeping track of the miles they walk or run and then recording them on a map of the city, state, or country. Some schools turn the event into a contest. A teacher will need to obtain maps of the geographic areas that he/she wishes to cover. The playground and gymnasium are often marked off so students are able to convert the number of laps around the playground or gymnasium into miles walked or run. Pedometers are instruments used to measure the distance a walker has covered in steps by measuring the length of his/her stride. Pedometers, when available, may be loaned to or purchased by students to help them keep track of the distance traveled. Paper slips are made available to students with such information as name, number of miles walked or run, and the date. The slips have to be signed by a teacher or staff member in order to verify that the student has actually walked that distance. This activity can be performed during recess, or before or after school. Parents may also become involved in the program in order to involve the whole family in a fitness activity. A map is then put on display at school and the number of miles are marked each day or week, in order to tally the number of miles traveled.

## Summary

You, as the classroom teacher, are the person responsible for the overall progress of your students for at least one year of their lives. You are the one to whom your students look for guidance and support. Modeling positive behaviors regarding physical activity, and providing opportunities for your students to be active on a daily basis, will give your students "the edge" when it comes to learning. Be creative and enthusiastic about learning through movement and moving through learning! Instill in your students a love for physical activity. In this way, you can "Link Your Classroom to Health Kids."

**Internet Source:**
http://www.cde.ca.gov/nr/ne/yr02/yr02rel37.asp

CHAPTER

# 16

# Evaluation in Physical Education

Every phase of a child's education undergoes evaluation within the parameters of education. Achievement tests measure levels of language arts and mathematics skills; unit tests measure mastery of content; quizzes measure progress toward mastery. All of these testing procedures fall under the cognitive domain. Evaluation is essential; results determine not only the child's cognitive abilities but also the effectiveness of teaching methods. Results also indicate the child's ability to move on to the next level. Grades seem to be "facts of life" in schools, although some systems do grade physical education in the elementary school on a satisfactory/unsatisfactory basis, and these determinations are often made on attitude and effort. If physical education is important, then it should be graded on mastery, just like math and reading is graded. Does a fitness level represent mastery? Does a skill level represent mastery? The answer to these questions is "yes and no." If it is a goal for the child to improve in fitness or skill levels, then mastery of this goal should be the basis for the grade. If a child is already physically fit and/or skilled, and maintains that level, should he/she also earn a high grade, even though he/she did not have to actively work to improve? Before we attempt to answer these questions let's look at the different areas of evaluation in physical education.

## Physical Fitness Assessment

Traditionally, testing in elementary physical education has been exclusively assessment of physical fitness levels. Most physical educators test children's fitness levels in the Fall at the beginning of the year, and in the Spring at the end of the school year. Comparisons between Fall and Spring scores are often made; however, improvement in fitness over a year of growing and maturing may be a factor of just that: maturation. It may not be indicative of progress made in fitness through physical education. As a matter of fact, it probably is definitely not a reflection of the physical education program. This testing procedure has been thoroughly addressed in the "Physical Fitness" chapter.

You know, from reading and studying about physical fitness, that differences can be made in physical fitness levels only if children participate in moderate to vigorous activity for a minimum of 20 minutes, a minimum of three non-consecutive days a week. And this is for the development of aerobic fitness, barely influencing muscular strength. Therefore, if differences do exist from

Fall to Spring, they may be purely maturational, or they may be factors of physical fitness work outside of the school program.

If you have a good, effective physical education teacher, he/she will most probably do this testing for all students in the school. If, for some reason, this is not the case, it would be very important for you to do the testing of your own class. Testing a large group in fitness is often a cumbersome task; asking for help from older students is always a good solution so that children are tested efficiently and time is not wasted. After all, good health affects cognitive learning: fitness should be a major factor in the education of young children. Once the testing is done, children (with your guidance) can develop individualized plans of activities that they enjoy in order to develop or maintain sound fitness levels. And, as you know, children should be encouraged to work on fitness at home.

We therefore conclude that physical fitness testing is definitely a form of assessment and evaluation that should occur in the school program, whether it be the responsibility of the physical educator or the classroom teacher. Parents should receive the results for their children along with suggestions to help their children increase and/or maintain good fitness levels.

## Motor Skill Assessment

You know that it is important to teach fundamental skills and refinement of those skills and variations throughout the child's education. Should we then grade the children on mastery of the skills? The answer to this question is "maybe." IF physical education is a five-day-a-week program taught by a certified physical education specialist, yes. Otherwise, no. Adequate time is not allocated to ensure skill development. Until physical education is recognized as important enough to be a daily occurrence, testing of skill mastery is fruitless. Classes are not grouped by skill levels, as they are in math and reading. Children range from truly uncoordinated to athletic and graceful. How difficult it would be to have all children reach the same levels of skill achievement under these conditions!

Skill tests abound: but it makes no sense to use them at the elementary level. Time is a factor as well as individual differences. As far as skill development goes, the teacher should be knowledgeable concerning each child's general abilities, and should make note of those children with motor deficits. Parents should be alerted, for home intervention may be the key to helping the uncoordinated child. You will recall that a child can display sound mature motor skill patterns by the age of 6 years, IF he/she has had developmentally appropriate experiences during the critical periods. Many children arrive at school without those experiences. It is time for them to play "catch-up." It does not seem fair, however, for them to be graded on a lack of mastery over which they had little control.

# Self Evaluation

---

**SELF EVALUATION**

Name _____ Date _____

Grade _____ Teacher _____

Answer each of the following questions, using the following ratings to evaluate yourself. Please be as honest as possible.

     1  Outstanding       2  Average       3  Needs Improvement

1. _____ I am prepared to participate in each class by wearing tennis shoes and appropriate clothing.

2. _____ I work well with others and work cooperatively when working with partners, groups, or on a team.

3. _____ I listen to and follow directions.

4. _____ I respect everyone, especially regarding individual differences.

5. _____ I participate to my best every day.

6. _____ I know the things I need to do to become physically fit.

7. _____ I participate in regular physical fitness activities outside of school.

8. _____ I put forth my best effort when performing physical activities in class.

---

If children are aware of the expected outcomes of the physical education class, they may be able to take part in their own assessment. Using a form such as that indicated below may allow the older child to really think about physical education and why it is important. Such an evaluation may prove to be very insightful for you as you see the children both in the classroom and in the gymnasium settings. Could the children be different in the various settings?

# The Best Solution

You have learned that physical education should contribute to the psychomotor, cognitive and affective domains of learning. You have read about skills and fitness, games and activities. You know that what may be developmentally appropriate for one child may not be so for a second child. You know that there is a great deal that goes into a good physical education program.

If you choose to issue a grade based on the child's fitness level, do you believe that children can be held accountable for fitness levels despite their genetic make-ups? Assuming your answer will be no, then you have to use those measured fitness levels on individual bases. For example, the child who improves is graded on the basis of degree of improvement; the child who is fit is graded on the basis of maintenance. If this is the chosen evaluation of physical education, grades would be issued only at the end of the school year, unless testing is done each grading period. Remember, testing takes a lot of time, and usually physical education is taught only 2–3 times per week. Of course with your supplementing the program so that children have physical education five days per week, this kind of testing per grade period might be possible.

You might ask, at this point, why you have spent all of this time learning about the skills that are essential to making children efficient and effective movers? Why not work toward high levels of physical fitness and ignore the skill development? The answer is simple. Efficient and effective movers can pursue good physical fitness levels more easily than those with coordination difficulties. The skills learned in the elementary years enable the child to participate in activities that will contribute to physical fitness. Imagine doing only exercises and jogging for the entire lifespan. Surely a variety of activities would be more stimulating, and the participant would be more likely to pursue physical activity in leisure times.

How are you going to grade each marking period? If fitness testing each time is not feasible, how will you grade? Let's remember that physical fitness development and maintenance has a huge cognitive factor. Written tests should be given to assess understanding of fitness principles. These written tests should be included in the grading process, whenever it may occur. So, if you still need an objective way to grade the students each marking period, what will you do?

Sometimes teachers grade on effort and participation. If this is the case, it seems that the importance of physical education is minimal. Looking only at factors of attitude demean the importance of physical education. Grading in physical education is certainly a dilemma; it always has been.

The answer to your grading problem lies within the format of your program. A daily physical education program, taught by a certified elementary physical education teacher should be graded on skill, fitness level, and cognitive knowledge. If you are teaching physical education, express your unwillingness to provide a grade each time, because you do not have the specialized background of a physical educator. You should, however, send a report home of fitness levels, graded or not, your choice.

If the principal says you MUST furnish a physical education grade, it seems appropriate for you to generate your grade based on attitude and effort. It will be important that you have a concrete and objective way of grading attitude and effort, so a daily record chart such as the following will

| Student | Cooperates with others | Helps Others | Praises Others | Plays Fair | Tries Hard |
|---------|------------------------|--------------|----------------|------------|------------|
| Alison | | | | | |
| Andrew | | | | | |
| Brian | | | | | |
| Jeffrey | | | | | |
| Jennifer | | | | | |
| Krista | | | | | |
| Martha | | | | | |
| Matthew | | | | | |

help to keep track of the children's performances in these areas in physical education. You may record a date when you have seen evidence of the quality listed, or a date and a "minus" when you observe a lack of that quality.

Send, with the report card, a form similar to the following:

---

**Date**

**To:**        Parents of Ms. Jones' Students

**From:**     Ms. Jones, Classroom Teacher

**Re:**        Physical Education Grades

As you are aware, I have the primary responsibility for teaching physical education to the students in my homeroom class. It is unfortunate that the school does not have a certified physical education specialist for this very important phase of your child's education, but budget factors make this impossible at this time.

In the Fall I sent you a written evaluation of your child's physical fitness. You will receive one again at the end of the year, telling of improvement or maintenance of good fitness levels. This is the only area of physical education that I feel comfortable in assessing. I do not have the extensive background of a certified physical educator, and do not feel qualified to assess your child's performance in physical education. Therefore, my grade for physical education is based on effort and participation, not on physical education mastery.

---

Sending a notice such as the above will help parents realize the importance of physical education to their children. It also demonstrates your respect for physical education.

# Summary

As you can see, evaluation in physical education is rather difficult. However, one should not assume that evaluation is unnecessary; only that in order to have evaluation, first the children must have the opportunity to learn and master the necessary skills. Once quality, daily physical education becomes a reality, then evaluation becomes a positive necessity. In order to assist children in realizing their responsibility and accountability for achieving and maintaining their own physical fitness, as well as their education from a physical perspective, the self evaluation is recommended. Children are generally rather honest in evaluating themselves. This tool can be helpful during parent conferences as well as in helping the teacher to see in which areas the students may need greater instruction or individual assistance.

# References and Suggested Readings

Anderson, A. & Goode, R. (1997). Assessment informs instruction. *Journal of Physical Education, Recreation and Dance,* 68(3), 42–49.
Melograno, V. J. (1997). Integrating assessment into physical education teaching. *Journal of Physical Education, Recreation and Dance,* 68(7), 34–37.

CHAPTER

# 17

# Intramural Activity and Field Days

If we choose to encourage participation in sport activities as crucial to a healthy lifestyle, it is necessary to extend the physical education experience in such a way that children have the opportunity to participate in wholesome activity programs, designed to foster appreciation for physical fitness maintenance through active participation. It is not simply enough to provide classes in physical education, but it is necessary to provide a laboratory setting in which the newly learned skills may be applied. A skill-based approach to physical education, as advocated in this text, would not be complete without the capstone: use of those skills in actual games and contests for leisure pursuit.

## Leisure Participation in Sport Activities

Physically educated people will pursue participation in sport activities during leisure time because they have learned about and value the benefits gained from such participation. In the elementary school we try to establish positive attitudes towards sports participation, and we do this by providing positive experiences with sports to encourage the development of those positive attitudes.

As you have learned, the content for elementary physical education is vast, and even with a 5-day-per-week program, teachers cannot cover the content as thoroughly as they might wish. Therefore, you are encouraged to provide additional programs in which the children can apply learned skills.

# Intramural Programs

Intramural sport programs take place within the school, usually on an after school basis. Some schools hold early bird intramural activities where children come to school before school officially begins for the day in order to play in these programs. The basic idea behind the intramural program is to provide a fun and exciting way to utilize and practice new and learned skills. The intramural program allows for much socialization, and teaches children about cooperation and teamwork. Children build allegiance to their teams; some learn about leadership in a captains role; others learn to follow cooperatively.

The structure of intramural programming is usually unit based: children stay after school on designated days to participate in playing the sport they are learning about in their physical education classes. For this reason, intramural activities are usually designed only for children in grades 4–6. However, it is strongly suggested that such a program should be offered at least once a week for the primary grade children and it should be designed around developmentally appropriate group games.

Traditionally the physical educator has been the person to assume responsibility for the intramural programs. With the rising awareness of the importance of physical education and fitness to our children, many classroom teachers are willing to take on the extra duties. When this occurs, several different groups can meet after school, depending on the availability of facilities. In most schools, teachers receive remuneration in addition to contract salary for running such programs.

# Competitive Intramural Activity

Competition involves the meeting of two or more individuals or two or more teams in a quest to demonstrate supremacy. While it is hard to imagine that competition would be intense at the elementary school level, you will find, in fact, that competition is tremendous motivation. In competitive intramural activity, teams are organized in, for example, soccer. The teams may be composed of children from one grade level only, or they may be a combination of fourth, fifth and sixth graders, boys and girls alike. Usually the team rosters are posted and captains are appointed. Sometimes children are encouraged to put together their own teams for the intramural unit; sometimes the teacher sets the teams from the names of the children who have signed up for the program.

Research tells us that children do not truly understand competition until approximately age 11 (Smoll, Magill, & Ash, 1988 in Plimpton & Regimbal, 1992). Therefore, the element of winning should be downplayed. Children should learn that cooperation is the key to competition, and that they need to be able to cooperate with other team members in order to have a good competitive team. Children should be taught about fair play so they can learn to appreciate effort and skill; winning should be secondary.

In competitive intramural activity, each day is a contest. Depending on facilities available, perhaps only two teams will play on that day. Team standings are kept and posted for the duration of the unit, and a championship team will emerge by the end of the program. Specific children should be recognized for cooperative team behavior. The children in the competitive intramural program should be those who want to compete, and who are capable of understanding that winning is not the only thing. Any child who wants to play should be allowed to do so, regardless of skill level, and each child should play an equal amount of time to every other player. The children must be willing to be accepting of each other and the differences of each individual. It is in the intramural program that the children learn the most about each other and about their own tolerance and patience.

It is in the competitive program that fair play must be discussed and implemented. Often children are told to be a good sport but no one tells them how to do this. It is important to teach children that a good sport appreciates the winner's skill and acknowledges the loser's effort. Team members should be taught to shake hands at the conclusion of every match, and any comments should be restricted to "good game." Any children that cannot participate under these conditions should be asked to take a time out from the intramural program.

The competitive program is for the child who enjoys the challenge of conquest, and who likes to be involved in contests with others.

## Cooperative Intramural Activity

What about the child who just wants to play and be active? The child who doesn't want to compete with and against others? The child who loves to play games for the sake of pure play, and is not concerned with winners and losers? For this child, the cooperative intramural program is ideal.

As mentioned above, in order for a team to be successful in competition, the members must first learn to cooperate with each other. Since we know that the majority of children do not understand the true meaning of competition until age 11, it seems logical that cooperative play programs would help to build the strength of cooperative skill and effort that should be the backbone of any competitive team.

The best plan for cooperative intramural activities would be a program designed for primary grade children once a week, and a program designed for older children once or twice a week, again depending on facilities available. The program should run like the competitive intramural activity in that children sign up to participate, and if groups are necessary, the teacher will decide the make-up of those groups. But here the similarity between the two ends. There are no team standings posted. The children come to have fun and play together. The teacher should plan a variety of games for the intramural hour. The children should be encouraged to make up games and present them to the group. It should be a pleasurable hour at the conclusion of which the children feel as if they have played for the sake of play itself.

## Round Robin Tournament

A round robin tournament is one in which every team has the opportunity to play every other team. This type of tournament can be used in all types of intramural activities, whether competitive or cooperative. If you have 8 teams in your intramural program, the following is an example of how you would set up a round robin tournament.

| ROUND ONE | ROUND TWO | ROUND THREE | ROUND FOUR |
|---|---|---|---|
| Team 1 plays Team 2 | Team 1 plays Team 3 | Team 1 plays Team 5 | Team 1 plays Team 7 |
| Team 3 plays Team 4 | Team 5 plays Team 2 | Team 7 plays Team 3 | Team 8 plays Team 5 |
| Team 5 plays Team 6 | Team 7 plays Team 4 | Team 8 plays Team 2 | Team 6 plays Team 3 |
| Team 7 plays Team 8 | Team 8 plays Team 6 | Team 6 plays Team 4 | Team 4 plays Team 2 |

| ROUND FIVE | ROUND SIX | ROUND SEVEN |
|---|---|---|
| Team 1 plays Team 8 | Team 1 plays Team 6 | Team 1 plays Team 4 |
| Team 6 plays Team 7 | Team 4 plays Team 8 | Team 2 plays Team 6 |
| Team 4 plays Team 5 | Team 2 plays Team 7 | Team 3 plays Team 8 |
| Team 2 plays Team 3 | Team 3 plays Team 5 | Team 5 plays Team 7 |

In order to set up a round robin tournament you would take the number of teams and set them in two equal columns. If you have an uneven number of teams one team called a bye is added to make the teams equal. The team scheduled to play a bye would not play that time. Always leave team one stationary moving the other teams in a clockwise position one place around team one. Refer to the above example.

## Field Days

Classified as intramural activity because it occurs within the school, the field day is an opportunity for children to use learned skills in a relaxed and fun environment. There are many formats used for field days, and the format used does depend greatly on the number of students in the elementary school, and the facilities available.

The purpose of a field day is to have fun while participating in game-like activities. In past years, physical education teachers have held field days that centered around track and field events. Winners were awarded ribbons in a school-wide assembly, and parents and family members came in droves to watch the games. If you are sensitive to children and their thoughts, you may be able to foresee the downside in this kind of field day. Children do not all enjoy track and field events. Since the competitions focus on the individual, children who are not as skilled as others may feel awkward and embarrassed to perform in front of such crowds. It is true that the majority of children would probably enjoy such an event (until the awards ceremony when only a few are declared winners) but for those who do not enjoy demonstrating their lack of skill, such a field day would be devastating to their developing attitudes toward physical activity. We suggest that a track and field competition be held each Spring, but that it be on an elective basis. Several elementary schools could take children who sign up to the area high school for such a competition. This would then become an *extra*mural activity, competing outside the school with others. Therefore, since the field day is to be fun and game-like, the following models are suggested.

The **whole school approach** is a large undertaking for the field day planner. Assuming a school with a K–6 population, the following organization would be highly effective:

1. Using the whole school roster, pair children so that sixth graders are with second graders, fifth graders are with first graders, fourth grades are with kindergarten children, and third graders are paired with third graders. Then divide the pairs equally into the number

of groups necessary so that there are no more than 14–16 pairs per group. There should be an equal number of 6–2, 5–1, 4–K, and 3–3 pairs in each group. Have the groups written out and distributed to each classroom teacher in the school so that the children will be told in advance the number of the group they will be in. On the field day, at a specific time children will report to the station on the field that has a flag representing their group number. They will then rotate to the next station in numerical order. The older children will be responsible for taking care of the younger children who are paired with them. In all activities involving partners, the children will work in the assigned pairs.

2.    Each elementary school teacher will be assigned to a game or activity station. The field day planner should distribute a listing describing each station activity well prior to the field day and ask the teachers to submit their first three choices for a station to run. Depending on the number of stations, there may be more adults available, and parents should certainly be welcome to help out as well. The persons chosen to run the stations should be familiarized with the activity well before the day of the contest.

3.    The field day planner must assume the responsibility for setting up the stations and being sure that all equipment is furnished and ready to go. Since most schools have field days on a half-day basis, usually afternoon, it is helpful to have some older children help in the setting up of the stations during the morning.

4.    Assuming, for this example, a school of 400 students, there would be about 24 stations necessary. The students would rotate stations every 10 minutes, and in an afternoon would probably rotate to 8 stations at the most, considering rotation time. Since even the most efficient field day could not possibly rotate to more than 12, stations may be repeated in the second 12 stations, making organization even easier.

5.    Typical station activities would include:

***Animal Noise***: The leader of the station has a set of cards on which there is a picture of an animal. There are two pictures of that animal in the set of cards Each child takes a card and on the signal to go moves in the play area making the sound of the animal on the card. This continues until all players have found their matches.

***Chariot Race***: Two chariots (automobile tire tube with a long hemp jump rope passing through the tire and held by the horse, the bigger of the partners) are at the station. The group is divided in half and runs a relay race in which the bigger partner tows the smaller partner who is sitting on the tire tube to a designated pylon and back.

***Dress and Run***: A set of large clothes, including shirt, pants, and shoes or boots is set at a goal line for each of the two teams. Each player in turn runs to the goal line, dresses in the clothes, runs back, takes the clothes off where the next person puts them on, runs to the goal line, takes them off, etc.

***Clown Faces***: Partners use the available paints to decorate each others faces.

***Elephant, Goat, Kangaroo***: Children stand in a circle with one child in the middle. The middle child spins around and stops, pointing to a child and says Elephant! the child pointed to holds his/her shoulder to his/ her nose so that the arm forms a trunk, and he/she waves the trunk up and down. The children to each side of the elephant head use their arms to form the ears of the elephant. The child spins again, points and calls Goat! The center child pretends to stroke his/her goatee, the side children pretend to milk the goat. Kangaroo: center child holds arms as a pouch, side children jump up and down; Duck: center person claps hand at mouth while saying quack, quack and the side people flap out wings.

*Jello Slurp:*   Each player is given a bowl of jello to place in front of himself/herself on a table. On the signal to go, the players bend over, face in the jello and eat, hands are held behind the back.

*Killer:*   All children hide their eyes and the group leader taps one child on the head who is to be the secret killer. On signal all children open their eyes and move within the play area, shaking hands with people. The killer taps the inside of each persons wrist with whom he/ she shakes hands. Anyone killed must first shake hands with two more people then fall down dead. The game continues until a player who has not been killed can guess who the killer is.

*Eskimo Walk:*   Teams are in relay formation and each set of partners will travel to a goal line and back. One child will be the Eskimo and one will be in charge of the snowshoes. The snowshoes are pieces of cardboard that the Eskimo must step on to advance. The snowshoe person moves the cardboard when the Eskimo lifts the foot and places the cardboard in front of the Eskimo to step forward.

*Lap Sit:*   Children form a circle, standing single file. When tightly together, they bend their knees slightly and sit on the lap of the person behind. When this balance is achieved they may attempt to walk forward with the leader giving signals for left foot, right foot.

*Marshmallow on a String*: Partners face each other and hold the end of a string in their mouths, off the middle of which hangs a marshmallow. On the signal to go, the partners, using only their mouths, eat their way forward on the string to be the first to get to the marshmallow.

*Mural Painting*: This station will have a huge roll of drawing paper where children will draw and color their own individual contribution to the mural. After the field day the mural will be displayed in the school halls. This station might also involve sidewalk chalk and children decorate the walks of the school.

*Parachute Play*: The leader performs a series of parachute games with the children at the station. Activities can be selected from Chapter Nine.

*Partner Tango:*   Partners hold whole lemons between their foreheads and travel to a goal line and back.

*Water Balloon Toss:*   Children work in their partner pairs. Partners face each other and on signal line #1 children toss the balloon to line #2 children. The leader continues to give signals for the toss. After each toss, each line steps backward one giant step. The game continues until only a few water balloons are left (others breaking on missed catches).

*Water Bucket Brigade:* The group is divided into two teams, each with its own full bucket of water, an empty bucket and a styrofoam cup. The full bucket is placed next to the team and the empty bucket 10 yards away. Each player in turn fills the styrofoam cup, carries it to the empty bucket, pours it in and returns to give the cup to the next player to repeat. Teams try to have the most water in the originally empty bucket.

*Whose Shoe?* All the children take off their shoes and put them in a pile at the goal line. On the signal to go, all run to the pile and pick up their own shoes giving them to one designated team player. They all go back to the starting point and sit in single file lines while the last person carries all the shoes back for the team, sits at the end of the line and passes one shoe at a time forward. When all shoes are on and tied the team is finished.

1.  It is a good idea to have a special activity at the end of the field day to tie things together. One would be a faculty-student tug o war; another might be a faculty-sixth grade volleyball game. Some teachers like to calm the children down with a short movie in the gymnasium where it is likely to be cooler, before they leave for the day. In this kind of a field day there are no awards—the children's reward is an afternoon of fun and unusual activities

2.  In the *grade level* approach to field day, half a day is usually designated to grades 1 and 2, half to 3 and 4, and half of the next day to grades 5 and 6. Kindergarten may or may not be included, but it is difficult to have them participate successfully in this format. There are several programming options in this type of field day:

3.  Station activities may be planned as designated in the *whole school* approach. Care must be taken to select those activities that are at the appropriate level for the grade levels involved. For example, the chariot race would not work with the smaller children as there will be no older and larger children to pull the chariots.

4.  A rotational system could be set around games so that the children would be arranged in teams, either by grade level or mixed, and each team would play 5 different games for twenty minutes.

5.  Competitive events can be held so that all children run the 50-yard-dash, jump in the running long jump, throw a softball for distance, and a class selected team can run a track-style relay. This is the format that field days of the past have used; many schools are moving away from this format because the competition model does not lend itself to the objectives of a final school week field day.

## Summary

Many children have the opportunity to participate in youth sport programs sponsored by community organizations. Children start participation in organized t-ball, soccer or ice hockey as young as 5 years of age. Many of these programs are good, depending on the coach's credentials and philosophy. But, many other children do not have the opportunity to play in such programs due to such factors as parents work schedules, music lessons, etc. The intramural program becomes very important to these children. It has been the expressed belief in this text that children in elementary school should not play the parent game in physical education classes. There is simply not enough time to give every child enough opportunities to respond with the learned skills. Thus the intramural program allows for participation in that parent game. Field days should be fun and exciting. This day should allow the children to enjoy the physical skills that they have learned during the year in an enjoyable atmosphere.

## References and Suggested Readings

Jackson, B. & Rokosz, F. (1995). Super kids day classic games: Two field days for elementary schools. *Journal of Physical Education, Recreation, and Dance,* 66(3), 56–63 and 71–72.

Plimpton, C.E. & Regimbal, C. (1991). Cooperative competition: A children's sport model. *Future Focus,* 12(2), 4–7.

# CHAPTER

# 18

# Playground Games

Many schools have time allotted during the school day for recess. Children love to play and move freely. Just as adults need time for recreation, relaxation and breaks in the daily workday, it is even more important for children to have these opportunities. Some children, however, are not as creative as others and do not know what to do during recess. Many teachers have indicated that they would like the physical education teacher to teach various play and movement activities to students, during physical education class, which may be used during recess. Cognitive applications of material learned in the classroom setting can also be reinforced during playground games. For these reasons, as well as for fitness purposes, a small unit covering playground games has been included in this chapter.

Most children are not given an opportunity to exercise at their target heart rate at least 3 times a week for 20 minutes on non-consecutive days during the 5-day school week. It has been found that in order to improve or maintain fitness, this amount of exercise is essential. Most elementary school students have physical education class for only 30 minutes, twice a week. Therefore, the recess time allotted each day may be used to help students improve their fitness levels while having fun. Eventually, all students will need to formulate and implement fitness plans for life. Performing some fitness activities during recess can assist students with this task as well as helping to improve fitness levels over a period of time. The physical education teacher can help them to formulate individualized fitness plans. Target heart rates as well as fitness in general are discussed in detail in the "Physical Fitness" chapter.

Most schools have a blacktop playground area with swings, slides, and other playground equipment in close to the blacktop. The court diagrams illustrated and explained in this section may either be painted on the blacktop in order to make them somewhat permanent, or drawn with chalk. It is suggested that all of the games be taught to the appropriate grade levels by the physical education teacher, in cooperation with the classroom teacher. Some of the playground games presented in this chapter require more activity than others. Several of the games presented work on improving the students' fine motor skills. All of the games may be adapted for maximum participation as well as to be developmentally appropriate. Several courts may be drawn for the same game in order that many games may be going on at the same time. Courts may be shortened or lengthened, equipment may be substituted, and instructions may be simplified or changed, to make these games developmentally appropriate.

# Playground Activities

Some of the playground games may be adapted in order to reinforce cognitive concepts learned in the classroom. General categories being studied in the classroom can be used in the games in place of the theme of the actual game. For example, in the game Kitty, before drawing a Kitty part in that rectangle the player must name one fact correctly in that category.

A large variety of items may be used for throwing, catching, and bouncing purposes: yarn balls, beach balls, foam balls, vinyl balls, playground balls, foam flying discs, and rag balls, to name a few. In games requiring markers or shooters, a player may use a beanbag, flat stone, bottle cap, poker chip, coin or some small flat game piece for a marker. Beanbags are recommended for safety purposes.

### *Kitty*
* Level: Grades 1 – 4
*Skills Enhanced:* Tossing for accuracy
*Equipment Needed:* Several beanbags and several pieces of colored chalk
Court: A Kitty Court
*Description*: Two or more players are needed. One player stands behind the starting line and attempts to throw his/her beanbag completely within an empty rectangle, not touching any boundary lines. If successful, that player may draw a Kitty head in that space. Each player is given a different color of chalk in order to keep track of his/her Kittens. Players take turns, one at a time, trying to get their beanbags to land in a rectangle. Several players may draw a Kitty's head in the same rectangle. However, he/she may only draw body parts to his/her own Kitty's head, which is identified by his/her color of chalk. Each time a player's beanbag lands in a rectangle where that player previously had a Kitty head, he/she may draw one of the Kitty's ears. The first thing drawn must always be the Kitty's head. A player whose beanbag lands within the KITTY rectangle may fill in every space with a Kitty head or draw the next Kitty part needed in each rectangle. In order to win the game, a player needs to have three completed Kittens in the same rectangle. A complete Kitty consists of a head, two ears, a body, and a tail. If desired two eyes, a nose, and a mouth may be required to make the game more challenging.

Fouls: If the following infractions occur the player's turn is over and no drawing occurs:
   • A beanbag lands on a line
   • A beanbag goes off the court
   • A player steps on or over the start line.

### *Skully*
- Level:  Grades 3 - 6

*Skills Enhanced*:  Tossing for accuracy

*Equipment Needed*:  a beanbag for each player

*Description*: Two or more players are needed. The object of the game is to toss one's beanbag in such a way that it lands in each rectangle from one to ten in numerical order. Players will number off and take turns in the appropriate order. The first player stands behind the start line, attempting to toss the beanbag into the rectangle marked number one. If the player is successful, the toss counts and that player then stands in rectangle one and continues to toss at number two.  When a player's turn is over, he/she leaves the beanbag where it landed and tosses from that spot on his/her next turn.

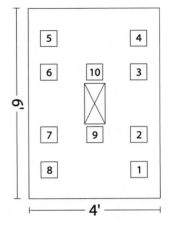

Bonus:  If the following occurs, the player gets one free turn and moves up one space.
- A beanbag hits another player's beanbag

Fouls:  If the following infractions occur, the player 's turn is over.
- A beanbag does not land in the appropriate rectangle (the beanbag is then left where it lands).
- A beanbag goes out of bounds (the beanbag is placed where it went out).
- A beanbag lands on the X  (beanbag is moved back one space).
- A player's beanbag goes out of bounds 2 times in a row (the player starts over from the beginning).
- A beanbag lands in the trap, not on the X (the player starts over from the beginning).

### *Pottsie*
- Level:  Grades 1 - 6

*Skills Enhanced*:  Ball handling skills, exercise skills, and cognitive reinforcement of classroom material

*Equipment Needed*:  a piece of chalk, a tennis ball, handball, or any other type of appropriate bouncing ball

*Description*:  Two or more players are needed. Before starting play someone using a piece of chalk draws or writes a subject heading or category in each rectangle, preferably related to present classroom material.  The first player then stands behind the starting line and attempts to bounce and catch his/her ball in space number one. He/she must identify an item related to the subject heading in rectangle one and then perform one jumping jack. The other players simultaneously perform one jumping jack. If correct, the same player continues to rectangle two; however, he/she must now bounce and catch the ball while answering the category correctly, and then perform two jumping jacks. All other players now perform two jumping jacks. The object of the game is to get through all ten rectangles in one turn.

| Nursery Rhymes |
| --- |
| Vegetables |
| Birds |
| Songs |
| Alphabet |
| Shapes |
| Flowers |
| Animals |
| Numbers |
| Colors |

*Variation*:  For younger children, the players may go back to the last space in which they were successful, but still lose the present turn. Categories for each grade level should be related to classroom work for that particular grade. More time may be provided for primary grades to answer categories. A variety of exercises can be used, such as toe touches, arm circles, etc.

*Fouls:* If one of the following infractions occur, the player's turn is over and he/she starts over from the beginning.
- The ball rolls out of the rectangle.
- A player stops for more than 3 seconds when attempting to answer a subject heading.
- A player does not have control of the ball.
- A player gives an incorrect answer.

### *Hopscotch*
- Level: Grades 3 - 6

*Skills Enhanced:* Hopping, jumping, tossing for accuracy

*Equipment Needed:* a beanbag per player

*Description:* There are numerous ways of playing hopscotch, as well as a wide variety of courts and patterns. Several diagrams of various Hopscotch Courts have been included in this chapter. Players take turns one at a time. One player stands behind the starting line and attempts to toss his/her beanbag in such a way that it lands inside rectangle number 1 without touching a boundary line. If successful, that player attempts to hop through the pattern of the court landing on one foot in a single rectangle and landing on two feet in a straddle position when there are side by side rectangles. The player then turns around at the rest rectangle hopping back to the beginning and retrieves the beanbag while returning to the

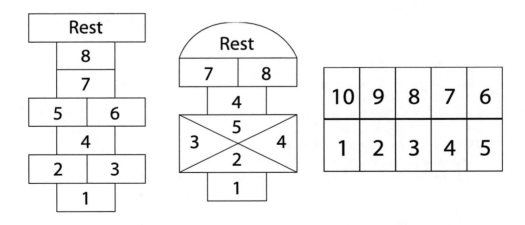

starting line. Whenever there is one rectangle in the pattern the participant hops on one foot in the rectangle. Player number one will take his/her next turn by attempting to toss the beanbag in rectangle two and repeat the pattern; however, this occurs only after all the other players have had their first turns. The first participant to throw his/her beanbag correctly in each rectangle, as well as to hop the pattern correctly is the winner.

- *Fouls*: A player loses his/her turn and must try to repeat the previous number. The following are considered fouls:
- A marker lands on the line.
- A marker does not land in the appropriate space.
- A player steps or jumps on a line.
- A player loses his/her balance and steps instead of hopping.

### Two Square

- Level: Grades 3 - 6

*Skills Enhanced*: Ball handling skills

*Equipment Needed*: A playground ball or any other appropriate type of bouncing ball and a piece of chalk

*Description*: Two players are needed. If there are several students who wish to play, several courts can be drawn. A two square court consists of two side by side squares approximately 4 1/2 feet by 4 ½ feet, or whatever space is 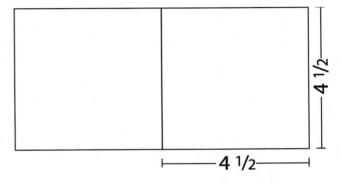 available. The courts may be made larger or smaller depending on the age and skill levels of the participants.

Players begin by standing outside the court. The server starts the game by bouncing the ball in his/her own box, and hitting it with the open palm of the hand into the opponent's court. A player may enter the court whenever he/she wishes, in order to return the ball. One bounce is allowed between each volley. Only the server may score. If an infraction is committed by the server, the receiving player wins the serve. A game consists of 21 points and the winner must have at least a two point lead.

*Fouls:* If one of the following infractions occurs the ball is considered to be dead:
- The ball goes out of bounds.
- A player is unable to return the serve or volley.
- More than one bounce occurs after the serve or volley..

### Four Square

- *Level*: Grades 3 - 6

*Skills Enhanced*: Ball handling and game strategies

*Equipment Needed*: A playground ball or any other appropriate bouncing ball

*Description:* Four players are needed for Four Square. Extra players may be substituted in during play or may start another game on another court. A court is made up of four squares approximately 41/2 feet by 41/2 feet each. The size of the court may vary. The court's squares can be numbered 1 through 4, or may be left blank. However, one square needs to be assigned as the server's square. The server stands just outside square one and the other three players each stand just outside one of the other three squares. The server begins play by bouncing the ball into square one and hitting it using the palm of his/her hand into any of the other three squares. The player in that box must hit it with an open hand into any other square. Play continues until someone misses; that player moves to square 4 and everyone else moves up one space. The object of Four Square is to attempt to reach square one, and stay there. Four Square is an ongoing game without points being scored. There are many different versions of Four Square with a wide variety of rules. The previous version is just one of many.

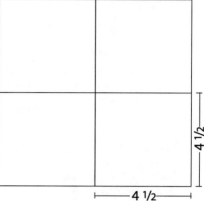

*Fouls:* A player committing a foul moves to square four and the other players move up one space to fill in the empty spaces. If the server commits the error he/she moves to the last box and everyone else moves up one square. If there are more than four players, the player committing the foul goes to the end of the waiting line, the first person in the waiting line moves into square four and everyone in the game moves up to the next empty square. The following infractions are considered fouls:

> The ball bounces more than once.
> A player hits the ball out of bounds.
> A player is hit by the ball.
> A player does not use an open palm to hit the ball.
> The ball hits the line.
> The server misses the serve.

### *Handball*
- Level: Grades 4 - 6

*Skills Enhanced*: Ball handling skills, game strategies
*Equipment Needed:* a handball, tennis ball, or other appropriate ball
*Description*: Either two or four players are needed, depending upon whether playing singles or doubles. The serving line for handball is usually around 15 to 17 feet from the wall, however the court may be drawn larger or smaller depending on the age and skill level of the participants. The server stands behind the serving line and bounces the ball once, hitting it with the palm of the hand in such a way that it rebounds off the wall and bounces on the other side of the serving line. Two attempts are permitted on the serve.

The receiving player hits the ball back against the wall either directly from the rebound off the wall or after allowing it to bounce once. Players attempt to continue volleying the ball off the wall. Only the server may score points. If the server commits an infraction the receiver wins the serve. If the receiver makes an error the server wins one point. When a player blocks another player from making a play, a foul is called. If the server was responsible for the block, the receiver wins the serve. If the receiver was responsible for the block, the serve is taken over. 21 points wins the game.

Doubles is similar to singles with the following exceptions:

> The player closest to the ball plays it.

Regarding the serving team, the non-serving player must stand outside the court until after the serve has been executed.

*Fouls:*  The following infractions are considered fouls:
- Blocking the other player from hitting the ball.
- An incorrect serve that does not bounce on the other side of the serving line.
- A player failing to hit the ball.
- The ball goes out of bounds

### *Tennis Handball*
- Level:  Grades 4 - 6

*Skills Enhanced*:  Ball handling skills and game strategies

*Equipment Needed*:  a handball, tennis ball, or any other appropriate bouncing ball

*Description*:  There are two teams with eight or more players on each team.  The average tennis handball court is usually about 20 feet by 40 feet and is divided in half.  However, the court may be drawn larger or smaller depending on the age and skill levels of the participants. Both teams will assign numbers to team members for the purpose of the serving order.  The ball may be served from anywhere within the serving team's side of the court.  The first server will bounce the ball once, and use an open hand to hit it into the opponent's court. The opponents try to hit the ball back to the serving team's court, also using an open hand. The ball may bounce several times before it is volleyed.  Only the serving team may score. If the serving team commits an infraction, the receiving team wins the serve.  If the receiving team makes an error, the serving team gets one point.  The ball is playable until it comes to a stop.  21 points wins the game.

*Fouls:*  The ball is considered dead when the following infractions occur:
- The ball stops bouncing.
- The ball goes out of bounds.

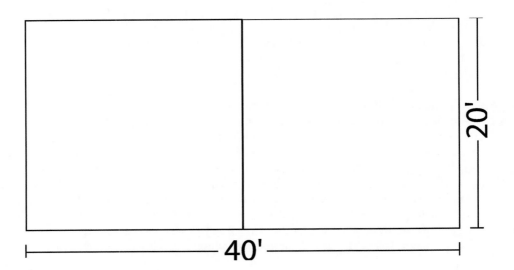

### *Danish Rounders*
- Level:  Grades 4 - 6

*Skills Enhanced*:  Running bases, throwing for accuracy, fielding the ball, and general softball skills

*Equipment Needed*:  a tennis ball, handball, or other appropriate ball

*Description*:  Eight or more players are needed.  The size of the court will depend on the ages as well as the number of participants.  A square somewhere between 18 to 20 feet on a side would be average.  The court is set up similar to a baseball diamond, in that there are three bases, home plate and a pitcher's mound.  Two teams are needed for Danish Rounders, an infield and an outfield team.  The outfield team will need a pitcher and a catcher and the remainder of the team will be fielders.  To begin the inning, the pitcher will pitch the ball high and the batter will attempt to hit the ball with the palm of his/her hand.  It does not matter if the batter hits the ball or misses it, or if the pitch is a bad pitch, the batter must run to first base.  Wherever the ball ends up, it is the job of the fielders or catcher to return the ball to the pitcher immediately.  As soon as the pitcher has possession of the ball, he/she tags the pitcher's mound with the ball, calling out "STOP."  Runners not on base when the pitcher calls "STOP" are out.  If the ball happens to be caught on a fly, the batter as well as any runners not on a base are out.  Teams trade places after three outs.  Just as in softball, whenever a runner makes it to home plate, a run is scored.  There can be several runners on the same base and runners may pass each other.  Runners may stay on a base indefinitely.  If all players are waiting on bases and there is only one batter left, he/she is allowed to bat three times in a row.  The winner will be the team having the most runs at the end of the game.

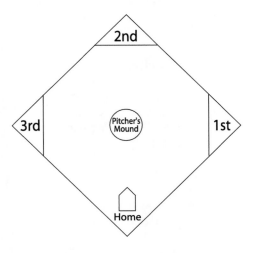

*Fouls:*  The following rule infractions result in an out.
- Any base runner not on a base when the pitcher calls "STOP."
- A hit ball is caught on a fly.
- Any base runners between bases when "STOP" is called.

### *German*
- Level:  Grades 3 - 6

*Skills Enhanced*:  Ball handling skills, fielding skills, and game strategies

*Equipment Needed:*  A tennis ball, handball, or other appropriate ball

*Description*:  Two or three players are needed for each team.  Divide the two teams into a batting team and an outfield team.  The court should be drawn next to a wall without windows, preferably on the blacktop or sidewalk.  The court is approximately 25 feet long and 5 feet wide.  The court may be shortened or lengthened depending on the age and skill level of the participants.  There are five rectangles drawn within the court each about 3 to 5 feet long, to represent bases.  The first rectangle is labeled "at bat," the second rectangle is labeled "single," the third "double," the fourth "triple," and the last "home run."  The outfield team assigns a player to each of the rectangles from 2 through 4; if there are only two players the outfielders will stand between two bases. The batter stands in the "at bat" box and throws the ball in such a way that it bounces off the wall into the court. Outfielders let the ball bounce one or more times before trying to catch it. The outfield player in the rectangle, who catches the ball will affect how many points the hit is worth. If the outfielder in the "single" rectangle catches it, the runner scores a single. If the outfielder in the "double" area catches it, the runner is awarded a double, etc. If all of the outfielders miss the ball, a home run is scored. The runner is to stand in the rectangle for which he/she received credit,

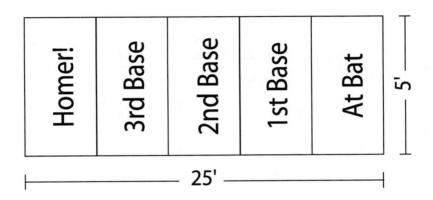

and may be advanced by the next batter. As an example, if the first batter scored a triple, the batter would stand in the "triple" box. If the next batter scores a triple, this would advance the first runner to home. If it is a batter's turn to hit and he/she is standing in a rectangle, that player may come up to the "at bat" rectangle and still score from the previous base; however, players must keep track of scores, positions on base etc. A time limit is determined before starting the game. The team with the most points at the end is the winner. After each player on the batting team has had two turns, the teams change places.

### One, Two, Buckle Your Shoe
- Level: Grades 1 - 6

*Skills Enhanced*: Ball handling skills
*Equipment Needed*: A tennis ball, handball, or any other appropriate type bouncing ball.
*Description*: One or more players are needed. Each player in turn will attempt to complete the following motions or activities while singing the following chant. Other activities may be substituted for the ten that follow.

Chant:
One, two buckle your shoe. Three, four open the door. Five, six pick up sticks. Seven, eight lay them straight. Nine, ten a big fat hen. Other jump rope rhymes or general rhymes may be used instead.

The motions are to be performed in order as chanting, while also always allowing the ball to bounce one time before catching it.
- Bounce the ball against the wall high, let it bounce and catch it
- Bounce the ball against the wall low, let it bounce and catch it
- Bounce the ball against the wall medium, let it bounce and catch it

- Bounce the ball against the wall, let it bounce, and catch it under 1 leg
- Bounce the ball against the wall, let it bounce and catch it under the other leg
- Bounce the ball against the wall, do 1 jumping jack, let it bounce and catch it.
- Bounce the ball against the wall, touch toes once, let the ball bounce and catch it.
- Bounce the ball against the wall clap hands once, let the ball bounce and catch it.
- Bounce the ball against the wall, clap hands 3 times, let the ball bounce once and catch it.
- Bounce the ball against the wall, turn around once, let the ball bounce once and catch it.

Instruct the participants to write down as many different activities as they can think of to perform to "One Two Buckle Your Shoe." Substitute their ideas and activities when appropriate.

### *Beanbag Toss*
- Level: Grades 1 - 6

*Skills Enhanced*: Throwing for accuracy

*Equipment Needed*: Several targets drawn or painted on the playground, several beanbags, and a piece of chalk

*Description*: Several targets are placed or drawn throughout the playground area. Students are divided into teams with each team being assigned a different target. For safety purposes students will number off and take turns in order. It is suggested that each student take a predetermined number of turns at one target before giving the next student a turn. It is further suggested that students move from one target to the next with his/her team, with all moving at the same time. Students when applicable should keep their own scores. Primary grade children will not keep track of their scores but rather stress that they hit the targets. If a beanbag lands on a line, no points are scored for that particular toss. The student with the most points at the end of a predetermined amount of time is the winner.

*Variations*: Older students can throw at the targets using the rules for darts. In one form of darts, the first player to hit each space in order and then hit the bullseye is the winner

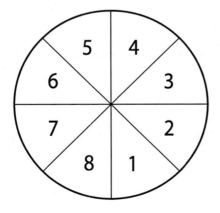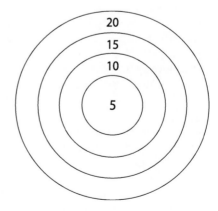

In another version, each box is assigned a point value with the bullseye being worth at least double any other box. The number of points needed to win the game is determined before

beginning play. The first player to reach that score wins. General categories being studied in the classroom can be drawn in chalk in each box on the target.

The following diagrams are illustrations of various beanbag targets.

## Other Playground Activities

There are many other activities that can be performed on the blacktop during recess. Long and short jump ropes, flying discs, and hula hoops, to name a few, can all be performed during recess if the appropriate equipment is available. Flying disc and hula hoop activities are described in detail in the "Manipulative Activities" chapter. Jump rope activities are described in the "Dance and Rhythmic Activities" chapter. Many of the games in the "Developmentally Appropriate Games" chapter are also appropriate for recess time.

## References and Suggested Readings

Bancroft, J. (1967). *Games for the playground, home, school and gymnasium.* New York,: MacMillan.

Brown, M. (1980). *Finger rhymes.* New York: E.P. Dutton.

Dieden, B. (1995). *Games to keep kids moving.* West Nyack: Parker.

Gabbard, C., LeBlanc, E. & Lowry, S. (1989). *Games, dance, and gymnastics activities for children.* Englewood Cliffs: Prentice Hall.

Graham, G., Holt/Hale, S., & Parker, M. (2001). *Children moving.* Mountain View: Mayfield Publishing Co.

Kamiya, A. (1987). *Elementary teacher's handbook of indoor and outdoor games.* West Nyack: Parker.

Maguire, J. (1990). *Hopscotch, hangman, hot potato & ha ha ha.* New York: Simon & Schuster, Inc.

Mulac, M. (1964). *Games and stunts for schools, camps, and playgrounds.* New York: Harper & Row.

Nelson, B. (1994). *Pickle, pepper, and tip in too.* New York: Simon & Schuster.

Nelson, E. (1975) *Movement games for children of all ages.* New York: Sterling Publishing.

Winn, M., Miller, A., & Kuskin, K. (1970). *What shall we do and allee galloo.* New York: Harper & Row.

Wiswell, P. (1987). *Kids games.* Garden City: Doubleday and Co.

CHAPTER

# 19

# Classroom Teacher and Physical Educator: A Dynamic Duo

Hopefully by now you have developed an appreciation for not only the course, physical education, but also for the person known as the physical educator. So often people assume that the physical educator needs less education than other teachers because "all they do is 'play' with children and young adults all day." These people see the physical educator's job as "soft" and they are often unkind with their shared perceptions. Unfortunately, some teachers encourage these perceptions when they do not do the job as it is to be done. If you do not

have an effective physical educator in your school, and instead have one of the "roll-out-the-ball" variety, you should also be critical. You know and understand the importance of physical education: be sure that your children receive the quality education they deserve. This text has been designed to give you information that is critical for you to be able to teach your own physical education to your own classroom group. It is, by no means, an acceptable text for a potential physical educator who would teach all levels, preK–6. Remember that the law concerning provision of physical education, which is applicable to many states, says that a minimum amount of

physical education will be provided to elementary school children. The school district may decide who will teach it, and, in most states, certified elementary physical educators are not required. Therefore, the task may come to you as the classroom teacher. Hopefully, however, you will have an effective physical educator to work with, and you can become a dynamic duo!

## Teacher Collaboration

Collaborative planning is a new buzz term in modern education. This term applies to the various disciplines coming together in order to plan for their integration with one another. In certain school systems several substitutes are hired to cover a variety of classes throughout the day in order to give classroom teachers, specialists, special education teachers, and other disciplines an opportunity to collaborate. This would be an excellent opportunity to work as the dynamic duo in the planning and implementing of creative ideas. In-service days offer another opportunity for the dynamic duo to meet, create, and collaborate.

It seems that many school systems, perhaps unknowingly, have fostered some isolationist approaches causing teachers to become competitive rather than cooperative. As you read in Chapter Fifteen in dealing with intramurals, cooperation is relevant to student learning. If teachers are forced to worry about job cuts, and pay incentives, perhaps they're not as willing to share significant ideas and programs. In the long run everyone loses, but most of all it is the students who lose. There is a fine line between working together as a team and interfering with an individual teachers creativity and right to teach in areas of choice. It has been heard often that sometimes what has proven to work for one teacher may not work for another. Teachers have their individual strengths as well as their weak areas, just as students have strengths and weaknesses. The question may be: "How can teachers work as a team and still keep individuality? A question both classroom teachers and physical educators need to ask themselves would be: "How can we work together for the best interests of our students?"

## Working as a Dynamic Duo

Let us assume for a moment that you do have an effective physical education teacher at your school. Physical education in this case is probably provided 2–3 (30) minute periods per week. In order for your children to develop good fitness as well as refined motor skills, you know that they need to have physical education more than the 2–3 times per week. As a matter of fact, you know that physical activity should be a daily regimen. Since you are going to be a very effective classroom teacher, you will want to work with the physical educator to promote sound levels of fitness and motor skills for your children. Since you will be so effective, you will manage time very well in your classroom, and you will be able to provide one-half hour of physical activity for your students on the days that they do not meet with the physical educator.

Perhaps you will be unable to have the gymnasium for your class, but you know how to provide good fitness activities either outside or in the classroom. You might propose to the physical educator that you will work on the fitness aspect, leaving the time for skill development to the teacher who has studied extensively in that area. It would be wonderful if you could manage your time so well that you could even do a 20 minute activity warm-up with the children at the beginning of every day! At any rate, you can supplement the physical education program by providing for fitness development.

Another way that you might work with the physical educator would be to leave the skill teaching to him/her and you play lead-up games on alternate days that give the students opportunities to practice the skills they have learned in a play situation. This would mean that you would have to do your planning with the physical educator but a cooperative venture would probably be an excellent idea.

So far you have two options to discuss with the physical educator. It seems that you're the one who is doing the giving, by supplementing the physical educator's program. What is the benefit to you?

Remember Chapter Five where we discussed the relationship of cognitive learning and physical education. You know that children learn well when they are moving. Why not talk with the physical educator about the classroom curriculum and see if you might do some teaching together; or, ask the physical educator if there is a way he/she can incorporate your curriculum into the physical education class. A simple example of that integration would be that you are teaching fractions to your students in mathematics. The physical educator could have the children keep track of points earned by allocating fractions instead of whole number points in a game or drill. The children can practice adding fractions while participating in physical activity. A folk dance unit might center on Greek folk dances because your class is studying Greece. Lessons in metric measurements might be complemented by participation in a track and field unit. Studying classical music might go nicely with creative dance to the same music. The possibilities are truly endless: only your own creativity and certainly that of the physical educator limit them.

You should be able to tell right away if you have an effective physical educator. Talk with him/her and let him/her know your understanding of physical education and its importance to the education of the child. Offer to work together to meet both his/her goals and your goals. Establish an alliance with the physical educator. He/she can be an excellent resource for you as well as someone who can often help you out in a tight situation. Suppose that your physical education class is canceled for an assembly. You were counting on that time to do some important paperwork but now you have to attend the assembly: if you have a good working relationship with the physical educator, he/she might cover your class at the assembly, OR he/she might even take your class for physical education experience during his/her free time! Unheard of? Hardly! There are many creative ways of working together as a duo. For example, in order for children to receive a greater amount of physical activity, all 3 fourth grades and their teachers may come to the gymnasium together once a week for a dance activity. The 3 classroom teachers may assist in supervising the large number of students, while the physical education specialist instructs the students regarding a variety of popular dances which are cardiovascular in nature. Another example might be that the physical education specialist and two of the fourth grade teachers assist in supervising the students, while the other fourth grade teacher instructs the students in a lesson using movement in order to learn about the movement of the planets in the solar system. The possibilities are limited only by the team's creative abilities. There is a great deal, which can be accomplished by a team approach.

The physical educator works with students from kindergarten through 6th grade. Therefore, the specialist is able to see the growth, maturity, and development of each individual child. The physical educator sees the students in a different arena than you do. Many times the physical educator can share important information regarding individual students and ways to assist in improving instruction and relationships with individual students. You also have important information regarding your students that can be of importance to the physical educator. You spend a great deal of time each day with the class and generally will know each individual student quite well. If the dynamic duo is able to share information and work together for the betterment of all students, this can be a powerful educational tool. If both you and physical education specialist ask what can be done to assist each other in making the students education more meaningful, great things can happen.

## Your Responsibilities to the Physical Educator

Just as the physical educator should respect your classroom contributions, you also have some responsibilities to the physical educator. Be sure that you arrive on time for physical education and that you pick your children up on time as well. Sometimes teachers use physical education as a punishment: "if your work isn't done, you can't go to physical education!" There is absolutely NO excuse for this. The children are required to be in physical education just as they are required to be in school. You do not have any right to take students away from the physical education class, nor from other special areas such as music and art. The physical educator will not hold your children for extra physical education; you owe him/her the same courtesy.

Another irritating habit that some classroom teachers have is that of leaving some children in the room to finish work and, when finished, the children come to physical education. When you are teaching do you enjoy reteaching each time a student enters the room late? Of course you don't. Develop a mutual respect with your physical educator.

## Unite for Success for the Students

There is an enormous amount that can be accomplished from an educational perspective if teachers and specialists work together for the betterment of the students. This seems to be especially true for the classroom teacher and the physical education specialist. Hopefully, you have come to realize how important your student's health and well-being is related to learning in general. Further, you have also come to realize how important exercise, fitness, and physical education are to the child's health and overall well being. A healthy child is more alert and receptive to learning than that same child would-be when ill or otherwise unhealthy. Therefore, the classroom teacher and the physical educator can become the dynamic duo, in assisting students towards improving health, fitness, and learning in general. And, to encourage parents to understand as well, the following letter may be sent home from you and the physical educator:

## Summary

It is truly important that you use the art of collaboration with all teachers in your school. Your relationship with your physical educator is particularly important, however, because both you and the physical educator now understand the importance of physical education to good health and, thus, to success in the classroom. Just imagine how the health problems in society would be reduced if all children received five days per week of good, sound, effective physical education! Physical fitness would be a constant in the lives of children and hopefully they would carry those learned values into their adult lives where they can participate in leisure activities for pleasure as well as for the health of it! Both you and the physical educator have the same goals for your children. Work together: be a dynamic duo!

Dear Parents,

We are writing to you regarding our endeavor to improve your child's health, physical fitness, and overall well being. The American Alliance for Health, Physical Education, Recreation and Dance recommends quality daily physical education for elementary students. Most situations call for the physical education specialist to teach 2–3, 30 minute classes of physical education per week, per grade. It is widely known that individuals need to participate in appropriate physical activity at least three non-consecutive days a week in order to affect their fitness levels. Therefore, the classroom teacher, physical educator, parents and students need to work together to assist and encourage students to achieve their best fitness levels. Please encourage your child to participate in fitness activities outside of school.

We also wish to let you know how we can work together for the betterment of your child. It is important that both the classroom teacher and the physical educator be informed of any conditions that your child may have which could restrict or affect your child's physical activity. We wish to be informed of any special considerations, first aid treatments, etc. that we may need to know in order to serve your child in the best way possible. It is especially important that your student wear tennis shoes and appropriate clothing in order to participate in physical activities. Appropriate wearing apparel contributes to safety as well as performance.

Students will be evaluated on their effort as well as their participation. Although each child is an individual with varying abilities, all children are strongly encouraged to do their best. Physical fitness will definitely be given consideration when evaluating your child. The classroom teacher and physical educator will be working together in an attempt to help students improve their health, fitness, and overall well being. Your support and cooperation are greatly appreciated.

## References and Suggested Readings

Petray, C.K. (1989). Classroom teachers as partners teaching health-related physical fitness. *Journal of Health, Physical Education, Recreation and Dance,* 60(7), 64–66

Pissanos, B.W. & Temple, I.G. (1991). Fitting together physical education specialists and classroom teachers. *Journal of Health, Physical Education, Recreation and Dance,* 62(7), 55–61.

# References and Suggested Readings

Allsbrook, L. (1992). Fitness should fit children. *Journal of Physical Education, Recreation and Dance*, 63(6), 47-49.

Anderson, A. & Goode, R. (1997). Assessment informs instruction. *Journal of Physical Education, Recreation and Dance*, 68(3), 42-49.

Anderson A. & Weber, E. (1997). A multiple intelligence approach to healthy active living in high school. *Journal of Physical Education, Recreation and Dance*, 68(3),42-49.

Bancroft, J. (1967). *Games for the playground, home, school and gymnasium*. MacMillan.

Bass, C.K. (1985). Running can modify classroom behavior. *Journal of Learning Disabilities*. 18(3), 160-161.

Bennett, J. G. & Murphy, D.J. (1995). Sit-ups and push-ups only-Are we heading for muscular imbalance? *Journal of Physical Education, Recreation and Dance*, 66(1), 67-72.

Block, M.E. & Etz, K. (1995). The pocket reference-A tool for fostering inclusion. *Journal of Physical Education, Recreation and Dance*, 66(3), 47-51.

Brown, M. (1996). *Finger rhymes*. Penquin Group (USA) Inc.

Brown, M. (1980). *Finger Rhymes*. E.P. Dutton.

Brzycki, M. (1996). *Youth strength and conditioning for parents and players*. McGraw-Hill.

Brzycki, M. (1995). *Youth strength and conditioning for parents and players*. Masters Press.

Butler, J. (1997). How would Socrates teach games? A constructivist approach. *Journal of Physical Education, Recreation and Dance*, 68(9), 42-47.

Capon, J. & Hallum, R. (1977). *Teachers guide: Get ready to square dance*. Educational Activities, Inc.

Clements, R.L. (1995). *My neighborhood movement challenges: Narratives, games, and stunts for ages three through eight years*. NASPE.

Cooper Institute for Aerobics Research Staff (2006). *FITNESSGRAM/Activitygram test administration manual*. Human Kinetics.

Cooper Institute for Aerobics Research (1992). *The Prudential FITNESSGRAM*. Cooper Institute.

Corbin, C.B. (1987). Physical fitness in the K-12 curriculum. *Journal of Physical Education, Recreation and Dance*, 15(7), 49-54.

Davis, M.G. (1996). Promoting our profession: The best of times . . . the worst of times. *Journal of Physical Education, Recreation and Dance*, 67(1), 48-51.

Dawson-Rodriques, K., Lavay, B., Butt, K. & Lacourse, M. (1997). A plan to reduce transition time in physical education. *Journal of Physical Education, Recreation and Dance*, 68(9), 30-33.

Deal, T.B. & Deal, L.O. (1995). Heart to heart: Using heart rate telemetry to meet physical education outcomes. *Journal of Physical Education, Recreation and Dance, 66(3)*, 30-35.

Deoreo, K. & Williams, H.G. (1980a). Characteristics of visual perception. In Corbin, C.B. (Ed.) *A textbook of motor development*. W.C. Brown.

Deoreo, K. & Williams, H.G. (1980b). Characteristics of kinesthetic perception. In Corbin, C.B. (Ed). *A textbook of motor development*. W.C. Brown.

Dieden, B. (1995) *Games to keep kids moving*. Benjamin-Cummings.

Dieden, B. (1995). *Games to keep kids moving*. Parker.

Eggen, P.D. & Kauchak, D. (1994). *Educational psychology: Classroom connections.* Merrill, Maxwell MacMillan International.

Eggen, P.D. & Kauchak, D. (1992). *Educational psychology: Classroom connections.* Merrill.

Gabbard, C.P. (2003). *Lifelong motor development.*Benjamin-Cummings

Gabbard, C.P. (1992). *Lifelong motor development.* Brown & Benchmark.

Gabbard, C., LeBlanc E., & Lowry, S. (1994) *Physical education for children, building the foundation.*Prentice-Hall.

Gabbard, C., LeBlanc E., & Lowry, S. (1987). *Physical education for children, building the foundation.* Prentice-Hall.

Gabbard, C. LeBlanc E. & Lowry, S. (1989). *Game, dance, and gymnastics activities for Children.* Prentice Hall.

Gallahue, D. (2005). *Developmental physical education for all children.* Human Kinetics.

Gallahue, D. (1997). *Developmental physical education for today's children.* McGraw-Hill.

Gallahue, D. (1987). *Developmental physical education for today's children.* Macmillan.

Gallahue, D. (2001). *Understanding motor development in children.* McGraw-Hill.

Gallahue, D.L. (1982). *Understanding motor development in children.* Wiley

Gilbert, A.G. (2000). *Teaching the three r's through movement experiences.* University of Washington.

Gilbert, A. G. (1977). *Teaching the three r's through movement experiences.* Burgess.

Graham, G., Holt/Hale, S. & Parker, M. (2003). *Children moving.* McGraw-Hill.

Graham, G., Holt/Hale, S., & Parker, M. (2001). *Children moving.* Mayfield Publishing Co.

Graham, G. (1990). Physical education in U.S. Schools. *Journal of Physical Education, Recreation and Dance*, 61(2), 35-39.

Gray, G.R. (1995). Safety tips from the expert witness. *Journal of Physical Education, Recreation and Dance* 68(9). 18-21.

Grineski, S. (1992). What is a truly developmentally appropriate physical education program for children? *Journal of Physical Education, Recreation and Dance.* 63(6), 33-35.

Grosse, S.J. (1995). Danger ahead for students with disabilities: Beware of the swinging pendulum. *Journal of Physical Education, Recreation and Dance*, 66(1), 4-5.

Hammett, C.T. (2001). PE Central http://db.pecentral.org/lessonideas.

Harris, J., Pittman, A., & Waller, M. (1994). *Dance a while: Handbook of folk, square, contra, & social dance.* Boston: Allyn and Bacon.

Hayes, E. (1980). *An introduction to the teaching of dance.* Krieger Publishing Co.

Hayes, E. (1964). *An introduction to the teaching of dance.* The Ronald Press.

Hipps, R. & Chappell, W. (1973). *World of fun.* Melody House Publishing Co.

Hipps, R. & Chappell, W. (1970). *World of fun.* MelodyHouse Publishing Co.

Issues. (1995). *Journal of Physical Education, Recreation and Dance*, 66(3), 10-13.

Issues. (1989). *Journal of Physical Education, Recreation and Dance*, 60(3), 14.

Jackson, B. & Rokosz, F. (1995). Super kids day classic games: Two field days for elementary schools. *Journal of Physical Education, Recreation and Dance* 66(3), 56-63 and 71-72.

Jackson, S. (1965). *All time favorite folk dances for children.* Dance Records, Inc.

Kamiya, A. (1995). *Elementary teacher's handbook of games.* Kendall/Hunt.

Kamiya, A (1987). *Elementary teacher's handbook of indoor and outdoor games.* Parker.

Kirchner G. & Fishburne, G.J. (2001). *Physical education for elementary school children.* McGraw Hill Higher Ed.

Kirchner G. & Fishburne, G.J. (1998). *Physical education for elementary school children.* McGraw Hill

Kirchner G. & Fishburne, G.J. (1995). *Physical education for elementary school children.* Brown and Benchmark.

Kirkpatrick, B. & Buck, M.M. (1995). Heart adventures challenge course: A lifestyle education activity. *Journal of Physical Education, Recreation and Dance*, 66(2),17-24.

Kraus, R. (1950). *Square dances of today and how to teach and call them*. Ronald Press.

Kraus, R. (1964). *Folk dancing*. Macmillan Co.

Kuhrash, C. (2001). http:db.pecentral.org/lessonideas.

Kulbitsky O. & Kaltman, R. (1959). *Teachers' dance handbook: Number one: kindergarten to sixth year*. Bluebird Publishing Co.

Kuntzelman, C.T. (1990). *Fitness discovery activities*. Arbor Press.

Kuntzelman, C.T. (1978). *Fitness discovery activities*. Arbor Press.

Kuntzelman, C.T., Kuntzelman, B., McGlynn, M. & McGlynn, G. (1984). *Aerobics with fun*. Fitness Finders.

Lambdin, D. (1989). Shuffling the deck, a flexible system for class organization. *Journal of Physical Education, Recreation and Dance*, 60(4), 25-28.

Langley, D.J. & Woods, A.M. (1997). Developing progressions in motor skills: A systematic approach. *Journal of Physical Education, Recreation and Dance*, 68(7), 41-45.

Maguire, J. (1990). *Hopscotch, hangman, hot potato, & ha ha ha*. Simon & Schuster, Inc.

Manross, D. & Templeton, C.L. (1997). Expertise in teaching physical education. *Journal of Physical Education, Recreation and Dance*, 68(3), 29-35.

McSwegin, P., Pemberton, C. Petray, C. & Going, S. (1989). *Physical best*.AAHPERD.

Melograno, V.J. (1997), Integrating assessment into physical education teaching. *Journal of Physical Education, Recreation and Dance*, 68(7), 34-37.

Mitchell, M. (1996). Stretching the content of your warm-up. *Journal of Physical Education, Recreation and Dance*, 67(7), 24-28.

Mosston, M. & Arnsworth, S. (2001). *Teaching physical education*. Benjamin-Cummings.

Mosston, M. & Arnsworth, S. (1986). *Teaching physical education*. Merrill

Mueller, L.M. (1990); What it means to be physically educated. *Journal of Physical Education, Recreation and Dance*, 62(4), 100-101.

Mulac, M. (1964). *Games and stunts for schools, camps, and playgrounds*. Harper and Row.

Murata, N.M. & Hodge, S.R. (1997). Training support personnel for inclusive physical education. *Journal of Physical Education, Recreation and Dance*, 68(9), 21-25.

National Association for Sport and Physical Education (NASPR) (1995). *Moving into the future: National standards for physical education*. Mosby.

Nelson, B. (1994). *Pickle, pepper and tip-in too*. Simon & Schuster.

Nelson, E. (1975). *Movement games for children of all ages*. Sterling Publishing.

Nichols, B. (2001). *Moving and learning. The elementary school physical education experience*. McGraw Hill.

Nichols, B. (1994). *Moving and learning. The elementary school physical education experience*. Times Mirror/Mosby.

Nichols, B. (1990). *Moving and learning. The elementary school physical education experience*. Times Mirror/Mosby

Nilges, L.M. (1997). Educational gymnastics-Stages of content development. *Journal of Physical Education, Recreation and Dance*, 68(3), 50-55.

Ogden, C L., Flegal, K.M., Carroll, M.D., & Johnson, C.L. (2002). Prevalence and trends in overweight among U.S. children and adolescents 1999-2000. *JAMA* 288: 1728-32. http://www.cdc.gov/nchs/products/pubs/pubd/hestats/overwght99.htm.

Orlick, T. (1996). *Cooperative games and sports*. Human Kinetics.

Orlick, T. (1996). *The cooperative sports and game-book*. Kendall/Hunt.

Pangrazi, R.P. (2006) *Dynamic physical education for elementary school children*. Benjamin-Cummings.

Pangrazi, R.P. (2003). *Dynamic physical education for elementary school children*. Benjamin-Cummings.

Pangrazi, R P. 1998). *Dynamic physical education for elementary school children*. Allyn and Bacon.

Pangrazi, R P, Dauer, V.P. (1995). *Dynamic physical education for elementary school children*. Allyn and Bacon.

Pangrazi, R.P., Dauer, V.P. (1992). *Dynamic physical education for elementary school children*. Macmillan.

Payne, V.G. & Isaacs, L.D. (2007). *Human motor development: A lifespan approach*. McGraw-Hill.

Payne, V.G. & Isaacs, L.D. (2001). *Human motor development. A lifespan approach*. Mayfield.

Payne, V.G. & Isaacs, L.D. (1995). *Human motor development: A lifespan approach*. Mayfield.

Payne, V.G. & Isaacs, L.D. (1991). *Human motor development: A lifespan approach*. Mayfield.

Petersen, S.C. (1992). The sequence of instruction in games: Implications for developmental appropriateness. *Journal of Health, Physical Education, Recreation and Dance*, 63(6), 36-39.

Petray, C.K. (1989). Classroom teachers as partners-Teaching health-related physical fitness. *Journal of Health, Physical Education, Recreation and Dance*, 60(7), 64-66.

Phillips, D.A. & Carlisle, C. (1987). *The physical education teaching assessment instrument*. Greeley: University of Northern Colorado.

Pica, R. (2001). *Wiggle, giggle, and shake*. Gryphon House Inc.

Pissanos, B.W. & Temple, I.G. (1991). Fitting together-Physical education specialists and classroom teachers. *Journal of Health, Physical Education, Recreation and Dance*, 62(7), 55-61.

Pittman, Anne M., & Waller, M. (2004). *Dance a while: Handbook for folk, square, contra, & social dance*. Benjamin-Cummings.

Plimpton, C.E. & Regimbal, C. (1991). Cooperative competition: A children's sport model. *Future Focus*, 12(2), 4-7.

President's Council on Physical Fitness and Sports. (1997). *The president's challenge physical fitness program packet*. The President's Challenge.

Ratliffe, T., Ratliffe, L. & Bie, B. (1991). Creating a learning environment: Class management strategies for elementary physical education teachers. *Journal of Physical Education, Recreation and Dance*, 62(9), 24-27.

Ray, O. (1997). *Encyclopedia of line dances: Country-Western volume 1*. Siddall and Ray.

Regimbal, C. (1998). Personal interview, University of Toledo, Toledo.

Sherrill, C. (2003). *Adapted physical activity, recreation and sport*. McGraw-Hill.

Sherrill, C. (1993). *Adapted physical activity, recreation and sport*. Brown & Benchmark.

Siedentop, D. & Tannehill, D. (2000). *Developing teaching skills in physical education*. McGraw-Hill.

Siedentop, D. & Tannehill, D. (2000). *Developing teaching skills in physical education*. Mayfield.

Sidentop, D. (1991) *Developing teaching skills in physical education*. Mayfield.

Siedentop, D., Herkowitz, J. & Rink, J., (1984). *Elementary physical education methods*. Prentice-Hall.

Siegenthaler, K.L. (1996). Supervising activities for safety. *Journal of Physical Education, Recreation and Dance*, 67(7), 29-30 and 36.

Solomon, G. (1997). Does physical education affect character development in students? *Journal of Physical Education, Recreation and Dance*, 68(9), 38-41.

Sorensen, J. (1990). *Aerobic dancing*. Universal Home Video.

Sorensen, J. (1981). *Aerobic dancing*. Macmillan.

Sorensen, J. (1979). *Aerobic dancing*. Rawson, Wade, Inc.

Sylwester, R. (1994). How emotions affect learning. *Educational Leadership*. October, 60-65.

U.S. Department of Health & Human Services. Centers for Disease Control and Prevention, March 1997, *Information Packet on Guidelines for School and Community Programs to Promote Lifelong Physical Activity Among Young People.*

Vannier, M. & Poindexter, H.B. (1976). *Individual and team sports for girls and women.* Holt, Rinehart, &Winston Inc.

Vannier, M. & Poindexter, H.B. (1968). *Individual and team sports for girls and women.* Saunders.

Wall, J. & Murray, N. (1993). *Children and movement. Physical education in the elementary school.* McGraw-Hill.

Wall, J. & Murray, N. (1989). *Children and movement. Physical education in the elementary school.* Brown and Benchmark.

Weikart, P. (2004). *Round the circle: Key experiences in movement for young children.* High/Scope Press.

Weikart, P. (2003). *Round the circle: Key experiences in movement for young children.* High/Scope Press.

Weikart, P. (2000). *Round the circle: Key experiences in movement for young children.* High/Scope Press.

Weikart, P. (2003). *Teaching movement & dance: A sequential approach to rhythmic movement.* High/Scope Press

Weikart, P. (1998). *Teaching movement & dance: A sequential approach to rhythmic movement.* High/Scope Press.

Weinberg, K. (2002). *Grocery bag fun.* http://db.pecentral.org/lessonideas.

Wickstrom, R. L. (1985). *Fundamental motor patterns.* Lea & Febiger.

Wickstrom, R.L. (1983). *Fundamental motor patterns.* Lea & Febiger.

Williams, H.G. (1983) *Perceptual and motor development.* Prentice-Hall.

Williams, N.F. (1996). The physical education hall of shame, part III: Inappropriate teaching practices. *Journal of Physical Education, Recreation and Dance*, 67(8), 45-48.

Winn, M., Miller, A. & Kuskin, K. (1970). *What shall we do and allee galloo.* Harper and Row Publishers.

Wiswell, P. (1987). *Kids games.* Doubleday and Co.


http:www.cahperd.org/images/pdf_docs/CDE_News_Release.pdf

http://www.cdc.gov

http://www.cdc.gov/mmwr/preview/mmwrhtml/mm5233al.htm

http://www.cdc.gov/nccophp/dash/physicalactivity/promoting-health/calltoaction.htm

http://www.cdc.gov/nchs

http://www.shapeup.org/sua/bmi/how.htm

http://wwwshapeup.org/sua/dated/071196.htm(http://www.cde.ca.gov/nr/ne/yr02/yr02rel37.asp).